Musica Poetica

Musica Poetica

Musical-Rhetorical Figures in German Baroque Music

Dietrich Bartel

University of Nebraska Press
Lincoln and London

Manufactured in the United States of America
♾ The paper in this book meets the minimum requirements of
American National Standard for Information Sciences—Permanence
of Paper for Printed Library Materials, ANSI Z39.48-1984.
Library of Congress Cataloging-in-Publication Data
Bartel, Dietrich.
Musica poetica: musical-rhetorical figures in German Baroque
music / Dietrich Bartel. p. cm. Rev. and enl. ed. of:
Handbuch der musikalischen Figurenlehre. Includes
bibliographical references and index.
ISBN 0-8032-1276-3 (cl : alk. paper)
1. Music and rhetoric. 2. Music—Germany—17th century—
Philosophy and aesthetics. 3. Music—Germany—18th century—
Philosophy and aesthetics. I. Bartel, Dietrich. Handbuch der
musikalischen Figurenlehre. II. Title.
ML3849.B289 1998
780'.943'09032—dc21
97-2450 CIP
MN

Contents

Part Three

Definitions and Translations of the Musical-Rhetorical Figures

Appendices

INTRODUCTION

Music has frequently been referred to as a universal language. As universal as organized pitch and rhythm might be, as common as some musical intervals and rhythmic patterns are to all cultures and civilizations, there are nonetheless a great many "dialects" of this language which not only distinguish one civilization from the next, but indeed distinguish different eras of the same culture from one another. The music of the Baroque era is just such a dialect, growing out of the language of Renaissance music, yet with a content fundamentally distinct from the aesthetics and semantics of Enlightenment or Romantic musical expression.

Throughout the twentieth century musicians and musicologists alike have concerned themselves with deciphering and interpreting the language of Baroque music. After generations of "enlightened" neglect and "romantic" misunderstanding, it became evident that objective insight into the Baroque musical idiom could only be gained if its grammar and its syntax—that is, its own unique compositional precepts and principles—were rediscovered and appreciated. This interest in authentic Baroque performance practice has revolutionized the interpretation of Baroque music, spawning countless performing groups and artists who further the cause of Baroque authenticity with Baroque bows, gut strings, and valveless horns, all tuned to appropriate Baroque pitch. Likewise, in the discipline of musicology, a great deal of scholarly energy has been invested into a myriad of historical and theoretical questions, resulting in a focus of increasing attention on the relationship between music and rhetoric during this period.

The call for a more systematic study of music and rhetoric, specifically regarding the musical-rhetorical figures, initially was issued by Schering in an article published shortly after the turn of the century.[1] The seed thus planted brought forth abundant fruit in the following generation of primarily German musicologists, particularly in the

1. Arnold Schering, "Die Lehre von den musikalischen Figuren im 17. und 18. Jahrhundert," *Kirchenmusikalisches Jahrbuch* 21 (1908): 106.

studies by Brandes, Unger, Gurlitt, and Schmitz.[2] In addition to these more general examinations of music, rhetoric, and the concepts of the musical-rhetorical figures as well as the affections, monographs on individual theorists and their treatises began to appear, including significant studies of Bernhard, Burmeister, Nucius, Thuringus, and Mattheson.[3] Furthermore, in addition to facsimile editions of numerous Baroque publications during this time, a few treatises which had remained in manuscript were made available in modern editions, notably those of Bernhard and the early compositional treatises by J. G. Walther and J. Scheibe.[4] As details of the various treatments of the musical-rhetorical figures were exposed, it became increasingly apparent that a unified or systematic Baroque doctrine of musical figures—as presented by Schering or Unger—could not be endorsed. There were simply too many discrepancies, contradictions in definitions, and varied bases of the concept of the figures to permit such a generally valid and unified teaching or "doctrine." Rather than one *Figurenlehre*, there appeared to be virtually as many *Figurenlehren* as there were music theorists. Just as performing artists could be exces-

2. Heinz Brandes, *Studien zur musikalischen Figurenlehre im 16. Jahrhundert* (Berlin: Triltsch & Huther, 1935); Hans-Heinrich Unger, *Die Beziehungen zwischen Musik und Rhetorik im 16.–18. Jahrhundert* (Würzburg: Triltsch, 1941; Hildesheim: Olms, 1969); Willibald Gurlitt, "Musik und Rhetorik," *Helicon* 5 (1944): 67–86; Arnold Schmitz, *Die Bildlichkeit in der wortgebundenen Musik J.S. Bachs* (Mainz: Schott, 1950).

3. Helmut Federhofer, "Die Figurenlehre nach Christoph Bernhard und die Dissonanzbehandlung in Werken von Heinrich Schütz," *Internationaler Musikwissenschaftlicher Kongreß Bamberg* (Kassel: Bärenreiter, 1953), 132–35; Martin Ruhnke, *Joachim Burmeister: Ein Beitrag zur Musiklehre um 1600* (Kassel: Bärenreiter, 1955); Fritz Feldmann, "Das 'Opusculum Bipartitum' des Joachim Thuringus (1625) besonders in seinen Beziehungen zu Joh. Nucius (1613)," *Archiv für Musikwissenschaft* 15 (1958): 123–42; Hans Lenneberg, "Johann Mattheson on Affect and Rhetoric in Music," *Journal for Music Theory* 2 (1958): 47–84, 193–236; George J. Buelow, "The *Loci topici* and Affect in Late Baroque Music: Heinichen's Practical Demonstration," *Music Review* 27 (1966): 161–76.

4. Johann Gottfried Walther, *Praecepta der musicalischen composition*, ed. Peter Benary, Ms. 1708 (Leipzig: Breitkopf & Härtel, 1955); P. Benary, *Die deutsche Kompositionslehre des 18. Jahrhunderts* (Leipzig: Breitkopf & Härtel, 1961), which includes Scheibe's early composition treatise *Compendium Musices*; Josef M. Müller-Blattau, *Die Kompositionslehre Heinrich Schützens in der Fassung seines Schülers Christoph Bernhard* (Kassel: Bärenreiter, 1963).

sively zealous in their application of newly discovered approaches to "correct" musical interpretation, so too could musicologists distort the portrayal of historical developments through strained associations or misconstrued conclusions.

Nonetheless, the fact remains that numerous German Baroque authors described compositional devices which deviated from the ordinary or regular manner of musical expression with terminology either borrowed from the discipline of rhetoric or formulated to emulate such terminology. Instead of matching a certain term with a single definition (or vice versa) as Unger has attempted, a clearer understanding of a term can be attained by tracing its use and development through the diverse *Figurenlehren*. H. H. Eggebrecht, a student of Gurlitt and my mentor at Freiburg University, developed this methodology in *Studien zur musikalischen Terminologie* (1968). Such a terminological approach to the subject avoids the pitfalls of the earlier systematic generalizations regarding the *Figurenlehre* and sheds further light on the growing relationship between rhetoric and music, as well as on steadily evolving artistic and aesthetic principles throughout the seventeenth and eighteenth centuries.

The rigorous application of rhetorical terminology and methodology to musical analysis and composition remained a predominantly German Baroque phenomenon. While rhetorical principles influenced musical composition in Italian, French, and English circles, only in Germany did this develop into an enthusiastic adoption and adaptation of rhetorical terminology, methods, and structures. This resulted in a veritable musical rhetoric, a "local German dialect" which flourished particularly in the writings of Lutheran *Kantors*. In the postscript to a reprinted article which examines the fundamental differences between Italian and German Baroque aesthetic principles, Eggebrecht acknowledges that the fundamental criteria for determining these differences are to be discovered in the unique and pervasive influences on German musical thought of the Protestant reformer Martin Luther.[5] At the very heart of Baroque musical concepts in Protestant Germany lies Luther's theology

---

5. Hans Heinrich Eggebrecht, "Über Bachs geschichtlichen Ort," *Johann Sebastian Bach* (Wege der Forschung 170, Darmstadt: Wissenschaftliche Buchgesellschaft, 1970): 247–89.

of music, which had significant influence on the development of German music throughout the sixteenth to eighteenth centuries. His theological understanding of music helps to explain the continued German acceptance of the scientific-mathematical significance of medieval music theory, the didactic rather than purely aesthetic intention of music, the increased importance of the rational accessibility to the musical craft, and the heightened significance of the rhetorical discipline, including the concepts of the affections and the musical-rhetorical figures.

The present study explores the framework, origins, and development of the concept of musical-rhetorical figures.[6] By examining the commonalities and differences between the various *Figurenlehren* in their divergent contexts, we are able to trace the development not only of the concept but also of Baroque musical thought. It will be observed that the concept of the musical-rhetorical figures grew out of a desire to identify and define with rhetorical terminology those expressive musical devices which deviated from conventional compositional norms, that the musical-rhetorical concept developed into a specific means of representing and arousing the affections, and that toward the end of the Baroque era, an age in which such systematic and objective principles contradicted the increasing emphasis on "enlightened" individualistic and subjective musical expression, such a concept would experience its inevitable decline. Frequently these developments will be observed in the various definitions of a single musical-rhetorical term.

Part 1 of this study seeks to present not only the necessary background to the concept of the musical-rhetorical figures but can serve as an introduction to German Baroque music theory in general, focusing on Luther's theology of music, the development of the German Baroque concept and discipline of *musica poetica*, the concept of the affections in German Baroque music, and the application of the principles and devices of rhetoric in compositional theory and practice. Regarding the chapters on *musica poetica*, the affections, and rhetoric, the discussion focuses chiefly on developments in Germany during the Baroque period,

---

6. Parts 2 and 3 of this study are based on the author's dissertation completed at the *Albert-Ludwigs-Universität*, Freiburg im Breisgau (1982), published as *Handbuch der musikalischen Figurenlehre* (Laaber: Laaber Verlag, 1985).

as this remained the almost exclusive locus of the systematic development of a "musical rhetoric," including the musical-rhetorical figures. Occasionally it will be necessary to provide some background information to these various developments and concepts. In such cases, it is the legacy of the historical background which will be of chief interest, rather than a thorough presentation of the historical developments leading up to the Baroque period. It should be remembered that in seventeenth-century Germany Cicero and Boethius were still being read, albeit at times in modified or amended versions, rendering these and other "ancient" sources authoritative and therefore "contemporary" to the Baroque student.

Considering the centrality of Luther's theological views on music to this subject, the study begins with a brief summary of Luther's theology of music. While this short chapter is not intended to present an exhaustive discussion of Luther's views on music but serves primarily as a foundation for the following material, it is fundamental to the German concept of *musica poetica*, and thus deserves its own separate albeit brief presentation. This is followed by a chapter on *musica poetica*, the uniquely German discipline of Baroque music which seeks to combine medieval music theory with Lutheran theology, inspired by Renaissance humanistic thought and seventeenth-century rationalism. The concept of the affections, which is central to the musical-rhetorical figures and has been associated with both music and rhetoric since antiquity, constitutes the subject matter of the third chapter. The fourth chapter concerns itself with rhetoric, predominantly in its application to Baroque musical composition.

Part 2 introduces the various *Figurenlehren* as presented in seventeenth- and eighteenth-century treatises and publications. After a cursory biographical sketch, each author's interpretation and classification of the figures is discussed. The diverse descriptions and categorizations resulted in some figures being classified as simple ornaments (*Manieren, figurae simplices*) by some writers and as musical-rhetorical figures by others. For this reason, *Figurenlehren* such as those of Printz, and the discussion of ornamental embellishments by authors such as Vogt, Walther, Mattheson, and Spiess, are also included, but a comprehensive terminological study of the relevant terms is not attempted.[7]

In part 3 the various authors' definitions of the musical-rhetorical figures are presented alphabetically with their original text with parallel English translations, accompanied by a discussion of the term's origin and development. Regarding the organization of this section, an alphabetical listing of the figures was considered the most appropriate and convenient method for a number of reasons: first, any other method of listing the figures (for example by category) would make looking up figures rather awkward, especially since there are many references to individual figures in parts 1 and 2 of the text, as well as numerous cross-references in part 3 itself; second, it renders part 3 most accessible as an independent reference resource; third, it preserves the methodology of a terminological study in which the term rather than its content is the determining criterium, a methodology which allows for a revised and corrected understanding of the *Figurenlehre* itself; finally, related to the last point, it avoids numerous figures needing to be placed in more than one category owing to frequent multiple meanings of the same term. Included in the appendices is a summary of the figures by category which groups the figures in various classifications, thereby aiding readers who wish to discover groupings of related figures.

While further examples in addition to those found in the sources which would demonstrate the use of a figure in various Baroque compositions would have added interest to this study, this was considered infeasible for a number of reasons: first, as a terminological study, the interest of the present text lies in exploring the origin, development, and understanding of a term rather than the content which the term names or describes; second, the fact that a single term often receives multiple definitions would lead to an unwieldy study far exceeding the intended compass of this volume; third, there presently exist numerous studies which explore the use of musical-rhetorical figures by specific composers or in specific compositions; finally, it is my hope that this present study, having contributed toward the clarification of the diverse understanding and development of musical-rhetorical figure terminol-

---

7. For a thorough discussion of such embellishing devices, the reader is referred to studies such as Frederick Neumann's *Ornamentation in Baroque and Post-Baroque Music* (Princeton: Princeton University Press, 1978, 1983).

ogy, will facilitate further work in the use of the figures by specific composers.

Each discussion of a figure begins with a summarizing definition, followed by a terminological explication. Wherever applicable, the term's literal meaning, rhetorical content, and musical application, interpretation, and development are discussed. Because individual authors are amply discussed in part 2 and all the musical definitions are listed with their translations, it was not considered necessary to recapitulate each author's understanding of the figure but rather to concentrate on matters concerning the linguistic and musical origins and development of the term. The musical definitions of a figure are preceded by rhetorical definitions of the respective term whenever possible, represented among others by classical (Quintilian), Renaissance (primarily Susenbrotus), and Baroque (Gottsched) sources. The musical definitions of each term are presented in chronological order, occasionally including definitions taken from sources other than a recognized *Figurenlehre* (e.g., Praetorius, Herbst). The source of a definition is indicated in parentheses following the name of the author through an abbreviation of the treatise and the appropriate page number, when possible. Should the treatise only be available in a modern edition, as in Bernhard's treatises[8] or Walther's *Praecepta*, the page numbers of the modern edition are used. All translations were prepared by myself, at times in consultation with previous translations. While the English translations remain relatively literal, the inclusion of the original texts permits certain liberties which facilitate a more fluent translation. The musical examples found in the treatises are occasionally omitted, such as when the examples in various treatises coincide or when an author includes numerous similar examples. In addition to the musical-rhetorical figures, the ornamental embellishments (*figurae simplices* or *Manieren*) which are included in the treatises of the various authors have also been incorporated. However, rather than discussing these embellishments comprehensively, they are considered only to the extent of their inclusion in the relevant treatises.[9]

---

8. In the case of Bernhard's treatises, the page numbers refer to the Müller-Blattau (1963) edition.

9. For an exhaustive study of such ornaments, see Neumann, *Ornamentation*.

The four appendices at the conclusion of this text provide various summaries and overviews of the musical-rhetorical figures, beginning with a listing of the figures in alphabetical order accompanied by a short definition, followed by a listing of the figures according to seven categories: figures of melodic repetition, figures of harmonic repetition (including fugal figures), figures of representation, figures of dissonance and displacement, figures of silence, figures of ornamentation, and miscellaneous figures.[10] As the classification of the figures varied widely in the seventeenth- and eighteenth-centuries, no modern attempt at classification can be considered definitive. Rather, the present categorization of the figures is meant both to assist in determining or locating related figures and to provide a tool with which more expediently to match a certain musical-compositional device or phenomenon with a specific term or figure. For this reason, the terms which were cross-referenced in part 3 and in appendix 1 are listed here along side the term under which the figure was defined in part 3. It is also in this appendix that the ornamental, "non-rhetorical" *figurae simplices* or *Manieren* can be most easily discerned. Appendices 3 and 4 provide summaries of the figures by author, appendix 3 listing the authors alphabetically and the figures defined or mentioned in their respective treatises in the order of their original appearance, and appendix 4 listing the figures alphabetically followed by the authors who define or mention them.

I would like to express my appreciation and gratitude to a few of the individuals who have encouraged and helped me throughout this entire project: to Prof. H. H. Eggebrecht, *Albert-Ludwigs-Universität*, Freiburg i. Br., Germany, who directed me toward this area of research and patiently advised and guided me in my original doctoral studies and research; to Prof. Rolf Dammann, *Albert-Ludwigs-Universität*, who inspired me to "think theologically" about German Baroque music; to Dr. Traugott Schächtele, who spent countless hours with me in Freiburg over Latin translations; to Prof. Gregory Butler, University of British Columbia, Vancouver, Canada, who introduced me to the area of music

---

10. These categories are an adaptation of the classifications found in George Buelow's article, "Rhetoric and Music," *New Grove Dictionary of Music and Musicians*, ed. Stanley Sadie (London: Macmillan, 1980), 15: 793-803.

and rhetoric and advised me in this present study; to Prof. Evan Kreider, University of British Columbia, who encouraged and advised me throughout this project; and above all, to my wife, Jocelyn, without whose support, advice, proofreading, but most of all patience and understanding, this project would not have seen completion.

Part One

Introduction to the Concepts

Luther on Music: A Theological Basis for German Baroque Music

For music is a gift and largesse of God, not a human gift. Praise through word and music is a sermon in sound. . . . In summa, next to the Word of God, the noble art of music is the greatest treasure in this world. Martin Luther

Martin Luther's outspoken comments on music are as legendary as they are colorful. Luther presented his fledgling church with much more than a random collection of passing thoughts on musical issues. Rather, in his writings one is confronted by a theology of music which not only outshines the musical musings of other church reformers but indeed, during the centuries that followed, provided Protestant musicians and music theorists alike with a fundamentally theocentric philosophy of music.

Music: A Divine Gift

Luther's views on music differed substantially from those held by his humanistically inclined contemporaries, including those of two other notable reformers, Jean Calvin and Ulrich Zwingli. Rather than viewing music as a primarily human innovation, Luther believed music to be essentially a divine gift to humanity, second only to the Word of God or theology. This divine origin of music established God as the author and source of the natural phenomenon of sound, including the world of tones. Speculative musical theory based on the numerical proportions of musical intervals did not become irrelevant conjecture, as it did for the more humanistically minded, but rather was germane to understanding music's divinely ordained power. This belief proposed that the very essence of God is revealed in and through the musical proportions. Through music the invisible becomes audible. The divine essence of music was underscored again and again by Luther in his numerous writings. In his foreword to Georg Rhau's *Symphoniae* (1538), Luther wrote: "I truly desire that all Christians would love and regard as worthy the lovely gift of music, which is a precious, worthy, and costly treasure given mankind by God. . . . In summa, next to the Word of God, the noble art of music is the greatest treasure in this world."[1] In an unfinished essay on music (1541), he stated: "For music is a gift and largesse of God, not a human gift. . . . After theology I accord to music the highest place and the greatest honour."[2] Not surprisingly, Luther regarded music as the most significant of the four mathematical disciplines of the seven liberal arts. Writing to Ludwig Senfl (1530), Luther maintained: "For this very reason the prophets cultivated no art so much as music in that they attached their theology not to geometry, nor to arithmetic, nor to astronomy, but to music, speaking the truth through psalms and hymns."[3] Throughout the Baroque, Lutheran writers continued to emphasize this speculative aspect of music theory, reinforcing rather than rejecting its metaphysical relevance.

Along with music per se, the discipline of musical composition was also viewed as a divine gift. Unlike his humanistic colleagues, Luther was not willing to abstract the art from the material. Both music and its associated discipline were God-given gifts. In the preface to the *Geistliches Gesangbüchlein* (1524), Luther wrote: "I desire that all arts, particularly music, be employed in the service of Him who has given and created them. I pray, therefore, that every pious Christian . . . if God has endowed him with the necessary talents and ability, help further the cause."[4] It is therefore most appropriate that Luther praise the fine compositions of musicians such as Georg Rhau: "However, when man's natural musical ability is whetted and polished to the extent that it becomes an art, then do we note with great surprise the great and perfect wisdom of God in music, which is, after all, His product and His gift; we marvel when we hear music in which one voice sings a simple

1. This and the following translated Luther quotations are taken from Walter Buszin, *Luther on Music*, ed. J. Riedel, Pamphlet Series No.3 (Saint Paul: Lutheran Society for Worship, Music and the Arts, 1958). The essay first appeared in *Musical Quarterly* 32 (1946).

2. Cited in Buszin, *Luther on Music*, 11.

3. Ibid., 7.

4. Ibid., 10.

melody, while three, four, or five other voices play and trip lustily around the voice that sings its simple melody and adorn this simple melody wonderfully with artistic musical effects, thus reminding us of a heavenly dance, where all meet in a spirit of friendliness, caress, and embrace. . . . A person who gives this some thought and yet does not regard it as a marvellous creation of God, must be a clodhopper indeed and does not deserve to be called a human being; he should be permitted to hear nothing but the braying of asses and the grunting of hogs."[5]

Music: Its Effect

Luther continued to embrace the concept of music's affective and formative power, based ultimately on a Christian interpretation of the Greek ethos teachings. The order of natural sound as defined through the mathematical proportions of the intervals was present from the moment of Creation and is thereby an attribute of the Creator. To further support both this "orderly" explanation of Creation and the phenomenon of music, most Lutheran music treatises of the sixteenth through the eighteenth centuries continued to quote a passage of scripture taken from the Apocryphal book, the Wisdom of Solomon (ch.11.20): "But thou hast ordered all things by measure and number and weight." The act of hearing music, of listening to ordered sound, is to resonate with Creation, of which the individual is a part. When the human ear perceives the various musical harmonies, it involuntarily recognizes the reality of the Creator's work. The human desire to participate in musical activity is not, therefore, so much a need for self-expression, as the humanists would have it, as it is a longing for and a reflection of a relationship with the Creator. This recognition also has affective and formative power on the human mind and body. Luther's views on music reflect Augustine's synthesis of Greek music theory with Christian dogma: music not only mirrors the order of the created universe through its own numerical order but can positively affect individuals by audibly "putting them in touch" with the greater order of Creation. The order or

5. Ibid., 6.

"music" through which God created the universe thus becomes a means of spiritual growth. Music becomes a theological statement which allows it to be used in the struggle against melancholy, depression, and powers of darkness. References to the metaphysical power of music are frequently encountered in Luther's writings. In the preface to a collection of part songs (1538), he wrote: "To you, my dear young man, I commend this noble, wholesome, and joyful creation, through which the feelings of your heart may at times be helped, especially when withstanding shameful lusts and bad company."[6] And from his unfinished essay concerning music: "Music drives away the devil and makes people happy; it induces one to forget all wrath, unchastity, arrogance, and other vices."[7] In one of his table talks, he claimed that "Satan is very hostile to [music], since it casts out many scruples and evil thoughts. The devil does not remain near it, for music is one of the finest of all arts. . . . Music drives away the spirit of sadness. Music is a taskmistress which makes people milder and more gentle, more civil and more sensible."[8] Luther had little patience for those individuals who did not appreciate this power of music: "Those who are not moved by this [contrapuntal music] are, indeed, unmusical and deserve only to hear some dunghill poet or the music of swine."[9]

Music: A Pedagogical Tool

In assigning music the preeminent position as theology's handmaid, with its role of praising God and edifying humanity, Luther also gave music a didactic purpose. Rather than being a human invention developed for the purposes of entertainment, recreation, and self-expression, God's gift of music could impart divine truth both to those who heard it and to those who performed or studied it. Youth in particular were to be trained in the musical discipline, Luther repeatedly pointed out. In the preface to the *Geistliches Gesangbüchlein* Luther

6. Ibid., 5.
7. Ibid., 11.
8. Ibid., 13.
9. Ibid., 5.

expressed his concern over the musical education of youth, particularly regarding the eternal parental anxiety over their instinctive musical preferences: "The music is arranged in four parts. I desire this particularly in the interest of the young people, who should and must receive an education in music as well as in the other arts if we are to wean them away from carnal and lascivious songs and interest them in what is good and wholesome. Only thus will they learn, as they should, to love and appreciate what is intrinsically good."[10] Again from his letter to Senfl: "It is necessary indeed that music be taught in the schools. A teacher must be able to sing; otherwise I will not as much as look at him. Also, we should not ordain young men into the ministry unless they have become well acquainted with music in the schools. . . . We should always make it a point to habituate youth to enjoy the art of music, for it produces fine and skillful people."[11] Thus music was to become an integral part of the Lutheran *Lateinschule* curriculum. In his *Letter to the Aldermen and Cities of Germany to Erect and Maintain Christian Schools* of 1524, Luther wrote: "Since youth must skip about and leap, or at least do something that affords pleasure, and since it would certainly not do to forbid this entirely, ought we not to furnish schools in which we could teach youth such art? . . . If I had children and would be able to carry it out, I would insist that they study not only the languages and history, but also singing music and all of mathematics."[12]

Not only music "and all of [the other] mathematics," but also the linguistic subjects were regarded as integral to the curriculum of the Lutheran *Lateinschule*. The new Lutheran emphasis on preaching the Word in worship services further encouraged the widespread "rediscovery" of the rhetorical discipline. Rhetoric was given a very specific task: the preacher was to use the persuasive art of oration to admonish and edify his congregation. Luther maintained that preaching also occurs specifically through music, particularly when music is combined with a sacred text. A musical composition could thus become a "sermon in

10. Ibid., 10.
11. Ibid., 8.
12. Ibid., 14.

sound."[13] Music could play both an indirect and a direct role in this process. First, it could move the listener to a receptive state for the spoken word: "[Music] can engender a calm and willing heart, making it receptive for God's Word and Truth."[14] Furthermore, music could lend the associated text a greater measure of emphasis and potency. While a spoken text might be understood intellectually, its text and affection could be expressed more emphatically through the addition of music. The musical expression of the text and the associated affection became the dominating concern for the following generations of Lutheran musicians and composers. Luther had given them the mandate not only to express the text and affections in their compositions, but to explain and expound on the meaning and significance of the words. He encouraged musicians to ensure that "all the notes and melodies center on the text."[15] In fact, in a proper musical setting, "the music will bring the text to life."[16] Music is therefore not just a passive reflection of the text but a tireless advocate of the text.

In the Latin preface to the Funeral Chorales (1542), Luther also maintained that "the addition of the singing voice [to the text] results in song, which is the voice of the affections. For just as the spoken word is understood intellectually, it is affectively perceived through song."[17] Both the heart and the mind were to be targeted by the composer. The affections were to be portrayed and aroused by the Lutheran composer not primarily to delight the audience, or to faithfully reflect and re-present the text, but rather, quite simply, to preach the Christian Gospel. Herein lies one of the significant differences between Italian and Protestant German Baroque music. Like the sermon, the musical composition was the "living voice of the Gospel," the *viva vox evangelii.*[18] And like the preacher, the composer was to use any artistic

---

13. "Das laudare verbo et musica ist eine sonora praedicatio." Oskar Söhngen, *Theologie der Musik* (Kassel: Johannes Stauda Verlag, 1967), 95.

14. Ibid., 96.

15. "Die Musica soll 'alle ihre Noten und Gesänge auf den Text richten.'" Ibid., 95. Significantly, this quote is also found in Michael Praetorius's *Syntagma musicum I.*

16. "Die Noten machen den Text lebendig." Ibid., 97.

17. "Sed vocem addendo fit cantus, que vox est affectus. Sicut ergo verbum est intellectus, sic vox ipsius affectus." Ibid., 96.

18. Ibid., 97.

means necessary to convince his listeners. The use of rhetorical devices and structures in music was one of these methods. Both its structuring steps and divisions as well as the expressive devices used in rhetoric were adopted by the Lutheran musicians in order to make them better "preachers." Specifically the musical-rhetorical figures became not simply unconventional or decorative musical phenomena, but rather musical devices which were developed to lend the composition a greater measure of exegetical capacity. The role of Lutheran music was clearly pedagogical, seeking to teach and edify. With both music and rhetoric accorded such prominent and related status in the *Lateinschule* curriculum, the path for their inevitable interrelationship was cleared. Although the new Italian musical idioms and styles were to be adopted by Lutheran musicians, these were always to be used primarily to explain and express the meaning and sense of the text, not just to imitate its affection.

In summary, through his continued adherence to the holistic medieval concept of music and his simultaneous emphasis on music's practical application, Luther prepared the way for a synthesis between *musica speculativa* and *musica practica*, ultimately leading to the uniquely German *musica poetica*. Through his concern over the education of youth coupled with his colleague Melanchthon's classical, humanistic interests, a curriculum for the new Lutheran *Lateinschulen* was to be established which would emphasize both the mathematical and the linguistic Latin disciplines. Through his emphasis on the importance of music as well as the spoken (and preached) Word, Luther stimulated the integration of the rhetorical and musical disciplines. And through his theological reinforcement of the traditional ethical view of music, Luther encouraged the combination of a musico-theological ethos with the concept of the affections based on the speculative science of the numerical proportions of the musical intervals.

Toward *Musica Poetica*: The Emergence of a German Baroque Music

Musica Poetica is that discipline of music which teaches how to compose a musical composition . . . . in order to sway the hearts and spirits of individuals into various dispositions. Joachim Burmeister (1606)

Music is a heavenly-philosophical and specifically mathematical science, which concerns itself with tones, with the intent to produce an agreeable and artful Harmony or consonance. Johann Gottfried Walther (1708)

Music is the science and art wisely to arrange proper and agreeable sounds in a correct manner, and to execute them pleasingly, in order to foster God's glory and all virtue through their consonance. Johann Mattheson (1739)

Two themes consistently receiving attention in German Baroque music treatises are music's speculative mathematical foundation and its intended edifying effect. Johann Gottfried Walther, J. S. Bach's cousin, friend, and colleague in Weimar, introduces his compositional treatise with the above definition of music which highlights both of these points. Although Walther's Italian contemporaries had abandoned the concept of music as a mathematical science, the understanding of music as a "heavenly-philosophical and specifically mathematical"[1] discipline remained prevalent in Lutheran Germany throughout most of the Baroque. While the philosophical basis for such an understanding is founded on the Lutheran theocentric philosophy of music, the historical basis for this phenomenon is rooted in classical and medieval concepts of music, influenced by Renaissance humanism and the revival of the linguistic and rhetorical disciplines. In order to gain a clearer and more thorough understanding of German Baroque music, it will be necessary to explore these classical and renaissance influences.

---

1. "Die Music ist eine himmlisch-philosophische, und sonderlich auf Mathesin sich gründente Wiβenschaft, welche umgehet mit dem Sono, so fern aus selbigen eine gute und künstl. Harmonie oder Zusammenstimmung hervor zubringen." J. G. Walther, *Praecepta*, 13.

The Classical Legacy

The Roman philosopher and mathematician Boethius (480–524) furnished the link between Greco-Roman and medieval music theory, and remained influential well into the Baroque era. Through his work the Pythagorean concept of music as a mathematical discipline became entrenched in medieval scholastic thought, establishing the primacy of the speculative science over the sensuously perceivable art of music making. The musical discipline was subdivided into three orders: *musica mundana*, *musica humana*, and *musica instrumentalis*. In all three categories the relationship between a microcosmic reflection of a macrocosmic reality becomes evident. The highest order of music, *musica mundana* (music of the spheres), deals with the "harmonic" and orderly motion of the stars and planets, the alternation of the seasons, and the organization of the elements. It is essentially a rational explanation of the macrocosm, presented through numerical proportions. The next order of music, *musica humana* (music of the human body and spirit), concerns itself with the "harmonic" relationship between the body and the soul, uniting the two in certain numerical proportions which are influenced by and reflective of the macrocosmic order of *musica mundana*. As such, the human body represents a microcosm of the larger order. Both are governed by the same numerical proportions and relationships. The third and lowest order of music, *musica instrumentalis*, deals with the physical properties of sound and focuses on the numerical proportions of the musical intervals. The audible intervals are determined by the same proportions which govern *musica mundana* and *musica humana*. In this order the numerical proportions become audibly perceptible through the physical application of the mathematical principles. The distinguishing feature between the two higher orders and the applied order lies in the fact that the former exist a priori while the latter is the result of human fabrication, using either musical instruments or the human voice. Medieval scholasticism placed much more confidence in intellectual *ratio* than in the emotional and consequently fallible *sensus*. It is therefore mathematical *ratio* which was always to correct aural *sensus*. With mathematical proportions determined through *ratio*, the music theorist (*musicus*) was considered superior to the practical musician or composer (*cantor*). *Musica instrumentalis* was regarded as a rational exercise rather than a creative or expressive act, with the instruments merely being tools which allowed scientific observation and practical application.

Throughout the Middle Ages music was accorded a place alongside its sister mathematical disciplines, arithmetic, geometry, and astronomy, these four subjects making up the *quadrivium* of the seven liberal arts. Consequently the instructor of this subject, the *musicus*, was a mathematics professor on the *quadrivium* faculty. The craft of musical composition had no place in this speculative concept of *musica*. The linguistic subjects of the *trivium* incorporated the other three liberal arts: grammar, dialectic, and rhetoric. It was as a member of the *trivium* faculty that the practical musician, the *cantor*, found his place. Applied music was considered a craft dealing with elocution or delivery, and was therefore more akin to rhetoric than to mathematics. In addition to directing school or church choirs and teaching the rudiments of music, the *cantor* was also frequently called upon to teach other subjects of the *trivium*, especially Latin and Rhetoric. This connection was to stand the Lutheran *Kantor* in good stead as rhetorical principles and methods became adopted by the musical discipline. While the linguistic disciplines were regarded as inferior or "trivial" next to the quadrivial subjects in the medieval ordering of the seven liberal arts, this ranking was to change with the dawn of the Renaissance. Rhetoric and poetry rather than *mathesis* would increasingly be regarded as music's "sister discipline." Gradually it was the composer who was to be regarded as the true *musicus poeticus*, albeit with a redefined mandate.

Numerical Proportions of the Intervals

The numerical proportions of the various intervals can be audibly and visually demonstrated through the use of the monochord, a single stringed instrument with a moveable bridge. This instrument became the "laboratory" of the musical science, the tool of *musica instrumentalis*. Given the continued significance of these principles in German Baroque music theory, the intervallic proportions will be explained in more detail. The first and simplest interval, the octave, is produced by dividing the monochord string into two equal portions. If the original string sounds a *C*, then one of the two portions would produce a *c*, the note one octave higher than the original note, resulting in the octave proportion 1:2. Octaves can therefore also be calculated by factoring by 2: the note c^1 can be represented by the relationship 1:4, the note c^2 by 1:8, etc. The fifth is created by dividing the string into three equal portions. One of these portions produces the note *g*, a twelfth higher than the original *C*, resulting in the relationship 1:3. Fifths can therefore be calculated by factoring by 3. To arrive at the proportion of the fifth, the numbers representing *c* (1:2) and *g* (1:3) are juxtaposed, resulting in the proportion 2:3. The interval of the fourth with its proportion 3:4 is derived by juxtaposing the numbers representing *g* (1:3) and c^1 (1:4). To arrive at the next fifth, d^2, the *g* (1:3) must again be divided into thirds, resulting in the relationship 1:9. To calculate the proportion of a whole tone, the numbers representing c^2 and d^2 are juxtaposed, resulting in the proportion 8:9. Through combining the calculations of fifths and octaves, all musical intervals can thus be given a specific numerical proportion, based on the number representing the desired new note juxtaposed against the appropriate octave of the original note. To establish the proportions of a major third, two further divisions by 3 of the note d^2 are required, resulting in the interval C–e^5 having the relationship 1:81, and c^5–e^5 generating the proportion 64:81. Throughout the fifteenth and sixteenth centuries, major and minor thirds were increasingly regarded as consonances, calling the validity of their high proportions and thus their implied dissonance into question. Renaissance music theorists were to demonstrate that in fact an e^1 could be generated on the monochord with the relationship 1:5, resulting in the consonant proportion 4:5 for the major third c^1–e^1, while 5:6 (e^1–g^1) was shown to produce the minor third.[2] With this justification, it becomes apparent that *sensus* rather than only *ratio* was being called upon to determine dissonance and consonance. The medieval distrust of

2. This "new" proportion of the major third (4:5 = 64:80) is indeed very close to the Pythagorean proportion 64:81. Being now so much closer to the unison, it could be defined as a consonance instead of a dissonance. The difference between these two thirds (80:81) was considered equal to one *comma.* Nine *commata* make up one whole tone (8:9 = 72:81; 81 - 72 = 9), with a major semitone consisting of 5 *commata* and a minor semitone consisting of 4. See also *Apotomia* in part 3, below.

the senses was being gradually modified by a new Renaissance "humanized" orientation. In summary:

Unison:	(*C*)	1:1	Minor Third:	(e^1–g^1)	5:6
Octave:	(*C*–*c*)	1:2	Major Sixth:	(g–e^1)	3:5
Fifth:	(*c*–*g*)	2:3	Minor Sixth:	(e^1–c^2)	5:8
Fourth:	(g–c^1)	3:4	Whole Tone:	(c^2–d^2)	8:9
Major Third:	(c^1–e^1)	4:5	Semitone:	(b^2–c^3)	15:16

Intervallic Proportions and Theological Symbolism

In the cosmo-theological understanding of the musical discipline, the relationship between the musical intervals and their divine origin did not remain vague speculation but was thoroughly explored by German Baroque music theorists. The unison, with its proportion 1:1, was considered the starting point of all music, much like the point of a line in geometry. It remained only a small step to make the connection between the perfection of the unison and the perfection of God, the "starting point" of creation.[3] For music, the mirror of the cosmos, has a perfect origin like the universe itself, with the unison standing above consonance or dissonance. From this "point" the perfect and imperfect consonances are derived. The intervals were ranked according to their proportions by the following principle: the closer a proportion is to the unison (i.e., the lower the numerals), the more consonant it will be. It is not surprising that in such a cosmological understanding of the intervals, numerology played a significant role. The composer and theorist Andreas Werckmeister went to some length to ascribe theological

3. "Denn wie die Unität von sich selber ist / und von keiner Zahl den Anfang hat / sondern der Anfang aller Numerorum selber ist / und kein Ende hat. Also ist Gott ein eintziges Wesen von Ewigkeit / der Anfang ohne Anfang / und Fortgang aller Dinge / deβen Wesen und Kraft sich in Ewigkeit erstrecket / und kein Ende hat." Andreas Werckmeister, *Musicalische Paradoxal-Discourse* (Quedlinburg, 1707), 92. "Gott selbst ist die Unität." J. H. Buttstett, *UT, MI, SOL*, 24, cited in Rolf Dammann, *Der Musikbegriff im deutschen Barock* (Laaber: Laaber Verlag, 1984), 38.

significance to the various intervallic proportions.[4] While the numeral 1 represents God the Father, 2 represents the Son, being one with the Father yet distinct, just as the two notes spanning an octave are the same yet distinct. Numeral 3, the fifth, represents the Holy Spirit, making up the Trinity. It is embraced by the octave (1:2 = Father:Son) and equals its sum. Numeral 4 is called an angelic or heavenly number, representing the angels who fulfill the will of God. As the "cosmic" number, it also represents the four elements, seasons, and temperaments. Furthermore, the fourth (3:4) unites the Trinity (1:2:3) with the triad (4:5:6). Numeral 5 represents humanity, the human having five senses and five appendages (head, feet, and arms). And only when placed within the Divine context, that is between the fifth (4:5:6; 4:6 = 2:3) does humanity find fulfillment. The minor third (5:6) remains forlorn on its own without the Divine reference point, 4. The numeral 7 does not appear in the proportions, for it is a "mysterious" and "holy" number. It "rests" as God rested on the Sabbath, the seventh day of creation.

Cosmological Musical Concepts

The speculative and expressive components of the musical discipline were brought into a balanced equilibrium in Lutheran musical thought during the Renaissance and Baroque eras. Fundamental to this concept of music is the assumption that God created all things according to the orderly principles of measure, number, and weight. This order becomes the underlying principle and governing force behind every element of creation. It reflects the image of God and provides the "common denominator" between God and the various elements of the universe, including both its macrocosmic and microcosmic components. God is thereby reflected in both the universal macrocosm and the human microcosm. The same cosmological relationships which exist between God and his creation are also to be found between the three musical orders. While the universal *musica mundana* is perceived as a macrocosmic reflection

---

4. Andreas Werckmeister, "Von der Zahlen geheimen Deutung," *Musicalische Paradoxal-Discourse* (Quedlinburg, 1707), 92ff.

of the Divine Creator, *musica humana* reflects God in the microcosmic human form, both of these musical manifestations being speculative and inaudible. Furthermore, humankind can use the divinely ordained natural laws to bring the numerical proportions to sound through *musica instrumentalis*. Music thereby becomes an audible manifestation of the Divine, reflecting the creative mathematical principles which lie at the heart of the universe as well as the proportions and relationships of the human mind, body, and spirit.

In addition to being a passive reflection of divine and universal numerical principles, music is also an active agent, affecting specifically the human spirit and body. This is accomplished through the audible expression of the numerical proportions which music has in common with the macrocosm and ultimately with God. "For the same musical proportions constitute the human soul and body, as we have heard. When a person perceives these proportions through sounding tones, his likeness is thereby correspondingly held before him, providing him with pleasure."[5] When the divine essence is audibly realized, the human being will naturally and involuntarily resonate accordingly, analogous to the principle of sympathetic vibrations: "For it cannot be otherwise, than that an individual's temperament is moved and controlled through well-written music. For an individual is both inwardly and outwardly, spiritually and physically a divinely created harmonic being. . . . Because he is a musical blueprint (a veritable formula of music), the individual will naturally find pleasure when his own likeness is presented to him through the musical proportions."[6] Music thereby acts as

---

5. "Darnach hat auch der Mensch die Gleichheit der Musicalischen Proportionen in seiner Seele / und äuβerlichen Gliedern / wie wir gehöret haben / wann nun der Mensch solche durch die Sonos vernimmt / so wird ihm dadurch ebenmässig sein Eben-Bild vorgestellet / an welchen er sich belustigen kan." Werckmeister, *Paradoxal-Discourse*, 25.

6. "Und es kann auch nicht anders seyn, als daβ Gemüth des Menschen durch eine wohlgesetzte Music muβ regieret und beweget werden. Denn ein Mensch ist so wohl innerl. als äuβerlich, geist- und leibl. ein von Gott erschaffenes harmonisches Wesen. . . . Weil nun der Mensch ein rechtes Formular der Music ist, so belustiget er sich freylich, wenn ihm sein Ebenbild durch musicalische Proportiones vorgestellet wird." Walther, *Praecepta*, 75. Similarly Werckmeister: "Wenn nun ein wohlgesinneter Mensch eine Music höret / so empfindet sein Gemüthe zwar die Lieblichkeit / so den Schöpfer geordnet / aber er weiβ doch nicht die Uhrsache / wo ihn nicht die Zahlen

an ethical force, influencing the individual through its reflection of the divine Creator. "Is it not marvelous to recognize that music finds its origin in God, and that as His image, we can harmonize with God!"[7] Furthermore, not only does music present an individual with his own likeness, "(namely that he is harmonically created), but God is also reminded of His own divine wisdom, providing Him with pleasure."[8] For this reason the human endeavor of music-making is a delight both to God and humankind.

Just as *musica practica* serves to praise God and edify the listener, so too do the speculations of *musica theoretica* serve to glorify God. Luther's familiar quote, "next to Theology, I give music the highest place," is not an empty statement in simple praise of music. Rather, it points to the importance of the speculative discipline of *musica theoretica* in uncovering and explaining the mysteries of the universe. The very role of music was to make arithmetic audible and could not therefore be simply a speculative exercise. Of this Leibnitz writes in 1712: "Music is a hidden arithmetical exercise which 'counts off' (*se numerare*) subconsciously in the soul."[9] In music's mathematical order, the order of creation is revealed, manifesting God's wisdom and creative power. In the words of Werckmeister: "Nothing of the natural order can be discovered in music unless *ratio*, that is *arithmetica* and *mathesis* first point out the right way."[10] Again Werckmeister: "We call that natural which can be comprehended by sense and ratio . . . in accordance with God's creation and ordering of all things."[11]

---

dahin gebracht hätten / und ihm die Proportiones harmonicas, welche von Gott geordnet / gezeiget hätten." *Paradoxal-Discourse*, 25.

7. "Ist das nun nicht ein groβes/ daβ wir wiβen wie die Music ihrem Uhrsprung aus Gott habe / und daβ wir als Ebenbilde Gottes / mit Gott harmoniren können." Ibid., 28.

8. "Denn durch die Music wird dem Menschen nicht allein sein Ebenbild (neml. daβ er harmonisch zubereitet sey) vorgelegt; sondern es wird auch Gott seine göttl. Weiβheit vorgehalten, darinnen Er sich belustiget." Walther, *Praecepta*, 14.

9. "Musica est exercitium arithmeticae occultum nescientis se numerare animi." Leibnitz, in a letter to mathematician Goldbach, cited in Dammann, *Musikbegriff*, 79.

10. "Es kann aber in Musicis nichts natürliches geschlossen und erkandt werden, wo nicht ratio, das ist Arithmetica und Mathesis vorher den rechten Weg zeigeten." Cited in Eggebrecht, "Über Bachs geschichtlichen Ort," 266.

11. "Wir nennen dasjenige natürlich / was unsere Sinne und Vernunfft begreifen können . . . wie Gott alle Dinge in der Welt geschaffen und geordnet hat." Andreas Werckmeister, *Musicae mathematicae Hodegus curiosus* (Frankfurt/Leipzig, 1686), 12.

Changing Priorities of Speculative and Practical Music Theory

The purely speculative Boethian concept of music slowly began to lose its dominating position at the dawn of the Renaissance. With the growing concern regarding musical notation and the craft of musical composition, a new categorization of music was introduced which gave greater prominence to matters concerning humanly conceived music. In his *Tetrachordum musicae* (1490) Adam von Fulda, an influential Renaissance music theorist from Wittenberg, redefined *musica instrumentalis* while retaining the categories of *musica mundana* and *musica humana* as two subcategories of *musica naturalis*. He listed as the latter's counterpart *musica artificialis*, under which he reintroduced *musica instrumentalis* and added *musica vocalis*. Thus *musica instrumentalis* graduated from the lowest manifestation of *musica* to one of two categories of *musica artificialis* or "skillfully crafted music," itself now at least on par with *musica naturalis*. Besides incorporating the structuring of intervals and modes, *musica artificialis* also included the various notational and compositional precepts. Throughout the Italian Renaissance the speculative science of music gradually lost ground to the more practical craft of musical composition. The two speculative orders of music, *musica mundana* and *musica humana*, were subsumed into one musical category, *musica theoretica* or *naturalis*, resulting in a bipartite division of the musical discipline into a theoretical and a practical category. In addition, the concept of science itself underwent a change during this period, increasingly referring to the realization of a concept rather than just the concept itself. A science was to be functional rather than purely speculative. It was to be applicable and pertinent to the individual in order to be relevant. The underlying reasons for this change are to be found in the very essence of the Renaissance world view. The human began to replace the Divine as both object and subject of the disciplines. To legitimize this shift in emphasis, the sciences were "humanized" while, at the same time, the arts were given greater credence through scientific explanations and justifications. Furthermore, the linguistic disciplines of the *trivium*, with their emphasis on human communication, became increasingly prominent. This permitted those theorists who chose to continue emphasizing the science of music to legitimately include its practical application. Thus Machaut could already declare: "And music is a science, whose purpose is to make people laugh and sing and dance."[12] The changing perception of the arts and transformed concept of science "humanized" the theory of music, while simultaneously "rationalizing" the craft of composition.

THE RISE OF *MUSICA POETICA*

Throughout the fifteenth and sixteenth centuries, the cosmological focus of *musica* revealed in the numerological abstractions of *musica theoretica* shifted to an anthropological focus revealed in the rhetorical powers of *musica poetica.* This paralleled the Renaissance shift in emphasis from the mathematical *quadrivium* to the linguistic *trivium.* In Italy, this change was accomplished at the dawn of the Baroque era. The musical composition was thus perceived aesthetically rather than speculatively. Music itself had become the language. While Italian Renaissance and Baroque writers tended to adhere to the bipartite divisions of music into *musica theoretica (naturalis, speculativa)* and *musica practica (artificialis)*, some German Lutheran writers began to promote a third category, *musica poetica.* This order of music combined the established truths of *musica theoretica* with the heightened Renaissance concept of the composer as artist, who is called upon to reveal the meaning of the text in and through his music. The speculative medieval tradition was not cast off but rather redefined in the Lutheran north. In reaction to the growing scepticism of medieval speculative music theory Adam von Fulda exclaimed: "The unfortunates! They do not seem to know that Boethius said in the XXXIII chapter of the first book of his Institutione: '*id musicus est, qui ratione perpensa*' (the musician is one who measures by reason)."[13] It was only few years later that Nicolaus Listenius introduced the term *musica poetica* as a genre of musical

12. Cited in Paul Henry Lang, *Music in Western Civilization* (New York: Norton, 1941), 162.

13. Ibid., 60.

composition.[14] In 1563 the term was first used as a title for a compositional treatise by Gallus Dressler,[15] establishing it as a description of both a genre and a discipline. By 1600 a systematic use of rhetorical principles and terminology, including the concept of musical-rhetorical figures, had been established in the *musica poetica* discipline through the writings of Joachim Burmeister.[16] This emphasis on persuasive communication was incorporated by expanding *musica practica* into two subcategories: the traditional *ars cantus*, focusing on the execution of a composition, and the new *musica poetica*, focusing on text-expressive composition. While some German theorists, such as J. G. Walther, included *musica poetica* as a subcategory of *musica practica*, thereby retaining the Italian bipartite classification, others, such as Andreas Herbst, defined it as an independent musical category. In either case, the theoretically informed composer was now given the highest ranking as the true *musicus poeticus*, replacing the medieval *musicus*-theorist. Werckmeister's explanations of the roles of theorist and practitioner clearly point to the superiority of one who has mastered both disciplines. While the theorist only knows the rules but cannot practically apply them (by playing or composing) and while the practitioner can compose or play according to the rules but cannot comprehend or explain them, the ideal musician is expert in both areas.[17]

The concept of divine order remained all important to the German Baroque musician, reflecting the increasing significance of natural rationalism in the context of the cosmologically and theologically

---

14. Nicolaus Listenius, *Rudimenta musicae planae* (Wittenberg, 1533). *Musica poetica* predates the introduction of the term *musica reservata* (first used by Coclico, *Compendium musices*, 1552) and becomes much more widespread and significant, particularly in German circles.

15. Gallus Dressler, *Praecepta musicae poeticae* (Magdeburg, 1563).

16. Joachim Burmeister, *Hypomnematum musicae poeticae* (Rostock, 1599); *Musica poetica* (Rostock, 1606).

17. "Ein Theoreticus kan die Natur der proportionen oder derer Fortschreitung wohl gründlich beschreiben / und gute rationes davon geben / es kan aber demselben an der invention der Zusammensetzung und manirlichen modulation fehlen; Ein Practicus aber kan aus den Regeln / welche ein Theoreticus vorgeschrieben / die manier und modulation auf allerhand Arth verändern / jedoch weiβ er keine rationes von seiner erbauten Harmonia zugeben. . . . Jedoch ist es umb so viel besser / wenn jemand ein Theoreticus und Practicus zugleich seyn kan." Werckmeister, *Musicae mathematicae*, 10.

anchored Protestant view of music. Intellectual understanding recognized order in Nature (arithmetic proportions), a natural order which the musical composition was to reflect. *Ratio* was to be used to discern the power of music, to structure musical compositions, and ultimately to control the affections of the listeners. Even the untrained ear would recognize the beauty of properly composed music, for when "truth" is experienced, it is recognized as such. Conversely, music which did not conform to the natural laws would confuse the ear and would be recognized as chaotic. The further the proportions strayed from the unison (i.e., from God), the more dissonant they would become, the infinite being considered reprehensible and confused.[18]

The Baroque discipline of music attempted to understand and control nature and its harmonic system through this objective rationalism, encouraging the taming of nature as did Baroque gardening, painting, and architecture. Nature itself was to be controlled and harnessed to become what it was destined to have been. Artistic devices, whether in gardening or in music, were to be employed to "correct" nature herself, particularly those aspects of nature where the uncontrolled had run amuck. Humankind, with its higher rationalist insight, could facilitate this. The result would be ultimate truth, the very core of nature. Thus human artful and rational improvements, reprojected upon nature, could illuminate the true essence of nature, realizing in the end that which the Creator had originally intended according to "measure and number and weight." It is in this light that the Baroque concept of the affections and the musical-rhetorical structures, with their mandate to arouse and portray the passions, can best be understood and explained. For just as nature could be tamed, so too could the human temperaments and passions be controlled through orderly and craftfully fashioned artistic devices, ultimately leading to a rhetorical and affective *musica poetica*.

---

18. ". . . so sind es numeri, welche in keine kleine Zahlen können gebracht werden / und bekömmet der Verstand des Menschen gleichsam ein Grauen vor solchen grossen Zahlen / weil sie nicht können begriffen und verstanden werden / darum heiset es hie auch wohl natura ab infinitis abhorret." Werckmeister, *Cribrum musicum oder musicalisches Sieb* (Quedlinburg und Leipzig, 1700), 7f. Also Werckmeister, *Musicae mathematicae*, 13. This rational naturalism, heightened to a dogma during this period, was considered unnatural toward the end of the Baroque era.

Musica Poetica: An Expression of Text and Affection

The objectives of *musica poetica* were summarized by Walther as follows: "*Musica Poetica* or musical composition is a mathematical science through which an agreeable and correct harmony of the notes is brought to paper in order that it might later be sung or played, thereby appropriately moving the listeners to Godly devotion as well as to please and delight both mind and soul. . . . It is so called because the composer must not only understand language as does the poet in order not to violate the meter of the text but because he also writes poetry, namely a melody, thus deserving the title *Melopoeta* or *Melopoeus*."[19] As this definition points out, *musica poetica* is essentially vocal music in which the "music-poet" was to present the text in a *Klang-rede* or musical oration. In order ultimately to move the listener to greater Godly devotion, music was to express both the text and its associated affections, two mandates which were either implied or emphasized in most *musica poetica* treatises. Luther had already established text expression as one of music's primary purposes: music is most powerful when united with the Gospel, for in combining the Word with music, God's two most powerful gifts to humanity are forged into one invincible force.[20] While the text convinces the intellect, the music persuades the passions. Furthermore, music was to be used both to express and to explain the text. Just as the sermon is the "living voice of the Gospel," so too is music to "bring the text to life."[21] Luther's interest in present-

19. "Musica Poetica, oder die musicalische Composition ist eine mathematische Wiβenschafft, vermöge welcher man eine liebl. und reine Zusammenstimmung der Sonorum aufsetzet und zu Papier bringet, daβ solche nachmahls kann gesungen oder gespielet werden, den Menschen fürnemlich zu eifriger Andacht gegen Gott dadurch zubewegen, und dann auch das Gehör und Gemüth deβelben zu ergetzen und zu vergnügen . . . wird sie genennet deswegen, weil ein Componist nicht allein die Prosodie so wohl als ein Poet verstehen muβ, damit er nicht wieder die quantitaet der Sylben verstoβe; sondern auch, weil er ebenfalls etwas dichtet, neml. eine Melodey, von welcher er auch genennet wird Melopoeta oder Melopoeus." *Praecepta*, 75.

20. Söhngen, *Theologie der Musik*, 91ff.

21. "Die rechte Predigt ist *viva vox evangelii* (= lebendige Stimme des Evangeliums), und auch die rechte Music is *viva vox evangelii*: *'Die Noten machen den Text lebendig'* (Tischreden Nr.2545b)." Ibid., 97. The reference to "bringing the text to life"

ing and teaching the Christian message through music also encouraged a German adoption of those styles of music which were limited to the theater in Italy. For it was the text-expressive *stylus theatralis*, including the *stylus recitativus*, which could depict and explain the text most effectively. This style of music also made the best use of the many text-expressive and affection-arousing devices which paralleled the rhetorical figures of speech and thought. The mandate to express and explain the text encouraged not only the development of the concept of musical-rhetorical figures but also led to the introduction of a musical *inventio*, *dispositio*, and *elocutio*, along with the associated rhetorical methods and devices. *Musica poetica* thus adopted literary and rhetorical concepts and language to describe and define its own mandate. The description of a composition and its expressive musical devices in such rhetorical terms first emerged in German circles during the sixteenth century, parallel to the establishment of Lutheran Protestantism. Throughout the seventeenth and eighteenth centuries, *musica poetica* then gradually embraced virtually all of rhetoric's principles and procedures.

While the focus of the musical-rhetorical figures was initially on the text, the expression of the affections through the figures gradually gained prominence, eventually replacing the text's dominating role. In the introduction to the musical-rhetorical figures in his *Musica Poetica*, Burmeister assured the student that "the text itself will present the rules" for their application.[22] In his list of figures Burmeister included such devices as *hypotyposis*, used to express the text in a realistic and life-like manner, and *pathopoeia*, which was most suitable for expressing the text and creating the associated affection. Johann Nucius listed over forty words to be musically expressed at the end of his chapter dealing with the musical-rhetorical figures.[23] The same list also appeared in Andreas Herbst's treatise.[24] Adopted from Nucius were the "affective words" (*verba affectuum*): rejoicing, weeping, fearing, wailing, mourn-

---

is unmistakably reminiscent of the rhetorical figure of speech, *hypotyposis*. See *Hypotyposis* in part 3, below.

22. See p.97, n.10, below.

23. Johannes Nucius, *Musices poeticae sive de compositione cantus* (Niesse, 1613), G3^{v}.

24. Johann Andreas Herbst, *Musica poetica sive compendium melopoeticum* (Nürnberg, 1643), 111.

ing, pleading, raging, laughing, pitying; "words of motion and place": standing, running, dancing, resting, leaping, lifting, lowering, ascending, descending, heaven, hell, mountain, abyss, heights, etc.; "adverbs of time and number": quickly, fast, soon, slowly, early, late, twice, thrice, four times, again, once more, often, rarely; and other words such as light, day, night, darkness. Herbst also included words describing human states: childhood, youth, old age; and human mores: haughty, humble, contemptuous, inferior, odious. By the end of the century, Daniel Speer would almost double Nucius's list of words.[25] A similar albeit much shorter list was presented by Bernhard in his introduction to the figures used in the *stylus theatralis*, a style most closely linked to the expression of the text.[26] Kircher repeatedly stressed affection and text expression both in his introductory comments and definitions of the figures, shifting the emphasis of the musical-rhetorical figures from an elaborative to an expressive concept. The text was to be depicted and made present and alive through the music. This concept of vividly expressing the "idea" of the text through the music was also underscored by Mauritius Vogt, who called his expressive musical-rhetorical figures *figurae ideales*. Like Nucius and Thuringus before him, Vogt encouraged the composer to emulate the painter, "placing the beautiful or frightful images life-like before the eyes of the listeners through the music."[27] Johann Ahle's discussion of the musical figures was based entirely on the literary figures. The composer was to reflect musically not only the syllables, accents, and caesurae but also the rhetorical figures which were found in the text. The natural expression of the text was also underscored by Mattheson, who devoted a number of chapters of his *Der vollkommene Capellmeister* to this matter. However, with Mattheson, and especially Scheibe and Forkel, the centrality of a text gave way to general affective expression, equally important and possible in purely instrumental music. By the early eighteenth century, *musica poetica*'s emphasis on text expression was superseded by the call to portray and arouse the affec-

---

25. *Vierfaches musikalisches Kleeblatt* (Ulm, 1697), 283. Nucius's and Speer's lists are cited in Hans-Heinrich Unger, *Die Beziehungen zwischen Musik und Rhetorik im 16.–18. Jahrhundert* (Würzburg: Triltsch, 1941), 38. See *Hypotyposis* for Speer's list.

26. See p.116, below. See also *Hypotyposis*.

27. See p.128, n.89, below.

tions, gradually giving way to the emerging Enlightenment mandate to express an individual's sentiments.

A Changing Musical Aesthetic

The *numerus*-oriented concept of seventeenth-century German Baroque music underwent a fundamental transformation during the following century. In music, as in all other artistic disciplines, the equilibrium between *sensus* and *ratio* which the Renaissance had established would be upset in the eighteenth century. In a Zeitgeist which sought to determine aesthetic principles on the basis of empirically discerned personal experience, the influential role of the speculative perception of music was increasingly called into question. The first indications of this change can be traced back to the sixteenth-century reevaluation of the legitimacy of the third as a consonance. While this modern approach determined the concept of music at the beginning of the Italian Baroque, resulting in an early rejection of an aesthetic based on *numerus*, the mathematical-theologically oriented understanding of music in Lutheran Germany held its own into the eighteenth century. Writing at the close of the seventeenth century, Wolfgang Caspar Printz still pointed to the authority of *ratio* over *sensus*: "Although we have two judges in music, *ratio* or the intellect and *sensus* or the ear, it is imperative that while they should agree, *ratio* retains the upper hand and does not allow the ear the freedom to judge independently, unless it is absolutely unavoidable. For if the ear is given the upper hand and is allowed the freedom to judge independently, then absolutely nothing could be verified with certainty in music."[28] Not only is this musical *ratio* still rooted in speculative mathematics, but so is its calculable effect, a point which Johann Kuhnau emphasized a few years later: "Music belongs among

28. "Wir haben zwar in der Music zween Richter / Rationem, die Vernunfft / und Auditum, das Gehöre / jedoch dergestalt / daß beyde mit einander übereintreffen / und doch Ratio die Ober-Hand behalte / und dem Gehöre niemahls die Freyheit gönne allein zu judiciren / es erfordere es dann eine unumbgängliche Nothwendigkeit. Denn wenn das Gehör die Ober-Hand und die Freyheit allein zu judiciren haben solte / so würde man in Musicis gantz nichts Gewisses schliessen können." Wolfgang Caspar Printz, *Phrynis Mytilenaeus, oder Satyrischer Componist* (Dresden/Leipzig, 1696), pt.3, 84.

the mathematical sciences and is therefore axiomatic."[29] However, Kuhnau's illustrious student Johann David Heinichen was of quite a different mind on this matter. As if arguing directly against Printz (and all others who shared Printz's views including his own teacher) Heinichen stated: "Musicians of the past, we know, chose two judges in music: Reason and the Ear. . . . It wrongly classed the two judges and placed the Ear, the sovereign of music, below the rank of Reason. . . . [Present-day musicians] return to the oppressed Ear the sovereignty of its realm; . . . but otherwise, [if] Reason differs in opinion, it must serve [the Ear] with complete obedience and employ all of its skill, not for the visual appearance on paper, but to give the Ear the satisfaction of an absolute ruler."[30] Walther's earlier definition of *musica poetica* as a "mathematical science" (*Praecepta*) was also noticeably revised in his *Lexicon*: "*Musica Poetica* . . . the name given to musical composition, or the art [!] of inventing melodies and arranging consonances with dissonances."[31] The changing concept of music in Germany was unequivocally and explicitly emphasized by Mattheson, who went to considerable length to discredit the speculative-mathematical concept of music: "I am therefore basically still of the same opinion, . . . namely that not a grain of musical substance can be found in arithmetic. . . . It is Nature which produces sound, including all the as yet undiscovered proportions. . . . Mathematics is like a pen, and the notes the ink, but Nature must do the writing. . . . Mathematics is only a human art; but Nature is a Divine power."[32] While still accepting a theological rele-

---

29. "Die Music gehöret unter die Mathematischen Wissenschaften und hat folgendlich unfehlbare Demonstrationes." Johann Kuhnau, *Musicalische Vorstellung einiger Biblischer Historien* (Leipzig, 1700; new ed. K. Stone, New York: Broude, 1953), xi.

30. Cited in George Buelow, *Thorough-Bass Accompaniment according to Johann David Heinichen*, revised ed. (Ann Arbor: UMI Research Press, 1986), 278f.

31. "Musica Poetica . . . also heisset die eigentlich also genannte musicalische Composition, oder die Kunst, Melodien zu erfinden, und die con- und dissonirende Klänge mit einander zu vermischen." Johann Gottfried Walther, *Musicalisches Lexicon* (Leipzig, 1732).

32. "Der Satz: Daβ die Mathematik bey der Musik nichts helffe, ist unrichtig, und bedarff einer guten Erläuterung . . . daβ die Mathematik der Musik Herz und Seele sey; daβ alle Gemüths-Veränderungen, so durch Singen und Klingen hervorgebracht werden, bloβ in den verschiedenen äusserlichen Verhältnissen der Töne ihren Grund haben, solches ist noch viel ärger und irriger, als obiger Ausspruch. . . . Des Herzens Bewegung hat demnach ihren Grund, d.i. ihre Ursache, ihren Ursprung nimmermehr in den blossen

vance of music theory, the mathematical explanation of music became subservient to the empirical realm of natural experience. This reorientation placed a subjective and individualistic slant on musical interpretation, consequently preparing the way for the eighteenth-century *Empfindsamkeit* aesthetic. Objectivity gave way to subjectivity, mathematics to nature, science to expression, and the Baroque to the Enlightenment.

In summary, throughout the seventeenth century, general musical thought in Lutheran Germany continued to revolve around theocentric, mathematical-scientific concepts inherited from medieval music theory. However, influenced by Renaissance thought and Lutheran theology, significant revisions of the purely speculative perception of music resulted in a "humanized" understanding of the discipline. The human *sensus* became as important as *ratio* in determining music's effects, illustrated by the admittance of the third as a musical consonance. The purpose of music as an effective as well as affective means of communication made the practical discipline of composition more prominent than its theoretical counterpart. But instead of dismissing the speculative acoustical science of music as irrelevant, German writers sought to incorporate Lutheran theology and Boethian mathematics into the flourishing understanding of music as a humanistic art form. With the growing Renaissance and Lutheran emphasis on the *trivium*, linguistic and rhetorical concepts became significant elements of musical composition, resulting in a uniquely German *musica poetica*. The Lutheran emphasis on exegesis of the Word coupled with the Renaissance emphasis on the linguistic disciplines resulted in a concept of music which elevated the expression of the text and its associated affections

---

Klängen und Wörtern. . . . Denn die Seele, als ein Geist, wird empfindlich gerühret. Wodurch? wahrlich nicht durch die Klänge an und für sich, noch durch ihre Grösse, Gestalt und Figur allein; sondern hauptsächlich durch deren geschickte, immer neuersonnene, und unerschöpfliche Zusammenfügung. . . . Ich bin also im Grunde noch eben der Meynung . . . daβ nehmlich in der Rechenkunst kein Schein des musikalischen Fundaments stecket. . . . Die Natur bringt den Klang, und alle seine, auch die grössesten Theils noch unbekannte Verhältnisse hervor. . . . Mathesis ist die Feder. Klänge sind die Dinte; aber die Natur muβ der Schreiber seyn. . . . Mathesis ist eine menschlich Kunst; Natur aber eine Göttliche Krafft." Mattheson, *Vorrede, Der vollkommene Capellmeister* (Hamburg, 1739), 16–22.

above all else. Although few authors went to quite the same length as Werckmeister in order to establish the relationships between theology, science, and art, the synthesis of these disciplines was a central element of *musica poetica*. It was now the art of composition rather than the discipline of *musica* which had become the mathematical science. Most authors of German music treatises were established and prominent musicians, holding positions as either Lutheran organists or *Kantors*, not simply theorists contemplating musical mysteries in ivory towers. It was the *musicus poeticus*, the theoretically informed composer and performer, who was now regarded as the ultimate musician. He was to use all available resources to portray and arouse the appropriate affections, including the various rhetorical procedures and devices. With all the theological, rhetorical, and musical tools at his disposal, the *melopoeticus* could move the affections of the listener at will, ultimately to the glory of God and to the edification of the listener.

Musica poetica remained a unique concept of music, one which sought to balance science and art, *ratio* and *sensus*, speculation and craft. Its primary purpose was rooted in moving the listener through affective text interpretation and through a musical representation of the cosmic order. The compositional emphasis of *musica poetica* solved the dilemma of focusing on the text while retaining the speculative nature of *musica theoretica* by assimilating the principles of rhetoric and mathematics. This synthesis of science and art not only laid the groundwork for the rational approach to the concept of the affections, subject matter which until then had remained in the domain of the *trivium* discipline of rhetoric, but allowed the inclusion of the concept of the temperaments, subject matter which was traditionally part of the medical discipline. Medieval cosmology, Protestant theology, and rhetorical artistry all combined to this end. Throughout the eighteenth century the governing mathematically oriented concept of music was called into question, resulting in the eventual replacement of *numerus* with *natura*. While affective and rhetorical principles became increasingly influential in musical construction, the speculative understanding of music lost its predominant position, preparing the way for the dawn of *Empfindsamkeit*.

The Concept of the Affections in German Baroque Music

Whereas all of music's pleasantness grows chiefly out of her ability to move heart and spirit . . . Johann Andreas Herbst (1643)

The composer always ought to work towards achieving the intended affection in his composition. Mauritius Vogt (1719)

In summary, everything that occurs without affections, means nothing, does nothing, and is worth nothing. Johann Mattheson (1739)

Since antiquity the concept of the affections has been associated with both music and rhetoric. While music's power over the human emotions was never denied throughout the medieval or Renaissance eras, the portrayal and arousal of the affections became the intended purpose, indeed, the very essence of all Baroque music. Werckmeister asserted that music "is ordered to arouse, correct, alter, and calm the passions."[1] At the height of German musical rhetoric, Johann Mattheson claimed that "the goal of all melody is none other than a gratification of the ear through which the affections of the soul are aroused."[2] Meinrad Spiess said of the affections: "to arouse and to still the same is music's one and only goal."[3] While the various Baroque styles and traditions throughout Europe shared this general concept of affective music, the specifically German view was based on an attempt to rationally understand and explain the underlying physiological phenomena, coupled with the singular interest in the structuring principles furnished by the

---

1. Andreas Werckmeister, *Musicalisches Send-Schreiben* (Quedlinburg, 1700), 11

2. "Weil inzwischen das rechte Ziel aller Melodie nichts anders seyn kan, als eine solche Vergnügung des Gehörs, dadurch die Leidenschafften der Seele rege werden." Mattheson, *Capellmeister*, 207, §31. In §30, Mattheson speaks of the difference between vocal and instrumental music, pointing out that although words become superfluous, instrumental music cannot dispense with the expression of the affections.

3. "Leidenschaften. Affectus. Bey denen Menschen zu erregen, oder zu stillen, ist der Music einziges Zihl." Meinrad Spiess, *Tractatus musicus compositorio-practicus* (Augsburg, 1745); cited in Dammann, *Musikbegriff*, 215.

rhetorical discipline in order to fulfill the mandate of *musica poetica.*

German music theorists and composers were of one mind regarding the centrality of expressing the affections but were less unanimous regarding specific methods of expressing them. As Buelow has pointed out, the assumption frequently encountered in modern music scholarship—that there existed a certain Doctrine of the Affections or *Affektenlehre*—becomes untenable when one examines the many Baroque sources.[4] Virtually every writer admonished the composer to examine the text which was to be set to music for affective words or implied affections. Many writers ascribed certain affective qualities to the various church modes, although few agreed on specific details. Others suggested that certain affections might be portrayed through specific dance genres, types of rhythm, or literary forms. The generally accepted affective nature of the various intervals also led some writers to suggest certain interval combinations for representing affections. While all of these suggestions were no doubt legitimate methods of expressing the affections, particularly for those writers who were suggesting them, a generally valid doctrine or *Lehre* cannot be discerned. What can be established, however, is the general principle of expressing the affections. The primary goal of Baroque music is defined by the composer's intent to objectively present a rationalized emotional state referred to as an affection, as diverse as this process may have been. This principle or concept of the affections is rooted in the rhetorical discipline, which was becoming increasingly influential, particularly in German compositional theory. The concepts of rhetoric and the affections were eventually to center on the musical-rhetorical figures, which were referred to as "the very language of the affections."[5] In order to elucidate this high calling of musical-rhetoric, it will be necessary first to discuss the concept of the affections, focusing primarily on general principles rather than on specific methods of their expression.

---

4. George Buelow, "Johann Mattheson and the invention of the *Affektenlehre*," *New Mattheson Studies*, ed. G. J. Buelow and H. J. Marx (Cambridge: Cambridge University Press, 1983), 393.

5. "Kann man wohl ohne sie die Gemüthsbewegungen erregen und ausdrücken? Keinesweges. Die Figuren sind ja selbst eine Sprache der Affecten." Johann Adolf Scheibe, *Der critische Musicus* (Leipzig, 1745), 683.

Music and the Affections

The original Greek term, *pathos*, was understood as an ailment or malady resulting in a passive condition of the person. The Latin translation of *pathos*, *affectus*, is rooted in the verb *adficere*, meaning to work upon, influence, affect.[6] Both Plato and Aristotle were concerned about the power of music and its influence on the human spirit, leading them to suggest specific uses of certain kinds of music based on the ethos of the specific Greek modes. Quintilian, whose *Institutio oratoria* became the most influential classical rhetorical source in the Renaissance, called for music that "excites generous feelings and calms disordered passions."[7] The Stoics retained the early Greek negative view of the affections, regarding them as unnatural. Desiring an impassioned stance or condition, Stoicism demanded complete mastery over the passions. Both terms, *passio* and *affectus*, were used by early Christian writers, including Augustine. Here the concept of the affections was expanded to include both constructive and destructive passions, including human virtues and sins. The ethical and healing power of music was promulgated in music treatises throughout the Middle Ages and into the Baroque era. Biblical stories describing music's power were added to the traditional classical myths, thereby blending Christian and Greco-Roman musical values.

With the increasing importance of the linguistic disciplines in the Renaissance and the simultaneous "humanization" of musical thought, a new emphasis on text expression began to replace the classical-medieval significance of speculative music. A long list of Renaissance writers advocated the musical expression of the affections discerned in a composition's text. As Zarlino pointed out, the primary concern

---

6. Both "affection" and "affect" have been used in English scholarship. "Affect" underscores the importance of the concept in German music theory (German: *Affekt*), while at the same time distancing this concept of rationalized emotional states from the modern meaning of "affection." However, recent scholarship has tended to favor the English term "affection," a usage which is adopted in this book.

7. *Institutio oratoria (De musica)*, i.11; cited in Claude Palisca, "Ut Oratoria Musica: The Rhetorical Basis of Musical Mannerism," *The Meaning of Mannerism*, ed. F. Robinson and S. Nichols Jr. (Hanover NH: University Press of New England, 1972), 39.

should be directed towards a proper and appropriate setting of the words, "so that everything may be done with proportion."[8] Through correct text declamation and sensitive text expression, words and music were to be brought into a balanced equilibrium. The concern of sixteenth-century writers and musicians was not so much to move the listener as to express the words. Renaissance theorists and composers alike regarded the text as the object of affective expression.

Baroque Music and the Affections

Although the affective role of music remained fundamental throughout both the Renaissance and the Baroque eras, the exhilarated spirit of the Baroque called for a heightened expressiveness. The Renaissance balance between text and music was disturbed, resulting in a musical mannerism which exaggerated the role of text expression beyond the limits of the Renaissance artistic ideal. While the Renaissance sought to portray a balanced view of the affections, the Baroque wanted to arouse and move the human spirit to its passionate extremes. Music was actively to create the intended affections, not just passively reflect them. Compositions were to both portray *and* arouse the affections in the listener. To the Renaissance *affectus exprimere* the Baroque added *affectus movere*. It was no longer enough simply to present the affection objectively through the music: the listener was to be drawn into the drama of the presentation, to be emotionally affected himself. The Baroque composer wanted to move the listener to a heightened emotional state. It was now the listener and not the text that had become the object of the composition.

---

8. "For if the poet is not permitted to write a comedy in tragic verse, the musician will also not be permitted to combine unsuitably these two things, namely, harmony and words. Thus it will be inappropriate if in a joyful matter he uses a mournful harmony and a grave rhythm. . . . On the contrary, he must use joyful harmonies and rapid rhythms in joyful matters, and in mournful ones, mournful harmonies and grave rhythms, so that everything may be done with proportion." G. Zarlino, *Le institutioni harmoniche*, 4, 32, as translated in Oliver Strunk, *Source Readings in Music History* (New York: Norton, 1950), 256.

The Affections and the *Numerus*

The move toward a greater affective musical expressiveness did not initially cancel the fundamental importance of the speculative mathematical understanding of music in Germany. Rather, the physical and psychological musical elements were to be in resonance with each other and with rationally discernable natural laws. Fundamental to this argument was the belief that all creation is rooted in, reflects, and longs for a natural order, the *unitas*, which is the essence of the Creator himself. Music would reflect this universal order by virtue of its harmonic proportions. When confronted with this truth, the human spirit would instinctively recognize it as such and resonate accordingly.[9] The controlling factor found in the numerical proportions of the musical intervals guaranteed a predictable reaction in the listener to the musically created affection. The subjective expression of a personal sentiment or feeling, so familiar to us through a nineteenth-century aesthetic, is quite foreign to this understanding of music. The intended affection remains an objectively conceptualized state of mind. At the very heart of the Baroque concept of the affections lay a quasi-Newtonian premise of law and order, action and reaction, mutually accepted by musician and audience. Based on such rational explanations, the Baroque composer could count on a calculated emotional response from the listener, thus controlling the emotional state of the listener through the music's power. He had a concrete and well-defined understanding of the affections. The desired affection could be presented and aroused through the appropriate mode or key, time signature and tempo, figure and cadence, along with the entire arsenal of rhetorical methods and devices.

The Lutheran *melopoeta* regarded it as his mandate to use this rhetorically motivated divine power of music appropriately to arouse and move the affections in the hearts of the listeners. Effective and affective musical text-setting would move the devout listener to greater

---

9. "Denn gleichwie aus Gott / als dem einigen Wesen alles Gute herfließet / und was dem an Nechsten verwandt / eine Harmoniam mit ihm machet: Und was gar zu weit von demselben entfernet / mit ihm gar nicht harmoniret. Also mercket daßelbe auch unser Gemüthe in der harmonia durch die Zahlen / wenn sie zum klange gebracht werden." Werckmeister, *Paradoxal-Discourse*, 92.

piety and Godly devotion. The music of the church was therefore not to limit itself to archaic or austere styles but rather to use those devices and styles which had been proven effective in stirring the affections in secular music, particularly in opera. In 1721 the Lutheran theologian Gottfried Scheibel published a music treatise, *Zufällige Gedancken von der Kirchenmusic*, in which he deplored the attacks of the *Zwingelianer* who were opposed to the inclusion of the modern *stylus theatralis* in church music. He valued music's role in moving the affections of the worshipers in harmony with the Word of God. He also supported the practice of parodying operatic music by substituting appropriate sacred words for the secular text, adding, "I do not understand why the opera alone should have the privilege to move us to tears, and why this is also not appropriate to the church."[10] The audience for its part did not assume an aesthetic-reflective or distanced and critical stance. The presented affection enveloped the listener, causing a direct and spontaneous reaction. He was not free to control himself; rather he was controlled by the realized affection, spontaneously breaking into laughter or weeping, sorrow or longing, rage or contentment. Numerous contemporary eyewitness accounts refer to the intensity and grand effect of such affection-arousing compositions, causing the entire audience to break spontaneously into sobbing and wailing.[11]

The Baroque affective musical devices were considered learnable and teachable, analogous to the mathematical and rhetorical-linguistic aspects of music theory. In order to have access to and take advantage of music's affective power, it was considered possible to undertake a rational analysis of music and to objectively identify its God-given power. The German Baroque composer still viewed the act of composition as a craft rather than an aesthetic undertaking. Like all other disciplines, music was taught by learning the rules, studying the established examples, and imitating the works of the masters. The triumvirate

---

10. George Buelow, "Scheibel," *New Grove Dictionary*, 16: 601.

11. "Die Bewegung ist oftmal so groß und hefftig / daß die auditores überlaut anfangen zu schreien / seufzen / weinen / sonderlich in casibus tragicis, daß auch in diesem Stück die heutige Music der alten nichts bevor gibt." Kircher, *Musurgia Universalis*, in the translation of Andreas Hirsch, *Artis magnae de consono & Dissono Ars Minor; Das ist / Philosophischer Extract* (Schwäbisch-Hall, 1662), 134; cited in Dammann, *Musikbegriff*, 228.

of *praeceptum, exemplum, et imitatio* was as important to the subject of music as it was to rhetoric. In order to master the discipline of composition, the Baroque composer therefore spent much time copying and then imitating the works of established masters. Together with the study and acquisition of theoretical knowledge, the composer also practiced his empirical skills by observing human behavior, recognizing as well as analyzing psychological phenomena on the basis of acquired theoretical knowledge. The Baroque composition was not a result of inspiration, subjective experience, or the "outpouring of a lonely soul." Rather, it was calculated "in cold blood," as Mattheson puts it.[12] Initially this was based on acquired knowledge, which could certainly include—but not necessarily—a past personal experience of the intended affection.

During the course of the eighteenth century, the need to have personally experienced the affection was increasingly emphasized to the point that, at the dawn of *Empfindsamkeit*, experience rather than rational knowledge of the affection was considered of paramount importance. Mattheson, who would put so much emphasis on a disciplined rhetorical approach to composition, sought to discover the root of the affection in its personal experience rather than in the *numerus*.[13] The musical-mathematical discipline became subservient to the empirical realm of natural experience. In a significant reversal of Werckmeister's understanding of music, Mattheson contended that "Mathematics is a human art; Nature, however, a Divine force."[14] This is also reflected in the determination of the source of the rhetorical figures: writers on rhetoric as well as music increasingly pointed to natural linguistic and musical expression as the source for expressive compositional devices rather than to traditional scholastic sources and writings.

---

12. "Die Erfindung will Feuer und Geist haben; die Einrichtung Ordnung und Maasse; die Ausarbeitung kalt Blut und Bedachtsamkeit." *Capellmeister*, 241. See also *Mimesis*, below, for an explication of *imitatio*.

13. "Denn niemand wird geschickt seyn, eine Leidenschafft in andrer Leute Gemüthern zu erregen, der nicht eben dieselbe Leidenschafft so kenne, als ob er sie selbst empfunden hätte, oder noch empfindet." Ibid., 108. "So wird mir ja niemand dieses Ziel treffen, der keine Absicht darauf hat, selber keine Bewegung spüret." Ibid., 207.

14. "Mathesis ist eine menschliche Kunst; Natur aber eine Göttliche Krafft." Ibid., *Vorrede*, 21. Furthermore, "Menschliche Gemüther sind gleichsam das Papier. Mathesis ist die Feder. Klänge sind die Dinte; aber die Natur muß der Schreiber seyn." Ibid., 20.

Thus rhetorical as well as musical expression became increasingly empirical and less theoretical. Human experience rather than dogmatic divine truth gradually became the foundation of a new music aesthetic.

The Affections and the Temperaments: A Musical Pathology

The mid–seventeenth century witnessed the publication of two widely read and influential texts on the subject of the human affections. René Descartes's *Les Passions de l'âme* (1649) was the first modern attempt to develop an all-encompassing, systematic theory of the affections. Not only the reasoning behind the process but the actual physiological process of bodily reaction to the represented affection was subject to rational explanation, resulting in a kind of musical pathology or *musica pathetica.* Only one year later, Athanasius Kircher's *Musurgia universalis* appeared in print in Rome. It is a synoptic, encyclopedic compendium of historic and contemporary musical thought, truly universal in nature. Kircher was a German Jesuit and former professor of sciences working in Rome. His work is a far more detailed and comprehensive tome than Descartes's, incorporating all facets of musical interest. Kircher devoted much of his *Musurgia* to the subject of *musica pathetica*, discussed at great length in the chapter entitled *Quomodo numerus harmonicus affectus moveat* ("How the harmonic numbers arouse the affections"). The desire to link mathematics, and the closely related discipline of medicine, with rhetoric is unmistakable, now in conjunction with the teachings of the four temperaments and humors.

The teachings of the temperaments, going back to Greek medical theory as formulated by Empedocles, Hippocrates, and Galen, remained authoritative into the Baroque era.[15] According to this ancient theory, there are four different human temperaments: melancholic, sanguine, choleric, and phlegmatic. Each temperament is associated with one of the four elements: earth, air, fire, and water. A temperament is deter-

15. Judith Pilszynski, "The Evolvement of the Humoral Doctrine," *Medical Times* 92, 10 (1964), 1009.

mined by a combination of two of the four primary attributes: hot and cold, wet and dry. Each temperament is also associated with a certain body fluid or humor, produced by an internal body organ. The following table summarizes the concept:

Temperament	Sanguine	Choleric	Melancholic	Phlegmatic
Humor & Organ:	Blood Heart	Yellow Bile Liver	Black Bile Spleen	Phlegm Brain
Elements & Planet:	Air Mercury	Fire Mars	Earth Saturn	Water Neptune
Attributes:	Hot & Wet	Hot & Dry	Cold & Dry	Cold & Wet
Season: Time of Day: Age:	Spring Morning Youth	Summer Noon Young Adult	Fall Evening Older Adult	Winter Night Aged
Affections:	Love, Joy	Anger, Fury	Sorrow, Pain	Peacefulness, Moderate Joy, Sorrow

Every human being is governed by a certain temperament according to the individual's physiology, which is determined, in part, astrologically at time of birth. A personality will reflect those affections associated with its corresponding temperament more prominently than other affections. An imbalance in the humors results in a pathogenic condition. Furthermore, an external affective stimulus (music or otherwise) will influence an individual with the corresponding affective inclination much more strongly than those individuals governed by contrasting temperaments. The individual is thereby inclined to suffer from some afflictions (due to an overemphasis of a particular affection) more easily than others.

An individual is moved to certain affections by a process which involves a change in balance of the four humors in the body. When appropriately aroused by external stimuli, the affected body organ produces its corresponding humor, which enters the blood stream in a gaseous state. The vaporous humor then combines with the *spiritus animalis* (Descartes: *esprits animaux*; German: *Lebensgeister*). Descartes considers these the smallest subparticles in the blood, a kind of ether. The "humored" *spiritus animalis* then rise from the blood and enter the nerves, described as hollow, tubular tissue. Thus they travel through the body, affecting all body functions and parts, including the humor-producing organs and the brain. These vapors also influence the soul, which was thought to be situated in the pineal gland.[16] This process would result in the corresponding affection, a physio-psychological condition which would last until another affection was evoked.

The effect of music on the human psyche was understood as just one of the affection-arousing stimuli. The numerical proportions, which are at the root of all created matter and life, are the same ones which are reflected by the musical intervals. Thus music, the audible form of the numerical proportions, facilitates an aural perception of the realities which lie at the root of all natural phenomena. The properties of the air which is set in motion through the music is analogous to the music itself, both consisting of the same proportions. These proportions then enter the body via the ear, thereby setting the corresponding physiological functions in process and resulting in the appropriate affection. The numerical proportions embodied in the music, the "outer air," sets the *spiritus animalis*, the "inner air," into motion, which in turn motivates the humors.[17] For this process to function satisfactorily, it is necessary that both the text and the accompanying music express the same affection, and not contradict each other. The quadrivial and the trivial

---

16. The pineal gland is situated near the hypothalamus, at the base of the brain. It presently has no known function, although its tiny follicles suggest a glandular function. It seems to have some calcium-containing bits that medical researchers have descriptively dubbed "brain sand." Although some aspects of the concept of the temperaments seem quite far-fetched to a modern mind, the similarity between the humors and the hormones is an intriguing one.

17. "Vorausgesetzt nun / daβ die einige proportion des numeri relati, in welchem die qualitates disponiret sind / das praedominium derer passionen oder Gemüths-Bewegungen machet / und daβ die unterschiedliche Vermischungen des numeri relati die Ursachen der unterschiedenen harmonien sind / so ist gar leicht zu schliessen / daβ eben dieselbigen proportiones, welche sich in denen qualitatibus befinden / auch in denen harmonien gesucht werden können; daher es dann kommt / daβ / wenn jemand eine gewisse disposition oder Ordnung harmonischer proportion höret / daβ sie mit denen übereinstimmen / in welcher in ihm bemeldte qualitäten disponiret sind / so ist gewiβ / daβ die passio, welche ihn überherrschet / dadurch gereitzet und vermehret wird / und zwar dieses um deswillen / weil gleich und gleich nach einander begierde trägt." Werckmeister, *Musicalisches Send-Schreiben*, 60. (This Werckmeister work is an expanded translation of Agostino Steffani's *Quanta certezza* [1659]). Cited in Dammann, *Musikbegriff*, 250.

principles must cooperate. Were a composer fully to comprehend and master these principles, he would be able to arouse any desired affection.

Listeners' different reactions to hearing the same music was also rationally explained. The varying temperaments of different individuals would predispose them to stronger reactions to different affections. For example, a melancholic person would react much more readily and vehemently to melancholic music than would someone of a choleric character. This is due to the fact that the melancholic temperament, along with the already dominant corresponding humor, would be that much more receptive to the arousal of an affection parallel to its own nature. This understanding prompted Morely to speak of "diverse men diversely affected to diverse kinds of music,"[18] and Werckmeister to assure that "the melancholic or passionate person very much appreciate the correct use of dissonance."[19] Not only would "diverse men" react differently to various affections, but they would also be attracted to music corresponding to their individual "temperamental" predispositions. In fact, an individual's predominant temperament could be discerned from his musical preference.[20] These variables also precluded a systematic and generally valid "Doctrine" of the affections. Those musical devices and idioms which might arouse a certain passion in one listener may not succeed to the same degree in another listener. This becomes particularly evident in the discussion of modal and tonal characteristics. A mode which may suggest a certain affection to one author (composer or listener) may not necessarily evoke the same affection in another.

---

18. Thomas Morely, *A Plaine and Easie Introduction to Practicall Musicke* (London, 1597; new ed., New York: Norton, 1952), 297.

19. "Melancholici und tieffsinnige Leute werden den rechten Gebrauch der Dissonantzen . . . sehr beypflichten." *Musicae mathematicae*, 84.

20. "Derowegen kan man so wohl eines Musici der da Music machet / als eines Zuhörenden Gemüthe / daher ziemlicher maβen erkennen. . . . Ein trauriger und Melancholischer / wird mehr auf traurige Music halten / als auf freudige und lustige Stücke / ein fröhlicher Mensch hingegen wird von der traurigen Harmonie nicht viel halten. Also, wenn einer ein Instrument berühret / so kan man seine Humor und Gemüthe ziemlich daraus erforschen." Werckmeister, *Paradoxal-Discourse*, 38.

The Affections and Modality/Tonality

Renaissance and Baroque theorists and composers frequently stressed that one of the primary considerations regarding the musical expression of the affections should be the choice of a composition's mode or key. Throughout the Middle Ages and the Renaissance, the various church modes had been assigned expressive characteristics analogous to the ethos of the Greek modes. As the Renaissance drew to a close, harmonic concepts were being significantly revised: major-minor tonality was beginning to replace modality, while the expressive characteristics of the modes or keys were being redefined. Although no theorist or composer would have suggested that modes or keys do not contain expressive power, many questioned the validity of associating specific affections with individual modes or keys as had traditionally been done.

Grounded on the assumption that the church modes had developed from Greek forerunners, humanistic zeal encouraged the application of the classical modes' affective ethos qualities to the church modes, resulting in substantial discrepancies between the Greek and the medieval modal characteristics. Unbeknown to Renaissance writers, their church modes had evolved from the Byzantine *octoechoi* rather than the Greek ethos-oriented modes. Not only were there discrepancies between the classical and Renaissance modal characteristics, but, as Mattheson indicated, "neither do today's musicians agree on the character of the keys, nor can any uniformity in the compositions be easily established in this regard, reinforcing the saying: 'Many heads, many minds.'"[21] At times an author might even change his mind on a specific mode's effect. As much as some musicologists may have tried to develop a unified doctrine of key-affections, there is little historical basis for such a thesis.

The changes to modal theory during the Renaissance were inspired not only through rediscovered classical music theory sources but through an evolving and changing harmonic aesthetic. By the sixteenth

---

21. "Gleichwie nun die Alten / also sind auch die heutigen Musici wol schwerlich einerley Meinung in dem was die Eigenschafft der Tohne betrifft / und kan auch nicht leichtlich eine Gleichförmigkeit in allen Stücken hierüber praetendiret werden / massen es wol dabey bleibet: Quot capita, tot sensus." Johann Mattheson, *Das neu-eröffnete Orchestre* (Hamburg, 1712), 231f., §6.

century, the eight medieval ecclesiastical modes had been expanded to twelve through Glareanus's addition of the Aeolian and Ionian modes (plus their plagals). Based on the *finalis* A (Aeolian) and C (Ionian), the two new modes were to become the prototypes for the major and minor scales. Two paths lead toward the gradually emerging major-minor tonality. Beginning with Zarlino, theorists increasingly pointed to two basic classes of modes which were determined by either a major or a minor third above the *finalis*, paralleling the major and minor scales. While the modes which generate a major triad over their *finalis* were to be used to express joyful sentiments, those with a minor triad could express sadder affections. Zarlino thus maintained that "certain compositions are lively and full of cheer, whereas others on the contrary are somewhat sad and languid. . . . Whereas in the first group the major third is often placed beneath the minor, in the second [group] the opposite is true."[22] Zarlino's differentiation between these joyful *modi laetiores* and sad *modi tristiores* was also propagated by Calvisius in his influential *Exercitatio Musica tertia* (1611).[23] It was Johann Lippius (*Synopsis musicae nova*, Strassburg 1612) who "first presented a comprehensive theory of major-minor polarity" differentiating between "two types of mode almost exclusively according to the quality of the 'tonic' triad."[24] In addition to referring to joyful and sad modes, Andreas Herbst at one point mentioned three qualitative differentiations of the modes (joyful, sad yet gentle, and harsh), just as Kircher had pointed to three fundamental affections: joy, pious submission, and sorrow.[25] Johann Kuhnau, J. S. Bach's Leipzig predecessor and Johann Heinichen's teacher, maintained that "the difference between the modes with the major third and the minor third is certainly clearly perceptible, in

22. Rita Steblin, *A History of Key Characteristics in the Eighteenth and Early Nineteenth Centuries* (Ann Arbor: UMI Research Press, 1983), 31.

23. Martin Ruhnke, *Joachim Burmeister: Ein Beitrag zur Musiklehre um 1600* (Kassel: Bärenreiter, 1955), 120f.

24. Joel Lester, "The Recognition of Major and Minor Keys in German Theory: 1680–1730," *Journal of Music Theory* 22 (1978), 65.

25. "Vor allen dingen aber / soll ein solcher modus, welcher mit der materi deß Textes / oder der Wort fein übereinstimmt / elegirt und erwehlet werden: Dann etliche Modi seynd frölich: als 1. 9. 11. Etliche aber traurig und gelind: als 4.6.10. Etliche hart und zornig: als Lydius der fünffte modus." Herbst, *Musica poetica*, 83.

that the former present something perfect and cheerful, while the latter portray a sad, melancholy, and longing spirit."[26] Mattheson also conceded that those "who wish to discover the secret of harmony's power in the major and minor third, with all minor keys being sad and major ones being joyful, are certainly not wrong on all accounts, although they still have much to learn."[27] Furthermore, the frequent additions of a B-flat or an F-sharp to the various modes resulted in transpositions either to the "major" Ionian or the "minor" Aeolian mode. Either way, major-minor tonality gained increasing acceptance throughout the seventeenth century, albeit not always without vociferous objections. It would be misleading to suggest that modes with a minor third above the *finalis* were consistently considered sad and those with a major third joyful. In fact, neither the Dorian nor the Aeolian were usually referred to as particularly sad modes. Conversely, the Lydian mode was frequently regarded as harsh, presumably because of the tritone between its *finalis* and subdominant note. However, if it is altered through the addition of a B-flat (as was frequently done), it would result in a joyful, transposed Ionian mode. Thus the placement of the semi-tone within the notes of the mode or scale of a key also determined its expressive quality.

Not only was the authority of the traditional modes being called into question, but so too was the principle of their distinctive expressive content. Burmeister had already admitted that he had failed to discover the specific power of the different modes as defined by older sources, but had noticed that a composer could express various sentiments using the same mode.[28] A similar opinion was expressed by Burmeister's contemporary, Calvisius.[29] Herbst also "senses, that a whole range of

---

26. "Sonderlich ist die Difference zwischen denen Tonis mit der Tertia majore, und denen mit der minore gar sehr empfindlich / indem jene etwas vollkommenes / und lustiges / diese aber etwas trauriges / melancholisches / und wegen des Mangels eines halben Commatis ohngefehr / oder andern kleinen Theilgens / was sehnliches vorstellen." Kuhnau, *Biblische Historien*, xii.

27. "Diejenigen / die da meinen / es stecke das gantze Geheimniß in der Tertia minore oder majore, und darthun wollen / daß alle molle Tohne / in genere davon zu reden / nothwendig traurig sind / hergegen aber / daß alle dure Tohne gemeiniglich eine lustige Eigenschafft hegen / haben zwar nicht in allen gar zu grosses Unrecht / sie sind aber in der Untersuchung noch nicht weit gekommen." Mattheson, *Orchestre*, 231, §3.

28. Ruhnke, *Burmeister*, 120f.

29. Ibid., 122.

affections can be expressed in one and the same mode or tone," for which reason he felt inclined to further elaborate on the expression of affective words.[30] Similarly, Kuhnau "is surprised, that many musicians and especially those who are familiar with the fundamentals of their art (including the otherwise inquisitive Athanasius Kircher) nonetheless in spite of mathematical principles adhere to the preconceptions of the past and continue to repeat in simple blind faith that each mode has a certain precise effect."[31] Kuhnau's student Heinichen also questioned the validity of specific modal effects, maintaining "that one can express the same words and affections in various and, according to the old theory, opposing keys. For that reason, what previous theorists have written and re-written about the properties of the modes are nothing but trifles, as if one mode could be merry, another sad, a third pious, heroic, war-like, etc. But even if these imaginary properties had any inherent correctness, the slightest change of temperament used for them (which can never be accurately done by the tuner of instruments) and even more changes of *Chorton*, *Kammerton*, French, and the extravagant Venetian tunings would cause continual shipwrecks. In my opinion, the ancient theorists erred in their research of modal characteristics, in the same way as we continue to err today in judging a musical work. . . . It remains the case, therefore, that every single key and all keys or musical modes without distinction are suited to expressing many opposing affections."[32]

Nonetheless, Baroque theorists continued to recommend a careful choice of mode or key in setting a text, frequently listing the expressive characteristics of the various modes, even if the validity of such a list

---

30. "Jedoch weil ich spüre / daß gleichwol inn einem jeden Modo oder Tono, allerley affecten deß Gemüths können exprimirt und außgedrucket werden / als hat mich vor gut angesehen / von dieser Sachen etwas mehrers in specie, und insonderheit zu tractiren und außzuführen. Erstlich müssen die Verba und Wort . . . / wol ponderirt und deroselben Natur und Eygenschafft fleissig in acht genommen und betrachtet werden." Herbst, *Musica poetica*, 111.

31. "Ich selber wundre mich / daß viel Musici, und sonderlich diejenigen / welchen das Fundament ihrer Kunst nicht unbekand ist (darunter ich auch den sonst curieusen Athanasium Kircherum finde) dennoch wider die Principia Matheseos in denen Praejudiciis derer Alten stecken bleiben / und in einem rechten Köhler-Glauben ihnen immer blindlings nachsagen / daß dieser Tonus praecise diese Wirckung ein ander eine andere habe." Kuhnau, *Biblische Historien*, xii.

32. Cited in Buelow, *Thorough-Bass Accompaniment*, 283.

was questioned in the same treatise. In his chapter on setting the text, Herbst elaborated on the expressive qualities of the modes, a topic he had already considered in his discussion of the *exordio*, *medio*, and *fine* of a composition (ch. 8). He suggested that the composer should first examine the meaning of the text and then choose a suitable mode, "for the *musicus poeticus* (should he not be well versed and experienced in musical composition) will not easily be able to express and re-present the affections required by the text in any mode; all modes are not suitable for all texts, for some have joyful and others have sad properties and qualities, and are thus perceived."[33] Herbst went to quite some length in describing the modes, presumably for those less "well versed and experienced in musical composition" and not able to express a certain affection in any mode. After dealing with the expressive characteristics of the twelve modes, Herbst then discussed the more significant musical elaboration of affective words. Vivid text expression rather than "correct" choice of mode became more important for the successful representation of the desired affection.

Most of the references to the modal characteristics point to a mode's general expressive properties rather than to an affection. A joyful or sad mode could be *used* to express a joyful or sad affection, without inherently *being* an expression of that affection. This allowed authors to describe the modes (or later keys) as possessing a certain character without limiting their use to a specific affection. Thus some theorists would continue to list the properties of modes while at the same time insisting that compositions in one mode could express a variety of contrasting affections. Instead of dogmatically imposing a specific and objective affection on a key or mode, the reference to a mode's character

33. "Zum ersten / soll ein Componist den Verstand deß Textes oder Sentenz wol in acht nemen / denselben wol examiniren und betrachten / in welchem Modo nemlichen er die Harmoniam oder den Gesang componiren und setzen will. . . . Also ein Musicus Poeticus (wenn er nicht wol versiret, und in setzung der Consonantien, sonderlichen exerciret und erfahren ist) wird nicht in einem jeden Modo, die jenigen affecten und Bewegungen / so der Text und Sententz erfordert / also leichtlichen herfürbringen / und an den Tag geben können: Denn sich nicht alle Text auff alle Modos schicken / weil etliche frölicher, etliche aber trawriger Proprietät und Eygenschafft seyn / und erfunden werden." Herbst, *Musica poetica*, 101. Among others, Kircher suggested a similar approach. Dammann, *Musikbegriff*, 315.

or property allowed for a wider spectrum of the mode's application and reception. Specific key characteristics were thus also closely linked to an individual's temperamental disposition rather than only to designated expressive attributes. After voicing his doubts regarding the composer's arbitrary powers over his audience, Kuhnau reminded his readers that the "temperaments of individuals are quite different. For the composer's ease or difficulty in executing his intentions will be determined by the temperament of the listener. A merry spirit can easily be led to joy or compassion, while the same is achieved with a melancholy or choleric temperament only with great difficulty."[34] When Heinichen discussed the criteria for choosing a certain mode or key for a composition, his first consideration was the inclination or temperament of the composer.[35] Similarly, Mattheson stressed that his suggestions regarding the expressive nature of the keys were only his personal interpretations, "allowing everyone complete freedom to construct a better arrangement according to their own sentiment, being fully aware that although they may seem satisfactory, they will not necessarily find favor with everyone else."[36] He repeated this concern at the end of this discussion of the key's expressive content: "the more one wishes to clarify the matter, the more contradictory it becomes. For the opinions regarding this matter are innumerable. I can only explain this on the basis of the human temperaments which must undoubtedly be the main cause for a certain mode to seem merry and lively to the sanguine temperament but troubled and sorrowful to the phlegmatic one. For that reason we will not dwell on

---

34. "Und wenn uns nichts anders zweiffelhafftig machen könte so wäre doch dieses einzige genug dazu / daβ die Complexiones der Menschen gantz unterschieden sind. Denn nach dem der Humeur der Zuhörer ist / nachdem wird auch der Musicus seine Intention schwer oder leichte erlangen. Ein lustiger Geist kan ohne Schwierigkeit zur Freude oder zum Mitleiden gebracht werden / da hingegen ein Künstler grosse Mühe haben wird / wenn er dergleichen bey einem Melancholico oder Cholerico ausrichten soll." Kuhnau, *Biblische Historien*, ix.

35. "However, the choice of these depends primarily on four basic conditions: (1) . . . on the inclination or in physical terms, on the temperament of the composer." Buelow, *Thorough-Bass Accompaniment*, 283.

36. ". . . dabey zugleich einem jeden seine völlige Freyheit lassen / nach seinem Sentiment eine andere und bessere Einrichtung hierin zu machen / von welcher er sich doch auch / wenn sie gleich noch so vollkommen / nicht wird versprechen können / daβ sie bey allen und jeden Ingress finden werde." Mattheson, *Orchestre*, 231, §6.

this any longer, but allow each one the freedom to ascribe certain qualities to the modes according to his own disposition."[37] Increasingly the *natura* of the composer and audience instead of the *scientia* of the music becomes the determining factor in the musical expression of the affections. Rather than limiting himself to musical artifices whose expressive content had been predetermined, the Baroque composer sought to express the textually or otherwise inspired affections with devices more closely tied to natural expression. These he found in the principles and procedures of rhetoric. For rhetoric was not only inextricably tied to natural speech but had been intimately associated with the expression of the affections since antiquity. Not surprisingly then, the humanistically oriented musical discipline found rhetoric to be the ideal framework for developing its affective expressiveness, rather than the frequently contradictory concepts of mode or key characteristics.

The Affections and Rhythm

Rhythm, meter, and tempo were also examined and explained according to their affective properties, for these too are numerical expressions. While the sanguine and the choleric personalities would generally prefer faster tempi, a serious and grave composition would find resonance in the temperament of a melancholic or phlegmatic character. Although the importance of rhythmic variety in a composition was emphasized in the Renaissance,[38] the reason for its importance lay in the desire to delight (*oblectatio*) the listener with a varied but balanced composition. As in

37. "Allein je mehr man sich bestreben wolte / etwas positives davon zu statuiren / je mehr contradicentes würde sich vielleicht finden / sintemahl die Meinungen in dieser Materie fast unzehlig sind / davon ich keine andere Raison, als den Unterscheid der Menschlichen Complexionen zu geben weiβ / als wodurch es Zweifels frey hauptsächlich geschehen mag / daβ ein Tohn / der einem Sanguinischen Temperament lustig und ermunternd scheinet / einem Phlegmatischen träge / kläglich und betrübt vorkommt / u. s. w. derowegen wir uns hierbey auch nicht länger auffhalten / sondern einem jeden nochmahls die Freyheit gerne lassen wollen / daβ er einem oder andern Tohn solche Eigenschafften beylege / die mit seiner natürlichen Zuneigung am besten übereinkommen / da man denn finden wird." Ibid., §25.

38. ". . . ita et in musica concentuum diversitas animam auditorum vehementer in oblectamentum provocat." Tinctoris, *CS* IV, 152, cited in Dammann, *Musikbegriff*, 309.

the other areas of Baroque compositional theory, the emphasis on rhythmic *varietas* shifted to a desire to portray and arouse the affections. Werckmeister spoke of the tempo indications such as *presto* or *adagio* primarily as indications of the affection. Should "changes be indicated within a composition governed by one affection, the different tempi are to be understood as proportional changes within the governing *tactus*."[39] Michael Praetorius supported this view when he suggested that the designations of *forte* or *piano*, *presto*, *adagio*, or *lento* serve to express the affection and stir the listener.[40] Mattheson also encouraged the composer to focus on the intended affection when choosing a tempo indication: "This purpose must always be visualized when a composer sets his adagio, andante, presto, etc. Then his work will be a success."[41] Both tempo indications and rhythmic characteristics of dance forms could help express the affection. Mattheson amplified this by elaborating on typical Baroque dance forms: the minuet typifies moderate delight (*mässige Lustigkeit*), the gavotte jubilant joy (*jauchzende Freude*), the bourrée contentment (*Zufriedenheit*), etc.[42] The various dance genres were to embody the affective characteristics in much the same way that the temperaments of individuals or stage actors typify a certain affection. Unlike the *varietas*-oriented Renaissance suite, the Baroque suite was thus a series of dance movements ordered and determined by affection. In an age where all musical composition was directed toward expressing and arousing the affections, the correlation between specific dances and their affections resulted in the dance form assuming a predominant role in structuring both sacred and secular, instrumental and vocal music.

---

39. Dammann, *Musikbegriff*, 310.

40. "Forte, Pian: Praesto; Adagio Lento . . . So deuchtet mir doch solche variation und umbwechselung / wenn sie fein moderate und mit einer guten gratia, die affectus zu exprimiren und in den Menschen zu moviren, vorgenommen und zu werck gerichtet wird / nicht allein nicht unlieblich oder unrecht seyn / sondern viel mehr die aures & animos auditorum afficire." Michael Praetorius, *Syntagma Musicum III* (Wolffenbüttel, 1619), 112.

41. *Capellmeister*, 233, §137.

42. Ibid., 224ff.

On Specific Affections

There seems to have been limited consensus regarding the number of affections which could be represented through music. Kircher suggested that the various affections could be categorized into three groups (joyful, pious/subdued, and sad), out of which all the other affections originate.[43] He then listed eight typical affections: *Amor* (love), *Luctus seu Planctus* (mourning or lamentation; also called *Dolor*: grief or sorrow), *Laetitia et Exultatio* (joy and exultation), *Furor et Indignatio* (rage and indignation), *Commiseratio et Lacryma* (pity and weeping), *Timor et Afflictio* (fear and pain), *Praesumptio et Audacia* (presumption and audacity), and *Admiratio* (admiration or astonishment). Other writers also summarized the different affections in two or three categories. The German philosopher Christian Wolff differentiated between agreeable and unpleasant affections, with the affection of longing being a mixture of the two extremes.[44] Mattheson mentioned over twenty different affections,[45] many of them being closely related. In spite of the different classifications, there seemed to be general agreement regarding the musical representation of at least the fundamental affections.

A sorrowful affection could be expressed through harsh or grating intervals and harmonies as well as through syncopated rhythms. Just as the human condition in this affection is far removed from the joy and contentment experienced in a wholesome and healthy situation, so too should the intervals be far removed from the image of perfection, the unison. The suggestion to use syncopations or suspensions rests on both harmonic and rhythmic irregularities. While the resulting suspensions will incur harmonic dissonances, the regular meter of the composition will be interrupted, thus causing uncertainty. The effect of the dissonant intervals and harmonies with their high numerical proportions will concur and sympathize with the human emotional state of this affection, thus ensuring the desired result. The dissonance of the semitone is considered useful for portraying the sadder affections, not only on

---

43. See p.109, n.38, below.

44. Walter Serauky, "Affektenlehre," *Musik in Geschichte und Gegenwart* (Kassel: Bärenreiter, 1955), 1: 113.

45. *Capellmeister*, 16–19, §56–82.

account of its "imperfect" and "dissonant" proportion but also because of its small scope or span. The various dissonances, particularly when moving slowly, also cause the *spiritus animales* to weaken and slow down, finally even causing their suffocation. This unnatural condition is reflected by an unnatural, slow, thin and weak pulse, resulting in an affection of sorrow or sadness.[46] Werckmeister continued this thought by explaining that the weakened *spiritus animales* find it more difficult to enter the senses and intellect.[47] The same intervals in a fast tempo would express and arouse the affection of rage.

A joyful affection requires the more consonant and perfect intervals, found in the major keys. The rhythm should be faster, and there are to be few dissonances and syncopations, the texture being closer to perfection both in harmony and rhythm. As an individual longs and strives for wholeness, that is for God, he strives toward the unison, resulting in joy and contentment. Thus the closer the numerical proportion of an interval is to the unison, the more joyous must be its effect. The major triad with its proportions of 4:5:6 is therefore considered more joyful than its minor counterpart, with the proportions of 10:12:15. The reason that compositions in the minor key were to end in a major triad or open fifth has much less to do with presenting a happy ending than with the longing and striving for perfection.[48] The tessitura should

46. "Die Traurigkeit hat auch gantz widerwärtige pulsus, nemlich gering / langsam / dünne und schwach / dardurch wird die Wärm ersticket / wegen Zertrettung deβ Geblüts / daher komt kält und Erstarren deβ gantzen Leibs; gleich wie nun in der Excessiv-grossen Freud die Geister zertrennet werden / daβ der Mensch sterben und verschmachten muβ / also gehets auch mit der Excessiv-grossen Traurigkeit / wegen der Erstickung der Geister." Kircher, *Musurgia universalis*, in the Hirsch translation, *Artis Magnae*, extr. 317; cited in Dammann, *Musikbegriff*, 274.

47. ". . . freylich also durch die unvollkommenen consonantien traurige affectus regen / und durch den rechten gebrauch der dissonantien noch mehr / denn sie ziehen nicht allein die Spiritus zusammen / sondern gehen schwerlicher in den Intellectum, und Sensum ein." Werckmeister, *Musicalisches Send-Schreiben*, 67.

48. "Jedoch wird der Gesang in Cadentien . . . sowohl in der Mitte . . . als auch im Final in die Tertiam majorem, ob schon der Gesang mollis ist / versetzet. Woraus wir sehen / daβ die Natur nach der Ordnung und Vollkommenheit / strebet / damit doch der Sensus zu letzt sein Vergnügen habe." Werckmeister, *Musicae Mathematicae*, 81. And similarly: "Clausula formalis ist in mancherley Partibus und Stimmen / durch allerhand liebliche Concordantien . . . da in deroselben final und Endschafft / entweder eine Ruh oder stillstand / oder eine perfection und Vollkommenheit erfordert wird." Herbst, *Musica poetica*, 58.

be relatively high, resulting in a brighter sound. Triple time, symbolizing the Trinity—and therefore perfection—is commonly used, especially in conjunction with faster moving dance forms. The swift, leaping consonances will effect a similar movement of the *spiritus animales*, coinciding with and thereby arousing the characteristics of these affections. It is a far more natural affection than sorrow because it is the "friend of life and health."[49]

The affection of love is characterized as a longing to appreciate the beauty of something or someone beloved. This affection will therefore include both longing and joy. Those who find themselves in this condition are unstable, at times vehemently stirred, at times languid, and at yet other times "agreeably tickled" (*suaviter titillantes*, Kircher). Mattheson refers to love as a dissipation or diffusion (*Zerstreuung*) of the *Lebens-Geister*, requiring the employment of intervals of similar nature.[50] The composer must find means to express these various and contrasting stirrings. Harmonic and melodic material should include both rousing and gentle intervals, both soft (i.e., semitone) and strange intervals. The tempo and rhythm should be calm, as with the sadder affections.

The other affections are evoked by using various combinations of consonant and dissonant intervals and harmonies, faster or slower rhythms or tempi, and different tessituras. The affection of rage and indignation should use faster, more vehement tempi and rhythms with a liberal use of dissonance. It is the affection closest to the choleric temperament. Monteverdi's *stile concitato* corresponds to this affection. The affection of pity and weeping would use slower tempi and smaller intervals, particularly the minor second. Fear and pain would be expressed through harsher harmonies and a moderate tempo. The affections of presumption or audacity and admiration or astonishment are determined by the text and the corresponding musical expression, including suitable musical-rhetorical figures.

---

49. Mattheson, *Capellmeister*, 17, §70. Mattheson continues by reminding the reader that the most appropriately used joyful music is directed toward the praise of God, for we continually have great reason and opportunity, to broaden (*ausbreiten*) the *spiritus animales* (*Nerven-Geister*).

50. Ibid., 16, §58.

The Text and the Affections

Throughout the seventeenth century, the musical representation of the affections was inextricably tied to text expression. Music theorists frequently included lists of words closely resembling lists of affections which were to receive particular attention in the composition. After discussing his musical-rhetorical figures, Nucius stated that "to these must also be added the other embellishments of the harmonia, beginning with the affective words: rejoicing, weeping, fearing, lamenting, bewailing, mourning, raging, laughing, and pitying, which are expressed and painted through the variety and sound of the notes."[51] A similar list was incorporated into the *pathopoeia* definition by Thuringus, a figure which, as Burmeister pointed out, expresses the text in such a manner "that no one remains untouched by the created affection."[52] The list of affective words reappeared in Herbst's *Musica Poetica*, preceded by introductory comments which again emphasized the expression of the affections: "Therefore, the beauty of music consists primarily in stirring the heart and the affections, which was demonstrated in the preceding discussion of the nature and properties of the modi. However, because I recognize that the various affections can be expressed in any one modus, I find it appropriate to be more specific and to elaborate on this matter. First, the words upon which the composition is to be based must be well pondered, their nature and properties being carefully observed and considered, beginning with the affective words."[53] While attributing

---

51. "Huc inferenda sunt alia Harmoniae quoque decora, ut sunt primum verba affectuum, Laetari, Gaudere, lacrymari, timere, ejulare, flere, lugere, irasci, ridere, Misereri, &: quae ipso sono & notarum varietate sunt exprimenda & pingenda." Nucius, *Musices poeticae*, G3ᵛ.

52. See *Pathopoeia* (Burmeister, *Hypomnematum*), below.

53. "Dieweil dann alle Liebligkeit der Music / mehrentheils in Bewegung der Herzen und Gemüther bestehet / wie solches kurz vorher von aller Modorum Natur und Eygenschafft ist angezeigt worden / und darauß nach der Länge kan gesehen werden: jedoch weil ich spüre / daß gleichwol inn einem jeden Modo oder Tono, allerley affecten deß Gemüths können exprimirt und außgedrucket werden / als hat mich vor gut angesehen / von dieser Sachen etwas mehrers in specie, und insonderheit zu tractiren und außzuführen. Erstlich müssen die Verba und Wort / nach welchen die moduli sollen fingirt und angestellet seyn / wol ponderirt und deroselben Natur und Eygenschafft fleissig in acht genommen und betrachtet werden / als da seyn: Verba affectuum bewegungs Wörter." Herbst, *Musica poetica*, 111.

certain expressive characteristics to the church modes, Herbst was quick to point out that no one mode was limited to a certain affection or vice versa. More important is the expressive representation of the words of a text using a variety of musical devices.

With Kircher the musical expression of the affections became more closely linked to rhetorical structures and devices. It was Kircher who introduced the rhetorical steps of *inventio*, *dispositio*, and *elocutio (elaboratio, decoratio)* into musical compositional theory, linking them to text expression. He equated the musical figures with their rhetorical counterparts, both being used to express diverse affections. In addition, Kircher was the first to consistently emphasize the expression of both the affections and the text in his figure definitions, frequently providing examples of both a suitable affection as well as appropriate words for a figure. Janovka not only adopted Kircher's affective understanding of the musical-rhetorical figures but also applied the list of affections which Kircher had used to describe the church modes now to describe the figures. Mauritius Vogt also linked the expression of both the affections and the text with the musical-rhetorical figures, which he called *figurae ideales*. He encouraged the composer vividly to paint the images found in the text through the music, "always to make it his goal that the intended affection be achieved in his composition; and furthermore, where there are no suitable affective words, he ought to grasp the sense of the text."[54] The admonition "to grasp the sense of the text" points to a growing concern in the eighteenth century to reflect the general affection of a composition instead of getting caught up in excessively specific or inappropriate word-painting. Heinichen was preoccupied with a similar concern. He also assumed a close relationship between affection and text expression: "What a bottomless ocean we still have before us merely in the expression of words and the affects in music. And how delighted is our ear, if we perceive in a well-written church composition or other music how a skilled composer has attempted here and there to move the emotions of an audience through his refined and text-related musical expression, and in this way successfully

54. See p.128, n.89, below.

finds the true purpose of music."[55] To assist the composer in "grasping the sense of the text," Heinichen suggested the application of rhetoric's *loci topici*, especially in those cases where the given text contained little affective material. The *loci topici* (discussed below) could assist in establishing a composition's affection, whether this be rooted in the text to be set or, should it be an "uninspired" one, in the surrounding texts.[56] Mattheson finally related virtually every aspect of composition to the expression of the affections. Only one of his countless references to affective text expression will suffice: "The greatest emphasis, most powerful expression, and exact observance of the words, that is the sense of the words, are rooted in the affections, and can no more exist without them as can a carriage without wheels."[57]

The most important Baroque genre for portraying and arousing the affections of a text was the aria, appearing at climactic points of operas, oratorios, or cantatas to comment or reflect on the proceedings of the libretto. Erdmann Neumeister, who provided numerous libretti for Bach's church cantatas, referred to the aria as "the soul of an opera."[58] The aria does not further the action in a Baroque opera but rather reflects upon it. The actor singing the aria does not seek to develop a character but rather aspires to portray the temperament of the character as he interacts with the various and changing situations in the plot. Of this Alessandro Scarlatti says that "the expression of the passion with which the characters speak . . . is the very most principal consideration and circumstance for moving and leading the mind of the listener to the diversity of sentiments that the various incidents of the plot of the drama unfold."[59] The temperament of a character is, of course, predetermined,

---

55. Johann David Heinichen, *Der General-Bass in der Composition* (Dresden, 1728), 24, as translated in George Buelow, "The 'Loci Topici' and Affect in Late Baroque Music," *Music Review* 27 (1966), 162.

56. See p.78, below.

57. "Der grösseste Nachdruck, starcke Gedancken, und die genaueste Beobachtung der Worte, d.i. des in den Worten steckenden Verstandes rühren ja ursprünglich von den Gemüths-Bewegungen und Leidenschafften her, und können eben so wenig ohne dieselbe bestehen, als ein Wagen ohne Räder." *Capellmeister*, 146.

58. Dammann, *Musikbegriff*, 264.

59. Mario Fabbri, *Alessandro Scarlatti e il Principe Ferdinando de' Medici* (Florence, 1961), 73; cited in Claude Palisca, *Baroque Music* (Englewood Cliffs: Prentice Hall, 1981), 236f.

and would remain unchanged throughout the plot. The sudden changes in the plot resulted in the character being plunged into frequently contrasting passions. Not a subjective, personal response, but an objective, universally valid reaction to a situation determined the resulting affection, "so that a character at any given moment of expression [was] for the time being simply the incarnation of a certain state of mind and feeling."[60] The coincidence of the two forces, the changing external situations and the constant temperament of the character would determine a whole spectrum of affections endured by the character throughout the story. He becomes the mirror of the human being as an actor on the "world stage."[61] Thus an aria represented the consequence of the character's temperament coupled with a particular situation in the plot, resulting in a highly stylized presentation of the single resulting affection. The reigning affection guaranteed musical unity of the aria, thereby thwarting any dynamic musical or character development. It was a rational fabrication of affection-typical unity, based on a single rhetorically derived nucleus. "The complete picture of the character is to be obtained by the synthesis of all these expressive moments rather than, as in modern drama, by the analysis of a complex of moods expressed in a single aria or scene."[62] The Baroque inclination to control the natural forces by means of an overarching and unifying form, which is also reflected in contemporary architectural or garden design, resulted in the static *da capo* aria impervious to any demands of dramatic realism.

The sixteenth-century compositional technique of episodic concatenation exemplified in the contrapuntal motet was replaced by a homogeneous structure based on a single rhetorical-textual idea and musical device representing the one, single affection. In his *Praecepta*, Walther states that "when an affection is to be expressed, the composer should

---

60. Donald J. Grout, *A Short History of Opera*, 2nd ed. (New York: Columbia University Press, 1965), 159.

61. The concept of Renaissance and Baroque drama (and opera) as a representation of the *theatrum mundi* is a well-known phenomenon. When Shakespeare pronounces that "All the world's a stage . . ." (*As You Like It*, II,7), he reinforces the belief not only that the individual is part of a cosmic drama but that this macrocosm is microcosmically reflected on stage.

62. Grout, *Opera*, 159.

focus on that, rather than on the individual words; not that the words should be completely disregarded, but rather that those words which contradict the affection should not be singularly expressed."[63] On the other hand, a situation in the plot may allow various responses by the character or indeed present contrasting or even opposing perspectives, frequently resulting in the use of the musical-rhetorical figure *antithesis*.[64] In certain situations, the contrasting affections suggested by the text could influence the overall form of the aria. In such cases, the central B section of a *da capo* aria might reflect on the action from a different perspective as the A section, thereby portraying antithetic affections. In numerous Bach cantata arias the contrast is rooted in a theologically derived parallelism frequently highlighting the difference between a worldly, existential view and a heavenly, eschatological perspective.[65] In such cases the second section can be exegetical in nature, interpreting and commenting on the primary, human reaction. The rhetorical process is thus combined with a theological and musical interpretation.

In summary, the concept of the affections remained authoritative throughout the Baroque era, determining virtually every aspect of musical composition. Rather than simply representing the affections found in the text, the Baroque composer sought to arouse and move the listener through music portraying and arousing the affections. The text and its affection replaced the *numerus* as music's subject, while the listener replaced the text as the object of music. An artful and craftful representation of the affections in the music could cause an involuntary and corresponding emotional state in the listener. Both the theories of the *numerus* as well as the teaching of the temperaments explained this

---

63. "Wenn aber eine Gemüths-Regung zu exprimiren ist, soll der Componist mehr auf dieselbe, als auf die eintzeln Worte sehen, nicht zwar, daβ er dieselben insonderheit gar nicht achten dörffte, sondern, daβ er nur die Worte, welche der Gemüths-Regung zu wieder sind, nicht absonderlich exprimiren solle." *Praecepta*, 158.

64. For example, in Bach's "I joyously await my death" (BWV 82, *Ich habe genug*), the rhythmic vitality expresses joy, while the C-minor tonality and other devices reflect death and sorrow. See also *Antithesis*, below.

65. In the aria "Es ist vollbracht" from his *St. John Passion*, Bach pits the opening pathos-laden lament over Jesus's death against the jubilant outburst over Christ's victory over Satan in the B section. Both are equally legitimate responses to Christ's act of self-offering.

process. In addition to harmonic and rhetorical principles, rhythm and meter were also used to express the desired affections. While the affective purpose of music remained constant throughout the era, the foundations for expressing the affections underwent a fundamental change. German musical thought was determined by the authority of the theological-mathematical concept of music throughout the seventeenth century, culminating in such speculative writings as those of Andreas Werckmeister. However, encroaching eighteenth-century Enlightenment thought fundamentally altered the orientation of the prevailing concept of music toward an empirical, natural aesthetic. Toward the end of the Baroque era, the dogmatic methods of explaining and portraying the affections were found increasingly unnatural and artificial. Enlightenment composers found the restrictions of such theologically informed and scientifically determined music far too oppressive; Enlightenment listeners preferred personal, subjective expressiveness and a pervading presence of the emotional utterance of the individual. An era with a radically altered philosophy of music was ushered in.

Principles of Rhetoric in German Baroque Music

. . . so we must conclude that there is only little difference between music and the nature of oration. Joachim Burmeister (1601)

. . . until the art of music has attained such a height in our own day, that it may indeed be compared to a rhetoric, in view of the multitude of figures.
Christoph Bernhard (late seventeenth century)

For the figures are themselves a language of the affections. Johann Scheibe (1745)

The humanists' renewed interest in the linguistic disciplines during the Renaissance was to have a profound effect on virtually all aspects of academic and artistic endeavor throughout Europe. Common to all European Renaissance and Baroque music traditions was the growing emphasis on musical text expression and general references to the relationship between music and rhetoric. Unique to the German *musica poetica* tradition was its thorough and systematic development of a secondary "musical rhetoric" corresponding to the contemporary linguistic rhetorical discipline.[1] Fundamental to this concept was the attempt to identify and define existing musical phenomena and devices

1. Brian Vickers's attempt to denounce a Baroque "musical rhetoric" ("Figures of Rhetoric/Figures of Music?" *Rhetorica*, 2, 1 [1984], 1–44) must be dismissed for various reasons. Besides being riddled with musical misunderstandings and inaccuracies, Vickers's argument refuses to allow the transfer of rhetorical methods to nonlinguistic disciplines: "but rhetoric is inalienably about communication, and can only use words, and meanings" (p.44). However, as George Kennedy points out, "the application of theories of rhetoric outside of the field of oral expression was not limited to literature" (*Classical Rhetoric and its Christian and Secular Tradition from Ancient to Modern Times* [Chapel Hill: University of North Carolina Press, 1980], 215). In addition to its adaptation by the musical discipline, rhetoric was also influential in painting (Kennedy, p.215). While this may be inconsistent with classical rhetorical concepts, the existence of this development cannot be repudiated. In order to discover the significance of a certain era's music, the musicologist must assume an unprejudiced historical perspective. Only through its unique, theologically informed, and rhetorically permeated character can the essence of German Baroque music be discovered and explained. To understand *musica poetica* one must accept its own tenets and language.

with terminology borrowed from rhetoric. It would be misleading to explain these developments by maintaining that *musica poetica* sought out rhetorical methods and devices and then constructed analogous musical forms. The German musician's primary point of departure was an existing musical expression or form which was to be analyzed to identify its components, making it available for both pedagogical and artistic purposes. Both *musica poetica* and rhetoric aspired to an emphatic and affective form of expression through the artful application of their respective techniques. In addition, both disciplines approached their respective subjects objectively and analytically. The one element which *musica poetica* lacked was a terminology which could articulate its intent and methods. With common didactic methods, expressive purposes, and related positions in the *Lateinschule* curriculum, the "rhetorization" of *musica poetica* was an inevitability.

The increased significance placed on language and the linguistic disciplines by contemporary humanist scholars resulted in a growing influence of rhetorical concepts on musical thought. The Lutheran emphasis on the Word as a means of revelation, education, and proselytization reflects the humanist influences on Protestant thought[2] and also points to the didactic function of music associated with a text. Both music and word were to teach; both stood in the service of proclaiming the Christian Gospel. In addition to facilitating a synthesis of *musica speculativa* and *musica practica*, as well as encouraging an ethico-theological interpretation of the concept of the affections, Luther's theology of music prepared the way for the unique and thorough German adaptation of rhetorical principles and procedures, including a systematic development of the concept of musical-rhetorical figures.

2. A widely read rhetoric text in the Renaissance, Rudolphus Agricola's *De Dialectica Inventione* (1479), which contended that "the first and proper objective of speech is to teach," was very influential in the writings of the Protestant leader and friend of Luther Philipp Melanchthon, who developed the curriculum for the Lutheran *Lateinschulen* (Kennedy, *Classical Rhetoric*, 208f). See also Wilfried Barner, *Barockrhetorik* (Tübingen: Niemeyer, 1970), 260.

Germany and Italy: Contrasting Philosophies of Music

Italian Baroque music was modeled after the art of oratory rather than the discipline of rhetoric. Its goal was to imitate the actor rather than the playwright, the orator rather than the rhetorician, reflecting a long-standing Platonic mistrust of rhetoric. Dramatic gesture and pathos-laden delivery was to supply the necessary inspiration for musical invention.[3] The Italian rejection of music's numerological and cosmological significance in favor of its direct affective and aesthetic effect led to a form of musical expression which focused on a modern aesthetic principle of expressing and stirring the affections rather than explaining the text. Although the text was central to musical composition, it became the springboard for musical expression rather than the object of the composition. The expressive musical devices which characterize the Italian *nuove musiche* were developed with an aesthetic rather than exegetic principle in mind. Instead of introducing an intermediate level of linguistic and theological significance to the musical phenomena as was done in Lutheran Germany, the Italians sought to speak directly and immediately to the senses. Thus Monteverdi's *Orfeo*, a paragon of Italian Baroque music, celebrates the power of music over physical and spiritual forces. While the compositional phenomena and devices may appear analogous to *musica poetica*'s musical-rhetorical figures as defined by German theorists, Italian writers and composers were not as

3. "When they [the musicians] go for their amusement to the tragedies and comedies that the mummers act, let them . . . be so good as to observe, when one quiet gentleman speaks with another, in what manner he speaks, how high or low his voice is pitched, with what volume of sound, with what sort of accents and gestures, and with what rapidity or slowness his words are uttered. . . . Let them observe the prince when he chances to be conversing with one of his subjects and vassals; when with the petitioner who is entreating his favour; how the man infuriated or excited speaks; the married woman, the girl, the mere child, the clever harlot, the lover speaking to his mistress as he seeks to persuade her to grant his wishes, the man who laments, the one who cries out, the timid man, and the man exultant with joy. From these variations of circumstance . . . they will be able to select the norm of what is fitting for the expression of any other conception whatever that can call for their handling." Vicenzo Galilei, *Dialogo della musica antica e della moderna* (Florence, 1581); cited in Strunk, *Source Readings*, 318.

interested in a linguistic articulation of naming and defining these musical devices. (The art of Italian vocal or French instrumental ornamentation, on the other hand, was developed much more thoroughly, owing to the Italian emphasis on delivery, on *actio* or *pronunciatio*, the last of the rhetorical structural steps and the one most important to the actor.) The spokesperson for the Florentine *Camerata*, Vicenzo Galilei, who decried the Aristotelian-scholastic emphasis on learned rhetoric,[4] recommended to composers that they observe human behavior, thereby empirically acquiring the methods for the musical portrayal of the affections. This precluded the discussion of a systematic application of rhetorical compositional techniques. Natural, affection-directed speech and its delivery rather than studied, rhetorical theory was to be the compositional model. Only toward the end of the German Baroque did this approach make inroads into German musical thought, championed by writers such as Mattheson, Scheibe, and Forkel. Although Mattheson and Forkel insisted that musical truth lay primarily in *natura*, they nonetheless recommended a rhetorically structured approach to musical composition. However, while Mattheson leaned more toward *musica poetica*'s artistic concepts, Forkel's thoughts sprang from the context of a post-Baroque (Enlightenment) aesthetic.

The situation in France corresponded to the Italian Baroque music aesthetic. While rhetoric seems to have been even more significant in French Baroque music, there is no evidence of the development of a systematic concept of musical-rhetorical figures, in spite of a promising beginning by Anonymous of Besançon.[5] Like the Italians, the French looked to the actor or orator for musical-rhetorical inspiration. In the words of Rameau, "a good musician should surrender himself to all the characters he wishes to portray. Like a skillful actor he should take the place of the speaker, believe himself to be at the location where the different events he wishes to depict occur, and participate in these events as do those most involved in them. He must declaim the text well, at least to himself, and he must feel when and to what degree the voice should rise or fall, so that he may shape his melody, harmony, modula-

4. Dammann, *Musikbegriff*, 107, 153ff.

5. Gregory Butler, "Fugue and Rhetoric," *Journal of Music Theory* 21 (1977), 53.

tion, and movement accordingly."[6]

In England there were also references to a correlation between music and rhetoric without the subsequent development of a systematic concept of musical-rhetorical figures. In his music treatise Charles Butler mentioned four "Graces or Ornaments: Consecution, Syncope, Fuga, and Formaliti," describing the proper progression ("consecution") of the intervals, the use of the suspensions, and the fugue, as well as the arrangement of a composition using these devices and cadences.[7] Even though he quoted Calvisius's reference to a composition's *exordium* and *finis*,[8] he did not elaborate on the musical-rhetorical implications as was done by Burmeister and his followers. The remaining English musical-rhetorical references occurred primarily in rhetorical rather than musical treatises.[9] Furthermore, they referred predominantly to technical fugal devices of repetition. While English rhetoricians continued to use rhetorical terminology in their discussions of the rhetorical figures of repetition, no conscious effort was made by music theorists to adopt similar terminology. Instead, terms such as *reply*, *revert*, *report*, and *counterchange of points* were employed. The similarity between the musical devices and the rhetorical figures was then emphasized by the rhetoricians instead of the musicians. Francis Bacon summed this up in his comment: "The reports and fugues have an agreement with the

---

6. *Traité de l'Harmonie réduite à ses Principes naturels* (Paris, 1722; trans. Ph. Gossett, New York: Dover, 1971), 156. Although Leslie E. Brown ("Oratorical Thought and the *Tragédie lyrique*: A Consideration of Musical-Rhetorical Figures," *College Music Symposium* 20 [1980], 99) makes a number of helpful references to the role of rhetoric in French Baroque music, the identification of the expressive musical devices which were employed by French composers as musical-rhetorical figures remains questionable. While the identified devices undeniably coincide with numerous expressions identified as musical-rhetorical figures by German writers, they were never referred to as such by French writers. Although a contemporary German musician, upon encountering the French music, may have defined the musical phenomena as musical-rhetorical figures, the lack of any such French references would seem to suggest that neither the French composer nor his audience would have jumped to the same conclusion.

7. Charles Butler, *The principles of musik* (London, 1636), 57. The treatise is largely based on Seth Calvisius's *Exercitationes Musicae Duae* (Leipzig, 1600).

8. Butler, *Principles*, 86.

9. For a discussion of this phenomenon, see Gregory Butler, "Music and Rhetoric in Early Seventeenth-Century English Sources," *Musical Quarterly* 66 (1980), 53.

figures in rhetoric of repetition and traduction."[10] Furthermore, as in France and Italy, there seems to have been little attempt made systematically to link the rhetorical figures and devices with text- and affection-expressive musical composition during the seventeenth and eighteenth centuries. There was no English advocate of "musical preaching" comparable to the Lutheran *Kantor*, the driving force behind the development of *musica poetica*. English Protestantism was fundamentally Calvinistic, a theology which rejected all forms of elaborate church music. While orthodox Calvinism allowed unaccompanied, unison congregational singing in worship, it frowned on the liturgical use of choral polyphonic music, which was associated with "popery" in England. The tone for Anglican church music was set by the "author" of the Book of Common Prayer, Thomas Cranmer, chaplain to Henry VIII and Archbishop of Canterbury (1533). In a letter to Henry VIII regarding a translation of the Great Litany, Cranmer suggested that "the song that should be made thereunto would not be full of notes, but, as near as may be, for every syllable a note, so that it may be sung distinctly and devoutly."[11] The Calvinist view of music as a humanistic recreational endeavor stood in sharp contrast to the Lutheran divinely ordered and ordained concept of music. Thriving in the historical

---

10. Francis Bacon, *Sylva Sylvarum; or, a naturall historie, in ten centuries* (London 1627), 38, 60.

11. Strunk, *Source Readings*, 351. Similar directives to specific cathedrals abound in the sixteenth century. In an injunction to the dean and chapter at York Minster in 1552 it was noted: "We will and command that there be none other note sung or used in the said church at any service there to be had, saving square note plain, so that every syllable may be plainly and distinctly pronounced, and without any reports or repeatings which may induce any obscureness to the hearers" (Peter le Huray, *Music and the Reformation in England 1549–1660*, Cambridge: Cambridge University Press, 1978, 25). During the Elizabethan period, similar strict controls were placed on church music, as is evidenced in the ban of contrapuntal music in Winchester Cathedral in 1571: "Item, that in the choir no more shall be used in song that shall drown any word or syllable, or draw out in length or shorten any word or syllable, otherwise than by the nature of the word it is pronounced in common speech, whereby the sentence cannot be well perceived by the hearers. And also the often reports or repeating of notes with words or sentences, whereby the sense may be hindered in the hearer shall not be used." Ibid., 38. The one oasis of contrapuntal church music during this era was the Chapel Royal, "which obstinately refused to be bound by the restrictions urged upon so many other centres of church music" (Eric Routley, *A Short History of English Church Music*, London: Mowbrays, 1977, 23).

association between music and rhetoric in the context of the *Lateinschulen*, Lutheran musical exegesis led to the text- and affection-portraying *musica poetica*, combining the disciplines of music and rhetoric more explicitly and systematically than any other European music tradition. Only on German soil did the theological, historical, and practical prerequisites for the development of such a musical rhetoric exist.

The German *musicus poeticus* first sought to analyze and define his linguistic source and then construct a parallel musical structure, instead of aspiring to draw directly on the source of the affection. The text was to be depicted and explained, reflected upon and taught. This process included a search for analogies between text and music, frequently involving complicated and at times obscure exegetical devices. A divinely ordered universe would guarantee the possibility of rationally explaining not only the mathematical and affection-arousing aspects of musical theory but also the rhetorical-linguistic principles of musical composition. In prescribing that a composition be "arranged in order and proportion," Mattheson juxtaposed theological and rhetorical terminology: the rhetorical "arrangement" (*Einrichtung* = *dispositio*) of a composition is to reflect the order and proportion of the created universe.[12] The Italians, in contrast to German writers, put less emphasis on theoretical and theological considerations, concentrating primarily on the effect of music.[13] Only the execution of the speech, the final two steps in the rhetorical process of oration (*memoria* and *pronuntiatio* or *actio*), were to be influential in music. Gesture and declamation were to be of prime consideration, not structure and form.

The Lutheran application of the traditional pedagogical method of *praeceptum, exemplum, et imitatio* (learning the rules, studying examples, and imitating established masters) reinforced the continued perception of musical composition as a craft rather than an aesthetic

---

12. See p.35, n.12, above.

13. The Italian emphasis, characterized by its empirical approach, is in part encouraged by a quasi-magical understanding of the power of music, parallel to a similar understanding of the power of oration to stir the affections. In his *Rationalis Philosophiae pars tertia*, Campanella devotes chapter 11 to *De oratoris instrumento magico*. And Monteverdi, the son of a physician, also concerned himself with alchemy. Dammann, *Musikbegriff*, 160.

undertaking. While the Italians highlighted "heavenly inspiration" (*celeste influsso et inclinatione*),[14] and argued that a composer must be a born composer, the Germans emphasized the teachable and learnable skill of composition. In his *Musica Poetica*, Andreas Herbst wrote: "Just as a builder or carpenter leaves a house or other building to posterity, so too and in like manner can a *musicus poeticus* or composer bequeath to following generations a musical composition which he constructed with great diligence, toil, and industry, thereby ensuring the abiding remembrance of his name."[15] In accounting for his musical accomplishments, J. S. Bach commented, "I had to work hard; anyone who is as industrious, can achieve the same level."[16] Bach's comment was not made simply out of bashful modesty but rather reflects the conviction that the craft of musical composition can indeed be learnt. That which was captured instinctively in the south was analytically unraveled, terminologically objectified, and systematically taught in the north.

The Discipline of Rhetoric

The ancient and distinguished discipline of rhetoric, the art of eloquent speech, originated in the fifth century B.C. as an oral skill used by lawyers and statesmen. Athenian rhetoricians and philosophers gradually produced systems of rules and regulations which were taught at the various schools and academies. With the rise of epideictic oration, which focused on rhetorical display, philosophers became wary of the discipline. From Plato to Aristotle, philosophers "either reject rhetoric altogether, or they treat it as a subordinate part of philosophy, claiming to treat the subject with greater competence than the professional

---

14. Ibid., 113.

15. "Dann gleich wie ein Werckmeister oder Zimmermann / ein Hauβ oder sonsten ein Gebäw / so von ihme verfertiget / hinter ihm verläst: Also auch und der gestalt kan ihme ein Musicus Poeticus oder Componist / ein dergleichen Musicalisches Wercklein / welches er mit grossem fleiβ / müh und arbeit / durch diese kunst zusammen gebracht / zu seines Namens immerwärendem Gedächtnuβ den Nachkömlingen hinderlassen." Herbst, *Musica poetica*, 1.

16. "Ich habe fleiβig sein müssen; wer ebenso fleiβig ist, der wird es ebenso weit bringen können." Cited in Dammann, *Musikbegriff*, 113.

rhetoricians were able to do."[17] With the rise of Christianity, scholars and writers of the Church adopted the classical rhetorical discipline from their Roman teachers who, in turn, had fully embraced Greek theory and practice. The art of public speaking lost its prominence in the Middle Ages. While medieval rhetoricians focused on the art of composing letters or official documents, the clergy cultivated rhetoric in the literary genre of the homily or sermon. Rhetoric, championed by the humanists along with all other classical disciplines, experienced a revival in the Renaissance, "and came to pervade all areas of civilization, as it had not been the case during the preceding centuries. . . . For the *studia humanitatis* included grammar and poetry, history and moral philosophy, as well as rhetoric. As a humanist enterprise, rhetoric was thus closely connected with all these other subjects, and the rhetoric of the humanists must be understood as an integral part of their widespread interests and activities."[18]

RHETORIC IN THE *LATEINSCHULE* CURRICULUM

Through the Lutheran school reforms pioneered by Luther's humanistically inclined associate, Philipp Melanchthon, the discipline of rhetoric received high priority in the parochial *Lateinschulen*, schools which virtually all German Lutheran musicians would have attended.[19] The *trivium*, which included rhetoric, formed the core of the curriculum both at the *Lateinschulen* and the universities. Indeed, *Kantors* teaching at *Lateinschulen* frequently found themselves teaching both music and Latin, which included grammar and rhetoric. This was also the case with Joachim Burmeister, the author of the first *musica poetica* treatise which systematically combined the disciplines of music and rhetoric. All course instruction was conducted in Latin. Furthermore, all conversation, whether in the classroom or on the playground, was to be in Latin.

17. Paul Oskar Kristeller, *Renaissance Thought and Its Sources* (New York: Columbia University Press, 1970), 219.

18. Ibid., 242f.

19. For an excellent and exhaustive study of rhetoric in the Baroque, see Barner, *Barockrhetorik*, especially 241–321.

(Although the exclusive concentration on Latin abated throughout the seventeenth century, it was not until the eighteenth century that the vernacular replaced Latin as the language of rhetoric.) Introductory rhetoric was only taught in the final one or two years of school, after the students had thoroughly mastered Latin grammar and syntax. The weekly curriculum of the advanced students included eight hours of Latin, three hours of dialectic (logic), two hours of rhetoric, and two hours of Cicero. In addition to other subjects, provision was also made for further private tutoring in rhetoric. The student was taught to prepare a given topic either in oral or written form according to the examples of classical authors. To this end the students used various textbooks which presented the general rhetorical concepts and techniques of the classical authors (Aristotle, Cicero, Quintilian) in a condensed form. Lossius, who was Burmeister's teacher, simplified the texts by Melanchthon and Erasmus for his own use. Rules of rhetoric were defined with examples from classical writings, providing material which the students could emulate. Classical authors were not read for their literary content but rather to determine linguistic rules. Like all other disciplines including Latin grammar and music, the subject of rhetoric was taught through *praeceptum, exemplum, et imitatio.*[20]

Rhetorical Structure

The process of rhetorical structuring traditionally comprises five steps: *inventio*, *dispositio*, *elocutio*, *memoria*, and *actio* or *pronunciatio*. While *inventio* concerns itself with determining the subject and gathering pertinent information, *dispositio* focuses on logically arranging the material. The third step, *elocutio*, translates the various ideas and thoughts into words and sentences, adding any necessary devices which would give the argument greater emphasis. The last two steps deal with memorization and delivery. The first three steps each receive further consideration according to the topic's generalities or ideas (*res*) and to the particulars and words (*verba*). To assist in finding a suitable theme,

20. See also *Mimesis*, below, for an explication of *imitatio*.

rhetorical *inventio* offers a long list of *loci topici* or "subject areas," including topics dealing with names, definitions, antecedent or subsequent causes, effects, comparisons, and contrasts.[21] Through the *dispositio* or arrangement and development of the subject matter, the oration is usually subdivided into six segments: *exordium* (introduction), *narratio* (factual account), *propositio* (the proposed argument or point to be made), *confirmatio* (supporting arguments), *confutatio* (rebuttals), and *peroratio* or *conclusio* (concluding comments). Regarding *elocutio*, its stylistic expectations are summed up in the four *virtutes elocutionis*: correct syntax (*puritas, latinitas*), clarity (*perspicuitas*), figurative language (*ornatus*), and suitability of form to content (*aptum, decorum*). It is in this third "virtue," *ornatus*, that the rhetorical figures and tropes find their home. Tropes are understood as metaphoric expressions, while figures are described as deviations from the normal choice, order, or structure of words and sentences. It is above all these figures of speech, which serve to embellish, amplify, and vividly portray the thoughts, that were considered the most useful tools in presenting and arousing the affections. The last two structural steps, *memoria* and *actio* or *pronunciatio*, deal with memorizing the oration and polishing the delivery, adding gestures and proper inflections. Because these two steps have little to do with the formulation of a properly ordered sermon or speech, they received only minor attention in the German context. Vossius, who wrote one of the most widely read rhetorical textbooks in Germany, focused on *inventio* in books 1 and 2, on *dispositio* in book 3, and on *elocutio* in books 4 and 5, appending only two short chapters on memorization and delivery at the end of book 5.[22] The preponderance of the first three rhetorical steps in German rhetoric was also reflected in the *musica poetica* tradition. The German context encouraged an emphasis on orderly and eloquent construction rather than on dramatic delivery. *Inventio*'s *loci topici*, the sectional *dispositio*, and *elocutio*'s rhetorical figures, rather than the rhetorical steps concerning delivery and performance, were to determine *musica poetica*'s concepts and

---

21. In his *Der grünen Jugend nothwendige Gedancken* (Leipzig, 1676), Christian Weise examined twelve *loci topici*, summarized in Unger, *Beziehungen*, 4.

22. For a detailed discussion of Vossius's *Commentariorum Rhetoricorum* (Leiden, 1606), see Barner, *Barockrhetorik*, 265ff.

structures. The composer sought to emulate the rhetorician rather than the actor, with the composition replicating an orderly rhetorical construction rather than mimicking an inspired theatrical presentation. Although there were minor variations in the number and presentation of the rhetorical structures, they can be summarized as follows:

a) *Inventio*, including the *loci topici*
b) *Dispositio*
  i) *exordium*
  ii) *narratio*
  iii) *propositio (divisio)*
  iv) *confirmatio*
  v) *confutatio (refutatio)*
  vi) *peroratio (conclusio)*
c) *Elocutio (Decoratio)*
  the four *virtutes elocutionis:*
  i) *puritas*, *latinitas*
  ii) *perspicuitas*
  iii) *ornatus*, including rhetorical figures and tropes
  iv) *aptum*, *decorum*
d) *Memoria*
e) *Actio*, *Pronunciatio*

The Rhetorical Figure

The Latin term *figura* is rooted in the verb *fingere* (to form or shape) and refers to a "modeled fabrication." While *figura* originally meant simply "shape" or "form," it later referred to the image of the original shape or form. Thus the term assumed the meaning of both an image or reflection of an object as well as an independent structure or conception. Greek rhetorical terminology used the term *schemata* to designate both rhetorical styles as well as the specific forms of expressive elaboration. This term was then translated into Latin as *figura* by Cicero (b. 106 B.C.), using it to designate certain rhetorical styles, and later by Fabius Quintilian (b. ca. A.D. 35) in his *Institutio oratoria*, with reference to the embellishing devices.[23]

Quintilian's teachings on the rhetorical figures are indisputably the most significant and influential writings on the subject, remaining authoritative throughout the medieval, Renaissance, and Baroque eras. In books 8 and 9 of his *Institutio oratoria* Quintilian discussed the tropes and figures at great length, explaining that while tropes and figures are used for the same purpose, namely "to add force and charm" to the oration,[24] the two types of embellishments should not be confused. While a trope is "the expressive alteration of a word or phrase from its proper meaning to another,"[25] he described a figure as "a conformation of our speech altered from the common and obvious usage. . . . A figure is therefore a new and artful manner of speech."[26] While the trope lends novel content to familiar language, the figure uses novel language construction. The various literal nuances of meaning of *figura* as *forma* and *imago* become evident in Quintilian's rhetorical use of the term. The term was used in reference to any "form" of verbal expression, as well as to an intentionally altered use of language from the ordinary and simple form.[27] Through this alteration (*mutatio*) the verbal expression is used to denote a deviating or illusory meaning, thereby being an implicit *imago* of that which is not explicitly stated. This rhetorical understanding of *figura* would later be transferred to music, as the musical figure through its unique structure becomes an expression of both the image (*imago*) of the text and the source (*forma*) of the intended affection.

The traditional classification of the figures into two groups, sentence

---

23. Erich Auerbach, "Figura," *Gesammelte Aufsätze zur romanischen Philologie* (Bern: Franke, 1967), 55.

24. ". . . usus quoque est idem: nam et vim rebus adiiciunt et gratiam praestant." Quintilian, *Institutio oratoria* ed. and trans. by H. E. Butler (London: Heinemann, 1921), IX.i.2, 349.

25. "Tropus est verbi vel sermonis a propria significatione in aliam cum virtute mutatio." Ibid., VIII.vi.1, 301.

26. "Figura . . . conformatio quaedam orationis remota a communi et primum se offerente ratione. . . . Ergo figura sit arte aliqua novata forma dicendi." Ibid., IX.i.4, 14, 350, 354.

27. "Nam duobus modis dicitur: uno qualiscunque forma sententiae, . . . altero, quo proprie schema dicitur, in sensu vel sermone aliqua a vulgari et simplici specie cum ratione mutatio." Ibid., IX.i.10, 11, 352.

figures and word figures, was also observed by Quintilian.[28] Words or phrases could be altered or repeated in various ways with the intent of lending the oration greater power and charm, for "there is no more effective method of exciting the emotions than an apt use of figures."[29] However, the specific figure was not to be confused with the affection to be expressed. While rage, pity, pain, fear, and other affections can be expressed through the figures, they are not figures themselves. Quintilian went to considerable length to clarify this point, citing long passages of Cicero's *Orator* and *De Oratore*. In addition to the tropes and figures, Quintilian also listed four kinds of amplification, including *incrementum* or *auxesis*, *comparatio*, *ratiocinatio*, and *congeries*. These *amplificationes* are closely related to various figures, resulting in their incorporation into the lists of figures by subsequent writers.

The Renaissance was marked not only by the humanistically inspired reappearance of many classical sources and texts but also by a surge in contemporary texts on rhetoric. A widely circulated collection of figures and tropes is found in the *Epitome* by Johannes Susenbrotus.[30] Susenbrotus defined a rhetorical embellishment, including both figures and tropes, as "a deviation from the simple or normal form of speech."[31] *Figura* was defined as an artful and novel form or manner of writing or speaking.[32] Susenbrotus then distinguished between grammatical and rhetorical figures. The grammatical figures were concerned with orthographic alterations to a word and syntactic changes to a sentence. A number of his syntactic figures had been defined as either tropes,

---

28. "Inter plurimos enim, quod sciam, consensum est duas eius esse partes, διανοίας, id est mentis vel sensus vel sententiarum, et λέξεως, id est verborum vel dictionis vel elocutionis vel sermonis vel orationis; nam et variatur et nihil refert." Ibid., IX.i.17, 356.

29. Ibid., IX.i.21, 358.

30. Johannes Susenbrotus, *Epitome troporum ac schematum et grammaticorum et rhetorum* (Antwerp, 1566). Henry Peacham the Elder (1546–1634) based his influential *The Garden of Eloquence* (London, 1593), also a collection of rhetorical figures and tropes, on Susenbrotus's *Epitome*.

31. "Figura est ratio quaedam, qua de recto ac simplici loquendi genere cum aliqua dicendi virtute deflectitur." *Epitome*, 6.

32. "Schema vel figura proprie, est aliqua novata et scribendi et dicendi forma. Vel est quaedam arte novata, tum scribendi tum dicendi ratio." Ibid. Susenbrotus uses the terms *figura*, *schemata*, *orationis lumina*, *exornatio*, and *color* interchangeably.

figurae verborum, or *figurae sententiae* by Quintilian. Just as Quintilian had done, Susenbrotus classified the rhetorical figures into word and sentence figures, additionally including Quintilian's methods of amplification as a third class of figures, forming the categories of *figurae dictionum*, *figurae orationum*, and *figurae amplificationis*.

According to Susenbrotus, the purpose of the figures was to "relieve the irritation of everyday and worn-out language, to lend the oration greater delight, dignity, and elegance, to add greater force and charm to our subject, and finally to fortify our writing or speaking in an unusual manner."[33] A significant aesthetic rather than functional reorientation concerning the purpose of the rhetorical figures can be observed in Susenbrotus's definition. Quintilian's concept of the figures was entirely rooted in their classical function, namely to move and convince an audience, be it the senate or a public crowd, through a heightened and enlivened form of oration. This utilitarian purpose was replaced by a primarily aesthetic and artistic one: to lend the oration greater delight and dignity, force and charm. Moreover, thanks to centuries of medieval rhetoric, it was not only the spoken but also the written language which benefitted from this uncommon expressiveness. Eloquently intensified composition rather than convincing political oration characterized the Renaissance purpose of the rhetorical figures. With this altered concept of the figures and of rhetoric in general, the groundwork had been prepared for music's adoption of rhetorical principles and techniques.

The philosophical currents of the seventeenth and eighteenth centuries spawned certain reforms and revisions in the rhetoric curriculum of the Lutheran *Lateinschulen*, significantly influencing the understanding of the rhetorical figures. With neo-Platonic thought replacing Aristotelianism, emphasis began to be placed more on natural, affective expression than on calculated composition. Influenced by a rising national identity and a call for an intuitive naturalness, the German language began to replace Latin. Rhetorical figures were not to be

---

33. ". . . ut quotidiani ac protriti sermonis fastidium levent, ut orationem aut iucundiorem, aut graviorem, aut elegantiorem efficiant, ut vim rebus adiiciant et gratiam praestent, et nos denique a vulgari, tum scribendi tum dicendi genere muniant." Ibid., 49. The phrase "ut vim rebus adiiciant et gratiam praestent" had already been used by Quintilian to describe the purpose of the figures (IX.i.2).

sought in ancient textbooks but rather in the inspired natural speech of the German citizen. The most significant German late Baroque rhetorician, Johann Christoph Gottsched (1700–1766), published numerous influential works on this subject, including his *Ausführliche Redekunst* and *Versuch einer Critischen Dichtkunst*, both texts undergoing multiple editions and printings. Gottsched also classified the figures into *figurae dictionis* and *sententiarum*, of which "the former are not all of equal value, for most of them are nothing but empty wordplay which produce nothing but a childish clatter and contain no fire of an affection."[34] Gottsched's concept of the rhetorical figures rests entirely on their capacity to express the affections: "One could even say, they are the language of the passions. Everyone who is possessed by a certain affection will naturally and involuntarily invent figures, for no one can express their affection without figures."[35] Gottsched further compared the figures to facial expressions, which, like language, are external reflections of internal activities or emotions. Furthermore, like the actions of the swordsman, figures could be used to startle, distress, delight, enrage, and elicit approval from an audience. The figures thus assumed a dual purpose: like facial expressions or the work of a painter, they could be used to portray the reigning affection; and like the combative endeavors of the fencer, they could arouse various affections in the listener. In his *Critische Dichtkunst*, the work which formed the basis of Johann Scheibe's concept of the musical-rhetorical figures, Gottsched maintained that "the entire power of an oration is rooted in the figures, for they possess a certain fire, and through their magic throw a spark into the heart of the reader or listener, and similarly set them aflame."[36] Although the arousal of the affections had been associated

---

34. "Die Figuren sind zweyerley, nemlich Dictionis und Sententiarum; d.i. entweder in einzelnen Worten, oder in ganzen Sätzen. Die ersten sind nicht alle von gleichem Werthe, denn die meisten darunter sind nichts, als kahle Wortspiele, die nichts, als ein kindisches Geklapper in den Ohren machen, aber kein Feuer eines Affectes in sich halten." Johann Christoph Gottsched, *Ausführliche Redekunst* (Leipzig, 1736), 276.

35. "Man könnte kürzer sagen, sie wären die Sprache der Leidenschaften: Weil alle Menschen, die im Affecte sind, von Natur, und ohne daran zu denken, Figuren machen; und niemand seinen Affect ohne Figuren recht ausdrücken kan." Ibid., 273.

36. "Die ganze Stärke einer Rede zeigt sich darinn, weil sie ein gewisses Feuer in sich enthalten, welches auch den lesern oder Zuhörern, durch eine geheime Kunst, Funken ins Herz wirft, und sie gleichergestalt entzündet." Johann Christoph Gottsched,

with rhetoric and specifically the figures since antiquity, only in the late Baroque was this elevated to the figures' primary purpose. While Quintilian regarded the figures as a means to convince an audience, and Susenbrotus focused on their decorative role in speech and literature, Gottsched sought to base his concept of the figures entirely on their affective nature and potential. A similar process can also be observed in the development of the musical concept of the figures.

TOWARD A RHETORICAL *MUSICA POETICA*

General comparisons have been drawn between music and rhetoric since antiquity. While Roman writers emphasized the usefulness of musical knowledge for the orator,[37] rhetoric was increasingly regarded as the model for musicians as early as the sixteenth century. Just as it was the intent of rhetoric to assist in captivating and convincing an audience, so too did it become expected of music that it should express the sentiment of the text in order to increase its effect on the listener. This could be accomplished through a musical reflection of the text's syntax, meter, and structure, as well as through a vivid representation of the text's images, affections, and ideas. As music adopted rhetoric's goals and intentions, namely to encourage audience involvement through the portrayal and arousal of appropriate affections in order ultimately to move and effect them, it is not surprising that references emphasizing a similar approach to composition are frequently encountered in music

---

Versuch einer critischen Dichtkunst, 4th ed. (Leipzig, 1751), 314.

37. In his *Institutio oratoria* (I, 165–177), Quintilian stressed the importance of an orator's knowledge of music: "It is by the raising, lowering, or inflection of the voice that the orator stirs the emotions of his hearers. Further, the motion of the body must be suitable and becoming or, as the Greeks call it, eurhythmic, and this can only be secured by the study of music. This is a most important department of eloquence. Still I think I ought to be more emphatic than I have been in stating that the music which I desire to see taught is not our modern music. No, I refer to the music of old which was employed to sing the praises of brave men and was sung by the brave themselves. Give me the knowledge of the principles of music, which have power to excite or assuage the emotions of mankind." Cited in George Buelow, "Teaching Seventeenth-Century Concepts of Musical Form and Expression: An Aspect of Baroque Music," *College Music Symposium* 27 (1987), 9.

treatises. While references to the corresponding goals of music and rhetoric are found in Italian, English, and French treatises, the development of a systematic musical rhetoric is limited primarily to Germany. Italian writers restricted their suggested guidelines to matters concerning correct text underlay, an appropriate musical realization of the textual structure, and general admonitions regarding the agreement between the sentiment of the music to that of the text.[38] In Germany, on the other hand, references to the relationship between rhetoric and music became much more specific and detailed, developed and taught appropriately in the context of the *Lateinschule* curriculum.

The *musica poetica* tradition did not attempt to establish a new musical order, as did the Italian *seconda prattica*, but rather fused quadrivial and trivial, mathematical and linguistic definitions and concepts of music into a musical order which served specific Lutheran needs instead of general aesthetic principles. Through the introduction of Lutheran liturgical practices, greater emphasis was placed on congregational involvement, which was realized musically primarily through the many new Lutheran chorales. Luther's theology of music also encouraged the inclusion of polyphonic choral music in the liturgy, with the choral leadership in the churches provided by the various parochial school choirs. Music was thereby given a greatly increased significance in both the liturgy and in the church's school curriculum. Simultaneously, the role and position of the *Kantor*, who directed the church choirs and taught music at the schools, also rose in stature. It was to be the Lutheran *Kantor* who would determine the direction of German Baroque music, culminating in the work of J. S. Bach.[39] With the

---

38. Zarlino, *Institutioni* 4, ch.32, 33.

39. The vast majority of German Baroque music treatises were penned by practicing church musicians, most of them Lutheran *Kantors*. Attempts have been made to devalue German Baroque music as provincial and secondary to contemporary French and Italian musical developments (esp. Suzanne Clercx, "Le 'Baroque' Musical," *Les Colloques de Wegimont* 4 [Paris, 1963], and Arno Forchert, "Musik und Rhetorik im Barock," *Schütz Jahrbuch* 7–8 [1985–86], 8). However, the undeniably progressive Italian and French influences on German music have little bearing on the discussion of a uniquely German musical rhetoric. To be modern does not necessarily mean to be better. It is, after all, the Lutheran *Lateinschule* tradition which produced one of the greatest musicians of Western music, Johann Sebastian Bach, Leipzig *Kantor* of third choice, provincial and outdated in the eyes of his sons and other German contemporaries

growing humanist interest in the classics and the increased significance of practical music-making in the parochial schools, the place of music in the liberal arts underwent an important change: while *musica speculativa* began to disappear from curricula, the applied musical discipline was promoted to a position comparable to the linguistic arts, becoming part of the core curriculum of the Lutheran *Lateinschulen*. Rhetoric would provide a paradigm for its sister discipline, music. In accordance with Luther's teachings, music itself was regarded as a heightened form of speech, becoming a rhetorical sermon in sound. Through the *Lateinschule* curriculum, rhetorical terminology and methodology was already familiar to students and teachers alike, expediting the musical adaptation of rhetorical terminology and concepts. In adopting ancient and distinguished rhetorical terminology and methods, the art of musical composition was given both a greater legitimacy and a clearly established rationale and objective.

Throughout the sixteenth century, numerous authors referred to rhetorical methods and techniques in their discussions of musical composition. While some explained musical terms in rhetorical language, others assigned rhetorical terminology to musical devices[40]: as early as 1536 Stomius referred to fugue as *mimesis*; Galliculus (1538) spoke of *schemata variorum colorum* ("figures of varying adornment") without, however, identifying any specific figures[41]; rhetorical figures used by grammarians were compared to various notational signs by Heyden (1540) and to musical ornamentation by Holthauser (1551). In discussing pauses, Dressler (1563) used pronounced rhetorical language: they were to be used for reasons of *elegantiae et suavitatis*; at times, all the voices might pause because of *emphasin* as well as the meaning of

---

(let alone the sophisticated and "modern" Italians and French), who learnt, knew, and taught the craft of music, regarded by a colleague and Leipzig professor of rhetoric, J. A. Birnbaum, as a great "musical orator."

40. For a comprehensive list of sixteenth-century rhetorical references in musical treatises, including the ones mentioned here, see Ruhnke, *Burmeister*, 135–38. As the present study focuses on the musical-rhetorical figures, only those references to rhetorical figures are listed here.

41. The fact that Galliculus uses both the terms *schemata* (the Greek term for rhetorical figures, otherwise not encountered in contemporary music theory) and *colorum*, traditionally also associated with the rhetorical figures, makes it almost certain that he was referring to rhetorical figures in music. See also Unger, *Beziehungen*, 32.

the words; he highlighted Clemens non Papa's use of suspensions, cadence, and fugue as three outstanding *ornamenti*. Hoffmann (1582) referred to the transgression of a mode's range as *redundantia* and *ellipsis*. Following these and other musical-rhetorical references by various German writers, the Lutheran *Kantor* and teacher Joachim Burmeister provided a detailed and systematic approach to musical composition which enshrined rhetorical terminology and methodology in the German *musica poetica* tradition at the beginning of the seventeenth century. Burmeister's efforts have been characterized as "the most significant consequence of combining music and rhetoric,"[42] profoundly influencing German compositional theory throughout the Baroque era.

Baroque Musical-Rhetorical Structure

References to rhetorically arranged music became more specific throughout the seventeenth century. Parallel to *musica poetica*'s gradual adoption of the concept and terminology of the rhetorical figures was its acceptance of rhetoric's structuring principles. Athanasius Kircher was the first to introduce the terms of the rhetorical structuring process, *inventio*, *dispositio*, and *elocutio* into musical compositional theory, preparing the way for a more explicit correlation between music and rhetoric. All three steps in this process were linked to text expression: while *inventio* refers to an appropriate musical adaptation of the corresponding text, the *dispositio* concerns itself with an "appropriate and pleasant" musical expression of the words. The musical *elocutio* then embellishes the entire composition through the use of tropes and figures.[43] This union between music and rhetoric was consummated in

42. Eggebrecht, "Über Bachs geschichtlichen Ort," 270.

43. "Ubi Rhetorica tribus constat partibus, inventione, dispositione et elocutione, ita et nostra Musurgica Rhetorica; Inventio Musurgicae Rhetoricae nihil aliud est, quam apta Musarithmorum verbis congruorum adaptatio; Dispositio vero est pulchra quaedam eorundem per aptas notarum applicationes expressio. Elocutio denique est ipsa Melothesiae onmibus numeris absolutae, tropis figurisque exornatae per cantum exhibitio." Athanasius Kircher, *Musurgia universalis sive Ars Magna Consoni et Dissoni* (Rome, 1650) II, L.8, ch.8, §4: "De Partibus Rhetoricae Musurgica," 143.

the writings of Mattheson, particularly in *Der vollkommene Capellmeister*. While the concept of the musical-rhetorical figures of the musical *elocutio* had taken firm root by the eighteenth century, Mattheson introduced the complete rhetorical structuring process to musical composition and with it the various particulars of that process, including all of *inventio*'s *loci topici* and the six steps of the *dispositio*.

MUSICAL-RHETORICAL *INVENTIO*

The first step in the rhetorical structuring process is *inventio*: determining a topic or subject. Although Kircher had introduced the concept of a musical-rhetorical *inventio*, he limited its application to the musical representation of the associated text. According to Kircher, the composer first chooses a theme or subject whose material is to become the basis and foundation for the represented and evoked affection.[44] Second, the key for the composition is chosen, again in consideration of the desired affection. Third, the composer decides upon the meter and rhythm for the composition, taking both text and its affection into consideration. This must all be done before the actual work of composition (*dispositio*) can begin. The "invention" of subject, key, and rhythm should be undertaken in such a way that the intended affection is established. Throughout the seventeenth century, composers were provided with lists of words of motion, place, affection, time, number, etc., which they were encouraged to "express and paint."[45] The musical expression of a word was frequently accomplished through the use of musical-rhetorical *hypotyposis*-figures, devices through which "the meaning of the words are enlightened in such a way, that they seem to spring to life."[46] With *inventio* thus linked to text-expression, this first step of the rhetorical process was directly linked to the third step,

---

44. Ibid., ch.3, *De locorum temporisque constitutione ad affectus concitandos ordinanda*. Dammann, *Musikbegriff*, 314.

45. ". . . quae ipso sono et notarum varietate sunt exprimenda et pingenda." Nucius, *Musices poeticae*, G3^{v}.

46. See *Hypotyposis* (Burmeister, *Musica poetica*), below. *Hypotyposis* devices, limited only by the composer's imagination, include figures such as *anabasis*, *catabasis*, and *circulatio*.

elocutio or *decoratio*, which traditionally concerned itself with the rhetorical figures.[47]

The flourishing genre of seventeenth-century instrumental music brought with it an expansion of the text-oriented concept of the musical *inventio*. Particularly fruitful in this regard was the incorporation of the *phantasia* technique, "used to refer to certain short, mechanical contrapuntal patterns, so called because they were the product of the composer's or player's imagination."[48] The correlation of *inventio* and *phantasia* is demonstrated by Mauritius Vogt when he gave the title "*De Phantasia et Inventionibus*" to the sixth chapter of his compositional treatise.[49]

With the rise of instrumental music and the growing concern regarding unity of affection, early-eighteenth-century composers were encouraged to make use of the *loci topici* in writing their music. By transferring the rhetorical *loci topici* to musical composition, Heinichen proposed that the composer might "derive a good idea from the given (and frequently unfruitful) text. But to lead our imagination, cannot, I believe, be better accomplished than through the oratorical *loci topici*. Even with the most uninspired text one can take just the three principal sources, namely *antecedentia*, *concomitantia*, and *consequentia textus*, and examine them according to the *locus topicus* by weighing carefully the purpose of the words, including the related circumstances of person, time, place, etc. Thus the inborn natural imagination . . . never lacks for the expression of valuable ideas or, to speak more clearly, skillful

---

47. See Unger, *Beziehungen*, 35ff.

48. Gregory Butler, "The Fantasia as Musical Image," *Musical Quarterly* 60, 4 (1974), 614.

49. Mauritius Vogt, *Conclave thesauri magnae artis musicae* (Prague, 1719). In a glossary at the beginning of the treatise, Vogt provides the following definition: "Phantasia, simplex & ordinatus processus sonorum, ex quibus variae fugae, themata, & passagio eliciuntur" (*Conclave*, 6). In addition to illustrating how a simple chord progression can be expanded into a longer passage, Vogt also includes some unconventional suggestions for musical invention. The composer might drop four hobnails bent in various shapes representing different *figurae simplices*, and then notate musical figurations imitating the patterns of the nails. Furthermore, the composer may want to use dice in determining the intervals to be used, or even resort to alcohol: "Et ut sim aptior ad inveniendum et componendum . . . generosi vitrellum vini non abjiciam." Ibid., 157.

inventions."[50] A composer could use the principle of the rhetorical *loci topici* and examine the texts surrounding the one which was to be set to music. Out of the context of preceding (*antecedentia*), parallel (*concomitantia*), or subsequent (*consequentia*) texts, the composer would be able to establish a suitable affection for even the "uninspired" text. Not only could such an application of the *loci topici* furnish the composer with ideas for his composition, but it would also discourage a preoccupation with particular words which might be contrary to the governing affection.[51] While Heinichen focused only on the *locus circumstantiarum*, Mattheson suggested that all *loci topici* be explored for their musical potential. Mattheson began his chapter on melodic invention with a discussion of melodic motives which might be used in structuring the melody.[52] Although he mentioned that a composer might "make a collection of all the pleasing motives which he has encountered, order them according to chapter and title, and when the need arises, gather counsel and consolation from them," he assured the reader that this would result in ragged patchwork.[53] Rather, the motives are to be kept in mind so that the composer can express himself comfortably "without constantly consulting a Lexicon for counsel."[54] Mattheson devoted the rest of the chapter to a discussion of the musical application of the *loci topici*. Even the *locus exemplorum*, which he interpreted as an imitation of other composers, can prove beneficial. However, even if this is the most frequently used source, the composer must take care that he not simply copy or steal another's work but "return it with interest. That is, one must arrange the borrowed materials in such a way, that they assume a more beautiful and improved expression than in their original context. . . . Even the greatest capitalists will borrow money if it is to their advantage or convenience."[55]

The Baroque compositional process was an objective one, in

---

50. Heinichen, *Der General-Bass*, 30, as translated in Buelow, "The 'Loci Topici' and Affect in Late Baroque Music," 162f.

51. If, for example, the composer were setting a text such as "death is swallowed up in victory," he would focus on a joyful affection instead of the word "death."

52. *Capellmeister*, pt.2, ch.4, "Von der melodischen Erfindung," 121.

53. Ibid., 123.

54. Ibid., §17.

55. Ibid., 131–32.

contrast to the subjective and individualistic one of later eras. The adaptation of a preexisting idea and the invention of a new theme were equally considered a part of the *inventio* process. The necessity of a personal and subjective experience as an inspired source for composition was foreign to the Baroque mind. All irrational, indefinite, or inaccessible musical thought was considered unworthy. This applied as much to *inventio* as to the other structural steps. The composition was conceived of and structured by rational principles of form and expression common to composer and audience alike. Thematic or subject material was in the public domain, common to all composers and comprehensible to all listeners. Whether or not a composer's disposition or "mood" coincided with the desired affection of a composition was immaterial: the composer was obligated to set a certain text to music (or provide instrumental music for a certain occasion) and looked to the given, objective material or situation for the predetermined affection. For the *musicus poeticus* such a rationally conceived and perceived composition would portray and arouse the desired affections called for by the text, always with the intention of glorifying God and edifying the listener.

Musical-Rhetorical *Dispositio*

The first musical reference which reflects the steps of the rhetorical *dispositio* can be found in Gallus Dressler's description of the *exordium*, *medium*, and *finis* of a composition.[56] Burmeister, who also espoused this tripartite organization, referred to the central section as "the body of the composition itself."[57] The *dispositio* order became a determining factor specifically in fugue composition. The opening statement of the fugal theme was referred to as "*la propositione della fuge*" by Angelo Berardi in 1690, a thought which is echoed by Dresden Capellmeister Johann Christoph Schmidt in a letter to Johann Mattheson in 1718. As Butler points out, Schmidt used the rhetorical *chria*, a simplified form

---

56. Ruhnke, *Burmeister*, 137.

57. "Haec tres habet partes, 1. Exordium, 2. Ipsum corpus carminis, 3. Finis." Burmeister, *Musica poetica*, ch.15: "De Analysi sive dispositione carminis musici," 72.

of the *dispositio*, to explain fugal structure.[58]

It remained for Mattheson to systematically apply all of the rhetorical *dispositio* steps to musical composition, now no longer applied primarily to the fugue.[59] The *exordium* introduces the composition, arousing the audience's attention and preparing them for that which is to follow. This might take the form of a prelude to a fugue or, as Praetorius indicated, an opening ritornello in an aria or concerto.[60] The *narratio* advances the intention or nature of the composition. This can be realized through the entry of the vocal part in an aria or the solo instrument(s) in a concerto. Just as the *narratio* is optional in rhetoric (it is omitted in the *chria*), it can be incorporated by the *propositio* in a musical composition. Besides being identified with the presentation of a fugal theme, the *propositio* is assigned the function of presenting the actual content and purpose of the composition. The following two sections, *confirmatio* and *confutatio*, can be considered as contrasting processes with the same ultimate purpose: to strengthen the proposition by either confirming the argument or by refuting or resolving any objections to it.[61] While the *confirmatio* employs varied and artful repetitions to reinforce the *propositio*, the *confutatio* makes use of suspensions, chromaticism, or contrasting passages which, when properly resolved, strengthen the original theme.[62] Finally, the *perora-*

---

58. "Denn eine Fuguam zu tractiren, muss ich die artificia so wohl aus der Oratoria, als bey dem Stylo moderno, nehmen. . . . Denn Dux ist Propositio: Comes Aetiologia, Oppositum ist inversio varia Fugae; . . . Confirmatio wäre wenn ich das subjectum canonisire; und Conclusio, wenn ich das subject gegen die Cadenze, in Imitatione, über eine natam firmam hören lassen." Butler, "Fugue and Rhetoric," 67, 69. Butler's study provides a most enlightening discussion of the rhetorical structure and interpretation of Baroque fugal composition, focusing primarily on the steps of the *dispositio*.

59. The details of the *dispositio* are discussed in *Capellmeister*, pt.2, ch.14: "Von der Melodien Einrichtung, Ausarbeitung und Zierde," 235ff. It is also primarily in this chapter that Mattheson deals with the musical-rhetorical figures, domain of the rhetorical *elocutio*.

60. Praetorius, *Syntagma Musicum III*, 151.

61. Frequently linked together under the term *contentio*, these steps seem to be reversible or alternating in a composition, explaining Mattheson's different ordering of the two in chapter 14, §4 and §10–11. G. Butler, "Fugue and Rhetoric," 70.

62. G. Butler lists a number of musical-rhetorical figures which are associated with these sections, including *congeries* (specifically mentioned by Burmeister), *incrementum (auxesis)*, *climax (gradatio)*, *distributio*, *confirmatio*, *hypallage*, *antistrophe*, *antimetabole*, *antithesis (contrapositum)*, *paronomasia*, and *schematoides*. Ibid., 79–97.

tio, the conclusion of the composition, is to end the composition emphatically. This may include a repetition of the opening *exordium* or ritornello. It may also make use of an elaborated pedal point, a device which is given the various names of *paragoge*, *manubrium*, or *supplementum*. The *climax* as defined by Nucius and Thuringus may also have been understood as a cadential figure, in which "we are diligent to detain the listener who eagerly awaits the end."[63]

Musical *Elocutio*: The Musical-Rhetorical Figures

The relationship between music and rhetoric was most frequently and concretely articulated through the concept of the musical-rhetorical figures. Although the musical and linguistic figures use contrasting expressive language unique to their respective discipline and medium, they agree in expressive principle, a phenomenon made possible through their common affective goal.[64] In the same way that an orator was to ornament and heighten his speech through rhetorical figures to lend it greater persuasive effect, so too could the composer portray and arouse the affections through comparable musical figures. And just as the rhetorical *elocutio* availed itself of figures of speech and thought, *musica poetica* would cultivate a concept of musical figures. Music thereby adapted one of rhetoric's most emphatic devices, beginning within a Renaissance aesthetic based on text expression and evolving throughout the Baroque era into a concept based on the expression and arousal of the affections in the listener.

---

63. See also *Climax*, below, especially Nucius and Thuringus.

64. The conflicts between the two disciplines which Vickers wishes to identify are the result of a misinterpretation both of *musica poetica*'s intentions and of the majority of literature dealing with the musical phenomenon. Vickers maintains that "all discussions of music and rhetoric assume that notes in music behave in the same way as do words in language" ("Figures of Rhetoric," 27). Upon closer examination of the sources, it becomes quite clear that music and rhetoric in the Baroque were assigned a common purpose, namely to express and arouse the affections, allowing the two disciplines to employ similar methods and strategies, without, however, the notes and the words behaving "in the same way."

The Aristotelian notion that phenomena must be terminologically identified and defined in order to be understood and taught encouraged the development of this concept of the musical figures. Only in naming the devices employed by past masters of vocal polyphony could their music be understood and explained. In order to accomplish this and make the art of composition an accessible craft to the student, it was necessary for the teacher to make these musical phenomena available for instruction, analysis, and composition. Through the concentrated emphasis on the linguistic disciplines in the *Lateinschulen*, rhetorical terminology was familiar and accessible to all students. The desire to identify preexisting musical phenomena with familiar but newly defined rhetorical terminology was explicitly affirmed by Burmeister, thereby opening up a new world of analytical possibilities.

The concept of the musical-rhetorical figures developed from an early Baroque *ornatus*-oriented understanding, in which figures were defined as aberrations from the simple or traditional compositional norms, primarily for the sake of variety, interest, and color, to a late Baroque, *movere*-oriented understanding in which the figures were defined as the primary agents for presenting and arousing the affections. A corresponding development of the rhetorical figures can be observed in the German Baroque. The rhetoric textbooks of the late seventeenth century were becoming increasingly cursory, reflecting the decline of the Latin rhetorical tradition and its classical sources of rhetorical figures. On the other hand, the growing popularization of German rhetoric based on natural speech by authors such as Christian Weise, Menantes, and Gottsched resulted in texts which increasingly emphasized rhetoric's role in directly moving the listener.[65] This led to a more affective rather than ornamental understanding of the figures. Rhetoric developed from an academic Latin discipline to a form of psychological examination of the relationship between the German language and the affections. Consequently the rhetorical figures became understood not so much as consciously applied artistic devices but as intuitive expressions found in natural speech. Such changes and developments in the rhetorical *Figurenlehre* correspond to similar developments in the discipline of music.

---

65. Forchert, "Musik und Rhetorik," 16.

THE DEVELOPMENT OF A MUSICAL *FIGURENLEHRE*

The large number of music treatises which are in one way or another indebted to Burmeister's *Figurenlehre* (Eggebrecht speaks of seventeen different authors producing twenty-seven treatises[66]) attests to the wide support and general acceptance of this rhetorical approach to music. Upon closer examination of the many different treatises, it becomes apparent that the development of the musical-rhetorical figures was anything but uniform. As Buelow points out, "there are numerous conflicts in terminology and definition among the various writers, and there is clearly no one systematic Doctrine of Musical Figures for Baroque and later music, notwithstanding frequent references to such a system by Schweitzer, Kretzschmar, Schering, Bukofzer and others."[67] Not only are there discrepancies between early- and late-Baroque *Figurenlehren*, but there are also substantial differences between authors of the same generation.[68] While some writers viewed the figures primarily as a legitimization of dissonance, others regarded their main function as the expression of the text and the affections.

In spite of the substantial differences between the various concepts of the musical-rhetorical figures, certain fundamental elements are common to all *Figurenlehren*. A musical-rhetorical figure was generally regarded as an artful and expressive musical device which digressed from either the simple, unadorned musical idiom or the established rules of counterpoint. The sixteenth century contributed both the first musical-rhetorical terminology as well as the musical sources for the first *Figurenlehren*. These early references to figures, including the writings of Burmeister, Nucius, and Thuringus, focused on text expression and *ornatus* in keeping with the Renaissance artistic ideal. Although text expression was inevitably associated with the expression of

---

66. Eggebrecht, "Über Bachs geschichtlichen Ort," 27.

67. George Buelow, "Rhetoric and music," *New Grove Dictionary*, 15: 794.

68. The term *Figurenlehre* is not used here to refer to a Baroque "Doctrine of Figures" as has been done in past scholarship, but rather only to the individual authors' concepts of the figures. As the discussion of the authors of the various *Figurenlehren* in the second part of this study will deal with the individual concepts of the musical-rhetorical figures, it will not be necessary to elaborate on the developments in great detail at this point.

the affections, this was not the primary concern of the early-seventeenth-century concepts of the figures. These early *Figurenlehren* were developed by musicians who thought, wrote, and composed in the style and context of sixteenth-century imitative counterpoint.

Throughout the seventeenth century, text-oriented modern Italian musical styles became increasingly popular in German circles, further encouraging the expression of the affections and the adaptation of rhetorical principles in musical composition. Nucius and Thuringus linked the musical figures to their rhetorical counterparts much more consciously than Burmeister had done, as evidenced in their classification of the purely musical *figurae principales* and the musical-rhetorical *figurae minus principales*. While the early *Figurenlehren* referred only periodically or indirectly to the figures' powers to evoke the affections, this function became increasingly important throughout the century. Athanasius Kircher, borrowing heavily from earlier German writers but also strongly influenced by the Italians, combined the theoretically motivated German concept with the empirically motivated Italian approach. This resulted in an increased emphasis on the portrayal of the affections. Christoph Bernhard's concept of musical-rhetorical figures rests not so much on the concern to introduce affective and rhetorical language and methods into the musical realm as it does on his efforts to bring together Italian praxis-oriented stylistic concepts with German contrapuntalism. This led to a *Figurenlehre* which concerns itself with explaining *seconda prattica* dissonances in the context of *stylus gravis* rules of counterpoint.

The growing relationship between music and rhetoric and the increasing emphasis on the affective nature of the musical-rhetorical figures continued into the eighteenth century. Ahle explained the figures in a purely rhetorical context, focusing on the literary figures found in a composition's text. In maintaining that these were to be musically expressed, he allowed a musical interpretation of virtually any rhetorical figure. With his unique classification of the musical-rhetorical figures as *figurae ideales*, Mauritius Vogt stressed that they should vividly portray not only the affection but the "idea" of a composition's text. Johann Gottfried Walther collected terms and definitions of the musical-rhetorical figures from various sources in his *Lexicon*, covering diverse *Figurenlehren* based on contrapuntal *ornatus* (Thuringus), expression of affections (Kircher, Janovka), ornamentation (Printz), dissonance use (Bernhard), and rhetorical figures (Ahle). Mattheson, like Ahle, also turned to the rhetorical figures as his source for the musical devices, regarding the musical figures as virtually identical to their rhetorical counterparts. Furthermore, through his insistence that musicians ought to turn to *natura* instead of *scientia* for their musical inspiration, Mattheson introduced a subjective and empirical element into his concept of the musical-rhetorical figures, which corresponded to parallel developments in contemporary German rhetoric.

Scheibe related his *Figurenlehre* more closely to a rhetorical concept of the figures than any previous author had done, directly modeling his discussion of the musical-rhetorical figures on Gottsched's *Versuch einer Critischen Dichtkunst*. Like Gottsched, he insisted that the figures were the very language of the affections. Both the literary and the musical expressive devices grow out of a common affection, the genesis of all human expression. The source of the musical figure is no longer the text but the affection which lies at the heart of the text. This facilitated a natural transfer of the musical-rhetorical figures to instrumental music, away from a primary focus on text-expressive vocal music. The textual orientation, a hallmark of *musica poetica* which still clearly determined Ahle's *Figurenlehre* and was beginning to weaken in the writings of Mattheson, virtually disappeared in Scheibe's *Figurenlehre*. Forkel's discussion of the figures brought the *musica poetica* and its concept of musical-rhetorical figures to its conclusion.[69]

69. The attempt has been made by some musicologists to project the concept of the musical-rhetorical figures onto music which would find such an approach quite foreign. In a series of articles, "Figurenlehre from Monteverdi to Wagner," *Musical Times* vol.120 (1979) and vol.126 (1985), Peter Williams not only points to musical-rhetorical figures in Baroque compositions but wishes to analogously define similar musical devices found in nineteenth-century Romantic music. Although his study identifies the expressive use of chromaticism, rests, and ornamental figuration in music beyond the Baroque confines, this does not legitimize the use of Baroque terminology to explain Romantic expressiveness. The absolute presuppositions of the *musica poetica*, complete with its concepts of the affections and the figures, would have been just as abhorrent to Wagner's musical taste as Baroque political absolutism was offensive to Wagner's political ideals. The concept and terminology of the *Figurenlehre* only makes sense when applied to music which was conceived, composed, and perceived in a corresponding aesthetic framework.

Although he had high praise for a musical rhetoric, his terminology betrays a concept of music which was foreign to *musica poetica.* Individualization, subjectivity, and feeling replaced the authoritative, objective, and affection-driven Baroque concept of music. Not insignificantly, Forkel's discussion of the figures no longer takes place in the context of a compositional treatise or music dictionary but in the foreword to a history of music.

The musical-rhetorical figures developed out of a need to identify and define expressive musical devices which were perceived to be more or less analogous to the rhetorical figures. The varying degrees of commonality between the musical and the rhetorical devices resulted in varying levels of overlap between their definitions. The terminology chosen to identify the musical devices was either adopted from rhetoric or newly coined to emulate a rhetorical term. The definitions which described the rhetorical or quasi-rhetorical terminology could be uniquely musical or could be modeled on the rhetorical definition of the term: first, a musical figure could be a technical, non-affective device with a unique musical, non-rhetorical name (e.g., *transitus*). Second, it could be an affective device with a newly coined musical but rhetorical sounding name. The choice of either a Greek or Latin term with the ring of a rhetorical term but no rhetorical precedent is explained by the desire to confer greater respectability on the musical device through its newly won association with the rhetorical discipline and to establish an association with the other musical-rhetorical figures. Upon closer examination of the chosen term, a literal description of the musical phenomenon is frequently found in the root of the Greek or Latin word (e.g., *heterolepsis*). Third, a figure could be an affective device with a newly defined rhetorical name. Frequently an existing rhetorical figure is not immediately adaptable to the musical context, in which case the familiar rhetorical term might be redefined with either a somewhat or a substantially altered musical definition, or even an entirely new musical content (e.g., *hyperbole*). The use of rhetorical terms with redefined musical content can lead to considerable confusion, especially when one writer attempts to establish a relationship between musical and rhetorical definitions while another author does not. One of the most involved examples of a mixture of redefined rhetorical terms and newly coined para-rhetorical terms is found in the definitions of the figures of repetition, *ana/epanalepsis* and *ana/epanadiplosis*.[70] Finally, it might be an affective musical-rhetorical figure, with name and content being common to both music and rhetoric (e.g., *exclamatio*).

In summary, classical rhetoric experienced a renewed vitality through the efforts of Renaissance humanists. This growing interest in the linguistic disciplines along with the "Word" orientation of Protestant Germany led to the development of a *musica poetica* which focused on a rhetorically structured, text-interpreting, and affection-arousing concept of music. While rhetorical influences are evident in Italian, English, and French Baroque music, only the *musica poetica* tradition developed a systematic albeit disparate concept of musical-rhetorical figures. This was the result of the German predilection to rank the rhetorical structure of a composition above its affective delivery. Instead of looking to the actor or orator for inspiration and guidance, the *musicus poeticus* turned to classical rhetorical structures. Rhetoric's structuring steps, *inventio*, *dispositio*, and *elocutio*, provided *musica poetica* with the necessary framework. *Inventio*'s *loci topici, dispositio*'s methodical precepts, and *elocutio*'s expressive devices, the rhetorical figures, all familiar to *Lateinschule* and university students and teachers, contributed the necessary methodology and terminology.

While early *Figurenlehren* reflected an *ornatus*-oriented understanding of the musical-rhetorical figures, later authors emphasized the figures' potential to express and arouse the affections. The move away from the academic classical Latin rhetoric to a vernacular German rhetoric in the *Lateinschulen* was reflected in the musical discipline through an increased emphasis on a personal experience of the affection which was to be musically presented. Germane to this development was the belief that the affection and its expressive devices were to be found in *natura* rather than in the textbook. While Forkel advocated rhetorical, affective expression in musical composition, his presuppositions were already quite foreign to *musica poetica* assumptions. Rhetorical figures "lie at the heart of human nature, and in normal speech they are the first expressions familiar to the uncultivated *Naturmensch*. . . . No doubt,

---

70. See Dammann, *Musikbegriff*, 141–44.

some of these were likewise the first forms of musical expression."[71] This aesthetic led to an eventual rejection both of *musica poetica*'s methodical expressive processes and its specific and calculated expressive devices. The natural and subjective expression of individualistic sentiments, a hallmark of an Enlightenment *Empfindsamkeit* aesthetic, no longer allowed for a calculated and objective presentation of generally accepted affections. Baroque *musica poetica* rhetoric, along with the concept of the musical-rhetorical figures, had thus become outdated and irrelevant.

71. Johann Nikolaus Forkel, *Allgemeine Geschichte der Musik* (Leipzig, 1788), 54.

Part Two

Treatises and Sources

Treatises and Sources

Joachim Burmeister

Joachim Burmeister (1564–1629) was born into a musical and literate family in Lüneburg. His four brothers all pursued artistic careers: Anton became *Kantor* at St. Michaelis in Lüneburg, Georg the rector at the *Lateinschule*, Johannes a respected poet and writer, and Franz an organist at St. Lamberti in Lüneburg. Joachim attended the local *Lateinschule* where his teachers included the *Kantors* Christoph Praetorius and Euricius Dedekind. Equally formative was his rhetoric instruction under the vice-rector, Lucas Lossius, whose textbooks on the subject were to become significant influences in Burmeister's later musical writings. In 1586 he began his studies at the Rostock University, where he completed a master's degree in the Faculty of Law in 1593. In addition to his post as *Kantor* at Rostock's principal church, St. Marien, he was also a teacher at the *Gymnasium*, holding both positions until his death.

Burmeister's responsibilities at the *Gymnasium* included not only musical activities but also Latin instruction for students up to the second last school year. His theoretical writings are more than merely "singing manuals, for it was his objective to regain for music its rightful place among the sciences."[1] It was Burmeister's intention to give the art of musical composition a place alongside the other humanistic disciplines. He considered himself a humanistically educated academic, and was therefore interested in raising the profile of compositional theory through the application of the distinguished discipline of rhetoric. At the same time, however, he also stood in the tradition of the Lutheran *Kantor*, with responsibilities to teach both music and Latin at the *Lateinschule*. His familiarity with both music and rhetoric, coupled with his responsibilities as a teacher in both disciplines, motivated him to devise a pedagogical approach which would combine these interests.

1. Martin Ruhnke, "Burmeister," *New Grove Dictionary,* 3: 485.

Burmeister was thus responsible for developing and systematizing an approach to musical analysis and composition through the application of rhetorical terminology and concepts which would remain decisive for the remainder of the Baroque *musica poetica* tradition.

Burmeister was the first in a long line of German authors to present a comprehensive list of expressive musical devices identified with terminology adapted from the rhetorical figures. Through his three publications, *Hypomnematum musicae poeticae* (1599), *Musica autoschediastike* (1601), and *Musica Poetica* (1606), he introduced a systematic concept of the musical-rhetorical figures, building on the numerous sixteenth-century references to rhetorical figures in music. It was his intention to identify established musical devices with rhetorical terminology and make them objectively accessible, as the foreword to his *Musica autoschediastike* clearly indicates: "Upon consideration of the manner in which music's wonderful 'ornatus' which surrounds the text shines forth, I must conclude, that more comprehensive and complete precepts can be provided. When we study the works of the great masters, we will rarely find one which does not exemplify some notable device. But we are bound to record our observations and gather them for future generations . . . in the form of rules and regulations. . . . And in careful and rational examination of music, we will undoubtedly conclude that there is but little difference between music and the nature of an oration. For the great power of oratory lies not in the simple aggregation of plain words or in the correct division of phrases and their unchanging and unadorned combination, but rather an oration appropriates its expressiveness through its *ornatus* and its use of significant words, including the use of emphatic expressions. In like manner, in addition to the combination of pure consonances, music also offers the listener a mixture of perfect and imperfect consonances as well as dissonances in a composition, thereby moving the heart. . . . This compilation is useful both for others and ourselves; for us because it is then no longer necessary to lecture as in past practice, and furthermore instead of using the works and rules of other writers we would have our own established forms according to which we could structure our lectures and which would guide us by the hand, as it were. Similarly these established forms would provide the listeners with terms for practically all musical devices, through which they could recognize and understand the musical devices. . . . In choosing these terms, we were moved by nothing other than our sincere desire to eliminate the lack of terminology. We believe that through these terms and designations it will be possible to become familiar with the musical material in its appropriate form."[2]

The various musical devices are given names which are either borrowed from rhetoric or coined to emulate rhetorical terms. Frequently this involves a transfer only of the literal meaning of the word rather than the rhetorical device associated with the term.[3] In other cases the rhetorical and musical contents of the term coincide. Burmeister's point of departure is always the musical composition and its expressive devices rather than the rhetorical term with a search for a corresponding musical expression. In their desire to establish a closer link between music and rhetoric, later authors would not only redefine some of Burmeister's terms with a musical content closer to the original rhetorical meaning (e.g., *anaphora*, *anadiplosis*) but would also include more figures which were common to both disciplines. While he does not consider his list of *ornamenta* exhaustive, Burmeister's musical-rhetorical figures are meant to provide a means to identify and then apply techniques which could be used in artful composition. To illustrate the application of these figures, Burmeister cites numerous examples from composers such as Clemens non Papa and Orlando Lassus, culminating in a complete analysis of Lassus's motet, *In me transierunt*.

Burmeister describes the musical figures, or *ornamenta* as he also calls them, with a definition similar to the description of the rhetorical figures. They are harmonic or melodic expressions which deviate from the simplest forms of musical expression, thereby enhancing the

---

2. A larger portion of the extensive foreword can be found in German translation in Ruhnke, *Burmeister*, 144f., which was also the source for the above translation.

3. An interesting adaptation of the rhetorical term *symploce* occurs in Burmeister's *Musica poetica*, where the term signifies a mixture of major and minor semitones. (See *Complexio*, below.) Burmeister's definition has nothing in common with the rhetorical definition of the figure, but rather is a fine example of his pursuit, in Olthoff's words: to "give everything appropriate and suitable terminology taken from rhetoric and other arts." Ruhnke, *Burmeister*, 147.

composition in a more artful manner.[4] The emphasis of this definition lies on the *ornatus* or *elegantia* function of the figure. Although the expression of the affections is not explicitly mentioned in the definition, it is tacitly included through the use of the term *periodus*. Burmeister "uses the terms period and affection interchangeably, for he defines musical affection (*affectio musica*) as 'a period in melody or harmony terminated by a cadence that moves and affects the souls and hearts of men.'"[5] Furthermore, *musica poetica*'s roles of *delectare* and *movere* are regarded as an inseparable unit, demonstrated both through Burmeister's definitions of some of his figures and his description of *poeticum decorum*. In his *Musica autoschediastike* he describes *poeticum decorum* as a most pleasant and ornate construction, a result of the consideration and interpretation of the text.[6] Rhetorical *elegantia* can be compared to this aspect of the figures. Through "*elegantia* the aesthetic expectation of the educated and fastidious listener was to be satisfied, while at the same time intentionally arousing specific affections. The chosen text for a composition presented the composer with the same expectations. . . . The two categories cannot be separated. Most of the figures can be explained both in terms of *elegantia* and word expression, for these categories were not yet distinctly separated."[7] In addition to assuming the role of text expression, a number of Burmeister's definitions also refer to the effect of the figure. The *noema*, for example, "has a sweetly stimulating and astonishingly soothing effect on the ear and spirit."[8] On the other hand, the *symblema minus* does not have the power to move the listener ("*non ita afficit*") because of its brevity, and is therefore not counted as one of the figures. The *pathopoeia* is singled

---

4. "Ornamentum, sive Figura musica est tractus musicus, tam in Harmonia, quam in Melodia, certa periodo, quae a Clausula initium sumit, & in Clausulam definit, circumscriptus, qui a simplici compositionis ratione discedit, & cum virtute ornatiorem habitum assumit & induit." *Musica poetica*, 55.

5. Palisca, "Ut Oratoria Musica," 41.

6. "Poeticum decorum est harmoniae ultra suavisonantem et harmonicam syntaxin ornatum ex textus explicandi exigentia addens." Ruhnke, *Burmeister*, 95. *Decorum* is rhetoric's fourth *virtus elocutionis*, following *ornatus*, that is, the application of the rhetorical figures and tropes.

7. Ibid., 148.

8. See *Noema*, below.

out as a particularly expressive device, defined as "an apt figure to express the affections."[9] While Burmeister's concept of the figures does not explicitly focus on affective expression as later *Figurenlehren* will, the domain of *movere* is nonetheless integral to his understanding.

As the definition of *poeticum decorum* indicates, it is the composition's text which is the determining factor in the application of the figures. This view is also articulated in the introductory comments to the figures in *Musica Poetica*: "If the student wishes to know when and where the composition is to be adorned with these figures, he is carefully to examine the text of a composition, especially one which uses the specific ornament, and then adorn a similar text with the same figure. Should he do this in such a manner, the text itself will prescribe the rules."[10]

Burmeister classifies his figures in three categories: harmonic, melodic, and harmonic-melodic figures (*figurae harmoniae*, *melodiae*, *tam harmoniae quam melodiae*). His categories are modeled after the rhetorical classifications of the figures. Rhetoric differentiated between those figures which were applied to individual words (*figurae dictionis* or *verbi*) and those which pertained to the entire sentence or structure (*figurae totius orationis*, *sermonis*, or *sententiarum*). Thus Burmeister draws a parallel between "word" and "melody" figures on the one hand, and "sentence" and "harmony" figures on the other. *Figurae harmoniae* are applied to all the voices of a composition, thereby affecting the entire structure or *harmonia*, analogous to rhetorical sentence figures.[11] The fugal figures, *fuga realis*, *metalepsis*, *hypallage*, *apocope*, the *noema* and related figures, *analepsis*, *mimesis*, *anadiplosis*, as well as

---

9. See *Pathopoeia*, below.

10. "Insuper et hoc addimus, si forte Philomusus sollicitus foret scire, quando et quo loco Harmoniae flosculis harum Figurarum sint exornandae, et quando ea adhibenda, ibi Philomusus textum alicujus Harmoniae, cujusdam autoris, et praesertim, quae alicujus ornamenti cultum et ornatum induisse videtur, probe consideret, arbitreturque, sibi similem textam eadem figura esse exornandum quo ille alterius Artificis textus est exornatus. Quodcum fecerit, textus ipse et praeceptorum instarerit." *Musica poetica*, 56.

11. "Harmoniae est, quo periodus aliqua Harmoniae ex quotenis etiam ea confecta sit vocibus, novum induit habitum, alienum a simplici consonantiarum absolutarum nexu." Ibid., 55.

symblema, *syncopa* or *syneresis*, *pleonasmus*, *auxesis*, *pathopoeia*, *hypotyposis*, *aposiopesis*, and *anaploce* belong to this category. A *figura melodiae* can be applied to either one or more voices but, like the word figures, does not necessarily alter the entire structure.[12] These figures are not, however, to be understood as mere "melodic ornaments," corresponding to the *figurae simplices* of Vogt or Printz. Burmeister uses the term *melodia* to refer to individual voices, while *harmonia* signifies the entire structure. The figures *paremobole*, *palillogia*, *climax*, *parrhesia*, *hyperbole*, and *hypobole* belong to this second category. To accommodate those musical figures which he considers both melodic and harmonic, he establishes his third category. The remaining figures, *congeries*, *Faux Bourdon*, *anaphora*, and *fuga imaginaria* make up these *figurae tam harmoniae quam melodiae*. Although more than one voice is affected through these figures, Burmeister does not count them as *figurae harmoniae*. These figures initially transform only individual voices through similar or identical structuring. Only through this process is the *harmonia* altered. Burmeister's classifications seem somewhat awkward at times, better suited to rhetorical than to musical figures. Nucius recognizes the difficulty with Burmeister's categories and develops a classification which is derived from the musical figures themselves and tailored to suit their specific needs. It was to be Nucius's grouping of the musical-rhetorical figures which would be adopted by subsequent writers. Not until Mattheson is the parallel between the musical-rhetorical figures and the *figurae dictionis* and *figurae sententiarum* again to be drawn, albeit in a very different context and with contrasting implications.

The originality of Burmeister's work is affirmed by his fellow musician Statius Olthoff, as well as by Johannes Simonius, the Rostock *Professor oratoriae*. In a letter to Olthoff, Simonius voices his approval regarding the application of rhetorical terminology not only to musical figures but to all parts of a composition: "Most learned Master Statius, I am returning to you the very scholarly book on *musica poetica* by M. Burmeister, a book directed at the well educated and not the student. I approve whole-heartedly of it. While I cannot allow myself judgement

---

12. "Melodia ornamentum est, quod unicae saltem voci ornatum addit." Ibid., 56.

on matters concerning *musica poetica*, I nonetheless recognize that he [Burmeister] employs grammatical and oratorical terminology to express valuable material on scales, notation . . . and the progression of musical consonances and dissonances in a most learned and subtle manner. . . . I find his teachings on the modi and the figures particularly attractive, and that in his discussion of the same he chooses from their infinite number only a few simple polyphonic examples and assigns them oratorical terminology."[13] Olthoff also acknowledges Burmeister's groundbreaking work, and encourages him to persist in his pursuits: "You not only teach composition, the syntactic rules of consonances, and the recognition of the musical modi with the help of certain figures and careful subdivisions, but you also give everything appropriate and suitable terminology taken from rhetoric and other arts, in order to avoid any misunderstandings or ambiguity. Although there will undoubtedly be those who will disapprove of these terms because of their novelty, I must nonetheless encourage you for the sake of the students to continue in your efforts and to ensure that these precepts be published and made available to all. May this art receive further research and clarification through similar studies."[14] It is quite unlikely that Simonius, Olthoff, or even Burmeister could have imagined how much "further research and clarification" the musical-rhetorical figures were about to receive, or how many "similar studies" on this art were to be written in the years to follow.

Johannes Nucius

Johannes Nucius (ca.1556–1620) was born in Görlitz, Silesia, where he attended the local *Gymnasium*. Here he came under the influence of the *Kantor*, Johannes Winkler, from whom he also received private lessons in composition. Nucius acknowledged the formative influences of the Lutheran Winkler in the introduction to his *Musices Poeticae*.[15]

13. Ruhnke, *Burmeister*, 147.
14. Ibid.
15. *Musices poeticae sive de compositione cantus praeceptiones* (Niesse, 1613).

Around 1586 Nucius entered the Cistercian monastery in Rauden as a monk, becoming a deacon in 1591. In the same year he was also named the abbot of a small monastery in Himmelwitz. A talented composer, Nucius published over one hundred motets in two volumes (1591, 1609).

Nucius's *Musices Poeticae* plays an important role in furthering the concept of the musical-rhetorical figures. While Burmeister's classification of the figures into *figurae harmoniae*, *melodiae*, and *tam harmoniae quam melodiae* was derived from rhetorical models, Nucius introduces two categories based on the content and function of the musical figures themselves. He distinguishes between *figurae principales* and *figurae minus principales*, a classification which was adopted by Thuringus, Kircher, and Janovka. Bernhard and after him Walther substitute the terms *figurae fundamentales* and *figurae superficiales* respectively for these two categories of figures. Nucius inaugurates a distinction between those musical figures which are essentially technical musical devices and those which are more closely linked to the text and affection-expressive rhetorical figures. In the years that followed, this latter category would receive increased attention and substantial additions.

Nucius classifies three figures, *fuga*, *commissura*, and *repetitio*, as *figurae principales*. Both *fuga* and *commissura* (the passing note) are among the oldest and most conventional methods of elaborating a musical composition. While fugal technique arose out of the repetition or imitation of a musical motive or phrase, the origin of the passing note can be found in the penultimate dissonances in early *organum*. Fugal imitation and passing notes are also fundamental to fifteenth- and sixteenth-century contrapuntal technique. These two compositional devices are unique musical phenomena, lacking rhetorical models for both their terminology and their content. And yet they are the first devices to be associated with the rhetorical figures. As early as 1477, Tinctoris had compared the passing dissonance to an *ornatus* used by grammarians.[16] Stomius (1536) had referred to fugue as a *mimesis*,

16. "Discordantiae parvae a musicis sicut rationabiles a grammaticis ornatus necessitatisve causa assumi permittuntur." Feldmann, "Das 'Opusculum bipartitum,'" 132.

while Dressler (1563) had maintained that, in addition to suspensions and cadences, fugues were one of Clemens non Papa's *ornamenta.*[17] Nucius stands in good company when he classifies these venerable musical devices as "principal" methods of elaborating a composition.

While *fuga* and *commissura* would be classified as "principal" or "fundamental" figures by later authors, Nucius's third *figura principalis*, the *repetitio*, was to be removed from this category. Thuringus, whose *Opusculum bipartitum* was published eleven years after the *Musices Poeticae*, adopted a great deal of Nucius's *Figurenlehre*. In addition to using the same figure categories, Thuringus also repeats Nucius's description of the role and purpose of the figures virtually verbatim. However, Thuringus would make two significant changes to the classification of the figures. Substantially increasing the number of musical-rhetorical *figurae minus principales* from Nucius's four (*climax*, *complexio*, *homioteleuton*, *syncopatio*) to fourteen, Thuringus also classifies the *repetitio* as one of these, while removing the *syncopatio* from this group and placing it among the *figurae principales*.

The introductory comments to the figures in the treatises of Nucius and Thuringus are virtually identical, and can therefore be discussed simultaneously. The explanation of the musical figures begins with a comparison between the visual and the musical arts: "Just as the painter will not merit great praise through an exact reflection of the bearing, state, or color of an image, but rather endows his images with their unique gestures, peculiar appearances, and distinct colors, thereby gratifying the eyes of the viewers, so too will a musical composition through uninterrupted similitude and lack of florid embellishments not only remain artless, but also bore the listeners."[18] Nucius then suggests that musical figures (*musica schemata*) could embellish and enhance a composition in the same manner that rhetoric uses figures and tropes. As deviations from the plain and ordinary musical idiom, the figures

17. Ruhnke, *Burmeister*, 135f.

18. "Sicut Pictor eodem habitu ac statu, eodemque colore pingens quascunque imagines tantam non meretur laudem, ac si singulis singulos gestus, peculiarem vultum, ac distinctos colores, quibus spectantium oculi pascuntur, tribuat. Sic Harmonia Musica, sui perpetuo similis, nec ullis ornata floribus, non modo indoctior habetur, sed etiam taedium auditoribus incutit." *Musices poeticae*, ch.7, F4^{r}.

would lend the composition greater "grace and variety."[19] The purpose of the figures as described by both Nucius and Thuringus centers more on *ornatus* than *movere*, more on delighting the listeners than on arousing them. The musician's work is compared to that of a painter rather than an orator. Unlike Burmeister, neither Nucius nor Thuringus refer to the expression of the affections in their introductory definition of the figures. However, following his discussion of the figures, Nucius adds various lists of words which are to be expressed musically in a composition. Included is a list of "affective words" (*verba affectuum*), consisting of rejoicing, weeping, fearing, lamenting, bewailing, mourning, raging, laughing, and pitying, all to be "expressed and painted through the variety and sound of the notes."[20] While Nucius appends this list to his discussion of the figures, Thuringus would incorporate the list in his definition of *parthopoeia*, as he spelled it, reintroducing Burmeister's figure into his own *Figurenlehre*. The figures' role of expressing the affections, explicitly encountered only periodically in the *Figurenlehren* of Burmeister, Nucius, and Thuringus, would become a distinguishing feature of the musical-rhetorical figures beginning with Kircher. A similar development can be observed in the development of the rhetorical figures throughout the seventeenth and eighteenth centuries.

In contrast to Burmeister, who justified the novelty of introducing musical figures by emphasizing the need for new terminology to aid in teaching analysis and composition, Nucius seems to be more concerned with the lack of established musical-rhetorical figures.[21] While Burmeister's *Figurenlehre* grew out of the musical material, assigning rhetorical terminology to the musical devices found in a composition, Nucius's grows out of a desire to establish a musical *Figurenlehre* analogous to the rhetorical concept of the figures. He suggests that it would not be

---

19. "Ut vero econtra Rhetorum orationes verborum sententiarumque luminibus ornatae, ac figuris ac Tropis variatae . . . gratiosae sunt ac auditoribus arrident. Sic contentus elegantiam, non parum Musica Schemata ornant atque juvant." Ibid.

20. "Huc inferenda sunt alia Harmoniae quoque decora, ut sunt primum verba affectuum, Laetari, Gaudere, lacrymari, timere, ejulare, flere, lugere, irasci, ridere, Misereri, &: quae ipso sono & notarum varietate sunt exprimenda & pingenda." Ibid., G3^{v}.

21. "Quare pauca de his quoque annotabimus." Ibid.

difficult to assemble a large catalog of musical figures in imitation of rhetoric.[22] Taking his own advice to heart, Nucius describes his *complexio* as a figure "*in imitation of the poets*."[23] While the authors of the various music treatises frequently refer to the similarity between the musical and the rhetorical *Figurenlehren*, only Nucius and Thuringus explicitly encourage a musical imitation of the rhetorical concept. However, the musical "parody" should be understood not simply as an imitation, but as an attempt to structure the musical "oration" parallel to its rhetorical counterpart, lending it greater *varietas* and *elegantia*. The fact that an extensive catalog of rhetorical figures was familiar to musicians who were intent on establishing a similar musical arsenal encouraged authors like Nucius, Thuringus, and many following writers to identify musical-rhetorical devices "*ad imitationem poetarum*." As Nucius reminds the reader, even the mediocre student was familiar with rhetorical figures,[24] suggesting not only their widespread recognition and use, but also their immediate adaptability. Like Burmeister, Nucius quoted musical examples taken from the motets of Clemens and Lassus, indicating that he is also intent on identifying preexisting musical devices rather than only encouraging the development of new musical expressions. Ultimately, Nucius is not so much only interested in introducing specifically rhetorical devices into musical composition as he is concerned with establishing a closer link between musical and rhetorical devices through a common terminology.

Joachim Thuringus

Joachim Thuringus, whose dates remain unknown, was presumably the son of a Pastor M. Thuringus in Fürstenberg, Mecklenburg.[25]

22. "Etsi ad Rhetorum imitationem non difficile erat ingentem figurarum Cathalogum coacervare." Ibid.

23. See *Complexio*, below.

24. "In his enim omnis latini sermonis delicias sitas esse, nemo est, vel mediocriter eruditorum, qui nesciat." Ibid.

25. Besides calling himself "S. S. Theol. et Lib. Art. Studiosus et P[oeta] L[aureatus] C[aesareus]," he was referred to as "Doctissimus Juvenis vir." Feldmann, "Das 'Opusculum bipartitum,'" 124.

Besides being a music theorist, Joachim Thuringus was well rounded in the humanities, his interests incorporating both theology and the liberal arts.

Thuringus stands under the influence of both Nucius and Burmeister, reflecting the *Figurenlehren* of both authors in his own treatise, *Opusculum bipartitum* (Berlin 1624). Thuringus's close association with the Burmeisters is attested to by the epigrams in his treatise by Joachim Burmeister's two brothers, Anton and Georg. Furthermore, Thuringus reintroduces many of Burmeister's figures which had not been included in Nucius's *Musices Poeticae*. However, Thuringus is indebted to Nucius for the substantial elements of his concept of the musical-rhetorical figures. The introductory comments which the treatises of the two authors have in common has already been discussed.[26]

Thuringus also adopts Nucius's classification of the figures into *figurae principales* and *figurae minus principales*. He no doubt recognized the importance of Nucius's new categories which divided the figures between primarily musical, technical-compositional devices, and musical-rhetorical expressive figures. However, Thuringus changes the classification of some figures and adds a substantial number to the second category. While retaining *fuga* and *commissura* in the first category, Thuringus reassigns the *syncopatio* to this group. Along with fugal technique and the passing note, the harmonic syncopation or suspension was an integral element of fifteenth- and sixteenth-century counterpoint. As early as 1563 Dressler had referred to the suspension as one of the expressive *ornamenta* used by Clemens.[27] While it is a common musical device, it appears only infrequently in rhetoric, where it refers to the omission of a letter in a word.[28] The *repetitio*, on the other hand, Thuringus moves from the first category to the *minus principales* figures. In contrast to the *syncopatio*, the *repetitio* is a figure frequently encountered in rhetoric, used by some rhetoricians as a collective name for all figures of repetition. By consistently applying Nucius's principles of classification, it becomes necessary for Thuringus

26. See p.101f., above.
27. Ruhnke, *Burmeister*, 137.
28. See *Syncopatio* (Susenbrotus), below.

to make these minor adjustments to Nucius's categorization of the figures, "thus achieving a distinction between the autonomous figures and the heteronomous musical-rhetorical *figurae minus principales*."[29] Thuringus's grouping of the figures is then adopted by Kircher and Janovka, as well as Bernhard and Walther, who were to rename the categories as *figurae fundamentales* and *figurae superficiales*. At the close of the Baroque era, these three principal or fundamental devices are still regarded as a unit, but are no longer regarded as figures. Scheibe would describe them as elementary rules of composition, having little or no affective potential.

In addition to interchanging the classifications of *repetitio* and *syncopatio*, Thuringus significantly expands the number of *figurae minus principales*. To Nucius's *climax*, *complexio*, *homioteleuton*, and now *repetitio*, Thuringus adds the *pausa*, *anaphora*, *catachresis* (*faux bourdon*), *noema*, *parthopoeia* [*sic*], *parrhisia*, *aposiopesis*, which included both the *homiaeoptoton* and *homioteleuton*, *paragoge*, and *apocope*. Except for *pausa*, all the figures which Thuringus adds are to be found in Burmeister's *Figurenlehre*. In cases where Nucius and Burmeister had supplied a term with different definitions (e.g., *climax*), Thuringus adopts the Nucius definition. Thuringus is the only writer to include both the *repetitio* and the *anaphora* in his *Figurenlehre*, adopting Burmeister's definition of *anaphora* and Nucius's definition of *repetitio*. In his discussion of the *pausa* and its applications, Thuringus leans on the writings of Dressler.[30] The *pausa* or musical rest had long been considered a text-expressive device, and was therefore traditionally linked to oration. Furthermore, all of Thuringus's *minus principales* figures apart from the *pausa* are assigned names adopted from the rhetorical figures, thereby dutifully increasing the "*cathalogum figurarum . . . ad Rhetorum imitationem.*" Thuringus changes the names of two Burmeister figures, calling Burmeister's *faux bourdon* "*catachresis*" and the *supplementum* (Nucius's *manubrium*) "*paragoge*," thereby ensuring a consistent use of rhetorical terminology in this group of figures.

---

29. Feldmann, "Das 'Opusculum bipartitum,'" 134.
30. See *Pausa*, below.

ATHANASIUS KIRCHER

Athanasius Kircher (1601–1680) was a German Jesuit theologian, mathematician, music theorist, and polyhistorian. He received his education in the humanities and sciences at various Jesuit schools and universities in Germany. In 1629 he was appointed professor of mathematics, philosophy, and oriental languages at the University of Würzburg. After some more studies at Avignon in the natural sciences, Kircher went to Rome in 1633, where he was appointed professor of mathematics, physics, and eastern studies at the Jesuit *Collegio Romano*, and remained until his death.

Kircher's *Musurgia Universalis*,[31] a "compendium of musical facts and speculation that is still essential to an understanding of 17th-century music and music theory . . . was drawn upon by almost every later German music theorist until well into the 18th century."[32] In this profound and all-encompassing tome Kircher, the historian, seeks to gather the entire body of both historical and contemporary, western and eastern musical knowledge and speculation. While he is not part of the north German Lutheran *Kantor* tradition, he shares many concerns and interests with the *Melopoeta*. Like most seventeenth-century Lutheran composers, Kircher, the mathematician, subscribes to the medieval, cosmological understanding of speculative music theory. As a natural scientist, Kircher has keen interests in the field of human pathology, including the study of the affections. And as a Jesuit scholar, the importance of the discipline of rhetoric is not lost on Kircher. It should come as no surprise that Kircher would highlight the speculative, affective, and rhetorical nature of music, as anachronistic as this might seem in a work published in Italy in 1650. Kircher's conservative yet rationalistic concept of music is much more rooted in the *musica poetica* tradition than it is in the Italian milieu. However, his *Figurenlehre* does not appear in a *musica poetica* treatise but rather in an encyclopedic and philosophical summary of musical concepts.

Kircher discusses the musical-rhetorical figures in two separate

---

31. *Musurgia universalis, sive ars magna consoni et dissoni* (Rome, 1650).
32. George Buelow, "Kircher," *New Grove Dictionary*, 10: 73.

places in his *Musurgia Universalis*. He begins *Liber* 5 *(De Symphoniurgia)*, chapter 19 (*De Figuris sive Tropis harmonicis in cantilenis servandis*) with a definition of the musical-rhetorical figures: "Our musical figures are and function like the embellishments, tropes, and the varied manners of speech in rhetoric. For just as the orator moves the listener through an artful arrangement of tropes, now to laughter, now to tears, then suddenly to pity, at times to indignation and rage, occasionally to love, piety, and righteousness, or to other such contrasting affections, so too music [moves the listener] through an artful combination of the musical phrases and passages. . . . There are, then, two classes of figures recognized in music: *principales* and *minus principales* figures."[33] Kircher's concept of the musical-rhetorical figures does not focus on the use of rhetorical language in musical analysis (Burmeister), nor on the figures' usefulness in lending a composition greater grace and variety (Nucius, Thuringus). Rather, Kircher highlights the figures' role as affective devices. While the expression of the affections was implied and periodically mentioned by the earlier authors, it now becomes the primary objective of the musical figures.

Following the definition, Kircher provides a list of musical figures based on Thuringus's *Figurenlehre*, after which he discusses only the *figurae principales*. He retains not only the classification of the figures as they were listed in the *Opusculum*, but even lists the figures in the same order as Thuringus had done. While *commissura*, *syncopatio*, and *fuga* make up the *figurae principales*, the *figurae minus principales* consist of *pausa*, *repititio*, *climax*, *complexum*, *anaphora*, *catachresis*, *noema*, *prosopopoeia*, *parrhesia*, *aposiopesis*, *paragoge*, and *apocope*. Besides some minor variations in spelling,[34] Kircher replaces Thurin-

33. "Figurae in Musurgia nostra idem sunt praestantque, quod colores, tropi, atque varii modi dicendi in Rhetorica. Quemadmodum enim Rhetor artificioso troporum contextu Auditorem movet nunc ad risum modo ad planctum; subinde ad misericordiam, nonnunquam ad indignationem & iracundiam, interdum ad amorem, pietatem & iustitiam, aliquando ad contrarios hisce affectus, ita & Musica artificioso clausularum sive periodorum harmonicarum contextu. . . . Sunt itaque duplices figurae a Musicis considerandae; Principales, & minus principales." *Musurgia universalis*, L.5, ch.19, 366.

34. Kircher was inconsistent in his own spelling of *repititio, complexum* (L.5) / *repetitio, complexus* (L.8), with *complexum* / *complexus* replacing Thuringus's *complexio*. He also used the more common spelling of *parrhesia* instead of Thuringus's *parrhisia*.

gus's *parthopoeia* with *prosopopoeia.* Kircher must have been concerned with more than the unique yet consistent (mis)spelling of *parthopoeia.* Having defined the figures as devices which generally express the affections, it was no longer necessary to include a figure whose primary purpose coincided with the general purpose of the *Figurenlehre.* Instead, Kircher chooses to include the *prosopopoeia*, a figure used to give inanimate objects life and action.[35] As such, the *prosopopoeia* is a "word-expressive" or *hypotyposis* figure. However, neither of these two figures are included in his list of defined figures in *Liber* 8. In place of these, Kircher defines specific *hypotyposis* figures, including *anabasis, catabasis, circulatio, homoiosis*, as well as other figures which could also be used for this purpose. With affection and word-expression subsumed into the general concept of the musical-rhetorical figures, these functions no longer require a specific figure.

Kircher later defines a number of musical-rhetorical figures in the eighth chapter of *Musurgia Universalis*'s *Liber* 8: *Musurgia Mirifica*, a chapter which he dedicates to the discussion of "musical rhetoric." The chapter, entitled *Musurgia Rhetorica*, begins with a few introductory paragraphs which emphasize the similarity in purpose and method between rhetoric and music. It is here that Kircher includes the introduction of a musical *inventio, dispositio*, and *elocutio*.[36] Dressler had already referred to the *exordium, medium*, and *finis* of a composition, the three fundamental sections of the *dispositio* which Burmeister also adopts. Building on this tradition, Kircher expands the concept of a musical rhetoric by introducing the three structural steps of rhetoric into musical composition. Throughout these paragraphs, and indeed the entire chapter, the importance of the expression of the affections is continuously stressed.[37] According to Kircher, the various affections could be classified in three general categories: joyful, pious or subdued,

---

35. Sonnino, *Handbook*, 54.

36. See p.76, n.43, above.

37. "Sicuti Rhetorica variis argumentis & rationibus veluti per figurarum troporumque varium contextum animum nunc delectat, nunc contristat, . . . denique peracta mentis commotione tandem ad id, quod Orator intendit, consentiendum Auditorem inclinat. Ita & Musica pro vario periodorum contextu tonorumque diversa dispositione, varie animum agitat." *Musurgia universalis*, L.8, ch.8, §2, 142.

and sad, out of which all the other affections originate.[38] Kircher then enumerates the twelve church modes, or *toni* as he calls them, with their associated affections. He not only associates the modes with certain affections, as was traditionally done, but also draws a parallel between the modes and the rhetorical tropes.[39] After discussing the musical *inventio, dispositio*, and *elocutio*, Kircher elaborates on the role of musical *ornatus*, the third *virtus* of *elocutio*, and home of the rhetorical figures. Once again the expression of both the affections and the words is of central importance.[40] The discussion and definitions of the musical-rhetorical figures follow. While adopting the rationale and terminology of rhetorical figures, Kircher is careful to note the difference between the musical and the rhetorical principles: "We perceive the figures in musical composition differently than do the rhetoricians, for we use tropes and figures for the same purpose. However, the rhetorical figure varies the same word. . . . But the rhetorical figures cannot serve our undertaking, so very distinct through its combination of voices in a composition, in quite the same measure. Nevertheless, this class of figures is well suited to the *stylus recitativus*, when namely only one voice has the greater advantage of expressing the words."[41]

---

38. "Movet autem animam nostram per tres potissimos affectus, ex quibus tanquam ex radice quadam alii postmodum nascuntur. Sunt autem hi tres affectus generales sequentes, primus est laetitia, quae sub se continet affectus amoris, magnanimitatis, impetus, desiderii, qui ex sanguine originem suam nanciscuntur, si vero laetitia dissoluta intemperataque fuerit, generat affectus proprie cholericos, irae, odii, indignationis, vindictae, furoris. Secundus remissionis affectus generalis cum tardo motu gaudeat, generat affectus pietatis, amoris in Deum, item constantiae, modestiae, severitatis, . . . Tertius est misericordiae affectus, sub qua manent omnes ii affectus qui a phlegmate & cholera nigra profluunt, uti sunt tristiae, planctus, commiserationis." Ibid.

39. "Nos tropos aliter sumentes, nihil aliud esse dicimus, quam certas Melothesiae periodos, certam animi affectionem connotantes; & tales iuxta duodecim tonorum diversitatem duodecim quoque constituimus; Nam hinc, & antiqui tonos non aliter ac tropos appellandos censuerunt; cum diversi diversos animi affectus denotent, & sunt proprii Musicorum." Ibid., §7, 144. The terms *modus* and *tropus* had been used interchangeably in rhetoric since antiquity. (Quintilian, *Institutio*, VIII.v.35, 300.)

40. "Ornatus Musurgiae nostrae in hoc consistit, ut notarum, intervallorumque contextus verborum significationi respondeat, ut si celerem animi motum significent verba, eum notis celeribus, si tardum, tardis apte exprimat." *Musurgia universalis* L.8, 144.

41. "Figuras in hac Musurgica arte nos aliter accipimus, ac Rhetores; Nam hic pro eadem re sumimus tropos & figuras. Consistit autem figura Rhetorica in varia eiusdem verbi additione, geminatione . . . . Que non ita commode nostro instituto servire possunt,

Kircher then defines the following figures: *pausa, stenasmus* (*suspiratio*), *anaphora* (*repetitio*), *climax*, *symploce* (*complexus*), *homoioptoton*, *antitheton* (*contrapositum*), *anabasis* (*ascensio*), *catabasis* (*descensus*), *kyklosis* (*circulatio*), *fuga*,[42] *homoiosis* (*assimilatio*), and *abruptio*. Of this list, the *pausa*, *repetitio*, *climax*, *complexus*, and *anaphora* are mentioned earlier in *Liber* 5. Two distinguishing features become evident in this list of figures and their definitions. Kircher seems to be intent on using Greek terminology wherever possible, including those figures or terms which were purely musical innovations without rhetorical antecedents, thereby linking the musical figures more closely to the ancient art of rhetoric. Secondly, in all of his definitions there is an explicit reference to the expression of either an affection or the text. Throughout his *Musurgia*, in every instance where Kircher mentions, discusses, or defines the musical-rhetorical figures, affection expression in a rhetorical context plays a significant role. Due to the vast, encyclopedic nature of the *Musurgia Universalis* and Kircher's concern to represent all current and past musical thought, it is inevitable that certain inconsistencies in terminology or content would arise. However, the orientation toward the concepts of rhetoric and the affections in Kircher's *Figurenlehre* remains unequivocal.

Kircher is the first author to identify specifically the *stylus recitativus* as a suitable musical style for the application of the musical-rhetorical figures. He thereby incorporates not only Renaissance choral polyphony but also contemporary musical styles into his concept of the figures. While Burmeister, Nucius, and Thuringus still thought, wrote, and composed in the context of imitative counterpoint, Kircher does not remain untouched by the modern Italian styles. He is thus prompted not only to apply the figures to these new musical forms of expression but

---

utpote vocibus concordantibus harmonice, nimium dissipatis: etsi stylo recitativo id genus figurarum melius quadret, dum videlicet uno vox maiorem commoditatem habet eas exprimendi." Ibid., §7.

42. *Fuga* in this context is more than simply an imitative device, but rather signifies a specific text-expressive use of fugue, reflecting a "chase" in the music. Even though the fugue had been thoroughly discussed earlier as a *figura principalis*, it is now explained in terms of its *hypotyposis* character, justifying its reappearance in this list of figures. In Janovka's definition, this distinction is clarified through the expression, *fuga in alio sensu* (fugue in another sense). See *Fuga*, below.

to emphasize musical expression itself, focusing so notably on *musica pathetica* and the concepts of the affections and temperaments. Significantly, it will be Christoph Bernhard, student and successor of Heinrich Schütz, who will apply the musical-rhetorical figures to the modern styles in the German context. Together Kircher and Bernhard signal *musica poetica*'s integration of affection and text expression with the new Italian styles, while still retaining the cosmological concept of music. While Kircher accomplishes this in a highly speculative and encyclopedic treatise on the accumulated store of musical knowledge, Bernhard will present his theories in German praxis-oriented compositional manuals.

Elias Walther

The numerous *musica poetica* treatises, music dictionaries, and encyclopedias are not the only sources for the musical-rhetorical figures. The 1664 dissertation by Elias Walther of Arnstadt provides us with an example of a young scholar's practical application of the *Figurenlehre*. Presiding at Walther's examination at the University of Tübingen was the illustrious poet and professor *Eloquentiae Historiarum et Poeseos* Christoph Caldenbach, a learned scholar of rhetoric. In his dissertation, Walther analyzes the motet *In me transierunt* by Orlando Lassus. In the final pages of the dissertation, Walther also discusses the musical-rhetorical figures found in the motet. In this section, he leans heavily on Burmeister's analysis of the same motet, found at the end of the *Musica Poetica*.[43] All of the figures identified by Walther are found in Burmeister's treatise. Neither does Walther provide any specific definitions of the figures, but rather seems to assume that they are familiar enough not to warrant further explanations. While his dissertation does not offer a new or distinct perspective on the *Figurenlehre*, it does establish the fact that rhetorical analysis of

43. For a complete translation of section 18 of the dissertation which deals with the musical-rhetorical figures in the motet, see Arnold Schering, "Die Lehre von den musikalischen Figuren," 109ff.

musical compositions did not only remain wishful thinking on the part of music theorists but indeed was applied and accepted by musicians and rhetoricians alike during the German Baroque era.

CHRISTOPH BERNHARD

Christoph Bernhard (1628–1692) was born in Kolberg, Pomerania (now Poland). In 1649, after attending the *Lateinschule* in Danzig, Bernhard was appointed singer and voice instructor at the electoral court in Dresden. Here he worked under Heinrich Schütz, who held Bernhard in high regard, recommending him as his deputy, a position which he finally assumed in 1655. In the 1650s Bernhard undertook two trips to Italy, where he is said to have studied with Carissimi. In 1663 he moved to Hamburg, where he was appointed *Kantor* at the *Johannisschule*, being responsible for the music at the city's four principal churches. He returned to Dresden in 1674 as vice-*Kapellmeister* and tutor to the elector's grandchildren. He held the position of *Kapellmeister* from 1681 until his death.

Bernhard's compositional treatises did not appear in print during his life-time. They include *Von der Singe-Kunst, oder Maniera*, *Tractatus compositionis augmentatus* (hereafter referred to as *Tractatus*), and *Ausführlicher Bericht vom Gebrauche der Con- und Dissonantien* (hereafter referred to as *Bericht*).[44] While *Von der Singe-Kunst* is a short and presumably early work on vocal ornamentation, the *Tractatus* (ca.1660) is the most comprehensive and detailed compositional treatise. The *Bericht* is a later abridgment of the *Tractatus*, which focuses primarily on the figures. His theoretical works were widely circulated, profoundly influencing the writings of J. G. Walther and Mattheson, among others.

---

44. The three treatises first appeared in print under the title *Die Kompositionslehre Heinrich Schützens in der Fassung seines Schülers Chr. Bernhard*, ed. Joseph Müller-Blattau (Leipzig: Breitkopf & Härtel, 1926; 2nd. ed. Kassel: Bärenreiter, 1963), translated into English by Walter Hilse as "The Treatises of Christoph Bernhard," *Music Forum* 3, ed. William Mitchell and Felix Selzer (New York: Columbia University Press, 1973), 1–196.

Bernhard introduces a new perspective to the concept of the musical-rhetorical figures. While Burmeister, Nucius, and Thuringus were primarily concerned with identifying devices of musical *ornatus*, and Kircher was intent on establishing a correlation between the figures and the affections, Bernhard's prime objective is to explain and legitimize the occurrence and use of dissonance in a musical composition through the application of the musical-rhetorical figures. In spite of their differences, germane to all of these *Figurenlehren* is the concept of a figure as an artful and irregular manner of musical text expression. In his *Tractatus*, Bernhard defines a figure as "a certain way of employing dissonances, which renders these not only inoffensive, but rather quite agreeable, bringing the skill of the composer to the light of day."[45] In the parallel section of his *Bericht*, Bernhard states that dissonances "should be avoided only when they are without a basis in musical rules, and hence unacceptable. To this end—namely, to exhibit the use of dissonances that much more clearly—I have sought out certain figures, which hopefully will not be without service."[46]

Bernhard considers all figures—whether they are time-honored contrapuntal techniques such as suspension and passing notes or more modern expressive devices—to be rooted in the rules of traditional counterpoint. It is the counterpoint of sixteenth century polyphony which is to form the basis of the modern style of composition.[47] Most of his numerous musical examples include both an example of the figure as well as an "un-figured" original version, which is invariably in the *gravis* style. Bernhard thereby demonstrates the corresponding relationship between the two styles rather than suggesting a breach between the

45. "Figuram nenne ich eine gewisse Art die Dissonantzen zu gebrauchen, daß dieselben nicht allein nicht wiederlich, sondern vielmehr annehmlich werden, und des Componisten Kunst an den Tag legen." *Tractatus*, ch.16, 3; Hilse, "Treatises," 77.

46. "So dennoch sind die Dissonantien, wenn sie kunstmäßig gebrauchet werden, die vornehmste Zierde eines Stückes und sollen dannenhero nur vermieden werden, wenn sie ohne Grund der musikalischen Regeln, und also ohne Annehmlichkeit seyn. Zu solchem Ende, nehmlich den Gebrauch der Dissonantien desto klärer zu zeigen, hab ich etliche Figuren erfunden, welche hoffentlich nicht undienlich seyn werden." *Bericht*, ch.10; Hilse, "Treatises," 77.

47. F. Fiebig, "Christoph Bernhard," *Hamburger Beiträge zur Musikwissenschaft* 22 (1980): 55. This point is also repeatedly made by Helmut Federhofer, "Christoph Bernhards Figurenlehre und die Dissonanz," *Musikforschung* 42 (1989): 110.

old and the new, the *prima* and *seconda prattica*. Any expressive devices or figures which cannot be explained on the basis of traditional counterpoint are not to be condoned: "Such figures and works, however, have the old masters as their foundation, and what cannot be excused through them must rightly be weeded out from composition as an abomination."[48]

Bernhard is also the first author to explicitly apply the concept of the figures to purely instrumental music. In emphasizing the use of dissonance instead of the expression of the text as the primary motivating factor for his *Figurenlehre*, Bernhard allows a transfer of the concept of the figures to music which is not text-bound. This understanding of the figures is mentioned a number of times in his treatises. The figures can be "found nowadays in vocal works—both church and table music—as well as in instrumental pieces."[49] Furthermore, composers were inspired to include figures in their compositions in emulation of the embellishments employed not only by singers but also by instrumentalists.[50]

Bernhard classifies the figures in his *Tractatus* according to the various styles of contrapuntal composition. The "*contrapunctus gravis* is the type consisting of notes which do not move too quickly, and of few kinds of dissonance treatment. It does not consider text as much as it does harmony; and since it was the only type known to composers of former ages, it is called stylus *antiquus*—as also *a cappella* and *ecclesiasticus*, since it is better suited for that place than for others, and since the Pope permits this type alone in his churches and chapel."[51] The

48. "Solche Figuren und Sätze aber, haben die alten Componisten zu ihrem Grunde, und was durch solche nicht kann excusiret werden, dasselbige soll billich aus der Composition als ein Ungeheuer außgemustert werden." *Bericht*, ch.13; Hilse, "Treatises," 91.

49. ". . . weil derselbe nunmehre in singenden, sowohl Kirchen als Taffel-Sachen, ingleichen denen Sonaten gefunden wird." *Tractatus*, ch.21; Hilse, "Treatises," 91.

50. "Nachgehends hat man observiret, daß künstliche Sänger auch Instrumentisten . . . von den Noten hier und dort etwas abgewichen, und also einige anmutige Art der Figuren zu erfinden Anlaß gegeben; denn was mit vernünfftigen Wohl-Laut kan gesungen werden, mag man auch wohl setzen." *Bericht,* ch.13; Hilse, "Treatises," 90.

51. "Contrapunctus gravis ist, welcher aus nicht allzugeschwinden Noten, wenig Arten des Gebrauchs der Dissonantzen besteht, und nicht so sehr den Text als die Harmonie in Acht nimmt, und weil dieses Genus allein den Alten bekandt gewesen, als wird er Stylus antiquus genennet, auch wohl a Capella, Ecclesiasticus, weil er sich dahin

figures belonging to this category consist of passing notes and suspensions (*transitus*, *quasi-transitus*, *syncopatio*, *quasi-syncopatio*). The *stylus modernus* on the other hand, makes use of "*contrapunctus luxurians*, the type consisting in part of rather quick notes and strange leaps—so that it is well suited for stirring the affections—and of more kinds of dissonance treatment (or more *figurae melopoeticae* which others call *licentiae*) than the foregoing. Its melodies agree with the text as much as possible, unlike those of the preceding type. This can again be subdivided into *communis* and *comicus*, the first being used everywhere, the second most of all in theatrical productions, although something recitative-like is also often employed in church or table music. No style succeeds as well in moving the heart as *theatralis*."[52] Before discussing the figures belonging to the two kinds of *stylus luxurians*, Bernhard again reminds the reader that this new style of composition employs a greater variety of dissonances or *licentiae* which "do not seem to be excused"[53] by the passing note or suspension. The figures belonging to the *stylus communis* are *superjectio*, *anticipatio*, *subsumtio*, *variatio*, *multiplicatio*, *prolongatio*, *syncopatio catachrestica*, *passus duriusculus*, *saltus duriusculus*, *mutatio toni*, *inchoatio imperfectae*, *longinqua distantia*, *consonantiae impropriae*, *quaesitio notae*, and *cadentiae duriusculae*. The most modern of musical styles, called the *stylus theatralis* (*comicus*, *recitativus*, *oratorius*), will often require dissonances to adequately express the text: "It is also at times called *stylus recitativus* or *oratorius*, since it was devised to represent speech in music, and indeed not too many years ago. . . . And since

---

mehr als an andere Orte schicket, und weil solchen der Pabst allein in seiner Kirchen und Capelle beliebet." *Tractatus*, ch.3; Hilse, "Treatises," 35.

52. "Contrapunctus luxurians ist, welcher aus theils ziemlich geschwinden Noten, seltzamen Sprüngen, so die Affecten zu bewegen geschickt sind, mehr Arten des Gebrauchs derer Dissonantzen (oder mehr Figuris Melopoeticis welche andere Licentias nennen) mehr aus guter Aria so zum Texte sich zum besten reimet, als etwan der obige, besteht. Dieser kan wieder in Communem et Comicum eingetheilet werden, deren der erste allenthalben, der andere aber meist auff Theatris gebraucht wird, wiewohl in Kirchen und Taffel-Music auch offt etwas recitativisches gebraucht, einen guten Effect in Bewegung der Gemüther (welchen Zweck kein Stylus so wohl, als Theatralis erreichet) zu veruhrsachen pfleget." *Tractatus*, ch.3; Hilse, "Treatises," 35.

53. ". . . weilen sie mit denen vorgemeldeten Figuris nicht scheinen entschuldiget zu werden." *Tractatus*, ch.21.

language is the absolute master of music in this genre, just as music is the master of language in *stylus gravis*, and language and music are both masters in *stylus luxurians communis*, therefore this general rule follows: that one should represent speech in the most natural way possible."[54] The exhortation to "represent speech in the most natural way" is then followed by a list of examples not unlike Nucius's, Herbst's, or later Speer's list of affective words.[55] The composer is to appropriately express joyful and sorrowful, swift and slow thoughts. Emphasized words as well as elevated or exalted thoughts should be set higher, while unemphasized words and low or dark thoughts should be set lower, not unlike the *hypotyposis* figures of *anabasis* and *catabasis*. Punctuation marks, in particular the question mark, should also be reflected in the music (*interrogatio*).[56] Various kinds of repetition can also be used, including unison sections (Kircher's *complexus*) and repetitions rising in pitch (Kircher's *climax*, *gradatio*). Bernhard then lists the figures which, in addition to those used in the other styles, can also be used in the *stylus theatralis*: *extensio*, *ellipsis*, *mora*, *abruptio*, *transitus inversus*, *heterolepsis*, *tertia deficiens*, and *sexta superflua*.

Bernhard's classification of the figures according to compositional styles proved to be unsatisfactory in his German setting. The stylistic differentiations proposed in his *Tractatus* are modeled after the Italian stylistic divisions of Marco Scacchi, who classified musical composition according to *stylus ecclesiasticus*, *stylus cubicularis*, and *stylus theatralis*.[57] The various styles' distinct characters, devices, and appro-

---

54. "Er wird auch sonst Stylus recitativus oder Oratorius genannt, weil er eine Rede in der Music vorzustellen erfunden worden, und zwar für nicht allzuvielen Jahren. . . . Und weil in diesem Genere die Oratio Harmoniae Domina absolutissima, so wie im Stylo gravi Harmonia Orationis Domina und in luxuriante communi sowohl Oratio als Harmonia Domina ist, also rühret daher diese General Regel, daβ man die Rede aufs natürlichste exprimiren solle." *Tractatus* ch.35; Hilse, "Treatises," 110.

55. See p.24f., above. See also *Hypotyposis*, below.

56. Although the *interrogatio* is not defined as a musical-rhetorical figure until Scheibe's *Figurenlehre*, the musical representation of the question was a well-established technique. Calvisius had already suggested a musical reflection of a question in the text. Unger, *Beziehungen*, 31.

57. *Cribrum musicum* (1643) and *Breve discorso sopra la musica moderna* (1649). Lorenzo Bianconi, *Music in the Seventeenth Century,* trans. David Bryant (Cambridge: Cambridge University Press, 1987), 47ff.

priate settings were not to be intermixed. Indeed, Scacchi's *Cribrum musicum* was an attack on some psalm settings of the north German Paul Seifert, particularly his use of the *basso continuo* and certain chromatic licenses in his church music.[58] For the Italians, the use of the *stylus theatralis* in ecclesiastical music was simply improper. However, while the differentiation between styles in Italy was made according to their appropriate locale of employment or performance (church, chamber, or theater), this clear-cut distinction could not be made in Germany.[59] German Baroque music sought a synthesis of the styles rather than a clear distinction between them, allowing the Lutheran *musicus poeticus* greater versatility and effectiveness in expressing the text through the music. Not only is this amply demonstrated in the music of Bernhard's mentor, Heinrich Schütz, but was in fact mentioned in Bernhard's own definitions of the *stylus modernus*. Therefore Bernhard drops these stylistic classifications of the figures in his *Bericht*, using instead the terms *figurae fundamentales* and *figurae superficiales*. The *figurae fundamentales* are those "which are to be found in fundamental composition, or in the old style, no less than in styles employed today. There are two such: *ligatura* and *transitus*."[60] Bernhard chooses the term *superficiales* to describe the expressive musical-rhetorical figures. With this he wishes to affirm their link to the "fundamental" style. Far from being "superficial," they are "formed upon" (*super facere*) the *figurae fundamentales*, and while "they do not seem to be excused,"[61] they in fact have "the old masters as their foundation."[62] Furthermore, these figures are *super-facies* in that they were adopted by composers only after their established use by singers and instrumentalists "until the art of music has attained such a height in our own day, especially in the newly established and lately continually further embellished *stylus recitativus*, that it may indeed be compared

58. Ibid.

59. See also Eggebrecht, "Über Bachs geschichtlichen Ort," 281.

60. "Figuras fundamentales nenne ich diejenigen, welche in der fundamental Composition oder im alten stylo nicht weniger als in den üblichen Arthen befindlich sind. Solche Figurarum Fundamentalium sind zwey; Nehmlich Ligatura und Transitus." *Bericht*, ch.10; Hilse, "Treatises," 77.

61. See n.53, above.

62. See n.48, above; also Federhofer, "Chrisoph Bernhards Figurenlehre," 112.

to a rhetoric, in view of the multitude of figures."[63] With these classifications, Bernhard also establishes a link between the *figurae principales* and *minus principales* of earlier *Figurenlehren* and his own categories. While *principales* and *fundamentales* refer to the principal structural, musical devices fundamental to the *stylus gravis*, *minus principales* and *superficiales* signify the affective and rhetorical, *ornatus*-oriented figures. In contrast to the earlier *figurae principales*, fugue is not included in Bernhard's *fundamentales* figures because it is not a device dealing specifically with dissonance, as do the passing note (*transitus*) and suspension (*syncopatio* or *ligatura*). The *superficiales* figures include *superjectio*, *subsumtio*, *variatio*, *multiplicatio*, *ellipsis*, *retardatio*, *heterolepsis*, *quasitransitus*, and *abruptio*. No longer listed as specific figures in the *Bericht* are *anticipatio*, *prolongatio*, *syncopatio catachrestica*, *passus duriusculus*, and *saltus duriusculus*, *mutatio toni*, *inchoatio imperfecta*, *longinqua distantia*, *consonantiae impropriae*, *tertia deficiens*, *sexta superflua*, *quaesitio notae*, *cadentiae duriusculae*, *extensio*, *mora*, and *transitus inversus*. While many of these are either subsumed under other figures or given new names, others are apparently not considered sufficiently irregular, rhetorical, or expressive to warrant special mention.

Bernhard's discussion of the musical-rhetorical figures updates the *Figurenlehre*, placing it squarely in the context of mid-seventeenth-century stylistic trends without breaking its ties to the past. He not only illustrates the correlation between the expressive or dissonant compositional devices of the *stylus luxurians* and the principles of the *stylus gravis* but seeks to provide the composer of modern music with expressive figures to affectively express a text. In this modernized *Figurenlehre*, the works of the great past masters of vocal polyphony as well as the compositional styles of contemporary composers such as Monteverdi, Carissimi, Cavalli, and Rossi are cited as appropriate models for imitation.[64] Bernhard presents a concept of the musical-

---

63. See n.50, above. The text continues: "Biß daß auff unsere Zeiten die Musica so hoch kommen, daß wegen Menge der Figuren, absonderlich aber in dem neu erfundenen und bisher immer mehr ausgezierten Stylo Recitativo, sie wohl einer Rhetorica zu vergleichen." *Bericht*, ch.13; Hilse, "Treatises," 90f.

64. *Tractatus*, ch.43.

rhetorical figures which focuses less on the analysis of vocal polyphony through the application of rhetorical concepts than on the composition of contemporary music through the use of modern expressive techniques. Kircher's reference to the suitability of the musical-rhetorical figures in the *stylus recitativus* is thus rigorously applied in Bernhard's *Figurenlehre*.

WOLFGANG CASPAR PRINTZ

Wolfgang Caspar Printz (1641–1717) was an important late-seventeenth-century composer, theorist, and music historian, whose works influenced writers of the next generation such as J. G. Walther and Mattheson. After attending the *Lateinschule* in Vohenstrauβ (Upper Palatinate), he went to Altdorf in 1659 to study theology at the university. His career as a Lutheran minister was cut short through the reconversion of the local aristocracy to Catholicism, at which point Printz decided to make music his profession. In 1662, during an extended trip through Italy, Printz encountered Kircher, "who was a major influence on his theoretical writing."[65] After his return, he eventually arrived in Sorau (now Poland), where he remained for the rest of his productive life, assuming the positions of *Kantor* as well as music director to the counts of Promnitz.

Much of Printz's theoretical writing concerns itself with questions regarding performance rather than composition. He is included in this study not only because of his influence on *musica poetica* theorists, but also because many of the embellishments discussed in his writings also appear in *Figurenlehren* of later authors. In his *Phrynis Mytilenaeus*[66] Printz specifically states that his intention is to describe musical embellishments, but not "those *variationes* which occur through the connection and arrangement of consonances and dissonances, of which

65. George Buelow, "Printz," *New Grove Dictionary,* 15: 274.

66. *Phrynis Mytilenaeus, oder Satyrischer Componist*, published in its entirety in 1696 (Dresden, Leipzig), was published earlier in three separate volumes (Quedlinburg, 1676–79).

you have been sufficiently informed through *musica poetica*."[67] His instructions are directed toward the performing musician, the *Musicant*, not the composer, who is compared to a cook rather than an orator: "Why should not also the musician, who is concerned with delighting the ear, apply as much effort as the cook or painter in discovering every variation in order to do justice to his calling? After all, music itself consists only of variations in sound, and everything which is repeated without change is an annoyance rather than a pleasure to the ear."[68]

The following diagram depicts Printz's classifications:

- silent figures: pauses
- sounding figures:
  - simple:
    - stepwise: *accentus, tremolo, groppo, circulo mezo, tirata meza*
    - stationary: *bombi*
    - leaping: *salto semplice, salti composti*
    - hovering: *trillo, trilletto*
    - mixed: *corta, messanza, suspirans*
  - composite:
    - running: *cirulo, tirata, bombilans, passagio*
    - hovering: *tremamento longo*
    - mixed: *mistichanza composta*

Printz defines an embellishment or *variatio* as "an artful modifica-

67. "Ich will aber hier nicht handeln de Variatione, so geschicht Coniunctionibus & Consecutionibus Consonantiarum & Dissonantiarum, und dergleichen / davon du genugsam berichtet bist aus der Musica Poetica, sondern de Variatione, aus welcher alle und jede Erfindungen eines Componisten fliessen." *Phrynis Mytilenaeus*, part 2, ch.8, §5, 46.

68. "Warumb solte denn nun nicht auch der Musicant, der das Gehör zu vergnügen beschäfftiget ist / gleiche Fleiβ (wie der Koch oder Maler) anwenden / alle und jede Varietaet und Abwechselung zu erfinden / umb seinem Ambte rechtschaffen vorzustehen / zumahl weil die Music an sich selbst in mera Varietate sonorum bestehet / und alles was offt in derselben wiederholet wird / dem Gehör mehr Verdruβ als Annehmlichkeit verursachet." Ibid., §3, 45.

tion of a given musical passage."[69] Although the terms *figura* and *manier* are brought together in a following definition, it is clear that Printz understands the term *figura* as a general heading for the embellishments, *manier* meaning simply "manner" rather than "ornament" as Mattheson would use the term: "A musical *figura* is a certain *modulus* which results through divisions of one or more notes and which is performed in an appropriate manner."[70] Of his embellishments, the *circulo* and *suspirans* appear in *musica poetica* treatises as musical-rhetorical figures. Kircher had already defined the *circulatio* and the *suspiratio* as such. Furthermore, the *tirata* and especially the *accentus* are also given text-expressive potential by some writers. However, Printz defines all of his embellishments as melodic ornaments, quite independent of their harmonic implications or expressive capabilities. His examples are without exception monodic, unlike Bernhard's, which were always placed in a harmonic context. This is particularly significant in the case of the *accentus*. While Printz explains this ornament simply as a melodic embellishment, other writers describe it in terms of its harmonic context and implications. The *suspirans*, described by others under the terms *suspiratio* or *stenasmus*, is simply defined as a three-note *figura corta* in which one of the notes is shortened through the insertion of a rest. Although the term itself suggests an expressive application (*suspirare*: to sigh, long for), there is no reference to this expressive content in Printz's definition. Printz goes to some length in his pursuit to define the various figurative constructions. For example, in enumerating the *salti composti*, a four-note combination of simple leaps, Printz arrives at one thousand possible combinations. With his use of the term *figura*, Printz introduces yet another method of differentiating the figures, namely, between ornamental embellishments and expressive musical-rhetorical figures. Mattheson refers to the embellishments as *figurae cantiones* or *Manieren*, while Vogt and Spiess call them *figurae simplices*. The musical-rhetorical figures, on the other hand, are referred to as *figurae cantus* by Mattheson, *figurae ideales* by

69. "In stricta Significatione aber is Variatio eine jede Veränderung eines Moduli, da man dieses allezeit in jener mercken und abnehmen kan." Ibid., §7, 46.

70. "Figura ist in Musicis ein gewisser Modulus, so entstehet aus einer / oder auch etlicher Noten Zertheilung / und mit gewisser ihm anständiger Manier hervor gebracht wird." Ibid., ch.9, §1, 47.

Vogt, and simply *figurae* by Spiess.

While Printz's discussion of the ornamental melodic *figurae* or *variationes* does not contribute directly to the development of the concept of musical-rhetorical figures, it does indicate a growing German interest in melodic rather than only contrapuntal principles. Parallel to the emphasis on modern expressive compositional devices in Bernhard's *Figurenlehre*, Printz's emphasis on melodic ornamentation reflects a gradual modernization or "Italianization" of German musical thought. It would remain for Mattheson to fully integrate the modern melodic orientation into a comprehensive rhetorical structure.

JOHANN GEORG AHLE

Johann Georg Ahle (1651–1706) was the son of the renowned organist Johann Rudolf Ahle, from whom he presumably received his musical education.[71] Born and raised in Mühlhausen, he succeeded his father as organist at St. Blasien at age twenty-three, a post he held until his own death. He was then succeeded by the young J. S. Bach. Ahle was not only an accomplished musician but also a distinguished poet, being crowned poet laureate by Emperor Leopold I in 1680 "on account of not only his virtue and wonderful capabilities, but especially his excellent scholarship in the noble art of German poetry, as well as his exceptional and graceful manner of musical composition."[72]

Ahle's musical-rhetorical *Figurenlehre* is presented in his *Sommer-Gespräche*, the second in a series of four publications covering the theory and history of music.[73] The prose of these texts is written in

---

71. The Lüneburg *Kantor* Michael Jacobi referred to Johann Rudolf Ahle as "the German Monteverdi." A. Adrio, "Ahle," *Musik in Geschichte und Gegenwart*, 1: 169.

72. Hartmut Krones, "Die Figurenlehre bei Bachs Amtsvorgänger Johann Georg Ahle," *Österreichische Musikzeitschrift* 40 (1985): 89, quoting E.L. Gerber, *Neues historisch-biographisches Lexikon der Tonkünstler*, vol.1 (Leipzig, 1812), 35.

73. The first of the series, *Johann Georg Ahlens musikalisches Frühlings-Gespräche, darinen fürnehmlich vom grund- und kunstmäßigen Komponiren gehandelt wird*, was published in 1695 (Mühlhausen). The following *Sommer-Gespräche*, *Herbst-Gespräche*, and *Winter-Gespräche* then appeared at two-year intervals. Ahle deals with consonances, dissonances, and cadences in the first volume, ending with the matter of text settings. This is taken up in the second volume under the musical-rhetorical figures;

humorous dialogue form, one of the characters being *Helian*, a pseudonym of the author derived from the letters of his latinized name, *Ahlenius*. After discussing the importance of observing a text's periods, commas, and colons through various cadences and pauses, Ahle focuses on the careful musical expression of a word's syllables and accents. He then proceeds to the topic of the musical-rhetorical figures. Ahle, the poet laureate, derives his concept of the figures directly from the rhetorical source. He suggests that the composer first study the rhetorical figures found in the text and then reflect these in the music, in the same manner that the cadences and accents of the text might be represented by the music: "Just as orators or poets use a great variety of rhetorical figures, so also do a number of *melopoets* use them in their musical discourse."[74] To demonstrate the musical application of the rhetorical figures, Ahle does not supply musical examples but rather, in keeping with his literary interests, simply illustrates the various figures through changing and rearranging a given text. He applies assorted repetitions, inversions, and additions to a psalm verse: "Rejoice in the Lord, all the earth; sing, glorify, and praise him. The intelligent song-poet will know how to construct various word figures out of this text."[75] While all of his examples are taken from the rhetorical emphasis figures, devices used to clarify and accentuate the text,[76] Ahle also stresses the figures' *ornatus* character: "And because the composer is aware that the oratorical and poetical embellishments are only used like sugar and spices, he figurates each statement different from the other, according to the most appropriate and useful manner."[77] Two rhetorical

---

the third volume includes a discussion of musical embellishments, including *accento*, *tremolo*, *groppo*, *circolo mezzo*, *cercare della nota*, and *tirata mezza*. The *Winter-Gespräche* deals with questions regarding poetry, the modes, and the musical intervals.

74. "Gleichwie die Redner in freier / und die Poeten in gebundener Rede allerlei Rhetorische Figuren gebrauchen; also bedienen sich auch mancher die Melopoeten in singender Rede." *Sommer-Gespräche* (Mühlhausen, 1697), 16.

75. "Im 98. Psalmen steht: Jauchzet dem HErren alle welt, singet, rühmet und lobet. Hieraus weis ein verständiger Sangdichter unterschiedliche Figuras λέξεως seu dictionis zu machen." Ibid.

76. Krones, "Die Figurenlehre bei Ahle," 93.

77. "Dän weil ihm bewust / daβ die Rednerischen und Poetischen zierligkeiten nur als zukker und gewürze zu brauchen; so figuriret er immer einen ausspruch anderst als den andern / nach dem er es tuhnlich und dienlich zu sein befindet." *Sommer-Gespräche*, 17.

figures which Ahle does discuss in their musical context are *antithesis* and *emphasis*. However, instead of defining them, Ahle cites an example in which the two rhetorical figures are ignored in their musical setting of the text: "For one day in Thy courts is better than a thousand elsewhere." After quoting a certain musical setting of this text, he launches into a critique of the anonymous composer's efforts: "Oh how silly that sounds! The malpoet (*melopoet*, I meant to say) has neither regarded nor expressed the *antithesin* or *emphasin*. For in this text the words *one day* and *a thousand* as well as *in thy courts* and *elsewhere* are juxtaposed: therefore he should have set the word *one* longer than *day* and *elsewhere* higher than *for*, as proper emphasis would dictate."[78]

Ahle includes not only those rhetorical figures which are easily applied to a musical composition (*epizeuxis*,[79] *anaphora*, *anadiplosis*, *climax*, *epistrophe*, *epanalepsis*, and *epanodos*) but also figures which will remain purely literary devices, such as *asyndeton* and *polysyndeton*.[80] His concept of the musical-rhetorical figures is a unique one. Ahle's point of departure is not the text-expressive musical phenomena, the explanation of dissonance, or even the expression of the affections through devices which music and rhetoric have in common. Rather, he begins with the rhetorical figures which are found in the text and which are then to receive musical expression or at least consideration. This would imply that the composer is to observe not only those figures

---

78. "Ei, wie läppisch klinget das! Hat doch der Schlimsetzer (Stimsetzer wollte ich sagen) weder die *Antithesin* noch *Emphasin* beachtet und ausgedrückt. Dän hier werden die wörter **ein Tag** und **tausend** / wie auch **in deinen Vorhöfen** und **sonst** gegen einander gesetzet: darum hätte er **ein** länger als **Tag** / und **sonst** höher als **dän** / wie beides der nachdruck erfordert / setzen sollen." Ibid., 31.

79. Ahle's assumption that the rhetorical figures be applied in the musical composition is clearly evident in a comment he makes about *epizeuxis*: it is the most common figure, "as composers use it in virtually all passages." ("Doch wie das salz die gemeinste würze ist; also ist die Epizeuxis die gebreuchlichste Figur: sintemahl sie von den Komponisten schier in allen commatibus angewendet wird.") Ibid., 17.

80. The *asyndeton* and *polysyndeton* refer to a lack or excess of conjunctions. Those figures which cannot be reflected in the music (*asyndeton*, *polysyndeton*, *synonymia*) would not be adopted by Walther in his *Lexicon*, who otherwise includes Ahle's figures, eventhough they were defined as purely rhetorical devices. Although Vogt would include the *polysyndeton* in his list of *figurae ideales*, he defines it as a purely musical, expressive figure, reflecting the term's literal meaning rather than its rhetorical content. See also *Polysyndeton* and *Synonymia*, below.

which in one way or other can be transferred from the literary to the musical medium but, indeed, all rhetorical figures found in the text. In addition, the composer is also to apply the rhetorical *Figurenlehre*, constructing literary figures in the text and then observing them in his setting of the words. Thus, Ahle's *Figurenlehre* implicitly embraces all of the rhetorical figures, even though he explicitly mentions only a few of them.

Tomáš Baltazar Janovka

Tomáš Baltazar Janovka (1669–1741) was a Czech organist and lexicographer. Like Kircher, Janovka received a Jesuit education, which emphasized not only the liberal arts in general but rhetoric in particular.[81] He received a masters degree in the liberal arts from Charles University in Prague in 1689. Two years later he accepted the post as organist at Tyn, Prague's principal church, a position he held for the following fifty years.

Janovka is remembered chiefly for his one published work, *Clavis ad Thesaurum*.[82] The *Clavis* is the first music dictionary to be printed in the Baroque era. While other authors included lists of defined terms in their composition treatises, Janovka devotes his entire publication to the definition of approximately 170 musical terms arranged in alphabetical order. In defining the terms, Janovka borrows from various older sources, Kircher's *Musurgia Universalis* in particular. In many cases, "his definitions are more correct and precise than those of Kircher."[83]

Kircher serves as the only source for Janovka's definitions of the musical-rhetorical figures, all listed under the term *Figurae Musicae*. In his introductory comments to the figures, Janovka, like Kircher, emphasizes their role in expressing the affections. Unlike Kircher, however, Janovka does not place the same emphasis on the affective

81. The Jesuit emphasis on the rhetorical discipline is detailed in Barner's *Barockrhetorik*, 321–66.

82. The *Clavis ad thesaurum magnae artis musicae* (Prague, 1701) was reprinted in 1715 as *Clavis ad musicam*. The facsimile edition (Amsterdam: F. Knuf, 1973) is a reprint of J. S. Bach's personal copy, bearing the composer's signature, dated 1705.

83. J. Clapham and T. Volek, "Janovka," *New Grove Dictionary*, 9: 501.

attributes of the church modes.[84] While Kircher had compared the rhetorical tropes to the twelve modes through which "specific affections of the soul are manifested,"[85] Janovka uses the same phrase in his definition of the figures, thereby combining Kircher's definitions of modes and figures in his one definition: "The musical figures function similarly to the tropes and the varied manner of speech in rhetoric. Furthermore, the musical figures consist of certain musical passages in which specific affections of the soul are manifested, for example, love, joy, ferocity, violence, dignity, modesty, moderation, piety, compassion, et cetera."[86] Janovka also classifies the figures according to *figurae principales* and *minus principales*. The *commissura*, *syncopatio*, and *fuga* belong to the first group,[87] while *pausa*, *anaphora*, *climax*, *semplica* (*complexus*), *similiter desinens Figura* (Kircher's *homoioptoton*), *antitheton*, *anabasis*, *catabasis*, *circulatio*, *fuga alio sensu*, *assimilatio*, and *abruptio* make up the latter group.

Three further terms associated either with the musical-rhetorical figures or the various melodic ornaments are defined by Janovka in other places in his dictionary. In his discussion of counterpoint, Janovka employs the terms *hyperbatus* and *hypobatus* to describe the placement of the countersubject in relation to the subject. Chordal chanting, known

---

84. Janovka discusses the church modes under the term *cantus*, where he briefly describes the eight modes and lists an associated affection for each one (*Clavis*, p.8). Under the term *tonus*, the word Kircher used for the modes, Janovka goes to some length to define the various major and minor keys, listing their common intervals and their individual key signatures. Janovka's harmonic concept is governed more by modern tonality than modality.

85. "Nos tropos aliter sumentes, nihil aliud esse dicimus, quam certas Melothesiae periodos, certam animi affectionem connotantes; & tales iuxta duodecim tonorum diversitatem duodecim quoque constituimus." *Musurgia universalis*, L.8, ch.8, §7, 144.

86. "Figurae Musicae idem praestant, quod Tropi, atque varii dicendi modi in Rhetorica. Sunt autem Figurae Musicae quaedam Melothesiae periodi, certam animi affectionem connotantes, puta: amoris, gaudii, ferociae, impetus, gravitatis, modestiae, temperantiae, religionis, compassionis &c." *Clavis ad thesaurum*, 46f.

87. Janovka's definition of *fuga* includes not only the *fuga totalis* (the canon, also called *fuga ligata*) and *fuga partialis* (the imitative fugue, also called *fuga libera, soluta*) but also various specific forms of fugue: *fuga inversa* or *contraria*, *fuga perpetua* or *longa*, *fuga reciproca*, and *fuga cancrizans*. Like Kircher, he also includes *fuga* (*in alio sensu*) in his list of *figurae minus principales*, referring there to the use of fugue in a text-expressive manner in which the literal meaning of *fuga* ("chase, flight") is reflected in both the words and the music. See *Fuga*, below.

as *falso bordone* (not to be confused with *faux bourdon*), is also called *pleonasmus* by Janovka. He mentions that Kircher used the term *isobatus* to describe the technique. In describing *hyperbatus*, *hypobatus*, and *pleonasmus* as purely technical devices without any affective characteristics, Janovka defines them outside of his list of the musical-rhetorical figures. Melodic embellishments, including the *accentus (Einfall)*, *colloratura (diminutiones* or *passagae)*, *coulé*, *harpegiatura*, *tirata*, *tremulo*, and *trilla* are also defined in the *Clavis* in their appropriate alphabetic order. Having described the *figurae musicae* as passages which are used to express the affections, the purely ornamental devices do not find a place among Janovka's musical-rhetorical figures.

Mauritius Johann Vogt

Mauritius Vogt (1669–1730), born in Königshofen, Bavaria, studied philosophy and theology at Charles University in Prague. It is not inconceivable that Vogt and Janovka, exact contemporaries who attended the same university, were acquaintances. After entering the Cistercian monastery at Plasy in 1692, he was ordained priest in 1698. Besides his music studies at the monastery, Vogt also traveled to Germany and Italy to study music. In 1724, after many years of musical activity as organist, composer, and music director in Plasy, Vogt was appointed Superior at the pilgrimage church Mariánská Tynice, where he remained until his death.

In 1719 Vogt published a comprehensive music treatise, the *Conclave thesauri magnae artis musicae*. The treatise is divided into three parts, each consisting of three to five sections (*tractatus*), which in turn are divided into anywhere from five to sixteen chapters. The first part of the treatise, which deals with historical and speculative matters, also includes a section on organ building. Part 2 concerns itself with Gregorian chant and the church modes. Part 3 comprises well over half of the treatise and discusses the composition of polyphonic music. The third section of this part begins with two chapters discussing instrumental and vocal ranges, keyboard fingering, and a long list of admonitions to composers, singers, and instrumentalists. Then follow two chapters on the musical figures: chapter three discusses the *figurae simplices* and chapter four the *figurae ideales* (*ad arsin, et thesin, et periodum*).[88] This section concludes with chapters on the affections, on *phantasia* and *inventio*, and on the parts of a composition. The last two sections then explain the principles and rules of counterpoint.

Vogt incorporates the vocal and instrumental embellishments into his *Figurenlehre*, resulting in his novel classification of the figures. He calls the embellishments *figurae simplices*, which include the *accentus*, *coulé*, *curta*, *groppo*, *harpegiatura*, *herbeccio*, *messanza*, *mezocirolo* (*circulus*), *tirata*, *tremula*, and *trilla*. Some of these ornaments are only mentioned, while others are explained through musical examples. Vogt also illustrates how the *figurae simplices* can be combined, resulting in "compound figures" (*figurae compositae*). This process, which he calls *phantasia*, generates a *variatio* composed of mixtures or *messanzae* of *figurae simplices*.

The strong correlation between the *figurae ideales* and the musical expression of both the text and the affections is repeatedly underscored in Vogt's treatise. In his earlier admonitions, Vogt had encouraged the composer "to be a poet, not only that he recognize the meter of the verse, but that his themes also be inventive. He ought to understand how to further intensify [the composition] imaginatively through the musical-rhetorical figures of *hypotyposis* and *prosopopoeia*, and like a painter, place the beautiful or frightful images life-like before the eyes of the listeners through the music. . . . He ought always to work toward achieving the intended affection in his composition; and furthermore, where there are no suitable affective words, he ought to grasp the sense of the text. . . . He ought to understand the *antitheses*, *prosonomasias*, and all the other rhetorical figures, which are used in music."[89] At the end of his explanation of the figures, Vogt notes that "there are many

---

88. "Figurae sunt simplices, aut compositae, aut ideales ad arsin, aut thesin, & periodum." *Conclave*, 147.

89. "Debet porro Componista esse Poeta, ut non solum norit quantitates terminorum, sed etiam inventiosus sit thematum. Debet esse ideosus, & quodammodo pictor, ut sciat per figuras musicas Rhetoricas hypotyposes, & prosopopaeias idealiter elevare amplius, ac res pulchras, vel horridas cantu vivaciter ante oculos audientium proponere. . . . Debet compositione semper eo tendere, ut propositum affectum assequatur; imo nullum, quantum fieri potest, textum arripere debet, ubi non sint verba ad affectus apta. . . . Debet scire antitheses, prosonomasias, aliasque figuras rhetoricas, quarum usus est in Musica." Ibid., 144.

figurae ideales, usually motivated by the text. . . . The texts deserving expression through the *figurae ideales* are innumerable."[90] The expression of the affections through the *figurae ideales* is mentioned again in a following chapter.[91] These figures are not only to reflect the text but to present the text's "idea" to the listener in a lifelike (*vivaciter*) and imaginative (*idealiter*) manner. Vogt lists two familiar musical-rhetorical figures, *hypotyposis* and *prosopopoeia*, which could be employed to this end. The *hypotyposis* had been mentioned by Burmeister, while Kircher had replaced Thuringus's *parthopoeia* with *prosopopoeia* in his list of figures. These are used in rhetoric to re-present either the situation, affection, or another person's words in an oration.[92] With the expression of text and affection determining Vogt's concept of the musical-rhetorical figures, the *hypotyposis* and *prosopopoeia* characterize the entire category of figures, which he calls *figurae ideales*. This is further supported by Vogt's definition of the *idea musica* as "the musical representation of something. The *idea* is namely that which is portrayed through *hypotyposis* figures."[93] Once again *idea* and *hypotyposis* are correlated. Vogt's choice of the verb *decantare* indicates that he is referring to vocal music. Furthermore, the plural formulation of *figurae hypothiposeos* suggests an entire class of *hypotyposis* figures. Music and words are to work together in a vivid representation of the ιδεα (literally, "that which is seen") of the text, using the "*hypothiposeos figurae ideales.*" Besides encouraging the use of *hypotyposis* and *prosopopoeia*, Vogt also mentions *antithesis* and *prosonomasia*. Of these four figures, only the *antithesis* is included in his list of defined figures. The *prosonomasia*, however, can be linked to another figure which Vogt does define in his list of figures, namely the *polyptoton*.[94]

---

90. "Plures figurae sunt ideales, quibus plerumque textus dat occasionem. . . . Tales sunt textus infiniti, qui idealibus figuris deserviunt." Ibid., 153.

91. "Ut figurae ideales suum faciant effectum, & affectum, permultum conducunt particulae affectionales." *De Affectione, Themate, Capriccio, et Psychophonia*. Ibid., ch.5, 154.

92. See *Hypotyposis* and *Pathopoeia*, below.

93. "Idea musica, imago rei decantatae. Idea haec idem, quod affectus figurae hypothiposeos." *Conclave*, 5.

94. Sonnino, *Handbook*, 24, 26. Quintilian's definition of *paronomasia* mentions two forms of the figure: the repetition of a word with a change of case ending, also known as *polyptoton*, and a repetition of a word with greater (but unspecified) emphasis.

Before defining the *figurae ideales*, Vogt points out that they can affect either a part of or the entire *periodus* or passage.[95] He suggests that some figures are used at the beginning of the *periodus* (*ad arsin*), such as the *antitheton* or *schematoides*, while others are used at the end (*ad thesin*), such as the *anaphora*.[96] Yet others can be used *in medio*, such as the *climax* or *tmesis*. However, in his definitions of these and other figures, Vogt does not limit their use to any specific part of the *periodus* or musical passage. Rather, his definition of *anaphora* suggests that the figure can be used throughout the composition, while a *climax* or *tmesis* would also be very effective at the end of a *periodus*. Presumably he simply wishes to indicate that the *figurae ideales* can be used in various parts of or throughout (*ad periodum*) the composition. The allusion to *ad arsin et thesin* would thus be understood as a general reference to rather than specific application of the *figurae ideales*.

Vogt then lists and defines twenty *figurae ideales*. All the figures are labeled with Greek terminology, reflecting his concern to establish a relationship between the ancient art of rhetoric and the musical-rhetorical tradition. In contrast, the "modern" *figurae simplices* are given contemporary Italian names. Vogt's list of *figurae ideales* does not suggest a dependence on any other specific musical *Figurenlehre*. Rather, he includes figures found in various preceding treatises, at times supplying them with divergent definitions. Half of Vogt's figures are mentioned for the first time in his *Conclave*: *antistaechon*, *apotomia*, *ecphonisis*, *emphasis*, *epanadiplosis*, *ethophonia*, *metabasis*, *polyptoton*, *schematoides*, and *tmesis*. Of these, *apotomia* and *schematoides* are

---

Peacham the Elder supplies another variation of the *paranomasia* [*sic*], namely as "a figure which declineth into a contrarie by a likelihood of letters, either added, changed, or taken away." *The Garden of Eloquence*, 56. Vogt may have been using the term *prosonomasia* in the more generic sense of various word repetitions, while specifying the *polyptoton* in his defined list of figures. See *Polyptoton* and *Paronomasia*, below.

95. "*Caput IV. De Figuris ad Arsin, et Thesin, et Periodum*. Figurae ad arsin, & thesin sunt, quae non concernunt totam periodum, sed solum in parte, & vel maxime in principio ponuntur; ut sunt antitheta, schematoides &c. Aliae obveniunt medio, ut climax, tmesis. Aliae veniunt ad finem, ut anaphorae &c." *Conclave*, 150.

96. Although Vogt relates *arsis* and *thesis* to the first and second part of a *tactus* in his introductory glossary ("Arsis, divisi tactus primum medium. Medium alterum dicitur thesis." *Conclave*, 2), he presumably uses the terms at this point to refer to the beginning and end of the *periodus* or musical passage.

purely musical terms while, of the rhetorical terms, *polyptoton* is defined as a purely musical device. The other seven terms are given definitions which correspond in some way to their rhetorical meaning. The remaining ten terms had all appeared in the *Figurenlehren* of either Burmeister, Kircher (Janovka), or Ahle. In some cases Vogt defines them as his predecessors did, while at other times he supplies the terms with new definitions. Five of these had been included by Burmeister in his treatises: *anadiplosis*, *anaphora*, *aposiopesis*, *climax*, and *synaeresis*. Vogt only retains Burmeister's definition of *aposiopesis*, while adopting Ahle's *anadiplosis* definition. Vogt shares with Kircher and Janovka both the terms and definitions of *anabasis*, *catabasis*, *anaphora*, *antitheton*, and *climax*. Janovka's influence can also be detected in Vogt's definition of *falso bordone*, found in the glossary at the beginning of the *Conclave*. In addition to using this Italian term to identify the *faux bourdon*, only these two authors describe it as a *pleonasmus* or *isobatus*, a form of chordal chanting. Two additional terms, *epanalepsis* and *polysyndeton*, had also been used by Ahle. In both cases, however, Vogt defines them differently. Many of Vogt's definitions were to appear in Walther's *Lexicon*. In addition, Vogt's *Figurenlehre* would significantly influence the writings of the Benedictine monk and music theorist Meinrad Spiess.

Johann Gottfried Walther

Johann Gottfried Walther (1684–1748) was born in Erfurt, where he also received his education. After graduating from the local *Lateinschule*, he matriculated at the Erfurt University to study law. Before he could complete his university education, Walther decided to devote all of his time to pursue a musical career. He became not only an outstanding organist and composer for that instrument but also a notable music theorist and lexicographer. In studying the treatises of such influential writers as Werckmeister, Fludd, Kircher, and Thiele, Walther acquired a comprehensive knowledge of past and contemporary music theory and history. Walther also became a good friend of Werckmeister, who was significantly to influence the younger musician's writings. In 1707 he accepted the post of organist at Weimar's principal church, *St. Petri und*

Pauli, a position he held until his death. Simultaneously, he was appointed music teacher to Prince Johann Ernst, nephew to the Weimar duke. Walther and his cousin, J. S. Bach, became close friends and colleagues during their common sojourn in Weimar (1708–1717). During these early Weimar years, Walther also wrote his *Praecepta der musicalischen Composition*.[97] Between the years 1726 and 1738 the organ at *St. Petri und Pauli* was under repair, allowing Walther more time to complete his *Musicalisches Lexicon*.[98]

Walther's *Praecepta* is largely a compilation of seventeenth-century *musica poetica* treatises. While the first part concerns itself with rudimentary musical concepts, notation, and terms, its second and most substantial part deals with the art of composition. Here Walther discusses the intervals and chords together with their proportions, voice leading and counterpoint, the church modes, the use of consonance and dissonance, together with the musical-rhetorical figures, and proper text-setting. He calls this part of his treatise *Musicae Poeticae*, referring both to his treatise and to the discipline which it describes.

Like Bernhard, Walther incorporates the musical-rhetorical figures into his discussion of dissonances, indicating however that his explanations of the dissonances are based on Calvisius. Through them "one can comfortably proceed from one interval to the other without leaps; one can inflame the composition through them, if it is required by the text; and one can vary and embellish a composition with them. In summary, variety delights."[99] Walther then proceeds to define the suspension (*syncopatio*, *ligatura*) and the passing note (*transitus*, *commissura*). Before defining the remaining figures, Walther states that the *syncopatio* and *transitus*, in addition to the *fuga*, constitute the *figurae fundamentales*. While Walther's main source for his *Figurenlehre* is Bernhard's *Bericht*, he deviates significantly from Bernhard by including

97. The *Praecepta der musicalischen Composition* is dated 1708 and is dedicated to his student, Prince Johann Ernst. The manuscript remained unpublished until 1955 (Leipzig: Breitkopf & Härtel), ed. Peter Benary.

98. *Musicalisches Lexicon, oder Musicalische Bibliothec* (Leipzig, 1732). Walther completed a revised manuscript of the dictionary, which has remained unpublished.

99. "Und zwar kann man vermittelst derselben 1) von einem Intervallo zum andern desto bequehmer, und ohne Sprünge kommen, 2) kann man eine Harmonie, wenn es neml. der Text erfordert, durch sie exasperiren, und 3) kann man eine Composition durch sie verändern und ausschmücken. In Summa: Varietas delectat." *Praecepta*, 140.

fugue among his fundamental figures. Here Walther's authority is not Bernhard but rather Thuringus and Kircher. Like them, Walther counts the three fundamental contrapuntal devices of imitation, suspension, and passing dissonance to this class of basic figures, while at the same time using Bernhard's terminology, *figurae fundamentales*, rather than the older term, *figurae principales*. Walther's concept of the musical-rhetorical figures is broader than Bernhard's, allowing him to incorporate the *Figurenlehren* of other writers as well. Thus Walther also makes reference to Ahle's purely rhetorical figures, albeit without definitions, when he discusses musical text expression: "A composer might also employ various rhetorical figures in elaborating a text . . . for example, the *epizeuxis*, which is the most common and emphatic, the *anaphora*, *synonymia*, *anadiplosis*, *epistrophe*, *epanalepsis*, and so on. However, care must be taken to avoid excess."[100] In defining the *figurae superficiales*, Walther adopts Bernhard's (*Bericht*) list of those figures: *superjectio*, *subsumptio*, *variatio*, *multiplicatio*, *ellipsis*, *retardatio*, *heterolepsis*, *abruptio*, and *quasi transitus*. Walther also frequently models both his definitions and examples on Bernhard's. Both authors understand their musical-rhetorical figures as dissonances in a composition resulting from composers emulating the embellishments which singers and instrumentalists were using in their performances. Furthermore, both affirm that contemporary music might be compared to rhetoric because of its multitude of figures.[101]

In his *Musicalisches Lexicon*, the first comprehensive German music dictionary, Walther seeks to incorporate the accumulated musical

---

100. "Es mag zwar wohl ein Componist in elaborirung eines textes unterschiedl. rhetorische Figuren anwenden (vid: Joh. Georg Ahlens musical. Sommer Gespräche pag: 16 u. 17) Z.E. die Epizeuxin, als die gebräuchlichste und emphatischste: die Anaphoram, Synonymiam, Anadiplosin, Epistrophen, Epanalepsin, u.s.f. doch soll er allezeit das 'Ne quid nimis!' vor Augen haben." Ibid., 158.

101. "Allein in 15 seculo, haben die Componisten allbereit angefangen, eines und das andere zu setzen, was denen vorigen unbekannt, auch denen Unverständigen unzuläßlich geschienen; guten musical. Ohren aber annehml. gewesen: denn nachdem sie observiret, daß künstl. Sänger und Instrumentisten von denen Noten hier und dort abgewichen, und also andere anmuthige Figuren angebracht, haben sie solche nachgehens auch gesetzet, daß nunmehr unsere heutige Music wegen Menge der Figuren fügl. einer Rhetorica zu vergleichen ist." Ibid., 152. See also p.114, n.50, and p.118, n.63, above.

terminology known in his day. As expressed on the title page, the *Lexicon* or "musical library" includes both biographies of musicians who have distinguished themselves through their theoretical or musical contributions as well as Greek, Latin, Italian, French, and German musical terminology, all ordered alphabetically and defined by Walther. In contrast to a compositional treatise, which aims to identify and describe those musical devices and phenomena necessary for musical composition, the content of the *Lexicon* is determined by the various terms used to identify the devices rather than the devices themselves. Walther is intent on defining musical terminology rather than musical devices.[102] As such, his *Lexicon* is the very first terminological and historical music dictionary.

For his definitions of the musical figures, Walther turns primarily to the writings of Thuringus, Janovka, Printz, Bernhard, and Ahle. These authors each had a distinctive concept of the musical-rhetorical figures, covering *Figurenlehren* based on contrapuntal *ornatus* (Thuringus), expression of affections (Janovka), ornamentation (Printz), use of dissonance (Bernhard), and rhetorical figures (Ahle). Unlike Janovka, who listed only Kircher's definitions under one term *Figurae Musicae* in his *Clavis*, Walther lists over fifty figures, all arranged alphabetically. His intention to define the myriad of terms employed by the various authors leads to an unavoidable duplication or repetition of definitions. For example, the terms *complexio*, *epanadiplosis*, and *epanalepsis* are all described as a passage which begins and ends with the same material. While Thuringus is his source for *complexio*, the terms *epanadiplosis* and *epanalepsis* are used by Vogt and Ahle, respectively. Similarly, the passing note is listed or defined under *celeritas*, *commissura*, *symblema*, and *transitus*. Frequently, although not consistently, Walther lists the divergent explanations assigned to a single term by various authors, as exemplified in his definitions of *anaphora* and *climax*. Also noteworthy is Walther's inclusion of purely rhetorical definitions of some of the figures. The *epanadiplosis*, *epanalepsis*, *epanodos*, *epistrophe*, and *epizeuxis* are described as literary rather than musical devices. This is not to suggest that Walther understands them

102. Hans H. Eggebrecht, "Walthers Musikalisches Lexikon in seinen terminologischen Partien," *Acta Musicologia* 29 (1957): 13.

only rhetorically but rather, like Ahle, assumes that the composer would express the rhetorical figure found in a text through the accompanying music. However, Walther does not include all of the rhetorical figures which were listed by Ahle. Omitted are Ahle's *synonymia*, *asyndeton*, and *polysyndeton*, rhetorical figures which can hardly be reflected in the musical composition.[103]

The term "musical-rhetorical figure" is first encountered in Walther's *Lexicon*. It is used in the explanation of *anaphora*, where Walther includes the definitions of Thuringus and Janovka. Repetition, the literal meaning of *anaphora*, is as fundamental to musical as it is to rhetorical composition. Furthermore, both disciplines use the term to describe a specific type of repetition, each growing out of its respective tradition. In describing the figure as "musical-rhetorical," Walther does not wish to indicate a dependency of music on rhetoric, but rather wishes to indicate that this figure, like many others, is legitimately both a rhetorical *and* a musical expressive device. The term *figura* is defined simply as "generally those musical signs which indicate the notes and their duration, pauses, and so on. . . . The figures which are formed through various combinations of notes also receive names according to their construction."[104] He then defines *figura bombilans*, *figura corta*, *figura muta*, and *figura suspirans*. These are not considered to be expressive or rhetorical figures, but rather simple "figurations," analogous to Printz's understanding of *figurae* or *variationes*.

Walther does not dismiss former *Figurenlehren* as antiquated, but blends the past with the present in his *Lexicon*. By integrating sixteenth- and seventeenth-century sources, he amasses a stock of musical terminology and definitions at the end of an era. Thus "the historical occidental concept of music remains operative and determinative: the past is yet present, without having becoming history."[105]

---

103. *Polysyndeton* and *synonymia* are listed by other authors, however, with musical definitions not strictly modeled on their rhetorical counterparts. See *Polysyndeton* and *Synonymia*, below.

104. "Figura . . . also werden überhaupt alle eintzele in der Music gebräuchliche Zeichen, so die Klänge, deren Geltung, die Pausen u.s.f. andeuten, genennt. . . . Die aus etlichen auf verschiedene Art zusammen gesetzten Noten bestehende Figuren, haben von ihrer besondern Gestalt auch besondere Nahmen." *Lexicon*.

105. Eggebrecht, "Walthers Musikalisches Lexikon," 13.

Johann Mattheson

Johann Mattheson (1681–1764) was born in Hamburg, where he also established himself as an accomplished opera singer, composer, church musician, music critic, and theorist. His formal education ended in 1693 with his graduation from the *Johanneum*, a Hamburg *Gymnasium*. Mattheson was extremely well read and continued to keep abreast of the musical literature throughout his life, contributing substantially to it himself. At the age of nine, he had already established himself as a fine singer and organist in Hamburg and was asked to join the Hamburg opera company, which he considered his "musical university."[106] In the following years he would distinguish himself both as a composer and conductor of the Hamburg opera. In 1706 Mattheson was appointed secretary to the English ambassador. Through his travels on diplomatic missions, Mattheson was able to meet many famous musicians and composers of his day, including Farinelli, Venturini, and Kuhnau. He was also a close friend of Handel, Telemann, and C. P. E. Bach. (In 1703 Mattheson traveled to Lübeck with Handel to investigate the organist position left vacant upon Buxtehude's death. Presumably because of the associated marriage to Buxtehude's eldest daughter, neither Mattheson nor Handel decided to take up the offer.) Mattheson's works number eight operas, twenty-six oratorios and passions, and, besides other miscellaneous vocal and instrumental works, over two dozen published books, articles, or editions.[107]

Mattheson's most important publication is his book *Der vollkommene Capellmeister* (Hamburg, 1739), a vast, encyclopedic presentation of all the musical knowledge which he considered essential to church or court musicians. Mattheson divides the text into three parts. The first part deals with fundamental historical and rudimentary matters. The second part focuses on the composition of melody, considered the basis of all musical composition by Mattheson. The third part discusses contrapuntal composition. It is in the second part that Mattheson presents his views on the concepts of musical rhetoric, the figures, and

---

106. George Buelow, "Mattheson," *New Grove Dictionary*, 11: 833.

107. Except for a few instrumental pieces, one early opera, and only one of his oratorios, all of his music was destroyed in the World War II bombing of Hamburg.

the affections. While he defines the ornamental embellishments, referred to as *figurae cantiones* or *Manieren* in the third chapter of part 2,[108] other musical-rhetorical figures or *figurae cantus* are discussed in chapters 8, 9, and 14. Chapter 8 focuses on *emphasis* or appropriate word expression, while chapter 9 deals both with musical *antithesis* and with the appropriate expression of punctuation found in the text, including caesurae, exclamations, questions, and parentheses. In the final chapter of part 2 Mattheson first explains the musical-rhetorical process and then discusses the musical-rhetorical figures. Mattheson puts much more emphasis on developing a rationalized framework for musical expression and composition than on presenting a systematized list of expressive musical devices. He explains the process and parts of a musical composition entirely through rhetorical procedures and terminology. Like the orator, the composer can arrange his composition through the process of *inventio*, *dispositio*, and *elaboratio* or *decoratio*. Having covered musical *inventio*—including the *loci topici*—earlier in this part of his treatise (chapter 4), he now turns to the other two musical-rhetorical steps. Like the oration, the musical *dispositio* can also have its *exordium, narratio*, *propositio*, *confirmatio*, *confutatio*, and *peroratio*, while the musical-rhetorical figures find their appropriate place in the musical *elaboratio* or *decoratio*.[109]

It has been pointed out that Mattheson presented a substantially modernized view of the musical discipline, speaking "as the rational man of the Enlightenment, a musician who believed in the progress of his art, . . . [who] honoured the musical past, but in general found very little in that past to preserve for the future."[110] For Mattheson, the power of music was rooted in nature rather than mathematics, in empirical observation rather than theoretical speculation, in melody, ultimately, rather than in counterpoint. It is not surprising, then, to find that Mattheson's concepts of the affections, figures, and musical rhetoric are tied to melodic rather than to contrapuntal composition.

With the eighteenth-century emphasis on "natural" melodic expressiveness, coupled with the influence of French and Italian ornamenta-

108. "*Von der Kunst zierlich zu singen und zu spielen*," *Capellmeister*, 109ff.
109. "*Von der Melodien Einrichtung, Ausarbeitung und Zierde*," Ibid., 235ff.
110. Buelow, "Mattheson," 834.

tion, the contrapuntal-oriented classification of the figures begins to give way to categories based on melodic *Empfindung* or sentiment. Except in the early writings of Walther, the classification of the figures into *fundamentales* and *superficiales* no longer appears relevant in the eighteenth century. These categories, like the *figurae principales* and *minus principales* before them, are based on a contrapuntal rather than a melodic understanding of musical composition. The contrapuntal devices used by the composer become understood merely as elementary compositional tools, while the ornaments applied by the performer are given an increasingly important expressive role. Vogt had already included the ornamental embellishments in his *Figurenlehre*, bringing together the *figurae simplices*, as he called them, with the musical-rhetorical figures, which he termed *figurae ideales*, instead of adopting one of the contrapuntally oriented classifications. Significantly, Mattheson includes his discussion of both *figurae cantiones* and *figurae cantus*, as he calls them, in part 2 of *Der vollkommene Capellmeister*, which deals with the composition of melody, rather than in part 3 which concerns itself with polyphonic and contrapuntal issues.[111] In choosing this terminology, Mattheson wishes to distinguish between the embellishing figures which are applied to the melody (*cantio*) by the performer, and the expressive musical-rhetorical figures which are integrated into the composition (*cantus*) by the composer.

Mattheson's strongest statements regarding the expression of the affections are also placed in his chapter *Von der Melodie*: "The principal element in musical composition is the art of constructing a good melody. . . . In setting a melody, our primary purpose is to establish the affection. . . . In summary, everything which occurs without praiseworthy affections signifies nothing, accomplishes nothing, and is worth nothing."[112] This is as valid for instrumental music as it is for vocal music: "But one must remember that even in purely instrumental, textless music, the intention of every melody without exception must be directed toward the presentation of the reigning affection, in order that

111. *Capellmeister*, 244, §50. (See p.142, n.128, below.) Both terms, *cantio* and *cantus*, are derived from the Latin verb *canere (cantare)*: to sing or play. In his *Lexicon*, Walther understands a *cantio* as a song ("Lied"), while he defines *cantus* as a composition ("ein Gesang").

112. Ibid., 133, 145, 146 (§2, §74, §82).

the instruments are allowed to speak intelligibly and understandably through their notes."[113] Mattheson acknowledges that his emphasis on melody as opposed to counterpoint was unconventional.[114] It reflects the growing importance of a new aesthetic, one based on naturalness and expressivity, on the importance of the performer rather than only the composer, on the expression of the affections through *pronunciatio* rather than only through *dispositio* and *decoratio*. Increasingly, the embellishments rather than only the composition assume a role in presenting the affections.[115] Throughout the following decades a new music aesthetic would replace the predominantly Lutheran, theologically determined and dogmatically objectified concept of music. The "sensitive" performer would begin to replace the informed *melopoeticus*, and *Empfindsamkeit* would take the place of *musica poetica*.

The musical adaptation of rhetorical terminology and processes was not simply the result of a musical imitation of rhetoric. Since antiquity both disciplines had shared the common purpose of expressing the affections. Music adopted rhetorical terminology throughout the Renaissance and Baroque to explain its own unique and distinctive expressive devices, highlighting those elements which it shared with rhetoric but not structuring itself to be aligned with rhetoric. These same principles which had already dictated Burmeister's *Figurenlehre* were now applied by Mattheson in his explanations of a rhetorically structured composition. He emphasizes that while a musical *dispositio* can be discerned in many compositions, just as in the speech of "a naturally gifted, unschooled orator, . . . most composers would sooner contemplate their death rather than such a structure."[116] For Mattheson, it was

113. Ibid., 127, §45.

114. Ibid., 133, §2–4.

115. The importance of ornamental embellishments in portraying the affections is one of the main points in C. P. E. Bach's *Versuch über die wahre Art das Clavier zu spielen* (Berlin, 1753, 1762).

116. "Es ist zwar den allerersten Componisten eben so wenig in den Sinn gekommen, ihre Sätze nach obiger Ordnung einzurichten, als den mit natürlichen Gaben versehenen ungelehrten Rednern, solchen sechs Stücken genau zu folgen. . . Dennoch aber ist nicht zu leugnen, daβ bey fleiβiger Untersuchung sowol guter Reden als guter Melodien, sich diese Theile, oder die meisten davon, in geschickter Folge wircklich darin antreffen lassen; obgleich manches mahl die Verfasser ehender auf ihren Tod, als auf solchen Leitfaden gedacht haben mögen, absonderlich die Musici." *Capellmeister*, 235.

natura rather than *scientia* which was the ultimate teacher. Instead of relying on theoretical treatises, the composer could model his compositions on the "naturally gifted, unschooled" folk music. In his own compositions, Mattheson "achieved a melodic and at the same time very expressive simplicity," taking care "in maintaining poetic meters and in general avoided long melismatic passages," with a "striking emphasis on folklike songs, often strophic in form."[117] The existence of the musical-rhetorical figures is taken for granted by Mattheson, not only because theorists had long since elaborated on them and composers had long since been using them, but because they were to be found in natural musical as well as linguistic expression. Assuming the reader's familiarity with the musical-rhetorical figures, Mattheson asks rhetorically: "What can be more common than the *anaphora* in melodic composition? . . . Who cannot be aware of the exclamation's use? . . . Where is the *parrhesia* more forceful than in melodic composition?"[118]

Mattheson begins his discussion of the musical *decoratio* (*Ausschmückung*) by reminding the reader that "this depends more on the ability and healthy discretion of the singer or instrumentalist than on the directives of the composer. However, the composer must include a certain amount of embellishment in his melodies. To this end, the many rhetorical figures or ornaments can prove most useful, if they are skillfully applied."[119] Like Ahle, Mattheson turns to the rhetorical figures as his source for the musical devices. Both the *figurae dictionis* (word figures) and the *figurae sententiae* (thought figures) could be employed in the musical composition. He maintains that the word figures "bear a striking resemblance to the variations in duration or placement of the notes."[120] In a footnote Mattheson states that these

---

117. Buelow, "Mattheson," 834.

118. *Capellmeister*, 243.

119. "Wenn wir endlich noch ein Wort von der Ausschmückung machen müssen, so wird hauptsächlich zu erinnern nöthig seyn, daβ solche mehr auf die Geschicklichkeit und das gesunde Urtheil eines Sängers oder Spielers, als auf die eigentliche Vorschrifft des melodischen Setzers ankömmt. Etwas Zierath muβ man seinen Melodien beilegen, und dazu können die häuffigen Figuren oder Verblümungen aus der Redekunst, wenn sie wol angeordnet werden, vornehmlich gute Dienste leisten." Ibid., 242, §40.

120. "Die Figuren welche man dictionis nennet, haben eine grosse Aehnlichkeit mit den Wandelungen der Klänge in lange und kurtze, in steigende und fallende etc." Ibid., 242, §41. This should not be construed to mean, as Vickers seems to imply, "that notes

figures consist of various word repetitions which can easily be applied to single notes. The *figurae sententiae*, on the other hand "affect whole sentences through their variations, imitations, repetitions, etc., etc."[121] In the footnote Mattheson points out that these figures, "through which the entire sentence is accorded a certain affection, . . . can be looked up in rhetoric textbooks, almost all of which can be applied to the melody."[122] Mattheson regards the musical figures as virtually identical with their rhetorical counterparts, being so closely related "and having such a natural position in the melody, that it almost appears as though the Greek orators derived their figures from the musical discipline."[123] As word figures Mattheson lists *epizeuxis* (*subjunctio*), *anaphora*, *epanalepsis*, *epistrophe*, *anadiplosis*, *paronomasia*, *polyptoton*, *antanaclasis*, and *ploce*. The only sentence figures he lists here are *exclamatio*, *parrhesia*, *paradoxus*, *epamothosis*, *paralepsis*, *aposiopesis*, and *apostrophe*. At this point Mattheson notes that he has already discussed the *Exclamationen* in an earlier chapter, indicating that he interprets those devices as well as the other punctuating caesurae such as pauses, questions, and parentheses as figures.[124] Of all the authors, Mattheson attributed the most significance to the musical expression of a text's punctuation. While composers had long since expressed both the words and punctuation of the text in their music, it remained for Mattheson to fully integrate these devices into a musical rhetoric, thereby increasing

---

in music behave in the same way as do words in language" ("Figures of Rhetoric," 27). Mattheson is clearly pointing to similar methods rather than to similar "behavior," the latter suggesting a semantic rather than only a procedural analogy.

121. Ibid.

122. "Spruch-Figuren, dabey der gantze Spruch eine gewisse Gemüths-Bewegung enthält, kommen entweder ausser, oder bey der Unterredung vor. Ihrer sind 17, die man in den Rhetoricken nachschlagen und fast alle in der Melodie brauchen kan." Ibid., 242, footnote. Mattheson mentions that there are twelve "Wörter-Figuren" and seventeen "Spruch Figuren." Unfortunately, he does not cite his source. Mattheson's contemporary, Johann Christoph Gottsched, lists twenty-one *figurae dictionis* and twenty-three *figurae sententiarum* in his *Ausführliche Redekunst*.

123. ". . . haben solche natürliche Stellen in der Melodie, daß es fast scheinet, als hätten die griechischen Redner sothane Figuren aus der Ton-Kunst entlehnet." Ibid., 243, §46.

124. "*Von den Ab- und Einschnitten der Klang-Rede*," ch.9. In addition, the *emphasis*, which is also a rhetorical figure, is dealt with in chapter 8. Scheibe lists both *exclamatio* and *interrogatio* as specific figures.

the correlation between the disciplines.

In addition to these *figurae cantus*, Mattheson briefly alludes to the "figures of amplification, which number around thirty, and which serve more as extensions, amplifications, ornaments, embellishments, or display than to thoroughly convince the spirit." Included here also is "the famous art-work of fugue, including the *mimesis*, *expolitio*, *distributio*, and other embellishments which are only rarely fruitful and find their home in this greenhouse of figures."[125] Both the rhetorical *expolitio* and *distributio* are figures which an orator employs to expand his argument, amplifying his point through various repetitions and divisions of his thesis. As such both the *expolitio* and *distributio* are not only figures but rhetorical processes which can also involve other figures.[126] These techniques can be used both in the rhetorical as well as musical *confutatio*. The relocation of the fugue from the *figurae principales* or *fundamentales* into the category of amplification figures is Mattheson's innovation. His concern to establish parallels between music and rhetoric again becomes evident through his desire to provide a rhetorical "residence" for the fugue.[127] Thus he abandons the distinction between the musically and rhetorically rooted expressive figures inaugurated by Nucius. Only the melodic embellishments, the *figurae cantiones* or *Manieren*, are understood as purely musical figures.

Mattheson wishes to distinguish clearly between the musical-rhetorical figures and the *Manieren*. The two classes of figures "have nothing in common and should not be mixed together."[128] In contrast to

---

125. "Noch eins ist zu erinnern, daβ nehmlich unter die grossen Erweiterungs-Figuren, deren etliche dreiβig seyn werden, und die mehr zur Verlängerung, Amplification, zum Schmuck, Zierrath oder Gepränge, als zur gründlichen Uiberzeugung der Gemüther dienen, nicht mit Unrecht zu zehlen ist das bekannte und berühmte Kunst-Stück der Fugen, worin die Mimesis, Expolitio, Distributio samt andern Blümlein, die selten zu reiffen Früchten werden, ihre Residentz, als in einem Gewächs-Hause, antreffen." *Capellmeister*, 244, §52.

126. See *Distributio*, below.

127. Forkel would remove the fugue altogether from the *Figurenlehre*, treating it as a highly expressive genre instead of an embellishment.

128. "Vor Zeiten haben unsre gelehrte Musici gantze Bücher in ordentlicher Lehr-Art, von blossen Sing-Manieren (die ich Figuras cantionis, so wie die vorhergehenden Figuras cantus nenne) zusammen getragen, welche mit den obangeführten gleichwol keine Gemeinschafft haben, und mit denselben nicht vermischet werden müssen." *Capellmeister*, 244, §50.

the musical-rhetorical figures, the "*Manieren* thoroughly ruin many a fine melody and, as much as I admire the French instrumental style, I can no longer excuse it, when they entangle and disfigure their variations to such a degree that one can simply no longer perceive the beauty of the original notes."[129] However, should the *Manieren* be judiciously applied, "they are not to be lightly esteemed, should they be included by the composer himself, be he a fine singer or instrumentalist, or be spontaneously added by the performer."[130] Mattheson deals with the *Manieren* early on in this part of the treatise (chapter 3), where he discusses the *accentus* (*Vorschlag, Überschlag*), *tremolo*, *trillo*, *trilletto*, *tenuta*, *groppo*, *circolo mezzo*, *tirata*, *ribattuta*, *transitus*, *mordant*, and *acciacatura.* Apart from the *transitus*, these ornaments were all regarded as *figurae simplices* (*variationes* or *Manieren*) by earlier authors. Although Mattheson includes the *transitus* (the passing note, also known as *commissura*, classified as one of the *figurae principales* or *fundamentales*), he treats it simply as a melodic embellishment, referring to its ornamental character as well as to its ornamentation, without discussing the resulting dissonances. Like Printz, Mattheson supplies only monodic examples of the *Manieren*, disregarding their harmonic implications. The *accentus* is the only *Manier* which is directly linked to the expression of the affections, while the *groppo* is considered most useful if the intended affection "consists of similar turns and twists."[131]

Mattheson's concept of musical rhetoric, including the musical-rhetorical figures, might be summarized as follows: just as music and rhetoric share common goals, so do they share common methodologies, structuring principles, and expressive devices. While these were initially defined and systematized by the rhetorical discipline, they are equally evident in and applicable to the musical art. These musical phenomena which are described in rhetorical terminology have a long standing history. And while it is helpful to articulate this musical-rhetorical material, it can also be gleaned both from well-composed music and from naturally gifted musical expression through empirical observation.

---

129. Ibid., 242, §41.
130. Ibid., §43.
131. See *Accentus*, *Groppo*, below.

Meinrad Spiess

Meinrad Spiess (1683–1761) was a Bavarian composer and theorist. After entering the Benedictine Abbey at Irsee in 1701, he was ordained a priest in 1708. Following four additional years of music study in Munich, he was appointed music director at the Abbey, a position which he held until his death. Although he seems to have done little traveling, he did stay in contact with other musicians. He was a member of Mizler's *Correspondierende Societät der musicalischen Wissenschaften* in Leipzig, along with J. S. Bach, Telemann, Graun, and Handel. Leopold Mozart was also part of his circle of acquaintances, frequently sending Spiess his compositions for correction.

In 1745 Spiess published his compositional treatise *Tractatus musicus*, in which, "based on the best past and recent authors, the fundamentals of musical composition are extracted, gathered, compared, explained, and clearly illustrated with examples."[132] The "past and recent authors" include Kircher, Vogt, Walther, Heinichen, Mattheson, and Scheibe, among many others. With this disparate list of sources, it is understandable that the concepts presented in the *Tractatus* would be eclectic in character. Spiess adopts the speculative mathematical explanation of music, characteristic of seventeenth-century *musica poetica*, "that music is nothing else but clearly sounding numbers, and is therefore reverberating Mathematics."[133] He also holds to the superiority of the twelve church modes over the major-minor tonal system. Being a treatise written primarily for the composition of "skillful, contrapuntal, serious and dignified church music (which is the primary purpose and only goal of my treatise),"[134] Spiess proves to be an ardent

---

132. "*Tractatus musicus compositorio-practicus*. Das ist, Musicalischer Tractat, In welchem alle gute und sichere Fundamenta zur Musicalischen Composition aus denen alt- und neuesten besten Autoribus herausgezogen, zusammen getragen, gegen einander gehalten, erkläret, und mit untersetzten Exemplen dermassen klar und deutlich erläutert werden." (Augsburg, 1745; 2nd printing, 1746).

133. ". . . daβ die Music nichts anders sey, als lauter deutliche thönende Zahlen, und ein klingende Mathematic." *Tractatus*, 3.

134. ". . . eine gute Contrapunctische / Gravität- und Majestätische Kirchen-Musik (von welcher hauptsächlich zu schreiben meine mehreste Absicht und gäntzlicher Endzweck ist)." Ekkehard Federl, "Der Tractatus Musicus des Pater Meinrad Spieβ (1683–1761)," *Festschrift Bruno Stäblein* (Kassel: Bärenreiter, 1967): 40.

advocate of the *a cappella* style. Although the *Tractatus* is liberally sprinkled with disparaging remarks regarding the modern musical styles, Spiess does recognize a *stylus mixtus*, which he defines as "a mixed Church-style, namely when a composition of one to four voices and concertizing instruments is advanced with arias, contrapuntal writing, and fugues, yet in such a manner that the bounds of dignity and modesty befitting church music are not overstepped."[135] The ideal composition is to be facile, clear, flowing, and charming: "Facile is that which is easily grasped and therefore quickly understood. If something is facile, it is also clear; and if a number of clear things are appropriately connected, we perceive them to be flowing; and that which is clear and flowing is usually charming."[136] Although Spiess warns against all excesses, he does admit that "something rousing, lively, and brisk can also be presented in churches, particularly if it is required by the text."[137] While ascribing to an essentially conservative concept of music, Spiess does not remain untouched by more modern musical thought. Also more progressive is his adoption of Heinichen's and Mattheson's concepts of an expressive musical rhetoric. Like them, Spiess also proposes the use of the *loci topici* in musical invention. Like Mattheson, Spiess both includes a chapter dealing with the caesurae in the text: "*Von denen Ein- und Abschnitten*" (ch.24), and advocates a musical structure analogous to the rhetorical "*Invention, Disposition, und Elaboration*" (ch.25).

Out of his concern to express the text in a "facile, clear, flowing, and charming" manner, Spiess includes a discussion of the musical-rhetorical figures in his *Tractatus* (ch.27). He begins his explanations

---

135. "Vermischter Kirchen-Styl ist, wann die Composition mit 1. 2. 3. 4. oder auch mehreren Stimmen und cuncertirenden Instrumentis theils Ariosè, theils auch mit untermengten Contrapunct, Fugen etc. solchergestalt fortgeführet wird, daβ man jedoch die Gräntzen oder Schrancken der kirchlichen Gravität und Modestiae nicht überschreite." *Tractatus*, 161; Federl, "Der Tractatus Musicus," 44.

136. "Leicht heisset man alles das, so deutlich in die Sinnen fällt; und dahero vom Verstand bald kan begriffen werden. Wann eine Sach leicht ist, so ist sie auch deutlich; und wann verschiedene leichte oder deutliche Ding gehörig verbunden werden, so heissen wir sie flieβend, und was flieβend und deutlich ist, das ist auch mehrentheils lieblich." Ibid.

137. "Etwas excitates, munteres, frisches, zumahlen es sonderlich der Text erfordert, kan man in der Kirchen auch wohl anbringen." Ibid.

by differentiating between the symbols of musical notation and the expressive-ornamental devices, both known as *figurae musicae*, stating his intention to elaborate on this second understanding of *figura*: "These musical figures accomplish the same thing as do the rhetorical *figurae verborum* and *sententiarum*. Just as the rhetorical figures enhance an oration, so do the musical figures provide no small delight to the refined ear."[138] This analogy to the rhetorical *figurae verborum* and *figurae sententiarum* is undoubtedly adopted from Mattheson.[139] Spiess does not, however, elaborate on the difference between these two classes of rhetorical figures, nor how they apply to the musical figures, which suggests that he wishes to apply them to music as an inseparable unit. He points out that there are two classes of musical figures. The first category, also known as *Coloraturen* or *Manieren*, are the embellishments which he wishes "to leave to the singers, fiddlers, pipers, etc., and experienced musicians to execute."[140] Spiess goes on to say that he wishes, however, "to write about some belonging to the second kind, which should be familiar to the composer."[141] He then defines the figures in alphabetical order. However, instead of restricting himself to the musical-rhetorical figures, Spiess in fact also defines many of the melodic embellishments. He describes *variatio* as an embellishment of the vocal or instrumental melody, thereby adopting the same term used by Bernhard, Printz, and Walther for melodic ornamentation.[142] He also mentions that these *variationes* were called *figurae simplices* by Vogt. Spiess then defines *curta*, *groppo*, *circolo* (*circolo mezzo*), *tirata*, *messanza* (*misticanza*), *tenuta*, *ribattuta*, *superjectio*, *trillo*, *mordent*, and *acciaccatura*. That these ornaments are in fact identical with those *Manieren* which he wanted "to leave to the musicians" is further

---

138. "Es thun diese unsere Figurae Musicae eben das, was bey den Wohlrednern die Figurae Verborum & Sententiarum. Gleichwie nun die Figurae Oratoriae einer vollkommenen Oration nicht ein schlechtes beytragen; also pflegen auch diese Figurae Musicae einem delicaten Gehör kein geringes Vergnügen zu verursachen." *Tractatus*, 155.

139. See p.140, above.

140. "Die erste, so in unterschiedlichen, ja tausendfältigen Coloraturen, oder sogenannten Manieren bestehet, wollen wir denen Singern, Singerinnen, Geigern, Pfeiffern etc. und wohl-geübten Musicanten zur Execution anheim stellen." *Tractatus*, 155.

141. "Von der anderen Art aber einige, und zwar die ein Componist wissen soll, hier zu Pappier bringen." Ibid.

142. See *Variatio*, below.

supported by his use of the term *Manier* in the definition of *superjectio* and in the sentence which follows that definition: "Other vocal and instrumental *Manieren* could also be mentioned here."[143]

In examining both Spiess's list of figures and their definitions, it soon becomes evident that he chooses Vogt as the primary source for his own *Figurenlehre*. Not only does he refer to the melodic embellishments as *figurae simplices*, as Vogt had done, but of his remaining sixteen figures, only the technical devices—*anticipatio*, *retardatio*, and *diminutio*—were not included in Vogt's list of figures. In addition, a number of figures are only listed by these two authors, including *antistaechon*, *ethophonia*, *metabasis*, and *tmesis*. The remaining of Spiess's figures can be found in Vogt's as well as other *Figurenlehren*: *abruptio*, *anabasis*, *catabasis*, *anaphora*, *antithesis*, *aposiopesis*, *accentus*, *emphasis*, and *imitatio*.[144] However, a further nine of Vogt's figures do not find a place in Spiess's list. Neither does Spiess adopt Vogt's unique term for the musical-rhetorical figures, *figurae ideales*. By defining all of his figures, including the *figurae simplices*, under the general heading of *figurae musicae*, Spiess considers it unnecessary to give the musical-rhetorical figures a classification of their own.

The use of the musical-rhetorical figures to express and arouse the affections is not emphasized in the *Tractatus*. Spiess simply mentions that the figures provide "no small delight" to the listeners. However, each of these figures is explained with reference to a text, either in the definition or in the musical example. In contrast, the *figurae simplices* are consistently explained in purely musical terms, without reference to a text in their definitions or examples. While the basis of the *figurae simplices* is an unadorned melody, the source for the musical-rhetorical figures is the text. Spiess thereby adopts *musica poetica*'s text-oriented concept of the musical-rhetorical figures, even if this is not explicitly stated. The distinction between the two classes of figures, through their capacity to express the text in addition to their use by either composer or performer, further links Spiess's concept of the figures to that of

---

143. "Hiehero gehören auch noch andere, sowohl im singen, als auf Instrumenten übliche Manieren." *Tractatus*, 157.

144. Vogt defines the *abruptio* in his glossary at the beginning of his *Conclave* instead of under the list of *figurae ideales*.

Vogt. Vogt's *figurae ideales* were also linked to text expression, while his *figurae simplices* were regarded as ornamental embellishments.

Although Spiess uses various treatises as sources for his own work, including those of Kircher and Walther, he does not adopt their classification of the fugue, passing note, and suspension as *figurae principales* or *fundamentales*. In this regard, he also reflects the more modern concept of the musical-rhetorical figures as exemplified in the works of Vogt and Mattheson. Like Vogt, Spiess discusses these compositional devices in separate chapters of the *Tractatus*.[145] The seventeenth-century ranking of these devices as the fundamental method of constructing an expressive composition no longer seems relevant. Instead, the affective and concretely text-expressive musical-rhetorical figures are defined as the ideal methods of setting a text to music. Throughout the eighteenth century the musical-rhetorical figures increasingly assume this affective purpose, at first being associated primarily with a text, subsequently being transferred to instrumental music, as in Scheibe's *Figurenlehre*. The *figurae principales* or *fundamentales*, on the other hand, find themselves treated as purely technical, compositional constructions.

Johann Adolf Scheibe

Johann Adolf Scheibe (1708–1776), the son of a well-respected organ builder, was born in Leipzig, where he also attended the Lutheran *Nickolaischule*. In 1725 he began studies in law and philosophy at Leipzig University, which he had to abandon prematurely. Nonetheless, he was at the university long enough to become acquainted with the influential Johann Christoph Gottsched, professor of poetry and rhetoric, whose books on rhetoric were significantly to influence his own writings on music. After leaving the university, Scheibe continued his musical studies on his own. During this time he penned a compositional treatise which remained unpublished in his lifetime.[146] He moved to

---

145. Spiess discusses suspensions and passing notes in chapters 16–18 and various kinds of fugue in chapter 26 of his *Tractatus*.

146. *Compendium musices theoretico-practicum, das ist Kurzer Begriff derer nötigsten Compositions-Regeln* (ca.1730), published in Peter Benary, *Die deutsche Kompositionslehre des 18. Jahrhunderts* (Leipzig: Breitkopf & Härtel, 1961). Scheibe

Hamburg in 1736 where, with Telemann's encouragement, he began the publication of his music journal, *Der critische Musikus*. By 1740 he had published seventy-eight issues, which were collectively published in Leipzig in 1745 under the same title. The title of the journal was influenced both by Mattheson's earlier Hamburg journal, *Critica musica* (1722–25), as well as Gottsched's *Versuch einer Critischen Dichtkunst*. Scheibe served as *Capellmeister* to Markgrave Friedrich Ernst of Brandenburg-Culmbach in 1739, and then to King Christian VI of Denmark from 1740–47. In later years he established a music school for children and served as composer for the Danish court.

Scheibe presents a musical *Figurenlehre* in *Der critische Musikus* which is directly modeled on Gottsched's rhetorical *Figurenlehre* contained in *Versuch einer Critischen Dichtkunst*. Scheibe emphasizes "that the musical figures provide the greatest emphasis and uncommon vigor. . . . The circumstances in music are the same as in oratory or poetry. These two Liberal Arts would be left with neither fervor nor rousing spirit, were they to lose their use of the figures. Could the affections be expressed and aroused without them? Certainly not. For the figures are themselves the very language of the affections, as Professor Gottsched has thoroughly instructed in his *Critische Dichtkunst* in accordance with P. Lamy."[147] Mattheson's suggestion that the figures "can be looked up in rhetoric books, almost all of which can be applied to the melody," is realized by Scheibe. Instead of consulting one of the many musical *Figurenlehren*, Scheibe turns to the writings of his former Leipzig professor, upon whose rhetorical figures he "wishes to

---

mentions four figures in this early treatise: *anticipatio*, *retardatio*, *variatio*, and *generum Verwechselung*, all more compositional devices than musical-rhetorical figures. While *anticipatio* and *retardatio* are forms of suspension, *variatio* describes ornamental embellishments, and *generum Verwechselung* refers to the enharmonic rewriting of a note.

147. "Man wird mir allerdings Recht geben, wenn ich behaupte, daβ die Figuren der musikalischen Schreibart den gröβten Nachdruck und eine ungemeine Stärke geben. . . . Es ist damit in der Musik eben so, als in der Redekunst und Dichtkunst, beschaffen. Diese beyden freyen Künste würden weder Feuer, noch rührendes Wesen behalten, wenn man ihnen den Gebrauch der Figuren entziehen wollte. Kann man wohl ohne sie die Gemüthsbewegungen erregen und ausdrücken? Keinesweges. Die Figuren sind ja selbst eine Sprache der Affecten, wie solches der Herr Professor Gottsched in seiner critischen Dichtkunst aus dem P. Lami ausführlich erinnert." *Der critische Musikus*, 683. Scheibe notes that Gottsched was influenced by Bernhard Lamy's *La Rhétorique; ou, l'art de parler* (4th ed., Paris, 1701).

base the explanations of the musical figures, choosing those figures which particularly belong to music."[148] The fact that Scheibe wishes to discuss those figures "which particularly belong to music" points to his belief that rhetoric will help explain those expressions already found in music but not construct new devices analogous to rhetorical ones. Just as Burmeister sought to define musical devices through rhetorical terminology and Mattheson wished to explain musical structure through rhetorical principles, Scheibe also aspires to establish a musical *Figurenlehre* parallel to the rhetorical one. Music theorists throughout the Baroque emphasized the similar goals of the "sister disciplines,"[149] justifying the employment of common devices and principles.

Scheibe applies the figures to instrumental music more consistently and extensively than any author before him. While he emphasizes the figures' role in expressing the affections, the traditional references to text expression are conspicuously absent in his definitions of the figures. He only rarely mentions that they can be used to express the words, his illustrations consistently being drawn from instrumental rather than vocal music. However, in his introductory comments Scheibe maintains that the origins of the musical-rhetorical figures are to be found in vocal music, just as "instrumental music itself is rooted in vocal music. Because vocal music concerns itself with a text which can indicate the specific affection, it can justifiably be said that the root of the figures through which the affections are expressed is also to be found in vocal music. Thus one learns to differentiate between the figures' form and content through vocal music. Only then can they be applied to instrumental music, which, concerning the expression of the affections, is nothing other than an imitation of vocal music."[150] Scheibe

---

148. "Ich will, mit Erlaubniß des Herrn Prof. Gottscheds, das in der critischen Dichtkunst befindliche Capitel, von den Figuren in der Poesie, zum Grunde meiner Erklärung der Figuren in der Musik legen, und daraus diejenigen Figuren anmerken, welche der Musik insonderheit eigen sind." Ibid., 685.

149. Ibid., 684.

150. "Aus der Vocalmusik muß man nur auf die Instrumentalmusik schließen. Weil wir in jener mit Worten zu thun haben, dadurch aber die Affecten entdecken, welche darinnen befindlich sind: so kann man auch mit Recht sagen, daß in der Vocalmusik eigentlich der Sitz der Figuren befindlich ist, durch welche man nämlich die Affecten ausdrücket. Und so lernet man folglich durch die Vocalmusik die Beschaffenheit der Figuren unterscheiden, und einsehen, und sie hernach auch in der Instrumentalmusik

is not suggesting that a figure assumes a specific, literal meaning in vocal music, which is then transferred to instrumental music. In fact, except in the case of the *dubitatio*, which is used to express doubt, the various figures are not limited to certain affections but can be used to heighten, repeat, alter, or vary musical expressions in various affections. While both instrumental music as well as the musical-rhetorical figures find their origins in vocal music, it would be as inappropriate to assign specific, literal content to a musical-rhetorical figure as it would to a piece of instrumental music. Figures were developed in vocal music as a result of composers seeking to express the affections prescribed by the text. These devices can be used in instrumental music similarly to express the affections. The *dubitatio*, for example, is used in vocal music to express the specific doubt implied by the text, while in instrumental music similar musical progressions would express general ambiguity; a figure used in vocal music to express a specific exclamation could be used in instrumental music with a more general "exclamatory" effect; the musical devices used to express questions in a text could be applied in instrumental music, resulting in a "questioning" musical expression; the various figures used to repeat, amplify, or intensify a text could also be used in instrumental music to achieve similar effects. The commonality of the figures' usages in vocal and instrumental music lies in their power to express and arouse the affections rather than in their potential to express specific, literal thoughts. Musical-rhetorical figures do not assume a specific, programmatic character but rather retain their affective expressiveness in instrumental music.

Before addressing the musical-rhetorical figures, Scheibe discusses the figurated melodic embellishments or *verblühmten Auszierungen.* Instead of dwelling on their application by the performer, as had traditionally been the case, Scheibe focuses on their use by the composer. Should he fail to do so, "the composer will neither demonstrate his cleverness nor achieve his desired purpose in attracting and keeping the listener's attention. Nevertheless adhering only to the rudimentary rules of composition, . . . why is it, that he conceived and composed so insipidly without coming close to attaining the desired goal? Certainly

---

gebührend anwenden: weil diese in Ansehung der Affecten nichts anders, als eine Nachahmung der Vocalmusik ist." Ibid., 685.

only because he was too ordinary, too dry, too lean, and therefore dull and loathsome."[151] Like the musical-rhetorical figures, the embellishments are also used to better express the affections. Through the use of appropriate and agreeable embellishments, the composer would be able to intensify his composition, "as though the notes had come alive. Even his textless melodies have to captivate and move the listeners. And so he must bring all the passions and affections under his control, continually being able to stir the listeners anew."[152] He then praises various composers for their extraordinarily expressive use of the embellishments, including Hasse, Telemann, and, in particular, J. S. Bach.[153]

Unique to Scheibe is the comparison of the embellishments to the rhetorical tropes, which are descriptions or elaborations using metaphorical, symbolic, or allegorical expressions. Just as rhetoric uses words which digress from their natural and simple meaning, "in music we also have the trope-like, symbolic, figurative embellishments, which digress from the natural and simple order and placement of a composition's notes."[154] In comparing tropes to embellishments, Scheibe wishes to equate the unadorned melody with the unadorned thoughts or words of a sentence. In a trope the metaphoric word's meaning is then symbolically transferred onto the object. In a musical embellishment the ornamental note's "literal meaning" is understood as representing another note. Just as the trope uses words symbolically, so too is a musical ornament based on a note or phrase which itself remains only implied. However, the underlying notes or words, melodies or thoughts, should always remain tacitly yet essentially understood, in spite of their

---

151. "Und der Componist wird dadurch weder seinen Witz zeigen, noch auch seinen Zweck bey den Zuhörern erhalten. Da er aber gleichwohl den gewöhnlichsten Regeln der musikalischen Zusammensetzung gefolget ist, . . . was muβ es dann seyn, daβ er so schläfrig gedacht und geschrieben, und auch keinesweges den gehofften Zweck erreichet hat? Gewiβ nichts anders, als daβ er zu eigentlich, zu trocken, zu mager, und folglich platt und niederträchtig gewesen ist." Ibid., 644.

152. "Er muβ seinen Tönen gleichsam ein wirkliches Leben ertheilen können. Seine Melodien müssen auch ohne Worte die Zuhörer bewegen und einnehmen. Und so muβ er also alle Leidenschaften und Gemüthsbewegungen in seiner völligen Gewalt haben, und immer eine neue Aufmerksamkeit erwecken können." Ibid., 643.

153. Ibid., 646.

154. "Man hat also auch in der Musik tropische, uneigentliche und verblühmte Auszierungen, die sich von der natürlichsten und einfältigsten Folge und Stellung der Töne eines Gesanges unterscheiden." Ibid., 642.

embellishments.[155] It is precisely for this reason that the embellishments are fundamentally different from the musical-rhetorical figures, which "alter the musical passage and therefore also particularly affect the harmony and the entire context of the composition."[156] The embellishments can vary individual notes or entire phrases. This might even include a substantial alteration of the phrase's form through its connection to a subsequent phrase, or the introduction of quite unexpected or foreign notes or harmonies, giving the passage an entirely different intensity. Even these embellishments are not to be understood as figures, however, "because at all times, in spite of all these variations, they refer to and flow out of the original melody notes. In contrast, the figures digress utterly and absolutely from the fundamental notes."[157]

Scheibe's concept of the musical-rhetorical figures is substantially different from that of Ahle or even Mattheson. While Ahle also begins with the rhetorical figure rather than the musical device, he explains the figures purely in terms of their musical text application: repetitions or variations in the text were to be musically expressed. Mattheson also explains the figures in terms of their text-expressive potential. His discussion of the *emphasis*, *exclamatio*, and *interrogatio* (he does not use the last term) are undertaken in the context of a chapter dealing with the caesurae and punctuation marks found in the text. In addition, his musical examples for these figures are all taken from vocal music. Although an instrumental application can also be understood in Mattheson's list of the *figurae cantus*, it is not expressly indicated or emphasized to the extent that Scheibe does. The text-bound orientation of

---

155. A simple trope would be the metaphor "That person is a fox." The unadorned thought is "person," who is described as having the attributes of a fox (sly, etc.) rather than actually being a fox. By analogy, a note might be embellished by turns, trills, runs, or other notes, all of which "describe" the melody note instead of actually "being themselves." The person, just like the original note, is always tacitly understood as the embellished object.

156. "Denn diese verändern auch sehr oft die musikalischen Perioden, und müssen folglich auch vornehmlich auf die Harmonie, und auf den ganzen Zusammenhang eines Stückes gehen." *Der critische Musikus*, 642.

157. "Dennoch aber geht sie von den Figuren im eigentlichen Verstande noch ab, weil sie bey aller ihrer Veränderung doch allezeit aus den gewöhnlichen Grundnoten fließen, und sich auf dieselben beziehen muß, da hingegen die Figuren insgemein von den Grundnoten ganz und gar abweichen." Ibid., 647.

musica poetica, which is still clearly determinative in Ahle's *Figurenlehre* and begins to weaken in the writings of Mattheson, has virtually disappeared in Scheibe's *Figurenlehre*.

Just as Gottsched had done in his *Versuch einer critischen Dichtkunst*, Scheibe first lists the German term followed by the Latin equivalent in his definitions of the figures: *Ausruf (exclamatio)*, *Zweifel (dubitatio)*, *Verbeißen (ellipsis)*, *Versetzung (hyperbaton)*, *Wiederholung (repetitio)*, *Verstärkung (paronomasia)*, *Zergliederung (distributio)*, *Gegensatz (antithesis)*, *Aufhalten (suspensio)*, *Frage (interrogatio)*, *Wiederkehr (epistrophe)*, and *Aufsteigen (gradatio)*. Further rhetorical figures defined by Gottsched but not adopted by Scheibe are: *correctio*, *aposiopesis*, *praeteritio*, *epizeuxis*, *anaphora*, *anadiplosis*, *epanalepsis*, *pleonasmus*, *synonymia*, *hypotyposis*, *descriptio*, *simile*, *comparatio*, *prosopopoeia*, *sermocinatio*, *epiphonema*, *apostrophe*, *communicatio*, *confessio*, *epitrophe*, *periphrasis*, and *jusjurandum*. While many of these figures could not be musically represented, many others had been defined or at least mentioned in earlier musical *Figurenlehren*, including *aposiopesis*, *epizeuxis*, *anaphora*, *anadiplosis*, *epanalepsis*, *pleonasmus*, *synonymia*, *hypotyposis*, *prosopopoeia*, and *apostrophe*. As *epizeuxis*, *anaphora*, *anadiplosis*, and *epanalepsis* were regarded as specific types of repetition, it can be assumed that Scheibe tacitly included these in his *repetitio*. In fact, Scheibe goes on at some length to describe the various kinds of repetition which a composer could employ, which suggests that he indeed incorporated Gottsched's various repetition figures without explicitly naming them. Gottsched had also pointed out that the *aposiopesis* can be considered a form of *ellipsis*, explaining both Scheibe's omission of the term, *aposiopesis*, and his explanation of *ellipsis* with two possible meanings, one of which was traditionally associated with *aposiopesis*. Furthermore, Scheibe does not consider his list of figures exhaustive. While asserting that most of Gottsched's figures "are applicable in music in certain situations or connections, I am obliged tacitly to exclude various figures due to the restrictions of this publication, and only explain those which can be defined without musical examples."[158] And at the end of his discussion

---

158. "Die meisten Figuren, welche dieser berühmte Mann [Gottsched] daselbst anmerket, sind zwar alle, nach gewissen Umständen und Bedingungen, auch in der

of the figures, Scheibe insists that "these are by no means all the figures. Rather, their number is so great that they cannot easily be counted. The clever composer will also continually invent new ones without always being aware of them or their names. His inspiration [*Feuer*] will soon lead him from the mundane to greater heights."[159] In this comment Scheibe's Enlightenment concept of music shines through once more. It is the composer's "fire" rather than a given text which would lead to the invention of new figures. The common *musica poetica* suggestion that a composer consult the compositions of past masters for examples of the figures and apply those in his own compositions would also be quite unfathomable for Scheibe. Being at the vanguard of the Enlightenment, Scheibe believed that musical invention is inborn rather than learned, and that melodic composition rests in "the imitation of nature 'which is the true essence of music as well as of rhetoric and poetry.'"[160]

In the final paragraph of his chapter discussing the musical-rhetorical figures, Scheibe briefly mentions the *Durchgang (Transitus)*, *Bindung (Ligatura und Sycopatio oder Syncope)*, and *Fuge*. He points out that these familiar devices do not need to be explained as "they actually belong to the general and elementary rules of composition, which I do not intend to explain in this publication."[161] These venerable compositional devices, so integral both to the art of Baroque contrapuntal composition and the many earlier *Figurenlehren*, is now relegated to footnote status. Not only are they of little help in expressing the affec-

---

Musik anzuwenden: da mir aber die Einrichtung dieser Blätter nicht erlaubet, Exempel in Noten anzuführen: so bin ich genöthiget, verschiedene Figuren voritzo mit Stillschweigen zu übergehen, und nur diejenigen zu erklären, welche sich, ohne besondere Exempel, erläutern lassen." Ibid., 686.

159. "Ich sage aber keinesweges, daβ dieses alle Figuren sind. Ihre Menge ist vielmehr so groβ, daβ sie auch nicht leicht bestimmet werden kann. Ein scharfsinniger Componist wird auch immer neue erfinden, ohne sie eben so genau zu kennen, oder ihre Namen zu bemerken. Sein Feuer wird ihn gar bald von der gemeinen Bahn auf eine höhere leiten." Ibid., 697f.

160. George Buelow, "Scheibe," *New Grove Dictionary,* 16: 600.

161. "Diese Arten der harmonischen Figuren sind aber den Musikverständigen bekannt genug, daβ ich also nicht nöthig habe, mich mit deren Erklärung allhier zu beschäfftigen. Auβer diesen gehören sie eigentlich zu den allgemeinen und ersten Compositionsregeln, die ich in diesen Blättern zu erläutern nicht gesonnen bin." *Der critische Musicus*, 699. In fact, Scheibe does give a brief definition of *transitus, ligatura,* and *syncopatio oder syncope* in a footnote to this final paragraph.

tions but could easily lead to a style of music which the musician of the mid–eighteenth century found excessively opulent and "unnatural."

Scheibe can be considered the legitimate heir to Mattheson's new music aesthetic, rejecting the theologically determined, speculative, and dogmatic concepts of music which had reigned throughout seventeenth-century Lutheran Germany. His concept of musical-rhetorical figures is rooted in a fundamentally transformed aesthetic of music, bearing little resemblance to that of a Burmeister, Bernhard, or Walther. Scheibe has been unjustifiably maligned for his criticisms of J. S. Bach's music.[162] Although he recognizes the great art of Bach, even drawing attention to it in his writings, his progressive, Enlightenment views on music also led him to be critical of those elements in Bach's music which contradicted the growing "good taste" in music. (It might be helpful to remember that Scheibe was much closer in age to C. P. E. Bach, Sammartini, and Stamitz than he was to J. S. Bach.) Through Scheibe's *Figurenlehre* the concept of the musical-rhetorical figures is removed from the *musica poetica* tradition and placed in the context of the Enlightenment. Although it was a valiant attempt by Scheibe to salvage the Baroque rhetorical concepts for the new music aesthetic, it was ultimately doomed to failure. For the coming age, intent as it was on an individualistic expression of subjective sentiment in "natural" melody, could not accommodate a concept which had evolved in and indeed was reflective of a fundamentally contradictory concept of music.

Johann Nikolaus Forkel

Johann Nikolaus Forkel (1749–1818) was born near Coburg, where he received his first musical training at the organ. He matriculated at the University of Göttingen in 1769 to study law, philosophy, philology, and mathematics, a university he was to remain associated with for the remainder of his career. He was appointed university organist in 1770, and in 1779 became the university's music director. In 1787 the university awarded Forkel an honorary doctorate for both his musical and

162. See also George Buelow, "In Defence of J. A. Scheibe against J. S. Bach," *Proceedings of the Royal Musical Association* 101 (1974–75): 85.

academic prowess. He is credited with stimulating the nineteenth-century Bach revival through his biography of the great Leipzig *Kantor*, much of his material coming from the Bach sons. His vast and largely self-acquired knowledge of the musical literature becomes apparent in his bibliography, *Allgemeine Litteratur der Musik* (Leipzig, 1792), with some three thousand entries covering writings on music from antiquity to his own day. Through his work in Göttingen Forkel modeled the scholarly study of music history as an academic discipline, earning him the distinction as the founder of modern musicology.

Forkel lived in an age which rejected the fundamental precepts held by the Baroque *musica poetica* tradition. The objective Baroque *ratio*-oriented concept of musical expression no longer remained relevant in an era which believed in subjective, individualized, and *empfindsam* musical expression. This new music aesthetic had its roots back in the seventeenth century: with Descartes's famous "*cogito ergo sum*," the individual rather than church, society, or an objective dogmatic system was to become the genesis of all cognition and perception. Descartes thereby established the presuppositions for Locke's empirical philosophy, which influenced philosophical and scientific thought throughout eighteenth-century Europe. While empiricism opened new horizons to scientific investigation, liberal philosophy also encouraged a new music aesthetic. Both in philosophy generally and in music specifically the value of the individual achieved greater significance, undermining the authority of the normative and generally valid Baroque doctrines and dogmas. Thus the end of the concept of *musica poetica*'s musical-rhetorical figures became inevitable. *Musica poetica*'s objectively discernable and teachable *precepta*, which had determined musical composition in Germany throughout the past centuries, were replaced by a freer and subjective concept of musical expression. With that, "the art of musical rhetoric is then gradually lost in the generation of Bach's sons, which replaced outlived oratorical formulas by the natural outpouring of the human heart."[163] *Musica poetica* was rooted in the expression of objective and generally valid affections instead of subjective and individualized feelings. Its purpose—to edify the listener to

---

163. Friedrich Blume, *Renaissance and Baroque Music* (New York: Norton, 1967), 105.

God's greater glory, a theologically relevant precept to which Mattheson still ascribed—was quite unacceptable to late-eighteenth-century positivist philosophy, which denied the existence of the metaphysical and limited itself to human experience. Furthermore, *musica poetica* stood in an inextricable relationship with the linguistically articulated discipline of rhetoric at a time when the linguistic and musical arts were increasingly going their own separate ways.

It was during this "new age" that Forkel also worked on the publication of his *Allgemeine Geschichte der Music* (Leipzig, 1788– 1801), the first German attempt to compile an objective and comprehensive history of music. He completed only two volumes of the colossal undertaking, but it was enough to establish him as the first modern musicologist. Rather than rigorously subscribing to the assumption of the Enlightenment that music always progresses from primitive to more sophisticated levels, he recognized the possibility of musical retrogression, regarding "his own time as one of decline in musical values, a descent from the high-point achieved in the music of Bach."[164] Furthermore, in rejecting the prominent Enlightenment view of music as a "superficial stimulant to the senses," he believed that "music was a serious expression of human feeling. Just as words and their combinations served as the language of the mind, so notes and musical structures conveyed the language of the heart."[165] In these historical-nostalgic and emotion-oriented views, he not only betrayed the gulf between his musical concepts and those of *musica poetica*, but foreshadowed a Romantic interpretation of music. The first volume of the *Allgemeine Geschichte* appeared in 1788: at the eve of the French Revolution, the year of C. P. E. Bach's death, the year that Mozart wrote his *Jupiter* Symphony, that Kant published his *Kritik der praktischen Vernunft*, that the American constitution proclaimed individual freedom and equality for all citizens, the year that Goethe wrote his *Egmont*, and David painted his *Paris et Helena*. Thus it appears somewhat anachronistic that the progressive and liberal thinker, Forkel, should once more discuss the musical-rhetorical figures. However, Forkel's discussion of musical rhetoric does not appear in a treatise on composition intended for contemporary

164. Vincent Duckles, "Forkel," *New Grove Dictionary*, 6: 707.
165. Ibid.

composers but in the introduction to a history of music. The musical-rhetorical figures have now moved from being relevant compositional tools to becoming music history.

Interestingly enough, Forkel considers musical-rhetorical concepts, including the figures, of significance to his contemporary composers. In fact, he believes that only in his day has music progressed to the stage where a musical rhetoric could even be realized: "Even though a musical rhetoric is undeniably the preeminent and veritable essence of music, it is to this day scarcely mentioned. . . . Here Mattheson was also the first . . . among the German authors to comment on this subject in the chapter on melody of his *Vollkommener Capellmeister*. However, in his day, or rather when *Der vollkommene Capellmeister* was published, musical composition was not yet at the stage where a coherent musical rhetoric could be reflected in the music. Not only did it lack elegance and taste, but especially that coherence of its parts which would result in a genuine sentiment-discourse through the interrelated development of its musical thoughts, the unity of its style, and so on."[166] Even in this preamble, terms such as "elegance and taste" (*Feinheit und Geschmack*) and the concepts of "the interrelated development of its musical ideas" (*Entwicklung der Gedanken aus einander*) point to a Zeitgeist which was foreign to a *musica-poetica* concept of musical rhetoric. Forkel wishes to be understood as the successor to Mattheson in this field.[167] However, while Mattheson held to the classical rhetorical structuring methods, Forkel introduces a significantly altered system, consisting of: (1) musical periodology, (2) musical styles, (3) musical genres, (4)

---

166. "Diese musicalische Rhetorik, ob sie gleich unläugbar die höhere und eigentliche Theorie der Musik ausmacht, ist doch bis jezt noch kaum dem Namen nach bekannt. . . . Mattheson ist auch hierin . . . unter den Deutschen der erste gewesen, der in seinem vollkommenen Capellmeister im Capitel von der Melodie, viele hierher gehörige Bemerkungen geliefert hat. Allein, zu seiner Zeit, oder vielmehr in der Zeit, in welcher der vollkommene Capellmeister erschien, war die Musik noch nicht von der Beschaffenheit, daβ sich eine zusammenhängende musikalische Rhetorik aus ihr hätte abstrahiren lassen. Es fehlte ihr nicht nur Feinheit und Geschmack, sondern auch vorzüglich derjenige Zusammenhang ihrer Theile, der sie theils durch die Entwickelung der Gedanken aus einander, theils durch die Einheit des Styls u.s.w. erst zu einer förmlichen Empfindungsrede machte." *Allgemeine Geschichte*, 37.

167. "Es ist indessen doch zu verwundern, daβ man bey nachheriger Verfeinerung und Vervollkommung der Kunst, diese Matthesonischen Winke so ganz ungenuzt gelassen hat. . . . So viel mir bekannt ist, bin ich der erste . . ." Ibid., 37f.

musical organization, (5) musical performance, and (6) music criticism.[168] Rhetoric and *musica poetica*'s first step is the *inventio*. While Mattheson considered the application of *inventio*'s *loci topici* valuable to the composer, their employment by Forkel and his contemporaries is quite unthinkable. Such a systematization of musical inspiration would contradict every tenet of late-eighteenth-century musical thought. Rather, Forkel replaces traditional *inventio* with guidelines on periodology, style, and genre. The second rhetorical step, *dispositio*, now appears as the fourth step in Forkel's ordering. He emphasizes "that the expression and portrayal of our own sentiments must be the primary purpose of all compositions,"[169] repeatedly reminding his readers that the "individualization of common sentiments" (*Individualisirung allgemeiner Empfindungen*) lies at the heart of a musical composition.[170] He expands the *dispositio* from six to eight parts by subdividing the *propositio* into three sections: primary, secondary, and contrary subject or material (*Hauptsatz*, *Nebensatz*, *Gegensatz*). Thus the rhetorical *propositio* becomes adapted to the sonata concept. While he wishes to establish an analogy between rhetoric and music, his "aesthetic organisation" rests "entirely on the manner and method in which the sentiments and ideas develop out of each other."[171] The qualities of aesthetics and "taste" first acquire significance in appraising a musical composition during this period. The associated subjectivity on the part

---

168. (1) *Die musikalische Periodologie*—musical phrase and period construction; (2) *Die musikalischen Schreibarten*—appropriate musical styles according to the desired affections; (3) *Die verschiedenen Musikgattungen*—the genres unique to certain styles (e.g., chorales in church music) and common genres (e.g., fugues); (4) *Die Anordnung musikalischer Gedanken in Rücksicht auf den Umfang der Stücke, die man auch die ästhetische Anordnung nennen kann, nebst der Lehre von den Figuren*—"the organisation of the musical thought with consideration given to the scope of the composition, which can also be called the aesthetic organisation, including the teaching of the Figures;" (5) *Den Vortrag oder die Declamation der Tonstücke*—in which Forkel refers to the writings of Sulzer, C. P. E. Bach, Quantz, and Tosi/Agricola; (6) *Die musikalische Kritik*—the first reference to music criticism in a "musical rhetoric." Ibid., 39ff.

169. "Daß Ausdruck und Schilderung unserer Empfindungen ein Hauptzweck aller Tonstücke seyn müssen, wird von niemand leicht bezweifelt." Ibid., 49.

170. Ibid., 51, 52.

171. "Diese ästhetische Anordnung der Gedanken gründet sich, wie schon gesagt worden, einzig und allein auf die Art und Weise, wie sich Empfindungen und Gedanken aus einander entwickeln." Ibid., 50.

of both the composer/musician and the listener stands in contrast to the generally objective concepts of Baroque music. The obsolescence of these concepts nullify the fundamental validity of the musical-rhetorical figures, for these were based on an analysis and imitation of past masters rather than on an individualization of sentiment. Terms such as aesthetics, taste, and individualization are rooted in the Enlightenment, not in the Baroque. Through his very choice of vocabulary, Forkel announces the end of the *Figurenlehre*.

Forkel also places the discussion and use of the musical-rhetorical figures in the *distributio* stage, thereby abandoning the musical *decoratio* or *elocutio*. He maintains that "the impressions of one of the senses can be transferred to another sense, indeed, can even be abstracted from sensual impressions, ideas, and concepts."[172] It is this "transfer of impressions from one sense to another" which "occurs foremost through the Figures. They are therefore expressions which embody the image of an impression according to its corresponding sense. There is no sentiment and no conception which the imagination cannot conceive in a visual form, because all of our conceptions are originally nothing but abstractions of concrete, visible objects."[173] The musical-rhetorical figure is therefore both image and source of an impression or sentiment. On one hand, it reflects those sentiments which were impressed on other than aural senses, thereby being their musical image. On the other hand, it is a musically realized abstraction of an impression which exists independent of its subsequent verbalization or visual portrayal, thereby being its musical source. The musical figure is therefore not an imitation of the rhetorical one, but rather exists as an analogous form of human expression. Just as the rhetorical figures "lie

---

172. "Da sich aber die Eindrücke eines Sinnes auf einen andern übertragen lassen, ja sogar von sinnlichen Eindrücken, Ideen und Vorstellungen abstrahirt werden können, so folgt daraus, daβ die Absicht der Tonsprache auf Empfindung zwar die nächste, aber nicht die einzige ist." Ibid., 54.

173. "Diese Uebertragung der Eindrücke von einer Kraft auf die andere geschieht vorzüglich durch die Figuren. Sie sind daher eigentlich solche Ausdrücke, welche die bildliche Form eines Eindrucks nach der eigenen Natur einer jeden Kraft enthalten, und von einer auf die andere übertragen. Es giebt keine Empfindung und keine Vorstellung, von welcher sich die Einbildungskraft nicht eine bildliche Form vorstellen könnte, weil alle unsere Vorstellungen ursprünglich nichts anders sind, als Abstrakte von körperlichen, sichtbaren Gegenständen." Ibid.

at the heart of human nature, and in normal speech would have been the first expressions which the yet uncultivated 'natural human' would have used," so too is it more than likely that "certain similar figures would have been the first forms of musical expression, at least at the point of the innovation of musical composition."[174]

Forkel divides the musical figures into two categories, those for the intellect and those for the imagination, of which the latter are considered by far the most important.[175] As in earlier eighteenth-century treatises, the *figurae principales* or *fundamentales* are not regarded as expressive musical devices. They are to be used with great care and only in connection with other more effective methods of musical expression. As examples, Forkel lists various kinds of complex contrapuntal structures. The fugue, however, is not listed as an expressive device or figure but rather as the crowning musical genre. It receives a novel and expressive justification: while a single melodic line of an aria expresses the sentiments of an individual, the numerous independent melodic lines of a fugue express the sentiments of a multitude, and is thereby both a faithful image and a fruit of Nature. For Nature has generated a multiplicity of both individual and collective sentiments, and has provided music with a multiplicity of devices to express these sentiments, all of which can be incorporated into the fugue. Just as the individual is only one member of a nation, so can the aria be considered as only one voice of a fugue: a nation incorporates many individuals, and a fugue many arias. It is therefore the grandest of all genres, just as the general consensus of an entire nation is the grandest of all sentiments.[176]

---

174. "Die sogenannten Figuren liegen daher tief in der menschlichen Natur, und in der eigentlichen Rede sind sie das erste, was der noch unkultivirte Naturmensch zu brauchen weiβ. Es ist mehr als wahrscheinlich, daβ einige derselben auch in der Tonsprache das erste Mittel des Ausdrucks werden gewesen seyn, sobald wenigstens auf irgend eine Art eine gewisse Zusammenstellung der Töne erfunden war." Ibid.

175. "Man muβ die Figuren in der Tonsprache, eben so wie die in der eigentlichen Rede, nach ihrer Absicht und Anwendung vorzüglich in Figuren für den Verstand, und für die Einbildungskraft eintheilen. Die Figuren für die Einbildungskraft sind die wichtigsten, und zur lebhaften Wirkung eines Tonstücks die beförderlichsten." Ibid.

176. "Ist sie nicht, diese mannichfaltige und künstliche Verwebung, eine getreue Abbildung der Natur, ist sie nicht der vollkommenste Ausdruck der mannichfaltig modificirten Empfindungen aller Glieder eines Volks, die erst nach und nach entstehen, sodann aber in einen Strom sich ergieβen? . . . sie ist eine Frucht der Natur. So wie diese in dem Herzen der Menschen vielartige Empfindungen erschaffen hat, so wie sie nicht

The expression of the sentiments is accomplished through the employment of the figures for the imagination. These can again be divided into two categories: those which realistically imitate an object or sound (e.g., thunder), and those which "depict the inner sentiments in such a manner, that they appear to become visible to the imagination."[177] In a footnote, Forkel states that it is this latter group which are most important, belonging not to "musical painting" but rather to musical expression in general. A composer should concentrate on expressing the sentiments which are aroused by external stimuli instead of attempting to depict the external object itself. As an example he cites a "Garden-sonata, which is to express that gentle feeling which we experience in breathing in the beneficent and soothing garden air."[178] Forkel warns against the use of musical *onomatopoeia*, devices frequently found with "tasteless and indiscrete" composers.[179] The figures are to imitate the sentiments rather than the objects and sounds found in nature. For example, in reflecting a mother's sorrow at the loss of a child, "only her inner impassioned sentiment of the loss rather than her natural outpouring of grief in whimpering, weeping, and sobbing"

---

blos einzelnen, sondern auch mehrern Menschen zugleich die Aeuβerung ihrer Empfindungen verstattet, so hat sie auch der Kunst vielartige Mittel zum Ausdruck derselben gegeben. Diese Mittel sind sämmtlich in der Fuge enthalten; sie ist daher unter den übringen Musikgattungen die prächtigste, vollkommenste und gröβte, so wie unter den verschiedenen Aeuβerungen unserer Empfindung, die allgemeine Uebereinstimmung eines ganzen Volkes, in dem Ausdruck eines Gefühls, das prachtvolleste, rührendste und gröβte Schauspiel ist. Was will ein einzelner Mensch gegen ein ganzes Volk? Eben so wenig als eine einzelne Arie gegen eine Fuge. Die Arie ist von der Fuge nur ein Theil, wie der einzelne Mensch vom Volke. Das Volk enthält viele Menschen, und die Fuge viele Arien." Ibid., 48.

177. "Unter die Figuren für die Einbildungskraft können eigentlich alle sogenannte musikalische Malereyen gerechnet werden, die im Grunde nichts anders, als hörbare Nachahmungen entweder blos sichtbarer Gegenstände, oder solcher sind, mit deren Bewegung ein Schall verbunden ist. Die Tonsprache hat aber auch Mittel, selbst innere Empfindungen so zu schildern, das sie der Einbildungskraft gleichsam sichtbar zu werden scheinen." Ibid., 53.

178. "Auf diese durch äuβere Gegenstände in uns erregte Empfindung gründet sich z.B. eine sogenannte Gartensonate, (im musikalischen Mancherley, S.125) die das sanfte Gefühl ausdrücken soll, welches wir in einem Garten durch das Einathmen der wohlthätigen und balsamischen Luft empfinden." Ibid., 55f.

179. "Solche Onomatopoien findet man bey Geschmack- und Urtheillosen Componisten sehr häufig." Ibid., 59.

should be musically represented.[180] The figures which Forkel defines are *Ellipsis*, *Wiederholung*, *Paronomasie*, *Suspension*, *Epistrophe*, *Gradation*, and *Dubitation*. Not only had these musical-rhetorical figures all been mentioned by Scheibe, but only Scheibe and Forkel list *paronomasia*, *suspensio*, and *dubitatio*. In all of his definitions, Forkel leans unmistakably on Scheibe's description of the figures.

Forkel's concept of the musical-rhetorical figures rests completely on the expression of human sentiments, a criterium through which the merit and virtue of a figure can be determined. Neither the illustrative onomatopoeic *hypotyposis* figures nor the technical compositional devices are appropriate for Forkel's purposes. Decisive is the aesthetic of the Enlightenment (and emerging Romanticism), focusing on the natural expression of individual sentiments rather than on the systemized Baroque concept of generally valid and objective affections. The concept of the *Figurenlehre*, itself such a systematization, is not to be mentioned again in composition treatises, nor will it be recommended by music theorists. With Forkel, the *Figurenlehre* has indeed departed from the realm of compositional theory to the annals of music history.

180. Ibid.

PART THREE

DEFINITIONS AND TRANSLATIONS OF THE MUSICAL-RHETORICAL FIGURES

DEFINITIONS AND TRANSLATIONS

ABRUPTIO: a sudden and unexpected break in a musical composition.

The *abruptio* is one among a number of musical figures of silence.[1] While it is not commonly encountered as a rhetorical figure, the term is used by Virgil to denote a breaking off in the middle of a speech.[2] *Abruptio* is introduced into the musical *Figurenlehre* by Kircher, who chooses this term instead of the familiar *aposiopesis*. While *aposiopesis* signifies a certain silence in a musical composition, *abruptio* refers to the actual and unexpected breaking off of a musical passage.[3] As such it is virtually identical with the *tmesis*, another figure of silence which emphasizes a break in the texture rather than the following silence. Vogt and Spiess list both *abruptio* and *tmesis*, defining the former as a break toward the end of the composition and the latter as short interruptions within the context of a composition, analogous to Kircher's *stenasmus* or *suspiratio*.[4]

In his *Tractatus* Bernhard lists the *abruptio* as one of the figures used in the *stylus recitativus*. Here it signifies either the cutting off of a note through a rest in the context of a passage or the premature ending of the melody line on the penultimate harmony of a cadence, omitting the expected resolution on the final harmony. Only this second explanation reappears in Bernhard's *Bericht*, a definition which Walther adopts in

---

1. Included among the musical figures of silence are also *aposiopesis*, *ellipsis*, *homoioptoton*, *homoioteleuton*, *tmesis*, *suspiratio*, and especially *pausa*.

2. "Abrumpo," *Cassell's Latin Dictionary*, 5th ed. (New York: Macmillan, 1968).

3. Kircher uses *pausa* to denote the ensuing silence and *stenasmus/suspiratio* to indicate short breaks within the musical texture instead of the more common *aposiopesis*,which had been in use since Burmeister. Presumably the questionable musical application of the rhetorical *homoioptoton/homoioteleuton*, musical figures associated with *aposiopesis* by Nucius and Thuringus, led Kircher to opt for the new term. He subsequently assigns *homoioptoton* a musical definition which is much closer to its rhetorical counterpart rather than defining it as a subspecies of *aposiopesis*. See *Homoioptoton*.

4. See *Tmesis*. Similarly, *homoioptoton* can signify a pause in the middle of a passage, while *homoioteleuton* is understood as a pause following a cadence.

his *Praecepta.* In contrast to Kircher's text-oriented application of the *abruptio*, Bernhard's definition focuses on the correct use of dissonance, the underlying concern of his concept of musical-rhetorical figures. In his *Lexicon*, Walther again includes the more general application of the *abruptio*, indicating its use both in relation to a text or due to "other circumstances" in instrumental music.

Kircher (*Musurgia* L.8 p.145)
Repentina abruptio est periodus harmonica, qua rem cito peractam exprimimus, & ut plurimum locum habet in fine, ut illud (Desiderium peccatorum peribit.)

The *abruptio* is an unexpected musical passage in which we express a rapidly completed thought. It occurs most frequently at the end of a composition, for example to the text "The longing after sinfulness shall cease."

Bernhard (*Tractatus* p.85)
Abruptio ist, wenn für erwartender Consonantz, so zur Ergäntzung erfordert wird, der Gesang zerriβen, oder gar abgeriβen wird. Zerriβen in der Mitte eines Contextus, wenn an statt eines Punctes eine Pause gesetzet wird.

The *abruptio* occurs when, instead of sounding the anticipated consonance which a resolution would require, the composition is torn apart or even broken off. It can be torn in the middle of the *contextus* when a rest is written instead of a note.

Gar abgeriβen in einer Cadentz, und zwar also, daβ die obere Stimme in der Quarte endiget, ehe der Baβ die letzte Note der Cadentz ergreift.

It can be broken off at the cadence in such fashion that the upper voice ends on a fourth [above the bass] before the bass completes the cadence.

Bernhard (*Bericht* p.152)

Abruptio heiβet Abreiβung, und ist, wann man in der Quarta der Cadenz, welche erst durch die Tertia solte resolviret werden, endiget, ehe der Baβ die Cadenz schlieβet.

Abruptio means tearing off, and occurs when one ends on a fourth in the cadence which should have been resolved through a third, before the bass ends the cadence.

Janovka (*Clavis* p.56)

Abruptio est Periodus harmonica, qua rem cito peractam exprimimus, & ut plurimum locum habet in fine.

The *abruptio* is an unexpected musical passage in which we express a rapidly completed thought. It occurs most frequently at the end of a composition.

Vogt (*Conclave* p.1)

Abruptio est, cum periodus musica in fine posita aliqua pausa abrumpitur.

The *abruptio* occurs when a musical passage is broken off at the end by the placement of certain pauses.

Walther (*Praecepta* p.156)

Abruptio oder eine Abreiβung ist, wenn man in der Quart der Cadenz (welche erst durch die Terz solte resolviret werden) endiget, ehe die Fundament-Note die Cadenz schlieβt.

The *abruptio* or tearing off occurs when one ends on a fourth in the cadence (which should have been resolved through a third) before the bass ends the cadence.

Walther (*Lexicon*)

Abruptio (lat.) eine Abreissung; ist eine musicalische Figur, da gemeiniglich am Ende eines Periodi die Harmonie plötzlich (wenn es nemlich der Text, oder in Instrumental-Sachen andere Umstände also erfordern) abgebrochen und abgeschnappt wird. s. Janovkae Clavem ad Thesaurum magnae artis Musicae, p.56. Im Stylo Recitativo entstehet diese Figur, wenn die Sing-Stimme gegen den Bass sich in der Quart endiget, und solche nicht erst durch die Terz resolviret, sondern den Bass die Cadenz alleine fertig machen läβt.

The *abruptio* or break is a musical figure which commonly occurs at the end of a passage when the composition is suddenly broken or snapped off. This is either demanded by the text or, in instrumental music, other circumstances. See Janovka, *Clavis ad Thesaurum*, p.56. In the *stylus recitativus* this figure occurs when the melody voice ends on a fourth above the [dominant] bass note without resolving to the third, allowing the bass to end the cadence alone.

Spiess (*Tractatus* p.155)
Abruptio. Abreissung, Abbrechung, ist, wann eine oder mehrere Stimmen zu Ende eines Periodi nach Erforderung des Texts die Harmoniam plötzlich, und zwar ohne Erwartung einer Cadenz abbrechen. In Stylo recit: ist diese Figur gemein.

Abruptio, a tearing or breaking off, occurs when one or more voices suddenly break off the passage toward the end of a composition without completing the cadence, according to the requirements of the text. This figure is common in the *stylus recitativus*.

ACCENTUS, SUPERJECTIO: a preceding or succeeding upper or lower neighboring note, usually added to the written note by the performer.

This embellishment or *figura simplex* is included by a number of authors in their lists of figures, although it is normally not considered one of the musical-rhetorical figures.[1] Should the *accentus* precede the written note, it can assume up to half of the latter note's value, in which case it is also called *Vorschlag*, *le port de voix* (Mattheson), or *Stimm-Einfall* (Spiess). An *accentus* succeeding the written note is also called *superjectio* (Bernhard), translated into German as *Überwurf* (Walther) or *Überschlag* (Spiess). Mattheson defines the *Überschlag* as an *accentus* in which an upper neighbor is appended to the first note of a falling fourth or fifth before the second, lower note is sounded. Printz, who does not differentiate between these two ornaments, also mentions the *varius* or *circumflexus*, which occurs when the written note is interrupted by an inserted *accentus*. The diverse terminology differentiates between the ornament's effect (*accentus*) and its structure (*Superjectio*, *Überwurf*, *Überschlag*). Like the other musical embellishments, its association with rhetoric is rooted in delivery or *pronunciatio* rather than in the *ornatus* of the *decoratio*. However, this does not lessen its potential to be a text- or affection-expressive device.[2] In discussing the *Überschlag*, Mattheson relates a performance in which the device was used to embellish the

1. Although Janovka mentions the ornament, he does not include it in his list of figures. For a comprehensive discussion of the *accentus*, see Neumann, *Ornamentation*, esp. 103ff.

2. See also *Emphasis*.

word "*beugen*" (bow) in such an effective manner "that it almost seemed to become visible, the ears becoming like eyes."[1] While some authors do not rule out the possibility of the composer placing the ornament in the score, others, like Mattheson, clearly regard the application of the device as the performer's prerogative. The ornament "is not to be notated, but, like other Manieren, is added at the discretion of the performer, and is particularly effective in compositions of lamentation or humility."[2]

Susenbrotus (*Epitome* p.18)
Hyperbole est cum dictio vel oratio fidem excendens augendi minuendive gratia ponitur. Superlatio, dementiens superiectio, Eminentia et Excessus etiam appellata.

The *hyperbole* occurs when the speech or oration exceeds the truth for the purposes of exaggeration or understatement. It is also called *superlatio*, *dementiens*, *superiectio*, *eminentia*, and *excessus*.

Bernhard (*Tractatus* p.71)
Superjectio welche sonst insgemein Accentus genennet wird, ist, wenn neben einer Con- oder Dissonantz im nächsten Intervallo drüber eine Note gesetzet wird, doch meistentheils wenn die Noten natürlich eine Secunde fallen sollten. Superjectio hat bey allen Consonantzen, ingleichen neben dem Tansitu, Syncopatione, quasi-Transitu, und Quasi-Syncopatione statt, als:

The *superjectio*, otherwise generally called *accentus*, occurs when a note is placed a step higher next to a consonance or dissonance. This usually occurs when the notes should naturally fall by a second. The *superjectio* can be applied to all consonances, as well as to the *transitus*, *syncopatio*, *quasi-transitus*, and *quasi-sycopatio*, as in the following:

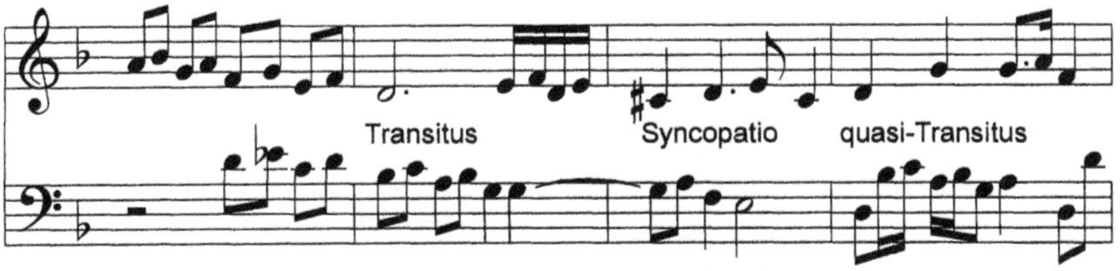

Welches Exempel natürlich also stünde:

1. *Capellmeister*, 113.
2. Ibid.

Diese Figur hat ihre Gültigkeit hergenommen aus dem Brauch der Sänger und Instrumentisten, welche im Stylo gravi zuweilen einen Accent genommen, welches hernach die Componisten gut befunden und also in ihren Sätzen imitiret haben.

This figure has been legitimized through its use by singers and instrumentalists, who occasionally added an *accent* in the *stylus gravis*, of which the composers subsequently approved and likewise imitated in their own compositions.

Bernhard (*Bericht* p.148)

Superjectio, insgemein Accentus genand, ist, wenn über eine Consonans oder Dissonanz eine Note im nechsten Intervallo drüber gesetzet wird. Dieser Accentus wird gebrauchet, wenn eine Stimme herunter gehet oder auch springet. Doch ist zu mercken, daß gleich wie das Fundament der Composition nicht zuläßt, aus einer Dissonans einen Sprung zu thun, also man auch nicht einen solchen übeln Sprung mit dem Accentu zieren oder entschuldigen könne.

The *superjectio*, generally called *accentus*, occurs when a note is placed a step above a consonance or dissonance. This *accentus* is employed when a voice descends by step or by leap. However, it should be noted that just as fundamental counterpoint does not permit a leap out of a dissonance, neither is it permitted to embellish or excuse such an offensive leap with an *accentus*.

Printz (*Phrynis Mytilenaeus* pt.2, p.47)

Accentus ist / wenn die Stimme gar sanfft hinauff oder hinunter in die nechste Linie oder Spatium gezogen wird. Er ist entweder auffsteigend oder absteigend / oder beydes zu gleich. Der erste wird Intendens, der andere Remittens, und der dritte Varius oder Circumflexus genennet. Ein jeder Accent gehet entweder in seine Principal Clavem, oder weicht ab von derselben / oder thut beydes zugleich. Der erste wird in einem musicalischen Stück nimmermehr ausdrücklich geschrieben / sondern von dem Musico nur zu rechter Zeit angebracht / der andere offt / nicht aber allezeit / und der dritte selten.

The *accentus* occurs when the voice is gently pulled into a neighboring higher or lower pitch. It is either ascending or descending or both together. The first kind is called *intendens*, the second kind *remittens*, and the third *varius* or *circumflexus*. Every *accent* either leads into its principal note, follows it, or does both simultaneously. The first kind is no longer explicitly notated, but is appropriately employed by the musician. The second kind is often but not always notated, while the third kind is seldom written down.

Walther (*Praecepta* p.152)

Superjectio. Insgemein Accentus genennet, ist eine Auf- oder Abschleifung von einer Consonanz in eine Dissonanz; oder von einer Dissonanz in eine Consonanz per secundam.

Superjectio. This figure, generally called *accentus*, is an up- or downward slide by a second from a consonance to a dissonance or from a dissonance to a consonance.

Der Accent soll nur angebracht werden bey solchen Sylben, so im Aussprechen lang fallen; doch werden die letzten Sylben etlicher Wörter, als welche es gar fügl. leiden, ausgenommen.

The *accent* is only to be applied in connection with accented syllables, except in those words where it is appropriate to accent the last syllable.

Walther (*Lexicon*)
Accento (ital.) Accent (gall.) Accentus (lat.) sc. musicus, ein musicalischer Accent, ist diejenige Art zu singen oder zu spielen, da man, ehe die auf dem Papier vorhandene Note exprimirt wird, die nächste drüber oder drunter, vorher touchieret. Ist also zweyerlei Gattung, davon die erste, wenn man nemlich aus einem höhern clave in den tiefern, z.E. aus dem c^2 ins h^1 gehet: Accentus descendens, oder remittens, der Absteigende Accent; und die zweyte, wenn aus einem tiefern clave in den höhern, z.E. aus dem d^2 ins e^2 gegangen wird: Accentus ascendens oder intendens, der Aufsteigende Accent heisset. . . . Wobey zu mercken: daß allerseits Arten nurgedachter Accente (welche sonsten auch Accentus simplices, d.i. einfache Accente heissen) der folgenden Note an ihrer Geltung manchmahl nur etwas weniges: als in den grössern Noten; manchmahl aber, und zwar in den kleinern, die Helffte abnehmen.

The *accentus musicus* or musical accent refers to a manner of singing or playing in which one sounds the neighboring higher or lower note before expressing the note written in the score. It is of two kinds. The first occurs namely when one moves from a higher to a lower note, for example from the c^2 to the b^1, and is called *accentus descendens* or *remittens*: the descending accent. The second occurs when one moves out of a lower note into a higher one, for example from the d^2 to the e^2, and is called *accentus ascendens* or *intendens*: the ascending accent. . . . It should be noted that all kinds of accents discussed here (which are otherwise also known as *accentus simplices* or simple accents) decrease the value of the following note at times only slightly, should it be a longer note, and at times by half, should it be a shorter note.

Accentus duplex ein doppelter Accent; ist die jenige Art zu singen oder spielen, da man von zweyen Gangs- oder Sprungsweise auf einander folgenden Noten, die zweyte der gestalt geschwinde zweymahl anschlägt, daß der ersten an ihrer Geltung die Helffte abgenommen, und hingegen die zweyte um so viel eher angeschlagen und gehöret wird. Beym Loulié p.80 seiner Elements oder Principes de Musique, ist die Einrichtung des Accents anders, und, so wohl der marque als der expression nach, folgende:

The *accentus duplex* is a double accent. It refers to a manner of singing or playing two subsequent notes, separated by step or by leap, in which the second note is rapidly sounded twice in such a way that the value of the first note is reduced by half, the second note being played and heard that much earlier. In Loulié's *Eléments* or *Principes de Musique*, p.80, the *accent* is defined differently, both in its marking as well as its performance, as follows:

Walther (*Lexicon*)

Superjectio ein Überwurf oder Accent, der einer längern Note aufsteigend noch gantz kurtz anhängt wird. s. Accento, und zwar des Hrn Loulié Meynung.

The *superjectio* is an ascending accent, which is quickly appended to a note of longer duration.

Mattheson (*Capellmeister* p.112f.)

Erstlich den sogenannten Accent, welcher bey einigen der Vorschlag, und in Frankreich le port de voix heisset, da die Stimme, ehe die folgende vorgeschriebene Note ausgedruckt wird, den nächst darüber oder darunter liegenden Klang vorher gantz sanfft, und gleichsam zweimahl sehr hurtig berühret.

The first [of the *Manieren*] is the *accentus*, which some call *Vorschlag* and is known as *le port de voix* in France. It occurs when, before expressing the following written note, the voice sounds the neighboring higher or lower note very gently, as if briefly touching it twice.

Es sind also die Accente theils auf- theils absteigend, einfach und doppelt: bey den einfachen wird von der nächstfolgenden Note nur ein weniges, bey den doppelten aber die Helffte der Geltung genommen, so daß die accentirende Note desto länger, und mit einer angenehmen Verzögerung gehöret wird, als worin offt die beste Lust besteht.

The accents can be ascending or descending, simple or double. The simple accents diminish the value of the following note by a small amount, the double accents by half its duration, so that the accenting note is heard that much longer, and with an agreeable retardation, wherein its most emphatic effect is frequently found.

Der neueste, und heutiges Tages starck eingeführte Gebrauch dieses Accents aber ist, daß er sowol im Spielen als im singen offt springend, von der Quart an bis in die Octav, auf und unterwärts

However, the newest and currently widespread use of this accent is found in vocal and instrumental music, where it is frequently employed in ascending and descending leaps of a fourth up to an oc-

Dienste thun muß: als wodurch insonderheit etwas spöttisches, sprödes, freches und hochmüthiges sehr natürlich ausgedruckt werden kan; wenn solches erfordert wird. Und auf solchen Gebrauch hat ohne Zweifel Heinichen gesehen, wenn es bey ihm heißt, es könne der Accent bey allen Intervallen angebracht werden.

tave, thereby very naturally expressing something scornful, obstinate, haughty, or arrogant, if necessary. It is undoubtedly this usage which Heinichen has in mind when he states that the accent can be applied to all intervals.

Eine noch unberührte Lehre von Accenten, die man billig Überschläge heissen könnte, so wie man jene Vorschläge nennet, muß ich doch hier mit Stillschweigen nicht vorüber gehen lassen. Es bestehen dieselben Accente oder Überschläge darin: wenn ein Fall in die Quart, Quint oder weiter herunter geschehen soll, daß alsdenn das erste Ende solcher Intervalle einen feinen und kurtzen Anhang oder Zusatz von dem nächst überliegendem Klange bekömmt, der nicht zu Buche stehen darff, sondern willkührlich ist, wie alle andre Manieren, und absonderlich in Sätzen, die was klagendes oder demüthiges haben, sehr artig zu hören ist. Z.E. der aufgeschriebene Satz wäre dieser:

A further unexplored teaching of the accents, which could simply be called *Überschläge*, must not be tacitly ignored. These accents or *Überschläge* occur when a small and short additional note is appended one step higher to the first of two notes separated by a fourth, fifth, or even more. This additional note is not notated but, like all *Manieren*, is added arbitrarily. It is appropriately employed especially in those passages which are sorrowful or humble in nature. For example, the passage written as follows:

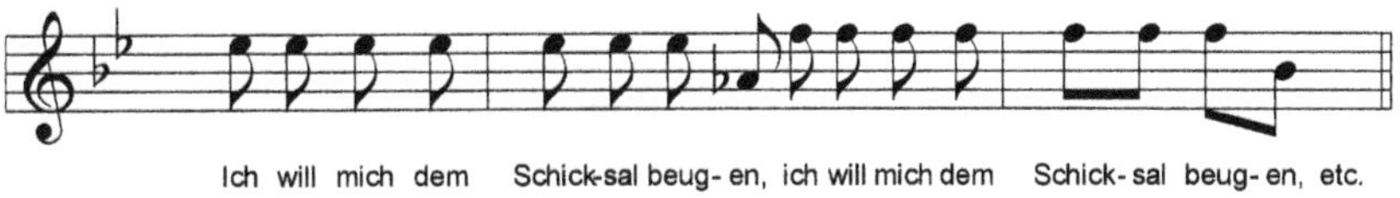

die berühmte Madame Keiser hat dieses beugen einst in der hiesigen Doms-Music so nachdrücklich herausgebracht, daß es fast sichtbar schien, und die Augen voller Ohren wurden; nur durch folgenden kleinen Zusatz und überschlagenden Accent:

was expressed by the famous Madame Keiser in a recent Hamburg Dom Music performance with such emphasis that it almost seemed to become visible, the ears becoming like eyes. This was achieved merely through the following small additional accent:

Spiess (*Tractatus* p.155)
Stimm-Einfall, ist die jenige Art zu sin-

The *Stimm-Einfall* is a manner of singing

gen, oder zu spihlen, da man, ehe die auf dem Pappier vorhandene Nota exprimirt wird, die nächste darüber, oder darunter, vorhero touchiret. Ist also zweyerley Gattung, davon die erste, wann man nemlich aus einem höheren Clave in den tiefferen gehet, Accentus Descendens oder Remittens, der absteigende Accent: und die anderte Art ist, wann aus einem tieferen Clave in einen höheren gegangen wird, so Accentus Ascendens, oder intendens, der aufsteigende Accent oder Vorschlag heisset. Beyde diese Vorschläg oder Accentus werden auch in Sprüngen (Saltibus) in der Terz, Quart, Quint, Sext, Sept und Octav angebracht. Der Componist gibt dißfalls seine Intention zu erkennen in Voransetzung eines Strichleins, oder auch kleinen Nötleins.

or playing in which the neighboring higher or lower note is sounded before the written note is expressed. It is of two kinds, the first being namely the progression from a higher to a lower note, called *accentus descendens* or *remittens*, the falling accent, and the second kind being the progression from a lower to a higher note, called *accentus ascendens* or *intendens*, the rising accent or *Vorschlag*. Both of these *Vorschläge* or *accentus* can also be applied to leaps (*saltibus*) of a third, fourth, fifth, sixth, seventh, and octave. The composer indicates his intentions for the accent's use by adding a small stoke or a small note before the note.

Spiess (*Tractatus* p.156)

Superjectio, der Überschlag, ist eine kleine, jedoch gratieuse Manier; geschiehet sonderheitlich bey aufsteigender Secund, allwo die 3th, 8te, 13te, und 18te Nota Superjecta genennet wird.

The *superjectio* or *Überschlag* is a small yet graceful embellishment. It occurs particularly at rising seconds, where [in the following example] the 3rd, 8th, 13th, and 18th notes are called *nota superjecta*.

ACCIACCATURA: an additional, dissonant note added to a chord, which is released immediately after its execution.

The *acciaccatura* is considered an ornamental embellishment and receives correlating definitions by the various writers. Of interest are the varying etymologies of the term. Heinichen wishes to find the root of the term in the Italian verb *acciaccare*, meaning to grind or squash (*zermalmen, zerquetschen*), which is to refer to the grinding effect of the dissonance. Although Walther mentions Heinichen's understanding of the term, he himself derives the term from the Italian *acciacco*, meaning "superfluous." Mattheson on the other hand rejects both of these origins in favor of *accia*, meaning "thread," by which the notes of the chord are "tied" together. In contrast to the *accentus* definitions, the various writers do not explicitly accord this embellishment great expressive potential.

Walther (*Lexicon*)

Acciaccatura (ital.) von acciacco, superfluus, überflüßig, übrig, entstehet: wenn z.E. nebst denen zum rechten Accord G. gehörigen Clavibus, d g h auch noch das fis, als ein zur Mordant dienlicher Clavis mitgegriffen wird; . . . Der seel. Hr. Capellmeister Heinichen derivirет es von acciaccare, welches zermalmen, zerquetschen, oder etwas mit Gewalt gegen einander stossen, bedeutet; daß demnach Acciaccatura eine gewaltsame Zusammenstossung unterschiedener neben einander liegenden clavium, die eigentlich nicht zusammen gehören, heisset.

The *acciaccatura* (from *acciacco, superfluus*, superfluous, remaining) occurs when, for example, in addition to playing the notes belonging to the G chord (d,g,b) the F-sharp is also included much like a mordant. . . . The blessedly departed *Capellmeister* Heinichen derives the term from *acciaccare*, which means to grind, squash, or forcibly strike together. Consequently *acciaccatura* would mean the violent collision of neighboring notes which actually do not belong together.

Mattheson (*Capellmeister* p.120)

Die Acciacatur ist endlich noch übrig, davon Gasparin, und aus ihm Heinichen, gewißlich mehr Wesens machen, als das Ding wircklich werth ist; in dem diese Manier weiter nichts, als der Mordant im gantzen Grad; sonst nirgend, als auf dem Clavier im General-Baß bey vollen Griffen gebräuchlich, und offt an vieler Unreinigkeit in der Harmonie des Spielens Ursache ist.

Finally the *acciacatur* remains, of which Gasparini and after him Heinichen certainly make much more than the thing is worth; for the *Manier* is nothing more than a whole-step mordant. It is used nowhere except in full-voiced *basso-continuo* keyboard realizations, frequently responsible for much harmonic untidiness in the playing.

Obbelobter Teutscher Verfasser ist der Meinung, das Wort Acciacatura komme her vom Zermalmen und zerquetschen. Behüte Gott für beissenden, zermalmenden Manieren! Walther hergegen schreibt, es entstehe von Acciacco, welches überflüßig oder übrig heisse. Es ist ein selbstgemachtes Kunst-Wort, und findet sich in keinem Veneroni.

The aforementioned German author is of the opinion that the word *acciacatura* is derived from "grinding" or "squashing." God save us from biting, grinding embellishments! In contrast Walther claims that it is derived from *acciaco*, which means superfluous or remaining. However, it is a homemade art word, not to be found in any venerable source.

Warum soll man aber das Ding so weit herholen? Heiβt nicht Accia ein Bindfaden, und kan nicht Acciacatura mit besserm Rechte eine Verbindung bedeuten, als eine Zerquetschung oder einen Überfluβ? da nehmlich mittelst eines solchen Mordants die Vollstimmigkeit der Clavier-Griffe desto fester und näher verbunden, oder so zu reden mit einander verknüpfft wird.

But why seek the source so far afield? Is not *accia* a string, and cannot *acciacatura* more justifiably signify a binding rather than a squashing or an excess? For, namely through the use of such a mordant, the full-voiced keyboard realizations are knit that much more tightly and closely, or are coupled together so to speak.

Spiess (*Tractatus* p.157)

Acciaccatura derivird Heinichen aus dem Gasparini von dem welschen Wort acciaccare, welches heiβt zermahlen, zerquetschen, oder etwas mit Gewalt gegeneinander stossen. Walther vermaynt, es möchte herkommen von Acciacco, welches überflüssig oder übrig heiβt. Mattheson aber haltet dafür man solle diese Wort-Forschung nicht so weit herholen, sondern weil Accia ein Bindfaden heiβt, könne man Acciaccatura mit so mehrem Recht eine Verbindung nennen, als sie in der That ist, und geschiet, wann E.g. in einem vollkommenen Griff auf dem Clavier mit beyden Händen so viel Claves, als Finger seynd, nidergedrückt werden; weil nur aber ein reiner Accord eines Ambitus nur 4. Claves erfordert, sc. 1. 3. 5. und Octavam; als muβ einer aus den 5. Fingern nothwendig sich inzwischen eindringen, und sich auf einen Dissonanten legen; es mag hernach dieser 5. Finger eine Quartam, Sextam, oder Secundam ausmachen. Diβ will man hier allein erinnert haben, daβ man nehmlich die falsche und dissonierende, und zum reinen Accord nicht gehörige Claves, oder diese Acciaccaturen nicht so lange hören lasse, sondern mit einem gelinden Harpeggio niderlegen, und bald wiederum fahren lasse, damit ja nicht gar zu grosse Unreinigkeit in der Harmonia verursachet werde.

Like Gasparini, Heinichen derives *acciaccatura* from the Italian word *acciaccare*, which means grinding, squashing, or forcibly striking something together. Walther claims it comes from *acciacco*, which means superfluous or remaining. Mattheson, however, believes one needn't go so far afield in this wordstudy but rather, because *accia* means string, justifiably call the *acciaccatura* a binding, which it in fact is. It occurs for example when, in a full chord on the keyboard, both hands depress as many notes as there are fingers. However, because a full chord spanning the scale requires only four notes—the tonic, third, fifth, and octave—then the fifth finger must necessarily insert an additional note, and depress a dissonance, be this added fifth note a fourth, sixth, or seventh. Above all one thing should be remembered, namely that the improper and dissonant notes which do not belong to the pure chord, in other words these *acciaccature*, should not be allowed to sound too long but should be played in a rapid *Harpeggio* and soon again released, so as not to cause too great an unclarity in the harmony.

ANABASIS, ASCENSUS: an ascending musical passage which expresses ascending or exalted images or affections.

The *anabasis* receives first mention with Kircher, the first author not only to define this as a specific figure, but also to consistently emphasize the affection-arousing role of the musical-rhetorical figures. Janovka, Vogt, Walther, and Spiess also include the figure in their *Figurenlehren*. However, Kircher is not the first to link the expression of ascending or elevated thoughts or images to the musical *Figurenlehre*. Certainly Burmeister's *hypotyposis* would be understood to include the expression of such words and images. Furthermore, Nucius appends various lists of words to be musically expressed to his discussion of the musical-rhetorical figures, including "words of motion and place, such as standing, running, dancing, resting, leaping, lifting, lowering, ascending, descending, heaven, hell, mountain, abyss, heights, and the like,"[1] a list which appears in an expanded version in Herbst's *Musica Poetica*. Similar lists are frequently encountered throughout the Baroque.[2] Although the *anabasis* does not find a rhetorical counterpart, Kircher endeavors to link it with the rhetorical figures by naming it with a Greek term. Much more than being simple wordpainting, the *anabasis* is used to musically recreate the effect of an ascending image or thought found in the text. It is therefore also useful in arousing "exalted, high, and eminent" affections (Kircher). For example, in Bach's setting of the text "*Et resurrexit*" (Mass in B Minor), the listener is not only aided in the visualization of the resurrection of Christ but is moved to joy and exaltation as a consequence of both the theological implications of the text and the accompanying "musical explanation." The figure is both descriptive and affective, describing the text and arousing the corresponding affection. Like so many of the musical-rhetorical figures, the *anabasis* can be both image and source of the affection.

---

1. "Secundo, verba motus & locorum, ut sunt stare, correre, saltare, quiscere, salire, extollere, deijdere, ascendere, descendere, Coelum, Abissus, montes profundum, altum & similia &c." *Musices poeticae*, G3r.

2. See *Hypotyposis*.

Kircher (*Musurgia* L.8 p.145)

Anabasis sive Ascensio est periodus harmonica, quam exaltationem, ascensionem vel res altas & eminentes exprimimus, ut illud Moralis (Ascendens Christus in altum etc.)

The *anabasis* or *ascensio* is a musical passage through which we express exalted, rising, or elevated and eminent thoughts, exemplified in Morales's *Ascendens Christus in altum.*

Janovka (*Clavis* p.56)

Anabasis sive Ascensio est Periodus harmonica, qua exaltationem ascensionem, vel altas eminentes res exprimimus ut in textu contingere posset hocce: Ascendens Christus in altum.

See Kircher for translation.

Vogt (*Conclave* p.1)

Anabasis, cum concentus valde in altum tendit.

Anabasis. A striving to the heights with great harmony of purpose.

Vogt (*Conclave* p.150)

Anabasis ascensus est, ut cum voce & textu ascendimus: ut ascendit in caelum.

The *anabasis* is an ascent which we express through the voice and the text, as in: He ascended into heaven.

Walther (*Lexicon*)

Anabasis (lat.) von ἀναβαίνω, ascendo, ich steige in die Höhe; ist ein solcher musicalischer Satz, wodurch etwas in die Höhe steigendes exprimiret wird. Z.E. über die Worte: Er ist auferstanden. Gott fahret auf. u.d.g.

Anabasis, from *anabaino*, *ascendo*, I ascend, is a musical passage through which something ascending into the heights is expressed. For example on the words: He is risen; God has ascended; and similar texts.

Spiess (*Tractatus* p.155)

Anabasis, Ascensus, Auffahrt. Geschiehet, wann man mit der Stimm nach Besag des Texts auch zugleich aufsteiget. v.g. Ascendit in Coelum.

Anabasis, *ascensus*, or ascent occurs when the voice also rises as directed by the text, for example: He ascended into heaven.

ANADIPLOSIS: (1) a repetition of a *mimesis*; (2) a repetition of the ending of one phrase at the beginning of the following one.

The *anadiplosis*, a term found in both rhetorical and musical *Figuren lehren*, is supplied with two musical definitions. Burmeister's prime concern is to establish a systematic musical terminology based on rhetoric which would aid in musical analysis and composition rather than to develop a collection of musical figures which simply mirror their rhetorical counterparts in terminology and content. In his search for terminology, Burmeister frequently chooses terms whose literal meaning rather than rhetorical content would best describe established musical devices. The *anadiplosis* is one of Burmeister's *noema* figures. The repetition of a *noema* (a homophonic section within a contrapuntal composition) at a different pitch Burmeister names *mimesis*. The repetition of a *mimesis* is then called *anadiplosis*, a four-fold repetition of a *noema*. Literally this term means "redoubling" (*ana*, again; *diploos*, double) and is thereby a precise description of the musical phenomenon: the repetition of a doubled *noema*.

While Burmeister uses *anadiplosis* to define a device unique to musical composition, Ahle, Vogt, and Walther lend the term a musical content analogous to its rhetorical meaning. Both a musical and a linguistic sentence or phrase could begin with the same material which ended the previous one. While Ahle describes the figure only in linguistic terms, it is clear from his *Figurenlehre* that he expects the composer to reflect the text's construction through the musical fabric. This expectation is reinforced by Walther, who includes *anadiplosis* in his *Musicalisches Lexicon* while omitting other rhetorical figures which do not allow such a musical transfer. The correlation between music and rhetoric is increasingly emphasized throughout the Baroque era, resulting in an ever closer correspondence between the musical and the rhetorical terminology and content of the figures. This correlation is explicitly emphasized by Mattheson, who maintains that the *anadiplosis*, among other figures of repetition, is rooted and familiar equally in music as in rhetoric and therefore requires no further explanation.

Susenbrotus (*Epitome* p.53)

Anadiplosis, Reduplicatio, est cum ultima prioris commatis dictio in sequentis initio iteratur: vel cum antecedentis membri exitum, consequentis initium facimus.

The *anadiplosis* or *reduplicatio* occurs when the last word of a preceding passage is repeated at the beginning of the following one or when we construct a subsequent opening out of the preceding close.

Gottsched (*Redekunst* p.280)

Anadiplosis. Wenn dasselbe Wort am Ende, und im Anfange des folgenden

Anadiplosis. When the same word is placed at the end of one sentence and at

Satzes zu stehen kömmt.

the beginning of the following one.

Gottsched (*Dichtkunst* p.323)
Oder man wiederhohlt zuweilen ein Wort, das am Ende eines Satzes gestanden, im Anfange des darauf folgenden, welches Anadiplosis heiβt.

Or one can repeat a word which ended one sentence at the beginning of the following one, which is called *anadiplosis*.

Burmeister (*Hypomnematum*)
Anadiplosis vicina Mimesi est, geminans id quod μιμετικῶς semel est introductum. Exemplum.

The *anadiplosis* is similar to the *mimesis*, repeating that which was first introduced through a *mimesis*.

Burmeister (*Musica Poetica* p.60)
Anadiplosis est talis harmoniae decus, quod constat ex duplici Mimesi & est hoc ornamentum Mimesi propinquum: geminat enim id, quod per Mimesin semel est introductum.

The *anadiplosis* is an embellishment of the *harmonia*, and is constructed out of a double *mimesis*. This ornament is similar to the *mimesis*, for it repeats that which was first introduced through a *mimesis*.

Ahle (*Sommer-Gespräche* p.17)
Setzet er: singet und rühmet / rühmet und lobet; so ist es eine Anadiplosis.

If he writes: sing and glorify / glorify and praise, it would be an *anadiplosis*.

Vogt (*Conclave* p.150)
Anadiplosis cum initium facimus ex praecedentis fine.

The *anadiplosis* occurs when we form a beginning out of the preceding ending.

Walther (*Lexicon*)

Die anadiplosis, von διπλῶς, duplex, Reduplicatio (lat.) ist: wenn das letzte Wort eines Commatis, wiederum das erste im folgenden Commate abgiebt. Z.E. Singet und rühmet / rühmet und lobet.

The *anadiplosis*, from *diplos*, *duplex*, *reduplicatio* (lat.), occurs when the last word of a passage appears again as the first word of the following passage. For example, sing and glorify / glorify and praise.

Mattheson (*Capellmeister* p.243)

Die Epanalepsis, Epistrophe, Anadiplosis, Paronomasia, Polyptoton, Antanaclasis, Ploce etc. haben solche natürliche Stellen in der Melodie, daβ es fast scheinet, als hätten die griechischen Redner sothane Figuren aus der Ton-Kunst entlehnet; denn sie sind lauter repetitiones vocum, Wiederholungen der Wörter, die auf verschiedene Weise angebracht werden.

The *epanalepsis*, *epistrophe*, *anadiplosis*, *paronomasia*, *polyptoton*, *antanaclasis*, *ploce*, etc., assume such natural positions in music that it almost seems as if the Greek orators borrowed these figures from the art of musical composition. For they are purely *repetitiones vocum*, repetitions of words, which are applied to music in various different ways.

ANALEPSIS: a repetition of a *noema* at the same pitch.

Although the term *analepsis* has the ring of a rhetorical figure, it is in fact only encountered as a musical figure. As one of his *noema* figures, Burmeister defines *analepsis* as a *noema* repeated at the same pitch, in contrast to his *mimesis*, which repeats a *noema* at a different pitch. It is Burmeister's intent to analyze and name musical devices using rhetorical terminology if possible, or to invent terms if necessary, which were literal descriptions of the musical device. As he had used the more general rhetorical terms referring to a repetition (*mimesis*, *anaphora*, *palilogia*) to describe other compositional devices, Burmeister constructs his own term for the repeated *noema*. Literally, the term means "re-take" (*ana*, again; *lambano*, to take) or simply "repeat." In choosing this term, Burmeister establishes a parallel between the terms *analepsis* and *anadiplosis*, both being forms of a repeated *noema*. And in both cases it is the literal meaning of the term rather than a rhetorical content which describes the musical device.

Burmeister (*Hypomnematum*)

Analepsis est quae conjunctarum vocum affectionem suavem ex merarum con-

The *analepsis* is a pleasant affect of united voices which consists in a uniform

sonantiarum syntaxeos aequabilitate constantem, iterat Noemati vicina.

syntax of pure consonances. It repeats a neighboring *noema*.

Burmeister (*Musica Poetica* p.59)
Analepsis est tractuli harmonici in aliquot vocum, syntaxi ex meris concordantiis contexti continua iteratio, sic Noematis repetitio & duplicatio, ac Noemati vicinum ornamentum.

The *analepsis* is an immediate repetition of a musical passage in certain voices whose united syntax consists of pure consonances. It is a repetition or duplication of a *noema* and thereby is an ornament related to the *noema*.

Walther (*Lexicon*)
Analepsis, von ἀναλαμβάνω, recipio, ist: wenn eine aus lauter Concordanzen bestehende kurze Clausul oder Formul noch einmal unmittelbar nach einander gesetzt und angebracht wird.

The *analepsis*, from *analambano*, *recipio*, occurs when a short clause or passage consisting of only consonances is immediately restated and reexpressed.

ANAPHORA, REPETITIO: (1) a repeating bass line; ground bass; (2) a repetition of the opening phrase or motive in a number of successive passages; (3) a general repetition.[1]

Both the rhetorical and the musical *anaphora* and *repetitio* are defined as specific as well as general forms of repetition.[2] In most cases authors choose only one of the two terms for their *Figurenlehre*. At times the terms are used interchangeably, while at other times an author assigns each term its own definition. Burmeister initially restricts the *anaphora* to the bass line but expands the definition in subsequent treatises to

1. These three definitions are referred to by number in the following table.
2. See also *Mimesis*, another term used for both a specific and a general form of repetition.

allow the repetition to occur in more than one but not in all voices.[1] Nucius then uses the term *repetitio* to denote a synthesis of the two Burmeister definitions: the repetition can occur in any one voice, but at different pitches. Thuringus again lists *anaphora* with the first Burmeister definition. In addition he includes *repetitio* with Nucius's expanded definition. Kircher, Janovka, and Walther use the two Greek and Latin terms interchangeably. While Kircher and Janovka define them as general forms of repetition, used in order to lend the composition greater expressivity, Walther lists both Kircher's and Burmeister's (ground bass) definitions under the terms. The remaining authors describe *anaphora* or *repetitio* with definitions analogous to the two rhetorical ones, Ahle and Mattheson using the above definition 2, Vogt and Spiess using definition 3 for the term *anaphora*, while Scheibe and Forkel use definition 3 for the term *repetitio*.[2] The following table illustrates the variety of combinations of term and content:

	anaphora	*repetitio*		*anaphora*	*repetitio*
Susenbrotus	–	2	Janovka	3	3
Gottsched	2	2, 3	Vogt	3	–
Burmeister	1, 1*	–	Walther	1, 3	1, 3
Nucius	–	1*	Mattheson	2	–
Thuringus	1	1*	Scheibe	–	3
Kircher	3	3	Spiess	3	–
Ahle	2	–	Forkel	–	3

Scheibe and Forkel mention that the *repetitio* is best used when combined with the *paronomasia*, a figure of repetition which alters the

1. This second understanding of the *anaphora* is indicated by 1* in the following table. The repetition of a phrase at the same pitch in one voice other than the bass Burmeister calls *palilogia*.

2. A further mention of the *anaphora* is made by Henry Peacham (the Younger): "Nay, hath not music her figures, the same which rhetoric? What [are] . . . her reports, but sweet anaphoras?" (*The Compleat Gentleman* 1622). Peacham's chapter on music is reprinted in Strunk, *Source Readings*, 331–37. In English Baroque terminology, a "report" is understood as an imitative entry of the subject: "Reporte is the Iterating or mainteining of a Point in the like motion, [per Arsin aut Thesin;] the Principal and Replie both Ascending, or bothe Descending" (Ch. Butler, *Principles of Musik*, 72). Peacham thereby compares the rhetorical figure which "beginneth diverse members, still with one and the same word" with a musical composition, in which the imitating voices begin in like manner.

passages it repeats, supplying additional material for the sake of emphasis.[1] In Scheibe's lengthy discussion of the *repetitio*, it becomes apparent that he understands the figure as a substantial form of musical construction, belonging to the musical *dispositio* as much as to the *decoratio*. The *repetitio* is not only used to repeat short passages, a point he also makes in his discussion of *epistrophe*.[2] Rather, it is also used to repeat entire sections of a composition, providing a musical-rhetorical device and explanation for *da capo* repeats and for musical recapitulations, "namely when the first part of an aria or another composition is repeated after the second part."

The various *anaphora* and *repetitio* definitions reveal the increasing importance placed on music's role to arouse the affections and the growing concurrence between musical and rhetorical definitions of the figures. While the early-seventeenth-century writers' definitions of the terms focus on musical techniques of composition, later authors' definitions repeatedly underscore the figure's rhetorical and emphatic nature.

Susenbrotus (*Epitome* p.51)

Repetitio est cum continenter ab uno eodemque verbo plurium membrorum prinicipia sumuntur. Vel est, cum eadem vox in plurium clausularum initio iteratur.

The *repetitio* occurs when the beginnings of numerous subsequent phrases are formed with one and the same word. Or it occurs when the same beginning phrase is repeated in numerous clauses.

Peacham (*Garden of Eloquence* p.41)

Epanaphora, or Anaphora, is a forme of speech which beginneth diverse members, still with one and the same word.

Gottsched (*Redekunst* p.279)

Anaphora. Wenn viele Absätze einer Rede auf einerley Art anfangen.

Anaphora. When numerous passages of an oration begin in like manner.

Gottsched (*Dichtkunst* p.322)

Die VIII. ist die Wiederholung (Repetitio) gewisser Wörter und Redensarten, wodurch die Rede einen sehr groβen Nachdruck bekömmt. Wenn nämlich das Gemüth in einer heftigen Bewegung ist,

The next figure is the repetition (*repetitio*) of certain words and expressions, through which the oration is given great emphasis. When the affection is intensely moved and calls for a concise argument,

1. See *Paronomasia.*
2. See *Epistrophe.*

und gern will, daβ man seine Meynung wohl fassen solle: so ist es ihm nicht genug, daβ er die Sache einmal sagt; sondern er sagts zwey, dreymal nach einander, damit man ja den Nachdruck seiner Worte recht einsehen möge. Es geschieht aber diese Wiederholung auf vielerley Art. . . . Zuweilen wiederhohlt man dasselbe Wort im Anfange etlicher Theile desselben Satzes, und das ist die Anaphora. . . . Zuweilen wiederhohlt man den Anfang eines Satzes in verschiedenen folgenden Sätzen, und das heiβt auch Anaphora.

it does not suffice to say something only once, but rather it should be repeated two or three times, thereby ensuring the proper understanding of the words' emphasis. This repetition occurs in numerous ways. . . . At times one repeats the same word at the beginning of numerous phrases, which is called *anaphora*. . . . At times one repeats the beginning of a sentence in numerous subsequent sentences, which is also called *anaphora*.

Burmeister (*Hypomnematum*)
Anaphora est ornamentum Palilogiae vicinum. Quia in solo Basso simile illi quid explet, quod in pluribus Palilogia.

The *anaphora* is an ornament related to the *palilogia* because, like it, the *anaphora* repeats something, yet only in the bass. Should this occur in more voices, it is a *palilogia*.

Burmeister (*Musica Poetica* p.65)
Anaphora est ornamentum, quod sonos similes per diversas aliquas, non aute omnes, Harmoniae voces repetit in morem Fugae, cum tamen revera non sit fuga. Ad Fugam enim requiruntur omnes Voces, si Fugae nomen harmonia moveatur.

The *anaphora* is an ornament which repeats the same notes through various diverse but not all voices of the composition in the manner of a *fuga* without being a true *fuga*. For a composition earns the name of *fuga* only if all the voices are involved.

Nucius (*Musices Poeticae* p.G2v)
Quid est Repetitio? Cum in Contrapuncto

What is the *repetitio*? When in florid or

florido seu fracto, thema in uno aliqua voce perpetuo iteratur, quantumvis mutatis locis. Exempla huius Schematis sunt in Missa super La Sol fa re mi. In Miserere mei Deus. In Fremuit Spiritus. Vana salus Hominis. Joh. Nucii. etc.

mixed counterpoint a theme is continually repeated in one and the same voice on however many different pitches. Examples of this figure can be found in *Missa super La Sol fa re mi*, in *Miserere mei Deus*, in *Fremuit Spiritus*, and in *Vana salus Hominis* by Joh. Nucius.

Thuringus (*Opusculum* p.126)
Quid est Anaphora? Est solius Basis aliquoties iterata repetitio.

What is an *anaphora*? It is a continued repetition only in the Bass.

Thuringus (*Opusculum* p.125)
Quid est Repetitio? Repetitio, quae Mimesis dicitur, est, cum in contrapuncto florido seu fracto, thema in uno aliqua voce perpetuo iteratur, quantum vis mutatis locis.

What is the *repetitio*? The *repetitio*, also called *mimesis*, occurs when in florid or mixed counterpoint a theme is continually repeated in one and the same voice at however many different pitches.

Kircher (*Musurgia* L.8 p.144)
Dicitur ἀναφορὰ sive repetitio, cum ad energiam exprimendam una periodus saepius exprimitur, adhibetur saepe in passionibus vehementioribus animi, ferociae, contemptus, uti videre est in illa cantillena nata: Ad Arma, Ad Arma, etc.

What is called *anaphora* or *repetitio* occurs when a passage is frequently repeated for emphasis's sake. It is often used in vehement affections such as ferocity or scorn, as exemplified in a composition based on the text: To arms! to arms!

Ahle (*Sommer-Gespräche* p.16)
Setzet er: Jauchzet dem Herren / jauchzet Ihm alle Welt / jauchzet und singet; so ist es eine Anaphora.

Were he to write: Rejoice in the Lord / rejoice in Him all ye lands / rejoice and sing; it would be an *anaphora*.

Janovka (*Clavis*)
Anaphora aliter Repetitio, cum ad energiam exprimendam una periodus, aut dictio saepius exprimitur, adhibetur que saepe in passionibus vehementioribus animi, uti ferociae, contemptus, ut si sit textus: ad arma ad arma etc.

See Kircher for translation.

Vogt (*Conclave* p.1)
Anaphora, cum terminum, vel figuram quandam ob energiam saepius repetimus.

Anaphora. When we frequently repeat a segment or certain figure for the sake of intensity.

Vogt (*Conclave* p.150)
Anaphora repetitio est. Fit non solum vera repetitio partis periodi, sed etiam

The *anaphora* is a repetition. It occurs not only as a repetition of a part of a pas-

figurarum simplicium.

sage, but also of the *figurae simplices*.

Walther (*Lexicon*)
Anaphora, von ἀναφέρω, refero, ist eine Rhetorisch-musikalische Figur, heisset so viel als Repetitio, und entstehet 1) wenn ein periodus, oder auch nur ein eintzeles Wort, absonderlichen Nachdrucks halber, in einer Composition öffters wiederholet wird, 2) wenn die Fundament-Noten etlichemahl (dergleichen in Ciaconen geschiehet) überein angebracht und tractirt werden.

The *anaphora*, from *anaphero*, *refero*, is a rhetorical-musical figure meaning repetition, and occurs (1) when a phrase or single word is frequently repeated in a composition for the sake of greater emphasis; (2) when the bass notes are repeated numerous times (as is the case in *Ciaconas*).

Mattheson (*Capellmeister* p.243)
Was ist wohl gebräuchlicher, als die Anaphora in der melodischen Setz-Kunst, wo eben dieselbe Klang-Folge, die schon vorgewesen ist, im Anfange verschiedener nächsten Clauseln wiederholt wird, und eine relationem oder Beziehung macht.

What is more common in melodic composition than the *anaphora*, in which an already introduced melodic fragment is repeated at the beginning of various following phrases, thus establishing a relationship?

Scheibe (*Critischer Musicus* p.689)
Die Vte Figure ist die Wiederholung (Repetitio) gewisser musikalischer Töne, Sätze und Gedanken, oder auch gewisser Wörter in Singesachen, wodurch der ganze Zusammenhang des Stückes, oder auch der Verstand der Rede selbst einen groβen Nachdruck bekömmt. . . . Was aber den Hauptsatz selbst betrifft, so ist es eine Nothwendigkeit, daβ dieser nicht zurück gesetzet, sondern bey aller Gelegenheit durch wohl ausgesonnene Wiederholungen von andern Neben- oder Zwischensätzen unterschieden werde. Die Wiederholungen aber dürfen nicht alle in einerley Tonart geschehen. Die Veränderung derselben erhebet auch die Stärke der Wiederholung. . . . Am besten aber geschieht sie, wenn sie mit der folgenden Figur, nämlich mit der Verstärkung verbunden wird. Sonst wird auch dieses zur Wiederholung gerechnet, wenn

The next figure is the repetition (*repetitio*) of certain musical notes, passages, or thoughts, as well as certain words in vocal music, through which the whole cohesion of the piece or the sense of the oration is lent greater clarity and emphasis. . . . Concerning the primary material of the composition, however, it is necessary that it not be ignored, but rather that it be differentiated at every opportunity through well devised neighboring or intervening passages. But the repetitions must not all be in the same key. The changes of the same also heighten the intensity of the repetition.

. . . The figure is best used in connection with the following figure, namely the *paronomasia*. In addition, the following is also considered among the methods of repetition, namely when the first part of

man den ersten Theil einer Arie, oder eines andern Stückes, nach dem Schlusse des zweyten Theiles wiederholet, oder auch, wenn man jeden Theil zweymal singt, oder spielet.

an aria or another composition is repeated after the second part, or when every part is sung or played twice.

Spiess (*Tractatus* p.155)
Anaphora ist, wann ein kurtzer Periodus oder Spruch: oder auch ein einziges Wort, absonderlichen Nachdrucks halben, in einer Musicalischen Composition öfften wiederholet wird.

The *anaphora* occurs when a short passage or saying, or even a single word is frequently repeated in a musical composition for greater emphasis.

Forkel (*Geschichte der Musik* p.57)
Die Wiederholung . . . erstreckt sich nicht nur auf einzelne Töne und ganze musikalische Sätze, sondern auch im Gesange auf Worte, die durch die Wiederholung einen verstärkten Nachdruck erhalten. Diese Figur ist in der Musik eine der gewöhnlichsten, und bekommt nur dann ihren meisten Werth, wenn sie mit der Paronomasie (Verstärkung) verbunden wird.

The repetition not only involves single notes and entire musical passages but also the text in vocal music which receives greater emphasis through the repetition. The figure is one of the most common in music, and only assumes its full potential when it is combined with the *paronomasia.*

ANAPLOCE: a repetition of a *noema*, particularly between choirs in a polychoral composition.

Both the term *anaploce* and the musical device which it describes are only encountered in Burmeister's *Figurenlehre*. This novel term is closely related to a familiar rhetorical one, *ploce*, which signifies the repetition of a word but with an altered sense (e.g., Boys will be boys; Let bygones be bygones).[1] Common to both figures is the element of repetition, a feature not reflected in the rhetorical term *ploce* (literally

1. In the treatise, *De Musica* (after 1559), Anonymous of Besançon uses the term *ploce* to define the fugue. Like Susenbrotus, he lists *copulatio* as the Latin translation of the Greek term. Various sixteenth-century authors used rhetorical terms of imitation or repetition to describe fugal composition. "Anonymous of Besançon is unique among the early music theorists who apply rhetorical precepts to music in the large number of figures he cites in his attempt to arrive at a clear and comprehensive delineation of the rhetorical concept of fugue." G. Butler, "Fugue and Rhetoric," 53.

"web, weaving"). While Quintilian's definition includes both elements of repetition and weaving (the *ploce* is a result of a "mixture of figures"), Susenbrotus and later Gottsched omit this feature while retaining the repetitive element of the figure. In adding the prefix *ana* (again), Burmeister modifies the term to include the repetition component. Thus the term describes a repeated (*ana*) *noema* which is "woven" (*ploce*) into a polychoral texture.

As he did with *analepsis*, another *noema* figure, Burmeister formulates this new term to define and elucidate a uniquely musical device for the purpose of analyzing and teaching musical composition rather than to force rhetorical terminology with its accompanying definitions into a musical framework. Although rhetorical terminology would frequently be admissible for his purposes, at times including more or less of the original content of the rhetorical term, of prime importance for Burmeister is the musical definition as it is reflected in the literal meaning of the term. This approach allows Burmeister to either adopt or adapt rhetorical terms without binding himself to predetermined definitions while still retaining a similar *ornatus*-oriented concept of the figures.

Quintilian (*Institutio* IX.iii.41)
Hanc frequentiorem repetitionem ploke vocant, quae fit ex permixtis figuris.

This frequent repetition is called *ploce* and consists of a mixture of figures.

Susenbrotus (*Epitome* p.55)
Copulatio sive Duplicatio, est cum idem verbum, cum emphasi quadam repetitur, hoc modo. Sed tandem ad illum diem Memmius erat Memmius.: posterius enim notat iam ante cognitos mores. Graeci vocant ploke. Differt ab Epizeuxis, quod haec principium geminat, illa finem.

The *copulatio* or *duplicatio* occurs when a word is repeated with a certain added emphasis, as in the example, "But on that day, Memmius was Memmius," the repetition referring to his previously familiar character. The figure is called *ploce* in Greek. It differs from the *epizeuxis*, which repeats the beginning word, while the *ploce* repeats the ending.

Gottsched (*Redekunst* p.276)
Ploce, wenn das wiederholte Wort zwar grammatisch dasselbe bleibt, aber doch seinen Verstand ändert. Z.E. Kinder sind Kinder.

Ploce, when the repeated word remains grammatically unchanged and yet changes its sense. For example, Children will be children.

Burmeister (*Musica Poetica* p.62)
Anaploce est in Harmoniis ex Octo praesertim vocibus, & duobus choris

The *anaploce* is a repetition [of a *noema*] in the same or neighboring musical

constantibus prope clausulam vel in ipsa etiam Clausula Harmoniae unius Chori in altero replicatio, repetitione ad binas ternasue vices inculcata. Exemplum est in Orlandi Deus misereatur nostri quo textus: Et metuant eum, expolitur.

clause by alternating choirs, specifically in an eight-part, double-choir composition. The two- or three-fold repeated alternation is often encountered toward the end of the composition, as in Orlando's *Deus misereatur* at the text *Et metuant eum*.

ANASTROPHE: see *HYPALLAGE*

ANTICIPATIO, PRAESUMPTIO: an additional upper or lower neighboring note after a principal note, prematurely introducing a note belonging to the subsequent harmony or chord.

The *anticipatio* is only to be found in musical *Figurenlehren*, describing a specifically musical device. However, in the definition of *anticipatio* in his *Lexicon*, Walther also includes the term *praesumptio* for the figure. This familiar rhetorical device is employed to anticipate and dismiss counter arguments to the main thesis of an oration.[1] While this rhetorical device can be a most forceful element in the argument, the musical device, closely related to the *accentus*, is considered more as an embellishment to be applied by the performer rather than a musical-rhetorical figure with affective, text-oriented power. Its inclusion in a musical *Figurenlehre* is justified through its explanation of a certain dissonance. While there is a technical similarity between the musical and rhetorical *anticipatio* or *praesumptio*, both devices being an anticipation of something to follow, the musical figure is more "grammatical" while the rhetorical figure is a powerful figure of thought.

It is Bernhard, whose concept of the musical figures rests on the correct and legitimate use of dissonance, who introduces the *anticipatio notae* as a musical figure. Bernhard lists the *anticipatio* only in his *Tractatus*. In his following treatise he expands the definition of *subsumptio*, incorporating the *anticipatio* along with its musical examples under

1. Susenbrotus uses the verb *anticipare* in his definition of *praesumptio*, both terms referring to similar concepts: to anticipate or presume.

subsumptio postpositiva.[1] In making this change, Bernhard states that the *subsumptio postpositiva*, used in either descending or ascending stepwise progressions, only makes use of the lower neighbor (*sub-sumere*). Only in a descending stepwise progression would the *anticipatio* and the *subsumptio* correspond. Should the progression rise, the anticipatory element is no longer present: the added note, still always a step lower, would need to leap by a third to the following ascending note instead of anticipating it. In his *Praecepta*, Walther also lists the *anticipatio* under *subsumptio*, defining it as the added lower neighbor without a reference to the following or anticipated note. In his *Lexicon*, however, Walther returns to the literal meaning of the term, and reestablishes the link between the added note with the following one. Scheibe and Spiess also include *anticipatio* in their *Figurenlehren*, lending the ornament its literal meaning of anticipation. While neither include *syncopatio* in their *Figurenlehre*, they employ the *anticipatio* and its antithesis, *retardatio*, to identify two forms of suspension. The former anticipates a note belonging to the subsequent harmony while the latter delays the entry of a note, allowing it to carry over into the subsequent harmony.[2] Scheibe also mentions that the device can be used to introduce the resolution of a suspension in one voice while the dissonant suspension is still sounding in another voice, thereby prematurely "anticipating" the resolution.

Quintilian (*Institutio* IX.ii.16)

Mire vero in causis valet praesumptio, quae πρόληψις dicitur, cum id quod obiici potest occupamus.

The *praesumptio* or *prolepsis* possesses great force and occurs when we deal with possible objections.

Susenbrotus (*Epitome* p.30)

Praesumptio, Praeoccupatio est quum id quod obiici, prius quam obiiciatur anticipamus.

The *praesumptio* or *praeoccupatio* occurs when we anticipate any objections before they are made.

Bernhard (*Tractatus* p.72)

Anticipatio Notae ist, wenn eine Stimme

The *anticipatio notae* occurs when a

1. Similarly, the *quaesitio notae* is defined separately in his *Tractatus*, but it is incorporated into the *subsumptio praepositiva* definition in the *Bericht*. See *Subsumptio*. For a more complete discussion of these various embellishments, see Neumann, *Ornamentation*, 103ff.

2. See *Retardatio*.

die im nächsten höhern oder tiefern Intervallo folgende Note [eher] anfänget, als eigentlich der natürliche Satz leiden wolle. Zu solchem Ende nimmt man etwas von dem Valore der vorhergehenden Note hinweg und setzet solches vor die folgende.

voice begins the neighboring upper or lower note earlier than the natural setting would allow. To this end durational value is taken from the preceding note and placed before the following one.

Walther (*Lexicon*)

Anticipatione della Nota, Anticipatio Notae, die Vorausnehmung einer Note ist: wenn sie im nächsten intervallo drunter oder drüber eher eintritt, und sich hören lässt, als eigentlich der ordinäre Satz sonsten thut. Diese Figur ist von dem Accentu duplici nur in so weit unterschieden, daβ solcher auch springend angebracht wird, welches die Anticipatio, so sonsten auch Praeceptio und Praesumtio heisset, nicht thun kan.

The *anticipatione della nota* or *anticipatio notae*, the anticipation of a note, occurs when the upper or lower neighboring note enters earlier than it normally would in the ordinary setting. This figure, also called *praeceptio* and *praesumptio*, differs from the *accentus duplex* only in that it is not to be used in leaps, which the *accentus duplex* may.

Scheibe (*Compendium* 3, §7)

Anticipatio ist, wenn ich wieder die in der andern Abtheilung und deβen 8ten Abschnitt §13 N.3 befindliche Regel: Es müβe diejenige Note, so die Dissonanz resolviret, niemals zugleich mit der Dissonanz in concentu reali stehen, die resolvierende Note zugleich unter der Ligatur in einer andern Stimme anschlagen laβe. Also daβ ich die Dissonanz und die resolvirende Consonanz zusammen höre, und also die Resolutio anticipire, oder vor der Zeit anschlage. In Ansehung der Melodie aber hat die Anticipatio einen neuen Nuzen und Gebrauch. Dieser nun bestehet darinnen, wenn ich Zierlichkeit halber einen oder zwo Thone zugleich, welche zum folgenden Accord gehören zum vorhergehenden noch mit anschlage, und also von den folgenden in voraus anticipirt.

The *anticipatio* occurs when a resolving note is heard against the suspended note in another voice, in other words when the dissonance and its resolving consonance are heard together, thereby anticipating the resolution or sounding it prematurely. This is contrary to the abovementioned rule found in chapter 8, §13.3, which states that the resolution of a dissonance and the dissonance itself are never to sound simultaneously. Regarding the melody, however, the *anticipatio* has a new use and application. This occurs for the sake of embellishment when one or two notes belonging to a subsequent chord are already played with the preceding one, thereby anticipating the following prematurely.

Spiess (*Tractatus* p.155)

Anticipatio, die Zuvorkommung, Vorausnehmung, Voranschlagung einer Notae, ist eine sehr übliche Figur, und geschiet wann eine Stimm im nächsten Intervallo drunter, oder drüber eher ein-

The *anticipatio*, anticipation or premature playing of a note, is a very common figure and occurs when a voice enters earlier with the neighboring higher or lower note and is heard before the actual or un-

tritt, und sich hören lässet, als es eigentlich der ordinäre Satz sonsten thut.

embellished setting would indicate.

Übrigens kann diese Figur mit- oder ohne Syncopa geschehen.

Furthermore, this figure can be employed with or without the *syncopa*.

ANTIMETABOLE: see *HYPALLAGE*

ANTISTAECHON: a substituted dissonance for an expected consonance, usually the result of the melody remaining on the same pitch while the bass implies harmonic changes.

The musical and rhetorical *antistaechon* describe a similar procedure, namely an exchange of certain notes or letters which would normally belong in the phrase or word with unexpected or foreign ones. Susenbrotus also employs the term *antithesis* for this figure, using this term to denote not opposing or contrasting ideas or thoughts but rather only the differing letters in a word. The musical *antistaechon* has a certain similarity to the *ellipsis*. However, whereas *ellipsis* refers to the omission of an expected consonance, the *antistaechon* points to the substitution of a consonance with a dissonance. In the example provided by Vogt and Spiess, "*Iam stat immobilis*" ("Now he stands unmoved"), the "immobility" of the melody through to the cadence over a moving bass line is an eloquent expression of the text. From the definitions and examples, it is not quite clear whether *antistaechon* refers to any such substitution or whether it is limited to such phrases in which the melody stays on one pitch instead of accommodating the harmonies implied by the bass. In the example, the figure is certainly used as a *hypotyposis* figure, vividly depicting the desired image. Furthermore, this "lining up" of the notes is reflected in the rhetorical term itself. *Antistaechon* literally means lining up in opposing rows (*anti*, against; *stoichos*, row), as, for example, combating soldiers might do. So too the melody "lines up" identical notes opposite the moving bass line.

Susenbrotus (*Epitome* p.24)

Antithesis (aptius Antistoechon). Est literae commutatio, hoc est cum litera pro litera ponitur. Vergil. Aen.1. Olli subridens hominum sator atque deorum, pro illi.

The *antithesis* or *antistoechon* signifies an exchange of letters, that is when one letter is substituted for another, as in Virgil's *Aeneid* where *Olli* replaces *illi*.

Vogt (*Conclave* p.150)

Antistaechon permutatio signi, literae, notae; ut cum in cadentia nota penultima non est tertia nec quinta, sed exotica ut quarta:

The *antistaechon* is an interchange of a sign, letter, or note, for example when the penultimate note in a cadence is not the third or fifth, but rather a strange interval such as the fourth:

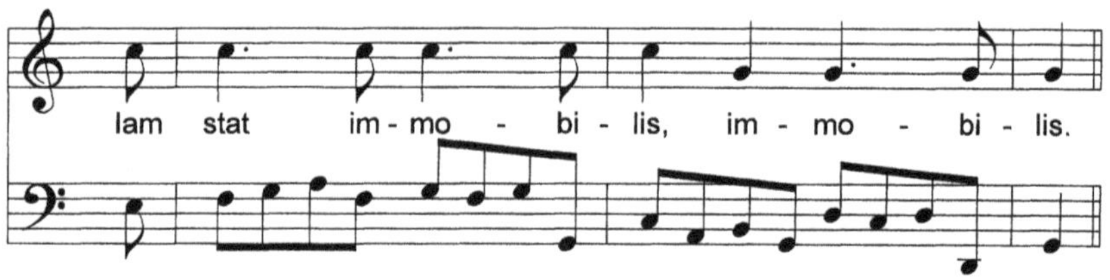

Maximus huius figurae usus est in solicíniis, ubi modus canendi frequentissime alias accipit notas, quam lineae habeant.

The greatest use of this figure is made in solo pieces, in which the performance practice most frequently introduces notes which differ from the written ones.

Spiess (*Tractatus* p.155)

Antistaechon wird als dann genennet, da die singende Stimm sich dem Bass in gebührenden Consonantien nicht accommodirt; sondern Texts halber ausser denenselben in den Dissonantien sich aufhaltet, v.g. in Exprimirung des Texts: Immobilis stat. Wo die Sing-Stimm immer in einer Zeil stehen bleibt, der Bass aber seine Gäng fortmachet.

The *antistaechon* is called such if the singing voice does not accommodate the bass with appropriate consonances but, rather than those, chooses dissonances instead in order to express the text. For example, in expressing the text "He remains unmoved," the vocal line remains on the same pitch while the bass proceeds in stepwise fashion.

ANTISTROPHE: see *HYPALLAGE*

ANTITHESIS, ANTITHETON, CONTRAPOSITUM: a musical expression of opposing affections, harmonies, or thematic material.

In both rhetoric and music, an expression of opposing ideas is called *antithesis* (*antitheton*) or *contrapositum*. This may refer to opposing affections (Kircher, Janovka, Scheibe), harmonies (Walther's *antithesis*, Spiess), or thematic material (Vogt, Walther's *antitheton*, Scheibe, Spiess). Only Walther chooses to differentiate terminologically contrasting harmonies and contrasting thematic material. The opposing musical ideas may occur successively or simultaneously: should two contrasting thoughts or words be expressed musically (e.g., "I sleep, but my heart wakes;" "They that sow in tears shall reap in joy"), contrasting harmonies be juxtaposed, or melodic material be inverted, a successive or linear *antithesis* is the result. However, should a fugue theme be highlighted through a contrasting counter-subject or should one text contain two contrasting affections (e.g., "In my anger, I relented"), a simultaneous or vertical *antithesis* can occur.

The *antithesis* is associated not only with vocal but also with purely instrumental music. The expression of musical opposites as well as thematic inversions is an important device in the elaboration of a subject in a musical composition. Burmeister had introduced the fugal inversion as *hypallage*, and Janovka mentions other forms of fugal inversion in his discussion of the *figura principalis*, *fuga*: besides the *fuga inversa seu contraria* (corresponding to *hypallage*), he also names the *fuga cancrizans* (retrograde) and the *fuga reciproca* (retrograde inversion). Walther defines similar fugal devices in his *Lexicon*. The aspect of musical opposites receives particular attention in Mattheson's discussion of the *confutatio*. Just as the *confutatio* serves to refute objections to the principal argument in rhetoric, so too can it be used to resolve "opposition" to the theme in music, particularly in fugal composition.[1] While these technical and contrapuntal forms of musical opposition remain of importance in eighteenth-century composition, the changing music aesthetic

1. G. Butler, "Fugue and Rhetoric," 85f.

looked at these "grammatical" devices with increasing suspicion. In discussing the rhetorical aspects of the fugue, Forkel reminds his readers that while contrapuntal inversions may be of interest to the "intellectual" listener, they should be used with great care: musical opposites (*Gegensätze*) could be useful in clarifying or "proving" the principal subject, particularly when combined with a fugue theme, a form of simultaneous *antithesis*, or they could appear successively, "especially when the main subject and the countersubject are so structured that they are easily remembered."[1] At the end of his discussion of the musical-rhetorical figures, Forkel also notes that "there are certain devices which are most useful in attracting the listeners' attention, such as new and unexpected changes as well as sudden modulations."[2] While the concept of the musical-rhetorical figures falls into oblivion with the passing of the Baroque period, the principle of the *antithesis* lives on in the very structure of the forms and methods of musical expression of the following era. The "unexpected changes and sudden modulations" of the *Sturm und Drang* as well as the fundamental principles of the sonata concept, with its positioning of tonic versus dominant keys and primary versus secondary material, all attest to this fact.

Quintilian (*Institutio* IX.iii.81)

Contrapositum autem vel, ut quidam vocant, contentio (ἀντίθετον dicitur) non uno fit modo. Nam et fit, si singula singulis opponuntur . . . et bina binis . . . et sententiae sententiis.

The *contrapositum*, also called *contentio* or *antitheton*, occurs in more than one manner. The contrast may be between single words, pairs of words, or entire sentences.

Gottsched (*Redekunst* p.283)

Antitheton. Wenn man viel wiedrige Dinge neben einander setzet, um sie durch die Gegeneinanderhaltung desto mehr zu erheben.

Antitheton. When many opposing things are placed next to each other in order to emphasize them through contrast.

Gottsched (*Dichtkunst* p.332)

Zum XVten folgt der Gegensatz, (Antithesis) wo man widerwärtige Dinge gegen einander stellt, um das eine desto mehr ins Licht zu setzen.

Next is the *antithesis*, in which opposing things are contrasted in order to highlight the one.

---

1. Forkel, *Allgemeine Geschichte der Musik*, 51, 54.
2. Ibid., 58.

Kircher (*Musurgia* L.8, p.145)

Antitheton, sive Contrapositum, est periodus harmonica, quam oppositos affectus exprimimus; sicut; illud Jacobi Carrissimi, quem Heracliti risum & Democriti planctum intitulat, & illud Leonis Leonii. Ego dormio, et cor meum vigilat.

The *antitheton* or *contrapositum* is a musical passage in which we express opposing affections, as Giacomo Carrissimi contrasted Heraclitus's laughing with Democritus's weeping, or as Leonus Leoni expressed: "I sleep, but my heart wakes."

Janovka (*Clavis* p.55)

Antitheton, sive Contrapositum est Periodus harmonica, qua oppositos Anaphorae affectus exprimimus ut in textu: ego dormio et cor meum vigilat fieri posset.

The *antitheton* or *contrapositum* is a musical passage through which (in contrast to the *anaphora*) we express opposing affections. The text "I sleep but my heart wakes" could be expressed in this manner.

Vogt (*Conclave* p.2)

Antithesis, figura musica, seu contrapositio.

The *antithesis* or contrast is a musical figure.

Vogt (*Conclave* p.150)

Antitheton oppositio tam fit in thematibus, contrathematibus, quam in oppositione dissonantiarum. Est communis.

The *antitheton* contrasts either a subject against a countersubject, or opposing dissonances. It is a common figure.

Walther (*Lexicon*)

Antithesis, heisset: wenn aus einer Clausula formali, gehling in eine frembde gegangen wird.

The *antithesis* signifies a direct progression from a *clausula formali* to a foreign one.

Antitheton, ist ein musicalischer Satz, wodurch solche Sachen, die einander contrair und entgegen sind, exprimirt werden sollen. Z.E. ich schlaffe, aber mein Herz wachet, u.d.g.

The *antitheton* is a musical passage in which contrary and opposite things are to be expressed, for example, "I sleep, but my heart wakes," and similar texts.

Mattheson (*Capellmeister* p.188)

Wenn ausdrückliche Gegensätze vorkommen, so verhält sich die Sache gantz anders. Denn der Worte Wiederstand erfordert daselbst auch ein gleiches in den Klängen. . . . Gegensätze können auf verschiedene Weise im Gesange ausgedruckt werden, es sey durch gewisse Klänge, die ihren Gang umkehren; durch Intervalle, die einander zuwieder lauffen; durch plötzliche Veränderung der Ton-Art, des Tacts etc.

When explicit opposites occur in the text, the matter is quite different. For opposition in the text demands a comparable expression in the music. . . . Opposites can be expressed in various ways in music, be it through certain notes which invert their progression, through intervals which oppose each other, through sudden changes of the key or the rhythm, etc.

Scheibe (*Critischer Musicus* p.693)

Der Gegensatz (Antithesis). Wenn man einige Sätze gegeneinander stellet, um den Hauptsatz dadurch desto deutlicher zu machen. Dieses geschieht vornehmlich in Fugen, da man dem Hauptsatze jederzeit noch andre Sätze entgegen setzet, um jenen desto besser auszuführen und zu erheben. Insonderheit aber gehöret zu dieser Figur, wenn man ganz fremde Sätze erfindet, die an sich selbst und einzeln genommen, im geringsten nicht mit dem Hauptsatze verbunden zu seyn scheinen. . . . Auch in solchen Singesachen, die zweyerley Affect enthalten, muβ diese Figur zum Ausdrucke derselben das meiste beytragen.

The *antithesis* occurs when a few passages are contrasted with each other in order to bring out the main subject that much more clearly. This occurs especially in fugues in which the main subject is continually contrasted with other subjects in order to better execute and amplify it. However, a particular aspect of this figure is the invention of completely foreign subjects which, taken individually on their own, seem to be not in the least related to the main subject. . . . It is also primarily this figure which must be used in expressing vocal music which contains two contrasting affections.

Spiess (*Tractatus* p.155)

Antithesis, Contrapositio, Gegensatz, geschiehet, wann einem Themati das Contrathema: oder denen erwartenden Consonantien die Dissonantien entgegen gesetzt werden. Wiederum so man aus einer Clausula formali gehling hinweg- und in eine fremde gehet. Dererley Antitheses oder Gegensätz ereignen sich auch zuweilen in dem Text selber. v.g. Ego dormio, et cor meum vigilat.

The *antithesis* or *contrapositio* occurs when a subject stands in contrast to a countersubject, or dissonances stand in contrast to expected consonances. It occurs, furthermore, when one leaves a *clausula formalis* and proceeds directly to a foreign one. Such *antitheses* or opposites occur at times in the text itself, for example in "I sleep, but my heart wakes."

Forkel (*Geschichte der Musik* p.51)

Die Gegensätze sind in der Musik das, was in der eigentlichen Rede die Beyspiele sind, wodurch wir den Zuhörer nöthigen, unsern Hauptsatz gleichsam eben so gegründet zu finden, als das angeführte ähnliche Beyspiel. Bisweilen werden sie mit dem Hauptsatze zugleich verbunden, wie in Fugen, oder überhaupt in der polyphonischen Compositionsart geschieht; bisweilen werden sie aber auch hintereinander angebracht, hauptsächlich, wenn Haupt- und Gegensatz so beschaffen sind, daβ sie leicht im Gedächnisse behalten werden können.

The musical *antitheses* are to music what the examples are to actual speech, through which we compel the listener similarly to perceive our primary theme just as well grounded as the cited similar example. In this respect they are a form of proof. At times they are combined with the primary theme, as in fugues and in general in polyphonic composition. At other times they are presented successively, especially when the primary and the contrasting themes are so fashioned, that they are easily remembered.

APOCOPE: an omitted or shortened final note in one voice of a composition.

The literal meaning of *apocope* (to "cut off") is reflected in both the rhetorical and the musical figure. While the rhetorical figure refers to cutting off a word's final letter or syllable, the musical figure is defined as a shortening of the final note in one voice of a fugue. Burmeister's concern to identify and name a specific musical device with a rhetorical term without necessarily adopting the associated rhetorical definition becomes evident once again. He uses the term to describe a prematurely ending voice which results in an incomplete *fuga*. Rather than referring only to the cutting off of the voice, Burmeister's *apocope* signifies the unfinished composition, prompting him to consider the figure as a *figurae harmoniae* along with the other fugal figures *metalepsis* and *hypallage*. Thuringus extends the figure's usage to any composition. Walther not only adopts Thuringus's definition but adds a reference to the *apocope*'s text-expressive potential: the note is to be quickly cut off at those words which would seem to demand such an interpretation. Neither Thuringus nor Walther differentiate between the cutting off of a single voice and the premature ending of the composition. In fact, in their definitions, they indicated that the entire *cantus* (Thuringus) or *periodus harmonicae* is cut off, resulting in a figure similar to the *abruptio* or *tmesis*.

Susenbrotus (*Epitome* p.22)

Apocope, est literae aut syllabae in calce dictionis abscisio.	The *apocope* signifies the dropping of the last letter or syllable of a word.

Burmeister (*Hypomnematum*)

Apokope est Fugae absolutio non integra.	The *apocope* is an only partially completed fugue.

Burmeister (*Musica autoschediastike*)

Apocope est Fugae, quae ex omnibus partibus, per omnes voces non absolvitur, sed in voce affectionis illius quae in fugam abrepta est, propter aliquam causam amputatio.	The *apocope* signifies a cutting off of the fugue for whatever reason. Instead of completing the fugue in all parts with all voices, one of its voices is broken off.

Burmeister (*Musica Poetica* p.59)
Apocope est Fuga, quae ex omni partie per omnes voces non absolvitur, sed cuius affectionis, quae in fugam abrepta est, propter aliquam causam in una aliqua voce fit amputatio, (ut in Legem pone mihi Domine Exordio Orlandi 5. vocum).

The *apocope* is a fugue which is not completed in all parts with all voices, but whose condition is broken off for a certain reason. It signifies a cutting off in one voice of the fugue.

Thuringus (*Opusculum* p.127)
Quid est Apocope: Est, cum finalis notula prorsus auffertur, & cum nota minima cantus terminatur, ut non erit finis.

What is an *apocope*? It occurs when the final note is substantially cut and the composition is ended with a *nota minima*, resulting in an incomplete ending.

Walther (*Lexicon*)
Apocope ist eine musikalische Figur, so entstehet: wenn bey der letzten Note eines Periodi harmonicae nicht ausgehalten, sondern behende abgeschnappt wird, und zwar bey solchen Worten, die solches zu erfordern scheinen.

The *apocope* is a musical figure which occurs when the last note of a musical passage is not completely held out but rather is quickly snapped off. It is used to express those words which seem to require such treatment.

APOSIOPESIS: a rest in one or all voices of a composition; a general pause.

Most authors define *aposiopesis* as a general pause, affecting all the voices of a composition. As the literal meaning of the term suggests (from *apo*, away, from; *siopesis*, silence), *aposiopesis* signifies a certain silence in a composition. This figure is related to the *abruptio*, a point which Spiess also emphasizes. However, while the *abruptio* denotes the sudden breaking off of a musical passage, the *aposiopesis* refers to an intentional and expressive use of silence in a composition. Furthermore, the *abruptio*'s break is normally described as sudden and unexpected, a characteristic not necessarily associated with the *aposiopesis*. In contrast, the rhetorical *aposiopesis* is defined as an unexpected break in the oration or an intentional suppression, thereby assuming a definition much closer to the musical *abruptio* or *ellipsis*. In fact, Gottsched mentions that the *aposiopesis* could be considered as a form of *ellipsis*. The *abruptio* on the other hand is not encountered as a rhetorical figure. Because rhetoric does not use silence as an expressive tool in the same manner that music does, it did not develop specific figures of silence. In contrast, the significance of silence in musical composition encouraged an entire group of figures which are used to express either silence or a break in the composition, including besides *abruptio*, *aposiopesis*, and *ellipsis* also *homoioptoton*, *tmesis*, *suspiratio*, and especially the *pausa*, which was associated with text-expression since the fifteenth century. Further differentiation between two kinds of *aposiopesis* is made by some authors with the figures *homoioptoton* and *homoioteleuton*. These are discussed under the corresponding terms.

The *aposiopesis* is frequently encountered in compositions whose texts deal with death or eternity.[1] In such cases it is the *aposiopesis* rather than the *abruptio* which is usually employed, expressing infinity or nothingness. In describing the various uses of the pause, Herbst includes its expressive use: it can be used at the composition's "end, when the loss, downfall, or destruction of something is to be expressed, for example [in the Magnificat text] 'He has scattered, He has sent them empty away,' or as J. Hassler expresses the text: 'I depart and die,' in which all the voices are silenced."[2] In a similar vein, Daniel Speer

1. See Unger, *Beziehungen*, 70ff.

2. ". . . als: am End / wann ein verlorne Sach / oder eines dings untergang soll angedeutet werden / nemlich / dispersit, dimisit inanes, und im J. L. Hasl. mit diesen Worten: Ich scheid und stirbe / da alle Stimmen stillschweigen." *Musica poetica*, 100.

encourages the expressive use of the pause: "The loss or destruction of something, as well as texts which imply a certain endlessness, such as 'The way of the Godless will vanish,' 'I have left you for only a moment,' 'Heaven and earth shall pass away,' 'Of peace there shall be no end,' or similar texts should be followed by pauses as the words demand, with all voices being cut off simultaneously."[1] In addition, the *aposiopesis* can be employed following rhetorical questions, where the ensuing silence allows the listener to supply the answer or to contemplate an unanswerable question. In such cases the figure is closely related to the *interrogatio*. But again, here, as with *abruptio*, the *aposiopesis* is used to express the silence following the question rather than the question itself. An example of such a use of the *aposiopesis* is provided in the musical example of Vogt's definition. Of interest here is the *basso continuo* part, which does not rest at the point of the *aposiopesis*. According to Vogt, the figure does not necessarily affect all the parts but only the vocal line(s), as determined by the text.

Quintilian (*Institutio* VIII.iii.85)

Absciditur per ἀποσιώπησιν quae, quoniam est figura, reddetur suo loco.

An omission is effected through the *aposiopesis* which, being a figure, will be dealt with later.

Quintilian (*Institutio* IX.iii.60)

Hanc quidam aposiopesin putant, frustra. Nam illa quid taceat incertum est aut certe longiore sermone explicandum.

This is wrongly regarded by some as an *aposiopesis*. For that which is omitted remains uncertain or requires a lengthy explanation.

Susenbrotus (*Epitome* p.27)

Aposiopesis, est quum ex affectu, aut alicuius interventu, aut etiam transitus ad aliud gratia, orationis pars aliqua praeciditur. Cicero Reticentiam et Praecisionem vocat, Celsus Obticentiam, nonnulli

The *aposiopesis* occurs when a part of the oration is cut off for the sake of the affection, other interruption, or even transition, or for some other reason. Cicero calls this *reticentia* or *praecisio*, Celsus

---

1. "Wenn eines Dinges Untergang oder eine Sache verloren gehet, oder wann die Textworte expresse ohne Ende sich ereignen, nemlich: 'Der Gottlosen Weg vergehet'; item: 'Ich habe dich einen kleinen Augenblick verlassen'; also auch 'Himmel und Erde vergehen'; oder 'Des Friedens kein Ende'. Bei solchen oder dergleichen Textworten sollen Pausen folgen, indem es der Text erfordert, daß zugleich mit allen Stimmen auf einmal abgeschnitten werde." Speer, *Vierfaches musikalisches Kleeblatt*, 283; cited in Unger, *Beziehungen*, 71.

Interruptionem. Ex affectu quidem, vel irae.

calls it *obticentia*, and others call it *interruptio*.

Gottsched (*Redekunst* p.289)
Aposiopesis, oder Reticentia. Wenn man den Anfang macht, etwas heraus zu sagen: Aber mitten in der Rede inne hält und abbricht.

Aposiopesis or *reticentia*. When one begins to make a statement but stops and breaks off in the middle of the sentence.

Gottsched (*Dichtkunst* p.320)
Die V. könnte zur vorigen gerechnet werden, und heiβt das Hemmen (*Aposiopesis*), wenn eine schleunige Veränderung des Entschlusses, der angefangenen Rede Einhalt thut.

The next figure, called the *aposiopesis*, could be included under the previous figure, the *ellipsis*. It occurs when a sudden alteration of intent interrupts the flow of the speech.

Burmeister (*Hypomnematum*)
Aposiopesis est totale omnium vocum silentium quocunque signo datum.

The *aposiopesis* is a complete silence in all voices and is indicated through a certain sign.

Burmeister (*Musica Poetica* p.62)
Aposiopesis est quae silentium totale omnibus vocibus signo certo posito confert.

The *aposiopesis* is a figure which causes a complete silence in all voices through the placement of a certain sign.

Thuringus (*Opusculum* p.126)
Quid est Aposiopesis? Est universale silentium in omibus Cantilenae partibus. Et est duplex: Homioteleuton & Homiaeoptoton.

What is an *aposiopesis*? It is a general silence in all parts of the composition. It is of two kinds: *homioteleuton* and *homiaeoptoton*.

Vogt (*Conclave* p.150)
Aposiopesis reticentia. Reticentia fieri debet, ubi alias necesse est cantari, ut it exemplo:

The *aposiopesis* indicates a silence. This silence ought to occur where it would otherwise be necessary to sing, as in the following example:

Walther (*Lexicon*)
Aposiopesis heisset in der Music: wenn eine Pausa generalis, oder ein durch-

In music the *aposiopesis* refers to a *pausa generalis*, or a complete silence in all

gängiges Stilschweigen in allen Stimmen und Partien zugleich vorkommt, welches auf zweyerley Art geschehen kan, als 1) Homoeoteleuton 2) Homoeoptoton.

voices and parts of the composition simultaneously. This can occur in two ways, through the *homoeoteleuton* and the *homoeoptoton*.

Spiess (*Tractatus* p.155)
Aposiopesis, verhalten, verschweigen, stillschweigen, ist, wann entweder mittelst einer General-Pausen alle Stimmen zugleich stillhalten: oder auch wann eine einzelne Stimm stillschweiget, und abbricht, da sie doch solte singen, und in gehörige Cadenz gehen. Hat im letzteren Verstand zimliche Gleichheit mit der Figura Abruptio.

The *aposiopesis*, suppression, concealment, silence, occurs when either all voices are silenced through a general pause, or when a single voice stops and breaks off when it should actually continue to sing and progress into the appropriate cadence. This second understanding corresponds to the *figura abruptio.*

APOTOMIA: an enharmonic rewriting of a semitone.

This rather obscure figure is only included in Vogt's *Figurenlehre*. Vogt is also quick to point out that the device is more frequently encountered in music theory than among the figures. In his *Lexicon* Walther defines the term in purely theoretical terms, without any reference to text interpretation or musical-rhetorical use. The term stems from Greek musical theory and is used to identify the major semitone. According to Pythagorean theory, a whole tone is subdivided into nine *commata*, resulting in a differentiation between a minor semitone, consisting of four *commata*, and a major semitone or *apotome*, consisting of five *commata*. Vogt defines the figure *apotomia* as the enharmonic rewriting of a minor semitone as a major semitone, resulting in enlarging the interval by one *comma* (intervallic proportion of 80:81).[1]

Vogt (*Conclave* p.151)
Apotomia Major pars semitonii. Spectat inter theoremata musicae amplius, quam inter figuras. Instruatur hic canens, ut ad # cruculam accipiat quinque commata, & non quatuor, similiter descendendo ad ♭ accipiat commata quinque prae quatuor,

The *apotomia* is the larger part of a semitone. It is encountered more frequently in music theory than among the figures. It is formed when the [ascending] semitone is increased from four to five *commata* through the addition of a sharp, or when

1. For a more thorough discussion of these numerical proportions, see above, p.12ff.

ut bene, & notabiliter durificet cruces, & bene emolliat ♭.

the descending semitone is similarly increased from four to five *commata* through a flat. Sharps cause an agreeable and noticeable brightening, while flats cause an agreeable softening.

Walther (*Lexicon*)
Apotome, von ἀποτέμνω, abscindo, ich schneide ab, also nannten die Grichen ihr in proportione super 139 parteinte 218 bestehendes Semitonium maius. s. Zarl. Vol.I. P.2. c.28. weil es ein abgeschnittenes Stück vom ganzen Tone ist.

The *apotome*, from *apotemno, abscindo*, I cut off, is what the Greeks called the major semitone proportion 139:218, because it is a part cut off from the whole tone. (see Zarlino, vol.1, part 2, ch.28.)

ASCENSUS: see *ANABASIS*

ASSIMILATIO, HOMOIOSIS: a musical representation of the text's imagery.

The *assimilatio* or *homoiosis* is only listed in the *Figurenlehren* of Kircher and Janovka. Their inclusion of this figure as an apparent alternative for Burmeister's *hypotyposis* indicates a changing concept of the musical-rhetorical figures.[1] As both the Latin and Greek terms indicate, the rhetorical *assimilatio* (*homoiosis*, *similitudo*) is a form of simile or parable. Through this figure the thought or significance of one expression is conferred onto another subject, thereby establishing a parallel. This process is applied to the musical context by Kircher. Through the musical "simile," the composer expresses the content of the text, whether it be an affection or other image, thereby establishing the parallel between the text and the music. However, this is more than mere musical word painting. A simile is another form of stating the same thing, not a reflection of something already said. Likewise, the musical *assimilatio* is a musical expression of that which the words expressed and not simply a musical "painting" of the text. The music re-presents (*referre*) the text instead of reflecting the words. The figure becomes not only the image of the text but, through its musical qualities, becomes the very source

1. See *Hypotyposis*.

of the affection which it is called to depict. The introduction of this figure by Kircher marks the general movement of the musical-rhetorical figures from reflecting the affections of a text to actually arousing them, from being an image to being a source of the affection. The *actiones* are to be expressed in actuality or "properly" (*proprie*: Kircher) rather than only "seemingly" (*videri*: Burmeister's *hypotyposis*). Not surprisingly, it is also Kircher who first highlights the figures' role as affection-expressive devices and moves the concept of the musical *Figurenlehre* fully into the Baroque world of moving the listener.

Susenbrotus (*Epitome* p.104)
Similitudo ὁμοίωσις Homoeosis, est cum aliquid ex re dispari simile ad rem quampiam traductur. Vel, est quando res cum re ex similitudine confertur.

The *similitudo* or *homoeosis* occurs when something is transferred from its context to a different but similar one. Or it occurs when one thing is associated with another because of their likeness.

Kircher (*Musurgia* L.8, p.145)
Ὁμοίωσις assimilatio est periodus harmonica, qua actiones rerum proprie exprimuntur, uti dum periodi singularum vocum diversa referunt, uti illud: (Tympanizant, Cytharizant, pulsant nobis fulgent stolis coram summa Trinitate) in hac cantilena basis Tympanum grave referet, coeterae voces omnis generis instrumenta.

The *homoiosis* or *assimilatio* is a musical passage through which the attributes of a certain thing are actually expressed, for example when individual voices in a passage depict different elements as in the text "*Tympanizant, cytharizant, pulsant nobis fulgent stolis coram summa Trinitate.*" In such a composition the bass represents the weighty *tympanum* while the other voices represent all kinds of other instruments.

Janovka (*Clavis* p.56)
Assimilatio est Periodus harmonica, qua actiones rerum seu verborum proprie exprimuntur, ut dum periodi singularum vocum diversa referunt, prout intextu illo: tympanizant, cytharizant, fulgent stolis coram summa Trinitate. In hac cantione Bassus tympanum grave referret, caeterae voces omnis generis instrumenta.

The *assimilatio* is a musical passage through which the attributes of a certain thing or word are actually expressed, for example when individual voices in a passage depict different elements as in the text "*tympanizant, cytharizant, fulgent stolis coram summa Trinitate.*" In such a composition the bass represents the weighty *tympanum* while the other voices represent all kinds of other instruments.

ASYNDETON: an omission of the appropriate conjunctions in a text.

The only music treatise which mentions the *asyndeton* is Ahle's *Musicalische Sommer-Gespräche*. In that work, Ahle does not provide or discuss musical examples of the figures but rather demonstrates the various possibilities of applying rhetorical figures to music by rearranging and modifying the text. He demonstrates the *asyndeton* by citing the text to be set to music and omitting all of its conjunctions, *und*. In this context, the *asyndeton* is not a musical but rather a rhetorical figure which a composer might employ in arranging a text for his composition. Walther omits this figure in his *Lexicon*, presumably because he did not consider it to be of musical significance. Other terms mentioned by Ahle but likewise omitted in Walther's *Lexicon* are *synonymia* and *polysyndeton*. In contrast, figures such as *epiphora* or *epizeuxis*, also defined as purely rhetorical figures by both Ahle and Walther, were included in the *Lexicon* because of the possibility of their musical application.

Gottsched (*Redekunst* p.278)
Asyndeton. Ein Mangel der Bindewörter.

Asyndeton. A lack of conjunctions.

Ahle (*Sommer-Gespräche* p.17)
Und / wän er das wörtlein "und" davon lässet / auch ein Asyndeton.

And should he omit the little word "and," an *asyndeton* results.

AUXESIS, INCREMENTUM: successive repetitions of a musical passage which rise by step.

In both music and rhetoric the *auxesis* or *incrementum* is understood as a growth through repetition, reflecting the literal meaning of the terms (growth, increase, offspring). Quintilian and Susenbrotus mention the possibility of an incremental intensification even beyond the superlative (e.g., being better than the best). As his musical example demonstrates, Burmeister understands the figure as a repeated *noema* (*conjunctis solis concordantiis*). Unlike other repetitions of the *noema* (such as *analepsis*—a repeated *noema* at the same pitch, and *mimesis*—a repeated *noema* at different higher *or* lower pitches), the *auxesis* is characterized by an incremental rise in pitch of a repeated *noema*. Walther is the only other author to include the *auxesis* or *incrementum* as a musical-rhetorical figure. Like Burmeister, he defines it as a continually rising repetition of a musical passage but does not restrict it to the *noema*.

Beginning with Kircher the musical device previously described by the terms *auxesis* or *incrementum* is identified as a *climax* or *gradatio*. Although earlier rhetorical and musical *Figurenlehren* (Quintilian and Susenbrotus, Burmeister and Nucius) included the *climax*, it was not understood as an expression of incremental growth. Rather, the *climax* or *gradatio* was described as an ascending *or* descending stepwise progression without requiring growth or increasing intensity, reflecting the literal meaning of the terms.[1] Kircher's description of *climax* with the *auxesis* definition (incremental growth) is then perpetuated by all subsequent authors. A similar development can be observed in the rhetorical *Figurenlehre*. In past musical scholarship, this differentiation between the *auxesis* and *climax* has been frequently overlooked. Attempts have been made to blend the various *Figurenlehren* into one homogeneous doctrine of musical-rhetorical figures, particularly by writers such as Brandes and Unger. Subtle and indeed substantial differences in the concepts and definitions of the various authors were ignored in order to create an artificial teaching of the figures. Not only did this result in a misconceived musical *Figurenlehre*, but the dynamic changes in the general emphasis of the concept throughout the Baroque era were not observed. Only by tracing the usages and definitions of the various terms is it possible to present the developments of the musical-rhetorical figures, as disparate as the concepts may at times appear.

Quintilian (*Institutio* VIII.iv.3f.,8)

Incrementum est potentissimum, cum magna videntur etiam quae inferiora sunt. Id aut uno gradu fit aut pluribus et pervenit non modo ad summum sed interim quodammodo supra summum . . . ut apud Verilium de Lauso: "quot pulchrior alter non fuit, excepto Laurentis corpore Turni." Summum est enim, "quo pulchrior, alter non fuit," huic deinde aliquid superpositum. . . .Crescit oratio minus aperte, sed nescio an hoc ipso efficacius, cum citra distinctionem in contextu et cursu semper aliquid priore maius insequitur.

The *incrementum* is a most powerful form [of amplification]: insignificant things are made to appear important. This is effected through either one or several steps and can be carried not only to the highest degree, but at times even beyond it, as in Virgil's description of Lausus: "for no one was fairer, except Laurentis Turnus." The superlative is expressed with "for no one was fairer," which is then further heightened. . . . The oration can be heightened less obviously but perhaps more effectively with an unbroken

1. See *Climax*.

series, in which each expression is continuously followed by a stronger one.

Susenbrotus (*Epitome* p.74)
Incrementum Auxesis, est quoties gradibus aliquot pervenitur, non modo ad summum, sed interim quodammodo supra summum.

The *incrementum* or *auxesis* occurs when something is advanced by step, not only to its highest degree, but at times in a way even beyond that.

Burmeister (*Hypomnematum*)
Auxesis est harmoniae, uni eidemque textui inservientis, incrementum.

The *auxesis* signifies a growth in the composition while using one and the same text.

Burmeister (*Musica Poetica* p.61)
Auxesis fit, quando Harmonia sub uno eodemque textu semel, bis, terve, & ulterius repetito, conjunctis solis Concordantiis, crescit, & insurgit. Exemplum est in Orlandi, Veni in hortum, ad textum: cum Aromatibus meis. Hoc Ornamento omnes fere cantiones, in quibus textus repetitur, ita, ut textus repetitionem, non Fugam, exigat, sunt repletae.

The *auxesis* occurs when the *harmonia* grows and increases with a single, twofold, threefold, or further repetition only of combined consonances [*noema*] using one and the same text. An example is found in Orlando's *Veni in hortum* at the text "cum Aromatibus meis." All compositions in which the text is repeated, but not in the form of a fugue, abound with this figure.

Walther (*Lexicon*)
Auxesis heisset: wenn ein Modulus, oder eine Melodie zwey- bis dreymahl wieder-

The *auxesis* occurs when a passage or a melody is repeated twice or three times,

holt wird, aber dabey immer höher steiget.

while at the same time, however, always rising higher.

BOMBUS, BOMBI, BOMBILANS: four identical notes in rapid succession.

The *bombus* and its grammatical/musical derivatives are considered ornaments or *Manieren* rather than musical-rhetorical figures. A series of *bombi* is referred to as *bombilans*. Walther maintains that the term *bombus* originally meant a movement of the hands resembling the sound of swarming bees, thereby explaining the German term for the ornament: *Schwärmer*. Although the "swarming" notes might prove useful in depicting the text, Walther restricts the figure to instrumental music. Should this occur in vocal music, Walther mentions that it is called *trillo*. The terms *trillo* and *tremolo* were frequently interchanged. Printz defines *tremolo* as rapidly alternating notes and *trillo* as a "trembling" embellishment on one pitch.[1] It is this understanding of *trillo* which Walther refers to when he applies the *bombus* to vocal music.

Printz (*Phrynis Mytilenaeus* pt.2, p.50)

Die einfachen bleibenden Figuren seyn / so in vier geschwinden in einer Clave bleibenden Noten bestehen: Sie werden Bombi oder Schwermer gennenet.

The simple stationary figures are those which consist of four rapid notes on one pitch. They are called *bombi* or *Schwermer*.

Walther (*Lexicon*)

Bombo, Bombus also hieβ ehemahls diejenige künstliche Bewegung der Hände, wodurch ein harmonisches, und den Bienen ähnliches Sausen gemacht wurde. . . . Anjetzo wird die aus vier geschwinden Noten bestehende, und in einem

A *bombo* or *bombus* formerly signified an artful movement of the hands which resulted in a beelike harmonic humming. . . . Nowadays a figure consisting of four rapid notes on one pitch (as in fig.3, no.7), that is a *Schwärmer*, is thus called.

1. In his definition of *tremolo*, Walther also mentions that the device is at times referred to as *trillo*. See *Tremolo*.

Clave bleibende und wie Tab.III No.7 aussehende Figur also, d. i. Schwärmer genennet. . . . Diese Figur wird in der Vocal-Music nicht gebraucht, so sie aber vorkommt, bedeutet sie nur ein trillo.

. . . This figure is not used in vocal music, but should it appear there, signifies only a *trillo*.

Printz (*Phrynis Mytilenaeus* pt.2, p.65)
Figura Bombilans ist / wenn lauter schwermende Figuren zusammen gesetzt werden. Ex. gr.

A *figura bombilans* occurs when numerous *bombi* are linked together.

Walther (*Lexicon*)
Figura bombilans ist, wenn lauter schwärmende Figuren zusammen gesetzt werden. s. Bombus.

A *figura bombilans* occurs when numerous *bombi* are linked together. See *bombus*.

Cadentia Duriuscula: a dissonance in the pre-penultimate harmony of a cadence.

This figure is encountered only in Bernhard's *Tractatus*. In keeping with his concern to legitimize the use of various dissonances inadmissible in the *stylus gravis*, Bernhard explains the dissonances as part of the cadential material, an explanation which can be traced back to the very beginnings of polyphonic music. In Bernhard's first example, a subdominant seventh is heard over the bar line. In his second example, a major seventh is created on the fourth beat of the first bar. These *duriusculus* or "hard" harmonies give the figure its name. The figure is no longer mentioned in his later *Bericht*, where Bernhard abandons the classification of the figures according to style. Indeed, the second example can be explained equally well through the *transitus irregularis*.

Bernhard (*Tractatus* p.82)

Cadentiae Duriusculae sind, welche etwas seltsame Dissonantzen vor denen beyden Schluß-Noten annehmen. Solche werden fast nur in Soliciniis und meistentheils in Arien und Tripeln angetroffen. Da aber einige in mehrstimmigen [Sachen] gefunden würden, so werden die übrigen Stimmen dermaßen gesetzt, daß solche keine Mißhelligkeit spühren lassen.

Cadentiae duriusculae are cadences in which some rather strange dissonances precede the final two notes. Such cadences occur almost exclusively in vocal solos and are most often found in arias and in triple meter sections. Should they occur in polyphonic works, however, the other voices must be set in such a manner that they do not allow any sense of disagreement.

CATABASIS, DESCENSUS: a descending musical passage which expresses descending, lowly, or negative images or affections.

The *catabasis* is used to depict musically either a descending or a lowly image supplied by the text, thereby creating the implied affection. The figure is first mentioned specifically by Kircher. However, as with its contrasting counterpart, the *anabasis*, the vivid musical expression of descending or lowly images had been linked to the concept of the musical-rhetorical figures since its inception.[1] In his definitions of the figures, Kircher emphasizes their role in expressing not only the text but also the associated affections. While Burmeister's *hypotyposis* was to be used to make the text or events "seem" (*videri*) present, Kircher's figures are to actualize the intended affection. The *catabasis*, like so many other musical-rhetorical figures, is called to do more than simply reflect the text: it is simultaneously image *and* source of the affection. In his definition of the figure, Walther mentions that the term is also used to describe a chromatically descending theme or *subjectum catabatum*. This would coincide with the description of Bernhard's *passus duriusculus*.

---

1. See *Anabasis*, *Hypotyposis*.

Kircher (*Musurgia* L.8, p.145)
Catabasis sive descensus periodus harmonica est, qua oppositos priori affectus pronunciamus servitutis, humilitatis, depressionis affectibus, atque infimis rebus exprimendes, ut illud Massaini: Ego autem humiliatus sum nimis, & illud Massentii: descenderunt in infernum viventes.

The *catabasis* or *descensus* is a musical passage through which we express affections opposite to those of the *anabasis*, such as servitude and humility, as well as lowly and base affections, as in: "I am, however, greatly humbled" (Massainus), or in "The living have descended into hell" (Massentius).

Janovka (*Clavis* p.56)
Catabasis sive Descensus est Periodus harmonica, qua oppositos Anabasi affectus pronunciamus, uti: servitutis, humilitatis, depressionis, infimarum denique verum, ut in textu: ego autem humiliatus sum nimis.

The *catabasis* or *descensus* is a musical passage through which we express affections opposite to those of the *anabasis*, such as servitude, humility, lowliness, baseness, and lastly truthfulness, as in the text: "I am, however, greatly humbled."

Vogt (*Conclave* p.150)
Catabasis descensus cum vox descendit, ut cum textu descendit ad infernos.

The *catabasis* or *descensus* occurs when the voice descends, as in the text: "He descended into hell."

Walther (*Lexicon*)
Catabasis, von καταβαίνω, descendo, ist ein harmonischer Periodus, wodurch etwas niedriges, gering- und verächtliches vorgestellt wird. z.E. Er ist hinunter gefahren. Ich bin sehr gedemüthiget. u.d.g. Daher heisset auch ein Ton-Weise, oder auch durch Semitonia ordentlich, und ohne einigen Sprung herunterwerts steigendes thema, ein Subjectum Catabatum.

The *catabasis*, from *katabaino, descendo*, is a musical passage through which lowly, insignificant, and disdainful things are represented, for example: "He has descended," "I am greatly humbled," and similar texts. For that reason a phrase or a theme which descends in semitones by step and without any leaps is called a *subjectum catabatum*.

Spiess (*Tractatus* p.155)
Cantabasis [sic], Descensus, Abfahrt. Heiβt in der Music, wann die Noten oder Sing-Stimmen, laut des Texts, mit den Worten absteigen. v.g. Descendit ad infernos.

The *catabasis, descensus*, or descent occurs in music when the notes or voices descend with the words, according to the text, as for example in "He descended into hell."

CATACHRESIS: see *FAUX BOURDON*

CELERITAS: see *TRANSITUS*

CERCAR DELLA NOTA: see *SUBSUMPTIO*

CIRCULATIO, CIRCULO, KYKLOSIS: a series of usually eight notes in a circular or sine wave formation.

The *circulatio* (*circulo*, *circolo*) is formed by positioning two opposite (rising and falling: *intendens* and *remittens*) *circuli mezzi* adjacent to each other in such a way that, were the two "half-circles" to be superimposed, a circle of notes would result. The figure is defined both as a text-explanatory musical-rhetorical figure as well as a simple ornament (*figura simplex*, *Manier*). This difference is further emphasized through the use of both Greek or Latin (Kircher, Janovka) and Italian terminology. Customarily, classical terminology is reserved for the musical-rhetorical figures while Italian is used for embellishing ornamentation and figurations. Only Kircher and Janovka explicitly correlate the *circulatio* with the expression of circular ideas or motion in the music's text. As a symbol of perfection, the musical circle has a long tradition of expressing not only circular concepts but also the eternal, infinite, and complete, ultimately symbolizing God.[1] Like virtually all of Kircher's figures, the *circulatio* is understood as a form of *hypotyposis*.[2] The remaining authors simply describe the motif's construction without referring to any text-expressive content. Even Walther, who frequently quotes Janovka in his *Lexicon*, does not mention the text-interpretive nature of the figure. Furthermore, he only defines the Italian term. While

---

1. W. Kirkendale, "*Circulatio*-Tradition, *Maria Lactans*, and Josquin as Musical Orator," *Acta Musicologica* 56 (1984), 69. In this exhaustive study of the musical circle's long history, Kirkendale points out that already "Hucbald understands by "*circulus*" a short group of notes which ends on the note with which it began, such as might be notated by the torculus neume." Ibid., 70, n.5. The suggestion that this musical device is to be linked with the rhetorical figure *circulus* (*circulo rhetorica*?) or the quite unrelated *redditio* is questionable, even though the terms may be related. Furthermore, there is no reason to believe that Nucius in his definition of *complexio* was describing the musical *circulatio* and not in fact a musical equivalent of the rhetorical *complexio*. While the *circulatio* is a short motif which returns to its beginning note, the *complexio* is a longer musical passage or phrase (Nucius says *Harmonia*) which opens and closes with the same material. See *Complexio*.

2. In a similar vein, Kircher defines *fuga* also as a text-expressive musical-rhetorical figure which can be used to depict a pursuit or flight, reflecting the literal meaning of the figure.

Vogt calls the figure by a Latin term, *circulus*, he includes it in his list of *Figurae simplices* and not among his text-expressive *figurae ideales*. Even though circular or infinite concepts are frequently expressed through a *circulatio*, such a content is not frequently associated with the figure itself.

Most writers (aside from Kircher and Janovka) explain the *circulo* as a formation out of two opposite *circuli mezzi*. While Vogt, Spiess, and Mattheson describe the *circulo mezzo* in accordance with Printz's definition, Walther's definition is based on Brossard, a description which agrees with Printz's *groppo* rather than *circulo mezzo*. In his definition of *groppo*, Walther explains that Brossard does not differentiate between *circulo mezzo* and *groppo*, both being four-note arching figures with common first and third rather than second and fourth notes.[1] Nonetheless, Walther's definition of the eight-note *circulo* is in agreement with that of the other authors, even though he describes it as two *circuli mezzi*. Mattheson defines only the *circulo mezzo*, but he adds a fifth note to the figure, presenting in fact an entire half-circle. In Spiess's example, two ascending and two descending *circuli mezzi* rather than one of each kind are adjoined, resulting in a figuration which does not agree with other *circuli*.

Kircher (*Musurgia* L.8, p.145)

Κύκλωσις sive circulatio est periodus harmonica, qua voces quasi in circulum agi videntur, servitque verbis actionem circularem exprimentibus, uti illud Philippe de Monte: Surgam et circumibo Civitatem.

The *kyklosis* or *circulatio* is a musical passage in which the voices appear to move in circular motion, and serves as an expression of words with a circular motion or content, as exemplified by Philippe de Monte in the text: "I will arise and surround the city."

Janovka (*Clavis* p.56)

Circulatio est Periodus harmonica, qua voces quasi in circulum agi videntur, servit que verbis actionem circularem exprimentibus, ut in hocce textu: surgam et circu[m]ibo civitatem.

The *circulatio* is a musical passage in which the voices appear to move in circular motion, and serves as an expression of words with a circular motion or content, as in the text: "I will arise and surround the city."

1. See *Groppo*.

Printz (*Phrynis Mytilenaeus* pt.2, p.49)

Circulo Mezo formiret im Schreiben einen halben Kreiβ / und bestehet in vier geschwinden ordentlich-gehenden Noten / deren andere und vierdte einerley / die erste und dritte unterschiedliche Stellen haben. Er ist entweder Intendens, so anfänglich auffsteiget / oder Remittens, so anfänglich absteiget.

The *circulo mezo* forms a half-circle in musical notation, and consists of four rapid notes moving by step, in which the second and fourth notes are on the same pitch while the first and third notes have different pitches. It is either *intendens*, beginning with ascending notes, or *remittens*, beginning with descending notes.

Printz (*Phrynis Mytilenaeus* pt.2, p.64)

Circulo ist / wenn zween Circuli mezi also zusammen gesezt werden / daβ Remittens dem Intendenti folge in der nechsten untern / oder Intendens dem Remittenti in der nechsten obern Clave.

The *circulo* occurs when two *circuli mezi* are combined in such fashion that the *remittens* follows the *intendens* one step lower or the *intendens* follows the *remittens* one step higher.

Vogt (*Conclave* p.148)

Alia vocatur circulus, ut.

Another [*figura simplex*] is called *circulus*, for example:

Walther (*Lexicon*)

Circolo, ein Circul oder Creyβ; also heisset 1.) die Art des doppelten CƆ oder ◯, so man noch in alten Musicalien nach dem clavi signata gesetzt antrifft. 2.) wenn zween Circoli mezzi also zusammen- und aneinander gehänget werden, daβ, so sie über einander gesetzt werden solten, sie einen vollkommenen Circul darstellen würden.

The *circolo* is a circle, and occurs: (1) as a form of a double CƆ or ◯, which is still encountered in old compositions as a time signature after the clef; (2) when two *circoli mezzi* are combined and follow each other in such fashion that, should they be superimposed upon each other, they would visually represent a complete circle.

Circulo mezzo ist eine aus vier Noten bestehende, und die Gestalt eines halben Circuls vorstellende Figur.

A *circulo mezzo* is a figure which consists of four notes and visually represents the form of a half-circle.

Printz aber . . . nennet dergleichen Figur, deren erste und dritte Note einerley, die zweyte und vierdte aber ungleiche Stellen haben, ein Groppo.

Printz, however, calls the same figure, whose first and third notes have the same pitch while the second and fourth notes have different pitches, a *groppo*.

Mattheson (*Capellmeister* p.116)

Der sogenannte Halb-Circkel, Circolo mezzo, ist fast dieser Art; doch etwa um die Helfte kleiner, als der Groppo, wenn die Gestalt der Noten, die gleichsam einen halben Circkel vor Augen stellet, betrachtet wird. Eigentlich ist es eine solche Figur, dadurch aus wenigen Grund-Noten gewisser maassen ihrer mehr, und kleinere gemacht werden.

The so-called half-circle or *circolo mezzo* is very similar to yet half as large as the *groppo*. It occurs when the formation of the notes depicts a half-circle, as it were. In fact, it is the kind of figure through which numerous smaller notes are formed out of a few fundamental notes.

Spiess (*Tractatus* p.156)

Circulo, ein Circul- oder Creiß-Figur, bestehend aus 8. geschwinden Noten; wird also genennt, weil sie gleichsam ein Circul formirt.

The *circulo* is a circle figure which consists of eight rapid notes. It is thus called because it forms a circle, as it were.

So sie aber 4. Noten hat, wird sie Circulo Mezzo oder Halbcircul-Figur benamset, wie Num.11 ausweiset; allwo auch der Unterscheidt zwischen einem Groppo, und einem Circulo Mezzo sich äusseret.

Should the figure consist of four notes, it is called a *circulo mezzo* or half-circle figure, as illustrated in no.11. This also illustrates the difference between a *groppo* and a *circulo mezzo*.

CLIMAX, GRADATIO: (1) a sequence of notes in one voice repeated either at a higher or lower pitch; (2) two voices moving in ascending or descending parallel motion; (3) a gradual increase or rise in sound and pitch, creating a growth in intensity.

A gradual shift in the definition of *climax* or *gradatio* throughout the seventeenth century is evident in both rhetoric and music. Quintilian and Susenbrotus use the term to describe a stepwise construction (*climax*, *gradus*: step, rung, ladder) of an oration in which a point is repeated and explained before proceeding to the next one. Although the series of expressions might be of increasing intensity, this is certainly not necessary. Such an incremental intensification is termed *auxesis* or *incrementum*. Gottsched no longer differentiates between the two rhetorical devices and therefore uses the terms *incrementum* and *gradatio* interchangeably. Reflecting the eighteenth-century emphasis on affective expression, he highlights the aspect of incremental growth in intensity. Gottsched thereby brings the elements of growth (*auxesis*, *incrementum*) and graduated progression (*climax*, *gradatio*) together in the one figure.

A similar development in the musical definitions of the *climax* or *gradatio* can also be observed. Burmeister, Nucius, and Thuringus define the figure simply as a graduated progression, parallel to the definitions of Quintilian and Susenbrotus. Burmeister describes the *climax* as the repetition of a certain sequence of notes at higher *or* lower pitches.[1] Nucius and Thuringus define two voices moving in ascending *or* descending parallel motion—at thirds or tenths—as a *climax* or *gradatio*. The use of the term *gradatim* in reference to simple stepwise melodic motion is encountered in most treatises of the time without any reference to growth or intensification.[2] The similarity between Burmeister and

1. In his *Hypomnematum* Burmeister describes the *palillogia* as a repetition of a theme at various pitches in different voices. In his later *Musica Poetica* he places limitations on these repetitions: they must occur in only one voice and at the same pitch. It is also in this treatise that Burmeister introduces the new figure *climax*, which repeats a theme at different pitches but in the same voice, thereby assuming in part the role of the old *climax*.

2. Similarly, Charles Butler described one of the forms of consecution (the progression from one interval to another) with the term *Gradation*: "But the continued Consecution of other Concords is allowed, as well ascending and descending, as immorant in the same place: especially of thirds and sixths in (1) Gradation, and (2)

Nucius's definitions is reinforced through their common choice of a musical example which demonstrates the figure, the motet *Maria Magdalena* by Clemens. Both early-seventeenth-century rhetorical and musical definitions reflect the literal meaning of the terms: both *climax* and *gradus* simply mean "step." In fact, the verbal root of *climax* (*klino*: to bow, turn away) suggests a downward rather than an upward or intensifying motion.

In Kircher's *Musurgia Universalis* the *climax/gradatio* is described as an affection- and text-expressive device for the first time, in accordance with Kircher's general understanding of the musical-rhetorical figures. Intensification takes precedence over graduated progression. This interpretation is then adopted by all subsequent authors. Only Walther's *Lexicon* still includes the older definition. With his terminological interests, Walther gathers together the diverse definitions of a term, including those which may no longer be current. He defines *climax/gradatio* first according to Ahle, second according to Nucius and Thuringus, third according to Burmeister but limiting the repetitions to ascending ones, and finally as an upwards-modulating canon. Scheibe and Forkel introduce the dynamic concept of *crescendo* into their definitions of the *gradatio*, applying the device on a much larger scale than previous authors had done. As such it becomes an appropriate description of the famous Mannheim Crescendo.

The combination of the *auxesis* and *climax* by Baroque authors has led to some confusion regarding the understanding of the two terms. Unlike Walther, some contemporary writers have chosen to define the terms together with only one definition. Any diverging definition of the terms is then described as "somewhat of an aberration."[1] Furthermore, in focusing on only one definition, the possibility of tracing a term's terminological development and providing insight into the historical context and developing aesthetic of musical concepts is severely hindered.

---

sometime in Skipping." *The Principles of Musik*, 57.

1. Unger regularly makes this mistake, resulting in numerous misunderstandings and questionable descriptions of figures, exemplified in his discussion of *Gradatio, auxesis, climax* (*Beziehungen*, 77). Instead of following the development of the terms, Unger seeks to match a certain compositional device with a term, thereby frequently disregarding the figures' diverse terminology and their ongoing development.

Quintilian (*Institutio* IX.iii.54)

Gradatio, quae dicitur κλίμαξ . . . repetit enim quae dicta sunt et, priusquam ad aliud descendat, in prioribus resistit.

The *gradatio*, also called *climax*, . . . repeats what has already been said and, before proceeding to something else, dwells on that which preceded.

Susenbrotus (*Epitome* p.84)

Gradatio κλίμαξ, est quum consequentia membra, ab iisdem ordiuntur est, quoties ita per gradus oratio distinguitur, ut dictio finiens particulam praecedentem, inchoet sequentem, hoc modo. Nam quae reliqua spes libertatis manet, si illis et quod libet, licet: et quod licet, possunt: et quod possunt, audent: et quod audent, faciunt: et quod faciunt, nobis molestum non est?

A *gradatio* or *climax* occurs when consequent phrases begin with the same words that ended the preceding phrase, frequently altering the case endings. Or it occurs when an oration is constructed by step in which a word which ends a phrase begins the following one, for example: For the remaining hope abides in freedom, and if it should please them, it is permitted; and whatever is permitted, they consider; and whatever they consider, they dare; and whatever they dare, they do; and whatever they do, does it not trouble us greatly?

Gottsched (*Redekunst* p.280)

Endlich kömmt noch Gradatio oder Climax, da man stufenweise von einem Wort auf ein anders, und von diesem noch auf ein stärkers fortschreitet.

And finally there is the *gradatio* or *climax*, through which one progresses by step from one word to the next, and from this to a yet more forceful one.

Gottsched (*Redekunst* p.284)

Incrementum s. Gradatio. Wenn man stufenweise von einer geringern Sache zu einer größern hinauf steiget.

Incrementum or *Gradatio*. When one progresses stepwise from a weak expression to a stronger one.

Gottsched (*Dichtkunst* p.344)

Man merke also zum XXX. das Aufsteigen (Gradatio), wenn man gleichsam stuffenweise von einer geringen Sache zu etwas höherm fortschreitet, und also immer was wichtigers sagt.

The next figure is the *gradatio*, through which one progresses by steps from a weak expression to a stronger one, thereby expressing thoughts of continually greater importance.

Burmeister (*Musica Poetica* p.63)

Climax est, quae per gradus intervallorum similes sonos repetit, ut hoc exemplum indicat.

The *climax* repeats similar notes but on pitches one step apart, as indicated in the following example:

Nucius (*Musices Poeticae* p.G2v)

Quid est Climax? Cum per Arsin & Thesin, binae voces similiter gradiuntur, ut cum Discantus & Basis in multis Decimis, aut Basis & Tenor in pluribus tertiis procedunt. Huius figurae usus circa finem Harmoniae potissimum spectatur, ubi auditorem avide finem expectantem, adhuc detinere studemus.

What is a *climax*? It occurs when two voices progress upwards or downwards in parallel motion, for example when the soprano and bass proceed in parallel tenths or the bass and tenor in parallel thirds. The use of this figure is most frequent at the end of a composition, to which we strive to engage the listener who eagerly awaits the conclusion.

Thuringus (*Opusculum* p.125)

Quid est Climax? Quae & gradatio dicitur, est cum per Arsin & Thesin, binae voces similiter gradiuntur, & cum Discantus & Basis in multis Decimis, & Basis & Tenor in pluribus tertiis procedunt: Huius Figurae usus circa finem harmoniae potissimum spectatur ubi auditorem avide finem &spectantem, adhuc detinere studemus.

What is a *climax*? This figure, which is also called *gradatio*, occurs when two voices progress upwards or downwards in parallel motion, for example when the soprano and bass proceed in parallel tenths or the bass and tenor in parallel thirds. The use of this figure is most frequent at the end of a composition, to which we strive to engage the listener who eagerly awaits the conclusion.

Kircher (*Musurgia* L.8, p.145)

Vocatur Climax sive gradatio, estque periodus harmonica gradatim ascendens adhiberique solet, in affectibus amoris divini & desideriis patriae coelestis, ut illud Orlandi. (Quemadmodum desiderat cervus ad fontes aquarum).

The *climax* or *gradatio* is a musical passage which ascends by step, and is often used in affections of divine love and yearning for the heavenly kingdom, as in Orlando's *Quemadmodum desiderat cervus* ("Like as the hart desireth the waterbrooks, so longeth my soul after Thee, O Lord.")

Ahle (*Sommer-Gespräche* p.17)

Setzet er aber: jauchzet und singet / singet und rühmet / rühmet und lobet; so ist es eine Climax.

But were he to write: Rejoice and sing / sing and glorify / glorify and praise; then it is a *climax*.

Janovka (*Clavis* p.55)

Climax sive Gradatio est Periodus Harmonica gradatim ascendens, adhiberique solet in affectibus amoris divini, & desideriis Patriae Coelestis, ut intextu fieret: quemadmodum desiderat cervus ad fontes aquarum, ita &c.

See Kircher for translation.

Vogt (*Conclave* p.151)

Climax, Gradualis ascensus. Figura est communis.

The *climax* is a widely used figure which ascends by step.

Walther (*Lexicon*)

Climax, oder Gradatio, κλίμαξ, ist 1) eine Wort-Figur wenn z.E. gesetzt wird: Jauchzet und singet, singet und rühmet, rühmet und lobet. 2) eine Noten-Figur, wenn nemlich zwo Stimmen per Arsin & Thesin, d.i. auf- und unterwerts gradatim Tertzenweise mit einander fortgehen. 3) wenn eine Clausul mit und ohne Cadentz etlichemahl immediate nach einander immer um ein Ton höher angebracht wird. 4) dörffte auch diesen Nahmen derjenige vierstimmige Canon verdienen, welcher, so offt zwo Stimmen von vorne wiederum anheben, allezeit um einen Ton hoher steiget, da inzwischen die andern beyden Stimmen noch im vorigen tieffern Tone sich aufhalten, und dennoch zusammen klingen.

The *climax* or *gradatio* is: (1) a word figure, for example when the words are set as follows: Rejoice and sing, sing and glorify, glorify and praise; (2) a musical figure which occurs when two voices progress upwards and downwards by step in parallel thirds; (3) when a passage with or without a cadence is immediately repeated several times at progressively higher pitches; (4) this term can also be given to a four-part canon in which, as the first two voices re-enter, each time one note higher, the other two voices remain in the previous key and yet still harmonize.

Scheibe (*Critischer Musicus* p.697)

Das Aufsteigen, (Gradatio), wenn man gleichsam stufenweise von einem schwächern Satze zu höhern Sätzen fortschreitet, und also den Ausdruck der Sache, oder die Stärke der Musik immer wichtiger und nachdrücklicher machet. . . . Wie schön ist es nicht, wenn der Anfang nur ganz schwach und fließend ist, die Folge aber immer höher steigt, und wenn daraus endlich die stärkste Melodie und Harmonie entsteht? Dieses rühret und setzet die aufmerksamen Zuhörer in Verwunderung.

The ascension (*gradatio*) occurs when one progresses by step from a weak passage to stronger ones, thereby gradually increasing the importance and emphasis of the expression or music. . . . Is it not delightful when the music begins most tentatively and, becoming progressively stronger and higher, finally evolves into the most powerful melody and harmony? This moves the attentive listener and causes wonder and amazement.

Forkel (*Geschichte der Musik* p.58)

Eine der schönsten und wirksamsten Figuren ist die Gradation (Steigerung). Man steigt gleichsam stuffenweise von schwächern Sätzen zu stärkern fort, und drückt dadurch eine immer zunehmende Leidenschaft aus. Die gewöhnliche Art, sie in der Tonsprache auszudrücken, geschieht durch das crescendo, womit man einen Satz vom gelindesten Piano an, bis zu dem stärksten Fortissimo fortführt. Eine bessere Art ist es, wenn diese Steigerung durch beständigen allmählichen Zuwachs an neuen Gedanken und

One of the most delightful and effective figures is the *gradatio* (intensification). This is a stepwise progression from weaker passages to stronger ones, thereby expressing an always increasingly powerful affection. The conventional musical expression of this figure employs the crescendo, progressing from the quietest *piano* to the strongest *fortissimo*. A superior form of the *gradatio* is achieved when this intensification combines a crescendo with a gradual and continuous growth in new ideas and modulations.

Modulationen bewerkstelligt, und dann
mit der ersten Art verbunden wird.

COLORATURA: see *VARIATIO*

COMMISSURA: see *TRANSITUS*

COMPLEXIO, COMPLEXUS, SYMPLOCE: a musical passage which repeats its opening phrase at its conclusion.

The first musical reference to this figure appears in a rhetorical text without specifying a distinct musical device. In describing the *symploce*, Henry Peacham the Elder mentions that the figure is "pleasant to the eare, which of some is called the Rhetoricall circle, and of others the Musicall repetition." At the end of the Baroque, Gottsched also comments on the musicality of this rhetorical figure, stating that "it is particularly pleasing in musical pieces." As Peacham indicates, the rhetorical *symploce* or *complexio* is a combination of two other figures, the *anaphora* and the *epiphora*. While *anaphora* signifies a common beginning of a number of subsequent sentences, *epiphora* signifies common endings of the same. The *symploce* or *complexio* ("combination, summary"; from *syn-*, *con-*, *cum-*, with, together; and *plectare* or *pleko*, to weave) weaves the two figures together into a new formation: common opening and closing words or phrases in a number of subsequent sentences or passages. The distinction between this figure and the *epanalepsis*, which signifies the repetition of the opening word(s) at the close of one sentence, is not maintained in the musical *Figurenlehren*.[1]

Burmeister is the first to mention *symploce*, but he does not define it as a figure. Rather it is a compositional error which occurs through the "simultaneous placing of the disparate signs of a flat and a sharp [in a chord], thereby disturbing the nature of the perfect consonances by

1. See *Epanalepsis*, *Epanadiplosis*.

mixing the properties of one harmony with that of another."[1] Burmeister is driven by a concern to clearly identify musical phenomena, both figures and other compositional devices, with familiar and suitable vocabulary. The use of rhetorical terminology to identify musical devices besides the *ornamenta* is recognized and commended by a fellow *Kantor*, Statius Olthoff.[2] Burmeister's choice of terminology is governed chiefly by a term's literal or general meaning rather than its specific rhetorical content. In choosing the term *symploce* he wishes to underscore not the interweaving of two distinct figures of repetition (the specific content) but rather of two harmonic species indicated by disparate accidentals.

Nucius, Thuringus, and Walther employ the Latin term *complexio* to identify a certain musical-rhetorical figure of repetition. Their definition, however, is not identical to the classical rhetorical understanding of the term but rather, like Gottsched's, describes *complexio* as the repetition of a passage's opening at its close. The specific reference in their definition that this musical device occurs "in imitation of the poets," indicates that Gottsched was not the first rhetorician to describe the *complexio* with an *epanalepsis* definition. Kircher, and after him Janovka, define the *complexus*, as they call it, with a divergent and more affective definition, a practice also to be observed in their definitions of *repetitio* and *climax*. However, it is not clear what is meant by their description of the figure. The reference to a musical passage in which all voices appear to "conspire as if they were one voice" may indicate a unison passage within a composition.[3] This would portray a literal rather than rhetorical meaning of the term. It is not likely that this refers

---

1. "Symploke est Disparatorum enunciandorum ♭ aut † & # appositio vel actu vel potentia permixta, omnem consonantiarum perfectarum, tum etiam suam ipsius naturam invertens, uniusque concentus naturam naturae alterius complicans" *(Musica poetica*, 30). In using both sharps and flats as accidentals in one harmony, the composer would be mixing major semitones (consisting of 5 commata) with minor semitones (having 4 commata). This procedure is later defined by Bernhard as a figure called *consonantia impropria*. See also *Apotomia*.

2. See above, 115f.

3. In his discussion of expressive composition in the *stylus theatralis*, Bernhard also suggests that the repetition of a text might occur "in *unisono* where elegance this allows" ("Die Wiederhohlung des Textes soll entweder garnicht, oder nur an den Orten, wo es die Zierligkeit zuläßt im *Unisono* gebraucht werden"). *Tractatus*, ch.35, §8.

to a homophonic passage, similar to a *noema*. The specification that the figure is used "only in affections of machination" seems to preclude the interpretation of *complexus* as the "pleasant and soothing" device which Burmeister and Thuringus describe.[1]

After Kircher's and Janovka's unorthodox definition of *complexus*, *epanalepsis* becomes the preferred term for this figure of repetition. In addition, Vogt also introduces the term *epanadiplosis* to describe the same device. In his *Lexicon*, Walther defines all three terms with similar definitions, reflecting his intent to catalog and define all known terms irrespective of possible contradictions or duplications.

Susenbrotus (*Epitome* p.54)
Complexio, Συμπλοκή est cum orationis alicuius membra idem principium eundemque finem sortiuntur.

The *complexio* or *symploce* occurs when subsequent parts of an oration are given the same beginning and ending.

Peacham (*Garden of Eloquence* p.43)
Symploce is a forme of speech which maketh many members or clauses following to have the same beginning & the same ending which the first had going before, comprising both the last ornaments [anaphora and epiphora] in one. . . . This figure may serve to any affection, and is a singular ornament, pleasant to the eare, which of some is called the Rhetoricall circle, and of others the Musicall repetition.

Gottsched (*Redekunst* p.280)
Symploce. Wenn Anfang und Ende vieler aufeinander folgender Absätze einerley sind.

Symploce. When a number of subsequent passages have the same beginnings and endings.

Gottsched (*Dichtkunst* p.324)
Hierher [repetitio] gehören denn auch die Wiederholungen, da man in ganzen Strophen die ersten Zeilen und Wörter, am Ende derselben noch einmal brauchet, welches sonderlich in musikalischen

Another form of the *repetitio* consists of a repetition of the opening lines and words of a stanza at its conclusion. This can be called a *symploce*, and is particularly pleasing in musical pieces.

1. See *Noema*. Unfortunately, I have not succeeded in locating the Clemens motet *Astiterunt Reges* (Psalm 2.2) referred to by Kircher, which would no doubt help clarify Kircher's understanding of the *complexus*.

Stücken angenehm fällt, und Symploce heiβen kann.

Nucius (*Musices Poeticae* p.G3)
Quid est Complexio? Cum Harmoniae initium in fine repetitur, ad imitationem Poetarum qui saepe uno eodemque vocabulo versum incipiunt & claudunt: ut Egl:7. Ambo florentes aetatibus, Arcades ambo. Huius Schematis multa sunt Exempla Musica, ut in Alleluja surrexit pastor bonus. Item in Noë, Noë & iterum Noë: Vitam quae faciunt Jacobi Vaët.

What is a *complexio*? It occurs when the beginning of a *harmonia* is repeated at the end, in imitation of the poets, who frequently begin and end a verse with the same word, as in, "Both in the flower of life, Arcadians both." There are many musical examples of this figure, such as *Alleluja surrexit pastor bonus* and *Noë, Noë & iterum Noë* by Jacobus Vaët.

Thuringus (*Opusculum* p.125)
Quid est Complexio? Cum harmoniae initium in fine repetitur, ad imitationem poetarum, qui saepe uno eodemque vocabulo versum incipiunt & claudunt.

What is a *complexio*? It occurs when the beginning of a *harmonia* is repeated at the end, in imitation of the poets, who frequently begin and end a verse with the same word.

Kircher (*Musurgia* L.8, p.145)
Συμπλοκή sive Complexus est periodus harmonica, qua voces quasi in unum si conspirare videntur, adhiberique solet in affectibus machinationum, ut illud Clementis non Papa, Astiterunt Reges terra adversus Dominum, & adversus Christum eius.

The *symploce* or *complexus* is a musical passage in which the voices appear to sound together as though they were one. It is only used in affections of machination, as in Clemens non Papa's *Astiterunt Reges* ("The kings of the earth take their stand, and the rulers take counsel together against the Lord and against His Anointed," Ps.2.2).

Janovka (*Clavis* p.55)
Complexus dicitur Periodus harmonica, qua voces in unum conspirare videntur, adhiberique solet in affectibus machinationum, ut si textus sit ille: Astiterunt Reges terra adversus Dominum, et adversus Christum eius.

The *complexus* is a musical passage in which all the voices appear to sound together in unison. It is only used in affections of machination, as in the following text: "The kings of the earth take their stand against the Lord and against His Anointed One." (Ps.2.2)

Walther (*Lexicon*)
Complexio heisset: wenn der Anfang eines harmonischen Satzes am Ende wiederholt wird, ad imitationem der Poeten, welche öffters mit einem Worte einen Vers anfangen, und mit demselben auch wiederum schlüssen. Z.E. Crescit amor nummi, quantum ipsa pecuma crescit.

The *complexio* occurs when the beginning of a musical passage is repeated at its end, in imitation of the poets, who frequently begin and end a verse with one and the same word.

CONGERIES, SYNATHROISMUS: an accumulation of alternating perfect and imperfect consonances, such as root-position and first-inversion triads.

Quintilian and Susenbrotus both define *congeries* as an accumulation of terms describing an object, a form of *amplificatio*. An object might be described through synonymous expressions or through more disparate ones. While Quintilian defines the figure as a collection of similar expressions, coinciding with Susenbrotus's *synonymia*, Susenbrotus defines *congeries* or *coacervatio* as a collection of varying terms, coinciding with Quintilian's *synathroismus*.

The musical *congeries* is included only in Burmeister's *Figurenlehre*. Three of the rhetorical terms, *congeries*, *synathroismus*, and *coacervatio,* appear in his definitions, the first two as identifying terms and the third as a description of the figure. The rhetorical accumulation of various terms is replaced with a musical accumulation of various types of consonances, thereby establishing a relationship between the rhetorical and musical content of the term, both reflecting its literal meaning (*congeries*, from *congerere*, to gather, accumulate). Musically, the description of an "object" (a certain harmony) is achieved through an "accumulation" (*congeries*, *coacervatio*) of perfect consonances (root-position triads with the proportions 3:4:5) and imperfect consonances (first-inversion triads with the proportions 5:6:8). These musical expressions are at once synonymous and disparate. Like the rhetorical *congeries*, the musical device is also used for purposes of amplification: "The *corpus* of the composition [i.e. *confutatio/confirmatio*], situated between the *exordium* and *finem* sections, comprises *congeries*, by whose texture, similarly to the varied arguments of the rhetorical *confirmatio*, minds are penetrated in order to clearly grasp and reflect on the sense [of the text]."[1]

Burmeister's inclusion of *congeries* in the *figurae tam harmoniae quam melodiae* is explained through the figure's relationship to the *faux*

1. "Corpus Cantilenarum est intra Exordium Finem affectionum sive periodorum comprehensa congeries, quibus textus velut variis Confirmationis Rhetoricae argumentis, animis insinuantur, ad sententiam clarius arripiendam & considerandam." *Musica poetica*, 72.

bourdon. This association is expressly mentioned in Burmeister's *faux bourdon* definition. While the *congeries* features an alternation between root-position and first-inversion triads resulting from continuous syncopations through suspensions in one of the voices "in which parallel motion has been abandoned," the *faux bourdon* features a series of first-inversion triads resulting from parallel motion between three voices at the third and the fourth. The *congeries* is thereby a *faux bourdon* with a syncopated upper voice. Thus both the *faux bourdon*, also termed *simul procedentia* (similar progression), and the associated *congeries* are not primarily descriptions of chord progressions but rather specific methods of voice leading which result in the described chordal textures. Burmeister's understanding of a musical composition is still governed by sixteenth-century imitative counterpoint rather than chordal, *basso continuo* texture, prompting him to classify the devices as both harmonic and melodic figures. While concerning themselves with individual voices or *melodiae*, the entire *harmonia* is affected. With the changing concept of music and the resulting redefinition of *faux bourdon* as *catachresis*, the justification of the *congeries* as a figure through its association with *faux bourdon* is removed, resulting in its omission in subsequent discussions of the musical-rhetorical figures.

Quintilian (*Institutio* VIII.iv.26,27)

Potest adscribi amplificationi congeries quoque verborum ac sententiarum idem significantium. Nam etiamsi non per gradus ascendant, tamen velut acervo quodam adlevantur. . . . Simile est hoc figurae, quam συναθροισμόν vocant, sed illic plurium rerum est congeries, hic unius multiplicatio.

The *congeries* or accumulation of words and sentences of identical meaning can also be regarded as a form of amplification. For although the expressions do not climax by step, they nonetheless heighten the argument through such an accumulation. . . . This is similar to the figure called *synathroismus*, except that while the later accumulates numerous different expressions, the former elaborates on only one thought.

Susenbrotus (*Epitome* p.75)

Congeries Coacervatio, est dictionum, res varias significantium enumeratio. Quale est illud ad Rom. 1. Plenos omni iniquitate malitia, dolo scortatione, avaritia, malignitate, contentione, etc. Differt a synonymia, quia in hac unius rei est multiplicatio, in illa multarum rerum congeries.

The *congeries* or *coacervatio* is a sequence of words with varying content, as exemplified in Romans, chapter 1: "being filled with all unrighteousness, wickedness, greed, evil, full of envy, murder, strife, deceit, malice, gossip, slander," etc. In contrast to the *synonymia*, which is an elaboration of one thought, the *congeries* is an accumulation of numerous different thoughts.

Gottsched (*Redekunst* p.288)
Cumulus. Wenn man viele Dinge zusammen häufet, und eine Menge kurzgefaßter Vorstellungen geschwinde hintereinander, gleichsam in einem Othem, heraus stößt, seine Zuhörer desto stärker zu rühren.

Cumulus. When a number of thoughts are amassed, and numerous short expressions are blurted out in rapid succession as if in one breath, in order to forcefully move the listeners.

Burmeister (*Hypomnematum*)
Congeries in tribus saltem vocibus tam perfectas, quam imperfectas concordantiarum species, vel in ascensum vel in descensum coacervat & per vices commutat.

The *congeries* amasses either ascending or descending perfect as well as imperfect consonances using at least three voices, causing an alternation in harmony.

Burmeister (*Musica Poetica* p.65)
Congeries Συνατρίσμὸς est coacervatio specierum concordantium tam Perfectarum, quam Imperfectarum, quarum par motus est concessus.

The *congeries* or *synatrismos* is an accumulation of perfect and imperfect consonances, in which parallel motion has been abandoned.

CONSONANTIAE IMPROPRIAE: false consonances, such as certain fourths, diminished or augmented fifths, augmented seconds, and diminished sevenths.

The use of the various augmented or diminished consonances is not normally allowed in the strict *stylus gravis*. Bernhard, whose concept of the figures is determined by an acceptable use of dissonance, justifies these intervals through passing notes (*transitus*) or suspensions (*syncopatio*), both devices permitted in *stylus gravis* composition. It is only in his *Tractatus* that Bernhard identifies the various irregular intervals as figures.[1] The *tertia deficiens* and its inversion, the *sexta superflua*, are listed as *consonantiae impropriae* but are also given separate consideration as figures only used in the *stylus theatralis*. However, these two intervals are notated not as thirds and sixths as their name would imply but rather as augmented seconds and diminished sevenths. In naming these intervals, Bernhard is not interested in their written form but in their harmonic construction. Mathematically, the augmented second is in fact smaller than the minor third, the same being true for the inverted intervals.[2] Therefore, these intervals cannot be written as forms of the third or sixth and are thereby "false." Because the second and seventh are not included in the list of consonant intervals, Bernhard classifies them as thirds and sixths. However, because of their extreme harmonic construction, they are not deemed to be "true" consonants and are therefore *impropriae*.

Bernhard (*Tractatus* p.79)

Consonantiae impropriae sind alle drei Species der Quartae, und Quinta deficiens und superflua, Sexta superflua, und Tertia deficiens. Die erste Species der Quartae nemlich die völlige, so aus 2 Tonis und einem Semitonio besteht, ist von denen Heutigen privilegiret, und für consonant angenommen worden, dergestalt, daß die auch loco impari bißweilen kann gebraucht werden, doch also daß sie (1) nicht in saltu sondern in gradu sey. (2) die tieffeste Stimme stille stehe, ehe die Quarta angehet, und biß eine andere Consonantz auch in Gradu vorüber sey. (3) Daß die Sexta darüber gebraucht werde [, als:]

The *consonantiae impropriae* include all three species of the fourth, the diminished and augmented fifth, the augmented sixth, and the diminished third. The first species of the fourth, namely the perfect, which consists of two tones and a semitone, is privileged by today's composers and accepted as a consonance, and can at times even be used on an uneven [strong] beat. However, (1) it must be approached by step and not by leap; (2) the lowest voice must remain sustained before the fourth is sounded and until another consonance likewise approached by step is sounded; (3) the sixth must sound above it, as follows:

---

1. Besides omitting the *consonantiae impropriae* in the *Bericht*, other figures explicitly mentioned only in the *Tractatus* include *prolongatio*, *syncopatio catachrestica*, *passus* and *saltus duriusculus*, *mutatio toni*, *inchoatio imperfecta*, *longinqua distantia*, *quaesitio notae*, and *cadentiae duriusculae*.

2. The major third minus the diatonic semitone is less than a minor third: $5:4 \times 15:16 = 75:64 < 6:5$.

Vor Quarta und Quinta sowohl deficiente als superflua daβ solche in Mittelstimmen vor Consonirend passiren, ist droben Cap.17 No.5 albereit gemeldet worden. . . . Sexta Superflua und Tertia deficiens wird nur in Stylo Theatrali zugelaβen, wovon drunten.

Regarding both diminished and augmented fourths and fifths, it has already been mentioned above (ch.14 no.5) that these are accepted as consonant in middle voices. . . . The augmented sixth and diminished third are only admitted in the *stylus theatralis*, discussed below.

Bernhard (*Tractatus* p.89)
Tertia deficiens ist ein Intervallum so noch nicht gar eine Tertia minor ist, und bestehet in folgenden clavibus:

The *tertia deficiens* [diminished third] is an interval which is not quite a minor third, and is written as follows:

Exempla wie sie gebraucht wird.

Examples of how it is used:

Sexta Superflua ist Sexta minor addito Semitonio majore, und bestehet in dergleichen clavibus.

The *sexta superflua* [augmented sixth] is a minor sixth with an added major semitone, and is written as follows:

CONTRAPOSITIO: see *ANTITHESIS*

CORTA: a three-note figure in which one note's duration equals the sum of the other two.

The *corta*, which simply means "short" in Italian, is a concise rhythmic figure which belongs to the species of ornamental *figurae simplices* (Vogt). The term does not refer to the duration of the entire figure, as this could be the same as the *bombus* or *circulo mezzo*. Rather, it refers to the number of notes employed to construct the figuration. Neither the term nor any accompanying definitions suggest an expressive content or application of the figure. However, due to the inherent rhythmic drive of a series of *cortae*, it is frequently used in compositions which wish to express agitated or joyful affections. The *corta* also forms the basis of Printz's *suspirans*, where the one longer note is subdivided into a rest and a note of equal value to the other two.

Printz (*Phrynis Mytilenaeus* pt.2, p.54)

Figura Corta bestehet aus dreyen geschwinden Noten / deren doch eine so lang ist / als die übrigen beyde zugleich.

The *figura corta* consists of three rapid notes, one of which has a duration equal to that of the other two combined.

Walther (*Lexicon*)

Figura corta bestehet aus drey geschwinden Noten, deren eine allein so lang ist, als die übrigen beyde.

The *figura corta* consists of three rapid notes, one of which has a duration equal to that of the other two.

Spiess (*Tractatus* p.156)

Curta, kurtze, kleine, geringe, wird sie vermuthlich darum genennet, weil diese Figur nicht aus 4. oder mehrern, wie alle andere Figurae, sondern nur aus 3. Noten bestehet.

The *curta*, meaning short, small, slight, is probably called such because it consists of only three rather than of four or more notes, like all the other *figurae* [*simplices*].

DEMINUTIO: see *TRANSITUS*

DESCENSUS: see *CATABASIS*

DIABASIS: see *METABASIS*

DIMINUTIO, MEIOSIS: (1) various elaborations of longer notes through subdivision into notes of lesser duration; (2) a restatement of thematic material in proportionally shorter note-values.

The *diminutio* has a long musical as well as rhetorical tradition. In both disciplines it is a form of elaboration which can lead to a fault if exaggerated. Quintilian uses the Greek term *meiosis* to describe such a fault, but indicates that the device can be used appropriately as a figure. Susenbrotus points out that the *diminutio* is an understated elaboration of something or someone for the purposes of expressiveness or decorum. Erasmus describes it as a "plentitude of words. Sometimes it has the savor of hyperbole as in 'shorter than a pygmy.'"[1]

The musical *diminutio* originates in eleventh-century florid *organum*, in which the melismatic *duplum* is regarded as a *diminutio* on the *cantus firmus*. In the early-fourteenth-century treatise *De diminutione contrapuncti* (*CS* III, 62ff.), the anonymous author explains how to set numerous notes in the counterpoint against one note of the *cantus firmus*. Gradually the practice of *diminutio* was expanded to incorporate the embellishment of a melodic line in counterpoint. During the Renaissance, the practice of *diminutio* "is not merely arabesque embellishment, but now also serves as a means of expressing the text and the affection."[2] *Diminutio* continued to refer to both an improvised addition to a composition and a consciously composed form of elaboration. The preferred terms for these embellishments are the Italian *passagio* and *coloratura*. While Praetorius does not present a systematic *Figurenlehre*, he does define various associated terms in his writings, including *diminutio*. Both he and Walther give *coloratura* as an alternative term.[3] Unique to Prae-

1. Sonnino, *Handbook*, 95.
2. H. Engel, "Diminution," *Musik in Geschichte und Gegenwart* 3: 493.
3. In his definition of *variatio*, Bernhard lists *passagio* and *coloratura* as alternative terms. The term *divisiones* or *divisions* is also used to refer to ornamentation. In his *Phrynis Mytilenaeus* (pt.2, 47) Printz uses the German translation of this term, *Zertheilung*, in defining the *variationes*.

torius is the distinction between the *diminutiones*, which move by step (*gradatim*) using the embellishments *accentus*, *tremulo* (defined as a trill), *groppo*, and *tirata*, and the *passagi*, which use ornaments moving by leap, step, or remaining on the same note. Although Walther also distinguishes between the *diminutiones* which move by step and those which move by leap, this differentiation is not reflected in his terminology. Under the *diminutio* (or *coloratura*) he lists all of the various *figurae simplices*. Spiess defines *diminutio* and *variatio* separately in his treatise. The *diminutio* can occur through an embellishment of the notes (*diminutio notarum*) or the theme (*diminutio subjecti oder thematis*). In his example of *diminutio notarum*, Spiess only uses embellishments which move by step and fill in the span between the intervals of the original melody, suggesting an adoption of the Praetorius understanding. This example, like those of his *figurae simplices*, is only melodic. The *diminutio subjecti* is not simply the ornamentation of a given melody but is an embellishment of the subject or theme through additional, faster-moving voices. Spiess illustrates this in a two-part setting in which the upper voice is a figurated counterpoint thematically based on the accompanying theme. He mentions that *diminutio subjecti* is also known by the Italians as *soggeto sminuito*. In the definition of this term in his *Lexicon*, however, Walther fails to make Spiess's differentiations, citing the terms *diminutione* and *double* as alternatives.[1] Spiess describes the *variatio*, on the other hand, as a device which can use both the *diminutio* and all of the *figurae simplices*. In fact, he defines all his *figurae simplices* under the term *variatio*. Similarly, Vogt describes a *variatio* as a combination of *figurae simplices*.[2]

Besides referring to the art of ornamentation, *diminutio* is also used to describe the proportional diminution of the note values of a theme.[3] In his definition of *imitatio*, Spiess again refers to the *diminutio*. Here

---

1. "Sminuito, diminuirt, kleiner gemacht, d.i. wenn an statt einer grossen und langen Note, etliche kleinere und kürtzere gesetzt werden; ist also eben so viel, als: Diminutione, Double."

2. See *Variatio*.

3. The *schematoides* is another figure which can signify metrical diminution. Furthermore, Scheibe explains that the *paronomasia*, an altered repetition of a theme, can also be used to repeat the music "with a changed or slower beat or with notes of double duration." See *Paronomasia*, *Schematoides*.

he mentions that, in contrast to freer imitation, "the progressions and leaps of the subject are presented through the diminution figures with faster notes but always in strict imitation."[1] This kind of metrical or durational diminution, widely used in Baroque fugal technique, has its origins in medieval mensural notation, where it "is used chiefly in order to introduce into perfect prolation short groups of duplets."[2] This change in time signature would result in a reduced duration of the notes, thereby effecting a *diminutio*. It is this understanding of the term which Walther appends to the end of his definition. This "early practice," as Walther calls it, is frequently encountered in canzona composition, where the theme is sectionally treated under varying time signatures. Durational *diminutio* is also an important device in sixteenth-century imitative polyphony, where the counterpoint to a theme could introduce the subject in proportionally reduced note durations, thus combining both forms of *diminutio*. One of the finest examples of this technique is found in J. S. Bach's *Canonische Variationen über Von Himmel Hoch* (BWV 769, 4: *Canon per augmentationem*). The soprano line is both a strict diminution of the bass line, as well as a figurated or embellished additional voice.

Quintilian (*Institutio* VIII.iii.50)
Vitari debet et μείωσις, cum sermoni deest aliquid, quo minus plenus sit; quanquam id obscurae potius quam inornatae orationis est vitium. Sed hoc quoque, cum a prudentibus fit, schema dici solet.

The *meiosis* ought to be avoided. It is a fault which consists of an inadequate form of expression, the oration characterized more by obscurity than a lack of ornaments. But should it be employed prudently, it is considered to be a figure.

Susenbrotus (*Epitome* p.81)
Diminutio μείωσις, est qua personam vel nostram aut rem aliquam venustatis, sive modestiae aut contemptus, interim etiam persuadende ac mitigandi gratia extenuamus.

The *diminutio* or *meiosis* occurs when we weaken the description of a person or thing for the sake of charm, modesty, contempt, or at times even persuasiveness or appeasement.

Praetorius (*Syntagma Musicum III* p.232)
Fürs ander muβ ein Sänger rechte

Second [in addition to a good voice], the

1. See *Mimesis*.
2. Willi Apel, *The Notation of Polyphonic Music* (Cambridge: Mediaeval Academy of America, 1953), 151.

Wissenschafft haben / die Diminutiones (so sonsten in gemein Coloraturen genennet werden) lieblich und Apposite zu formiren. Diminutio aber ist / wenn eine grössere Nota in viel andere geschwinde und kleinere Noten resolviret und gebrochen wird. Dieser sind nun unterschiedliche Arten und Modi: Deren etliche Gradatim nacheinander folgende / geschehen: als / Accentus, Tremulo, Gruppi und Tirata.

singer must possess the expertise to appropriately and graciously execute the *diminutiones*, otherwise generally called *coloraturen*. *Diminutio* signifies a dissolving or breaking up of a longer note into numerous faster and smaller notes, and can occur in various forms and methods, including in successive stepwise fashion, as for example the *accentus*, *tremulo*, *gruppi*, and *tirata*.

Walther (*Lexicon*)

Diminutio ist eben was Coloratura, wenn man nemlich eine große Note in viel kleine zertheilet. Es gibt deren vielerley Arten, als: 1) gradatim gehende, dergleichen die Trilli, Tremoli, Tremoletti, Groppi, Circoli mezzi, Fioretti, Tirate, Ribattuti di gola, u.s.f. sind 2) Saltuatim eingerichtete, nemlich um eine Terz, Quart, Quint, u.s.f. springende. Ehemahls hieß auch Diminutio, wenn der Tact um den dritten Theil, oder um die Helffte geschwinder, als ordinair gewöhnlich, gegeben wurde.

The *diminutio* has the same meaning as *coloratura*, namely the division of a long note into numerous shorter ones. This can be accomplished either through the many stepwise ornaments, such as *trilli*, *tremoli*, *tremoletti*, *groppi*, *circoli mezzi*, *fioretti*, *tirate*, *ribattuti di gola*, and similar figures, or through figures which leap by a third, fourth, fifth, etc. Previously, *diminutio* also referred to the acceleration of the established *tactus* by a third or a half.

Spiess (*Tractatus* p.156)

Verkleinerung, Verminderung, hat ein doppelte Bedeutnuß in der Music: eine wird genennet Diminutio Notarum, die andere Diminutio Subjecti oder Thematis. Die erste geschiehet, wann aus einer Nota eines grösseren Valoris, v.g. aus einer Noten eines gantzen oder halben Tacts mehrere und kleinere gemacht werden. Diminutio Subjecti oder Thematis, welches die Italiäner Soggeto Sminuito nennen, ist, wann das Subjectum, so in langgültigen Noten bestehet, durch andere neben-Stimmen durch kleinere Noten mit- und fortgeführet wird; welches meistens zu geschehen pflegt, da das Musicalische Stuck vollstimmig zu Ende getrieben wird.

Diminution or reduction has a twofold musical meaning: one is called *diminutio notarum*, the other *diminutio subjecti* or *thematis*. The first occurs when a longer note such as a half or whole note is divided into numerous shorter notes. *Diminutio subjecti* or *thematis*, called *soggeto sminuito* by the Italians, occurs when a subject which consists of longer notes is accompanied and extended by shorter notes in the other voices. This usually occurs when a composition is being concluded with a full-voiced texture.

DISTRIBUTIO: a musical-rhetorical process in which individual motifs or phrases of a theme or section of a composition are developed before proceeding to the following material.

Only toward the end of the Baroque era does the *distributio* find a place among the musical-rhetorical figures. It is first mentioned by Mattheson as a figure of amplification which, together with *mimesis* and *expolitio*, can be used in fugal composition.[1] None of the figures are explained, however, suggesting their general familiarity and wide-spread use. While the rhetorical *mimesis* and *expolitio* signify methods of varied and embellished repetition, the *distributio* is used to subdivide the general argument into its particulars and discuss each one individually. Both the rhetorical *expolitio* and *distributio* can make use of further figures, and can therefore be considered processes of elaboration or amplification as much as individual figures.[2] Just as *distributio* and *expolitio* are absolutely fundamental to the rhetorical process, being indispensable to the *confutatio* and *confirmatio*, so too are they essential in musical composition. In singling out these figures, Mattheson not only points to fundamental musical-rhetorical devices but to the process of fugal composition itself. Having established the musical-rhetorical compositional steps of *inventio*, *dispositio*, and *elocutio*, complete with all the accompanying

1. *Capellmeister*, 244. Of interest is Thuringus's use of the word *distributio* in his definition of *fuga* ("Quid est fuga? Est . . . artificiosa distributio"), suggesting a much earlier link between the rhetorical and musical compositional devices. See *Fuga*.

2. "Expolitio, when we abide still in one place, and yet seem to speake diverse things, many times repeating one sentence, but yet with other words, sentences, exornation, and figures" (H. Peacham, *Garden of Eloquence*, 193). "Distributio is a generall word, comprehending diverse special kindes. . . the first distribution is by division of the generall [diaresis or divisio], the second by partition of the whole [partitio], the third by enumeration of the subjects [enumeratio]. There are besides divers other figures which are kinds of distribution, but yet differing from these three" (123).

structural devices, the rhetorical *distributio* can also be transferred to the musical context.

It is Scheibe and Forkel who elaborate on the musical *distributio*. Both authors point to various methods of "dissecting" a theme. Scheibe highlights thematic fragmentation both of a fugal theme and of a concerto's or aria's opening material (*propositio*). Forkel discusses the *distributio* under the *dispositio* or arrangement of a musical composition, rather than under *elocutio*, the residence of the musical-rhetorical figures. Expanding on the *distributio*'s concept of going from generalities to particulars, he includes the elaboration on a chord or harmony in addition to thematic fragmentation. Indicative of his Enlightenment, even romantic aesthetic, is Forkel's description of this device as an "individualization of general sentiments." Not only a fugal subject but even a simple chord can be considered a general musical expression. This is lent beauty and vitality through the process of individualization, for "the individualization [of general expressions] is nothing but a form of *distributio*." He also indicates that the *distributio* can make use of various other musical devices or figures, including synonymous expressions, various descriptions, and exchanges.[1]

Susenbrotus (*Epitome* p.96)

Distributio μερισμός, Est cum genus vel totum vel subiectum, per enumerationem specierum, partium sive accidentium dilatamus.	The *distributio* or *merismos* occurs when we completely or partially extend the *genus* through an enumeration of the *species*, the parts, or the sections.

Gottsched (*Redekunst* p.282)

Distributio. Wenn man was vielfaches in seine Theile zergliedert, um seinem Leser einen ausführlichen Begriff von der Sache zu geben.	*Distributio*. When a multifarious thought is subdivided into its parts in order to provide the reader with a thorough understanding of the argument.

1. In using the term *Versetzung*, it is unlikely that Forkel is referring to Janovka's technical understanding of *hyperbaton*. In his discussion of the *Figuren für den Verstand*, which he equates with rhetorical-grammatical figures and musical-contrapuntal intricacies, he makes various disparaging remarks on the ineffectiveness of such "musical inversions" (*Allgemeine Geschichte der Musik*, 54, n.29). Scheibe translates *hyperbaton* with "Versetzung" but lends it a much more general and affective definition. Forkel undoubtedly was thinking of Scheibe's *hyperbaton* in his discussion of the contrapuntal devices, as Scheibe also related his *hyperbaton* to fugal technique. See *Hyperbaton*.

Gottsched (*Dichtkunst* p.330)

Die XIV. mag die Zergliederung (Distributio) heiβen, und besteht aus einer ausführlichen Erzählung aller Theile, die bey einer Sache vorkommen; wodurch denn dieselbe dem Gemüthe sehr deutlich und ausführlich vorgestellet wird.

The next figure might be called subdivision (*distributio*), which consists of a thorough discussion of every aspect of a thought, thereby allowing it to be clearly and thoroughly perceived.

Scheibe (*Critischer Musicus* p.692)

Die VIIte Figur ist die Zergliederung. (Distributio.) Diese geschieht, wenn man einen Hauptsatz eines Stückes auf solche Art ausführet, daβ man sich bey jedem Theile desselben nach einander besonders aufhält. Wenn man etwa ein Thema zu einer Fuge, das etwas lang wäre, zergliedern wollte, daβ man zuerst einen Satz, oder Takt, und alsdann auch das übrige gleichsam zertheilet, ausführte, und folglich all Theile des Hauptsatzes, als besondere Sätze betrachtete, und durch eine verschiedene Ausführung von einander absonderte. . . . Man kann einen Hauptsatz eines Concerts, oder einer Arie, auf diese Art zergliedern, und da in diesen Stücken der Hauptsatz ohnedieβ aus gewissen Abtheilungen besteht: so thut die Zergliederung derselben dabey vortreffliche Wirkung, vornehmlich, wenn man die Sätze durch die Veränderung der Stimme unterscheidet, also, daβ der Zuhörer bald diesen, bald jenen Satz besonders vernehmen kann. Auch in Singesachen lassen sich die Worte sehr gut zergliedern. Man kann dadurch eine Arie deutlicher machen, und ihren Inhalt gleichsam erklären.

The next figure is subdivision (*distributio*). This occurs when the principal theme of a composition is presented in such a manner that each of its parts is successively and thoroughly elaborated. For example, a lengthy fugue theme can be subdivided in such fashion by first treating only one phrase or measure and thereafter similarly treating and subdividing the remaining theme. Consequently, all parts of the principal theme are considered individually, separated from each other through their differentiated treatment. . . . The principal theme of a concerto or aria can also be subdivided in this manner. Because in such pieces the principal theme already contains certain subsections, its subdivision is extraordinarily effective, especially if the phrases are differentiated through a change in voice in such a manner that the listener particularly perceives now this phrase, now that one. In vocal music the text can also be subdivided very effectively, thereby clarifying an aria and explaining its content, as it were.

Forkel (*Geschichte der Musik* p.51)

Die Zergliederungen eines Hauptsatzes dienen dazu, ihn von allen seinen verschiedenen Seiten und Gesichtspunkten zu zeigen. Man bedient sich derselben hauptsächlich dann, wenn der Hauptsatz zu groβ oder vielseitig ist, um auf einmal ganz übersehen und begriffen werden zu können. Die Absicht eines Tonstücks kann seyn: eine individuelle, oder eine allgemeine Empfindung zu schildern. In

The subdivisions [*distributio*] of a principal theme serve to examine the musical material from all sides. They are primarily used when the principal theme is too long or diverse to be grasped and appreciated all at once. A composition's intention is to express either an individual or a general sentiment. In both cases the relationships and circumstances are so diverse that the sentiments cannot be suf-

beyden Fällen sind der Beziehungen und Verhältnisse so viele, daß die Empfindung ohne Auflösung in ihre einzelne Theile nicht deutlich genug werden kann. Man bedient sich zu dieser Auflösung eben so wie in der Sprache, mehrerley Mittel; wir haben z.B. auch in der Musik synonymische Ausdrücke, Umschreibungen verschiedener Arten, Versetzungen u.s.f. ja sogar eine Individualisirung allgemeiner Empfindungen läßt sich in den musikalischen Ausdrücken denken. . . . Folgender vierstimmige Accord kann ein solcher allgemeiner Ausdruck seyn:

ficiently clarified without dissolving them into their separate parts. Such a dissolution employs devices similar to linguistic ones: for example, in music we also have synonymous expressions, diverse forms of paraphrase, replacements [*hyperbaton*], and so on. Even an individualization of general sentiments can be musically expressed. . . .

The following chord might be such a general expression:

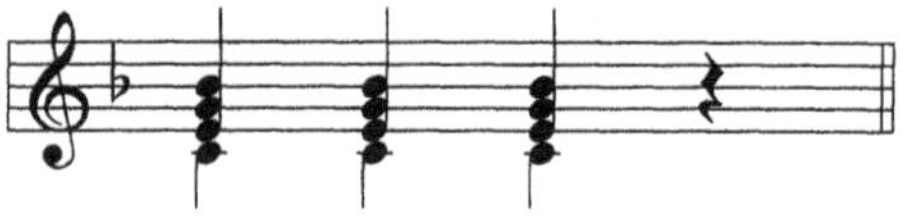

und jedes geübte Ohr empfindet zwar seine Bedeutung eben so gut, als der Kenner einer Sprache abstrakte Ausdrücke versteht; allein Lebhaftigkeit und Schönheit des Ausdrucks gewinnt ungemein, wenn diese auch bisweilen aufgelöset und individualisirt werden, und folgende Individualisirung obiger Accorde:

and every practiced ear perceives its meaning just as well as anyone who understands a language also understands its abstract expressions. However, the expression is given exceptional vitality and beauty only if the general expressions are also periodically dissolved and individualized, such as the following individualization of the above chords:

ist daher unstreitig weit lebhafter als der allgemeine Ausdruck. Man sieht übrigens, daß diese Individualisirung nichts als eine Art der Zergliederung ist.

which is unquestionably far livelier than the general expression. Moreover, it becomes apparent that this individualization is nothing but a form of subdivision.

DUBITATIO: an intentionally ambiguous rhythmic or harmonic progression.

A musical "doubting" can be caused by ambivalence or unclarity in either harmony or rhythm. This seems to be the only example in which affection and figure directly correspond. Both the musical-rhetorical device and its intended affection share terminology and content. While this rhetorical figure has been recognized since antiquity, it is only mentioned in musical treatises toward the end of the Baroque era. With the growing eighteenth-century emphasis on natural affective expression and the associated psychological examination of music's expressiveness, the element of doubt could be introduced into musical composition. Expressions of uncertainty or ambiguity, even though they be deliberate, would not have been acceptable to the seventeenth-century *musicus poeticus*. In fact, the *dubitatio* would have been considered quite unnatural, for "nature abhors the infinite."[1] However, with an increased call for composers to express their own feelings, which Forkel formulates as an "individualization of general sentiments,"[2] the expression of uncertainty becomes quite acceptable.

Quintilian (*Institutio* IX.ii.19)
Adfert aliquam fidem veritatis et dubitatio, cum simulamus quaerere nos, unde incipiendum, ubi desinendum, quid potissimum dicendum, an omnino dicendum sit.

The *dubitatio* can lend an expression a sense of truthfulness, and occurs when we pretend to question where to begin or end, what is most important to say, or what should be left unsaid.

Susenbrotus (*Epitome* p.67)
Dubitatio Graece ἀπορία, est cum perplexi animique dubii haesitamus, quidnam potissimum inter duo plurave decendum sit aut faciendum.

The *dubitatio*, which the Greeks call *aporia*, occurs when we hesitate out of doubt or confusion, especially when choosing or differentiating between two or more thoughts.

Gottsched (*Dichtkunst* p.317)
Die andre Figur ist der Zweifel, (Dubitatio) womit man entweder bey sich ansteht, ob eins oder das andre zu glauben, oder zu thun sey; oder sich doch so stellet, als ob man sich nicht entschließen könnte. . . . Zuweilen zweifelt man zwar selber nicht; will aber durch einen verstellten Zweifel die Zuhörer zum Nachsinnen bewegen.

The next figure is doubt or *dubitatio*, through which one either questions whether one thing or another is to be believed or done, or at least pretends to be undecided. . . . At other times one is not in doubt oneself but wishes to move the listener to reflection through an apparent doubt.

---

1. "Natura ab infinitis abhorret." Werckmeister, *Musicae mathematicae*, 13. See p.21, n.18, above.
2. See *Distributio*.

Scheibe (*Critischer Musicus* p.686)

Die IIte Figur ist der Zweifel. (Dubitatio.) Sie bemerket eine ungewiβheit, sich zu entschlieβen, und ist in der Musik von besonderer Wichtigkeit, weil sie fast in allen Gattungen vollständiger Stücke statt findet. Wenn die Verbindung und der Zusammenhang der Melodie und der Harmonie die Zuhörer gleichsam ungewiβ machen, welchen Fortgang sie nehmen, und in welchen Ton sie zuletzt fallen werden: so ist solches ein Merkmaal, daβ der Componist den Zweifel geschickt auszudrücken gewuβt hat. . . . Der Zweifel muβ dem Componisten nicht die Ordnung seiner Gedanken, oder den wohleingerichteten Zusammenhang seiner Sätze verwirren, und ihn also selbst zweifelhaft machen; er muβ nur die Zuhörer auf eine sinnreiche Art verführen, damit sie in der Folge der Sätze, oder der Töne ungewiβ werden, und seine Meynung nicht leicht errathen können.

The next figure is doubt or *dubitatio.* It indicates an uncertainty or indecision and is particularly important in music, for it is found in almost all genres of complete compositions. Should the combination and correlation between the melody and harmony result in the listeners' uncertainty regarding the music's progression and ultimate conclusion, it is an indication of the composer's adept expression of the *dubitatio.* . . . However, the *dubitatio* must not confuse the composer's own arrangement or the proper coherence of his music, thereby creating doubt in his own mind; rather he must only meaningfully lead the listeners astray so that, becoming uncertain regarding the order of the music or the notes, they cannot easily guess his intent.

Forkel (*Geschichte der Musik* p.58)

Die Dubitation (Zweifel) zeigt eine Ungewiβheit in der Empfindung an. Sie wird in der Musik auf zweyerley Art ausgedrückt: 1) durch eine zweifelhafte Modulation, z.B.

The *dubitatio* (doubt) indicates an uncertain sentiment. It is musically expressed in two forms: (1) through an indecisive modulation, for example:

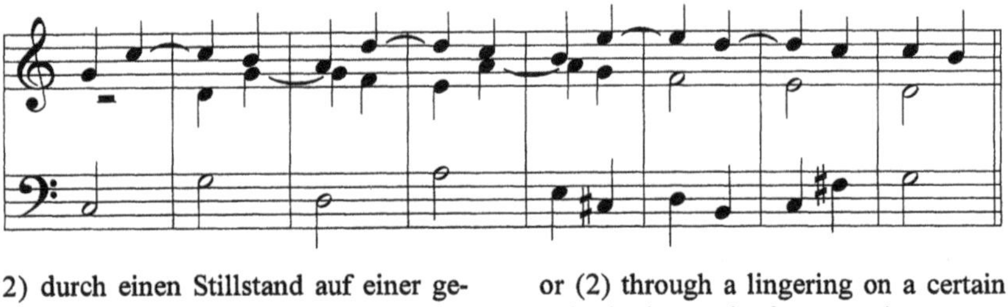

2) durch einen Stillstand auf einer gewissen Stelle eines Satzes, z.B.

or (2) through a lingering on a certain point in the music, for example:

Auch der Ausdruck der Unentschlossenheit muβ hierher gerechnet werden,

The expression of indecision must also be included here, of which C. P. E. Bach

wovon uns C. Ph. Em. Bach im musikalischen Allerley S.43. unter der Ueberschrift; l'irresoluë, ein schönes Beyspiel gegeben hat. Hier ist der Ausdruck dieser Figur durch Verlängerung des Rhythmus bewerkstelligt.

provided a fine example in his *Musikalisches Allerley* (p.43) under the title *l'irresoluë*. Here the expression of this figure is achieved through a prolongation of the rhythm.

ECPHONESIS: see *EXCLAMATIO*

ELLIPSIS, SYNECDOCHE: (1) an omission of an expected consonance; (2) an abrupt interruption in the music.

The *ellipsis* undergoes a semantic change in both rhetoric and music. Quintilian refers to the omission of an expression which is nonetheless understood in context as a *synecdoche*. Should the omitted expression remain unintelligible, it is regarded as an error (*vitia*), which he terms *ellipsis*. Whereas the term *ellipsis* simply means "leave away, omission," *synecdoche* means "with sequence (consequence), intimation, suggestion." Quintilian uses the two terms to differentiate between an unintelligible omission and the omission of an expression which, however, can be discerned through suggestion or intimation in the context of the oration.

Susenbrotus also uses the two terms but considers both of them to be figures.[1] Whereas his *eclipsis* refers to the omission of an expression which is understood in context, he defines *synecdoche* as a figure in which "one thing is understood through another by whatever means." Thus he calls Quintilian's *synecdoche* an *eclipsis*, while describing *synecdoche* as a figure which implies a content beyond the literal meaning of the words. This he clarifies through numerous examples supplied in his definition.

With Gottsched *ellipsis* assumes a different nuance in meaning. The emphasis is not on the figure's reference to an unspoken yet generally understood content but rather on the omission or suppression of the references. He translates the Greek term with *Verbeißen*, *Abbrechen*

1. The terms *ellipsis* and *eclipsis* can be used interchangeably.

(suppression, breaking off), resulting in a definition closely related to that of the *aposiopesis*. In fact, Gottsched explicitly links the two figures, mentioning that the *aposiopesis* can be considered a form of *ellipsis*.[1]

The first musical reference to the *ellipsis* is already encountered in the sixteenth century, when Eucharius Hoffmann uses the term to describe a transgression of the normal *ambitus* of a mode.[2] Bernhard is the first author to include the *ellipsis* in a *Figurenlehre*. Bernhard and Walther define the term in a manner analogous to Susenbrotus's understanding of the figure: it is an omission (of a consonance) which is nonetheless understood in the context of the composition. In Bernhard's first example (*Tractatus*) the syncopated d^1 in the melody (b.2) is not resolved but remains at the fourth above the bass note. However, through the dominant function of the bass, the listener understands a C-sharp, even though it is not sounded. This form of the *ellipsis* is explicitly explained both in Bernhard's *Bericht* and in Walther's *Praecepta*. Vogt's *antistaechon* signifies a similar musical device. However, while *ellipsis* refers to the suppression of a consonance, *antistaechon* denotes the substitution of a dissonance for an expected consonance. In the other example, the expected consonance, f^1, is replaced with a rest, the following e^1 forming the dissonant tritone with the bass. The e^1 is understood as a passing-note (*transitus*) from f^1 to d^1, with the f^1 being replaced by a rest but nonetheless understood in the context.[3] In his *Tractatus* Bernhard lists the *ellipsis* as a figure used in the modern *stylus theatralis* or *recitativus*. The "suppressed" d^1 would therefore be heard in the realized *basso continuo* part.

As a consequence of adopting Gottsched's *Figurenlehre* as his model, Scheibe supplies the *ellipsis* with a definition much closer to its affective, rhetorical—rather than its traditional musical—understanding. Unlike Gottsched, however, Scheibe does not link the *ellipsis* with the

---

1. See *Aposiopesis*.

2. E. Hoffmann, *Practica modorum explicatio* (1582); cited in Ruhnke, *Burmeister*, 137. This musical device is termed *hyperbole* and *hypobole* by Burmeister, *licentia* by Herbst, and *modus superfluus* (a form of *mutatio toni*) by Bernhard. See *Hyperbole*.

3. It is this explanation of the dissonance following the rest in Monteverdi's *Cruda Amarilli* (b.13) which is put forward by Signor Luca in Artusi's *L'Artusi, ovvero, Delle imperfezioni della moderna musica* (Strunk, *Source Readings*, 393), where the dissonant a^2 is described as the upper neighbor to the "suppressed" yet understood g^2.

aposiopesis. The rhetorical *aposiopesis* is associated with an omission or interruption, as is the *ellipsis*, making their correlation a natural one. The musical *aposiopesis* customarily refers to a silence or general pause, which might follow an interruption but is not considered identical to it. This specific musical differentiation leads to those figures of silence which signify a break in the music, such as *abruptio* or *tmesis*, and those which indicate a silence, including *aposiopesis*, *pausa*, and *suspiratio*. Scheibe and Forkel describe the *ellipsis* as such a break, after which the music subsequently continues in an unrelated or unexpected manner, thereby incorporating interruption, silence, and continuation in the one figure.

Quintilian (*Institutio* VIII.vi.21)

Quidam synecdochen vocant et cum id in contextu sermonis quod tacetur accipimus; verbum enim ex verbis intelligi, quod inter vitia ellipsis vocatur.

Some use the term *synecdoche* when something is suppressed but nonetheless assumed in the context of the speech. A word might be understood through another word, which is called an *ellipsis* when it leads to a fault in the oration.

Quintilian (*Institutio* IX.iii.58)

συνεκδοχῆ . . . cum subtractum verbum aliquod satis ex ceteris intelligitur.

The *synecdoche* occurs when the omitted word is clearly understood out of the context of the other words.

Susenbrotus (*Epitome* p.26)

Eclipsis, id est dictionis sive oratiunculae ad legitimam constructionem necessariae in sensu defectus. In hac dictio vel clausula, aut consuetudine autorum, id est, eruditorum consensu, subaudiri solet, aut ex caeteris verbis in orationis clausula expressis, certa est. Mancinellus: Dicitur unius verbi defectus Eclipsis.

The *eclipsis* signifies an omission of words or parts of speech which the correct construction requires. In this figure the omitted word or clause is ascertained either through the established usage of past authors, that is, through the consensus of the learned ones' usages, or through the other words in that clause of the oration. According to Mancinellus, the omission of a word is called an *eclipsis*.

Susenbrotus (*Epitome* p.8)

Synecdoche Intellectio, est quoties aliud ex alio quocunque modo intelligitur. Vel cum ex uno plura intelliguntur: ut, Romanus praelio victor, pro Romani victores. Vel ex parte totum: ut mucro pro gladio, tecum pro domo, Retroque: ut ingens

The *synecdoche* or *intellectio* occurs when one thing is understood in one way or another through something else: when the plural is understood out of the singular, as in Roman victor instead of Roman victors; when the whole is understood out

avertice pontus, id est, procella et unda ponti: et fontemque ignemque ferebant, id est, partem fontanae aquae. Vel ex species genus . . . Vel cum ex materia res confecta significatur . . . Vel ex praecedentibus sequentia. . . . Breviter quoties aliud ex alio intelligitur.

of the part, as in blade instead of sword or roof instead of house; or conversely, as in a huge sea instead of storm and waves . . . ; when the *genus* is understood out of the *species*, the product out of the raw material, the following out of the preceding, in short, when anything is understood out of something else.

Gottsched (*Redekunst* p.278)
Ellipsis. Die etwas ausläßt, so sich aber leicht verstehen läßt.

The *ellipsis* omits something which is nonetheless easily understood.

Gottsched (*Dichtkunst* p.319)
Die IV. ist das Verbeißen, (Ellipsis) oder Abbrechen einer Redensart, die man nur anhebt, aber nicht völlig endiget. Sie entsteht, wenn der Affect so heftig ist, daß der Mund und die Zunge den geschwinden Gedanken der Seele nicht folgen kann, und also mitten in einem Satze abbrechen, und dem neuen Gedanken des Geistes plötzlich folgen muß.

The next figure is the suppression or *ellipsis*, consisting of breaking off a manner of speech which one only begins but does not completely finish. It occurs when the affection is so vehement that the mouth and tongue cannot keep up with the rapid thoughts of the soul, therefore breaking off in the middle of a sentence and suddenly continuing with the new thought.

Bernhard (*Tractatus* p.84)
Ellipsis ist eine Auslaßung der sonst erforderten Consonantz. Und rühret entweder her aus Veränderung der Syncopation oder des Transitus. Ellipsis so aus der Syncopation herrühret, ist gar gebräuchlich wo die Quarta durch die drauff folgende Tertie in denen Cadentiis solte resolviret werden, und 1) entweder die Tertie gar ausgelaßen, oder 2) an deren Stelle eine andere Consonantz genommen wird.

The *ellipsis* is an omission of an otherwise required consonance, arising from an altered *syncopatio* or *transitus*. An *ellipsis* arising out of a *syncopatio* commonly occurs in cadences where a fourth should resolve to a third, but instead the third is either omitted altogether, or another consonance takes its place.

Ellipsis aus dem Transitu herrührend ist eine Verschweigung der Consonantz so in Transitu für der Dissonantz sonst

An *ellipsis* arising out of a *transitus* is the suppression of a consonance which is normally required before the passing dis-

erfordert wird.

sonance of a *transitus*.

Bernhard (*Bericht* p.151)
Ellipsis heiβet Auβlaβung und ist eine Verschweigung einer Consonans. Und geschiehet auff zweyerley Weise 1) wenn an stad der Consonanz eine pausa stehet und darauf eine Dissonanz folget.

Ellipsis means omission and signifies a suppression of a consonance. It occurs in two ways: when a *pausa* replaces a consonance and is followed by a dissonance:

Und wenn in einer Cadenz die Quarta durch die Tertia nicht resolviret wird, sondern stehen bleibet. Alβ:

or when in a cadence the fourth is not resolved by the third but rather remains stationary, as follows:

Walther (*Praecepta* p.154)
Ellipsis. Ist eine Auslaβung oder Verschweigung einer Consonanz welches geschicht 1) wenn an statt der Consonanz eine Pause stehet, und auf diese eine Dissonanz folget. 2) Wenn in einer Cadenz die 4ta durch die 3tia nicht resolviret wird, sondern unbeweglich liegen bleibet.

The *ellipsis* is an omission or suppression of a consonance which occurs (1) when a *pausa* replaces a consonance and is followed by a dissonance; (2) when in a cadence the fourth is not resolved by the third but rather remains stationary.

Walther (*Lexicon*)
Ellipsis [lat.] ἔλλειψις [gr.] von ἐλλείπω, praetermitto, deficio; ist eine

The *ellipsis*, from *elleipo* or *praetermitto*, *deficio*, is an omission or suppression of

Auslassung oder Verschweigung einer Consonanz, und entstehet, wenn an statt dieser eine Pause gesetzt wird, worauf eine Dissonanz folget.

a consonance and occurs when a pause is substituted for a consonance which is followed by a dissonance.

Scheibe (*Critischer Musicus* p.687)
Die IIIte ist das Verbeißen, (Ellipsis,) oder das Abbrechen eines Satzes, den man nur anhebet, aber nicht völlig endiget. Sie geschieht auf zweyerley Art. Erstlich, wenn man in dem heftigsten Affecte und mitten in einem angefangenen Satze unvermuthet abbricht und stille hält, endlich aber mit einem ganz fremden Gedanken aufs neue wieder anhebt. Oder auch, wenn man am Schlusse eines Satzes den gewöhnlichen Schlußton verändert, und in einen ganz fremden und unerwarteten Accord fällt. Dieses letztere nennen die Componisten: das Ausfliehen der Cadenz. Je heftiger aber der Affect ist, oder seyn soll, desto fremder muß auch der Accord seyn, in den man die gewöhnliche Cadenz verändert. Die erste Art dieser Figur ist die schönste, und erfordert wegen des Abbrechens, und weil man zugleich dem ganzen Satze Einhalt thun muß, viel Geschicklichkeit, Feuer und Stärke so wohl in der Melodie, als Harmonie.

The next figure is the suppression or *ellipsis*, or the breaking off of a passage which one only begins but does not completely finish. It occurs in two forms. First, one can suddenly break off and remain silent in the middle of a passage in a vehement affection. Or one can alter the expected ending notes of a passage and proceed to a completely foreign and unexpected chord. This second method composers call evading the cadence. The more vehement the affection, the more foreign the chord must be which alters the expected cadence. The first form of this figure is the more congenial one and, because of the abrupt silence and interruption of the entire passage, requires great facility, imagination, and power both in the melody as well as in the harmony.

Forkel (*Geschichte der Musik* p.56)
Eine auffallende Art von Aeußerung einer Empfindung ist die, wenn sie, nachdem sie nach und nach zu einem hohen Grad von Stärke angewachsen, auf einmal plötzlich stille steht, und abbricht. Diese Figur wird Ellipsis genannt. Die Kunst, die diese Art von Aeußerung ausdrücken will, muß sie daher so in ein Bild zu bringen suchen, daß dadurch der Gang der Leidenschaft für die Einbildungskraft gleichsam sichtbar werden kann. Sie kann es auf zweyerley Art bewerkstelligen, nemlich 1) wenn ein nach und nach zu einer großen Lebhaftigkeit angewachsener Satz unvermuthet abbricht, sodann aber mit einem ganz veränderten Gedanken aufs neue wieder

A notable form of expressing a sentiment occurs when its expression is suddenly suspended and broken off after a gradual and successively intensifying growth. This figure is called *ellipsis*. The art expressed by this device must seek to illuminate the path of the affections for the imagination, as it were. This can be achieved by two methods: first, when a gradually intensifying passage which has grown to great vehemence is unexpectedly interrupted, only to resume anew and proceed with an entirely altered thought. This form of *ellipsis* is found in the following Bach sonata:

anfängt, und weiter fortgeht. Von dieser Art ist folgende Ellipsis in einer Bachischen Sonate:

2) Wenn ein ebenfalls nach und nach sehr lebhaft gewordener Satz bis zu einer Art von Cadenz fortgeführt wird, anstatt aber diejenige Cadenz zu machen, die sich aus der vorhergehenden Modulation hätte erwarten lassen, in eine sogenannte ausfliehende Cadenz fällt, und dadurch den Faden der Modulation abreiβt, z.B.

Second, it occurs when a likewise gradually intensifying passage progresses to a form of cadence but, instead of proceeding to the expected cadence based on the preceding harmonies, proceeds to a so called evaded cadence, and thereby breaks the thread of the modulations, as in the following example:

Je heftiger aber die Empfindung ist, deren Lauf schleunig unterbrochen werden soll, desto fremder und entfernter muβ auch die Cadenz seyn, in welche die gewöhnliche verändert wird.

The more intense the sentiment which is to be abruptly interrupted, the more foreign and remote must also be the cadence which replaces the expected one.

EMPHASIS: a musical passage which heightens or emphasizes the meaning of the text through various means.

The rhetorical *emphasis* is similar to the *ellipsis* or *synecdoche*. [1] In both

---

1. Scaliger (*Poetices libri septem*, Heidelberg 1581) even lists the *emphasis* under *eclipsis*. Sonnino, *Handbook*, 200.

cases the oration wishes to convey more significance than is literally expressed. While the *ellipsis* signifies a certain omission, the *emphasis* highlights an additional yet unspoken connotation of the text.

The *emphasis* enters musical treatises as a figure relatively late. This can be explained by the fact that the discipline of *musica poetica* in general might be understood as a form of *emphasis*: it is the role of music to heighten or explain the meaning of the text above and beyond the literal meaning of the words. Music is to add the additional emphasis which the text on its own cannot provide. Early Baroque authors of musical treatises would find it redundant to include this figure. On the other hand, those writers who sought to mirror a rhetorical *Figurenlehre* in their musical treatises either omit the figure (Scheibe) or supply the term with a definition not entirely based on the rhetorical figure (Mattheson).

Vogt is the first musician to include the term in a list of musical figures. His comment that the figure can be executed by the singer without it being written into the composition suggests that Vogt may have had an *accentus* or similar ornament in mind. Although he mentions the *accentus* under his ornamental *figurae simplices*, Vogt may have wanted to highlight the figure's text-expressive potential. He therefore includes it in his list of musical-rhetorical *figurae ideales*, supplying it with an appropriate rhetorical term which reflects its function: to highlight and emphasize the text.[1] Spiess also limits the figure to an emphasis of particular words. Although he advises the composer to carefully set the words to be emphasized and the singer to execute them equally carefully, Spiess does not go into greater detail regarding the musical setting or the devices to be employed.

Mattheson devotes the entire eighth chapter of his *Capellmeister* (part 2), *Vom Nachdruck in der Melodie*, to the use of the *emphasis*. A variety of devices are regarded as part of the *emphasis*, including the correct stress of words and syllables, the use of appropriate ornamentation, and effective repetition of both text and music. Above all, the *emphasis* is to heighten the meaning of the entire text, "as though it were

1. Vogt furthermore describes the *polysyntheton*, another of his *figurae ideales*, as a successively repeated *emphasis*. The understanding of the *emphasis* as an *accentus* would be most appropriate in that definition as well. See *Polysyndeton*.

pointing out the intended affection, illuminating the sense and meaning of the work." Mattheson wishes to clearly distinguish between the *accentus* and the *emphasis*, which suggests that the two devices were commonly not only associated but equated. Rather than emphasizing the content of the entire text, the *accentus* focuses on the accentuation of specific words. Through clarifying and interpreting the text, the musical *emphasis* points beyond the text itself, adding a significance which the words on their own cannot provide. Herein lies both the commonality between the rhetorical and the musical figure, as well as the essence of a *musica poetica*.

Quintilian (*Institutio* VIII.iii.83)
Vicina praedictae sed amplior virtus est ἔμφασις, altiorem praebens intellectum quam quem verba per se ipsa declarant. Eius duae sunt species, altera, quae plus significat quam dicit, altera, quae etiam id quod non dicit.

A similar but more outstanding virtue [than *brachology*] is *emphasis*, through which a deeper understanding is revealed than is actually expressed by the words. It is of two kinds: either more is meant than is said, or something is meant which is not said at all.

Quintilian (*Institutio* IX.ii.64)
Est emphasis etiam inter figuras, cum ex aliquo dicto latens aliquid eruitur.

The *emphasis* is considered a figure when a hidden meaning is revealed through some other expression.

Susenbrotus (*Epitome* p.47)
Emphasis ἔμφασις, est cum altior subest intellectus ac maior significantia, quam verba per seipsa declarant. Haec plurimum adfert iucunditatis orationi, nonnumquam et dignitatis acrimoniaeque non parum. Mancinellus: Altior est sensus quoties quam quem tibi verba declarant, vel quam dicis plus significatur. Aut etiam quod non dicis, scito Emphasim esse.

The *emphasis* occurs when an expression is given a deeper understanding and greater significance than the words themselves express. This figure is frequently employed in entertaining speeches, at times also in speeches of praise or vehement speeches. In the words of Mancinellus, the *emphasis* results in a deeper understanding than the words themselves express, or when more is understood than is either said or even suppressed.

Vogt (*Conclave* p.151)
Emphasis. Hanc figuram ponit Melotheta, vel etiam sine eo illam canens efficit.

Emphasis. This figure can be either notated by the composer or extemporized by the singer.

Mattheson (*Capellmeister* p.174)
Die Emphatic (Ab ἐν, in; & φάσις,

The *emphasis* ([footnote:] from *en*, in;

apparitio, dictio: Die Lehre von den sonderbar hervorscheinenden Wörtern einer Rede. Emphasis est, cum vocabulum adhibitum singularem habet vim & efficaciam: so lautet die Beschreibung der Redner, welche man leicht auf den Klang deuten kan.), welche vom Nachdruck der Gedancken, Klänge und Wörter handelt, denselben erläutert und deutlich vor Augen leget, erfordert ein reiffes Nachsinnen und hat hauptsächlich mit folgenden vier Betrachtungen zu thun.

and *phasis*, manifestation: the teaching of the exceptionally prominent words of a speech. "*Emphasis* occurs when certain expressions are given singular power and efficacy." This rhetorical description can easily be applied to music.), which deals with the emphasis of thoughts, music, and words, explaining and vividly illustrating them, demands a thorough examination, and is primarily concerned with the following four observations.

Erstlich erweget man die eigentliche Emphasin, d.i. den Ton und Nachdruck der Wörter, an und für sich selbst. . . . Zum andern kömmt diejenige lange oder kurtze Aussprache der Sylben hiebey nothwendig in Erwegung, welche man den Accent nennet. Drittens ist der Artickel von den Passaggien, oder zierlichen Läuffen im Gesange zu untersuchen. Viertens beobachtet man die Wiederholungen nicht nur der Wörter, sondern auch der Klang- und Sang-Weisen, der Gänge, Fälle und Führungen in der Melodie, in so fern in denselben und in den vorigen Umständen ein gewisser Nachdruck erfordert wird. Dieses alles gehöret zur Emphatic.

First, the actual *emphasis* itself should be considered, that is the sound and stress of the words. . . . Next, the length of pronunciation of the syllables or the accent must be considered. Third, the *passaggi* or embellishing runs in the music are to be examined. Fourth, the repetition not only of the words but also of the harmonic and melodic passages are to be observed, particularly regarding the need for a certain accentuation in this and the preceding circumstances. This is all part of *emphasis*.

Ehe wir aber ein jedes Stück ins besondre vor uns nehmen, muß mit wenigen gewiesen werden, welcher Gestalt die eigentliche Emphasis von dem Accent zu unterscheiden sey. . . . Erwehnter Unterschied bestehet demnach vornehmlich in folgenden Eigenschafften. Erstlich fällt die Emphasis immer auf ein gantzes Wort, nicht nach dem Klange desselben, sondern nach dem darin enthaltenen Bilde des Verstandes; der Accent hergegen hat nur mit blossen Sylben, nehmlich mit deren Länge, Kürtze, Erhebung oder Erniedrigung im Aussprechen zu schaffen. . . . Dritens richtet der Accent seine Absicht bloß auf die Aussprache; die Emphasis hergegen zeiget gleichsam mit Fingern auf die Gemüths-Neigung,

Before dealing with each of these points in greater detail, a few words of explanation are required to point out the differences between the *emphasis* and accentuation. . . . These differences consist of the following. First, the *emphasis* concerns an entire word, focusing not on its pronunciation but rather on its literal content or meaning. Accentuation on the other hand deals only with the syllables' length and stress in verbalization. . . . The intention of accentuation is directed only on pronunciation; the *emphasis*, in contrast, illuminates the sense or meaning of the presentation as though it were pointing out the intended affection.

und beleuchtet den Sinn oder Verstand des Vortages.

Spiess (*Tractatus* p.155)
Emphasis, Nachdruck, sondere Expression, und Ausdruckung eines Worts in dem Klang oder Music muβ sowohl von dem Componisten gescheit gesetzt: als auch von dem Singer geschickt und eindringlich in jenen Wörtern angebracht werden, in welchen der absonderliche Enthalt, Nachdruck, Kraft, Macht, Vis, Efficacia, Energia eines Periodi oder Rede enthalten ist.

The *emphasis*, an exceptional expression of a word through the music, must be both cleverly set by the composer as well as skillfully and effectively executed by the singer. It is applied to those words containing the exceptional content, emphasis, power, strength, force, efficacy, or vigor of a passage or text.

EPANADIPLOSIS, REDUPLICATIO: a restatement of the opening of a passage or phrase at its close.

The term *epanadiplosis* does not appear in rhetorical treatises prior to the eighteenth century. A more common figure with a synonymous term, the *anadiplosis*, signifies a restatement of the close of one sentence at the beginning of the following one, rather than a common opening and close of the same sentence. The Latin term for this figure, *reduplicatio*, is mentioned in both musical and rhetorical definitions of *anadiplosis* (Susenbrotus and Walther). Walther also lists *reduplicatio* as an alternate term for *epanadiplosis*, which he describes in accordance with Vogt's definition. The rhetorical device which signifies a common opening and ending of a sentence is known as *epanalepsis*.[1] It is Vogt, then, who introduces the new term with a borrowed definition into the catalog of musical-rhetorical figures. Unger's explanation that this rearrangement "might be attributed to a misspelling on Vogt's part or a misprint by the printer" is questionable.[2] A more probable explanation is suggested by Dammann: "Pseudo-Rufinian also broke with tradition when he called

1. To confuse the matter even more, Walther also supplies *epanalepsis* with the same definition as his *epanadiplosis*. The *complexio* was also understood as a figure comparable to the *epanadiplosis* by some authors. See *Complexio*, *Epanalepsis*.

2. Unger, *Beziehungen*, 77.

the cyclical repetition-figure *epanadiplosis*."[1] Although this rhetorical reference postdates Vogt's writings, it does allow for the possibility of a common musical and rhetorical definition. Because Vogt defines *epanalepsis* as a different form of repetition, this term is not available to him for the designation of the cyclical figure. Having adopted the traditional definition of *anadiplosis* and Quintilian's repetition definition of *epanalepsis*, Vogt must find a different term for the cyclical definition of *epanalepsis*, his choice falling on the synonymous *epanadiplosis*. Walther then includes this choice of term and definition in his *Lexicon*. The duplications in his dictionary are explained through his desire to catalog all known terms and definitions in true terminological tradition irrespective of possible ensuing contradictions.

Vogt (*Conclave* p.150)
Epanadiplosis est, cum finis est, ut initium; ut si cum cadentia inciperes periodum, & cum eadem cadentia finires.

The *epanadiplosis* occurs when the ending is identical to the beginning; for example when a musical passage begins with a *cadentia* and ends with the same *cadentia*.

Walther (*Lexicon*)
Epanadiplosis, gr. ἐπαναδίπλωσις, Reduplicatio ist eine Wort-Figur, so entstehet, wenn in einer Sentenz das Anfangs- und Schluß-Wort einerley ist, oder überein heisset.

Epanadiplosis or *reduplicatio* is a word figure which occurs when the opening and closing words of a sentence are the same or agree.

EPANALEPSIS: (1) a frequent repetition of an expression; (2) a restatement of the opening of a passage at its close.

Epanalepsis is given two definitions, each featuring a different form of repetition. Quintilian and Susenbrotus use the term to specify a frequent repetition of an opening expression throughout the oration. The more specific form of repetition, namely the restatement of the opening words of a sentence at its close, is also called *epanalepsis* by Susenbrotus. It

1. Dammann, *Musikbegriff*, 142f. Dammann locates this source in *De schematibus lexeos*, ed. C. Halm, in *Rhetores latini minores* (Leipzig, 1863), 48ff.

is this latter definition which reappears most frequently in later rhetorical sources, including Gottsched.

Similarly, two definitions also exist for the musical *epanalepsis*. Vogt adopts Quintilian's more general form of repetition as the definition for his *epanalepsis*. In specifying that it be used to repeat an *emphasis*, Vogt suggests that the *epanalepsis* is a form of emphatic repetition. Having thus defined *epanalepsis*, he introduces a new term, *epanadiplosis*, to signify the second and more specific definition of *epanalepsis*.

By the eighteenth century, *epanalepsis* is generally explained with the second definition in both rhetorical and musical treatises. While the restated opening of a passage at its close is termed *epanalepsis* by Ahle and Walther, and *epanadiplosis* by Vogt and Walther, this musical device is defined as a *complexio* by Nucius, Thuringus, and Walther.[1] Walther's inclusion of all three terms for the one device is explained by his desire to terminologically catalog all known musical terms and definitions irrespective of possible ensuing duplications. Like Susenbrotus, he also provides the Latin term for *epanalepsis*: *resumptio*. Whether on account of the confusion surrounding the various terms associated with this technique of repetition or whether out of an assumption that the device is a subcategory of the *repetitio* (*anaphora*), other eighteenth-century authors either list one or more of the terms without definitions (Mattheson) or simply omit them altogether (Spiess, Scheibe, Forkel).

Quintilian (*Institutio* VIII.iii.50)

ταυτολογία, id est eiusdem verbi aut sermonis iteratio. . . . Interim mutato nomine ἐπανάληψις dicitur, atque est et ipsum inter schemata.	*Tautology* is a frequent repetition of a word or phrase. At times it is given the alternate name of *epanalepsis*, and as such is included among the figures [instead of errors].

Susenbrotus (*Epitome* pp.32, 52)

Epanalepsis, ἐπανάληψις est quando post aliquam multa, vel claritatis vel alia quapiam causa orationi interposita, id	The *epanalepsis* occurs when something is frequently inserted into the oration by repeating what was expressed in the be-

1. The rhetorical *complexio* or *symploce* distinguishes itself from the *epanalepsis* in that the former signifies common beginnings and endings of a number of subsequent sentences, while the latter signifies common beginning and ending words in one sentence. See also *Complexio*, *Epanadiplosis*.

quod in principio est collocatum, repetitur, ἐπανάληψις, Latine Resumptio, superiorum repetitio.

ginning for the sake of clarity or for some other reason. The *epanalepsis*, *resumptio* in Latin, was formerly called *repetitio.*

Epanalepsis ἐπανάληψις est cum eadem dictio et initum et finem occupat.

The *epanalepsis* occurs when the same expression is placed at the beginning and at the end of a sentence.

Gottsched (*Redekunst* p.280)
Epanalepsis wenn derselbe Ausdruck, so den Anfang zu einem Satze gemacht hat, denselben auch beschließet.

Epanalepsis. When the same expression which began a sentence also closes it.

Gottsched (*Dichtkunst* p.324)
Oder umgekehrt, das, was am Anfange eines Satzes gestanden, kömmt am Ende desselben zu stehen, und wird Epanalepsis genannt.

Or conversely [to *anadiplosis*], that which appeared at the beginning of a sentence reappears at the end, which is called *epanalepsis.*

Ahle (*Sommer-Gespräche* p.17)
Setzet er dan: singet / rühmet und lobet / ja lobet / rühmet und singet; so ist es eine Epanalepsis und Epanodos.

Were he to write: sing / glorify and praise / yea, praise / glorify and sing, it would be an *epanalepsis* and *epanodos.*

Vogt (*Conclave* p.151)
Epanalepsis. Repetita emphasis. Figura communis est.

Epanalepsis. A repeated *emphasis.* It is a common figure.

Walther (*Lexicon*)
Epanalepsis, gr. ἐπανάληψις, Resumtio (lat.) von ἐπαναλαμβάνω, repeto; ist eine Rhetorische Figur, nach welcher ein, oder mehr Worte, so zu Anfange eines Periodi u.d.g. stehen, auch am Ende desselben wiederhohlt werden.

The *epanalepsis* or *resumtio*, from *epanalambano*, *repeto*, is a rhetorical figure through which one or more words which began a phrase or passage are also repeated at the end of the same phrase or passage.

Mattheson (*Capellmeister* p.243)
Die Epanalepsis, Epistrophe, Anadiplosis, Paronomasia, Polyptoton, Antanaclasis, Ploce etc. haben solche natürliche Stellen in der Melodie, daß es fast scheinet, als hätten die griechischen Redner sothane Figuren aus der Ton-Kunst entlehnet; denn sie sind lauter repetitiones vocum, Wiederholungen der Wörter, die auf verschiedene Weise angebracht werden.

The *epanalepsis*, *epistrophe*, *anadiplosis*, *paronomasia*, *polyptoton*, *antanaclasis*, *ploce*, etc., assume such natural positions in music that it almost seems as if the Greek orators borrowed these figures from the art of musical composition. For they are purely *repetitiones vocum*, repetitions of words, which are applied to music in various different ways.

EPANODOS, REGRESSIO, REDITUS: the retrograde repetition of a phrase.

The rhetorical *epanodos* (literally: retreat) can signify two forms of "regressive" repetition. Through the Latin translation of the Greek term, *regressio* or *reditus* (to go back, return, regress), the procedure of the rhetorical device is specifically described. Two kinds of rhetorical regression are possible: first, an oration can return to a previously mentioned thought and expand on it, as described by Quintilian and Susenbrotus. Second, an author might repeat an expression "in regression" or in reverse order, as described by Gottsched.

Epanodos is mentioned in musical writings only twice, with a definition analogous to Gottsched's description of the term. In both cases the definitions only refer to the setting of the text rather than the music. Walther explicitly mentions that the device is a word figure. However, Walther includes only those rhetorical figures and their definitions in his *Lexicon* which are applicable to a musical setting of the text. In other cases, rhetorical figures defined without reference to the musical setting by Walther are included by other writers as musical figures (e.g., *epiphora*). Furthermore, in Ahle's general discussion of the figures, it becomes quite apparent that the composer is to apply the rhetorical figures contained in the text to his musical setting. The possibility of a "regressive" repetition is particularly well suited to musical composition. Indeed, a *fuga cancrizans* or *contraria* with its retrograde statement of the subject seems to be the most literal realization of an *epanodos*.

Quintilian (*Institutio* IX.iii.35)

Est et illud repetendi genus, quod simul proposita iterat et dividit. Επάνοδος dicitur Graece, nostri regressionem vocant.	Another form of repetition occurs when previously stated thoughts are repeated and simultaneously distinguished from each other. This figure which our authors call *regressio* is called *epanodos* in Greek.

Susenbrotus (*Epitome* p.86)

Regressio Επάνοδος, est cum semel propositum iteratur ac diversum quiddam in partibus divisis significatur.	The *regressio* or *epanodos* occurs when the repetition of a previously stated thought assumes a different meaning through its division into different parts.

Gottsched (*Redekunst* p.280)
Epanodos. Wenn man zwey Wörter nach einander besonders wiederholt; doch so, daβ das letzte zuerst, und das erste zuletzt kömmt.

Epanodos. When two words are subsequently repeated in a particular manner, namely that the last comes first and the first last.

Ahle (*Sommer-Gespräche* p.17)
Setzet er dän: singet / rühmet und lobet / ja lobet / rühmet und singet; so ist es eine Epanalepsis und Epanodos.

Were he to write: sing / glorify and praise / yea, praise / glorify and sing, it would be an *epanalepsis* and *epanodos*.

Walther (*Lexicon*)
Epanodus, gr. ἐπάνοδος, Reditus (lat.) von ἐπὶ und ἄνοδος, via sursum ferens; ist eine Wort-Figur, so entstehet, wenn die Worte einer Sentenz umgekehrt oder rückwerts wiederholt werden. Z.E. Singet, rühmet und lobet; lobet, rühmet und singet. idem ibidem.

The *epanodus* or *reditus*, from *epi* and *anodos*, the returning route, is a word figure which occurs when the words of a sentence are repeated in reverse order, as in the example: sing, glorify, and praise; praise, glorify, and sing, or similar passages.

EPIPHORA, EPISTROPHE: a repetition of the conclusion of one passage at the end of subsequent passages.

Both music and rhetoric define *epiphora* or *epistrophe* similarly. In addition, the terms *conversio* and *antistrophe* (both meaning a turning around or against, a return) are also used in rhetoric to name this device. While the terms *epistrophe*, *antistrophe*, and *conversio* all highlight the return to a previously expressed thought, *epiphora* (addition, extension) emphasizes an addition, namely of a common ending. A somewhat similar rhetorical figure is the *homoioptoton*, which refers to common word endings or final syllables rather than common final words in subsequent sentences or passages. While *epiphora* is a figure of repetition, *homoioptoton* is a grammatical figure of rhyme. Nonetheless, Kircher chooses this grammatical term to define the common endings of subsequent musical passages.[1]

1. *Homoioptoton* had been assigned a different definition by Nucius, who described it as a form of the general pause, the music ending at the same time rather than in the same manner. In compiling his *Lexicon*, Walther includes *homoioptoton* under *aposiopesis*, retaining Nucius's definition, while listing this figure of repetition under *epiphora*. See also *Homoioptoton*.

Epistrophe is first mentioned by Ahle, and becomes the preferred term for the musical figure in the eighteenth century. Only Walther lists both *epistrophe* as well as *epiphora* as names for the figure. While Ahle's and Walther's definitions focus on the textual application of the figure, they would assume that a figure found in the text be reflected in the accompanying music. This is specifically stressed by Mattheson, who maintains that the *epistrophe*, among other figures, is rooted and familiar equally in music as in rhetoric and therefore requires no further explanation. In contrast, Scheibe goes into considerable detail regarding the *epistrophe*'s extensive musical application. The importance of this device in eighteenth-century composition is further illustrated through Forkel's listing of this figure.

Susenbrotus (*Epitome* p.54)

Conversio ἀντιστροφή, est quando continenter ad unum atque idem verbum plura membra exeunt. . . . Hanc Rutilus ἐπιφόρα nominavit.

The *conversio* or *antistrophe* occurs when numerous subsequent passages conclude with the same word. . . . Rutilus called this *epiphora*.

Gottsched (*Redekunst* p.279)

Epiphora. Welche das Ende eines Absatzes in der Rede etliche mal wiederholet.

Epiphora, through which the ending of one passage is repeated a number of times [in subsequent passages] throughout the oration.

Gottsched (*Dichtkunst* p.341)

Zum XXV. kömmt die Wiederkehr (Epistrophe) da man die Schlußworte des einen Satzes etlichemal am Ende anderer Sätze wiederholet.

The next figure is the *epistrophe*, through which the concluding words of one sentence are repeated several times at the end of following sentences.

Ahle (*Sommer-Gespräche* p.17)

Setzet er: singet dem Herren / rühmet den Herren / lobet den Herren; so ist es eine Epistrophe.

Were he to write: sing to the Lord / glorify the Lord / praise the Lord, it would be an *epistrophe*.

Walther (*Lexicon*)

Epiphora, ἐπιφορὰ, oder Epistrophe, ἐπιστροφὴ, ist eine Rhetorische Figur, da ein oder mehr Worte zu Ende der Commatum, Colorum, u.s.f. wiederholt werden.

The *epiphora* or *epistrophe* is a rhetorical figure in which one or more words are repeated at the end of numerous phrases, elaborations, or similar passages.

Mattheson (*Capellmeister* p.243)

Die Epanalepsis, Epistrophe, Anadiplo-

The *epanalepsis*, *epistrophe*, *anadiplosis*,

sis, Paronomasia, Polyptoton, Antanaclasis, Ploce etc. haben solche natürliche Stellen in der Melodie, daß es fast scheinet, als hätten die griechischen Redner sothane Figuren aus der Ton-Kunst entlehnet; denn sie sind lauter repetitiones vocum, Wiederholungen der Wörter, die auf verschiedene Weise angebracht werden.

paronomasia, polyptoton, antanaclasis, ploce, etc., assume such natural positions in music that it almost seems as if the Greek orators borrowed these figures from the art of musical composition. For they are purely *repetitiones vocum*, repetitions of words, which are applied to music in various different ways.

Scheibe (*Critischer Musicus* p.696)
Die XIte Figur ist die Wiederkehr. (Epistrophe.) Diese besteht darinnen, wenn man die Schlußmelodie des ersten Satzes am Ende anderer Sätze wiederholet. Ich will dieses deutlicher machen. Man pfleget sehr oft in Concerten den Satz, mit welchem die Concertstimme den ersten Schluß machet, am Ende, da sie in den Schlußton schließt, in der Concertstimme wieder anzubringen. Dieses pflegt man auch in der Mitten des Concerts zu thun. Und dieses geschieht auch in Sonaten von zwo Stimmen, wie auch in Concerten von einer Stimme, als in Clavierconcerten. Auch in ordentlichen starken Arien mit Instrumenten wiederholet man in der Mitten, und am Ende derselben den Schlußsatz des ersten Rittornells. Man machet ferner Recitative, die mit Instrumenten begleitet werden, und in welche man bey verschiedenen Abtheilungen kurze Chöre einrücket, die aber allemal auf einerley Art gesungen werden. Man muß aber diese Figur nicht mit der Wiederholung verwechseln. . . . [Die *epistrophe*] bezieht sich nur auf den Schluß eines gewissen Nebensatzes, der an den Hauptsatz angeschlossen, und nur zu einer gewissen Zeit, und nach einer bestimmten Ordnung wiederholet wird, imgleichen auch sehr oft auf einen kurzen, doch vollständigen Satz, der auf solche Art wiederholet wird.

The next figure is the *epistrophe*. This occurs when the ending of one melodic passage is repeated at the end of other passages. I wish to clarify this. In concertos the ending passage of the first solo entry is frequently repeated in the tonic key in the solo voice at the conclusion of the movement. This restatement can also be encountered in the middle of the concerto, and can occur either in sonatas with two voices or in concertos with one voice, such as piano concertos. In quite forceful arias accompanied by instruments the final section of the first ritornello can also be repeated in the middle or at the end. Furthermore, the figure is also employed in recitatives accompanied with instruments which include short choral interjections all sung in similar manner. However, this figure must not be confused with the *repetitio*. . . . [The *epistrophe*] refers only to the repetition of the ending of a secondary passage which is connected to the principal theme and which is repeated only at a specific time according to the particular order of the principal theme. Similarly, it frequently occurs in a short yet complete passage which is repeated in like manner.

Forkel (*Geschichte der Musik* p.57)
Die Epistrophe (Wiederkehr) besteht darin, daß man den Schluß des ersten Satzes einer Melodie am Ende anderer Sätze

The *epistrophe* (return) consists of a return of the conclusion of the first melodic passage at the end of other passages. It is

wiederkehren läßt. Sie ist eine Art der Wiederholung, nur mit dem Unterschied, daß die eigentliche Wiederholung ganze Sätze, diese aber nur den Schluß eines Satzes angeht.

a form of the *repetitio* with the following difference: while the *repetitio* concerns itself with entire passages, the *epistrophe* is only concerned with the ending of a passage.

EPIZEUXIS: an immediate and emphatic repetition of a word, note, motif, or phrase.

This figure of repetition, which rhetoricians also call *subiectio* (Susenbrotus), *subjunctio*, or *adiectio*,[1] is given the same definition in both musical and rhetorical disciplines. Walther translates the Greek term literally with the Latin *adjunctio*. This term however signifies a grammatical figure which occurs when a single verb is used in connection with more than one sentence.[2] Walther's definition has nothing in common, however, with the rhetorical *adjunctio* but rather cites Ahle's description and examples of the *epizeuxis*.

As evidenced in numerous other Ahle/Walther definitions, both authors describe the figure in rhetorical terms with the understanding that they be employed musically. This is emphasized at the conclusion of Ahle's discussion of the figures, where he states that the *epizeuxis* is "the most common figure, since it is used by composers in virtually all passages." The widespread application of the figure is also underscored by Mattheson, who asked rhetorically: "What is more common, for example, than the musical *epizeuxis*?" Based on these comments, the figure is as common in instrumental music as in vocal compositions.

Although a systematic application of the rhetorical concept of figures to the musical art of composition remains a German phenomenon, hints of a similar approach can periodically be found in other traditions. In England, "almost without exception, references linking rhetorical elements to music appear not in music treatises, but in various non-musical sources."[3] Henry Peacham the Elder compares the rhetorical *epizeuxis* to the musical quaver or shake, stressing their common "function and

1. Sonnino, *Handbook*, 174.
2. Ibid., 22.
3. Butler, "Music and Rhetoric," 53.

effect when reiterated repeatedly without a break—namely that of a vehement and powerful stress on that particular unit with its attendant powerful impact on the listener."[1]

Susenbrotus (*Epitome* p.53)

Epizeuxis ἐπίζευξις Subiectio, est eiusdem dictionis, citra morem cum impetu pronunciationis ac maioris vehementiae gratia, geminatio: fit vel amplificandi gratia.

The *epizeuxis* or *subjectio* is a contiguous and passionate repetition of the same word for the sake of greater vehemence or amplification.

Peacham (*Garden of Eloquence* p.47)

Epizeuxis is a figure whereby a word is repeated, for the greater vehemencie, and nothing put betweene: and it is used commonly with a swift pronunciation. . . . This figure may serve aptly to expresse the vehemencie of any affection, whether it be of joy, sorrow, love, hatred, admiration or any such like, in respect of pleasant affections it may be compared to the quaver in Musicke, in respect of sorrow, to a double sigh of the heart, & in respect of anger, to a double stabbe with a weapons point.

Gottsched (*Redekunst* p.279)

Epizeuxis. Wenn dasselbe Wort gleich hinter einander im Anfange eines Satzes wiederholet wird.

Epizeuxis. When the same word at the beginning of the sentence is immediately repeated.

Gottsched (*Dichtkunst* p.322)

Es geschieht aber diese Wiederholung auf vielerley Art. Zuweilen wird im Anfange ein und dasselbe Wort zweymal gesetzet, und das heiβt Epizeuxis.

The *repetitio* can occur in many forms. At times one and the same word is set twice at the beginning of a passage, which is called an *epizeuxis*.

Ahle (*Sommer-Gespräche* p.16, 17)

Dän setzet er: Jauchzet / jauchzet / jauchzet dem Herren alle Welt; so ist es eine Epizeuxis. Setzet er aber Jauchzet / jauchzet dem Herren alle / alle Welt; so ist es eine doppelte. . . . Doch wie das salz die gemeinste würze ist; also ist die

Were he to set: Rejoice / rejoice / rejoice in the Lord all the earth; it would be an *epizeuxis*. And were he to set Rejoice / rejoice in the Lord all / all the earth; it would be a double *epizeuxis*. . . . But just as salt is the most common seasoning, so

1. Ibid., 55.

Epizeuxis die gebreuchlichste Figur: sintemahl sie von den Komponisten schier in allen commatibus angewendet wird.

too is the *epizeuxis* the most common figure, since it is used by composers in virtually all passages.

Walther (*Lexicon*)
Epizeuxis, gr. ἐπίζεῦξις, Adjunctio, von ἐπιζεγνυω, adjungo; ist eine Rhetorische Figur, nach welcher ein oder mehr Worte sofort hinter einander emphatischer Weise wiederholt werden. Z.E. Jauchzet, jauchzet, jauchzet dem Herrn alle Welt; setzet man aber: Jauchzet, jauchzet dem Herrn alle, alle Welt; so ists eine doppelte Epizeuxis.

The *epizeuxis* or *adjunctio*, from *epizegnuo*, *adjungo*, is a rhetorical figure through which one or more words are immediately and emphatically repeated, for example: Rejoice, rejoice, rejoice in the Lord all the earth. And were one to set Rejoice, rejoice in the Lord all, all the earth; it would be a double *epizeuxis*.

Mattheson (*Capellmeister* p.243)
Denn, was ist z.E. gewöhnlicher, als die musicalische Epizeuxis oder Subjunctio, da einerley Klang mit Hefftigkeit in eben demselben Theil der Melodie wiederholet wird?

What is more common, for example, than the musical *epizeuxis* or *subjunctio*, where the same note is vehemently repeated in the same portion of the melody?

ETHOPHONIA: see *MIMESIS*

EXCLAMATIO, ECPHONESIS: a musical exclamation, frequently associated with an exclamation in the text.

The musical *exclamatio* is virtually always used to express an exclamation in the accompanying text. As such, it might employ a variety of specific musical-rhetorical figures, depending on the nature of the exclamation. The relatively late and not particularly frequent listing of one of the most obvious musical-rhetorical devices is explained by the fact that many composers as well as authors used more specific figures in expressing exclamations. As early as the fifteenth century, Dunstable employs the *noema* in his motet *Salve regina* at the exclamation: "*O clemens, o pia*," further heightened through the addition of fermatas over each syllable. Praetorius, who does not develop a systematic catalog of musical-rhetorical figures, concerns himself with the related question of effective text interpretation. He discusses the *exclamatio* in the context of performance practice rather than musical composition. Here he underscores three requirements of the singer: the need for a pleasant and "moderately trembling" voice, good breath control, and a suitable vocal range. In addition, the singer must be knowledgeable regarding *intonatio*, "that is, how to begin a piece" (referring to the use of an opening *accentus*) and regarding *exclamatio*, "that is, the proper method of moving the affections." He associates the *exclamatio* with a rapidly descending dotted passage, calling for the vocalist to express the text appropriately. His emphasis on affection and text expression clearly points to the close relationship between the common understanding of the musical device and the concept of the musical-rhetorical figures. To portray and move the affections is the primary concern of both *musica poetica* and the musical as well as rhetorical figures themselves.

Vogt is the first author to include *exclamatio* as a specific musical-rhetorical figure. In keeping with all of his musical-rhetorical *figurae ideales*, he chooses the Greek term, *ecphonisis*, instead of the more common Latin *exclamatio*. In doing so, Vogt consciously establishes the relationship between the ancient art of rhetoric and his own musical-rhetorical interests. Walther then lists both Greek and Latin terms, suggesting the use of an upward-leaping minor sixth to express the exclamation found in the text. Mattheson and Scheibe both underscore the wide variety of techniques and devices which might be employed to realize a musical *exclamatio*. While Mattheson attempts to identify the various possibilities, Scheibe acknowledges that "its properties are as diverse as its origins, causes, or effects." Although Mattheson lists the figure as a *Spruch-Figure*,[1] he discusses it in the chapter dealing with the parts and caesurae of a musical oration.[2] Furthermore, the title and content of this chapter point to the eighteenth-century intention to develop an understanding of the figures which parallels the rhetorical discipline, even though the respective musical devices and methods had

---

1. *Capellmeister*, 243.

2. "*Von den Ab- und Einschnitten der Klang-Rede*," *Capellmeister*, ch.9, 180ff. Here he also discusses the musical question (*interrogatio*) and musical expressions of the *parenthesis*, all three being indicated in the text through specific punctuation marks.

long since been established compositional tools.

Quintilian (*Institutio* IX.ii.27)
Quod exclamationem quidam vocant ponuntque inter figuras orationis. Haec quotiens vera sunt, non sunt in ea forma, de qua nunc loquimur, at simulata et arte composita procul dubio schemata sunt existimanda.

Some call this *exclamatio* and place it among the figures of speech. When they are genuine exclamations, they do not belong to our present discussion. However, when they are simulated and artfully constructed, they can without doubt be regarded as figures.

Susenbrotus (*Epitome* p.64)
Exclamatio, est quae conficit significationem aut doloris aut indignationis per hominis, aut urbis, aut loci, aut temporis, aut rei cuiuspiam compellationem.

The *exclamatio* expresses an indication of anguish or indignation over a person, city, place, time, or any other such thing.

Gottsched (*Redekunst* p.286)
Exclamatio. Wenn man aus einer starken Gemüthsbewegung einen Ausruff thut.

Exclamatio. When an exclamation is uttered out of a vehement affection.

Gottsched (*Dichtkunst* p.316)
Lami fängt die Figuren mit dem Ausruffe (Exclamatio) an; weil diese die natürlichste ist, und in vielen Affecten zuerst hervorbricht. Denn es giebt einen Ausruf, in der Freude, Traurigkeit, Rachgier, imgleichen im Schrecken, Zagen, Verzweifeln, Trotzen, u.d.gl. Nun giebt es zwar gewisse Formeln, die eigentlich dazu bestimmt sind, als Ach! O! Weh! Wohlan! Hey! Sa, Sa! Ha! u.a.m. Allein es werden so viel andre Redensarten dazu gebraucht, daß ihre Zahl nicht zu bestimmen ist.

Lamy begins his list of figures with the *exclamatio*, because it is the most natural and first to be uttered in many affections. For there are exclamations in joy, sorrow, vengeance, similarly in fear, trepidation, despair, defiance, and similar affections. And there are also certain formulations which are intended for such expressions, such as *Ach! O! Weh! Wohlan! Hey! Sa, Sa! Ha!* and others. Indeed, the number of expressions used for this purpose is far too great to specify.

Praetorius (*Syntagma Musicum III* p.231)
Exclamatio ist das rechte Mittel die affectus zu moviren, so mit erhebung der Stimm geschehen muß: Und kan in allen Minimis und Semiminimis mit dem Punct / descendendo angebracht und gebraucht werden. Unnd moviret sonderlich die folgende Nota, so etwas geschwinde fortgehet / mehr affectus, als die Semibrevis, welche in erhebung und verringerung der Stimm ohn Exclamation mehr stadt findet / auch bessere gratiam hat.

The *exclamatio* is the proper method of moving the affections and is achieved through raising the voice. It can be employed in descending passages of dotted *minimae* or *semiminimae*, thereby causing the following faster note to be more passionate. In contrast, a heightened and shortended *semibrevis* is not used in connection with the *exclamatio* because it is less passionate and also more graceful.

Vogt (*Conclave* p.151)

Ecphonisis. Inclamatio, ut o, proh dolor, &c.

Ecphonisis. An exclamation, such as "O, what pain!" etc.

Walther (*Lexicon*)

Exclamatio (lat) ἐκφώνησις (gr.) ist eine Rhetorische Figur, wenn man etwas beweglich ausruffet; welches in der Music gar füglich durch die aufwerts springende Sextam minorem geschehen kan.

The *exclamatio* or *ecphonesis* is a rhetorical figure which signifies an agitated exclamation. This can be realized very appropriately in music through an upward-leaping minor sixth.

Mattheson (*Capellmeister* p.193f.)

Sollte nun wol iemand meinen, daß, gleichwie in den Fragen ein zweifacher Unterschied ist, also in den Ausrufungen ein dreifacher wäre? welches sich doch, bey der Untersuchung, gantz richtig befindet, und den Componisten allerdings verpflichtet, sothane Ausbrüche auch auf eben so vielerley Weise zu bearbeiten, obgleich nur einerley Zeichen (!) dazu gebraucht wird. Die erst Art begreifft eine Verwunderung, einen freudigen Zuruf, oder einen aufmunternden Befehl. . . . Und hiebey spielt die Freude allemahl Meister; sie ist die herrschende Leidenschafft: Daher denn lauter lebhaffte und hurtige Klangführungen dabey gebraucht werden müssen; absonderlich aber grosse und weite Intervalle.

Should someone now suggest that, just as a twofold differentiation is made in the *interrogatio*, there is similarly a threefold differentiation in the *exclamatio*, they would, upon further examination, be proven correct. The composer is also obliged to express such outbursts in as many different ways, even though they are indicated by one and the same sign: (!). The first type consists of an astonishment, a joyous shout, or an encouraging command. . . . Here joy is always master and the ruling affection. Therefore only lively and brisk musical expressions are used in such cases, and particularly large and leaping intervals.

Die zweite Art der Ausbrüche oder Exclamationen hält alles Wünschen und hertzliches Sehnen in sich; alle Bitten, Anrufungen, Klagen; auch Schreckniß, Grauen, Entsetzen, etc. Die letztern erfordern eine melodische Hefftigkeit, so am besten durch geschwinde oder doch hurtige Klänge auszudrücken stehet; das Sehnen aber und die übrigen Eigenschafften haben die Betrübniß allemahl zur Mutter. . . . Da müssen, nach Befinden der Umstände, bald grosse, doch nicht gemeine, bald kleine und ausserordentliche Intervalle angebracht werden. Die Zärtlichkeit herrschet darin vorzüglich.

The second type of outburst or *exclamatio* expresses all kinds of desire and fervent longing, all pleading, beseeching, complaining, as well as frightening, fearing, dreading, etc. The latter require a melodic vehemence best expressed through rapid or at least brisk notes. However, sorrow and grief is the mother of longing and the other sentiments. . . . Therefore the composer will use uncommon intervals, now large ones, now small ones, according to the circumstances. At all times tenderness is of particular importance.

Die dritte Art der Ausruffungen gehet auf

The third type of *exclamatio* consists of

ein rechtes Geschrey, so aus äusserster Bestürtzung, Erstaunung, aus schrecklichen, gräulichen Vorfällen entspringet, die den höchsten Gipffel der Verzweiffelung offt ersteigen. . . . Hier ist nun lauter desperates Wesen, und darff man also auch lauter verworrene Intervalle, die eine unbändige Eigenschafft wieder einander haben, als grosse und kleine Tertzen zusammen etc. auf die Bahn bringen, und zu dem ruchlosen, lästerlichen Geschrey, ein wütendes Getümmel, Gegeige und Gepfeiffe zur Begleitung wehlen.

a veritable scream resulting from extreme dismay or astonishment because of horrifying or atrocious events frequently of the highest order of despair. . . . Here desperation reigns supreme, which therefore also permits a fallacious use of intervals which exhibit an unruly character when brought together, such as simultaneous major and minor thirds. To accompany such vicious and scandalous screaming, one may choose a raging turmoil of fiddling and piping.

Scheibe (*Cirtischer Musicus* p.686)

Die erste Figur ist also der Ausruf. (Exclamatio.) Die Eigenschaften desselben sind so verschieden, als die Ursachen, wodurch er entsteht, oder als die Wirkungen, die ihn hervorbringen. Inzwischen ist dieses überhaupt dabey zu merken, daβ er insgemein aufwärts geschehen muβ, und daβ er bey freudigen Begebenheiten, oder Gemüthsbewegungen durch consonirende Sätze, bey traurigen aber durch dissonirende auszudrucken ist. Dieses ist nun, so wohl in Ansehung der Melodie, als in Ansehung der Harmonie, zu verstehen. Durchaus aber muβ er deutlich seyn, und sich von der Begleitung der Instrumente wohl unterscheiden. Bey der Verzweiflung und bey den heftigsten Regungen ist noch zu merken, daβ man den Ausruf am besten durch enarmonische Sätze, sie mögen in der Melodie, oder Harmonie, bestehen, ausdrücken kann.

The first figure is the *exclamatio*. Its properties are as diverse as its origins, causes, or effects. It should be generally noted that it is commonly expressed through an ascending passage, using consonances in joyous events or affections and dissonances in sorrowful ones. This applies in regard to both melody and harmony. The *exclamatio* must always be distinctly discernible and clearly distinguishable from the accompanying instruments. It should also be noted that, in passages expressing despair or other vehement passions, the *exclamatio* is best expressed through enharmonic melodic or harmonic passages.

EXTENSIO: a prolongation of a dissonance.

In accordance with his concept of the musical-rhetorical figures as devices which legitimize the unorthodox use of dissonance, Bernhard defines *extensio* as a figure through which a certain dissonance is prolonged or extended. Although the *extensio* is very similar to and is frequently used in connection with the *multiplicatio*, the former refers to an "extension" of a dissonance's duration while the latter underscores the "multiplication" of the (extended) dissonant note into numerous shorter ones. Bernhard lists *extensio* as one of the *stylus theatralis* or *recitativus* figures. Because of the *basso continuo*–accompanied monodic musical texture, this "modern" style permits a freer use of dissonance than the older contrapuntal style. In addition to allowing greater harmonic licence, the freer meter of the *stylus theatralis* also permits greater rhythmic freedom.[1] Thus, even if a dissonance were to be extended into an otherwise strong beat, the resulting irregularity would not be perceived as acutely as in other styles of music. A similar dissonance occurring in the *stylus luxurians communis* is called *prolongatio*, another figure found only in Bernhard's *Tractatus*.[2] In contrast to the *extensio*, the dissonance incurred through a *prolongatio* is explained in the context of a *transitus* or *syncopatio*, with reference to the durational relationship between the dissonance and the preceding consonance.

Walther's definition of *extensio* does not mention the figurative understanding of the term but rather describes a Greek compositional species also known as *agoge*. Neither does Bernhard mention the term again in his *Bericht* but rather incorporates the device (along with the *prolongatio*) under *multiplicatio*: "The extended or prolonged *multiplicatio* occurs when the dissonances are of longer duration than the preceding consonances."[3]

Bernhard (*Tractatus* p.83)

Extensio ist einer Dissonanz ziemlich lange währende Veränderung. Sie ist gemeiniglich mit der Multiplication vereiniget.

The *extensio* is a rather considerable prolongation of a dissonance. It is usually combined with the *multiplicatio*.

---

1. In his definition of another *stylus theatralis* figure, the *transitus inversus*, Bernhard notes that the dissonance incurred by this figure is permitted in the *stylus theatralis* because this style "does not observe a strict meter" ("welcher darum im Stylo recitativo zugelaβen, weil darinnen kein Tact gebraucht wird"). See *Transitus*.

2. See *Prolongatio*.

3. See *Multiplicatio*.

Walther (*Lexicon*)

Extensio (lat.) τονὴ (gr.) sonsten auch ἀγωγὴ τοναῖα genannt. s. Calvisii Melopoeiam c.8. war bey den Griechen die vierdte Gattung oder species ihrer Melopoeiae, und gestund darinn, daß die Stimme immer in einerley Tone lag.

The *extensio tone*, otherwise called *agoge tonaia* (see Calvisius, *Melopoeia*, ch.8), was the fourth *species* of Greek compositional theory, and consisted of the voice remaining in the same tone.

FAUX BOURDON, CATACHRESIS, SIMUL PROCEDENTIA: a musical passage characterized by successive sixth-chord progressions.

The early origins of the term *faux bourdon* are to be found in the fifteenth-century English *faburdon* practice, originally signifying an additional and improvised lower voice to the *burdon* or *cantus firmus*.[1] While the *faburdon* accompanies the *burdon* at the lower third, a *discant* is added a fourth above the *burdon*, resulting in a progression of successive sixths surrounding the *cantus firmus* or *burdon*. A similar and presumably related term, *faux bourdon*, is also encountered in France in the fifteenth century. Although it signifies a similar successive three-part sixth-chord progression, the *cantus firmus* appears in the upper

1. D. Hoffmann-Axthelm, "Faburdon / fauxbourdon / falso bordone," *Handwörterbuch der musikalischen Terminologie* (Wiesbaden: F. Steiner, 1972). In his article, Hoffmann-Axthelm has significantly clarified the confusion surrounding the origins, development, and interdependence of these terms.

voice. Furthermore, instead of only being considered a form of improvisation, *faux bourdon* also signifies the corresponding compositional technique.[1] The term *falso bordone* is used as a translation of the French *faux bourdon* in sixteenth-century Italy, signifying the parallel three-part compositional technique. Furthermore, it is expanded to include four-part chordal harmonizations of psalm tones, usually with the root of the chord in the bass voice. By the end of the sixteenth century the terms *faux bourdon* and *falso bordone* seem to be used interchangeably.

Burmeister originally adopts both the term *faux bourdon* and its content into his first *Figurenlehre*. In this case he does not find it necessary to supply a rhetorical term for the familiar musical device but, in his concern to identify compositional phenomena for the purposes of instruction and analysis, uses established terminology. With the further development of his concept of the musical-rhetorical figures, Burmeister does introduce alternative terminology. He chooses to name the figure with the descriptive term *simul procedentia*, meaning "simultaneous progression," and also supplies the Greek translation of the Latin term. Although this is not a rhetorical term, it is a conscious paralleling of rhetorical nomenclature. Through it he no longer emphasizes the archaic "contra-bass" understanding of this harmonic progression, but rather the contrapuntal "error" (or license, as Vogt later points out) of the resulting parallel fourths. Burmeister places the device among the *figurae tam harmoniae quam melodiae*. His understanding of musical composition is governed by sixteenth-century imitative counterpoint and not a chordal, *basso continuo* texture, prompting him to classify the figure as "both harmonic as well as melodic." He thereby underscores the parallel motion (*simul procedentia*) of the individual voices (*figurae melodiae*),

---

1. In northern Middle-English, *fa* means opponent and *burdon* signifies the *cantus firmus* as found in the lowest voice. While *bourdon* in the French term presumably parallels the English *burdon*, the prefix *fa* is replaced with *faux* (false). The various attempts to identify a semantic compositional "falseness" in the fifteenth-century context of the term have proven imaginative yet unconvincing. While the first reference to the French term is found in a manuscript of Dufay's *Missa Sancti Jacobi* (ca.1430), it is not clear whether it refers to a "fauxbourdoning" voice or to the entire *faux bourdon* passage. Only at the very end of the century is an elaboration on the incorrect musical syntax of parallel fourths encountered, namely in Adam Fulda's *Musica* (1490), thereby clearly establishing the term as a reference to an irregular compositional device.

with the resulting contrapuntal irregularity which is only realized in the polyphonic context (*figurae harmoniae*).[1]

In his conscious effort to develop a concept of musical-rhetorical figures which is analogous to its rhetorical counterpart, Thuringus predictably chooses a term for the *faux bourdon* technique which not only appears to be a rhetorical term but, in fact, is one. Although the rhetorical figure of *catachresis* (Latin, *abusio*) can hardly be musically realized, the term is useful in referring to the "abuse" of parallel fourths in counterpoint. This contrapuntal irregularity, which had already been discussed by Adam Fulda, among many others, is then clearly explained in Walther's definition of *catachresis*, which he defines with respect to parallel fourths and also other harmonic irregularities, such as harsh resolutions of dissonances.

The expanded Italian understanding of the *falso bordone*—to include a four-part homophonic harmonization of a chant or psalm tone—leads to the introduction of another rhetorical term, the *pleonasmus*, literally, "abundance, excess." Besides being used by Burmeister for a musical figure, this rhetorical term, which signifies an overabundance of modifying words,[2] is applied to the *falso bordone* technique to indicate an overabundance of syllables or words which are to be sung to a single note, a feature of psalm-tone incantation. This understanding of the term does not appear in any *Figurenlehre*, but it is listed by Vogt in the introductory glossary of his *Conclave* and appears in Janovka's *Clavis* as an independent entry under *falso bordone*. While Janovka explains the term only in this restricted understanding, Vogt supplies *falso bordone* with the two differing definitions. This twofold understanding of the interchangeable terms, *falso bordone* and *faux bourdon*, is already evident with Praetorius and appears again in Walther's definitions of the terms.

A further nonrhetorical Greek term, *isobatus*, meaning "same path" or "same progression," is employed by Kircher to describe the harmonized chant. The introduction of the terms *isobatus* and *pleonasmus* for harmonized psalm tones can be explained by the fact that this com-

1. See also *Congeries*, a figure which Burmeister understands as a modified *simul prodedentia*.

2. See *Pleonasmus*.

positional device no longer featured the harmonic irregularities which justified the term *faux/falso bourdon/bordone*. As Praetorius already points out, "now that the bass is always sung a fifth lower than the tenor, the harmony is corrected and completed." Therefore, some authors seek to distinguish between the two musical devices by introducing differentiating terminology. While some choose to underscore the harmonic irregularities of the sixth-chord progression with the term *catachresis*, others wish to highlight the overabundance of words to be sung in harmony to one chant note with the terms *pleonasmus* and *isobatus*. Simultaneously, *faux/falso bourdon/bordone* is also used to identify both musical devices.

Quintilian (*Institutio* VIII.vi.34)

Eo magis necessaria catachresis, quam recte dicimus abusionem, quae non habentibus nomen suum accommodat quod in proximo est.

This necessitates the *catachresis*, correctly translated as *abusio*, which adopts the nearest available term for something which has no name.

Susenbrotus (*Epitome* p.11)

Abusio, est quae non habentibus nomen suum, accommodat, quod in proximo est.

The *abusio* occurs when the nearest available term is adopted for something which has no name.

Burmeister (*Hypomnematum*)

Faux Bourdon fit quando Tertiae, Quartae, & Sextae simili motu seruntur, ad modum ferme congeriei.

The *faux bourdon* occurs when thirds, fourths, and sixths are combined in parallel motion, very much in the manner of the *congeries*.

Burmeister (*Musica Poetica* p.65)

Simul Procedentia, sive mota, ὁμοστιχάοντα vel ὁμιοκινεόμενα, vel aut gallico nomine vocata Faux Bourdon, est in tribus vocibus sub eodem motu & pari quantitate Ditonorum vel Semiditonorum & διατεσσάρων compositio. Exemplum est in Orlandi Omnia quae fecisti nobis Domine, ad textum: peccavimus tibi.

Simul procedentia or [*simul*] *mota*, that is *homostichaonta* or *homiocineomena* [simultaneous progression], known as *faux bourdon* in French, consists of a progression of major or minor thirds and fourths in three voices, all of the same duration and moving in parallel motion. An example is found in Orlando's *Omnia quae fecisti nobis Domine* at the text *peccavimus tibi*.

Praetorius (*Syntagma Musicum III* p.9)

Falso Bordone. 1. Fürs erste werden die Psalmen / so im anfang der Vesper / als Nota contra Notam in einer reige nach einander in unisono gesetzet seyn / Psalmi Falsi Bordoni genennet: Wiewol in denselben nunmehr der Baß in der Quinta unter dem Tenor allezeit gefunden wird / so die Harmoniam gut und Complet machet.

Falso Bordone. First, the Psalms at the beginning of Vespers which are set homophonically in successive note against note fashion are called *Psalmi Falsi Bordoni.* But now that the bass is always sung a fifth lower than the tenor, the harmony is corrected and completed.

2. Bey den Italis aber ist FALSO Bordone, welches die Frantzosen FAULX BOURDON nennen / wenn ein Gesang mit eitel Sexten nacheinander gesungen wird / also daß der Alt vom Discant eine Quarta, und der Tenor vom Alt eine Tertia niedriger / und also oben eine Quart, und unten ein Tertia respectu mediae Vocis ist. Erat autem veteribus receptum, ut iucundissimae harmoniarum excursiones interdum hac ratione instituerentur. Sed cum veram Basin non habeant, & Bordone Italis chordam, quae ὑπάτην seu maximam in Testudine proxime sequitur, significet, Falso Bordone appellatur. Denn die Tertia hat ihren natürlichen Sitz nicht in sonis gravibus & inferioribus, besondern in sonis acutis & superioribus.

Second, what the French call *faux bourdon* is also called *falso bordone* by the Italians. This occurs when a composition features only successive sixths in such fashion that the alto is a fourth lower than the soprano and the tenor a third lower than the alto, resulting in an upper fourth and a lower third between the voices. In the past it was also accepted that most delightful passages of the composition could occasionally be introduced by this method. But as these passages in fact lack the bass or *bordone*, and indicate a chordal progression which proceeds in the upper or next highest voices, it is called *falso bordone.* For the third by nature is not situated in the lower but rather in the upper voices.

Thuringus (*Opusculum* p.126)

Quid est Catachresis? Catachresis seu Faux Bourdon est, quando plures sextae & Tertiae ascendendo simul progrediuntur.

What is *catachresis*? The *catachresis* or *faux bourdon* occurs when numerous sixths and thirds ascend in parallel motion.

Janovka (*Clavis* p.42)

Falso bordone, alias Pleonasmus, aut ut Pater Kircherus habet Isobatus, dicitur, dum in aliquo cantu multae syllabae, vel vocabula sub una nota canuntur, quod contingit in quibusdam de OO. SS. Litaniis.

Falso bordone, also known as *pleonasmus*, or *isobatus* as Kircher calls it, occurs when numerous syllables or words are sung to one note in a *cantus*, as in certain litanies.

Werckmeister (*Hypomnemata Musica* p.7)

Damit wir nun weiter auf die progression der quartae kommen / so haben die Alten die Continuation derselben nur in gewissen progressionen zugelassen / doch hat sie ihren locum, n.p. superiorem behalten: Dieses haben sie genennet falso bordon und haben damit etwa einen traurigen affectum exprimiren wollen.

Continuing now with the *progressio* of the fourth, it should be noted that in the past its successive use was only allowed in certain passages and specific instances. This they called *falso bordon* and used it, for example, to express a sorrowful affection.

Vogt (*Conclave* p.4)

Falsobordone primo Pleonasmus est, & Isobatus, cum sub una magna nota plures syllabae, vel verba, uno, eodemque tono canuntur. Falsobordone secundo est recto motu consecutio plurium quartarum; & inter licentias locum habet. Hoc modo fiunt quartae illae.

First, *falsobordone*, or *pleonasmus*, *isobatus*, signifies a passage in which numerous syllables or words are sung on one pitch to one long note. Second, *falsobordone* signifies a passage of numerous fourths in orderly motion and is considered a *licentia* [an exception to contrapuntal rules]. These fourths occur in the following fashion:

Walther (*Lexicon*)

Catachresis, gr. κατάχρησις, heisset so viel als abusio, ein Mißbrauch, oder uneigentlicher Gebrauch. Dergleichen entstehet, wenn eine Dissonanz nicht auf ordentliche, sondern ausserordentliche und harte Art resolvirt wird. Der Progressus vieler auf einander folgenden Quarten, welche durch den Bass klang- und brauchbar gemacht werden, heisset auch also; weil nach der Pythagoräer Meinung solche auch unter die vollkommene Consonanzen mit gehören, und demnach immediate einander nicht folgen sollen.

The *catachresis* means *abusio*, an abuse or incorrect use. This occurs when a dissonance is resolved in an unusual and harsh manner. The progression of numerous successive fourths which are made acceptable through the bass is also called a *catachresis*. According to the Pythagoreans, fourths are also considered perfect consonances and therefore are not permitted to immediately follow each other.

Walther (*Lexicon*)

Falso bordone, heisset 1.) wenn auf eine Maximam, d.i. achtschlägige Note, viele Sylben und Wörter in Unisono gesungen werden. . . . 2.) werden diejenigen Sätze einer Composition also genennet, worinnen die Ober-Stimme gegen die Untere lauter Sexten, die Mittlere aber gegen die

Falso bordone occurs (1) when numerous syllables and words are sung *unisono* to a *maxima*, that is a note of eight beats. . . . (2) in a passage of a composition in which the upper and lower voices form successive sixths, the middle and lower voices thirds, and the middle and upper

untere Tertien, und gegen die obere Quarten machet; weil solcher gestallt jedem Satze das rechte und ordentlich Fundament, die wahre Stütze, oder das eigentliche Ende der Harmonie und des Accords mangelt. . . . 3.) Wenn die Melodie eines Cantus firmi nicht in den extrem. sondern in den Mittel-Stimmen (so gemeiniglich im Tenor geschiehet) angebracht und geführet wird, wozu die übrigen Stimmen figuriren.

voices fourths. It is thus called because such a passage lacks the proper and correct foundation, the true support, or the fulfilled harmony and completed chord. . . . (3) when the *cantus firmus* melody is not placed in the outer but rather in the middle voices (normally in the tenor), the other voices being free to figurate.

Walther (*Lexicon*)
Faux-Bourdon ist eben was Falso bordone. Beym Furetiere ist Faus-Bourdon auch so viel, als Contrepoint simple.

Faux bourdon means the same thing as *falso bordone*. Furetiere understands *faus bourdon* to mean simple counterpoint.

FUGA: (1) a compositional device in which a principal voice is imitated by subsequent voices; (2) a musical passage which employs *fuga* to vividly express chasing or fleeing.

Fugal composition is one of the first musical devices to be associated with the rhetorical discipline.[1] An indication of a rhetorical understanding of *fuga* appears as early as 1536 with the reference by Stomius to *fuga* as a *mimesis*, a rhetorical figure of repetition.[2] This seems to be the first known intentional application of specific rhetorical-figure terminology to a musical device. Dressler mentions *fuga* as one of the most important *ornamenta* (i.e., figures) used by Clemens non Papa.[3] In the treatise *De Musica* (after 1559), Anonymous of Besançon uses the term *ploce* to define *fuga*.[4] The common sixteenth-century understanding of

---

1. For a comprehensive discussion of the relationship between fugal technique, rhetorical procedures, and their common structural processes and devices, see G. Butler, "Fugue and Rhetoric," 49ff.

2. See also *Mimesis*.

3. Besides the *fuga*, Dressler also mentions *syncopatio* and *clausula*. It is also Dressler who suggests that the rhetorical organization of *exordium, medium,* and *finis* be adopted for a motet. Ruhnke, *Burmeister*, 137.

4. Quintilian defines *ploce* as a frequent repetition consisting of a mixture of figures. Like Anonymous of Besançon, Susenbrotus also translates the Greek term with the Latin *copulatio* as well as *duplicatio*. See *Anaploce*.

fuga is a form of strict canon, which Dressler calls *fuga integra.*[1] This is also clearly the case in the definitions of Stomius and Anonymous of Besançon. As numerous writers indicate, the term *fuga* is derived from the Latin *fugare*, meaning flight or chase, a vivid description of the imitative activity between the voices. Other forms of canon are also known by terms which feature the same meaning as *fuga*, namely the French *chase*, the English *catch*, and the Italian *caccia*. Freer forms of imitation are also regarded as *fugae*. Here Dressler differentiates between a *semifuga* (the successive entries of the voices at the beginning or during the course of a composition) and a *fuga mutilata* (general imitative counterpoint). Normally only a differentiation between canon and imitative counterpoint is made, referring to them as *fuga ligata* (*integra, mera, totalis*) and *fuga soluta* (*libera, partialis, semifuga*) respectively.[2]

The adoption of *fuga* into the family of musical-rhetorical figures is explained not only by the fact that it had long since been regarded as an embellished form of composition or as an *ornamentum* (as Burmeister also called his figures) related to the rhetorical figures, but that, as a frequent repetition of a theme, *fuga* is considered an aberration from the ordinary or common form of musical expression which could be explained through the concept of musical rhetoric. Regarding this Bernhard writes, "One should not repeat the same phrase too frequently. Yet Fugues and imitations retain their value."[3] Furthermore, the various specific forms of rhetorical repetition, which are also considered deviations from the simple form of expression, find a natural place in musical composition. Thus Burmeister heads his list of figures with *fuga*, followed by specific forms of fugal variation which include the figures *metalepsis*, *hypallage*, and *apocope*.

Burmeister introduces the terms *fuga realis* and *fuga imaginaria* to differentiate between the free and the strict *fuga* or canon, respectively.

---

1. Tinctoris also defines *fuga* in terms of a canon: "A *fuga* is an agreement between the voices of a composition regarding the duration, name, form, and at times also placement of their notes and rests." ("Fuga est identitas partium cantus quo ad valorem, nomen, formam, et interdum quo ad locum tonarum et pausarum suarem.") Coussemaker, *Scriptorum de musica medii aevi*, vol.4 (Paris, 1876), 184.

2. Ruhnke, *Burmeister*, 149.

3. "Man soll nicht oft einerley Modulation wiederbringen, doch bleiben die Fugen und Imitaiones in ihrem Werthe." *Tractatus* ch.2, §8, 41.

Of interest is his reversal of traditional nomenclature: the sixteenth-century canon or "real" *fuga* (*mera*, *integra*: pure, whole) now becomes the "apparent" or *imaginaria* one. Burmeister wishes to differentiate between those *fugae* in which voices are not identical but only imitate each other and those in which the voices are identical. Should the voices be identical, the composition in fact consists of only one voice and is only seemingly (*imaginaria*) a polyphonic composition. This also explains why Burmeister places the two forms of *fuga* in different figure categories. In his *Musica Poetica* the *fuga realis* is listed as one of the *figurae harmoniae*. These are the figures which affect all the voices of a composition. While the different voices may be similar, they are not identical.[1] The *fuga imaginaria*, on the other hand, is listed as one of the *figurae tam harmoniae quam melodiae*. As this form of *fuga* in actuality consists of only one voice, it is a *figura melodiae*. However, because the canonic device determines the formation of the remaining voices or the entire *harmonia*, it is *tam harmoniae quam melodiae*.

Nucius adopts different nomenclature for the two forms of *fuga* in his list of figures: the canon is called *fuga totalis*, while freer imitation is called *fuga partialis*. With this terminology he preserves the more traditional understanding of the two forms of imitation. While *totalis* refers to a complete or whole imitation (*mera*, *integra*), *partialis* signifies a "fractured" (*mutilata*, *soluta*) form of *fuga*. Nucius also introduces the categories of *figurae principales* and *figurae minus principales*, whereby he wishes to differentiate between the purely musical and the musical-rhetorical figures. Bernhard replaces this terminology with *figurae fundamentales* and *figurae superficilaes*. *Fuga* is listed under the *principales*—and later the *fundamentales*—figures, as it has no rhetorical parallel and yet is a fundamental musical device. Thuringus and Kircher both adopt Nucius's classifications as well as his *fuga* terminology. Kircher and Janovka include an additional definition of *fuga* (*in alio sensu*, as Janovka puts it). Kircher, who emphasizes the text- and

---

1. This understanding is reinforced through Burmeister's use of the terms μίμημα and μεμιμημένος, meaning to mimic or impersonate, in describing the *fuga realis*. The rhetorical figure *mimesis* refers to mimicking the voice of another person, frequently in derision. In such an imitation, the reference to the original must be clear yet at the same time remain distinct from it.

affection-expressive nature of the musical-rhetorical figures, explains this "other sense" of *fuga* as a figure which is used to express a text containing words or ideas related to the literal meaning of *fuga*: to flee or chase. This figure would consequently fall under the category of the rhetorically related *figurae minus principales*. This interpretation is again listed at the end of Walther's numerous entries under *fuga* in his *Lexicon*.

Because Bernhard's concept of the figures is determined by a justifiable use of dissonance in a composition, *fuga* finds no place in his list of figures. However, he includes the two species of *fuga* together with their traditional terminology in other appropriate chapters of his treatise. In addition, he also lists some alternative names: the *fuga partialis* is also called *soluta* while the *fuga totalis* is also known as *ligata*. In his *Lexicon* Walther lists the various terms for the two types of *fuga*: the canon is known as *fuga ligata*, *mera*, *integra*, *totalis*, and *universalis*, while the freer form of imitation is called *fuga fracta*, *libera*, *partialis*, or *soluta*. In all of the terms referring to the canon, an understanding of perfection or completeness of the figure is evident. In contrast, freer imitation is understood as an interrupted or liberated form of *fuga*. Burmeister's unique terminology does not find a place in this list of terms.

The relationship between rhetorical and musical composition focuses specifically on fugal devices in late Renaissance and early Baroque English treatises.[1] Francis Bacon refers to *fuga* in rhetorical terms when he states, "The reports [i.e., repetitions] and fugues have an agreement with the figures in rhetoric of repetition and traduction." The rhetorical *traductio*, also known as *polyptoton*, is a figure of repetition in which a word is repeated with alterations in emphasis, case, tense, or other parts of speech.[2] Butler suggests that the application of this term to *fuga* "may

1. G. Butler, "Music and Rhetoric," 53ff. As Butler notes, virtually all references to the relationship between music and rhetoric in England appear in treatises not on music but on rhetoric. Little attempt seems to have been made in England to transfer text- or affection-expressive rhetorical devices to musical composition.

2. Sonnino, *Handbook*, 178. See also *Polyptoton*. Peacham the Elder defines *traductio* as follows: "Traductio is a forme of speech which repeateth one word often times in one sentence, making the oration more pleasant to the eare. . . . This exornation is compared to pleasant repetitions and divisions in Musicke, the chiefe use whereof is, either to garnish the sentence with oft repetition, or to note well the importance of the word repeated" (*Garden of Eloquence*, 49). Peacham does not highlight grammatical

in fact reflect an attempt . . . to come to grips rhetorically with the current broadening of fugal practice in which the subject undergoes numerous slight alterations in the course of the work, including slight melodic changes (as in the tonal answer), rhythmic changes (as in the canzona), and a greater change in transposition."[1] In his treatise Charles Butler includes *fuga* in the section "Of the Ornaments of Melodi and Harmoni," where he also discusses the *reply*, *report*, and *revert*.[2] While these techniques have a similarity to imitative devices which are supplied with rhetorical terminology in German treatises, no attempt seems to have been made on the part of English music theorists to adopt explicit rhetorical terminology.[3] In fact, tonal and real fugal answers are identified with rhetorical terminology in German treatises. While a fugal subject is changed to accommodate a tonal answer through the *repercussio*, the *polyptoton* and *palilogia* can be understood as real fugal answers.[4] Bernhard also links the alteration of a fugal theme with his *Figurenlehre*, but explains it in terms of altering the *modus*. He lists *mutatio toni* as one of the figures used in the *stylus luxurians*. Later, in discussing these "mutations," Bernhard explains the tonal answer with the *consociatio modi*, a combination of the authentic and its associated plagal mode, and the real answer with the *aequatio modi*, an alteration of the mode to accommodate a real answer beginning on the fifth note of the mode.[5]

Mattheson still regards fugal writing central to the art of composition but classifies it as a figure of amplification "which serves more to prolong, amplify, and adorn a composition than to thoroughly convince the passions." As such, this novel classification of *fuga* is parallel to earlier practices of classifying the *fuga* as a *principales* or *fundamentales* figure rather than a figure more closely related to text- and affection-expres-

changes in the repeated word, but rather an increased emphasis through repetition.

1. G. Butler, "Music and Rhetoric," 62.

2. *The Principles of Musik*, 71ff.

3. It is Henry Peacham the Younger who makes this association when he asks rhetorically: "Nay, hath not music her figures, the same which rhetoric? What is a revert but her antistrophe? her reports, but sweet anaphoras? her counterchange of points, antimetaboles?" *The Compleat Gentleman*; cited in Strunk, *Source Readings*, 337.

4. See *Repercussio*, *Palilogia*, *Polyptoton*.

5. See *Mutatio toni*.

sion. It is an expanded concept of *fuga*, however, marking the end of its importance as a musical-rhetorical figure and its increased significance as an independent musical genre, the fugue. Mattheson specifically associates three additional figures with the fugue, *mimesis*, *expolitio*, and *distributio*, which "find their home in this greenhouse of figures." Unlike Burmeister's fugal figures, Mattheson's are not specific fugal devices but rather general procedures, each in themselves giving rise to other devices. While *mimesis* signifies the general principle of free, imitative counterpoint, *expolitio* and *distributio* are figures which an orator employs to expand his argument, amplifying his point through various repetitions and divisions of his subject.[1] As an independent genre, the fugue grows in stature to the point that Forkel, who on the one hand seems to think very little of intricate contrapuntal devices, on the other hand describes the fugue as the crowning musical genre. It also receives a novel and expressive justification: while a single melodic line of an aria expresses the sentiments of an individual, the numerous independent melodic lines of a fugue express the sentiments of a multitude, being thereby both a faithful image and a fruit of Nature. Just as the individual is only one member of a nation, the aria (the previously discussed genre) is only a part of a fugue: a nation incorporates many individuals, and a fugue, many arias. It is therefore the grandest of all genres, just as the general consensus of an entire nation is the grandest of all sentiments.[2]

---

1. Of interest is Thuringus's use of the word *distributio* in his *fuga* definition ("Quid est fuga? Est . . . artificiosa distributio"), suggesting a much earlier link between the rhetorical and musical devices. See *Distributio*, *Mimesis*.

2. "Ist sie nicht, diese mannichfaltige und künstliche Verwebung, eine getreue Abbildung der Natur, ist sie nicht der vollkommenste Ausdruck der mannichfaltig modificirten Empfindungen aller Glieder eines Volks, die erst nach und nach entstehen, sodann aber in einen Strom sich ergießen? . . .Sie ist eine Frucht der Natur. So wie diese in dem Herzen der Menschen vielartige Empfindungen erschaffen hat, so wie sie . . . auch mehrern Menschen zugleich die Aeußerung ihrer Empfindungen verstattet, so hat sie auch der Kunst vielartige Mittel zum Ausdruck derselben gegeben. Diese Mittel sind sämmtlich in der Fuge enthalten; sie ist daher unter den übringen Musikgattungen die prächtigste, vollkommenste und größte, so wie unter den verschiedenen Aeußerungen unserer Empfindung, die allgemeine Uebereinstimmung eines ganzen Volkes, in dem Ausdruck eines Gefühls, das prachtvolleste, rührendste und größte Schauspiel ist. Was will ein einzelner Mensch gegen ein ganzes Volk? Eben so wenig als eine einzelne Arie gegen eine Fuge. Die Arie ist von der Fuge nur ein Theil, wie der einzelne Mensch vom Volke. Das Volk enthält viele Menschen, die Fuge viele Arien." Forkel, *Allgemeine Geschichte*, 48.

During the course of the eighteenth century, *fuga* is dropped from the lists of musical-rhetorical figures. Not only is the device increasingly understood as an independent musical genre, but it no longer fits into the affection-oriented emphasis of the late-Baroque concept of the figures. As the figures are increasingly understood and defined according to their text expressive and affective potential, *fuga* loses its place to more expressive, rhetorical devices. The class of figures which were *minus principales* and *superficiales* in the seventeenth century now become the most significant ones. Scheibe mentions *fuga* merely in passing at the end of his discussion of the musical-rhetorical figures, calling it only a harmonic figure—he has also dropped the significant *figura principalis* or *fundamentalis* terminology—which "actually belongs to the common and basic rules of counterpoint."[1] The *fuga*, which was all important in the *decoratio* of a composition in the sixteenth and seventeenth centuries, and was even referred to as the *ornamentum ornamentorum*,[2] loses its preeminent position in the following century. As in other artistic disciplines, structure is de-emphasized in favor of expressiveness in the eighteenth century, sounding the death knell for the Baroque era and laying the cornerstone for the age of *Empfindsamkeit.*

Stomius (*Prima instructio* C2ᵛ)

Ingeniosa, quas mimeses seu fugas appellant: ubi eadem vox a pluribus, sed certis temporum spaciis intervenientibus, consequenter canitur.

Mimeses or *fugae* are ingenious constructions, in which one and the same voice is successively sung by other voices which are delayed by a specified interval of time.

Anonymous of Besançon (*De Musica* 206b)

Prima Graecis dicta est πλόκή: Latinis copulatio. Sed vulgus nunc cantorum fugam nominat. Est autem ploce, vocum repetitio similium aliquo modo parallela, hoc est, partium collatione aequali, vel

The first is called *ploce* by the Greeks and *copulatio* in Latin. However, among singers it is now generally referred to as *fuga*. The *ploce* is a parallel repetition of the same voice in a certain fashion, that

1. "Diese Arten der harmonischen Figuren [*transitus*, *syncopatio*, *fuga*] sind aber den Musikverständigen bekannt genug, daβ ich also nicht nöthig habe, mich mit deren Erklärung allhier zu beschäfftigen. Auβer diesen gehören sie eigentlich zu den allgemeinen und ersten Compositionsregeln, die ich in diesen Blättern zu erläutern nicht gesonnen bin." *Critischer Musicus*, 699.

2. Ruhnke, *Burmeister*, 149.

simili, sibi inter se respondentium.

is, through a combination of equal or like parts which in themselves correspond to each other.

Burmeister (*Hypomnematum*)

Fuga est Melodiae alicuius τö μεμιμημένον paribus vel iisdem intervallis expressum. Fuga duplex est Realis et Imaginaria. Fuga Realis expressis diversis vocibus, vel etiam similibus τö μίμημα exsequitur.

Fuga is the mimicking of the parts or same intervals of any *melodia*. There are two kinds of *fuga*: *Realis* and *Imaginaria*. *Fuga realis* accomplishes this mimicry by constructing diverse or similar voices.

Fuga Imaginaria Melodiam unica solum voce exponit, cuius imitamen aliae voces Melodiam imaginando expediunt, nonnunquam in iisdem intervallis, nonnunquam in similibus. Fuga Imaginaria tam multiplex fit, quam varie melodia ad distantias datur ruminanda, quae ex unisono fit, ex iisdem fit intervallis, eaque efformari ad plures voces potest. Quae Fugae ex alia distantia ruminantur, ut plurimum ex duabus constant vocibus, & nomen suum exinde (videlicet ex distantia) sortiuntur.

The *fuga imaginaria* presents the *melodia* through only one voice, through whose imitation the other voices then untangle the *melodia*, at times with identical intervals, at times with like ones. The *fuga imaginaria* occurs as frequently as it reappears in the various voices at a certain distance apart. It can occur at the unison using the same intervals and can be formed out of numerous voices. These *fugae*, which usually consist of two voices, are reiterated at various distances apart, this distance also giving them their specific name.

Burmeister (*Musica Poetica* p.57)

Fuga Realis φυγή οὐσιώδης est talis Harmoniae habitus, in quo omnes Harmoniae voces aliquam alicuius vocis in suo conjugio affectionem imitantur intervallis iisdem vel paribus. Quam compositionem velut μεμιμημένος, tam in exordiis cantilenarum, quam in medio exhibere liberum est. . . . In Fugis Vox alia dicitur προφωνεούσα; alia ὑστερόφωνος. Vox, quae Melodiam producit in Fugam convertendam, est illa, quae dicitur προφωνεούσα, ut ea, quae primo loco Fugae affectionem adornat. Quae autem inter reliquas, προφωνεούσα sit,

The *fuga realis* or *phuge housiodes* is a form of composition in which all the voices of the *harmonia* imitate a certain state of another specific voice in relation to the same intervals and phrases. One is free to use this musical mimicking either in the beginning or the middle of the composition. . . . In *fugae*, one voice is called *prophoneousa* (sounding before), the other *hysterophonos* (sounding after). The voice which introduces the *melodia* which is to be turned into a *fuga* is the one called *prophoneousa* and prepares the formulation of the *fuga* through its

perinde est. Ὑστερόφωνος est, quae affectionem Fugam parantem, ruminat, ut ea quae posterior editur. Ὑστερόφωνος tam multiplex fit, quam multas Fuga representat voces, quarum prima dici potest πρῶτη, subandi ὑστερόφωνος vox; Secunda δευτέρα; tertia τρίτη etc.

leading position. Among all the voices, it is the one which sounds first. *Hysterophonos* is the voice which imitates the prepared fugal structure and is introduced later. *Hysterophonos* can be as numerous as the number of imitating voices in the *fuga*, the first of which can be called *prote*, the second *deutera*, the third *trite*, etc.

Burmeister (*Musica Poetica* p.65)
Fuga Imaginaria φυγὴ φάντασtικὴ est Vocis unius existentis Melodia quam alia unica ex eodem sono, aut ex diverso, vel etiam plures voces ad ruminandum, abripiunt. Hoc fit in exiguis Melodiae portionibus, quae lusus gratia, nontam usus, & ita affinguntur, ut de novo ad placitum possint aliquoties iterari.

Fuga Imaginaria or *phuge phantastike* is a *melodia* which consists of a single voice, which is then imitatively taken up by more voices beginning on the same note or on different ones. The points of imitation occur at short portions of the *melodia*, the indication of these portions for the sake of execution not always being used. The additional voices are formed in such fashion that they can be repeated from the beginning at will.

Fuga Imaginaria est duplex ομόφωνος, unisona. Πάμφωνος multisona, ομόφωνος Fuga Imaginaria est Melodia in omnibus Vocibus una & eadem, hoc est, Voces ὑστερόφωνοι Melodiam per eosdem intervallorum gradus imitantur. . . . Πάμφωνος Fuga Imaginaria, est Melodia, quam ὑστερόφωνος imitatur non in iisdem intervallorum gradibus, sed per similes in distantia certa. Πάμφωνος Fuga imaginaria est tam multiplex, quam multiplices sunt distantiae intervallorum, in quibus Melodia unius vocis, ab altera voce ruminari potest.

The *fuga imaginaria* is of two kinds: *homophonos* or *unisona*, and *pamphonos* or *multisona*. The first occurs when the *melodia* is one and the same in all the voices, that is when the following voices imitate the *melodia* at the same pitch and intervals. . . . The second kind occurs when the *melodia* which the following voices imitate does not reappear exactly, but rather with the same intervals at a pitch a specified distance away. The formulations of *fuga imaginaria* can be as numerous as the distances of intervals at which the *melodia* of one voice can be repeated by another voice.

Nucius (*Musices Poeticae* G1v)
De Fugis. Quid sunt Fugae? Fugae nihil sunt aliud, quam eiusdem thematis per distinctos locos crebrae resultationes Pausarum interventu sibi succedentes. Dictae sunt autem a fugando, quia vox vocem fugat, idem melos depromendo. Porro haec figura apud Musicos in tanto est precio, ut non pro artificiosa Cantione ea habeatur, quae non laboratissimis abun-

Of *Fugae*. What are *fugae*? *Fugae* are nothing else but frequent, successive repetitions of the same theme in diverse voices, separated by pauses. This definition refers to flight, because one voice chases the other, thereby producing the composition. Furthermore, this figure is invoked by composers to such an extent that no composition is considered artful

dat & referta est fugis. Atque sane ex hac figura a omnium maxime Musicum ingenium aestimandum est, si pro certa Modorum natura aptas fugas eruere atque erutas bona cohaerentia rite jungere sciat. Quare omnino elaborandum est, ut Harmonia elegantibus fugis constet, quod si difficilius per omnes voces videbitur, quoniam magis exercitatorum est illud, in tribus tamen vel duabus vocibus Tyroni periculum est faciendum.

if it is not filled to overflowing with *fugae*. However, the ingenuity of a composer in the use of this figure is to be held in very high regard if he understands how to construct appropriate *fugae* according to the specific nature of the *modi* and to properly connect these in good coherent fashion. Therefore one should always strive to structure the *harmonia* through elegant *fugae*. Should this appear to be too difficult to accomplish in all voices, which takes a great deal of practice, the proof of Tyronius can be accomplished in three or even two voices.

Quotuplices sunt Fugae? Totales: & Partiales. Quid sunt Totales Fugae? Cum duae aut plures voces, ex eodem themate procedentes, juxta certi alicuius Canonis inscriptionem usque ad finem Harmoniae concinnunt. Tales Canones sunt Fugae in Unisono, Fuga in Epi vel Hypodiatessaron, fuga in ἐπι vel ὑποθιῶπεντε, fugae in ἐπι vel ὑποδιαπασον. Quid sunt fugae Partiales? Hae partes tantum sunt totalium, ideo & fractae fugae appellantur, ut cum eiusdem thematis resultatio in omnibus vocibus tandem in perfectam consonantiam aut formalem clausulam abit. Harum in omnibus Cantionibus, quas Motetas vocant, uberrimus est usus.

Which are the kinds of *fuga*? *Totales* and *Partiales*. What are *fugae totales*? When two or more voices, proceeding out of the same theme, unite to the end of the *harmonia* according to the specific inscription of the *canon*. Such *canones* can be a *fuga* at the unison, the upper or lower fourth, the upper or lower fifth, or the upper or lower octave. What are *fugae partiales*? These are frequently partial *fugae totales*, and are therefore called *fractae* [fractured] *fugae*. Here the repetition of the same theme in all voices finally resolves to a perfect consonance or *clausula formalis*. The use of this figure is most fruitful in those compositions called Motets.

Thuringus (*Opusculum* p.102)
Haec figura apud musicos, quae etiam principalis dicitur, in tanto est precio, ut non pro artificiosa cantione ea habeatur, quae non laboratissimis abundat & referta est fugis. Atque sane ex hac figura omnium maxime musicum ingenium aestimandum est, si pro certa modorum natura aptas fugas eruere, atque erutas bona cohaerentia rite jungere sciat. Quare omnino per omnes voces videbitur, quoniam magis exercitatorum est illus, in tribus tamen vel duabus vocibus Tyroni periculum est faciendem.

This figure, one of the *figurae principales*, is invoked by composers to such an extent that no composition is considered artful if it is not filled to overflowing with *fugae*. However, the ingenuity of a composer in the use of this figure is to be held in very high regard if he understands how to construct appropriate *fugae* according to the specific nature of the *modi* and to properly connect these in good coherent fashion. Therefore one should always strive to structure the *harmonia* through elegant *fugae*. Should this appear to be too difficult to accomplish in all voices, which takes a great deal of prac-

tice, the proof of Tyronius can be accomplished in three or even two voices.

Quid est fuga? Est unius & eiusdem clausulae in diversis cantilenae partibus successiva repetitio & artificiosa distributio. Vel: Est ejusdem melodiae in reliquis vocibus iteratio jucunda. Unde dicuntur? A fugando, quod una vox propter similitudinem notularum alteram quasi fuget & insequatur.

What is a *fuga*? It is an artful *distributio*, a successive repetition of one and the same *clausula* in various parts of the composition. Or, it is a delightful repetition of one and the same *melodia* in other voices. Whence comes the name? From *fugare*, because one voice appears to chase and follow the other voice due to the similarity of their notes.

Quid sunt Fugae Totales? Cum duae vel plures voces, ex eodem themate procedentes, juxta certi alicuius canonis inscriptionem usque ad finem harmoniae concinnunt. Dicitur fuga Ligata, integra vel mera, ubi necesse est omnia accidentia cantus quoad tempus & figuras observari, ut ex unico duce scripto comites eius intelligi & cani possint: ut:

What are *fugae totales*? When two or more voices, proceeding out of the same theme, unite to the end of the *harmonia* according to the specific inscription of the *canon*. The *fuga* is called *ligata*, *integra*, or *mera* when it is necessary to observe every accidental of the *cantus* regarding both the *tempus* and the notes, in order that numerous *comites* can be perceived and sung out of one notated *dux*, as in the following:

Kircher (*Musurgia* L.5, p.368)
De Melothesia fugata, sive De fugis artificiose instituendis. Principalis figura apud Musicos Fuga est, quae tanto in precio habetur, ut non pro artificiosa cantilena habeatur, quae non laboratissimis referta sit fugis; Et ita ne quemadmodum ex figurarum artificioso contextu in Oratoria facultate Rhetoris elucet ingenium, ita & Musici ingenium felix ex fugarum longe pulcherrima serie aestimandum est.

Of *Melothesia Fugata*, or the artful construction of *fugae*. The *fuga* is a *figura principalis* which is invoked by composers to such an extent that no composition is considered artful if it is not filled to overflowing with *fugae*. It does not present itself in the same manner as the ingenuity of an orator, namely through the artful combination of figures in an oration. Rather the ingenuity of the composer is held in esteem through his ability to construct a most delightful and long series of *fugae*.

Est autem fuga unius & eiusdem clausulae in diversis cantilenae partibus suc-

Furthermore, a *fuga* is an artful *distributio*, a successive repetition of one and

cessiva, quaedam repetitio, & artificiosa distributio. Prima vox dicitur Phonagogus sive dux, italice la guida, sive vox antecedens, altera consequens. Est autem generice loquendo fuga duplex, totalis & partialis. Totalis ext, cum duae vel plures voces ex eodem themate progredientes iuxta certi alicuius canonis inscriptionem a principio usque ad finem harmoniae continuantur. . . . Partialis fuga sive libera & soluta est, cuius consequens dicit easdem notas antecedentes, non a principio usque ad finem; sed aliquo usque. . . . Fugae partiales, sive imitantes sunt, quae supra notas alicuius cantus plani, vel altero subiecto indifferenti constituuntur.

the same *clausula* in various parts of the composition. The first voice is called *phonagogus* or *dux*, *la guida* in Italian, or the *vox antecedens* (foregoing voice), the other the *consequens* (following voice). The *fuga* can be of two kinds: *totalis* and *partialis*. The *totalis* occurs when two or more voices, proceeding out of the same theme, are coupled from the beginning to the end of the *harmonia* according to the specific inscription of the *canon*. The *fuga partialis*, also called *libera* or *soluta*, occurs when the *consequens* does not follow the *antecedens* from beginning to end, but introduces other notes. *Fugae partiales* or *imitantes* are constructed on a *cantus planus* or other subject.

Kircher (*Musurgia* L.8, p.145)
Φυγή sive fuga periodus harmonica est, verbis fugam indicantibus apta, cuiusmodi illud: Fuge dilecte mi; servit quoque actionibus successivis exprimendis, cuius quidem omnium frequentissimus usus est.

The *fuga* is a musical passage which is furnished with a *fuga* according to the requirements of the text, such as "*Fuge dilecte mi*." It also serves to express successive actions, for which it is most frequently used.

Janovka (*Clavis* p.56)
Fuga (alio nempe sensu, quam superius inter Principales Figuras sumpta) est Periodus harmonica, verbis fugam indicantibus apta, cuius modi est illud: fuge dilecte mi.

The *fuga* (now in a different sense than the previously cited figure among the *figurae principales*) is a musical passage which is furnished with a *fuga* according to the requirements of the text, such as "*Fuge dilecte mi*."

Walther (*Lexicon*)
Fugha, Fuga (ital.), Fuge (gall.), Fuga (lat.), φυγή (gr.) eine Fuge, ist ein künstlich Stücke, da eine Stimme der andern, gleichsam fliehend, mit einerley themate in verschiedenem Tone nacheilet. s. Niedtens Musical. Handleitung zur Variation des G.B. p.11, oder, nach Mathesonii Beschreibung, Crit. Mus. T.1, p.265. in der Anmerkung: eine Haupt-Figur, bestehend in einer gewissen Wiederhohlung und künstlichen Vertheilung einer eintzigen festfürgesetzten Clausul (auch wohl mehrer, wenn sie doppelt ist) welche man in verschiedenen

The *fuga* . . . is an artful composition in which one voice chases the other, as it were, using the same theme at different pitches. See Niedt's *Musicalische Handleitung*, p.11, or Mattheson's explanation in his *Critischer Musicus* 1: p.265, where he writes: "a principal figure, consisting of a certain repetition and artful distribution of a single predetermined *clausula* (possibly more, should it be a double *fuga*), which is alternately heard in various parts of the composition, be it of two, three, four or more voices." It receives its name from *fugare*, because one voice

Theilen, des Gesanges, er sey mit 2. 3. 4. oder mehr Stimmen, wechselsweise zu hören bekommt. Hat den Nahmen a fugando, weil eine Stimme die andere gleichsam jaget.

chases the other, as it were.

Fuga fracta (lat.) ist mit der partiali einerley.

Fuga fracta is the same as *partialis*.

Fuga impropria (lat.ital.) Fuga irregolare (ital.) Fuga irregularis (lat.) eine uneigentliche, unrichtige Fuge, ist nichts anders, als Imitatio.

Fuga impropria . . . or *irregularis*, a false or incorrect *fuga*, is nothing other than *imitatio*.

Fuga libera (lat.) eine freye, ungebundene oder ungezwungene Fuge, Fugue libre oder déliée (gal.) ist: wenn die anfangende Stimme von den Folge-Stimmen nur so lange und weit wiederholt wird, als das thema gewähret, ehe diese eingetreten.

Fuga libera, a free, unbound, or unconstrained *fuga*, *fugue libre* or *déliée* in French, occurs when the beginning voice is repeated by the following voices only up to that point of the theme where they themselves entered.

Fuga ligata (lat.) Fuga legata (ital.) Fugue liée (gal.) ist: wenn eine oder mehr Folge-Stimmen der anfangenden nicht nur ihr thema, d.i. den von Anfange bis auf die zweyte eintretende Stimme gemachten Satz, sondern auch alle andere, nach der eingetretenen zweyten oder Folge-Stimme, vorkommende Noten durchgängig nachmachen. Heisset deswegen auch Fuga mera und integra (lat.) obligata (lat., ital) Fugue obligée (gal.).

Fuga ligata . . . occurs when one or more subsequent voices completely imitate not only the theme of the first voice, that is its notes up to the entry of the second voice, but also all its following notes after the entries of the subsequent voices. It is therefore also called *fuga mera*, *integra*, *obligata*, and *obligée*.

Fuga partialis (lat.) ist eben so viel als libera; heisset auch bey einigen Particularis.

Fuga partialis is the same as *fuga libera*. Others also call it *particularis*.

Fuga sciolta (ital.) Fuga soluta (lat.) ist mit der libera einerley.

Fuga sciolta or *soluta* is the same as *fuga libera*.

Fuga totalis (lat.) Reditta (ital.) ist eben was Fuga ligata. . . . Heisset auch bey andern: Fuga universalis.

Fuga totalis or *reditta* is the same as *fuga ligata*. . . . Others also call it *fuga universalis*.

Fuga bedeutet auch einen solchen musicalischen periodum, welchen man bey Worten, die eine Flucht anzeigen, anbringet, und die Sache, so viel nur möglich, in Aehnlichkeit vorstellet. s. Janovkae Clavem ad Thesaurum magnae artis Musicae, p.56.

Fuga also refers to a musical passage which is employed when the words indicate a flight, thereby illustrating their content in as like manner as possible. See Janovka's *Clavis*, p.56.

Mattheson (*Capellmeister* p.244)

Noch eins ist zu erinnern, daβ nehmlich unter die grossen Erweiterungs-Figuren,

And finally it should be remembered that the well-known and famous art work

deren etliche dreiβig seyn werden, und die mehr zur Verlängerung, Amplification, zum Schmuck, Zierath oder Gepränge, als zur gründlichen Uiberzeugung der Gemüther dienen, nicht mit Unrecht zu zehlen ist das bekannte und berühmte Kunst-Stück der Fugen, worin die Mimesis, Expolitio, Distributio samt andern Blümlein, die selten zu reiffen Früchten werden, ihre Residentz, als in einem Gewächs-Hause, antreffen. An seinem Orte wird davon mehr Unterricht folgen.

called fugue is appropriately numbered among the large figures of amplification. There are approximately thirty of these figures, which serve more to prolong, amplify, and adorn a composition than to thoroughly convince the passions. Included in the fugue are figures such as *mimesis*, *expolitio*, *distributio*, and other embellishments which are rarely fruitful and find their home in that greenhouse of figures. More instruction regarding this will be given at the appropriate place.

GRADATIO: see *CLIMAX*

GROPPO: a four-note motif with a common first and third note.

In early-seventeenth-century Italian treatises, an entire trill which ends with a four-note turn is termed *groppo*, *groppolo*, or *gruppo* by Conforto, Cavalieri, and Caccini, respectively.[1] In later German sources, the term is used to specifically identify the ending four-note configuration. The *groppo* is an ornamental *figura simplex* which is very similar to the four-note *circulo mezzo*. Most authors agree that the *groppo* has common first and third notes while the *circulo mezzo* has common second and fourth notes. However, Brossard does not distinguish between the construction of the two ornaments, describing them both as having common first and third notes. While Walther defines the *circulo mezzo* according to Brossard's description, Walther's *circulo* (two adjacent but opposite *circuli mezzi*) agrees with the other authors' definitions. In order to clearly distinguish between the eight-note *circulo* and the *groppo*, Walther then suggests that the *groppo* only does justice to its name (roller, ball) if it consists of two such four-note motifs, resulting in two distinct eight-note configurations. Mattheson also describes the *groppo* as an eight-note figure. However, he justifies this through a different etymology of the term: it is to signify a whole cluster of notes instead of only four. In order to clarify this understanding of the term, Mattheson beams the

1. Neumann, *Ornamentation*, 287.

eight notes together, visually portraying a grapelike cluster of notes.

Printz (*Phrynis Mytilenaeus* pt.2, p.48)

Groppo ist eine geschwind-lauffende Figura, so sich überwaltzet wie eine Kugel / daher sie auch den Nahmen hat / und formiret im Schreiben einen halben Creiß: Sie bestehet in vier geschwinden Noten / deren erste und dritte einerley / die andere und vierdte unterschiedene Stellen haben. Sie ist entweder auffsteigend oder absteigend.

A *groppo* is a rapidly moving figure which appears to revolve as if it were a ball, thereby suppling its name. It consists of four rapid notes which form a half-circle, the first and third being the same, the second and fourth having different positions. It can be either ascending or descending.

Walther (*Lexicon*)

Groppo, oder Gruppo, pl. groppi, gruppi (ital.) grouppe (gall.) ist in der Music eine Diminutions-Gattung grosser und langer Noten, und bestehet ordinairement aus vier Achteln oder Sechzehntheilen, deren erstes und drittes in einerley Tone, das zweyte und vierdte aber in verschiedenen Tonen sich befinden. Steiget die vierdte Note in die Höhe, so ists ein Groppo ascendente; steiget sie aber abwerts, so ists eine Groppo descendente. Diese diminution wird öffters auf der penultima einer Cadenz, um das trillo zu endigen, gebraucht. s. Bross. Diction. Weil nun solcher gestalt diesem Auctori ein Circolo mezzo, p.20. und ein Groppo, p.43. einerley ist; halte ohnmaßgeblich dafür: daß diese letztere Figur alsdenn erst den Nahmen einer Kugel oder Waltze meritiret, wenn vorgemeldte vier Noten zweymahl angebracht werden.

The *groppo* . . . is a form of *diminutio* used to ornament notes of longer duration, and normally consists of four eighth or sixteenth notes with a common first and third note, the second and fourth having different positions. Should the fourth note ascend, it is called a *groppo ascendente.* Should it descend, however, it is called a *groppo descendente.* This *diminutio* is frequently used on the penultimate note of a cadence in order to end a *trillo.* See Brossard's *Dictionnaire.* Because Brossard does not differentiate between a *circulo mezzo* and a *groppo,* I believe that the *groppo* can only be regarded as a ball or roller if the four-note figure is set twice successively.

Mattheson (*Capellmeister* p.115f.)

Die ehmaligen Sangmeister machten viel Wesens von einer Ausschmückung, welche sie Groppo hiessen. Nach meiner Verteutschung ist das so viel, als ein Knauff in Trauben-Gestalt, und ich kan nicht begreiffen, wie es möglich sey, daß dieses Wort, Groppo, im Welschen eine

Previous songmasters made a great deal out of the embellishment which they called *groppo.* According to my German translation, this word means grapelike cluster, and I simply cannot understand how it is possible that this word, *groppo,* should mean roller or ball, even though

Waltze oder Kugel bedeuten könne; ob es gleich Printz, Walther und viele andre in ihren Büchern so auslegen. Es kömmt gantz gewiβ her von Grappo, eine Traube, die im Frantzösischen und Engländischen Grape heiβt, und bezeichnet alles dasjenige, sowol im eigentlichen als figürlichen Verstande, was wir im Niedersächsischen und Engländischen (als Alt-Teutschen) ein Kluster nennen, nehmlich z.E. viele kleine Beeren oder andre Dinge, die dicht zusammen gefüget sind oder sich häuffen: wie hier, bey dieser Manier, die an einander geschlossene Schreib-Noten thun. Wir . . . können die Groppen theils ausserordentlich, als einen blossen zufälligen Zierrath, theils förmlich oder wesentlich gar wol mit in die Melodie bringen, und gantze Läuffe daraus bilden: welche keinen geringen Wol-Laut mit sich führen, falls die Leidenschafft, so man ausdrücken will, dergleichen Dreh- und Wendungen vergönnet.

Printz, Walther, and many others define it as such in their books. It is undoubtedly derived from *grappo*, which means a grape, even in French and English. It denotes all those things, both literally and figuratively, which are referred to as clusters, both in Lower Saxony and England (as well as in old High German), namely many small berries or other items which are clustered together just as the notes in this *Manier*, which are all bound together. These *groppi* can be applied either periodically as simple coincidental embellishments or can be used to substantially structure the melody, forming entire runs. These runs can contribute in no small part to the musical expression, should the expression of the desired affection permit such turning and revolving.

Spiess (*Tractatus* p.156)
Groppo, heiβt bey dem Printz und Walther eine Waltze oder Kugel. Bei Veneroni ein Hauffen gemahlter Köpf, oder Figuren auf einer Tafel. Matthesoni will weder das erste noch das andere gefallen, sondern sagt, es komme gewiβ her von Grappo, eine Traube; in dem es alles dasjenige bezeichne, was von dieser in eigentlichem und Figurlichem Verstand könne gesagt werden. Wir wollen da diesen unnützen Wort-Streit nicht decidieren, sondern den eigentlichen Zierrath dieser Figur Groppo vor Augen legen.

Printz and Walther call the *groppo* a roller or ball. In the past it has also meant a group of illustrated figures or heads. Mattheson is pleased with neither definition, saying rather that it is derived from *grappo*, a grape, because it refers to all that which this term can literally or figuratively signify. We do not wish to settle this useless word war but rather illustrate the actual embellishment called a *figura groppo*:

Es bestehet aber der Groppo allzeit in 4. kleinen Noten, deren die erste und dritte in einem Ton: die anderte und vierte Nota aber in einem anderen Ton zu stehen kommen.

The *groppo* always consists of four short notes, the first and third being of the same pitch while the second and fourth notes are set at different pitches.

HETEROLEPSIS: an intrusion of one voice into the range of another.

The term *heterolepsis* is unique to the musical *Figurenlehre*. It is a descriptive term of a musical phenomenon, denoting an appropriation (*lepsis*) by one voice of notes which belong in the range of another (*heteros*). This can occur through a leap to a dissonance which might otherwise have been approached through a passing note by another voice, or through a leading note falling to the dominant at a cadence rather than rising to the tonic. Although the term is mentioned only by Bernhard and Walther, Mattheson's *parenthesis* as well as Spiess's and Vogt's *metabasis* are similarly defined. While the *parenthesis* might be expressed through a voice leaping from its own range to that of another voice, *metabasis* denotes voice crossing. In these two cases, however, the chosen terms have rhetorical antecedents and are descriptive of the textual allusion rather than the musical phenomenon. Scheibe also describes a similar musical device in his definition of *hyperbaton*. He refers to it as a *Verwechselung* (exchange) which occurs "when a note belonging to a higher voice is set in a lower one" or vice versa.[1] Bernhard's intention to explain a freer use of dissonance through his figures results in a choice of terms and definitions which emphasize compositional rather than text-expressive devices.

Bernhard (*Tractatus* p.87)

Heterolepsis ist eine Ergreiffung einer anderen Stimme und ist zweyerley. Erstlich, wenn ich nach einer Consonantz in eine Dissonantz springe oder gehe, so von einer andern Stimme in transitu könte gemacht werden.

The *heterolepsis* signifies the seizing of another voice and can occur in two ways: first, if a consonance moves by step or leap to a dissonance which could have been reached through a *transitus* from another voice:

1. See *Hyperbaton*, *Metabasis*, *Parenthesis*.

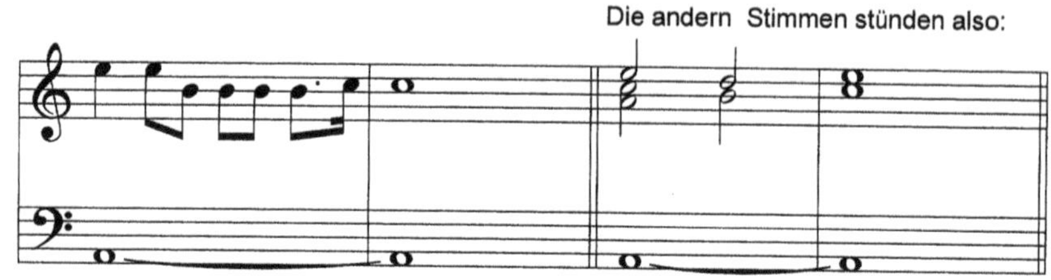

Zum andern, wenn bey einer syncopirten untern Stimme, die obere in einer Quarta begriffen nicht eine Secunde steiget, sondern eine Tertia fället.

Second, when an upper voice which forms a fourth with a lower syncopated voice does not rise a second, but rather falls a third:

Bernhard (*Bericht* p.152)
Heterolepsis heiβt einer andern Stimme Nehmung und geschicht, wenn ich 1) aus einer Consonanz [in eine Dissonanz] schreite, so von einer andern Stimme in Transitu könte gemacht werden. 2) Geschicht solche Nehmung, wenn in einer syncopirten Quarta die unterste Stimme sich endet, und die obere eine Tertia fället, da sie eine Secunda steigen solte.

Heterolepsis means the taking of another voice and occurs (1) when a consonance moves to a dissonance when this could have been accomplished by another voice through a *transitus*; (2) when a lower syncopated voice resolves and the upper voice which had formed a fourth falls a third where it should have risen a second.

Walther (*Praecepta* p.155)
Heterolepsis ist, wenn eine Stimme aus einer andern bisweilen einen Clavem hinweg nimmet, und den ihrigen unter-[?] daβ jener beraubten Stimme zukommen läβet: diese Figur, als welche sich einer groβen Freyheit anmaset, wird mehrentheils in sola voce, zu welcher etl. Instrumenta accompagniren, gebrauchet.

The *heterolepsis* occurs when one voice takes something from another voice or even another clef and adds to itself that which rightfully belongs to the other voice. This figure, which assumes a great deal of liberty, most frequently occurs in vocal solos accompanied by various instruments.

HOMOIOPTOTON, HOMOIOTELEUTON: (1) a general pause in all voices (*aposiopesis*), either interrupting the composition (*homoioptoton*) or following a cadence (*homoioteleuton*); (2) similar endings of a number of subsequent passages.

In rhetoric these figures signify either similar case endings (*homoioptoton*) or similar final syllables (*homoioteleuton*). In both cases, the term is a literal description of the device: while *homoios* refers to the similitude, *ptosis* signifies a specific case ending and *teleute* signifies an ending in general. The terms are first encountered in the musical *Figurenlehren* of Nucius and Thuringus to signify two forms of the general pause. Nucius chooses *homoioteleuton* to signify the figure which Burmeister termed aposiopesis. It is not the rhetorical definition but rather the literal meaning of the term which influences his choice. The musical "similar ending" describes a simultaneous ending of all the voices rather than a similar structural relationship between the voices. Of the two terms, Nucius elects the more general one rather than the term which is specifically related to case endings. Thuringus reintroduces Burmeister's *aposiopesis*, and adopts *homoioptoton* in addition to Nucius's *homoioteleuton* to distinguish between two different placements of a general pause. This distinction is clarified in Walther's *Lexicon*: whereas *homoioteleuton* is understood as a general pause following a cadence, *homoioptoton* does not require such a preceding ending. Walther presumably makes this differentiation on the basis of the terms *generalis pausa* for *homoioptoton* and *finale silentium* for *homoioteleuton* found in Thuringus's definitions. A *finale silentium* requires a corresponding *Final-Cadenz*, while the *generalis pausa* does not.

Kircher adopts a definition for *homoioptoton* more closely related to the rhetorical understanding of the term, describing it as a similar ending of a number of phrases. His Latin translation, *similiter desinens*, in fact serves as the translation of the rhetorical *homoioteleuton* rather than *homoioptoton* (Susenbrotus). As Kircher and Janovka do not understand the figure as a general pause and therefore do not differentiate between the two terms, the fine distinction between the words is not necessary. The use of the *homoioptoton* to express a question as described by Thuringus is consequently included in Kircher's definition of *pausa*, a function of this figure of silence which Thuringus did not include in his own *pausa* definition. Kircher's choice of *homoioptoton* might be explained by his indebtedness to Thuringus's *Figurenlehre* terminology, where *homoioptoton* is encountered for the first time as a musical term. Although Kircher mentions the *aposiopesis* in *Liber* 5 of his *Musurgia*, the term, like a number of other figures adopted from Thuringus, is not included in his figure definitions found in *Liber* 8. Instead, Kircher defines *pausa* and *stenasmus/suspirans* as figures of silence. The rhetorical definition given to *homoioptoton* is similar to that of *epiphora/epistrophe*, terms which then replace *homoioptoton* in the musical *Figurenlehre* toward the end of the seventeenth century.

Quintilian (*Institutio* IX.iii.77ff.)

Secundum, ut clausula similiter cadat, syllabis iisdem in ultimam partem collatis vocant ὁμοιοτέλευτον similem duarum sententiarum vel plurium finem.Tertium est, quod in eosdem casus cadit, ὁμοιόπτωτον dicitur.

Second, it occurs when clauses end similarly, the same syllables being placed at the end of each one. A similar ending of two or more sentences is called *homoioteleuton*. Third, when the same case ending is used, it is called *homoioptoton*.

Susenbrotus (*Epitome* p.58)

Similiter cadens ὁμοιόπτωτον, est quando iisdem casibus dictiones aut sententiae efferuntur, hoc modo: Moerentes, flerentes, lachrymantes, commiserantes.

Similiter cadens or *homoioptoton* occurs when words or sentences are expressed in the same case, as in *Moerentes, flerentes, lachrymantes, commiserantes.*

Similiter desinens ὁμοιοτέλευτον, est quum dictiones vel sententiae similter exeunt. Ennius Eos deduci, evehi, quam deseri malui.

Similiter desinens or *homoioteleuton* occurs when words or sentences end similarly, as in the example.

Gottsched (*Redekunst* p.276)

Homoeoteleoton und Homoeoptoton, wenn man mit den letzten Sylben, oder mit den Fallendungen spielet.

Homoeoteleoton and *homoeoptoton* occur when one plays with the last syllables or with case endings.

Nucius (*Musices Poeticae* G3ʳ)

Quid est Homioteleuton? Cum post communem vocum concursum Semibrevis aut minimae Pausae interventu generale silentium indicitur ac Harmonia interrumpitur. Hac figura Itali & Galli in Choreis, Galiardis, Madrigalis, Passamezis & similibus crebro utuntur. Recentiores quoque in Dialogis, & interrogationibus: Vide nostrum Quo celeras:

What is *homioteleuton*? It occurs when the *harmonia* is interrupted and a general silence is indicated with *semibrevis* or *minima* rests after the voices have run together. The Italians and French frequently use this figure in choruses, galliards, madrigals, passamezzi, and similar pieces, and contemporary composers in dialogues and in questions. . . . Previous

aliorumque hoc Schema usurpant: Veteres quasi attentionem excitaturi in motetis hanc figuram adhibuerunt.

composers employed this figure in motets in order to arouse attention.

Thuringus (*Opusculum* p.127)

Quid est Homioptoton? Est, cum generalis pausa atque nota vel semibrevis vel minima vel semiminima cantioni in omnibus vocibus simul inseritur. Hac figura Itali & Galli in Choreis, Galiardis, Madrigalis, Passamezis, Canzonettis, Couranti, Balletten, Auffzügen, Intraden, Paduanen, &c. crebro utuntur; Recentiores quoque in Dialogis & interrogationibus. Veteres quasi attentionem excitatur in motetis hanc figuram adhibuerunt.

What is *homioptoton*? It occurs when a general pause is simultaneously inserted in all the voices of the composition through *semibrevis, minima*, or *semiminima* rests. The Italians and French frequently use this figure in choruses, galliards, madrigals, passamezzi, canzonetti, courants, balletti, Auffzügen, intradas, paduanas, etc., and contemporary composers in dialogues and in questions. Previous composers employed this figure in motets in order to arouse attention.

Quid est Homioteleuton? Est finale silentium in medio cantionis. Vel: cum post communem vocum concursum semibrevis aut minimae pausae interventu generale silentium indicitur, ac harmonia interrumpitur.

What is *homioteleuton*? It is a complete silence in the middle of the composition. Or it occurs when the *harmonia* is interrupted and a general silence is indicated with *semibrevis* or *minima* rests after the voices have run together.

Kircher (*Musurgia* L.8, p.145)

Ομοιόπτωτον sive similiter desinens figura, est periodus harmonica quae similiter desinit in saepius repetita, adhiberique solet in seria alicuius rei affirmatione, negatione, aut increpatione, ut illud Prenestini (Nos insensati).

Homoioptoton or *similiter desinens figura* is a musical passage in which numerous repetitions are ended similarly. It is customarily used in a subsequent affirmation, negation, or emphasis of a certain thought, as in Palestrina's *Nos insensati*.

Janovka (*Clavis* p.55)

Similiter desinens Figura, est periodus harmonica, quae similiter desinit in saepius repetita, adhiberique solet in seria rei alicuius affirmatione, negatione, aut increpatione. ex. gr. in textu: non dimiatam te, donec benedixeris mihi.

The *similiter desinens figura* is a musical passage in which numerous repetitions are ended similarly. It is customarily used in a subsequent affirmation, negation, or emphasis of a thought, as in: "I will not dismiss you until you have blessed me."

Walther (*Lexicon*)

Aposiopesis heisset in der Music: wenn eine Pausa generalis, oder ein durchgängiges Stilschweigen in allen Stimmen und Partien zugleich vorkommt; welches auf zweyerley Art geschehen kan, als: 1.) wenn in der Mitte eines Stücks, vermittelst einer vorhergehenden final-Cadenz,

In music the *aposiopesis* refers to a *pausa generalis*, or a complete silence in all voices and parts of the composition simultaneously. This can occur in two ways: (1) through a complete silence indicated by a whole- or half-*tactus* rest in the middle of a composition following a

und drauf folgenden gantzen oder halben Tact-Pause, dergleichen gemacht wird; welche Art so dann insonderheit Homoeoteleuton heisset. 2.) wenn gleichfalls, vermittelst einer gantzen, halben, oder Viertels-Tact-Pause, ohne aber dabey einen formalen Schluß oder Cadenz zu machen, dergleichen Stillschweigen angebracht wird; diese Gattung heisset insonderhiet Homoeoptoton. s. Joach. Thuringui Opusc. P.2 c.18.

finalis cadence, which is called *homoeoteleuton*; (2) when a similar silence occurs in the middle of a composition through a whole-, half-, or quarter-*tactus* rest without a preceding ending or cadence, which is called *homoeoptoton*. See J. Thuringus's *Opusculum*, part 2, ch.18.

HOMOIOSIS: see *ASSIMILATIO*

HYPALLAGE: an inversion of the fugal theme.

The rhetorical *hypallage* is defined as a certain exchange of parts, either through substitution (Quintilian) or through inversion (Susenbrotus). Susenbrotus's understanding of the term coincides with Quintilian's *anastrophe*. Peacham uses both terms to denote an inversion, either of two words, called *anastrophe*, or of sentence order, called *hypallage*.

Burmeister chooses the term *hypallage* to identify a fugal inversion. Although the literal meaning of this term ("exchange") is less specific than the meaning of *anastrophe* ("reversal"), through Peacham's definitions it becomes apparent that the *anastrophe* is limited to two words while the *hypallage* is applied to the entire sentence. It would therefore be more appropriate to use the sentence- rather than word-figure in a musical application to a fugal theme. Burmeister not only adopts a definition similar to that of Susenbrotus but even uses the same terminology in his definition. Susenbrotus's *converso rerum ordine* becomes *converso intervallorum ordine* in Burmeister's *Musica Poetica*. In addition, the Latin term *submutatio* is also used by both authors. However, while the rhetorical figure refers to a linear inversion, the musical *hypallage* signifies a vertical inversion of the intervals rather than a retrograde form of the *fuga* subject.

Although the contrapuntal technique of inversion remains a standard device in the Baroque art of *fuga*, the term *hypallage* is not encountered again. Instead, authors use specific qualifying descriptions of *fuga*, such

as *fuga contraria* or *repercussio*.[1] In England a fugal inversion is referred to as a *revert*.[2] Henry Peacham the Younger associates the rhetorical *antistrophe* with the musical *revert*: "Nay, hath not music her figures, the same which rhetoric? What is a revert but her antistrophe? . . . her counterchange of points, antimetaboles?"[3] Peacham's choice of *antistrophe* for a fugal inversion is an interesting one. It is not the *antistrophe* but rather the *anastrophe* which signifies an inversion of word order in rhetoric.[4] It seems most likely that Peacham mistakenly used the closely related term, exchanging the prefix *ana* for *anti* in his definition. The only musical reference to *antimetabole* is also found in Peacham's essay. Here he compares the rhetorical figure to contrapuntal inversion, known in England as *counterchange of parts*, which occurs "when the Principal (that is the thing as it is first made) and the Reply (that is it which the Principal, having the parts changed, doth make) are sung, changing the parts in such manner as the highest part may be made the lowest and the lowest part the highest."[5] The elder Peacham defined the *antimetabole* as "a forme of speech which inverteth a sentence by the contrary, thus: It behoveth thee to eate that thou maist live, and not to live that thou maist eate."[6] This form of rhetorical inversion is used to express an opposing thought by exchanging the placement of the words.

---

1. In his *Lexicon*, Walther describes *fuga contraria* and *fuga inaequalis motus* as inversions of the fugal subject, while *fuga cancrizans* signifies a retrograde form of the subject. Unger's reference to Janovka's use of the term *hypallage* (*Beziehungen*, 79) must be corrected. It is probable that he based his conjecture on a reference by Brandes: "Janovka . . . bezeichnet die Hypallage als: Fuga inversa seu contraria." (*Studien zur musikalischen Figurenlehre*, 11). While Janovka defines the inverted *fuga*, he does not use the term *hypallage*. Brandes neglects to distinguish between term and definition, apparently leading to Unger's misunderstanding. Regarding *repercussio*, one of Mattheson's explanations of the term points to its use in identifying the inversion of intervals in a fugal answer. See *Repercussio*.

2. "Revert is the Iterating of a Point in contrari Motion, [*per Arsin & Thesin*;] the Replie mooving *per Thesin*, if the Principal Ascend, and *per Arsin*, if the Principal descend." Ch. Butler, *The Principles of Musik*, 72.

3. Strunk, *Source Readings*, 337.

4. The *antistrophe* refers to a repetition of the same word at the end of several successive phrases, also known as *epiphora* or *epistrophe* (Sonnino, *Handbook*, 63). See also *Epiphora* (Susenbrotus).

5. Thomas Morely, *A Plaine and Easie Introduction to Practicall Musicke* (London, 1597; new ed., New York: Norton, 1952), 188.

6. *Garden of Eloquence*, 164.

Likewise, the contrapuntal exchange results in a musical passage which assumes an opposite identity, albeit in a different sense from a linguistic opposite. Such a fugal inversion is also described in Scheibe's definition of *hyperbaton*: "when one works with more than one voice and exchanges the location in which the particular voices normally appear."

Quintilian (*Institutio* VIII.vi.23, 65)
Nec procul ab hoc genere discedit metonymia, quae est nominis pro nomine positio, sed, ut ait Cicero, hypallagen rhetores dicunt. Verum id cum in duobus verbis fit, ἀναστροφὴ dicitur, reversio quaedam.

The *metonymia* is related to [the *synecdoche*] and consists of a substitution of one name for another. As Cicero tells us, rhetoricians call this *hypallage*. When this [transgression, *hyperbaton*] affects two words, it is called *anastrophe*, which signifies their reversal.

Susenbrotus (*Epitome* p.36)
Hypallage ὑπαλλαγή est quoties oratio converso rerum ordine profertur. Latine Submutatio sive subalternatio.

The *hypallage* occurs when the oration is advanced through a reversed order of things. In Latin this is known as *submutatio* or *subalternatio*.

Peacham (*Garden of Eloquence* F3v, Gir)
Anastrophe, a preposterous order, or a backward setting of wordes.
Hypallage, when a sentence is sayde with a contrary order of wordes.

Burmeister (*Hypomnematum*)
Hypallage est Fugae submutatio.

The *hypallage* is an inversion of the *fuga*.

Burmeister (*Musica Poetica* p.58)
Hypallage est quando Fuga converso intervallorum ordine introducitur.

The *hypallage* occurs when a *fuga* introduces an inverted order of the intervals.

HYPERBATON: a transfer of notes or phrases from their normal placement to a different location.

The term *hyperbaton* (like its counterpart, *hypobaton*) is used in music theory prior to its adoption as a musical-rhetorical figure. In describing two-part counterpoint, Janovka defines the upper voice—be it the subject or the countersubject—as *hyperbatus*, while the lower voice is called *hypobatus*. In thus defining the relationship between the two voices, he retains the literal meaning of the terms, namely the "overpassing" (*hyperbatus*, *supergradiens*) or "underpassing" (*hypobatus*, *infragradiens*) of one voice in relation to the other.

Hyperbaton enters the musical *Figurenlehre* in Scheibe's *Critischer Musicus*, the only source where it is specifically mentioned as a musical-rhetorical figure. Rather than adopting the established musical-theoretical definition of the term, Scheibe adapts Gottsched's rhetorical definition. The rhetorical transfer of a word or thought from its natural location is applied to the transfer of a note or a phrase from its natural location to another. In the first case, "namely when a note which belongs in a higher voice is set in a lower one, or when a note which belongs in a lower voice is set in a higher one," the definition of *hyperbaton* coincides both with Bernhard's *heterolepsis* as well as Mattheson's example of a *parenthesis*, which signify similar note displacements. However, while Bernhard is primarily concerned with a proper use of dissonance, Scheibe's interest focuses on affective expression through a dramatic relocation of words, notes, or phrases. Forkel also mentions the use of the *Versetzung*, the term which Scheibe used to translate *hyperbaton*, now in connection with the musical *distributio* instead of the musical-rhetorical figures.[1] Rather than explaining its use, Forkel simply states that "the *Versetzungen* are easily understood"[2] before going on to discuss his interpretation of the individualization of general musical sentiments.

Quintilian (*Institutio* VIII.vi.62, 65)

Hyperbaton quoque, id est verbi transgressionem. . . . At cum decoris gratia	*Hyperbaton* is the transposition of a word. . . . But only when this is a far re-

1. Unger's conjecture that the *hyperbaton* is mentioned as a figure by Forkel (*Beziehungen*, 152) must therefore be revised.

2. "Was Versetzungen sind, läßt sich leicht begreifen." *Allegemine Geschichte*, 52.

traiicitur longius verbum, proprie hyperbati tenet nomen.

moved transposition for the sake of ornament can it properly be called a *hyperbaton.*

Susenbrotus (*Epitome* p.33)

Hyperbaton, ὑπέρβατον Transgressio, est cum dictionum clausularumve legitimus ordo immutatur.

The *hyperbaton* or *transgressio* occurs when the proper order of the words or clauses is altered.

Gottsched (*Dichtkunst* p.321)

Die VI. ist die Versetzung (Hyperbaton) eines Worts oder Gedankens von seiner natürlichen Stelle; die aber nicht aus der Unfähigkeit des Poeten, sondern aus der Heftigkeit des Affects herrühret, der dem Gemüthe nicht Zeit läßt, an die ordentliche Wortfügung zu denken.

The next figure is the transference (*hyperbaton*) of a word or thought from its natural position. This occurs not because of the incompetence of the poet but rather out of the vehemence of the affection, which does not allow sufficient time to consider proper word order.

Janovka (*Clavis* p.31)

Alius est contrapunctus solus, alius replicatus. Solus iterum duplex: vel enim ponitur supra Subjectum, & tunc Hyperbatus, id est supergradiens vocatur: vel infra subjectum procedit, & tunc Hypobatus, seu infragradiens dicitur. Subjectum vero in priori Hypobatum, in posterior Hyperbatum nuncupatur.

The *contrapunctus* is either *solus* or *replicatus. Contrapunctus solus* is also of two kinds. The *contrapunctus* is placed either above the *subjectum*, in which case it is called *hyperbatus*, that is, proceeding above, or below the *subjectum*, in which case it is called *hypobatus*, that is, proceeding below. Subsequently the first would have a *subjectum hypobatus* and the second a *subjectum hyperbatus.*

Scheibe (*Critischer Musicus* p.688)

Die IVte Figur kann die Versetzung (Hyperbaton) seyn. Sie geschieht, wenn man entweder einen Ton, oder auch einen ganzen Gedanken von seiner natürlichen Stelle an einen andern Ort versetzet. Im erstern Falle kömmt sie mit der Verwechselung der Harmonie überein, wenn man nämlich einen Ton, der in eine höhere Stimme gehöret, in eine niedrige setzet, oder auch, wenn man einen Ton, der in eine niedrige Stimme gehöret, in eine höhere Stimme setzet. . . . In Ansehung einer ganzen Gedanke aber geschieht diese Figur, wenn man mit mehr Stimmen, als mit einer Stimme arbeitet, und man verändert die Stellen, welche in diese Stimme gehören, daß sie in eine andere Stimme zu stehen kommen. Die-

The next figure is the transference or *hyperbaton.* It occurs when either a note or an entire thought is transferred from its natural position to a different one. In the first case it agrees with the harmonic exchange, namely when a note which belongs in a higher voice is set in a lower one, or when a note which belongs in a lower voice is set in a higher one. . . . Regarding an entire thought, this figure occurs when one works with more than one voice and exchanges the location in which the particular voices normally appear. This frequently occurs in fugues. . . . The *hyperbaton* also occurs in arias when the order of the normal melody is altered, its familiar and preceding progression being modified and interrupted

ses trägt sich sehr oft in Fugen zu. . . . Die Versetzung geschieht auch in Arien, wenn man die Folge der natürlichen Melodie verändert, und die gewöhnliche und schon vorausgesetzte Folge derselben verwechselt, und sie durch ungewöhnliche Zwischensätze unterbricht, die ordentlichen Sätze aber an einem andern Orte unvermerkt wieder anbringt. Man hat auch noch eine andere Gattung dieser Figur, welche mit den Worten einer Arie selbst geschieht. Man verändert nämlich die poetische Einrichtung und Folge derselben also, daβ man ein Wort, auf welches sich die ganze Rede bezieht, von seiner gewöhnlichen Stelle an einen andern Ort versetzet. . . . In Ansehung der Zergliederung eines Textes ist die Versetzung eine der schönsten Figuren, und zum verständlichen und nachdrücklichen Ausdrucke desselben, wie auch zur Erregung der Affecten auf das vortrefflichste geschickt.

with unusual interjections, eventually to return, however, in its unaltered form in another location. There is yet another form of this figure which affects the words of the aria themselves. The poetic arrangement and order of the words can be altered in such fashion that a word which is the focus of the entire text is transferred from its ordinary location to another place. . . . Regarding the *distributio* of the text, the *hyperbaton* is one of the most pleasing figures and is exceptionally appropriate for a clear and emphatic expression of the words as well as for the arousal of the affections.

Forkel (*Geschichte der Musik* p.54)
Man muß aber die eigentlichen contrapunktistischen Künste nicht mit solchen Spielwerken verwechseln, die sich nicht mit einzelnen Buchstaben und Worten, sondern mit der Modification ganzer Gedanken und Sätze beschäfftigen. Wer wird z.B. die Inversion in der Sprache, wodurch ein ganzer Satz aus seiner gewöhnlichen Stelle genommen, und an eine andere gestellt wird, für ein Spielwerk Halten? Fast die meisten contrapunktistischen Künste gründen sich auf eine solche Inversion musikalischer Gedanken, und sind daher in der Musik eben so wenig für Spielwerke, oder unnützen Schulzwang zu halten, als die Inversion in der Sprache, wenn beyde nicht gemißbraucht werden.

However, genuine contrapuntal artistry, which concerns itself with the modification of entire thoughts and passages rather than with individual letters and words, must not be confused with such trifles. Who, for example, would regard such linguistic inversions, through which an entire sentence is moved from its normal place to another, as a triviality? The vast majority of artistic contrapuntal devices are grounded on similar inversions of musical ideas and are therefore not to be regarded as trivialities or useless exercises any more in music than inversions are in rhetoric, given that in both cases they are not abused.

HYPERBOLE, HYPOBOLE: a transgression of the range or *ambitus* of a *modus*.

Burmeister's *hyperbole* and *hypobole* illustrate his intention to provide familiar musical devices with rhetorical terminology, even if the accompanying rhetorical definitions are not applicable. Here once more it is the literal meaning of the terms which determines his choice of names. The musical *hyper-* (over) *bole* (throw) oversteps the upper *terminus* or boundary of a mode's *ambitus* or range rather than the boundaries of truthfulness. The opposite rhetorical figure, called *litotes* (simplicity or modesty), is clearly not a suitable term for the opposite musical figure. Burmeister coins the related term, *hypo-* (under) *bole*, to signify a progression which exceeds the lowest *terminus* of a mode's *ambitus*. Just in case the reader misses the relationship between the two terms, Burmeister points to their contrary content.

Burmeister's concept of the figures is based on ornamental deviations from the simple *ratio* of musical composition. The *ambitus* in his definitions refers to the range of a composition's corresponding *modus*.[1] The transgression of a mode's *ambitus* was a well-established text-expressive compositional device in the sixteenth century. Indeed, Eucharius Hoffmann uses the rhetorical terms *redundantia*[2] and *ellipsis*[3] in his description of the device.[4] Rather than being simply a technical procedure, it is considered effective in portraying particularly "unheard of, monstrous, and abhorrently unnatural" thoughts.[5] While Burmeister does not explicitly mention the affective potential of these figures, they can

---

1. Burmeister, *Musica poetica*, 41. See also Ruhnke, *Burmeister*, 158. Both Brandes (*Studien zur musikalischen Figurenlehre*, p.18) and Unger (*Beziehungen*, 80) erroneously understand *ambitus* and *terminus* as references to the upper and lower staff lines, thereby explaining the figure as a purely superficial device in which a composer resorts to ledger lines instead of staying within the lines of the staff.

2. *Redundantia* is also known as *pleonasmus*, and indicates an overabundance or superfluity of words. Sonnino, *Handbook*, 156.

3. The later musical definition of *ellipsis* in the context of Bernhard's *Figurenlehre* stands much closer to the term's rhetorical understanding. See *Ellipsis*.

4. Ruhnke, *Burmeister*, 137. Although Hoffmann does not develop a systematic concept of musical-rhetorical figures, his use of rhetorical terminology makes the analogy between the two disciplines quite obvious.

5. Thuringus, *Opusculum*, 90. For a thorough and enlightening discussion of this device, see Siegfried Meyer, "Abweichungen von den Normen eines Modus als Mittel der Wortausdeutung," *Musica Disciplina* 42 (1988): 199–215; also Bernhard Meier, *The Modes of Classical Vocal Polyphony* (New York: Broude Brothers, 1988).

"be considered as some of the most expressive ones."[1]

J. A. Herbst also suggests a connection between the musical-rhetorical figures and the transgression of a mode's range. He associates the ornaments which others considered to be *figurae principales*, namely *fuga* and *syncopatio* in addition to the cadence, with the chromaticism which results from exceeding the mode's *ambitus*: "The *colores* in music are various kinds of fugues, suspensions, and gracious cadences, which, like pleasant phrases, assume and adopt notes above and below the natural and proper ones belonging to that *modus* or *tonus*."[2] Herbst later clarifies this in his discussion of the modes. After defining the term *ambitus*, he proceeds to discuss a transgression of the mode's *ambitus*. He calls this device *licentia*,[3] a familiar rhetorical figure meaning freedom (of speech), used to either flatter someone or to understate a disagreeable or abhorrent thought in such fashion that it becomes palatable.[4] As such, the *licentia* is very similar to *hyperbole*.[5]

A further musical-rhetorical reference to the transgression of a mode's *ambitus* is encountered under Bernhard's *mutatio toni*. This he

---

1. Ruhnke, *Burmeister*, 158.

2. "Colores seynd in der Music mancherley Art von Fugen, Syncopationen, liebliche Clausulen und Cadentien, welche gleichsam schöne Phrases seyn / so ein jeder Modus oder Tonus, neben seinen natürlichen und rechtmässigen Clausulen drüber und drunter assumirt und annimme." Herbst, *Musica poetica*, 5.

3. The *licentia* is also known as *parrhesia*, a term which appears in the *Figurenlehren* of Burmeister, Thuringus, and in Walther's *Lexicon*. It signifies the addition of various kinds of dissonances to a consonant setting. Burmeister lists another figure, the *pathopoeia*, as a device used to insert notes into a composition which do not belong to the modus. But whereas the *hyper-* and *hypobole* introduce notes which exceed the range of the mode, the *pathopoeia* adds notes which belong "neither to the modus or the genus of the composition." (See *Pathopoeia*.) As such, the *pathopoeia* is closer to the *parrhesia*, both being devices used to introduce dissonances.

4. Sonnino, *Handbook*, 127.

5. Bernhard links the term *licentia* to the general use of dissonance. In the context of his *Figurenlehre*, which concerns itself chiefly with the proper use of dissonance, he therefore equates the musical-rhetorical figures with *licentia*. This is clarified in his introductory description of the modern *contrapunctus luxurians*, "welcher aus . . . mehr Arten des Gebrauchs derer Dissonantzen (oder mehr Figuris Melopoeticis welche andere Licentias nennen) . . . besteht" (*Tractatus*, 42f.). In his introduction to the figures used in the *stylus luxurians*, he reiterates this thought: "Die andere Species Styli inaequalis ist luxurians, welche ich so nenne wegen derer vielerley Arten des Gebrauchs derer Dissonantzen, welche andere Licentias nennen, weilen sie mit denen vorgemeldeten Figuris nicht scheinen entschuldiget zu werden." Ibid., 71.

lists as one of the figures used in the *stylus luxurians (communis)*. In his definition of this figure, he refers ahead to the chapters dealing specifically with the modes and their various alterations. After defining *modus* (or *tonus*) and *ambitus*, Bernhard points out that some voices either do not fulfill the *modus*, which he calls *modus deficiens*, or exceed the mode's *ambitus*, which he calls *modus superfluus*: "*Modus superfluus* occurs when the octave [i.e., the eight notes of the *ambitus*] is exceeded by either a second or a third above or below the *ambitus*."[1] Later he lists various further alterations or exceptions to the modes, including *consociatio modi* (the combination of an authentic mode with its plagal counterpart; should only the tenor *cantus firmus* venture into the related mode, it is termed *mixtio modi*), *extensio modi* (which allows the points of imitation to begin on any degree of the *modus* in addition to the *finalis* and dominant, thereby leading to an "extension" of not only the mode but also the composition), and *alteratio modi* (a composition beginning in one mode and ending in another).[2] None of these variations or alterations involve the specific use of dissonance, explaining why Bernhard discusses the "mutations" under the modes rather than the figures, and why they are omitted altogether in his later *Bericht*.

Quintilian (*Institutio* VIII.vi.67)

Hyperbolen audacioris ornatus summo loco posui. Est haec decens veri superiectio.

I have kept the *hyperbole* for the end because of its bold nature. It is an acceptable overstatement of the truth.

Susenbrotus (*Epitome* p.18)

Hyperbole ὑπερβολή est cum dictio vel oratio fidem excendens augendi minuendive gratia ponitur. Mancinellus: Transcensus veri manifestus Hyperbola fiet. Superlatio, dementiens superiectio, Eminentia et Excessus etiam appellata.

The *hyperbole* occurs when the words or oration exceed the truth for the sake of over- or understatement. According to Mancinellus, a transgression of the actual truth occurs through the *hyperbole*. It is also called *superlatio, dementiens superjectio, eminentia*, or *excessus*.

Gottsched (*Redekunst* p.252)

Endlich werden zur Synecdoche auch noch die Hyperbole, und Litote gerechnet. Jene ist eine Vergrösserung diese

And finally the *hyperbole* and the *litote* are considered forms of the *synecdoche*. The former is an augmentation, the latter

1. Bernhard, *Tractatus*, ch.44, 91.
2. See *Mutatio Toni* for Bernhard's complete text.

eine Verkleinerung des Dinges, davon die Rede ist. Sie sagen also entweder mehr oder weniger, als in der That wahr ist, und bestehen also allemal aus einer Unwahrheit. Doch ist die Absicht dabey nicht, die Zuhörer zu betrügen, oder in Irrthum zu stürzen.

a diminution of the item under discussion. They thereby express either more or less than in fact is truthful and therefore consist of an untruth. However, it is not their intention to deceive the listeners or to lead them astray.

Burmeister (*Hypomnematum*)
Hyperbole tum fit quando Melodia terminos suos excedit.

The *hyperbole* occurs when the *melodia* exceeds its boundaries.

Burmeister (*Musica Poetica* p.64)
Hyperbole ὑπερβολή est Melodiae supra supremum eius terminum superlatio. Exemplum est in Orlandi Benedicam ad textum: Semper laus ejus. Consideretur ejus Harmoniae vox Bassus.

The *hyperbole* is an overstepping of the *melodia* beyond its uppermost *terminum* [boundary]. An example is found in Orlando's *Benedicam* at the text: *semper laus ejus*. The bass voice of the composition will be examined here:

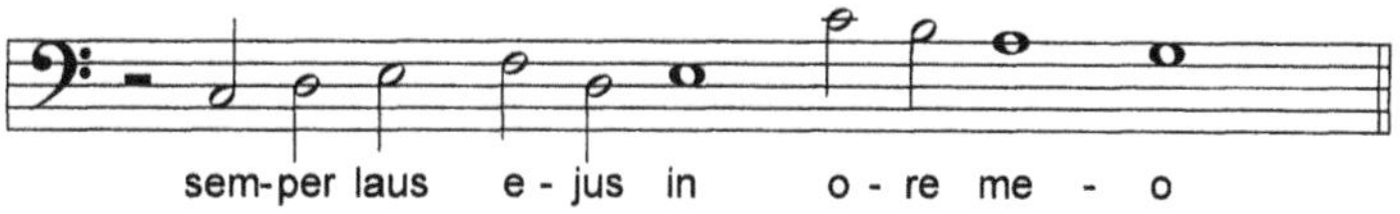

Hypobole ὑποβολή est Melodiae infra ejus infimum Ambitus terminum subjectio. . . . Unde colligitur ornamentum hoc contrarium esse Hyperbole.

The *hypobole* is an understepping of the *melodia* under the lowest *terminum* of the *ambitus*. . . . As is apparent, this figure is opposite to the *hyperbole*.

HYPOTYPOSIS: a vivid musical representation of images found in the accompanying text.

The *hypotyposis* is given the same task in music as in rhetoric: to vividly and realistically illustrate a thought or image found in the text. As such it might even be considered the most important and common text-expressive compositional device of Baroque music, for it is *musica poetica*'s mandate to delight and move the listener through a musical presentation of the text. Such musical word painting becomes a hallmark of Baroque music, being found in virtually every Baroque vocal composition. Already Burmeister laments the fact that not all composers used the device judiciously. Literally the term means an imitation or reproduction, from *hypo*, "under" (re-); *typosis*, "form, construct." Both music and rhetoric use this figure to reflect an image rather than to express an affection.

While Burmeister lists *hypotyposis* as a figure which reflects images, it is his *pathopoeia* which is to be used to musically express the affections.[1] Neither Nucius nor Thuringus include *hypotyposis* in their *Figurenlehren*. However, appended to his discussion of the figures, Nucius includes various lists of words which were to be expressed through the music, including affective words as well as words of motion, place, time, and number.[2] A similar and expanded list also appears in Herbst's *Musica Poetica*.[3] The list of words to be musically illustrated in Daniel Speer's treatise at the close of the seventeenth century is almost double the size of Nucius's list.[4]

In the two listings of figures in his *Musurgia*, Kircher includes similar figures. The list of undefined figures in *Liber* 5 is taken from Thuringus's *Opusculum* with very few changes. Only Thuringus's *pathopoeia* is replaced with *prosopopoeia*, a rhetorical figure which is used to give inanimate objects life, or mute things fictitious personalities, or deceased or absent persons a voice.[5] In his list of defined figures in *Liber* 5, Kircher includes yet another figure, *homoiosis* or *assimilatio*. Although this figure is very closely related to the *hypotyposis*, the *homoiosis* is to present the text's images in actuality or *proprie* rather than only reflect them *videri*, as in Burmeister's *hypotyposis*.[6] While

1. See *Pathopoeia*.

2. Thuringus reintroduces Burmeister's *pathopoeia* and includes a list of affective words very similar to Nucius's *verba affectuum*.

3. See above, under "*Musica Poetica*: An Expression of Text and Affection," p.25.

4. "Item die folgende Wörter müssen auch mit dem Satz übereinkommen als: Himmel / Erde / hoch / tief / schlecht / recht / gut / bös / gehen / stehen / lang / kurz / geschwind / oder behend / seufzen / laufen / jagen / laut / still / ein / 2 / 3 / alle miteinander / eins ums ander / Kyrie eleison / Alleluja / Amen / immer / ewig / stets / ruhen / springen / erheben / erniedrigen / aufsteigen / neiderfallen / Aufgang / Niedergang der Sonnen / prächtig / demütig / lieblich / rauh / schwarz / weiβ / scharf / gelind / Abgrund / Berg / bald / wiederum / abermal / oft / selten / Gott der Höchste / Engel / Mensch / Kindheit / Mann / Wieb / Magd / veracht / gering / beschwerlich / zwingen / frei / gebunden / wenig / nichts / genug / bloβ / schwer / hart / gebrochen / ich harre / ich rede / verfolge / nachfolgen / nacheilen / wiederkehren oder wiederkommen; solche und dergleichen vorkommende Text und Wörter müssen wohl observieret und mit der Harmonie oder mit dem Satze übereinkommende komponiert werden." Speer, *Vierfaches musikalisches Kleeblatt*, p.283; cited in Unger, *Beziehungen*, 38.

5. Sonnino, *Handbook*, 54.

6. See *Assimilatio*.

hypotyposis is an image of an idea, *homoiosis* recreates the idea itself.

The term *hypotyposis* is encountered once more in Vogt's *Conclave*. Vogt does not include it in his list of figures but rather uses the term to generally characterize his *figurae ideales*. These figures are not only to express the affections but are to present the text's *idea* in a lifelike (*vivaciter*) and imaginative (*idealiter*) manner. To this end, the composer is to use *hypotyposis* and *prosopopoeia* figures. With these instructions Vogt typifies his category of *figurae ideales*. The plural formulation of *figurae hypothiposeos* suggests an entire class of such figures. This understanding is supported by Vogt's earlier definition of *idea musica* as "that which is portrayed through *hypotyposis* figures." Music and words are to work together in a vivid representation of the ιδεα ("that which is seen") of the text, using *hypotyposeos figurae ideales*.

Although only Burmeister explicitly includes *hypotyposis* in his list of musical-rhetorical figures, virtually all other musical-rhetorical figures can be used as forms of *hypotyposis*, as suggested by Vogt. In fact, most specific text-expressive figures can be understood as specific forms of *hypotyposis*, including the various figures of silence. Even the ornamental *accentus* is understood as a form of *hypotyposis* by Mattheson when he describes its use by Madame Keiser, who applied it to the word "*beugen*" in such fashion, "that it almost seemed to become visible, the ears becoming like eyes."[1] As *musica poetica* increasingly emphasizes graphic and tangible text- and affection-representation, *hypotyposis* and *pathopoeia* are regarded more as principles of composition than specific figures. This explains their limitation to early treatises, even as they remain fundamental to musical composition throughout the Baroque.

Quintilian (*Institutio* IX.ii.40)

Ab aliis ὑποτύπωσις dicitur proposita quaedam forma rerum ita expressa verbis, ut cerni potius videatur quam audiri.	Others call *hypotyposis* a presentation of a thought which is expressed through the oration in such fashion that it is perceived as though it were seen rather than heard.

Susenbrotus (*Epitome* p.90)

Hypotiposis ὑποτύπωσις, est quando persona, res, locus, tempus, aut aliud quidpiam tum scribendo tum dicendo ita	*Hypotyposis* occurs when a person, thing, location, time, or anything similar is depicted through written or oral expression

1. See *Accentus* (Mattheson).

verbis exprimitur, ut cerni potius ac coram geri, quam legi, quam audiri videatur. Haec etiam Energia, Evidentia, Illustratio, Suffiguratto, Demonstratio, Descriptio, Effictio, Subiectio sub oculos appellatur. Hoc schema ad orationis evidentiam, ad iucunditatem, ad quoscunque etiam affectus movendus confert.

in such fashion that it is perceived as though the described person was present or the event was personally experienced. This is also called *energia*, *evidentia*, *illustratio*, *suffiguratto*, *demonstratio*, *descriptio*, *effictio*, *subiectio sub oculos*. It is employed to clarify and embellish the oration as well as to move the affections.

Gottsched (*Redekunst* p.283)
Hypotyposis s. descriptio. Darinn man eine ausführliche Abbildung von einer Sache giebt, und sie dem Zuhörer gleichsam vor Augen malet.

Hypotyposis or *descriptio*. Through which one provides a detailed description of something, seemingly painting it before the eyes of the listener.

Gottsched (*Dichtkunst* p.327)
Die XII. Figur kann auf deutsch eine Schilderung (Hypotyposis s. Icon) heissen, weil sie einen so lebhaften Abriß von einer Sache macht, als ob sie wirklich vorhanden wäre.

The next figure can be translated as a depiction (*hypotyposis* or *icon*), because it presents such a lifelike portrayal of something that it actually seems to be present.

Burmeister (*Hypomnematum*)
Hypotyposis est textus illa explicatio, qua quae ἄψυχα sunt, videantur ἔμψυχα ad oculum statuta, vel deumbrata.

Hypotyposis is an explication of the text through which lifeless things are clarified and appear to come alive before the eyes.

Burmeister (*Musica Poetica* p.62)
Hypotyposis est illud ornamentum, quo textus significatio ita deumbratur, ut ea, quae textui subsunt & animam vitamque non habent, vita esse praedita, videantur. Hoc ornamentum usitatissimum est apud authenticos Artifices. Utinam eadem dexteritate ab omnibus adhiberetur Componistis.

Hypotyposis is a figure through which the meaning of the text is clarified in such fashion that those words without life or spirit of the underlying text appear to have been given life. This figure is most commonly used by real artists. O that it were applied skillfully by all composers!

Vogt (*Conclave* p.5)
Idea musica, imago rei decantatae. Idea haec idem, quod effectus figurae hypothiposeos.

The *idea musica* is the musical representation of something. The *idea* is namely that which is portrayed through *hypotyposis* figures.

Vogt (*Conclave* p.144)
Debet esse ideosus, & quodammodo pictor, ut sciat per figuras musicas Rhetoricas hypotyposes, & prosopopaeias idealiter elevare amplius, ac res pulchras, vel horridas cantu vivaciter ante oculos audientium proponere.

[The composer] ought to understand how to further intensify [the composition] imaginatively through the musical-rhetorical figures of *hypotyposis* and *prosopopoeia* and, like a painter, place the beautiful or frightful images lifelike before the eyes of the listeners through the music.

IMITATIO: see *MIMESIS*

INCHOATIO IMPERFECTA: an omission of the opening consonance in the melody which is supplied by the *basso continuo* realization.

The fact that this figure is encountered only in Bernhard's *Figurenlehre* is explained through his unique interest to identify all conceivable permissible uses of dissonance through his musical-rhetorical figures. However, unlike the *ellipsis*, which also signifies an omitted consonance, the *inchoatio imperfecta* does not identify an otherwise unexcused dissonance but rather only an irregular or *imperfecta* beginning of the composition (*inchoatio*, from *incohare*, to start, to begin an oration). In the case of the *ellipsis*, the omitted consonance is followed by a dissonance, which is explained as a passing note or suspension related to the tacitly understood preceding omission.[1] In contrast, the omitted consonance of an *inchoatio imperfecta* is supplied by the realized *basso continuo* accompaniment and has nothing to do with resultant dissonances. For this reason, presumably, the *inchoatio imperfecta* is not listed as a figure in Bernhard's *Bericht*, while the *ellipsis* is included in this later version of his *Figurenlehre*.

---

1. See *Ellipsis*.

Bernhard (*Tractatus* p.79)

Eodem Capite [§ 11] ist gesagt daß die Perfectae anheben sollen, welches auch heute nicht so rigorosè erfordert wird, daher entstehet Inchoatio imperfecta. . . . Beyde diese letztern Figuren, als Inchoatio imperfecta und Longinqua distantia werden wegen des General Baßes zugelaßen, indem der Organist über den fürgegebenen Baß wo es möglich ein richtiges Quatuor schlagen soll, daher denn die am Anfange der Composition ausgelaßenen perfecta von dem Organisten ersetzet und durch seine Mittel-Partheyen die hohe Stimme der Composition mit dem tieffen Baße dergestalt vermittelt wird, daß das Gehör dadurch die weite Distantz nicht so sehr observiret.

In chapter 7, §11, it was stated that a composition is to begin with perfect consonances, something which is not as rigorously enforced nowadays, giving rise to the *inchoatio imperfecta*. . . . Both of these figures, the *inchoatio imperfecta* and the *longinqua distantia*, are permitted through the thorough bass, because the organist is to play a proper four-part harmony above the given bass whenever possible. The omitted perfect consonances at the beginning of the composition are thereby supplied by the organist, and the high voice of the composition is connected with the low bass through the organist's middle voices, in such fashion that the ear does not notice the great distance between them quite as much.

INCREMENTUM: see *AUXESIS*

INTERROGATIO: a musical question rendered variously through pauses, a rise at the end of the phrase or melody, or through imperfect or phrygian cadences.

"After all, who does not recognize the necessity and charm of the question in all musical compositions?" With this rhetorical question Scheibe ends his discussion of the *interrogatio*. Although the musical *interrogatio* is not mentioned specifically in the various *Figurenlehren* until well into the eighteenth century, evidence of the musical representation of a question can already be found in Gregorian chant.[1] In discussing cadences, Seth Calvisius suggests the use of an imperfect cadence ending on the dominant to express a question.[2] The earliest reference to the musical expression of a question in a *Figurenlehre* is encountered in Thuringus's definition of *homoioptoton*, where he mentions that contemporary composers use the general pause in dialogues and questions (*in*

1. Unger, *Beziehungen*, 21f.
2. Ibid., 31.

Dialogis & interrogationibus).[1] Kircher, who adopts a great deal of Thuringus's *Figurenlehre*, redefines *homoioptoton* with a definition much closer to its rhetorical counterpart. In his description of the *pausa*, he expressly includes its potential to express a question as well as a response, a property of the *pausa* not mentioned by Thuringus.[2] Bernhard's reference to a musical rendering of a question in the text can in fact be understood as a musical-rhetorical figure. It appears in the context of his discussion of the figures at the point where he introduces the figures used in the *stylus theatralis* or *recitativus*.[3] Mattheson discusses the musical question at some length in his chapter *Von den Ab- und Einschnitten der Klang-Rede*, where he discusses the sections and caesurae of the musical oration. Moreover, the title and content of this chapter point to the eighteenth-century intention to develop an understanding of the figures which parallels the rhetorical discipline, even though the respective musical devices and methods had long since been established compositional tools. It is in this same chapter, immediately following the discussion of the question, that Mattheson treats the musical *exclamatio*, signified by yet another punctuation mark. This device he in fact later lists as a musical-rhetorical figure.[4]

Scheibe finally assigns the rhetorical term to the musical device. In addition to expressing the given text, Scheibe also points to the *interrogatio*'s use in purely instrumental music. He understands the *interrogatio* in much broader terms, applying its use to consequent and subsequent phrases. Furthermore, an imperfect or half cadence which terminates a slow movement, thereby posing the *interrogatio*, can be answered most effectively by a following fast movement. Thus the *interrogatio* can be applied to passages within a phrase, to entire phrases, or indeed to whole movements. Scheibe's discussion of the figure is an enlightening example of the transfer of a musical-rhetorical figure's semantic significance,

---

1. See *Homoioptoton*.
2. See *Pausa*.
3. After stating that the composer is to ensure "that the text is to be most naturally expressed" ("daβ man die Rede aufs natürlichste exprimiren solle"), Bernhard elaborates this by describing various musical devices which concur with musical-rhetorical figures found in other *Figurenlehren*, including the description of such figures as *anabasis*, *catabasis*, *hypotyposis*, *repetitio*, and *gradatio*.
4. See *Exclamatio*.

which was gained through its specific text association, not only to purely instrumental music but to larger musical-compositional structures.

Quintilian (*Institutio* IX.ii.6)

Quid enim tam commune quam interrogare vel percontari? Nam utroque utimur indifferenter, quanquam alterum noscendi, alterum arguendi gratia videtur adhiberi. At ea res, utrocunque dicitur modo, etiam multiplex habet schema.

And what is more common than to ask or inquire? For both terms are used similarly, although one is used for the sake of inquiring, the other for proving a point. But nonetheless, which ever term is used, that which it represents admits numerous figures.

Susenbrotus (*Epitome* p.60)

Interrogatio diducitur in Simplicem et Figuratam. Simplex est, quae solu, sciscitandi ac a respondente discendi gratia, cum spiritu quodam interrogantis profertur. Figurata vero, quae sciscitandi gratia non assumitur, sed percontando variis servit affectibus. Asseverationi, miserationi, instantiae, indignationi, admirationi, dubitationi, quae Fab. exacte persequitur.

The *interrogatio* is classified as either a simple or a figurative question. The simple *interrogatio* is only used for the sake of inquiring and obtaining a response, in the spirit of its use. The figurative *interrogatio*, however, is not used for the sake of inquiring but helps to strengthen various affections through questioning, such as affections of vehement assertion, pity, perseverance, indignation, admiration, and doubt, which Fabius [Quintilian] has precisely described.

Gottsched (*Redekunst* p.285)

Interrogatio. Wenn man vielmal hinter einander seiner Zuhörer Gedanken mit Fragen herauszulocken bemühet ist.

Interrogatio. When one elicits the thoughts of the listeners through numerous successive questions.

Gottsched (*Dichtkunst* p.339)

Es folgt XXIII. die Frage, (Interrogatio) die sich von sich selbst versteht, und so zu reden, die gemeinste; aber auch eine von den kräftigsten Figuren ist. Zuweilen ist sie nur einfach, und dann hat sie so viel Nachdruck nicht, als wenn sie vielmal hinter einander gesetzt wird.

The next figure is the question or *interrogatio*, which explains itself and is the most common, so to speak. But it is also one of the most powerful figures. At times it is used only once and has not nearly as much emphasis as when it is used numerous times successively.

Bernhard (*Tractatus* p.83)

Die Fragen werden gemeinem Brauche nach am Ende eine Secund höher als die vorhergehende Sylbe gesetzt.

Questions are commonly expressed by ending the phrase a second higher than the foregoing note and syllable.

Mattheson (*Capellmeister* p.192f.)

Die Fragen in der Klang-Rede, so mit dem bekannten Zeichen (?) im Text ange-

Questions in a musical oration, which are expressed with the familiar (?) in the text,

deutet werden, folgen nun in ordentlicher Betrachtung, und sind entweder eigentlich oder verblümt. Viele Setzer stehen steiff in den Gedancken, es müsse das Fragzeichen nothwendig allemahl im Singen, durch eine oder andre Erhöhung der Stimme, ausgedruckt werden; aber man darff solchen Ausspruch keines Weges für unfehlbar halten. Zwar ist in gemeiner Rede und Aussprache die Erhebung der Stimme iederzeit bey einer Frage mehr oder weniger vermacht; allein in der Melodie gibt es viele Umstände, die hierunter eine Ausnahm nicht nur zulassen, sondern offt erheischen. Uiberdis trifft man viele figürliche Fragen in Versen an, dabey gar kein Zweifel vorwaltet, obs so, oder anders sey. Der Zweifel aber ist das wahre Kennzeichen einer eigentlichen Frage. Derohalben muß ein melodischer Setzer die eine von der andern billig wol unterscheiden, und darnach seine Noten einrichten . . . welcher alhie noch beizu-fügen stehet: daß die unvollkommenen Consonantzen am geschicktesten dazu sind, wenn die Frage z.E. in eine Sext schließt; man gerathe nun steigend oder fallend darauf: das macht es nicht allemahl aus, absonderlich im Recitativ. In einer Arie setzt Gasparini die Frage: Warum glaubst du nicht? wie No.1 hierunter angezeiget wird, nehmlich fallend, und in der Sext aufhörend. An einem andern Orte braucht er die tägliche Formel, No.2, und höret in der Quint auf. Es ist auch gut, und wir wollen solches keines Weges tadeln; aber es kan doch auch so angehen, wie No.3 stehet, durch die Sext, und ist nicht so gemein, als jenes.

are now to be considered. The questions can be either actual or figurative. Many composers are convinced that a question mark can only be expressed in vocal music through a raising of the voice in one form or other. But this should not be considered infallible. It is true that in common speech the raising of the voice at a question is more or less a given. But there are many circumstances specifically in music which not only allow for exceptions to the rule but often require them. Furthermore, figurative questions are frequently encountered in poetry, leaving no doubt whether or not they should be treated in this way. Doubt is the true sign of an actual question. Therefore the composer must clearly distinguish between the two forms of the question, and compose his music accordingly . . . and to this should be added, that imperfect consonances are most suitable [in expressing a doubting question without raising the voice at the phrase ending], for example, when the question ends with a sixth. It makes little difference whether the sixth is approached from below or above, especially in recitatives. In one of his arias, Gasparini expresses the question, "Why do you not believe?" as illustrated in example 1, namely ending with a sixth. Somewhere else he uses the conventional formula and ends with a fifth, as in example 2. There is nothing wrong with that, and we in no way wish to reprimand him. But it can also be expressed through a sixth as illustrated in example 3, which is not as mundane as the others.

Scheibe (*Critischer Musicus* p.695)
Die Xte Figur ist die Frage. (Interrogatio.) Die Eigenschaft derselben und ihre Stellung in Noten ist bereits allen Musikverständigen so bekannt, daβ ich auch fast nicht nöthig habe, etwas davon zu gedenken. . . . Sie kann in allen Instrumentalstücken überaus gut gebrauchet werden. . . . Ein Stück, das weitläuftig und mit vielen an einander hangenden Melodien ausgeführet ist, muβ an vielen Orten durch diese Figur in einem angenehmen Zusammenhange erhalten werden. Die Sätze aber, welche darauf folgen, müssen hingegen auch gleichsam einer deutlichen Antwort ähnlich seyn. Es kann ferner diese Figur sehr gut verdoppelt werden, und so können mehr als eine Frage unmittelbar auf einander folgen. Sie kann auch am Ende eines langsamen Satzes stehen, und da wird sie gewiβ mit dem besten Nachdrucke angewendet. Ueberall aber muβ sie sich auf einen gewissen Zusammenhang und auf eine unentbehrlich Folge von Melodien beziehen; man müβte denn eine Arie, der Worte wegen, ganz und gar damit beschlieβen, um bey den Zuhörern ein Nachdenken zu hinterlassen. . . . Wer sieht übrigens nicht die Nothwendigkeit und die Schönheit der Frage in allen musikalischen Stücken?

The next figure is the question or *interrogatio*. Its properties and musical expression are already so familiar to the musically literate that it is hardly necessary to consider it here. . . . It can be particularly useful in instrumental music. . . . A lengthy piece which is constructed out of numerous connected melodies retains a pleasant cohesion through a frequent application of the *interrogatio*. The subsequent passages must also provide clear answers in response, as it were. Furthermore, the figure can very well be doubled, resulting in numerous successive questions. It can also be employed at the end of a slow movement, where it is used with the most emphasis. In any case however, it must result in a certain cohesion and an indispensable succession of melodies. Consequently, an aria would ultimately end with an *interrogatio* in accordance with the text, in order to leave the listeners in reflection. . . . After all, who does not recognize the necessity and charm of the question in all musical compositions?

KYKLOSIS: see *CIRCULATIO*

LICENTIA: see *HYPERBOLE, PARRHESIA*

LIGATURA: see *SYNCOPATIO*

LONGINQUA DISTANTIA: a distance between two neighboring voices of a composition in excess of a twelfth.

In the second chapter of his *Tractatus*, Bernhard makes the following point: "The voices are not to be placed too far from each other, that is, not more than a twelfth apart. For that reason, composers of former days did not compose duos for soprano and bass, which today's composers frequently do in their dialogues, etc. Therefore this rule is also not very binding."[1] With the dawn of the *basso continuo* era, this rule of counterpoint is no longer as relevant or as strictly observed as in the sixteenth century. In realizing the bass line, the keyboard player fills in the gap between the voices "in such fashion, that the ear does not notice the great distance between them quite as much." Bernhard describes the *distantia* between soprano and bass as *longinqua* ("distant, foreign"). This latter term not only describes the "long" interval separating the voices, but also signifies the "foreignness" or "strangeness" of the resulting interval. Like a number of his other figures, including the *inchoatio imperfecta*, this figure is only found in Bernhard's *Tractatus*. This device was freely used in contemporary composition and did not technically define a dissonance but rather a compositional irregularity. In keeping with his intention to focus on the proper use of dissonance, he no longer considers it necessary to list this technicality as a figure in his *Bericht*. Neither is the figure encountered in any other *Figurenlehre*.

Bernhard (*Tractatus* p.79)

So ist oben in demselben Cap. No.13 der weite Unterscheid einer Stimme von der andern verbothen worden, wiewohl mit schon angehängter Erklärung, daβ heute solches nicht selten vorkomme, und solches heiβe ich sodann Longinquam distantiam.

In the same chapter [2], no.13, above, the wide separation of one voice from the other was forbidden. But as already explained, this occurs not infrequently nowadays, and I therefore call it *longinqua distantia*.

Beyde diese letztern Figuren, als Inchoatio imperfecta und Longinqua distantia werden wegen des General Baβes zugelaβen, indem der Organist über den fürgegebenen Baβ wo es möglich ein richtiges Quatuor schlagen soll, daher denn die am Anfange der Composition

Both of these figures, the *inchoatio imperfecta* and the *longinqua distantia*, are permitted through the thorough bass because the organist is to play a proper four-part harmony above the given bass whenever possible. The omitted perfect consonances at the beginning of the com-

1. "Die Stimmen sollen nicht zu weit oder nicht über eine Duodecimam von einander stehen, daher man nicht findet, das die Alten Canto e Basso solo componiret haben, welches zwar die Heutigen in denen Dialogis etc. thun, daher auch diese Regel nicht so gar sehr bindet." *Tractatus*, 41.

ausgelaßenen perfecta von dem Organisten ersetzet und durch seine Mittel-Partheyen die hohe Stimme der Composition mit dem tieffen Baße dergestalt vermittelt wird, daß das Gehör dadurch die weite Distantz nicht so sehr observiret.

position are thereby supplied by the organist, and the high voice of the composition is connected with the low bass through the middle voices in such fashion that the ear does not notice the great distance between them quite as much.

MANUBRIUM: see *PARAGOGE*

MESSANZA: a series of four notes of short duration, moving either by step or by leap.

Messanza is defined both as a simple ornamental figure as well as a song genre more commonly known as a *quodlibet*. In both cases, the literal meaning of the word, "mixture," is embodied in the musical devices. It is a mixture either of various different melodies or of various different intervals. Unlike the *figurae simplices* such as the *corta*, *groppo*, or *circolo*, this embellishment is not limited to a certain formation but can result in a myriad of different figurations. According to Printz, the total number of different four-note *messanzae* comes to six hundred.

Printz (*Phrynis Mytilenaeus* pt.2, p.57)

Messanza ist eine vermengte Figur, so aus vier geschwinden Noten bestehet / welche entweder zum theil bleiben / und zum Theil sich bewegen / oder theils springen / und theils ordentlich gehen.

The *messanza* is a mixed figure consisting of four rapid notes of which either some remain stationary while others move or some leap while others move by step.

Walther (*Lexicon*)

Messanza, (ital.) ist eine vermengte Figur, so aus vier geschwinden Noten bestehet, welche entweder zum theil bleiben, und zum theil sich bewegen, oder theils springen, theils ordentlich gehen. Beym Praetorio T.3. c.5. ist Messanza oder Mistichanza so viel, als ein Quodlibet; wenn nemlich aus vielen Motetten und Madrigalien, weltlichen und possier-

The *messanza* is a mixed figure consisting of four rapid notes of which either some remain stationary while others move or some leap while others move by step. In Praetorius's [*Syntagma*] vol.3, ch.5, *messanza* or *mistichanza* is defined as a *quodlibet*: namely when a half or a whole line of text with its melody is taken from a number of motets, madri-

lichen Liedern, eine Halbe oder gantze Zeile Text, sammt den Melodien, herausgenommen, und aus solchen Fleckgen und Stückgen wiederum ein gantzes Lied gemacht wird.

gals, or secular or lighthearted songs and these portions are fashioned into another entire song.

Spiess (*Tractatus* p.156)
Messanza, oder Misticanza, Mixtio, Vermischung, ist eine mit obigen Läuffen vermischte Figur, bestehet meistens in unterschiedlichen Sprüngen. Diese Figur wird in Passaggien, Phantasien, und sonderbar in Variationibus viel gebraucht.

The *messanza* or *misticanza*, also known as *mixtio* or mixture, is a figure consisting primarily of various leaps and is mixed with the above runs [*corta*, *groppo*, *cicolo*, *tirata*]. This figure is frequently used in *passaggi*, *phantasiae*, and especially in *variationes*.

METABASIS, TRANSGRESSIO: a crossing of one voice by another.

The terms cited by Vogt and Spiess for this figure, *metabasis* or *diabasis* and *transgressio*, are assigned different rhetorical definitions. *Transgressio* is the Latin term for *hyperbaton* and indicates a rearranging of the proper word or phrase order.[1] *Meta-* or *diabasis*, translated with the Latin *transitio*, refers to a transition from one thought to another.[2] The literal meaning of both *metabasis* and *transgressio* incorporates the sense of stepping (*basis*, *gressus*) over or through (*meta*, *trans*) something else.

Both Vogt and Spiess adopt the rhetorical terms *metabasis/trans-*

1. See *Hyperbaton*.

2. Although Mattheson generally uses the related term *transitus* in its common musical understanding, namely, of a passing note, in his discussion of the musical *dispositio* the term *transitus* is used to indicate "a transition, through which the foregoing is connected to the following" ("Da ist ein Transitus oder Uibergang, Krafft dessen das vorige mit dem folgenden an einander gefüget, und von jenem zu diesem herüber getreten wird." *Capellmeister*, 238). Here he refers to a specific bass note immediately repeated an octave higher following a cadential note marked with a fermata and forming an upbeat to the following phrase. The repeated note thereby "recalls" what has just been uttered, while at the same time introducing the subsequent thought, an exact parallel to the rhetorical *metabasis* or *transitio*.

gressio to indicate voice crossing.[1] The definition and example which Vogt provides (and Spiess duplicates) reflects the literal understanding of the term rather than its rhetorical content. The voices "step over" each other, creating in fact a two fold "transgression." First, such voice crossing is considered a compositional irregularity in traditional counterpoint. As Bernhard points out, "upper voices must seldom pass under lower ones, and lower ones seldom over higher ones."[2] Second, a visual transgression or crossover is created with this device. In the example, the figure is effectively used to vividly illustrate the text, "take me with you; seize me in your [arms]." As the voices intertwine, one voice "seizes" the other and "drags" it along.

Susenbrotus (*Epitome* p.88)
Transitio μετάβασις est quum paucis monemus quid dictum sit, et quid postea simus dicturi.

The *transitio* or *metabasis* occurs when we briefly recall what has been said and anticipate what is to follow.

Vogt (*Conclave* p.152)
Metabasis, vel Diabasis. Trangressio, ubi una vox alteram transgreditur: ut in exemplo:

The *metabasis* (or *diabasis, transgressio*) occurs when one voice crosses over the other, as in the following example:

Spiess (*Tractatus* p.156)
Metabasis, oder Diabasis, Transgressio, Uberschreitung, ist, wann immer eine Stimm die andere übersteigt.

The *metabasis* (or *diabasis, transgressio,* a transgression) occurs whenever one voice crosses over the other.

---

1. Although the specific technique of voice crossing is not mentioned in other *Figurenlehren*, a related compositional device is identified through *heterolepsis* and *hyperbaton*. These figures indicate an intrusion of one voice into the range of another. Thus the rhetorical device of *transgressio* finds its way into the musical *Figurenlehre* under its Greek name, *hyperbaton*, while the rhetorical *transitio* is identified as a *transgressio* in music. See *Heterolepsis, Hyperbaton, Parenthesis*.

2. "Die hohen Stimmen sollen selten unter die Tieffen und die Tieffen über die Hohen steigen." *Tractatus*, 42.

METALEPSIS, TRANSUMPTIO: a *fuga* with a two-part subject, the parts alternating in the composition.

The rhetorical *metalepsis* is supplied with two related definitions: two unrelated terms can be correlated through a third, intermediary, or transitional term, or a thought can be clarified with either a preceding or a subsequent thought. It is the latter understanding of *metalepsis* which is adopted into Burmeister's *Figurenlehre*. His somewhat enigmatic definitions are elucidated through his examples: soprano and alto voices begin with the entire subject, while tenor and bass voices enter with only the second part of the subject (to the text *procedit mel*). Finally the second tenor enters, now with the entire subject. The "missing" first part of the subject in the tenor and bass entries is supplied by the preceding and subsequent entries of the subject in the context of the composition, thereby completing both the musical and the textual thought. The musical *metalepsis* consequently concurs with both the rhetorical and the literal meaning of the term: the meaning of the musical (and textual) expression is clarified "through" (*meta/trans*) the "addition" (*lepsis/sumptio*, adoption, assumption) of a further reference. The meaning of *metalepsis* as "exchange" is also found in Burmeister's definition when he speaks of the voices being *vertuntur*. The Latin term for *metalepsis*, *transumptio*, appears in the definition as the verb *transumere*, referring to a "taking up" of two motives in the composition.

Like the other fugal figures *hypallage* and *parembole*, the *metalepsis* only appears in Burmeister's *Figurenlehre*. The various fugal techniques are not listed as separate figures after this but are included in general discussions of counterpoint or listed as variants of *fuga*.[1]

Quintilian (*Institutio* VIII.vi.37,38)

Superest ex his, quae aliter significant, metalepsis, id est transumptio, quae ex alio tropo in alium velut viam praestat; . . . Est enim haec in metalepsi natura, ut inter id quod transfertur et in quod transfertur sit medius quidam gradus, nihil ipse significans sed praebens transitum.

The *metalepsis* or *transumptio* is the last of the [tropes] involving a change of meaning and signifies a transition from one trope to another. . . . It is the nature of the *metalepsis* to form a certain intermediate step between a transferred term and that to which the term is transferred,

1. See *Fuga*.

Nam id eius frequentissimum exemplum est cano canto, canto dico, ita cano dico. Interest medium illud canto.

taking on no meaning itself, but only providing a transition. The most common example is the following one: if *cano* is replaced with *canto*, and *canto* with *dico*, then *cano* can be replaced with *dico*, the intermediate step provided by *canto*.

Susenbrotus (*Epitome* p.11)
Metalepsis, μεταλήψις Transumptio, est ubi gradatim itur ad id quod ostenditur. Vel est cum aliqua vox aliud proprietate significationis suae ex his quae praecesserunt, denotat. Tropus poeticus ac omnino rarus.

The *metalepsis* or *transumptio* occurs when something is revealed in stepwise fashion. Or it occurs when a certain utterance adopts a meaning other than its literal one because of that which preceded it. It is a rare poetic trope.

Vossius (*Commentatorium Rhetoricum*, 2, p.162)
Metalepsis vocatur tum quando ex antecedente intellegitur consequens aut ex consequente antecedens.

The *metalepsis* occurs when the subsequent is understood from the antecedent, or the antecedent from the subsequent.

Gottsched (*Redekunst* p.249)
Die Metalepsis, der Zustandswechsel, und dieser ist zweyerley. 1) Das vorhergehende fürs nachfolgende. Z.E. Man sagt: Er hat gelebet, an statt, er ist gestorben. . . . 2) Das Nachfolgende fürs Vorhergehende. Er hat nicht viel vergessen, an statt, er hat nicht viel gelernet.

The *metalepsis* or transformation is of two kinds: (1) the preceding can be stated instead of the subsequent, as in "He has lived" instead of "He died"; (2) or the subsequent instead of the preceding, as in "He has forgotten little" instead of "He has learned little."

Burmeister (*Hypomnematum*)
Metalepsis est Fuga duplex, in qua vocum, quae simili, in Modorum conjugio, sunt Ambitu circumscriptae, altera alterius Melodiam in fugam abripit, cui mox alterarum similiter ruminando adjicit.

The *metalepsis* is a double *fuga* in which one voice partially introduces the subject of another, namely its second part, into the *fuga*, which it thereupon completes through repetition of the whole subject. The range of the voices are similarly limited through the *ambitus* of their common *modus*.

Burmeister (*Musica Autoschediastike* p.13^r)

Metalepsis μετάληψις est talis habitus Fugae, in qua voces duae, vel ex reliquis aliae voces inter se modulaminis initium sive simul, sive per intervallum facientes, diversas proferunt melodias, quas reliquae voces una cum illis primis duabus in harmonia hinc inde transsumunt & in fugam vertunt, ut apud Orlandum in De ore prudentis.

The *metalepsis* is a form of *fuga* in which two or more of its voices, beginning either simultaneously or after a certain interval, introduce different subjects. The remaining voices together with the first two then adopt now one, now the other of the subjects and alternate them in the *fuga*, as in Orlando's *De ore prudentis*.

Burmeister (*Musica Poetica* p.58)

Metalepsis μετάληψις est talis habitus Fugae, in quo duae Melodiae in Harmonia hinc inde transsumuntur & in fugam vertuntur. Exemplum luculentissimum est apud Orlandum, in De ore prudentis.

The *metalepsis* is a form of *fuga* in which two subjects are alternately adopted in the *harmonia* and alternate in the *fuga*. A most splendid example is found in Orlando's *De ore prudentis.*

MIMESIS, ETHOPHONIA, IMITATIO: (1) a repetition of a *noema* at a different pitch; (2) an approximate rather than strict imitation of a subject at different pitches.

The rhetorical *mimesis* or *ethopoeia* signifies a contemptuous imitation of someone by mimicking their speech, mannerisms, and gestures in an oration. As such it is distinct from the *prosopopoeia*, which can be used to represent the speech of a deceased or absent person in a lifelike manner.[1] While *mimesis* is an imitation which is clearly distinct from the original through its mocking repetition, the *prosopopoeia* wishes to present someone's words as if that person were in fact present.

1. Sonnino, *Handbook*, 54.

The first musical use of *mimesis* occurs in Stomius's definition of a canon or *fuga*. This also appears to be the first time that rhetorical figure terminology is consciously applied to a musical device. Stomius wishes to identify the repetition of the canon or *fuga* subject with this term to distinguish between the original voice and the imitating voices.[1] Although the sense of mocking cannot be present in a musical *mimesis*, the distinction between the original and the imitation is retained. While the imitating voices reproduce the original subject, they are nonetheless perceived as autonomous and distinct voices.

Burmeister uses *mimesis* terminology both to define a *noema* figure and to describe *fuga*, in particular his *fuga realis*. In his *Musica Poetica* the *fuga realis*, a freer form of fugal imitation in contrast to the canonic *fuga imaginaria*, is listed as one of the *figurae harmoniae*. These are the figures which affect all the voices of a composition. While the different voices may be similar, they are not identical, just as an imitation remains distinct from its original. This understanding is reinforced through Burmeister's use of the *mimesis* terminology, *mimema* and *memimemenos* (μίμημα and μεμιμημένος), in describing the *fuga realis*. In such an imitation, the reference to the original must be clear yet at the same time remain distinct from it. The *fuga imaginaria* on the other hand is listed as one of the *figurae tam harmoniae quam melodiae*. As Burmeister describes this form of *fuga* as consisting of only one voice, it is a *figura melodiae*. However, because the canonic device determines the formation of the remaining voices or the entire *harmonia*, it is *tam harmoniae quam melodiae*. Thus Burmeister switches the use of *mimesis* terminology from describing strict imitation or canon, as Stomius had done, to describing freer and independent imitation. Similarly, the repetition of a *noema*, a homophonic passage within a contrapuntal composition, at different higher or lower pitches is specifically called a *mimesis* by Burmeister, while a repeated *noema* at the same pitch is termed *analepsis*. Here again Burmeister wishes to distinguish between an exact repetition and a similar but varied imitation.

Thuringus lists *mimesis* as an alternative term for *repetitio*, which he defines as a continuous repetition of a theme in one voice but at

---

1. See *Fuga*.

different pitches. He thus adapts Burmeister's varied repetition of a *noema* to the varied repetition of a theme.[1] This definition of *mimesis* is also given by Walther, who additionally lists *imitatio* rather than *repetitio* as an alternative term. However, he defines *imitatio* as an imitation of a theme at intervals other than the unison, fourth, fifth, or octave, indicating that this device does not refer to real or tonal fugal answers but rather to freer imitation. Burmeister's and Thuringus's conditions regarding the *mimesis* or *imitatio* are thus simplified to indicate freer imitation at various pitches. At the end of the final chapter of the second part of his *Capellmeister* (which deals with the musical *dispositio* and *decoratio*), Mattheson mentions *mimesis* as one of the figures used in fugal composition, also indicating an understanding of the device as freer imitation. He then places his discussion of *imitatio* (translated by the German *Nachahmung*, meaning mimicry) in the third part of his *Capellmeister*, which deals with the technical aspects of composition. The last variant of his threefold definition of the term also signifies a free form of imitation, emphasized through his bold print of *mit aller* (with all), in reference to the liberties taken in imitation.

Of all the musical *mimesis* definitions, Vogt's curious description is closest to its rhetorical counterpart. According to Vogt (and after him, Spiess), a *mimesis* can occur when women's voices are imitated by men. While the rhetorical sense of mimicking is most evident in Vogt's definition, he makes no mention of specific voices or intervals of imitation, being more concerned with the figure's effect rather than its technical requirements. Both Vogt and Spiess also list *ethophonia* as an alternative term for *mimesis*. While *ethophonia* does not appear in rhetorical *Figurenlehren*, Quintilian lists *ethopoeia* as an alternative to *mimesis*. In adapting the term to the musical context, Vogt replaces the literary *poeia* with the musical *phonia*, resulting in a closely related derivation. Spiess, like Walther, also lists *imitatio* as an alternative term for *mimesis* and *ethophonia*. And, like Walther, he also defines *imitatio* separately as a method of freer imitation. This form of imitation can occur either by reducing the durational value of the subject's notes while preserving the original intervals, known as *diminutio notarum* or *subjecti*, or

---

1. See *Anaphora*.

through a varied repetition of the subject.

Spiess begins his discussion of *imitatio* with the comment that he does not at that point wish to discuss the term in the sense of imitating the music of past masters, "which is in itself a praiseworthy undertaking, as long as this does not lead to outright musical plagiarism." This formulation again displays Spiess's indebtedness to Mattheson (among others), who uses this explanation in his second definition of *imitatio*. Burmeister dedicated the last chapter of his *Musica Poetica, De Imitatione*, to this topic, where he states that "*imitatio* is the striving and endeavor to dexterously reflect upon, emulate, and construct our musical compositions through the analysis of artful examples."[1] Included in this chapter is also a list of composers whose works Burmeister considers worthy of imitation. Such a process of analysis and imitation forms the very core of Renaissance and Baroque pedagogy, which consisted of learning the rules, studying the examples of past masters, and imitating their work, commonly summed up in the phrase *praeceptum, exemplum, et imitatio*. This understanding of *imitatio* is equally common in rhetoric and music.[2] It also lies at the heart of Burmeister's endeavor to identify and label compositional devices with familiar rhetorical terminology. In keeping with this tradition, Bernhard includes the chapter *Von der Imitation* in his *Tractatus*, where he also lists various composers who should be emulated.[3] Regarding *imitatio*, Bernhard states: "For the imitation of the most distinguished writers in the musical profession, as in all the other arts, is not only a useful but a necessary part of the praxis, without which all precepts are useless."[4]

(Quintilian *Institutio* IX.ii.58)

Imitatio morum alienorum, quae ἠθο-	The imitation of someone else's voice is

---

1. "Imitatio est studium & conamen nostra carmina musica ad Artificium exempla, per analysi dextre considerata, effingendi & formandi." *Musica poetica*, 74.

2. Ruhnke, *Burmeister*, 166.

3. Bernhard lists the various composers according to the musical styles. Included are not only Flemish and Roman masters (under *stylus gravis*) but also modern masters such as Monteverdi, Carissimi, and Rossi (under both kinds of *stylus luxurians*), as well as Scacchi, who strongly influenced Bernhard's stylistically oriented discussion.

4. "Denn doch die Imitation der vornehmsten Authorum dieser Profession nicht weniger als in allen andern Künsten nützlich ja nöthig ist, als ein Theil der Praxeos, ohne welche alle Praecepta ohne Nutzen sind." *Tractatus*, 90.

ποιΐα vel, ut alii malunt, μίμησις dicitur, iam inter leniores adfectus numerari postest; est enim posita fere in eludendo, sed versatur et in factis et in dictis.

called *ethopoeia* or *mimesis*, and is counted among the figures used to arouse gentler affections. It is used in a mocking manner, and concerns itself with deeds and with words.

Gottsched (*Redekunst* p.254)
Mimesis. Ist eine spöttische Wiederholung der Worte dessen, den man verspotten will.

The *mimesis* is a mocking repetition of the words of the person who is to be mocked.

Stomius (*Prima instructio* p.C2[v])
Ingeniosa, quas mimeses seu fugas appellant: ubi eadem vox a pluribus, sed certis temporum spaciis intervenientibus, consequenter canitur.

Mimeses or *fugae* are ingenious constructions in which one and the same voice is successively sung by others delayed by a specified interval of time.

Burmeister (*Hypomnematum*)
Mimesis fit, quando vocum quarundam propinquissime conjunctarum suavis affectio imitatione quadam ab aliis repetitur.

A *mimesis* occurs when the neighboring structure of pleasantly combined voices [i.e., a *noema*] is repeated by an imitation of the other voices.

Burmeister (*Musica Poetica* p.59)
Mimesis μίμησις est quando in plurium vocum combinatione aliquae voces maxime propinquae aliis silentibus Noema introducunt, & hoc eae, quae silent & sibi invicem vicinae sunt ac propinquae

A *mimesis* occurs when a number of voices in a polyphonic composition introduce a *noema*, while the other immediately adjacent voices are silent. They are imitated then in turn by the adjacent

depressius vel altius sublimiusve imitantur, ut apud Orlandum in Omina quae fecisti nobis Domine 5 vocum, ad textum: Misericordiam tuam &c.

voices at a higher or lower pitch, as in Orlando's five-voiced *Omnia quae fecisti nobis Domine* at the text *Misericordiam tuam*.

Thuringus (*Opusculum* p.125)
Quid est Repetitio? Repetitio, quae & Mimesis dicitur, est, cum in contrapuncto florido seu fracto, thema in una aliqua voce perpetuo iteratur, quantum vis mutatis locis.

What is the *repetitio*? The *repetitio*, also called *mimesis*, occurs when in florid or mixed counterpoint a theme is continually repeated in one and the same voice at however many different pitches.

Vogt (*Conclave* p.151)
Ethophonia, vel Mimisis. Cum aliquis alterius vocem imitatur, ut mulieris.

The *ethophonia* or *mimesis* occurs when someone imitates the voice of another, for example [when male voices imitate the voices] of women.

Walther (*Lexicon*)
Mimesis [lat.] μίμησις [gr.] imitatio, heisset in einer Composition: wenn ein gewisses thema in einer Stimme immer wiederholt wird. s. Thuring. P.2 c.18.

The *mimesis* or *imitatio* occurs in a composition when a certain theme is consistently repeated in one voice. See Thuringus, [*Opusculum*] part 2, ch.18.

Imitatione, oder Imitazione [ital.] Imitation [gal.] Imitatio [lat.] eine Nachahmung, Nachmachung, ist: wenn eine Stimme die Melodie einer andern in der Secund, Terz, Sext, oder Septima nachmachet.

The . . . *imitatio* is a mimicry or reproduction and occurs when one voice imitates the melody of another at the second, third, sixth, or seventh.

Mattheson (*Capellmeister* p.244)
Noch eins ist zu erinnern, daβ nehmlich unter die grossen Erweiterungs-Figuren, deren etliche dreiβig seyn werden, und die mehr zur Verlängerung, Amplification, zum Schmuck, Zierath oder Gepränge, als zur gründlichen Uiberzeugung der Gemüther dienen, nicht mit Unrecht zu zehlen ist das bekannte und berühmte Kunst-Stück der Fugen, worin die Mimesis, Expolitio, Distributio samt andern Blümlein, die selten zu reiffen Früchten werden, ihre Residentz, als in einem Gewächs-Hause, antreffen. An seinem Orte wird davon mehr Unterricht folgen.

And finally it should be remembered that the well-known and famous art work called Fugue is appropriately numbered among the large figures of amplification. There are approximately thirty of these figures, which serve more to prolong, amplify, and adorn a composition than to thoroughly convince the passions. Included in the Fugue are figures such as *mimesis*, *expolitio*, *distributio*, and other embellishments which are rarely fruitful and find their home in that greenhouse of figures. More instruction regarding this will be given at the appropriate place.

(*Capellmeister* p.331)
Denn, gleichwie eine Unterredung, da zu allen Vorträgen blosserdings Ja oder Nein gesaget, und keine Untersuchung vorgenommen, keine Behauptung angebracht, keine Gegenrede verspüret, kein kleiner freundlicher Streit erreget, ja, gar keine Mühe genommen wird, es einander nach oder auch zuvorzuthun, gar bald schläfrig macht, und schlechte Freude erwecket: also erfordert auch eine jede Harmonie, wenn sie gleich nur aus zwo Stimmen bestünde, eben solche Erörterung, Einwürffe, Beisprüche und Luftgefechte in den Klängen, die man durch kein bessers Mittel, als durch die so genannte Nachahmung, welche mit ihrem Kunstworte, Imitatio, vel potius Aemulatio vocum heisset, vorstellig machen kan. Diese Nachahmung nun hat in der Music dreierley zu bedeuten. Denn erstlich finden wir Gelegenheit, dergleichen Uibung mit allerhand natürlichen Dingen und Gemüths-Neigungen anzustellen, worin schier das grösseste Hülfsmittel der Erfindung bestehet, wie an seinem Orte gesaget worden ist. Fürs andre wird diejenige Bemühung verstanden, so man sich gibt, dieses oder jenen Meisters und Ton-Künstlers Arbeit nachzumachen: welches eine gantz gute Sache ist, so lange kein förmlicher Musicalischer Raub dabey mit unterläufft. Drittens be-

For, just as a discussion in which every statement is answered with only Yes or No, in which no inquiry is undertaken, no assertion is presented, no counterargument is discerned, no small friendly contest is provoked, yea, not the slightest effort is made to imitate or to excel, will soon become tiring and cause ill will, in like manner every composition, even if it were to consist of only two voices, also requires such explications, objections, analogies, and arguments in the music which are achieved through no better method than through so-called *Nachahmung* (mimicry), known also as *imitatio* or *aemulatio vocum*. Such mimicry has a threefold meaning in music. First, we have opportunity to imitate all sorts of natural things and affections, which is undoubtedly the greatest help for the *inventio*, as has already been discussed above. Second, it refers to the trouble one takes to imitate one or another master's or composer's work, which is in itself a praiseworthy undertaking, as long as this does not lead to outright musical plagiarism. Third, it refers to that agreeable competition fought *with all* freedom between the various voices over certain motifs, passages, or phrases.

mercket man durch die Nachahmung denjenigen angenehmen Wettstreit, welchen verschiedene Stimmen über gewisse Förmelgen, Gänge oder kurtze Sätze *mit aller* Freiheit unter einander führen.

Spiess (*Tractatus* p.156)
Ethophonia, oder Mimisis, Imitatio, Nachahmung, wird alsdann genennet, wann einer des andern Stimm imitirt. v.g. eines Weibs. Vogt fol. 151. Walther sagt, es heisse in einer Composition, wann ein gewisses Thema in einer Stimm immer wiederholet wird.

The *ethophonia* (or *mimesis, imitatio*, or mimicry) occurs when someone imitates the voice of another, for example [when a male voice imitates the voice] of a woman. Walther claims it occurs in a composition when a certain theme is consistently repeated in one voice.

Imitatio, Nachahmung, ist hier nicht zu verstehen von der Bemühung, so man sich gibt, dieses oder jenes Meisters preiβliche Arbeit nachzumachen, welches an sich selbsten ein gantz lobwürdige Sache ist, so lang kein formlicher Musicalischer Raub darbey mit unterlaufft; sondern Imitatio heiβt so viel, als Aemulatio vocum, Nacheifferung, Nachaffung der Stimmen, da sie sich anlassen, das Subjectum oder Thema nach Möglichkeit mit solch ihren Gängen und Sprüngen, so dem Subjecto immer gleichförmig scheinen, und seyn können, nachzuahmen und nachzumachen. Es geschiehet dieses meistens per Diminutionem Notarum so wohl, als auch Subjecti, doch mit diesem notablen Unterscheid, daβ in Figura Diminutionis jederzeit in jene Gäng und Sprüng des Subjecti, wiewohl nur mit geschwinden Noten, doch legaliter eingetretten werde, welches in der Imitation nicht geschiehet, sondern nur quomodocunque, wie es immer seyn und geschehen könne, das Subjectum oder Thema von anderen Neben- und Mittel-Stimmen imitirt und nachgeaffet wird. Exempla seynd allenthalben genugsam.

The *imitatio* or mimicry is here not to be understood as the endeavor to imitate one or the other master's worthy work, which is in itself a praiseworthy undertaking, as long as this does not lead to outright musical plagiarism. Rather *imitatio* means *aemulatio vocum*, the emulation or mimicry of the voices, resulting from an imitation or reproduction of the subject or theme with all its steps and leaps if possible, thus always appearing similar to the subject. This commonly occurs through the two forms of *diminutio*, *notarum* as well as *subjecti*, with one notable difference, however: the progressions and leaps of the subject are presented through the *diminutio* figures with faster notes but always in strict imitation, while the *imitatio* mimics the subject or theme in neighboring or middle voices only *quomodocumque*, that is, in what ever way possible. There are certainly enough examples of this figure.

MISTICANZA: see *MESSANZA*

MORA: a rising resolution of a suspension when a falling one is expected.

The term *mora* (literally, "delay") is only encountered in Bernhard's *Tractatus*. The choice of this term for an unexpected upward resolution of a suspension points to a twofold delay. First, the sounding of the expected consonance is delayed through the suspension. Second, in both of Bernhard's examples the initial rising resolution is followed by a falling melody line, thereby delaying the expected resolution that much longer. Although the term is not found in his *Bericht*, he introduces a related figure with the same literal meaning, the *retardatio*.[1] This figure signifies a delayed but expected upward resolution of a suspension. It is the *retardatio* which is then listed in Walther's *Lexicon*, as well as in the treatises of Scheibe and Spiess.

Bernhard (*Tractatus* p.85)

Mora ist eine umgekehrte Syncopatio, indem nehmlich die auff die rückende Dissonantz folgende Consonantz nicht eine Secunde fället, sondern steiget.

The *mora* is an inverted *syncopatio* which occurs when the consonance which follows the shifted dissonance rises rather than falls a second.

MULTIPLICATIO: a subdivision of a longer dissonant note into two or more notes.

In choosing the term *multiplicatio* for this figure, Bernhard focuses on a "multiplication" of one longer dissonance into numerous notes of shorter duration, the sum of which equals the duration of the original dissonant note. Because the *multiplicatio* does not actually introduce but

1. See *Retardatio*.

only modifies a dissonance, it is always used in conjunction with a different, dissonance-producing figure. In his definition of *multiplicatio*, Bernhard points to its use in conjunction with the *transitus* and the *syncopatio*. Elsewhere in his treatise he mentions other figures which are commonly associated with it. The *extensio*, a figure used to prolong the duration of a dissonance, frequently has the extended dissonance subdivided into shorter notes through the *multiplicatio*.[1] And in his *Tractatus* definition of the *quasi-transitus*, a passing note with the dissonance falling on the strong instead of the weak beat, Bernhard comments that this form of *transitus* always occurs in conjunction with the *multiplicatio*.[2] Although Bernhard omits many of the figures listed in his *Tractatus* in his later *Bericht*, presumably because they do not in fact incur or explain dissonances in a composition, the *multiplicatio* is retained because of its close association with the dissonance figures. Walther adopts the term along with its definition in his *Praecepta* but not in his *Lexicon*. Nor does the figure appear in any of the other affection-oriented *Figurenlehren* of subsequent authors. Scheibe does include this device in his early composition treatise but not in the *Figurenlehre* found in his *Critischer Musicus*. He identifies it as *variatio*, a term normally used to describe a general embellishing of a melodic passage.[3]

Bernhard (*Tractatus* p.75)

Multiplicatio ist einer Dissonatz /: sie sey in einer Syncopation oder Transitu :/ Zertheilung in 2 oder biβweilen mehr Theile.	The *multiplicatio* is the division of a dissonance (occuring either through a *syncopatio* or *transitus*) into two or more parts.

1. See *Extensio*.
2. See *Transitus*.
3. See *Variatio*.

Bernhard (*Bericht* p.150)

Die Multiplication ist eine Verkleinerung einer Dissonanz durch mehrere Noten in einem Clavis. Und ist zweyerley; Die Rechtmäßige und die Verlängerte. Die Rechtmäßige ist, welche aus dem Transitu Regulari herrührend oder auch aus der Syncopatione, nicht länger alß die vorhergehende Consonanz währet.

The *multiplicatio* is the subdivision of a dissonance through numerous notes on the same pitch. It is of two kinds: regular and extended. The regular *multiplicatio* emanates out of the *transitus regularis* or the *syncopatio* and does not last longer than the preceding consonance.

Die Verlängerte ist, wenn die Dissonanzen länger währen alß die vorgehenden Consonanzen.

The extended *multiplicatio* occurs when the dissonances last longer than the preceding consonances.

Walther (*Praecepta* p.154)

Multiplicatio. Ist einer Dissonanz Verkleinerung durch mehrere Noten in einem Clavi. Solche ist zweyerley, nem. 1) die rechtmäsige und 2) die verlängerte. Die rechtmäsige Verkleinerung ist diejenige, welche nicht länger währet, als die vorhergehende Consonanz. Die verlängerte ist, wenn die Dissonantien länger währen, als die vorhergehende Consonantien.

The *multiplicatio* is the subdivision of a dissonance through numerous notes on the same pitch. It is of two kinds, namely regular and extended. The regular *multiplicatio* is one which does not last longer than the preceding consonance. The extended *multiplicatio* occurs when the dissonances last longer than the preceding consonances.

MUTATIO TONI: an irregular alteration of the mode.

Changes to or of the mode within a composition are considered text-expressive musical devices long before the seventeenth-century *Figurenlehren.*[1] Hoffmann refers to the transgression of a mode's *ambitus* with the rhetorical terms *redundantia* and *ellipsis*. This musical device entered Burmeister's *Figurenlehre* as *hyperbole* and is called *licentia* by Herbst.[2] Furthermore, a composer might introduce chromatic notes which are foreign to the mode in order to express the text or affection, a figure known as *pathopoeia.*[3] Bernhard lists the *mutatio toni* as one of the figures used in the *stylus luxurians*. In discussing the figure, he mentions the practice of mixing authentic and associated plagal modes, as well as leaping to an unrelated mode in the middle of a composition. He then adds that this is all to be explained in greater detail under his discussion of the modes. In his introduction to the modes Bernhard then lists the *modus superfluus* and *mixtio modi*, both methods of extending the mode beyond the limits of its *ambitus* into the related plagal (or authentic) mode. While *modus superfluus* extends the range by one or two notes, *mixtio modi* is used to extend the tenor by a greater interval, thereby "mixing" the authentic and plagal modes. Before discussing each particular mode, Bernhard mentions that there are five further mode "characters" (*affectiones*), which he defines later. The *transpositio modi* (transposition of the mode) allows the composer to set the appropriate mode in a desired range, which requires a change in key signature. The *consociatio modi* (connection of the mode) signifies a use of both authentic and related plagal modes in all voices, as opposed to only the tenor voice as described by the *mixtio modi.* Its most common application is found in fugal composition where, in order to facilitate a tonal answer to the fugal theme, the intervals are adjusted to accommodate the related plagal (or authentic) mode.[4] The *aequatio modi* (equalization or adjustment of the mode) is used to effect a real rather than tonal fugal answer. The two modes are "equalized" by employing the same intervals in an answering

1. For a thorough discussion of this phenomenon, see Siegfried Meyer, "Abweichungen von den Normen eines Modus," and Bernhard Meier, *The Modes of Classical Vocal Polyphony*.

2. See *Hyperbole, Parrhesia*.

3. See *Pathopoeia*.

4. This device is also associated with the *repercussio*, which can refer to either the altered interval or the entire tonal answer. See *Repercussio*.

voice as in the fugal subject. Instead of adjusting the intervals to accommodate the mode, the mode is adjusted to accommodate the intervals.[1] The *extensio modi* (extension of the mode) is used to explain fugal entries on the various pitches of a mode's notes, along with the associated additional accidentals. This is only to occur after the fundamental mode has been adequately established. As Bernhard mentions, this device not only extends the mode but also extends or prolongs a composition through various modulations to other modes. Finally, should a composition end in a mode other than the opening one, it is termed *alteratio modi.*

Of the seven methods of *mutatio toni*, only *modus superfluus* modifies a given mode without involving a different one. The remaining alterations all incorporate either related plagal (or authentic) modes, or unrelated modes or key signatures. While deviations from the mode were traditionally associated with affective text expression, Bernhard is primarily concerned with discussing rules of counterpoint and their exceptions, without delving into the text-related reasons for the deviations. Like numerous other devices defined as figures in his *Tractatus* but not clearly associated with dissonance, *mutatio toni* is not included in the list of figures in Bernhard's *Bericht.*

The alteration of a mode is discussed by Walther in his *Lexicon* under the term *mutatio*. The various forms of *mutatio* listed here also include the *mutatio per modum* or *tonum*, the comparable device to Bernhard's various forms of *mutatio toni.* In contrast to Bernhard, Walther focuses on a sudden change in tonality or key rather than in mode. While Bernhard wishes to reconcile antiquated contrapuntal rules with modern expressive devices, Walther focuses entirely on the expression of the text and the affections, using modern tonal language. Thus the *mutatio per modum* or *tonum* signifies a shift from a major to a minor, or minor to a major key, provoked by the text or affection.

Bernhard (*Tractatus* p.79)

Im andern Capitel No.7 ist gebothen, daβ eine jede Stimme sich nach einen derer 12 Modorum richten solle. Von solcher

In the second chapter, no.7, it was stated that every voice of a composition must conform to one of the twelve modes. To-

1. The *polyptoton* as well as Burmeister's early description of *palilogia* can be understood to signify a similar device. See *Palilogia, Polyptoton.*

Regel schreiten die heutigen Componisten nicht selten ab, indem sie nicht allein /: welches auch die Alten gethan :/ authenticum cum suo plagali vermengen, sondern auch aus einem authentico oder plagali in einen andern in der Mitte der Composition springen, woran bey der Erklärung der Tonorum mit mehrerm sol gedacht werden.

day's composers frequently depart from this rule in that they not only mix an authentic mode with its plagal (which composers of the past also did), but also leap from a plagal or authentic to another mode in the middle of a composition. This will be discussed more fully at the explanation of the modes.

(*Tractatus* p.91f.)

Modus superfluus ist, wenn die Octave überschritten wird, also, daβ sich entweder ober oder unter derselben eine Secunde auch wohl Tertie findet. . . . Zu denen Superfluis gehören auch die Mixti, wenn nehmlich ein Tenor nicht allein die Octave um eine Secunde oder Tertie übertrifft, sondern auch gar zur Quarte unter dieselbe, oder zur Quinta drüber gehet. . . . Werden daher Mixti genennet, weil Modus authenticus und plagalis darinnen zu spüren, davon bald unten.

Modus superfluus occurs when the octave [i.e., the eight notes of the *ambitus*] is exceeded by either a second or a third above or below [the *ambitus*]. The *mixtio modi* also belongs to this form and occurs when the tenor exceeds the octave not only by a second or third but even goes a fourth below or a fifth above it. They are called *mixti* because both the authentic and the plagal *modi* are perceived in them. This will be discussed below.

(*Tractatus* pp.93, 97)

Affectiones Modorum sind 1) Transpositio 2) Consociatio 3) Aequatio 4) Extensio 5) Alteratio. . . . Weil die Toni nicht alle so beschaffen, daβ sie im Tenor bequemlichen Sitz haben können, als haben die Musici durch die Transposition derer Semitoniorum, Quarten und Quinten solcher Ungelegenheit abgeholffen und die Liebligkeit ziemlich befördert.

The different characters of the *modi* are *transpositio*, *consociatio*, *aequatio*, *extensio*, and *alteratio*. . . . Because the *modi* are not all constituted in such fashion that they comfortably lie in the tenor, musicians have remedied this through the *transpositio* of the mode's semitones, fourths and fifths, thereby considerably increasing their charm.

(*Tractatus* p.98)

Und ist Consociatio Modorum eine Vereinigung des Authentici mit seinem Plagali, und des Plagalis mit seinem Authentico in 2. 3. oder mehr Stimmen gegen einander gehalten. Consociatio ist unterschieden von der Mixtione, davon droben. Weil Mixtio im Tenor oder einer Stimmen allein, Consociatio aber in mehrern bestehet.

Consociatio modi is a combination of the authentic with its plagal or plagal with its authentic mode, occuring in two, three, or more juxtaposed voices. *Consociatio* is distinct from *mixtio*, which was discussed above, in that the *mixtio modi* only occurs in the tenor or another single voice, *consociatio modi*, however, in more voices.

(*Tractatus* p.102)

Aequationem Modi nenne ich: wenn einer Quartae, Quintae, Sextae oder Octa-

Aequatio modi occurs when, in order to maintain a fourth, fifth, sixth, or octave

vae zu gefallen, die andere Stimme einer Fuge nicht in dero nächsten verwandten, sondern in einem solchen Tenor fortführet, welche der ersten nur ratione der Quartae oder Quintae ähnlich ist.

[of the subject], the second voice of a *fuga* does not proceed in the nearest related mode, but rather proceeds in such a mode that it is similar to the subject only on account of the fourth or fifth.

(*Tractatus* p.106)
Extensio Modi ist einer Composition Verlangerung, nachdem solche den Tonum genugsam geformiret, geschehend durch alle Sonos der Octave. Zumahl durch die Dominantes. Und wird dem Judicio und der Gelegenheit des Compositoris anheim gestellet, wie bald er sich der Extension gebrauche, und wie lange er durch dieselbe außer denen eigentlichen Schranken des Modi bleiben wolle.

Extensio modi is the extention of a composition after its *modus* is well established, and occurs through all the eight notes of the *modus*, especially the fifth one. How soon he employs the *extensio* and how long he uses it to remain outside the boundaries of the *modus* is left to the judgment and opportunity of the composer.

(*Tractatus* p.108)
Alteratio Modi ist, wenn ein Stück sich in dem einen Tono anfänget, und in einem andern endiget.

Alteratio modi occurs when a composition begins in one mode and ends in another.

Walther (*Lexicon*)
Mutatione (ital.) mutatio (lat.) bedeutet 1.) in der Solmisation die Verwechselung der Sylben, wenn z.E. im g-Clave bald ut, bald re, bald sol gesungen werden muß. 2.) eines derer Accidentium, so in Ordnung der Klänge, welche eine Melodie oder Gesang ausmachen, vorkommen; welches Accidens durch eine Veränderung auf viererley Weise geschiehet und verrichtet wird:

Mutatione or *mutatio* means: (1) the exchange of syllables in solmization; when for example now an *ut*, now a *re* or a *sol* is sung on the same line in the G clef; (2) when an accidental is added to the notes of a melody or composition. Such an accidental is added because of an alteration, which can occur in four forms:

a) Da man das Genus verändert, d.i. aus dem Genere Diatonico ins Chromaticum oder Enharmonicum, und umgekehrt, aus dem Chromatico ins Diatonicum gehet, etc. dieses heisset: Mutatio per Genus.

(a) when the *genus* is altered, that is when the *genus diatonicum* is changed to the *chromaticum* or *enharmonicum* or, conversely, the *chromaticum* into the *diatonicum*, etc. This is called *mutatio per genus*.

b) Wenn man einen Gesang aus einem sehr hohen Klange in einen tieffen absteigen lässet, um einige Text-Worte zu exprimiren. Z.E. qui in altis habitat & humilia respicit in coelo & in terra. Dieses heisset: Mutatio per Systema.

(b) when a voice is allowed to fall from a very high pitch to a low one, in order to express the words, as in the text: "who dwells on high, and considers the lowly, in heaven and on earth." This is called *mutatio per systema*.

c) Wenn, um einigen Affect zu exprimiren, aus einem Modo in einen andern gegangen wird; z.E. aus dem Modo minore in majorem, & vice versa. Dieses heisset: Mutatio per Modum aut Tonum.

(c) when the affection is expressed by progressing from one mode to another, for example from the minor to the major, or major to the minor. This is called *mutatio per modum* or *tonum*.

d) Wenn man von einer Manier, z.E. männlich und starck zu singen, so maniera distendente heisset, ab- und in eine angenehmere, ohnmächtigere, weichere und weibische, so maniera restringente genennet wird, gehet; oder in eine ruhige und stille, so das Mittel zwischen gedachten beyden ist, und maniera quieta heisset, gehet. Diese Veränderung wird genennet: Mutatio per Melopoeiam.

(d) when one digresses from a certain musical manner, for example a masculine and strong one, called *maniera distendente*, to a more pleasant, gentle, feminine one, called *maniera restringente*, or to a gentle and peaceful one halfway between the above two, called *maniera quieta*. This alteration is called *mutatio per melopoeiam*.

NOEMA: a homophonic passage within a contrapuntal texture.

The musical *noema* reflects both the literal meaning of the term as well as its rhetorical content. The focus on a significant thought (*noema*) effects a recognition (*noeo*) of the idea's significance. The rhetorical *noema* refers to an expression which carries a greater significance than the words appear to have. This "recognition of thought" is distinct from those figures which intentionally omit or suppress thoughts or words (*aposiopesis*, *ellipsis*), for the thought is not suppressed through the *noema* but is expressed in an obscure fashion.[1] This obscurity is also unlike the rhetorical *emphasis*, in which an implied meaning is not hidden but is clearly understood in context. An orator uses this figure to imply the unspoken through some obscure parallel reference.

The *noema* is defined as a homophonic passage by Burmeister, Thuringus, and Walther.[2] It is to contain no dissonances but rather is to

---

1. The following is an example of the *noema*, provided by Susenbrotus: Hortensius denied being reconciled to his mother or sister; what is meant, however, is that his relationship with them was never broken.

2. Burmeister also lists four additional *noema* figures. These include the *analepsis*, a *noema* repeated at the same pitch; the *mimesis*, a *noema* repeated at a different pitch; the *anaploce*, an echoed *noema* in polychoral music; and the *anadiplosis*, a repeated *mimesis*, or a four fold *noema*.

consist of a collection of bare or unadorned (*nudus*) consonances. Ernesti mentions that the rhetorical *neoma* can be recognized through its unique construction, which is differentiated from the rest of the oration. This understanding of the figure applies equally to the musical *noema*. In his definition in *Musica Poetica*, Burmeister explicitly states that the *noema* can only be recognized in the context of the composition. It does not refer to a homophonic passage per se but rather only to such a passage within a contrapuntal context. The homophonic section stands in contrast to the surrounding texture, thereby lending it and the associated text greater emphasis and significance. The obscurity of the rhetorical figure is not a characteristic of the musical figure. Brandes has clearly demonstrated the widespread application of this device going back as far as Dufay.[1] The device is consistently used to underscore particularly significant phrases in the text of the mass or in motets. Burmeister's examples also reveal that the *noema* consistently coincides with the climax of the text.[2] Furthermore, the figure is used to highlight expressions of invocation or salutation, for example of the Trinity, Christ, the Blessed Virgin, or of various saints. As such, the *noema* can be used as a form of *exclamatio*.[3]

Quintilian (*Institutio* VIII.v.12)

Est et, quod appellatur a novis noema qua voce omnis intellectus accipi potest; sed hoc nomine donarunt ea quae non dicunt, verum intelligi volunt.	There is also a figure called *noema* by modern rhetoricians through which everything can be understood through the speech. However, they use this term to signify those things which are not said but can in fact be understood.

Susenbrotus (*Epitome* p.101)

Noema Nόημα est quum tecte significamus, quod auditor ex sese divinet. Vel est obscurum dictum alicui appositum.	The *noema* occurs when we make veiled allusions which the listener will decipher on his own. Or it is an obscure but closely related expression of something.

Ernesti (*Lexicon Graecorum*)

Vulgari et passim obvia significatione νοήματα dicuntur sententiae, quatenus	Expressions are called *noemata* on account of their common and widely under-

1. Brandes, *Studien zur musikalischen Figurenlehre*, 30ff.
2. Ruhnke, *Burmeister*, 151.
3. See *Exclamatio*.

τοῖς πράγμασι constant et ab elocutione, ἑρμηνείᾳ differunt.

stood meaning, in as much as they are constructed specifically for these purposes and differ in meaning from the rest of the oration.

Burmeister (*Hypomnematum*)
Noema est collectio nudarum concordantiarum quae suavissime aures afficit, unica vice ad eas delata.

The *noema* is a collection of pure consonances in a unique alteration which stimulates the ears most agreeably.

Burmeister (*Musica Poetica* p.59)
Noëma νόημα est talis harmoniae affectio, sive periodus, cujus habitus voces conjunctas habet in eadem sonorum quantitate, aures, imo & pectora suaviter afficiens & mirifice demolcens, si tempestive introducitur. . . . Hoc ornamentum, prout ornamenti partes explet, non ex nudis hisce exemplis notescet, sed ex ipso integri carminis contextu. Quocirca perlustrandus erit ejus integer contextus, vel integra Harmonia suis vocibus decantanda, ac tum demum se hoc manifestabit ornamentum.

The *noema* is a condition of the *harmonia* or *periodus* characterized by united voices with the same number of notes. It is most agreeably stimulating and wonderfully soothing on the ears and spirit if it is appropriately introduced. . . . Because of how it completes the parts, this *ornamentum* is not recognized through isolated examples but rather in the context of the entire composition, wherefore the entire context of the composition must be examined or the whole composition must be sung with all its voices.

Only then will the *ornamentum* manifest itself as such.

Thuringus (*Opusculum* p.126)
Quid est Noema? Est collectio nudarum concordantiarum una vice suavissime in Motetis prolata.

What is a *noema*? It is a collection of pure consonances, most agreeably revealed in motets through a singular alternation.

Walther (*Lexicon*)
Noema, heisset in Joach. Thuringi Opusculo Bipartito, P.2 c.18 so viel, als collectio nudarum concordantiarum uno vice suavissime in Motettis prolata, d.i. ein solcher Satz, worinn lauter Consonanzen auf einmahl gehört und hervor gebracht werden.

The *noema* is defined by Thuringus . . . as a collection of pure consonances, most agreeably revealed in motets through a singular alternation, meaning a passage in which pure consonances are simultaneously heard and produced.

PALILOGIA: a repetition of a theme, either at different pitches in various voices or on the same pitch in the same voice.

The *palilogia* is described in music and in rhetoric as both a general and a specific form of repetition. In addition to being an alternative term for *anadiplosis*, *palilogia* also signifies a more general repetition of a word for the sake of emphasis.[1] Peacham also suggests a similar understanding when he supplies the alternate term, *Rhetoricall Eccho*. His further comment, "that it carrieth the resemblance of a rebounded voice, or iterated sound," is particularly applicable to a musical figure.

Burmeister supplies two definitions for this figure. In his *Hypomnematum* he discusses the device among the other fugal figures, *hypallage*, *apocope*, and *paremoble*. The repetition of the theme occurs in all the voices at various pitches, as is clearly illustrated in his example. As such it is a more general form of repetition. In his later *Musica Poetica* Burmeister places two limitations on the repetition: it must occur in only one voice, and it must be at the same pitch. Simultaneously, Burmeister introduces a new figure into his *Figurenlehre*, the *climax*, which also

1. Heinrich Lausberg, *Elemente der literarischen Rhetorik* (Munich: Huebner, 1960), 43.

repeats a theme in the same voice but at different pitches. It thereby assumes at least in part the role of the "old" *palilogia.* The *palilogia* no longer appears with the other fugal figures in the category of *figurae harmoniae* but rather among the *figurae melodiae*, along with the *climax*. Apart from Walther, who defines the figure in purely rhetorical terms, *palilogia* is not mentioned in other musical *Figurenlehren*. Rather the device is replaced with other figures such as *anaphora*, *repetitio*, and *mimesis* or *imitatio*.

Susenbrotus (*Epitome* p.53)
Anadiplosis, Reduplicatio, est cum ultima prioris commatis dictio in sequentie initio iteratur. . . . Haec etiam παλιλογία nominatur.

The *anadiplosis* or *reduplicatio* occurs when the last word of a preceding passage is repeated at the beginning of the following one. . . . This is also called *palilogia*.

Peacham (*Garden of Eloquence* p.47)
This exornation [anadiplosis] doth not onely serve to the pleasantnesse of sound, but also to adde a certaine increase in the second member. Of some this figure is called the Rhetoricall Eccho, for that it carrieth the resemblance of a rebounded voice, or iterated sound.

Burmeister (*Hypomnematum*)
Palillogia est affectionis τοῦ μέλεος non in iisdem perpetuo locis iteratio.

The *palilogia* is a continual repetition of the structure of the *melos* but not at the same pitch.

Burmeister (*Musica Poetica* p.63)
Palillogia παλιλλογία est ejusdem τοῦ μέλεος affectionis sive tractuli in iisdem sonis, nonnunquam omnibus, interdum vero initialibus, in una eademque voce intercalatis quibusdam pausis, vel etjam nullis, iteratio, quae in unica saltem fit voce.

The *palilogia* is a repetition of either the entire or only the beginning of the structure of the *melos* or theme on the same pitch in the same voice, occurring with or without intervening rests in all events in one voice.

Walther (*Lexicon*)
Palilogia heisset; wenn einerley Worte allzuofft wiederhohlt werden.

The *palilogia* refers to an all-too-frequent repetition of the same words.

PARAGOGE, MANUBRIUM, SUPPLEMENTUM: a cadenza or coda added over a pedal point at the end of a composition.

The terms *paragoge*, *manubrium*, and *supplementum* all refer to the same musical device: an extended embellishment of the final harmony through figurative elaboration in two or more upper voices. The device only gradually made its way into the musical *Figurenlehre*, at which point it was also given a rhetorical name. Burmeister does not discuss his *supplementum* among the figures but rather chooses to place it in the preceding chapter of his *Musica Poetica* dealing with the ending of a composition. Although Burmeister chooses a nonrhetorical and rather pedantic term for this musical device, it is of interest that he associates the embellishment with the *expolitio* ("*Supplementum . . . est . . . expolitio*"). The rhetorical *expolitio* occurs by dwelling on a certain topic for some time, continually repeating it in various forms or through various expressions.[1]

Nucius appends the ornamental device to his *Figurenlehre*, expressly stating that it should be added to the above figures. He replaces Burmeister's term with *manubrium*, which is likewise a nonrhetorical term and is not adopted by following writers. *Manubrium*, meaning "handle,"

1. Sonnino, *Handbook*, 93. Mattheson also mentions the *expolitio* in his discussion of the fugue. See *Fuga*.

is also used to refer to the neck of a plucked instrument[1] as well as to the draw knobs on an organ.[2] Whether Nucius seeks to relate an organ's draw knobs to the pedal point in the figure or simply wishes to refer to the ornament as an added *cauda* (appendage, handle) remains conjectural.

Thuringus finally integrates the device into his *Figurenlehre* and supplies it with a rhetorical term, *paragoge*. This rhetorical figure, like its musical counterpart, also signifies an extension, specifically that of a word through additional letters or syllables. Like Nucius, Thuringus also points to the frequent use of the device in motets. Walther lists the figure only under *paragoge* in his *Lexicon*, where he defines it as an improvised cadenza rather than as the compositional *cauda* described by earlier authors. Being a well-known and accomplished organist himself, he would have been intimately familiar with the technique of improvising over a pedal point at the final cadence. The musical substance of the figure still coincides with that described by the other authors, even though he allows for the performer to add a *paragoge* extemporaneously.

Susenbrotus (*Epitome* p.22)

Paragoge Diductio, est literae vel syllabe in fine dictionis additio. Literae, ut apud Plautum, hostis pro hosti. Syllabae, Et Summa dominarier arce.

The *paragoge* or *diductio* is an addition of a letter (*hostis* instead of *hosti*) or syllable (*Et Summa dominari*[*er*] *arce*) at the end of a word.

Burmeister (*Musica Poetica* p.53)

Fine dato, nonnumquam adiecta reperitur affectio sive tractulus, qui vocem unam, vel plures voces inter plurimas, ad quas Harmonia excrevit, in sono illo qui Fini dando competit, sive hic Primarius, sive Secundarius sit, habet consistentes, & a modulamine quiescentes, circa quas reliquae voces in Harmonia circumcirca ambulant ad duos, tres, quatuor pluresve tactus: nihil autem aliud praestant, quam ut variationes harmonicas, quae uni sono attribui possunt, ostendant, finemque

At the end [of the *harmonia*] an added structure or passage is sometimes found in which one or more among the voices of the *harmonia* end and rest in their final notes, be this in the *primarius* or *secondarius*, while the remaining voices elaborate around them for two, three, four, or more measures. They present nothing more than harmonic variations which could be assigned to one note and thereby most clearly fashion the introduced ending. . . . This passage is called *harmoniae*

1. Janovka, *Clavis ad Thesaurum*.
2. Walther, *Lexicon*.

introductum esse maxime planum faciant. . . . Hunc tractulum vocant Harmoniae Supplementum, quod est Finalis soni vocis consistentis cum variis secum consonantibus sonis reliquarum vocum cum se in harmoniam unitarum expolitio, finem carmini musici illatum esse, & datum docens.

supplementum, that is, an *expolitio* or embellishment of the ending stationary voices with various in themselves harmonizing notes of the remaining united voices, the ending of the musical composition thereby being introduced and given clarification.

Nucius (*Musices Poeticae* p.G3[v])
Huc quoque Manubrium pertinet, quod est cum in fine Harmoniae duae aut plures voces cauda adijciunt. Huius compositionis usus & imitatio, cum fere in omnibus Motetis sit hodie frequentissimus, docebunt.

The *manubrium* also belongs here, which occurs when two or more voices add an appendage (*cauda*) at the end of the *harmonia*. The use and imitation of this compositional device are presented here because it is applied most frequently nowadays in virtually all motets.

Thuringus (*Opusculum* p.127)
Quid est Paragoge? Est, cum in fine harmoniae duae vel plures voces caudam adiiciunt, quod hodie fere in omnibus cantionibus fieri solet.

What is the *paragoge*? It occurs when at the end of the *harmonia* two or more voices add an appendage (*cauda*), which is nowadays usually employed in all compositions.

Walther (*Lexicon*)
Paragoge παραγογή heisset: wenn in einer Cadenz noch etwas angehänget wird, so nicht expresse vom Componisten hingesetzet worden, sondern vom Executore angebracht wird; von παρὰ praeter, und ἄγω, duco.

The *paragoge* occurs when something is appended to the cadence which was not, however, expressly included by the composer but rather added by the performer.

PAREMBOLE, INTERJECTIO: a supplementary voice in a fugue which fills in the harmony by proceeding parallel to one of the fugue's regular voices.

Both the musical and the rhetorical *parembole* signify an interjected passage which is not considered essential to the structure or meaning of the original passage. While Quintilian warns that the interjection can lead to confusion if it is not kept short, Ernesti underscores the independence of both the interjection as well as the original thought: both are able to stand on their own without the other.

The meaning of the musical *parembole* is clearly discernable both from Burmeister's definition and his example. The added voice begins only at the second entry of the theme, at that point filling in the harmonic structure. However, like the rhetorical *parembole*, the additional voice does not affect or alter the fugal *ratio* or structure. Were it to be omitted, the *fuga* would nonetheless remain intact. For this reason Burmeister includes the device among his *figurae melodiae*. It is neither one of the fugal figures, all considered to be *figurae harmoniae*, nor is it considered among the *tam harmoniae quam melodiae* figures. Rather than significantly structuring or altering the harmony through the addition of another melody, it simply fills in the harmonies which are already implied.

Quintilian (*Institutio* VIII.ii.15)

Etiam interiectione (quo et oratores et historici frequenter utuntur, ut medio sermone aliquem inserant sensum) impediri solet intellectus, nisi quod interponitur breve est.

Furthermore, through the *interiectio* (which orators and historians frequently use to insert another thought into the middle of a sentence), the understanding of a passage can be impeded if the interruption is not kept short.

Ernesti (*Lexicon Lat. Rhet.*)

[Parembole] Haec fit inserta aliqua sententia, quae per se consistit, ut si eam tollas, cetera salvo maneant.

The *parembole* signifies a certain insertion in a sentence which can stand on its own but, were it removed, would leave the remaining thought intact.

Burmeister (*Hypomnematum*)

Parembole est sonorum quorundam a voce aliqua ad alias, Fugae affectionem aemulantes, ad mixtorum interjectio, nihil ad fugam conferens.

The *parembole* is an interjection (*interjectio*) of certain notes through an additional voice, emulating the fugal structure without being a part of the *fuga*.

Burmeister (*Musica Poetica* p.62)

Parembole παρεμβολὴ est quando duabus vocibus vel etiam pluribus, fugae affectionem ab initio cantus persequentibus, admiscetur alia vox, quae cum

The *parembole* occurs when another voice is added to two or more voices of the *fuga* structure at the beginning of the composition. The added voice proceeds

illis alteris pariter procedit, nihil ad Fugae naturam vel rationem conferens, sed tantum vacua concordantiarum loca inter illas voces Fugae μίμημα exsequentes, replens.

alongside the other voices without changing the nature or sense of the *fuga*, but rather only filling in the missing consonances in the space between the voices of the *fuga* by mimicking their progression.

PARENTHESIS: a musical representation of parentheses in the text.

The representation of punctuation marks found in the text of a composition is certainly not new or unique to Baroque composers. The Renaissance practice of structuring a motet according to the caesurae in the text is a well-known device. Numerous sixteenth-century authors emphasize the artistic value and expressive content of the pause and the cadence.[1] Mattheson discusses the *parenthesis* in the chapter of his *Capellmeister* which deals with the sections and caesurae found in the composition's text. Like generations of writers before him, Mattheson recommends that the composer pay close attention to the text's punctuation marks. Included in this chapter are also discussions on the musical representation of questions and exclamations. While these two forms of expression and punctuation are included in other *Figurenlehren*, the *parenthesis* is only mentioned by Mattheson.[2] His concern in this chapter is not to identify and discuss specific musical devices but rather to encourage the composer to be resourceful in setting the text. As such, each punctuation mark of the text could be given a unique musical interpretation, depending on the text itself. After quoting a certain text which includes parentheses, Mattheson suggests that this particular text might be expressed through a drop in the melody "to the point of sounding like another voice, for example dropping at least a fourth or fifth from the middle of the soprano to the middle of the alto." Although this is only one possible musical realization of parentheses in the text, it does bear a striking resemblance to Bernhard's *heterolepsis* and Scheibe's *hyperbaton*.[3]

1. Ruhnke quotes excerpts from Gallicus (1520), Listenius (1537), Rhau (1538), Dressler (1563), and Calvisius (1592) regarding the observance of pauses in music and text (*Burmeister*, 135ff.). See also *Pausa*.
2. See *Exclamatio*, *Interrogatio*.
3. See *Heterolepsis*, *Hyperbaton*.

However, while Bernhard and Scheibe wish to explain certain musical devices, Mattheson wishes simply to describe possible methods of expressing the text. Thus the *heterolepsis* or *hyperbaton* become various means of expressing the *parenthesis*.[1]

Quintilian (*Institutio* IX.iii.23)

Unum quod interpositionem vel interclusionem dicimus, Graeci παρένθεσιν, παρέμπτωσιν vocant, dum continuationi sermonis medius aliqui sensus intervenit.

One of these figures we call *interpositio* or *interclusio*, which the Greeks call *parenthesis* or *paremptosis*. This occurs when the flow of the oration is interrupted in the middle by another thought.

Mattheson (*Capellmeister* p.194)

Gleichsam par parenthese ein Paar Worte von der Parenthesi selber zu machen, dürffte sich hier vieleicht, zum Beschluß dieses Haupt-Stückes, nicht übel schicken. Dieser Einschnitt ist ein Zwischen-Satz, da gewisse Worte, die von den übrigen gleichsam durch einen solchen Einschluß ( ) abgesondert sind, den Lauff des Zusammenhanges im Vortrage ein wenig unterbrechen. Das Ding ist eben nicht sehr musicalisch, und mögte meinentwegen gerne aus der melodischen Wissenschafft Urlaub haben. Weil es aber doch bisweilen in Arien, mehr und öffters aber im Recitativ mit besserm Fuge, vorkömmt, so darff derjenige, der mit solchen eingeschlossenen Worten richtig verfahren will, nur erwegen, ob sein vorhabender Zwischen-Satz viel oder wenig von dem Hauptzweck der Rede abweichet: maassen die Melodie nach solchen Umständen auch wenig oder viel unterbrochen werden muß. . . . Sollte solches gesungen werden, so müste wol der Gesang so weit herunter treten, als etwa aus der Mitte des Soprans in die Mitte des Alts, wenigstens eine Quart oder Quint, als wenns eine andre Stimme wäre.

It would not be inappropriate to say a few words regarding the *parenthesis* in parenthetical fashion here at the close of the chapter. This caesura is an interjection occurring when certain words, which are separated from the others by the brackets ( ), interrupt the flow of the oration's cohesion somewhat. This device is certainly not very musical and, as far as I am concerned, could take leave from melodic composition. However, because it does at times appear in arias, more frequently and successfully in recitatives, the composer who wishes to deal with such bracketed words properly must only consider to what degree the proposed interjection digresses from the main thought. The melody should then also be interrupted either more or less according to the circumstances of the text. . . . Should such a text be sung, the melody should drop to the point of sounding like another voice, for example dropping at least a fourth or fifth from the middle of the soprano to the middle of the alto.

1. In another example, Mattheson suggests that the parenthesis in a text for a choral composition be sung by a soloist, after which the choir returns. He also warns against the use of pauses to express the *parenthesis*.

PARONOMASIA: a repetition of a musical passage, with certain additions or alterations, for the sake of greater emphasis.

This figure of repetition enters the musical *Figurenlehre* relatively late. Mattheson is the first to mention the figure in a musical context. He maintains that the *paronomasia*, among other figures, is rooted and familiar equally in music as in rhetoric and therefore requires no further explanation. Scheibe adapts Gottsched's *paronomasia* as described in his *Critische Dichtkunst*, a definition which is then adopted by Forkel. Although the term literally means "additional name," and signifies a repetition of words with changes in case endings in classical rhetoric, Scheibe also adopts Gottsched's translation of the Greek term with "amplification" (*Verstärkung*). Both the rhetorical and the musical *Figurenlehren* gradually evolve into concepts which emphasize the expression of affections above all else. Concern regarding technical devices give way to a preoccupation with affective expression. Simple repetition "assumes its greatest benefit only when it is combined with the *paronomasia*." The repetitions can involve additional notes or changes in dynamics or rhythm. However, in all cases "the repetition must strengthen the emphasis of the expression and must lend it a singular beauty." The figure suggests a new music aesthetic, one which is no longer satisfied with the stationary dynamics and constant texture of Baroque music but wishes to express the "individualization of general sentiments," as Forkel puts it, through dynamically fluctuating and evolving musical expression.[1]

---

1. One might also speculate whether *paronomasia* played a role in Vogt's choice of *prosonomasia* and *polyptoton* in his discussion of the musical-rhetorical figures. All three terms signify altered repetitions of words. Furthermore, *paronomasia* is used as an alternative term for both *polyptoton* and *prosonomasia* (Sonnino, *Handbook*, 24, 26). *Paronomasia* can signify either a general altered and emphasized word or a specific alteration of the case ending or other syllables. Vogt defines *polyptoton* as one of his *figurae ideales*, while suggesting that composers should use *prosonomasia* (in addition to *hypotyposis*, *prosopopoeia*, and *antitheton*) to express the text in an earlier chapter. (See p.151, above.) Vogt is possibly referring to the more general meaning of *paronomasia* with the term *prosonomasia* in the earlier reference while using the term *polyptoton*, signifying the more specific meaning of *paronomasia*, in his definitions of the *figurae ideales*: a repetition at various pitches. See *Polyptoton*. Thus *paronomasia* becomes the unspoken combining link (a *metabasis*) between the other two figures.

Quintilian (*Institutio* IX.iii.66,67)
Hinc est παρονομασία, quae dicitur adnominatio. Ea non uno modo fieri solet: ex vicinia quadam praedicti nominis ducta casibus declinat, . . . et cum verbo idem verbum plus significans subiungitur.

The *paronomasia* or *adnominatio* also belongs here. It consists of more than one form: similar subsequent words can be in different cases, . . . or the same word can be repeated with greater meaning.

Gottsched (*Redekunst* p.276)
Paronomasia, wenn sich die Worte nur reimen.

Paronomasia, when the words only rhyme.

Gottsched (*Dichtkunst* p.324)
Die IX. ist die Verstärkung, (Paronomasia) wenn man zwar ein Wort oder eine Redensart, die schon da gewesen, wiederholet; aber mit einem Zusatze, der noch einen besondern Nachdruck verursachet.

The next figure, the *paronomasia*, occurs when a word or saying is repeated but with an addition which produces an exceptional emphasis.

Mattheson (*Capellmeister* p.243)
Die Epanalepsis, Epistrophe, Anadiplosis, Paronomasia, Polyptoton, Antanaclasis, Ploce etc. haben solche natürliche Stellen in der Melodie, daβ es fast scheinet, als hätten die griechischen Redner sothane Figuren aus der Ton-Kunst entlehnet; denn sie sind lauter repetitiones vocum, Wiederholungen der Wörter, die auf verschiedene Weise angebracht werden.

The *epanalepsis*, *epistrophe*, *anadiplosis*, *paronomasia*, *polyptoton*, *antanaclasis*, *ploce*, etc., assume such natural positions in music that it almost seems as if the Greek orators borrowed these figures from the art of musical composition. For they are purely *repetitiones vocum*, repetitions of words, which are applied to music in various different ways.

Scheibe (*Critischer Musicus* p.691f.)
Die VIte Figur ist die Verstärkung. (Paronomasia.) Diese ist insgemein mit der vorhergehenden Figur, nämlich mit der Wiederholung, verbunden. Sie geschieht, wenn man einen Satz, ein Wort, oder eine Redensart, so schon da gewesen, mit einem neuen, besondern und nachdrücklichen Zusatze wiederholet. Sie wird in der Instrumental- und Vocalmusik mit gleichem Nachdrucke gebrauchet. Die Arten ihres Gebrauches aber sind auch mancherley. Man wiederholet sehr oft ein paar einzelne Noten eines Satzes, und zwar mit einem besondern und neuen kurzen Zusatze, der auch nur aus einer einzigen Note bestehen kann.

The next figure is amplification or the *paronomasia*. It is generally used in conjunction with the previous figure, namely the *repetitio*. The *paronomasia* occurs when an already expressed sentence, word, or saying is repeated with a new, singular, and emphatic addition. It is used in instrumental and vocal music with equal emphasis. Very frequently a few notes in a passage are repeated with a special and new short addition which might only consist of one note. Furthermore, certain passages can be repeated with the specification soft (*piano*) or strong (*forte*). Similarly the last notes of a passage which were played by all parts

Man wiederholet ferner einige Sätze, mit der Bezeichnung: gelinde (piano) und stark (forte.) Imgleichen wiederholet man auch die letztern Noten eines Satzes, der vorher von allen Stimmen gespielet worden, nur mit einer, oder zwo Stimmen allein. Es geschieht auch die Wiederholung einiger wenigen Noten mit verändertem und langsamerm Takte, oder mit noch einmal so viel geltenden Noten. Allemal aber muß solches den Nachdruck der Sache verstärken, und ihr eine besondere Schönheit ertheilen. Mit den Worten in Singesachen pflegt man auch sehr oft dergleichen Verfahren mit sehr guter Art anzuwenden.

can be repeated with only one or two voices. Repetitions of only a few notes can also occur with a changed or slower beat or with notes of double duration. In any case, however, the repetition must strengthen the emphasis of the expression and must lend it a singular beauty. Similar repetitions are frequently applied to the text in vocal music with very satisfactory results.

Forkel (*Geschichte der Musik* p.57)
Diese Figur ist in der Musik eine der gewöhnlichsten, und bekommt nur dann ihren meisten Werth, wenn sie mit der Paronomasie (Verstärkung) verbunden wird, die einen Satz nicht blos so, wie er schon da gewesen, sondern mit neuen kräftigen Zusätzen wiederholt. Diese Zusätze können theils einzelne Töne betreffen, theils aber auch durch einen stärkern oder verminderten Vortrag bewerkstelligt werden.

This figure [*repetitio*] is one of the most common in music and assumes its greatest benefit only when it is combined with the *paronomasia* (amplification). The *paronomasia* does not repeat a passage just as it already occurred but rather with new and powerful additions. These additions might apply either to single notes or can also be effected through a stronger or a weaker delivery.

PARRHESIA, LICENTIA: the insertion of a dissonance such as a cross relation or tritone on a weak beat.

Through the rhetorical *parrhesia* a reprehensible thought is introduced into the oration in such fashion that it does not offend the listener. This device is linked to the license an orator or author can take in freely expressing himself, which explains the Latin alternative for the figure, *licentia*. The Greek term refers specifically to free speech (from *pan*, all, everything; *rhesis*, speech, conversation). Susenbrotus provides the following example: "Pardon me if it appears that I speak freely."[1] Like-

1. "Ignoscite, si videbor aequo liberius dicere." *Epitome*, 69.

wise the musical *parrhesia* introduces ignoble elements into a composition, namely forbidden dissonances, in such a manner that they do not cause offense.

The term *licentia* is used to describe both general and specific dissonances in music. In his discussion of the modes, Herbst refers to the transgression of the eight notes of a mode's range or *ambitus* by any one voice as *licentia* or "musical freedom." This definition of the term corresponds to Burmeister's definition of *hyper-/hypobole* and to Bernhard's understanding of various forms of *mutatio toni*.[1] Bernhard links *licentia* to the general use of dissonance. In the context of his *Figurenlehre*, which concerns itself chiefly with the proper use of dissonance, he equates the term with the musical-rhetorical figures in general. This is clarified in his introductory description of the modern *contrapunctus luxurians*, "which consists of numerous forms of dissonance use (or more *figurae melopoeticae* which others call *licentiae*)." In his introduction to those figures used in the *stylus luxurians*, he reiterates this thought. The name of the compositional style itself is determined by its use of dissonance, "which others call *licentiae*, because the dissonances do not appear to be excused with the already mentioned figures." Up to this point, Bernhard had defined the passing dissonance (*transitus*) and the suspension (*syncopatio*). The remaining figures consist of certain freedoms or *licentiae* taken with these two basic forms of embellishing the music and only appear to be independent forms of ornamentation or text expression.

Burmeister introduces both terms, *licentia* and *parrhesia*, into his *Figurenlehre*. While he names the figure *parrhesia*, the term *licentia* is used to describe the device in his *Hypomnematum*. The *parrhesia* is a brief dissonance falling on a weak beat in only one voice. It is therefore numbered among the *figurae melodiae* rather than among the structural *figurae harmoniae*. In his definition of the passing dissonance, the *symblema*, Burmeister mentions that the *symblema minus*, which occurs only in the middle of a *tactus*, is not considered among the *figurae*

---

1. See *Hyperbole, Mutatio Toni*. In his discussion of the modes, Praetorius similarly uses the term *licentia*: "Cujuslibet autem Modi Ambitus naturalis consistit quidem intra Diapason: verum per licentiam, modo Tonus, modo Semitonium cum inferiori tum superiori loco adsciscitur." *Syntagma Musicum III*, 48.

harmoniae because it does not significantly affect the listener.[1] When such fleeting cross relations, tritones, or any of the other dissonances enumerated by Burmeister occur in the middle of a *tactus*, they are counted among the *figurae melodiae* as a *parrhesia*. Thuringus summarizes the dissonant intervals mentioned by Burmeister with the phrase *mi contra fa*, which could signify tritones, other augmented or diminished intervals, and cross relations.[2] Burmeister, Thuringus, and Walther all agree on the brevity of the figure: it is to be employed in such fashion that no discord results, in the same manner that the rhetorical figure is to be used without offending the listener.[3]

Quintilian (*Institutio* IX.ii.28)

Quod idem dictum sit de oratione libera, quam Cornificius licentaim vocat, Graeci παρρησίαν. Quid enim minus figuratum quam vera libertas? Sed frequenter sub hac facie latet adulatio . . . sed hoc eum demeretur, cuius mala fuerat.

The same is true in freedom of speech, which Cornificius (*Auct. ad Herennium*) calls *licentia* and the Greeks call *parrhesia*. For what is less figurative than true liberty? However, adulation frequently is hidden under this device . . . and it obliges him whose cause was evil.

Susenbrotus (*Epitome* p.69)

Licentia (παρρησίαν loquendi libertas) est cum in oratione libertate veluti abutentes, autoritatem nobis et fidem concilare studemus. Praestat haec ne offendat libertas. Unde et in hoc adhibetur, ut mitiget liberius dicta, ne offendant auditorem.

The *licentia* (*parrhesia*, freedom of speech) occurs when we strive to gain authority and trust through full freedom in our speech. It is better if this freedom does not offend. This figure is used to mitigate the freely expressed words so that they do not offend the listener.

Gottsched (*Redekunst* p.286)

Parrhesia. Wenn man eine verhaβte Sache zwar frey heraus saget, aber doch auf eine erträgliche Art vorträgt und etwas zu lindern suchet.

Parrhesia. When a despised thought is freely expressed, yet in an acceptable manner which attempts to soften the thought.

---

1. See *Transitus*, Burmeister's definition of *symblema* (*Musica Poetica*).

2. "Mi-fa," *The New Harvard Dictionary of Music* (Cambridge: Harvard University Press, 1986), 493.

3. The introduction of dissonances into a composition which significantly affect the music's expressiveness is called *pathopoeia* by Burmeister. Although the same intervals may be involved as in the *parrhesia*, the *pathopoeia* is distinguished precisely through its capacity to "leave no one untouched by the created affection." Furthermore, on account of its role in altering the nature of the entire musical texture, the *pathopoeia* is included among the *figurae harmoniae*. See *Pathopoeia*.

Burmeister (*Hypomnematum*)
Parrhesia fit, quando Consonantia Quinta quae omnibus suis partibus plena & perfecta esse debet, imperfecta concentibus ex mera licentia commiscetur, sicut & Septima vel alia Discordantia.

The *parrhesia* occurs when intervals such as a seventh or other dissonances are freely mixed into a harmonizing texture, such as a fifth, which is to be complete and perfect in all its parts, making it imperfect.

Burmeister (*Musica Autoschediastike*)
Parrhesia παρρησίαν est commiscere cum reliquis concentibus Diapente, h.e. Quintam non perfectam & plenam, vel Diapente cum semitono vel Ditono, hoc est Septimam tam plenam quam non plenam. Plenum intervallum vel concentum intelligimus illum, qui potest citra jacturam harmoniae, augmentum non assumere aut decrementum pati: non plenum, qui semitonio potest vel adimpleri, vel cui potest semitonium demi, quales concentus sunt Semiditonus; Tonus; Diapente cum Tono; cum semitonio; cum semiditono cum Ditono.

The *parrhesia* occurs when an interval such as an imperfect or incomplete fifth, a minor sixth, or a major or minor seventh is mixed into the other harmonizing voices. Perfect intervals are understood as those which can be neither increased nor decreased without sacrificing the harmony. Imperfect intervals are those which can be increased or decreased through a semitone, such as the minor third, the second, the major or minor sixth, and the major or minor seventh.

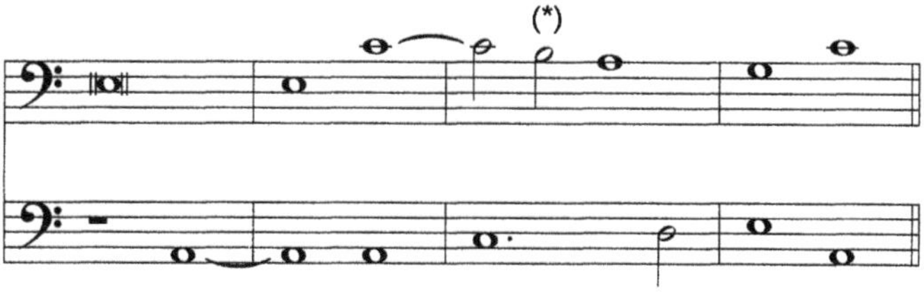

Burmeister (*Musica Poetica* p.64)
Parrhesia παρρησίαν est commiscere cum reliquis concentibus Dissonantiam unicam, eamque ad dimidium totius, quo ipsi reliquae voces in tactu respondent.

The *parrhesia* is an intermixing of a certain dissonance with the other harmonizing voices. It is placed in the middle of a beat in order that the other voices can resolve it within the beat.

Thuringus (*Opusculum* p.126)
Quid est Parrhisia? Est cum Mi contra Fa in quarta, quinta, vel semptime ita in

What is the *parrhisia*? It occurs when *mi* is set against *fa* in the fourth, fifth, or sev-

contrapuncto inseratur, ut nullam discordantiam pariat.

enth in such a manner that no discord becomes evident.

Herbst (*Musica Poetica* p.49)
Was ist Licentia, oder Musicalische Freyheit? Licentia ist / wenn ein Componist in dem Gesang (wenn es sonderlich der Text erfordert) nach seinem belieben und gefallen / entweder die Octav nicht erfüllet / oder aber über dieselbige etliche Noten schreitet / entweder zu oberst eine Terz, oder zu unterst eine Secund, in der Octav der Melodey hinzu setzet / daher gemeiniglich jedweder Modus durch die licenz oder Freyheit / die decimam im auff- und nidersteigen erfüllet / auch je zu Zeiten wol drüber kompt.

What is *licentia* or musical freedom? *Licentia* occurs when a composer either does not fulfill or exceeds the eight notes of a mode's *ambitus* according to his wishes and because of the particular needs of the text. He might add an additional third higher or a second lower to the *octav* of the melodic part, thereby allowing the mode normally to encompass a tenth through the *licentia* or Freedom, and at times even beyond that.

Bernhard (*Tractatus* pp.42, 71)
Contrapunctus luxurians ist, welcher aus theils ziemlich geschwinden Noten, seltzamen Sprüngen, so die Affecten zu bewegen geschickt sind, mehr Arten des Gebrauchs derer Dissonantzen (oder mehr Figuris Melopoeticis welche andere Licentias nennen) mehr aus guter Aria so zum Texte sich zum besten reimet, als etwan der obige, besteht.

The *contrapunctus luxurians* consists in part of somewhat rapid notes and strange leaps, which are suitable for moving the affections, of numerous kinds of dissonance (or more *figurae melopoeticae* which others call *licentiae*), and is more concerned with an appropriate agreement between the melody and the text than the foregoing [*contrapunctus gravis*].

Die andere Species Styli inaequalis ist luxurians, welche ich so nenne wegen derer vielerley Arten des Gebrauchs derer Dissonantzen, welche andere Licentias nennen, weilen sie mit denen vorgemeldeten Figuris nicht scheinen entschuldiget zu werden.

The other species of the *stylus inaequalis* is *luxurians*, which I give that name on account of the numerous forms of using dissonances, which others call *licentiae*, because the dissonances do not appear to be excused with the already mentioned figures.

Walther (*Lexicon*)
Parrhesia heisset beym Thuringo Part.2. Opusc. Bipart. wenn das mi contra fa in einer musikalischen Composition also angebracht wird, daß es keinen Übellaut verursachet.

Parrhesia is defined by Thuringus . . . as a setting of *mi contra fa* in a musical composition in such a manner that it causes no discord.

PASSAGGIO: see *VARIATIO*

PASSUS DURIUSCULUS: a chromatically altered ascending or descending melodic line.

The *passus duriusculus* is only encountered in Bernhard's *Tractatus*, as are the related *saltus duriusculus* and *cadentia duriuscula*. Like these other two figures, *passus duriusculus* is not a rhetorical term, but rather a vivid description of the musical device: it is a "hard" or "harsh" (*duriusculus*) "step" or "passage" (*passus*), musically realized through various uses of the semitone. The familiar device of a chromatic or chromatically altered ascending or descending voice is not only frequently encountered in Baroque compositions but is also specifically mentioned in Walther's definition of *catabasis* as a *subjectum catabatum*.[1] In addition, a number of musical-rhetorical figures expressly refer to chromatic alteration, including *parrhesia* and *pathopoeia*. The *passus duriusculus* indeed could just as well be explained as a form of *pathopoeia*.

The expressive content of a chromatically descending fourth, a familiar and widely used specific form of the *passus duriusculus* (*subjectum catabatum*), has been explored by a great many composers.[2] Eggebrecht points to the use of this form of the *passus duriusculus* as a musical expression with a specific significance or semantic content.[3] As Heinrich Schütz's pupil and assistant in Dresden, Bernhard was deeply influenced by the music of his teacher and mentor. Although Bernhard's *Figurenlehre* focuses on the appropriate use of dissonance, it is always to be understood in the context of the Lutheran *musica poetica* tradition, which strives to express the text and arouse the appro-

---

1. See *Catabasis*.

2. Peter Williams provides ample examples of the use of the descending chromatic fourth throughout music history in his articles, "Figurenlehre from Monteverdi to Wagner," *Musical Times* 120 (1979): 476–79, 571–73, and "Encounters with the Chromatic Fourth," *Musical Times* 126 (1985): 276–78, 339–43. However, to link the *Figurenlehre* of *musica poetica* with the music of Beethoven, Verdi, and Wagner is simply a gross misunderstanding of the concept. That is not to say that the use or expression of such a musical device throughout music history is unrelated. A clear distinction must be made however, between the Baroque concept of musical-rhetorical figures or *Figurenlehre* and the musical devices which these figures describe or embody.

3. "Zum Figur-Begriff der Musica poetica," *Archiv für Musikwissenschaft* 16 (1959): 57–69.

priate affections, thereby teaching and edifying the listener. This is the intended goal of the music of Schütz and the purpose behind the writings of Bernhard. In establishing the *passus duriusculus*'s adoption of a specific pathos-laden significance, Eggebrecht reveals how a figure can be used as an exegetical tool. Not only can it reflect musically a particular text but it can represent the adopted significance in combination with other texts or in textless contexts. In the same manner that the spoken sermon is to teach and edify the listener, so too is *musica poetica* to preach rather than simply entertain. Should a musical-rhetorical figure be sufficiently specific to take on a definite extramusical significance, it can become both an expressive device and an exegetical and interpretive tool. Eggebrecht therefore differentiates between the more general *pathopoeia*, which aims at *movere*, and the *passus duriusculus*, whose goal is also "a certain teaching, admonishing, and pointing out of the meaning."[1]

Bernhard (*Tractatus* p.77)

Passus duriusculus, einer Stimmen gegen sich selbst, ist, wenn eine Stimme ein Semitonium minus steiget, oder fället.	The *passus duriusculus* within one voice occurs when a voice rises or falls a minor semitone.

Welcherley Gänge einige für chromatische Art Sätze gehalten, mit was vor Gründe aber, solches mögen sie ausfechten. Oder wenn der Gang zur Secunde allzugroß oder zur Tertie zu klein, oder zur Quarta und Quinta zu groß oder zu klein ist.	These progressions some have held as chromatic ones, the reasons for which they can fight out amongst themselves. It can also occur when the step to a second is augmented, to a third is diminished, or to a fourth or fifth is augmented or diminished.

1. Ibid., 66.

PATHOPOEIA: a musical passage which seeks to arouse a passionate affection through chromaticism or some other means.

As the term suggests, *pathopoeia* (*pathos*, passion, affection; *poeia*, presentation, expression) signifies a vivid representation of an intense or vehement affection. In both rhetoric and music the figure is not limited to pathetic or anguished affections but can be used to arouse joyous as well as melancholic or sorrowful affections, as evidenced in the definitions of both Peacham and Thuringus. While Burmeister does not explicitly limit the use of the *pathopoeia* to the pathetic affections, his reference to the use of chromatic notes foreign to the *modus* of the composition does imply such an interpretation. Furthermore, his numerous examples of words or phrases in compositions where the figure can be found would support such an understanding.[1] Other Burmeister figures, such as the *hyper-/hypobole* and *parrhesia* also permit an introduction of notes which do not belong to the given *modus*. The first signifies a transgression of a mode's range, while the latter is a brief, passing dissonance. The terminology used to identify them points more to their technical structure ("transgression," "licence") than to the "pathos representation" of the *pathopoeia*. Significantly, the *pathopoeia* is considered a *figura harmonia* while the others number among the *figurae melodiae*.[2] Although Burmeister periodically refers to the effect of a figure (for example, *noema*) or even the lack of effect (*symblema minor*) in other definitions, the *pathopoeia* is the only one of his figures whose definition contains an explicit reference to the portrayal and arousal of affections.[3]

In contrast to Burmeister, Thuringus includes the whole range of affections in his definition of *pathopoeia*, or *parthopoeia* as he spells it.

---

1. Texts in compositions which exemplify the *pathopoeia* are *mori dignatus est*, *Heu quantus dolor*, *crudelem mortem*, *dolose agebant*, *mulier quia ploras*, and *flebant*.

2. It is precisely the brevity of the *parrhesia* which excludes it from being counted among the *figurae harmoniae*, in spite of introducing the same dissonances as those employed in the *pathopoeia*. See *Parrhesia*.

3. The "affectiveness" of the musical-rhetorical figures becomes increasingly important in following *Figurenlehren*. While Burmeister considers a figure an *ornamentum* which deviates from the simple compositional norm, Nucius and Thuringus unambiguously compare the musical figures with their rhetorical counterparts, and Kircher explicitly underscores the figures' affective properties.

Analogous to the rhetorical definitions, Thuringus understands the figure as a general representation of the affections, moving both musicians and audience alike. With this generalization of the figure, the specific reference to chromaticism is omitted. It is this general understanding of the figure which is at the root of Kircher's *prosopopoeia*. In listing but not defining the various *figurae minus principales* in his *Liber* 5, Kircher adopts Thuringus's list of figures, exchanging only *pathopoeia* with *prosopopoeia*, a rhetorical figure through which inanimate objects or absent persons are given life and action. Henry Peacham the Younger similarly uses the term *prosopopoeia* in reference to music's "passionate airs" instead of adopting his father's *pathopoeia*.[1] The "inanimate object" of the *prosopopoeia* becomes the affection which is given life and action through the music. Vogt also mentions the *prosopopoeia* without specifically defining it. He refers to this figure along with the *hypothyposis*, similarly lacking a definition in his *Conclave*, in his general admonitions to the composer to vividly express the *idea* of the text through the *figurae ideales*.[2] Vogt seems to suggest that the *hypotyposeos* figures are used to vividly portray the text while the *prosopopoeia* signifies the arousal of the affections, thereby replacing the *pathopoeia*. Instead of isolating a specific figure to signify affection portrayal in his list of defined figures, Kircher includes such references in virtually all of his definitions. On the other hand, he assigns the role of vivid text expression to the *assimilatio/homoiosis*.[3]

Neither *pathopoeia* nor *prosopopoeia* are mentioned in subsequent *Figurenlehren*. As the general concept of the musical-rhetorical figures increasingly focuses on expressing and arousing the affections, the specific figures which signify this intent become redundant. Instead, the discipline of *musica poetica* and specifically its *Figurenlehre* is in itself a *pathopoeia*. A similar fate faces the *hypotyposis*. Although Burmeister also includes this figure in his *Figurenlehre*, most subsequent writers omit it, presumably because its function also coincides with the general

---

1. "Nay, hath not music her figures, the same which rhetoric? What . . . [are] her passionate airs, but prosopopoeias?" *The Compleat Gentleman*; cited in Strunk, *Source Readings*, 337.

2. See *Hypotyposis*.

3. See *Assimilatio*.

purpose of a text- and affection-expressive *musica poetica*. Thus both vivid (*hypotyposis*) and affective (*pathopoeia*) text expression is assimilated into the general concept and definition of *musica poetica*.

Susenbrotus (*Epitome* p.66)
Denique tota πάθοποεία affectuum motio ac varietas. Qui quidem affectus a circumstantiis, ab habitu, aetate, fortuna, loco, tempore, causa, modo, materia, et personis peti solent.

And finally the entire force and variety of the affections can be expressed through the *pathopoeia*. These affections are usually elicited because of the circumstances, conditions, era, fate, location, time, cause, manner, matter, and persons.

Peacham (*Garden of Eloquence* p.143)
Pathopeia, is a forme of speech by which the Orator moveth the minds of his hearers to some vehemency of affection, as of indignation, feare, envy, hatred, hope, gladnesse, mirth, laughter, sadnesse or sorrow.

Prosopopoeia, the faining of a person, that is, when to a thing sencelesse and dumbe we faine a fit person, or attribute a person to a commonwelth or multitude. . . . Sometime to Cities, townes, beastes, birdes, trees, stones, weapons, fire, water, lights of the firmament, and such like things he attributeth speech, reason, and affection, and to no other end then to further his purpose and to confirme and make his cause evident.

Burmeister (*Hypomnematum*)
Pathopoeia fit quando textus semitoniis ita explicatur, ut quod affectus creet nihil ejus intentatum relinqui videatur.

The *pathopoeia* occurs when the text is expressed through semitones in such fashion that no one appears to remain unmoved by the created affection.

Burmeister (*Musica Poetica* p.61)
Pathopoeia παθοποιία est figura apta ad affectus creandos, quod fit, quando Semitonia carmini inseruntur, quae nec ad Modum carminis, nec ad Genus pertinent, sed unius beneficio in aliud introducuntur: Tum quando semitonia carminis Modo congruentia saepius extra morem attinguntur.

The *pathopoeia* is an apt figure to create affections. It occurs when semitones are inserted into a composition which neither belong to its *modus* or *genus* but are introduced into a composition's *modus* from another. It occurs when semitones are frequently added to the *modus* of a composition in an extraordinary fashion.

Thuringus (*Opusculum* p.126)

Quid est Parthopoeia? Est, quae dictiones affectuum, doloris, gaudii, timoris, risus, luctus, misericordiae, exultationis, tremoris, terroris, & similies ita ornat, ut tam cantores quam auditores moveat.

What is the *parthopoeia*? It occurs when the passage is enhanced with affections of sorrow, joy, fear, laughter, mourning, mercy, exultation, fright, terror, and similar affections in such a manner that it moves both singers and listeners.

PAUSA: a pause or rest in a musical composition.

Musical figures of silence can be divided into two categories: those signifying a breaking off or rupture of the musical line (*abruptio*, *ellipsis*, *tmesis*) and those signifying the ensuing silence (*aposiopesis*, *homoioptoton*, *homoioteleuton*, *suspiratio*). The *pausa* is either considered among the latter group or understood simply as a notational sign. As a musical expression, pauses can serve three distinct purposes: first, they are essential for technical reasons, facilitating a clearly articulated and differentiated musical structure; second, they serve to clarify the general structure of the text; and third, they can be used to express specific words, thoughts, and images found in the text.

The structuring of Renaissance motets according to the caesurae found in the text is a well-known phenomenon. Numerous sixteenth-century authors emphasize the artistic merit of the pause in a musical representation of the text. Ruhnke cites references by Gallicus (1520), Listenius (1537), Rhau (1538), Dressler (1563), and Calvisius (1592), regarding the observance of pauses in music and text.[1] Dressler explicitly emphasizes the "elegant" and "agreeable" attributes of pauses, particularly when all voices fall silent to emphasize and clarify the text.[2] This

1. Ruhnke, *Burmeister*, 135ff.

2. "Quinto elegantiae et suavitatis causa inseruntur pausae et non raro omnes voces propter emphasin et vocabulorum significationem." *Praecepta musicae poeticae*, ch.10; cited in Ruhnke, *Burmeister*, 137.

close association with text expression provides the basis for the various figures of silence to be included in the concept of musical-rhetorical figures, even though they would not all possess rhetorical counterparts.

Burmeister only includes the general pause under the term *aposiopesis* in his *Figurenlehre*. Thuringus includes not only the *aposiopesis* and the related *homoioptoton* and *homoioteleuton*, but also includes rests in general under the term *pausa*. His definitions of this figure are modeled on Dressler's discussion of the device.[1] With the inclusion of the *pausa* in his *Figurenlehre*, Thuringus establishes a rhetorical understanding of all musical figures of silence.

Kircher begins his list of defined figures with the *pausa*, emphasizing its property as a text-interpretive device. It is of particular usefulness in expressing questions in music. Kircher adopts a great deal of Thuringus's *Figurenlehre*, listing all but one of Thuringus's figures in *Liber* 5 of his *Musurgia*. In his defined figures, Kircher redefines *homoioptoton* with a definition much closer to the figure's rhetorical counterpart. While Thuringus ascribes the property of expressing a question to his *homoioptoton*, Kircher now assigns this task to his *pausa*. This attribute is not explicitly included by Thuringus in his description of the *pausa* but rather is found in his *homoioptoton* definition.[2] As part of his *pausa* definition, Kircher also lists the *stenasmus* or *suspiratio*, a "musical sigh."

The *pausa* is also mentioned by Printz and Walther. Neither mention the figure's rhetorical or affective use. Printz is primarily concerned with figurative embellishments rather than with text- or affection-expressive devices. Both his *suspirans* and *pausa* are described as purely technical devices rather than as expressive figures of silence. Walther similarly regards the *figura muta* or *pausa* simply as a sign in music notation. After defining *pausa* in his *Lexicon*, Walther defines further rests according to their durational value. Even his *pausa generalis* is described simply as a rest in all voices without any reference to the musical-rhetorical figures of similar description. These he lists under their respective terms, *abruptio* and *aposiopesis*.

---

1. Feldmann, "Das 'Opusculum Bipartitum,'" 135.
2. See *Homoioptoton*, *Homoioteleuton*, *Aposiopesis*.

Thuringus (*Opusculum* p.114)

Quid est Pausa? Est signum taciturnitatis, secundum notae quantitatem cui appropiatur constitutum. Quis est earum Usus?
1. Primo prosunt ad respirationem Canentium.
2. Ad varietatem & dulcedinem cantus; Cum enim nulla cantio suavis & artificiosa existimetur, nisi sit fugis ornata, necessario inventae sunt pausae, quo fugae constitui possent.
3. Ad vitandes concurrentes perfectas consonantiarum species, ne duae invicem ejusdem speciei immediate se sequi cogantur, cum se offerunt, & vitari difficulter possunt.
4. Ad vitanda prohibita intervalla Tritonum semidiapente, & semi diapason, quae arte vitari commode, nisi pausis intervenientibus vel vocibus positis fictis, non possunt.
5. Tollendae difficultatis causa: Cum enim duae vel tres cantilenae partes ita conglutinatae sint, ut plures addere perquam difficile sit, Pause commode poni possunt quo ad illa difficultas finem habeat.

What is a *pausa*? It is a sign of silence whose duration is determined according to a certain note. When are they used?
1. To allow the singer to breathe.
2. To add variety and charm to the composition. Since no composition can be regarded as charming and artful unless it is adorned with *fugae*, pauses are necessarily introduced in order for *fugae* to be constructed.
3. To avoid parallel perfect consonances, so that two of the same species do not immediately follow each other. Thus placed, the difficulty can be avoided.
4. To avoid prohibited intervals such as the tritone or major seventh. These dissonances are strictly and appropriately avoided through intervening *pausae* and a realignment of the voices.
5. To remove other difficult situations. For example, when two or three parts of the composition are combined in such fashion that the addition of more voices becomes difficult, appropriately placed *pausae* can be used until those difficulties are past.

Kircher (*Musurgia* L.8, p.144)

Παῦσις idem quod quies est, Pausa tunc commode adhibetur, cum una persona non multi censentur loqui; fitque tunc oportune; cum quis, vel interrogat, vel ad interrogata respondet, ut fit in dialogis harmonicis Viadanae.

Pausis is the same as silence. The *pausa* is appropriately used when one person instead of many are allowed to speak. It is suitably applied when someone asks a question or responds to a question, as in the musical dialogues of Viadana.

Printz (*Phrynis Mytilenaeus* pt.2, p.68)

Die schweigenden Figuren werden Pausae genennet. Es ist aber eine Pausa, wie dieses Wort allhier gebraucht wird / ein sehr kurtzes Stillschweigen / oder vielmehr nur eine Mäßigung der Stimme / die immer stiller und gelinder wird / zwischen geschwinden Noten.

Figures of silence are called *pausae*. A *pausa*, in the sense of its use here, is a very short silence, or rather only a moderation of the voice which becomes softer and gentler between notes of rapid succession.

Janovka (*Clavis* p.51)

Pausa, idem est quod quies, & tunc commode adhibetur dum una persona non vero multae censentur loqui, fit que tunc

The *pausa* is the same as silence. It is appropriately used while one person rather than many are allowed to speak. It is

opportune, dum quis vel interrogat, vel ad interrogata respondet, ut fit in Dialogis harmonicis.

suitably applied while someone asks a question or responds to a question, as in musical dialogues.

Walther (*Lexicon*)

Figura muta [lat.ital.] pl. Figure mute [ital.] Figurae mutae [lat.] Figure muëtte, pl. figures muëttes [gall.] eine Stumme Figur, Stumme Figuren, hierdurch werden die Pausen gemeynet.

Figura muta . . . a figure or figures of silence. These terms refer to pauses.

Pausa [lat. ital.] Pause [gall.] παῦσις [gr.] eine Ruhe, Stillhalten in der Music, so durch ein gewisses Zeichen angedeutet wird.

Pausa . . . refers to a rest or silence in the music, which is indicated by a certain sign.

PLEONASMUS: (1) a prolongation of passing dissonances through suspensions; (2) four-part harmonized chant; *falso bordone*.

Both the rhetorical and the musical *pleonasmus* signify a certain excess (Quintilian: ". . . *id est abundans*"; Burmeister: "*Pleonasmus est . . . abundantia*"), thereby reflecting the literal meaning of the term (from *pleonazo*, be in abundance, exaggerate). Burmeister introduces the term into the musical *Figurenlehre*, defining it as a passing dissonance (*symblema*) which is prolonged through a suspension (*syncopa*) before resolving. Both the *symblema* and the *syncopa* introduce dissonances into the harmonic structure of a composition. This results in the intended exaggeration or abundance, namely of dissonances. The combination of passing note and suspension extends not only a dissonance but can create yet another delay: should numerous *pleonasmoi* be linked together, the cadence might be extended over two, three, or more measures.

Janovka and Vogt list *pleonasmus* as an alternative term for *falso bordone*, the Italian translation of *faux bourdon*. *Falso bordone* signifies not only the familiar *faux bourdon* progression, but is expanded to include four-part chordal harmonizations of psalm tones with the root of the chord in the bass.[1] The "falseness" or irregularity of the three-part *faux bourdon* progression is considered eliminated through the addition

1. See *Faux Bourdon*.

of the bass voice, thereby encouraging the introduction of an alternative terminology. In performance of harmonized chant, each voice sings numerous syllables or words to a single note. This "overabundance" of words per syllable is compared to the excess of modifying words which characterizes the rhetorical *pleonasmus*. A further Greek, albeit non-rhetorical term, *isobatus* (literally, same path or progression), is used by Kircher to identify harmonized chant.

Quintilian (*Institutio* VIII.iii.53)
Est πλεονασμὸς vitium, cum supervacuis verbis oratio oneratur.

Pleonasmus is an error which occurs when the oration is overburdened with superfluous words.

Quintilian (*Institutio* IX.iii.46)
Hoc Caecilio πλεονασμὸς videtur, id est abundans super necessitatem oratio, sicut illa "Vidi oculos ante ipse meos."

Caecilius understands *pleonasmus* as an oration characterized by a wealth of words beyond necessity, such as "I have seen it with my own eyes."

Susenbrotus (*Epitome* p.31)
Pleonasmus, est cum supervacuis bis orationis contextus vel affirmationis vel Epitaseos gratia oneratur.

The *pleonasmus* occurs when the structure of the oration is frequently overburdened with superfluous words for the sake of assertion or emphasis.

Gottsched (*Redekunst* p.279)
Pleonasmus. Wenn man überflüssige Beywörter braucht die Sache noch desto nachdrücklicher zu geben. Z.E. Die heiße Glut, der grosse Riese, der kleine Zwerg.

Pleonasmus. When superfluous modifying words are used to render a thought with yet greater emphasis, as in hot embers, the large giant, or the small dwarf.

Gottsched (*Dichtkunst* p.325)
Die X. Figur ist der Ueberfluß, (Pleonasmus) wenn man viel mehr sagt, als nöthig ist. Sie entsteht wiederum aus der Heftigkeit des Affectes, welcher alles zusammen nimmt, die Leser oder Zuhörer aufs handgreiflichste zu rühren und zu überzeugen.

The next figure is superfluity (*pleonasmus*), which occurs when much more is stated than is necessary. It also occurs out of the vehemence of the affection which employs everything in order to tangibly stir and convince the readers or listeners.

Burmeister (*Hypomnematum*)
Pleonasmus ex Symblemate & Syncopa conflatur, potissimum sub introductione clausulae alicujus.

The *pleonasmus* is forged out of a *symblema* [passing dissonance] and *syncopa* [suspension], occurring most frequently in the beginning of a cadence.

Burmeister (*Musica Poetica* p.61)
Pleonasmus πλεονασμὸς est Harmoniae, in formatione Clausulae praesertim in ejus Medio abundantia, quae ex Symblemate & Syncopa conflatur, sub duplici, triplici, & ultra, tactus, &c.

The *pleonasmus* is a compositional excess in the formation of a cadence, most frequently in its middle, and is forged out of a *symblema* and *syncopa* over two, three, or more *tactus*.

Janovka (*Clavis* p.42)
Falso bordone, alias Pleonasmus, aut ut Pater Kircherus habet Isobatus, dicitur, dum in aliquo cantu multae syllabae, vel vocabula sub una nota canuntur, quod contingit in quibusdam de OO. SS. Litaniis.

Falso bordone, also known as *pleonasmus*, or *isobatus* as Kircher calls it, occurs when numerous syllables or words are sung to one note in a *cantus*, as in certain litanies.

Vogt (*Conclave* p.4)
Falsobordone primo Pleonasmus est, & Isobatus, cum sub una magna nota plures syllabae, vel verba, uno, eodemque tono canuntur.

First, *falsobordone* (or *pleonasmus*, *isobatus*) signifies a passage in which numerous syllables or words are sung on one pitch to one long note.

POLYPTOTON: a repetition of a melodic passage at different pitches.

The earliest reference to an association between the rhetorical *polyptoton* and a musical application is found in an English treatise. Puttenham describes *traductio* with a definition analogous to that of the *polyptoton*.[1]

1. Sonnino, *Handbook*, 179.

Henry Peacham in his *Garden of Eloquence* then compares the *traductio* to the repetitions and divisions [alterations] in music.[1] Although this general reference is found in an English rhetorical treatise, far removed from the German *Figurenlehre* both in substance and place, it does point to the growing correlation between the rhetorical figures and their musical application.

The well-known rhetorical figure is defined only in Vogt's musical *Figurenlehre*. Although the repetition of a musical passage might be considered a technique covered by the *anaphora*, Vogt chooses to bestow the device with a specific rhetorical name.[2] He specifies that the *polyptoton* repeats a passage in diverse *clavi* or pitches.[3] This would parallel the grammatical repetition of a word in diverse cases. Vogt does not clearly indicate which part of a composition is to be repeated, stating only that the *polyptoton* repeats a *colon* or section of the composition. This could be interpreted as a section of either a certain voice or the larger musical structure. However, Vogt consistently uses the terms *vox* and *voces* when discussing figures concerned with individual voices. As such Vogt defines the term *homophonia* in his glossary as a fugal *vox* which enters on the same pitch (*clavis*) as the previous statement of the theme,[4] or the *ethophonia* as an imitation of one *vox* by another.[5] It is therefore unlikely that Vogt wishes to identify the entry of a specific voice at a different pitch with *polyptoton*. On the other hand, Vogt normally employs the common designation of *periodus* when referring to a larger section of a composition. In all likelihood, *colon* simply refers to a melodic phrase, similar to its grammatical use. In this case, the *polyptoton* would signify the repetition of a melodic passage at different pitches, not unlike the *imitatio* of Walther, Mattheson, or Spiess.

---

1. "Traductio is a forme of speech which repeateth one word often times in one sentence, making the oration more pleasant to the eare. . . . This exornation is compared to pleasant repetitions and divisions in Musicke." *Garden of Eloquence*, 49.

2. His *anaphora* is described as a general form of repetition, either of a part of a *periodus*, or of a *figura simplex*. See *Anaphora*.

3. In his introductory glossary, Vogt defines *clavis* as "Quiscunque ad quemcunque tonus" (p.3), clearly associating *clavis* with the pitches of the *modus* or *tonus* rather than with the placement of the voice in different registers or staves.

4. "Homophonia primo voce sola. secundo cum voces in fuga eadem clavi successive incipiunt." *Conclave*, 4.

5. See *Mimesis*.

Mattheson mentions but does not define *polyptoton*. He includes it in a list of rhetorical figures of repetition which are rooted and familiar equally in music as in rhetoric and therefore require no further explanation.

Susenbrotus (*Epitome* p.56)
Hoc Schema poetis nominatur πολύπτωτον Polyptoton, hac est, multitudo casuum varietate distincta. Mancinellus: Datque Polyptoton varios casus retinendo.

This figure is called *polyptoton* by poets and is distinguished through a variety of different case endings. According to Mancinellus, it is marked by the repetition of a word in various cases.

Gottsched (*Redekunst* p.276)
Polyptoton, wenn ein Wort in seiner grammatischen Abänderung wiederholt wird.

Polyptoton occurs when a word is repeated with grammatical alterations.

Vogt (*Conclave* p.151)
Polyptoton. Cum colon in diversa clavi repetitur.

Polyptoton. When a passage is repeated at various pitches.

Mattheson (*Capellmeister* p.243)
Die Epanalepsis, Epistrophe, Anadiplosis, Paronomasia, Polyptoton, Antanaclasis, Ploce etc. haben solche natürliche Stellen in der Melodie, daβ es fast scheinet, als hätten die griechischen Redner sothane Figuren aus der Ton-Kunst entlehnet; denn sie sind lauter repetitiones vocum, Wiederholungen der Wörter, die auf verschiedene Weise angebracht werden.

The *epanalepsis*, *epistrophe*, *anadiplosis*, *paronomasia*, *polyptoton*, *antanaclasis*, *ploce*, etc., assume such natural positions in music that it almost seems as if the Greek orators borrowed these figures from the art of musical composition. For they are purely *repetitiones vocum*, repetitions of words, which are applied to music in various different ways.

POLYSYNDETON: an immediate repetition of an *emphasis* (*accentus*) in the same voice.

Ahle is the first author to list *polysyndeton* in the context of a musical *Figurenlehre*. In keeping with all of his explanations, he retains the rhetorical definition of the term. Walther, who adopts only those of Ahle's figures which are easily transferred to music, excludes *polysyndeton*, *asyndeton*, and *synonymia* from his *Lexicon*, all rhetorical figures which are not easily represented through the accompanying music.

Vogt is the only author to supply *polysyndeton* with a musical definition. Because his definition of *emphasis* is not entirely clear, the meaning of *polysyndeton*, which he describes as a repeated *emphasis*, is also indefinite.[1] Should Vogt's *emphasis* in fact signify a text-expressive *accentus*, his *polysyndeton* would be understood as a series of notes connected through numerous *accentus*. Such an upper or lower neighbor can either precede or follow a consonant note and can function as a "conjunctive" *transitus* or passing note. A series of *accentus* or *emphases* would thereby connect the principal notes. Vogt's *polysyndeton* thus connects (*syndeo*) both multiple (*poly*) *emphases* as well as principal notes of a composition.

Quintilian (*Institutio* IX.iii.50)

Contrarium illud est schema, quod coniunctionibus abundat. Illud ἀσύνδετον, hoc πολυσύνδετον dicitur.

Opposite to that one is a figure which signifies an excess of conjunctions. The former is called *asyndeton*, and this one *polysyndeton*.

Susenbrotus (*Epitome* p.39)

Polysyndeton, Πολυσύνδετον, id est, varie ac multipliciter coniunctum, est quum oratio multis coniunctionibus vel eisdem vel diversis abundat. Vel est multis nexa coniunctionibus oratio. Mancinellus: Diversas Voces coniunctio plurima si fert.

Polysyndeton signifies numerous and varied conjunctions, and occurs when the oration is overburdened with many either like or diverse conjunctions. Or it is an oration connected through numerous conjunctions. According to Mancinellus, it consists of a connection of numerous diverse phrases.

Gottsched (*Redekunst* p.278)

Polysyndeton. Wenn man gar zu viel Bindewörter braucht.

Polysyndeton. When too many conjunctions are used.

Ahle (*Sommer-Gespräche* p.17)

Hergegen aber / wän er solches noch mehrmal hinzutuht, ein Polysyndeton, als: jauchzet und singet und rühmet und lobet.

In contrast, were the composer to add [the conjunction *and*] numerous times, a *polysyndeton* results, as in "rejoice and sing and glorify and praise."

Vogt (*Conclave* p.151)

Polysyntheton. In similibus partibus periodi continuata emphasis.

The *polysyntheton* occurs when an *emphasis* is repeated successively in the same parts of a passage.

---

1. See *Emphasis*.

PROLEPSIS: see *ANTICIPATIO*

PROLONGATIO: a passing dissonance or suspension of longer duration than the preceding consonance.

According to strict rules of counterpoint, a dissonance which is incurred through a passing note or a suspension is not to be of longer duration than the preceding consonance. The *prolongatio* provides an exception to this rule. This purely musical figure is only mentioned in Bernhard's *Tractatus*, where it is included among the figures used in the *stylus luxurians communis*. It is virtually identical to the *extensio*, a figure used in the *stylus luxurians theatralis* or *stylus recitativus*. The distinction between the two devices lies not so much in the nature of their dissonances as in the place of their use. In addition to permitting greater harmonic license, the rhythmic freedom of the *stylus recitativus* negates a number of the contrapuntal requirements regarding dissonance and meter or duration, a condition which is underscored in Bernhard's definition of the *transitus inversus*.[1] Thus Bernhard simply mentions the *extensio*'s property of prolonging a dissonance and its customary combination with the *multiplicatio*, without making any reference to the durational relationship between the dissonance and the preceding consonance. The *prolongatio* in contrast is used in the *stylus luxurians communis*, a compositional style which combines expressive text interpretation with traditional counterpoint. Bernhard links the *prolongatio* to the *stylus gravis* through both his implied reference to traditional rules of counterpoint and his explicit reference to the two *stylus gravis* figures, *transitus* and *syncopatio*. His examples of the *prolongatio* are also contrapuntal, in contrast to the recitative examples of the *extensio*. While the *prolongatio* links this dissonant device with past compositional practice, the *extensio* points ahead to modern, expressive composition. Neither *prolongatio* nor *extensio* are included among the list of figures in Bernhard's later *Bericht*, but are subsumed under the definition of the *multiplicatio*, specifically its second, extended or prolonged (*Verlängerte*) form.[2]

---

1. See *Transitus*.
2. See *Multiplicatio*.

Bernhard (*Tractatus* p.76)

Prolongatio ist wenn eine Dissonantz sich länger aufhält, als die vorhergehende Consonantz, in Transitu sowohl als in Syncopatione. In Transitu sind folgende [Exempel] nur selten.

The *prolongatio* occurs when a dissonance is of longer duration than the preceding consonance, in the context of either a *transitus* [passing dissonance] or a *syncopatio*. Following examples are found in *transitus*, occuring only rarely.

In Syncopatione ist sie bräuchlicher doch vornehmlich bey der Quarta.

The *prolongatio* is more common in a *syncopatio*, particularly at the fourth.

PROSOPOPOEIA: see *PATHOPOEIA, HYPOTYPOSIS, MIMESIS*

QUAESITIO NOTAE: see *SUBSUMTIO*

QUASI TRANSITUS: see *TRANSITUS*

REPERCUSSIO: (1) a modified interval in a tonal fugal answer; (2) a tonal, inverted, or other modified fugal answer.

The *repercussio* is associated with a fugal answer, signifying either the interval altered to achieve a tonal answer or other variant of the subject (Walther) or the fugal answer itself (Mattheson).[1] As Walther's defini-

1. Spiess also employs the term *repercussio*, but uses it to signify the "repercussion" of a trilling note in a *ribattuta*. See *Ribattuta*.

tion suggests, this modification can entail the introduction of the related plagal mode, a procedure which Bernhard identifies as *consociatio modi*, a form of *mutatio toni*.[1] While Walther relates *repercussio* to the specific modified interval, Mattheson consistently identifies the entire modified answer with the term throughout his *Capellmeister*. In fact, even an inverted statement of the subject can be called a *repercussio*. Mattheson does not wish to limit these modified answers to fugal composition but suggests that they are especially useful in developing and amplifying the principal subjects (*Haupt-Sätze*) in "other pieces."

Mattheson also mentions that the *repercussio* is equivalent to the rhetorical figure *refractio* or *reverberatio*. This becomes particularly graphic in an inversion of the theme which "undertakes a contrary movement."[2] The rhetorical *refractio* signifies the repetition of a word yet with contrary meaning.[3] Similarly the tonal answer repeats the subject with certain contrasting changes. Not only are intervals modified or even inverted, but the contrapuntal role of a fugal answer stands in contrast to that of the opening subject, one being the leader (*dux*), the other the follower (*comes*); one leading away from the *finalis* or tonic, the other leading back to it. Thus the repetition and simultaneous contrast identified by the rhetorical *refractio* also appears in the musical *repercussio*.

Walther (*Lexicon*)

Repercussio also heisset dasjenige intervallum, welches in einer Fuge der Dux und Comes dem Modo gemäß, gegen einander formiren.

Repercussio signifies the particular interval which the *dux* and *comes* of a *fuga* form in opposition to each other, according to the *modus*.

In diesem Exempel, welches Modi Dorii ist, springet der Dux aus dem Final-Clave in die Quint; hingegen der Comes aus

In this example in the Dorian mode, the *dux* leaps from the *finalis* to the fifth; in contrast, the *comes* leaps only a fourth,

1. The *aequatio modi*, another form of *mutatio toni*, is used to accommodate a real or exact fugal answer. See *Mutatio Toni*.

2. Earlier, Burmeister had identified the inversion of a fugal subject as *hypallage*. See *Hypallage*.

3. Sonnino, *Handbook*, 158.

dem, unter den Final-Clavem, vermöge des Ambitus Modi Hypodorii (welches der Comes eben observiren muß) gehenden a nur in die Quart. Weil nun diese zwey intervalla, wenn noch mehr Stimmen darzu kommen, alterniren, so wird ein solcher processus Repercussio, oder der Widerschlag genennet.

proceeding out of the A below the *finalis*. This is determined by the range which the *comes* must observe, namely the *ambitus* of the Hypodorian mode. Should more voices be added, these two intervals alternate, a process called *repercussio* or *Wiederschlag* (repercussion).

Mattheson (*Capellmeister* p.124f.)
Der dritte Weg, darauf uns diese Notations-Quelle der Erfindung führet, begreifft die Wiederholungen, mit ihrem Kunst-Worte clausulae synonymae genannt, oder was man sonst in fugirten Sachen den Wiederschlag nennet, d.i. wenn ich einen gewissen Satz in andre Höhe oder Tiefe versetze. Durch dieses Hülffs-Mittel werden sehr viele hübsche Themata oder Haupt-Sätze, nicht nur zu Fugen, sondern vornehmlich zu andern sachen erfunden, und sehr geschickt durch- oder ausgeführet: zumahl wenn die eine Modulation durch etliche zwischenkommende abgelöset, und hernach wiederum so geschickt angebracht wird, daß es läßt, als ob sie gerufen käme. Der Wiederschlag heisset repercussio, wenn eine Stimme der andern nicht in blosser Wiederholung derselben Klänge, sondern in verschiedenen, entweder höhern oder tiefern, mit einer Gleichförmigkeit antwortet, und kan solches auch in einer eintzigen Stimme geschehen.

The third method suggested by this notational source [*locus notationis*] of *inventio* encompasses the repetitions, known by the art word *clausulae synonymae*, or what is otherwise called *Wiederschlag* (repercussion) in fugal pieces, that is when a certain passage is transferred to higher or lower placements. With this aid many attractive themes or principal subjects, not only in fugues but especially in other pieces, are very cleverly developed or amplified, particularly when a passage is interrupted by a number of intervening ones, after which it is again returned in such a clever manner that it seems as though it were summoned. The *Wiederschlag* is called *repercussio* when one voice answers another by repeating not only the same notes but also similarly structured higher or lower ones. This can even occur in the same voice.

(*Capellmeister* p.239)
Ferner folget ein frischer Wiederschlag, oder eine repercussio in der Quinte des Haupt-Tons, welche Figur in der Rede-Kunst, und zwar in den Figuris dictionis mit dem Nahmen refractio seu reverberatio beleget wird: doch so, daß die Singstimme diesesmahl nicht nachfolget, sondern vielmehr eine Gegen-Bewegung vornimmt.

Next follows a fresh *Wiederschlag* or a *repercussio* in the fifth of the main key, known as a rhetorical figure among the *figurae dictionis* as *refractio* or *reverberatio*. However, the voice does not follow this time but rather undertakes a contrary movement.

REPETITIO: see *ANAPHORA*

RETARDATIO: (1) a suspension which is prolonged or which resolves by rising; (2) a delayed rather than anticipatory suspension.

The *retardatio* is defined similarly in Bernhard's *Bericht* and Walther's *Praecepta.* In both treatises, which feature identical musical examples, it is understood as a suspension which initially resolves by rising. In his *Tractatus* Bernhard calls the same device a *mora.* Although both figures share one musical example, there is a slight difference in the two definitions. The *retardatio* is the result of a prolongation of a note which would normally rise a step, causing the suspension. In contrast, the *mora* signifies a rising resolution of a suspension when a falling one is expected.[1] While the *mora* can be characterized as an irregularly resolved suspension, the *retardatio* is a delayed upward resolution; the *mora* is an "inverted suspension," the *retardatio* is "devised in imitation of the suspension."

In his *Lexicon* Walther defines *retardatio* simply as a delayed or extended resolution, referring to the example under *resolutio mediata.*[2] Both Scheibe and Spiess include the *retardatio* in their treatises with a similar understanding.[3] Neither Scheibe nor Spiess include *syncopatio* in their *Figurenlehren.* Instead they use the two figures *anticipatio* and (its antithesis) *retardatio* to identify two forms of suspension. The former anticipates a note belonging to a subsequent harmony, allowing it to sound prematurely in the preceding harmony, while the latter delays a note, allowing it to sound belatedly in the subsequent harmony. Neither of these definitions differentiate between a rising or falling resolution of the dissonance, thereby permitting either form.

Bernhard (*Bericht* p.151)

Retardatio ist eine Versäumung, wenn	The *retardatio* is a hesitation, namely,

1. See *Mora.*

2. His second example, taken from Stierlein, coincides with the examples found in his *Praecepta* and Bernhard's *Bericht.*

3. Scheibe includes *retardatio* in his early compositional treatise, *Compendium musices,* but does not list the device in his *Critischer Musicus,* where he deals only with expressive musical-rhetorical figures adopted from Gottsched's rhetorical treatises.

nehmlich eine Note eine Secunda steigen solte und sich zu lange vor dem Steigen auffhält. Sie ist aber erfunden zur Imitation der Syncopation mit diesem Unterscheide, daβ, wo sich die Syncopation herunterwerts löβet, so thut solches die Retardatio auffwerts.

when a note which should rise a second tarries too long before rising. This figure was devised in imitation of the *syncopatio*, with this difference: while the *syncopatio* resolves by descending, the *retardatio* resolves by ascending.

Walther (*Praecepta* p.155)
Retardatio ist eine Versäumnung oder Aufhaltung, wenn neml. eine Note, so um eine Secunde steigen solte, sich zu lange vor dem steigen aufhält. Diese Figur ist ad imitationem syncopationis mit diesem Unterscheid erfunden worden, daβ, wo die Syncopation sich herunter läβet, so thut solches die Retardation hinaufwarts.

The *retardatio* is a hesitation or delay, namely, when a note which should rise a second tarries too long before rising. This figure was devised in imitation of the *syncopatio* with this difference: while the *syncopatio* resolves by descending, the *retardatio* resolves by ascending.

Walther (*Lexicon*)
Resolutio mediata welche—vermittelst anderer darzwischen stehenden Noten zwar eine Zeitlang aufgehalten, dennoch aber und endlich auf gebührende Art noch angebracht wird.

The *resolutio mediata* delays a resolution through other intervening notes for a time, but nonetheless finally resolves in the proper fashion.

Walther (*Lexicon*)
Retardatio ein Auffenthalt. s. das Exempel unter Resolutio mediata. Ein anders aber giebt Stierlein in seinem Trifolio Musicali, p.20, also aussehend.

Retardatio, a tarrying. See the example under *resolutio mediata*. Stierlein provides a different example in his *Trifolio Musicali*, as follows:

Scheibe (*Compendium*)

Retardatio ist der Anticipatio entgegen gesezt, und geschiehet ebenfalls auf zweyerley weise 1) in Ansehung der Resolution der Dissonanz 2) in Ansehung und Auszierung der Melodie. (1) Wenn ich dieselbe so lange verzögere, biß erstlich eine neue Dissonanz daraus entstehet, welche in keinen membro auch nicht durch die Verwechselung der Harmnonie mit der vorhergehenden Gemeinschafft hat. (2) Wenn ich in einem Thon der eigentlich zum ersten Accord gehört, bey dem folgendem Accord noch halten laße, und also denjenigen, der ordentlicher Weise dazu gehöret, zurückhalte, und die Anschlagung deßelben verzögere.

The *retardatio* is opposite to the *anticipatio* and also occurs in two forms, concerning, namely, the resolution of the dissonance and the embellishment of the melody. Regarding dissonance, it occurs when the dissonance is delayed so long that a new dissonance results which in no way has anything in common with the preceding dissonance, even if the harmonies were to be exchanged. Regarding embellishment, it occurs when a note which belongs to the preceding chord still sounds with the following chord, thereby detaining and delaying the sounding of the note which properly belongs to the following chord.

Spiess (*Tractatus* p.155)

Retardatio, Auffenthalt, Verzögerung, ist der Anticipation schnurgerad zuwider in deme, daß, wie jene zu frühe- diese zu späth in ihr gebührendes Intervallum einfället. Es ist die Retardation nichts anderes eigentlich, als eine aus allzulanger Aufhaltung der vorhergehenden Notae entstandene Dissonanz, welche zum folgenden Accord nicht gehöret, und nicht resolvirt werden mag. Das Exempel gibt die Sach klar.

The *retardatio*, a tarrying, delay, is directly opposite to the *anticipatio* in that it introduces the correct interval too late rather than too early. The *retardatio* is really nothing else than a dissonance resulting from an excessively delayed preceding note which neither belongs to the following chord nor is resolved. The example clarifies this.

RETICENTIA: see *APOSIOPESIS*

RIBATTUTA: an accelerating trill in dotted rhythm, used to embellish a *tenuta* or a note of extended duration.

The *ribattuta*, an embellishment commonly used to ornament a note of long duration called a *tenuta*, is counted among the *Manieren* (Mattheson) or *figurae simplices* (Spiess). Like other figurative embellishments, Italian rather than Latin or Greek terminology is used to identify this device, clarifying the distinction between the musical-rhetorical figures and the purely ornamental "simple figures."

Mattheson (*Capellmeister* pp.115, 118)

Die Welschen hergegen schlagen ihre gemeine Triller sehr geschwind, starck und kurtz, fast wie Trilletten; ausser dem Fall, wenn etwa auf einem oder andern Ton lange auszuhalten ist, welches sie eine Tenuta, und die Frantzosen tenuë nennen. . . . Bisweilen werden auf solchen Tenuten auch wol langsame Triller mit geschwinden untermenget und abgewechselt.

The Italians, in contrast [to the French], execute their ordinary trills very quickly, strong, and short, almost like *trilletti*, except in cases where one or another note is to be sustained for a long time. This they call a *tenuta*, or *tenuë* in French. . . . At times fast and slow trills are included and alternated on these *tenute*.

Die Ribattuta ist endlich noch wol werth, daβ man ihrer mit wenigem gedencke: sie bestehet in einer punctirten und bedächtlich-abgestossenen Umwechselung zweener neben einander liegenden Klänge, dabey man immer auf den untersten, und längsten, als einen Ruhe-Punct, wiederkehret und Fuβ fasset. Das Wort bedeutet eine Zurückschlagung, und braucht keiner weitern Auslegung; findet sich aber weder in musicalischen Wörterbüchern, noch in andern gewöhnlichen Unterrichtungs-Schrifften für Sänger. . . . Die Tenuta, deren wir oben erwehnet, wird gar füglich mit einer Ribattuta angefangen, welche, nachdem sie allmählig etwas geschwinder schläget, sich endlich in ein förmliches langes Trillo endiget, etwa auf folgende Art:

The *ribattuta* finally deserves mentioning. It consists of two neighboring notes in dotted rhythm which are deliberately executed in alternation as if one were returning to the lower, longer note as a point of rest and foothold. The word means repercussion and needs no further explication. However, it is found neither in music dictionaries nor in other common instruction manuals for singers. . . . The above mentioned *tenuta* is often begun with a *ribattuta*, which after a gradual acceleration finally ends in a proper long trill, as in the following example:

Spiess (*Tractatus* p.156)

Tenuta, Aushaltung, ist, wann eine Stimm lang in einem Ton aushalten muß; fanget gemeiniglich an mit einer Ribattuta, Repercussion, oder wieder Zuruckschlagung, und endiget sich gar wohl mit einem Trillo.

A *tenuta* or sustaining occurs when a voice must sustain a note for a long time. It commonly begins with a *ribattuta*, a *repercussio* or repercussion, and ends very well with a trill.

SALTI COMPOSTI: a four-note figuration consisting of three consonant leaps.

The *salti composti*, like all of Printz's figures, is an ornamental device used in figurative music. The leaping intervals used in the construction of this embellishment consist of the five consonant *salti semplice*: thirds, fourths, fifths, sixths, and octaves. Printz calculates that three leaps using the five intervals allows for 125 formations ($5^3 = 125$). This multiplied by the eight configurations results in one thousand variations, excluding transpositions.

Printz (*Phrynis Mytilenaeus* pt.2, p.50)

Salti Composti bestehen in vier geschwinden Noten und dreyen Sprüngen. Die Variatio der Salti Composti geschicht durch die unterschiedliche Bewegung / und unterschiedliche Intervalla. Die Bewegung ist achterley: Denn 1. gehet der erste Sprung hinauff / der andere hinunter / und der dritte wieder hinauff: 2. gehet der erste Sprung herunter / der andere hinauff / und der dritte wieder herunter: 3. gehet der erste Sprung hinauff / die letzten beyde herunter: 4. gehet der erste Sprung herunter / die letzten beyde hinauff: 5. gehen die ersten beyde hinauff / der letzte herunter: 6. gehen die ersten beyde herunter / der letzte hinauff: 7.

The *salti composti* consist of four rapid notes and three leaps. The *variatio* of these *salti composti* are formed through the different movement and size of the intervals. The movement is eightfold: (1) the first leap ascends, the second descends, the third ascends again; (2) the first leap descends, the second ascends, the third descends again; (3) the first leap ascends, the last two descend; (4) the first leap descends, the last two ascend; (5) the first two ascend, the last descends; (6) the first two descend, the last ascends; (7) all three leaps ascend; and (8) all three leaps descend. . . . Therefore [through the different intervals] each

gehen alle drey Sprünge hinauff / und 8. gehen alle drey Sprünge herunter. . . . Also hat man in jeder Bewegung hundert und fünff und zwanzig Variationes, welche zusammen tausend machen / ohne diejenigen / so ex Transpositione in alias Claves entstehen.

movement has one hundred twenty-five *variationes*, which altogether make one thousand, without counting those derived out of transposition into different pitches.

Walther (*Lexicon*)
Salti composti bestehen aus vier geschwinden Noten, und dreyen Springen.

Salti composti consist of four rapid notes and three leaps.

SALTO SEMPLICE: a consonant leap.

The "simple leap" signifies one of the five consonant leaps: thirds, fourths, fifths, sixths, and octaves. In keeping with his concept of figures, Printz employs the leaps in a purely technical manner, especially in the formation of larger, composite configurations. Even his reference to the application of the leaps in vocal music in order to extend a syllable is not correlated with text emphasis or expression.

Printz (*Phrynis Mytilenaeus* pt.2, p.50)
Salto Semplice ist einer Sylbe Dehnung durch ein sprüngendes Intervallum, in Sachen / so einen Text haben: Auf Instrumental Sachen aber bestehet er in zweyen Fusen / oder auch geschwinden Noten / so keiner andern Figur zugethan seyn. Er ist entweder Intendens, oder Remittens, jener springet über sich / dieser unter sich. Diese Sprünge seyn unterschiedlich / nachdem die Scala ist / in der sie geschehen. . . . Sagen demnach / daß ein jeder Sprung geschicht entweder in Tertiam oder in Quartam oder in Quintam, oder in Sextam, oder in Octavam.

The *salto semplice* is an extension of a syllable through a leaping interval in vocal music. In instrumental music it consists of two eighth or other rapid notes not covered by other figures. It is either *intendens* or *remittens*, the former ascending, the latter descending. The various leaps are determined by the key in which they occur. . . . It is said accordingly that every leap occurs either to the third, fourth, fifth, sixth, or ocatve.

Walther (*Lexicon*)
Salto semplice ist einer Sylben-Dehnung durch ein springendes Intervallum.

The *salto semplice* is an extension of a syllable through a leaping interval.

SALTUS DURIUSCULUS: a dissonant leap.

The specific identification of a dissonant leap as a distinct figure is encountered only in Bernhard's *Figurenlehre*. The harshness of the leaps is conveyed through the word *durus*, meaning not only "hard, harsh" but also "rough, brazen." This negative connotation is particularly well suited to express a text, as Bernhard's example illustrates.[1] The word *falsch* (false) is expressed through a falling diminished seventh. Not only is the text effectively expressed through the dissonance, but an added significance of "harshness, shamelessness" is implied through the literal meaning of a *duriusculus* leap. Like the *passus duriusculus*, this figure can also assume an added explicative dimension, lending it the potential to signify more than even the text might imply.[2] Although the *saltus duriusculus* is defined only in his *Tractatus*, Bernhard discusses forbidden leaps (*verbohtene Sprünge*) in the ninth chapter of his *Bericht*, where he suggests that they might be used in the *stylus recitativus*, "where they might be admitted to accommodate certain affections."[3]

Bernhard (*Tractatus* p.78)

Droben Cap.2 No.6 ist gesaget worden, daβ man sich für unnatürlichen Gängen und Sprüngen hüten solle. In stylo luxuriante communi aber werden etliche derselben zugelaβen. Der Saltus hexachordi minoris ist bey denen Alten nicht bräuchlich gewesen, als nur zwischen re, fa und mi, fa; Heute aber sind folgende auch zugelaβen:

Above in ch.2 no.6, it was said that unnatural progressions and leaps are to be avoided. In the *stylus luxurians communis*, however, a number of these are permitted. The leap of a minor sixth was not used by previous composers except either between *re* and *fa* or *mi* and *fa*. However, nowadays the following are also permitted:

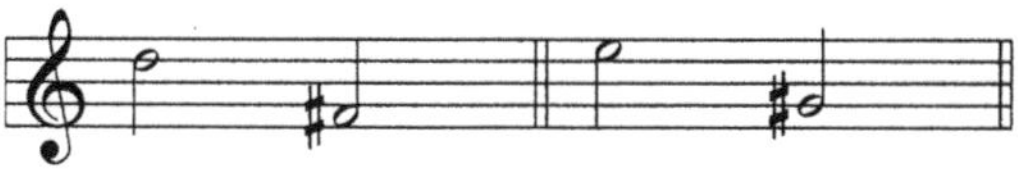

1. The second musical example of his definition is one of the few examples in Bernhard's treatises which includes a text. Other musical examples with text are found in his definitions in the *Tractatus* of *passus duriusculus*, *transitus inversus*, *heterolepsis*, and in his definition in the *Bericht* of *subsumtio*.

2. See *Passus Duriusculus*.

3. "Eine andere Beschaffenheit hätte es in Stylo Recitativo, wo sie vielleicht etlicher affecten zu gefallen zugelaβen werden." *Bericht*, 144.

Saltus Quartae deficientis im hinauff und heruntergehen, Saltus Quintae deficientis herunterwärts werden heute auch passiret. Saltus Septimae irregularis so vom Hexachordo minore und Semitonio majore bestehet, ist auch bißweilen, wiewohl fast nur in Soliciniis anzutreffen, doch nur descendendo.

The ascending or descending leap of a diminished fourth as well as the descending leap of a diminished fifth are also permitted today. The leap of a diminished seventh, consisting of a minor sixth plus a major semitone, is also periodically encountered, albeit almost exclusively in vocal solos, and then only descending.

Saltus Septimae regularis sowohl Nonae als anderer Intervallorum so über die Octave sind, setzet man itzo auch kühner als vor Alters, zumahl in Baß-Stimmen welche wohl Disdiapason herunter springen.

Leaps of a regular seventh and ninth in addition to intervals exceeding an octave are also employed more boldly today than previously, especially in bass voices which can even leap down two octaves.

SCHEMATOIDES: a figure which restructures a previous passage or configuration, either through changing text underlay or through durational augmentation or diminution.

The *schematoides* is described as various methods of restructuring a motive or figure by both Printz and Vogt. *Schema* is the general Greek term for "form" or "model," also meaning specifically rhetorical formulation or figure. As such it is translated into Latin with *figura* or *modellum*. As a rhetorical term, *figura* or *modellum* refers to a configuration similar to an architect's model of a structure which reflects the proportions of the structure in a smaller scale.[1] Likewise, the musical *schematoides* (from *schema to ios*, in like form) presents a formulation similar to the original *figura* or *schema*.

Although a great variety of musical-rhetorical figures are used to effect various harmonic and melodic structural changes, the *schematoides* is unique in its concentration on durational or rhythmic manipulation. If the original notes and duration are retained it is termed *perfectus*,

1. Sonnino, *Handbook*, 100.

indicating that the form remained whole or intact. The altered or *minus perfectus* form of the *schematoides* can be either more (*magis*) or less (*minus*) congruous to the original figuration, depending on how closely the relative proportions of the notes' durations are retained. Vogt refers only to durational changes incurred by a *schematoides*, specifically to rhythmic diminution. It is the only one of his figures which he describes as a "composite" figure (*figura composita*), even though he suggests in his introduction to the figures that this is a separate classification. Although *figurae compositae* do not receive separate attention, Vogt supplies examples of various *figurae simplices* (*groppo*, *messanza*, *circolo*, *tirata*) which are "compounded" in a *phantasia*.[1] The *schematoides* is not listed, however, under the ornamental *figurae simplices* but rather among the expressive *figures ideales*. Vogt thereby wishes to underscore the expressive potential of rhythmic diminution, which can be applied to any musical configuration. The *schematoides*, equally useful for restructuring *simplices* or *ideales* figures, thus compounds both categories of figures while retaining its expressive property.

Printz (*Phrynis Mytilenaeus* pt.2, p.69)
Schematoides ist ein Modulus, so einer Figur zwar / denen Intervallen nach / gleichet / aber doch Prolatione, oder an der Arth hervor zu bringen / von derselben unterschieden ist. Schematoides ist entweder Perfectus oder Minus Perfectus. Schematoides perfectus ist / wenn die Noten und Intervalla durchaus einer Figur gleich seyn / iedoch nicht in einer / sondern vielen Sylben hervor gebracht werden: Und dieses ist allein in Stücken / so einen Text haben / zu finden.

Schematoides is a figuration constructed out of the same intervals of a certain figure, but it differs either in duration or in the manner of execution from the same. The *schematoides* is either *perfectus* or *minus perfectus*. It is *perfectus* when the notes and intervals are the same as those of a figure but is sung to numerous syllables instead of only to one. This is to be found only in vocal music.

1. "Componuntur etiam ad passagio quadruplicis ordinis figurae; ut supra hanc phantasiam: . . ." *Conclave*, 149.

Schematoides minus perfectus ist / wenn die Intervalla zwar gleich / die Prolatio aber langsamer geschicht. Dieser ist entweder magis Congruus, oder minus Congruus. Magis Congruus Schematoides ist / wenn die Intervalla einerley / und die Noten zwar langsamer als in der Figur, iedoch aber mit den Noten der Figur Proportionales seyn. Schematoides minus Congruus ist / wenn die Intervalla zwar gleich seyn einer Figur, die Noten aber nicht mit einander Proportionales seyn.

The *schematoides minus perfectus* occurs when the intervals are the same but of longer duration. This is either *magis congruus* or *minus congruus* [with more or less correspondence]. *Magis congruus schematoides* occurs when the intervals are the same and the notes are slower and yet in equal proportion to the notes of the figure. *Schematoides minus congruus* occurs when the intervals are the same as those of a figure, but the duration of the notes are not of equal proportion to those of the figure.

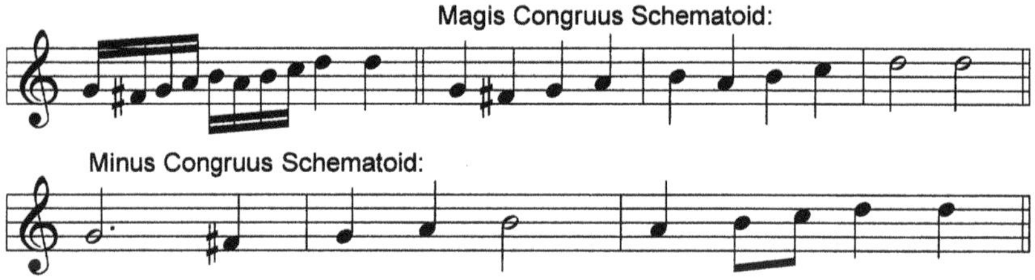

Vogt (*Conclave* p.151)
Schematoides. Figura composita est, cum idem modulus a voce una proportione longa, ab alia tardius incipiente proportione brevi tandem confluit: ut exemplum est in una nostra Missa ad tres choros:

The *schematoides* is a *figura composita*, occuring when the same *modulus* which appears in longer note values in one voice is introduced confluently by another voice beginning somewhat later in shorter note values. An example can be found in one of my masses for three choruses:

SECTIO: see *TMESIS*

SEXTA SUPERFLUA: see *CONSONANTIAE IMPROPRIAE*

SIMUL PROCEDENTIA: see *FAUX BOURDON*

STENASMUS: see *SUSPIRATIO*

SUBSUMPTIO, QUAESITIO NOTAE (CERCAR DELLA NOTA): various additions of lower neighboring notes.

The various methods of adding lower neighboring notes, to which the *anticipatio* could also be added, can be summarized as follows: (1) a lower neighbor can be appended to a principal note at the end of its duration before moving on by step or leap to the next principal note; (2) a lower neighbor can be appended to a principal note moving by step, thereby halving its duration and prematurely introducing the subsequent note if the stepwise progression descends, which is also known as *anticipatio* or *subsumptio postpositiva*; (3) the duration of a principal note can be halved by appending to it the lower neighbor of the following principal note, which is also known as *cercar della nota*, *quaesitio notae*, or *subsumptio praepositiva*. Bernhard lists the three related figures *anticipatio*, *quaesitio notae*, and *subsumptio* separately in his *Tractatus*.[1] All three figures share two common elements: a lower neighbor is added between two principal notes of a voice; the duration of the first principal note is shortened to compensate for the additional note. The term *subsumptio* itself signifies one of the various figures' common elements, namely the addition (*sumere*) of a lower (*sub*) neighbor. Presumably on account of these similarities, the various figures are all incorporated under one figure in Bernhard's *Bericht*. The condition (in the *Tractatus*) that the *subsumptio* only be used in stepwise ascending passages (or the *anticipatio* in stepwise descending ones) does not appear in the *Bericht*, thereby permitting the new variants of *subsumtio*. Furthermore, the reference in *Bericht* that the *subsumptio* is also called *cercar della nota*, Italian for *quaesitio notae* (which is only encountered in the *Tractatus*), also underscores Bernhard's intention to merge the related figures.

To differentiate between the variants of *subsumptio* in the *Bericht*, Bernhard introduces the modifiers *postpositiva* and *praepositiva*. In both instances, the added note is appended to and affects the duration of the first of two principal notes. However, while *postpositiva* signifies the

---

1. See *Anticipatio*.

lower neighbor of the preceding, shortened note, *praepositiva* refers to the lower neighbor of the subsequent, unaltered note. The pre-positioned *subsumptio*, which can be used in passages moving by step or leap, seems to be "searching" for the subsequent note, lending it the name *cercar della nota*, or *quaesitio notae* in Latin. The *subsumptio post-positiva* is limited to passages which ascend *or* descend by step, thereby incorporating the prerequisites in the *Tractatus* for both the *anticipatio* and the *subsumptio*. An anticipation of a note can only be realized if the post-positioned lower neighbor to the preceding note occurs in a step-wise descending passage. In a passage ascending by step, the post-positioned lower neighbors would need to leap up a third to the following notes rather than anticipating them, paralleling the *subsumptio* definition in the *Tractatus*.

Walther's definition of *subsumptio* in his early treatise includes all the variants in terminology, using the Italian *cercar della nota* instead of the Latin *quaesitio notae*. However, he does not restrict the figure to the second part of a note's duration but states that the additional neighboring note can be added to the beginning or the end of a note. Thus he uses the term *praepositiva* to refer to an added neighbor positioned at the beginning of a note or on the beat of the affected principal note. His example indicates that he does not even wish to limit the added note to a lower neighbor. This expansion (or misinterpretation) of Bernhard's *praepositiva* leads him to describe a figure which is virtually indistinguishable from the *accentus*, a fact which he explicitly mentions. Although his *subsumptio post positiva* is closer to Bernhard's figure of the same name, he does not restrict it to a passage moving by step. As his example reveals, in employing the figure in a line which descends by thirds, the *subsumptio* appears more like a rhythmically altered passing note or an added *accentus* than a melodic anticipation. The only remaining way of effecting an anticipation is to anticipate the following text syllable instead of note, a procedure which Walther incorporates with the term *anticipatione della syllaba*. Walther avoids all the confusion in his *Lexicon* by listing only *anticipatio* and *cercar della nota*.

Bernhard (*Tractatus* p.81)

Quaesitio Notae ist, wenn einer vorhergehenden Note etwas abgebrochen wird, daß solches für die folgende im nächsten

The *quaesitio notae* occurs when the part which is broken off of a preceding note is placed in front of the following note one

untern Intervallo gesetzet wird, dadurch denn gleichsam die folgende Note gesuchet wird. Sie wird gar offt in heruntersteigenden Noten, selten aber hinauffwärts gebraucht, es wäre denn in einem Passagio.

degree lower, thereby searching for the subsequent note, as it were. This is frequently employed in descending passages but seldom in ascending ones, except in a *passagio*.

Bernhard (*Tractatus* p.72)
Subsumtio ist, wenn ich einer natürlichen Note, deren folgende eine Secunde steiget, etwas dergestalt nehme, daβ ich solches der ersten im nächsten Intervallo unten anhänge. Subsumtio hat mehr Platz an dem Orte wo 2 Consonantien auffeinander folgen als irgends im Transitu oder Syncopatione.

The *subsumptio* occurs when a regular note which is followed by a note a second higher has a portion of its duration subtracted in such fashion that this portion is appended to the first note one step lower. It is more suitable where two consonances follow each other than in conjunction with a *transitus* or *syncopatio*.

Bernhard (*Bericht* p.148)
Subsumtio von den Italiänern Cercar della nota genennet, ist, wenn ich einer Note im nächsten Intervallo etwas unterwerts hinzusetze. Und ist zweyerley: Denn man entweder dem Anfange oder

The *subsumptio*, called *cercar della nota* by the Italians, occurs when something is added to a note at the next lower pitch. It is of two forms: the next lower note can be appended either to the beginning or to

dem Ende der Note unten etwas anhenget. Wenn man dem Anfange unten etwas anhenget, so könte man sie Subsumtionem praepositivam nennen wie in diesem Exempel.

the end of the note. If it is appended to the beginning, it can be called *subsumptio praepositiva*, as in this example.

Wenn man der Note am Ende eine anhänget, so könte man sie Subsumtionem postpositivam nennen: In singenden Sachen heiβen sie die Italiäner zuweilen Anticipatione della Sillaba, zuweilen Cercare, alβ:

If it is appended to the end of the note, it can be called *subsumptio postpositiva*. In vocal music the Italians at times call this *anticipatione della sillaba*, at times *cercare*, as:

Auβ diesem Exempel ist zuersehen, daβ die Subsumtio postpositiva nur allein stattfindet, wenn die Noten eine secunda fallen oder steigen. Die Subsumtio prae-

From this example it becomes evident that the *subsumptio postpositiva* only occurs when the notes rise or fall a second. The *subsumptio praepositiva* is,

positiva wird aber auch oft über Intervallen gefunden so da springen.

however, also frequently found with leaping intervals.

Walther (*Praecepta* p.153)
Subsumptio. Von denen Italiaenern Cercar della nota, d.i. ein Suchen der Note genennet, ist zweyerley. 1) Wenn man dem Anfange einer Note, oder 2) dem Ende einer Note etwas unten anhänget. Die erste Art kann genennet werden Subsumptio praepositiva oder Anticipatione della nota. Z.E.

Subsumptio, which the Italians call *cercar della nota*, that is a searching of the note, is of two forms, namely when something is appended to the beginning or the end of a note at the next lower pitch. The first form can be called *subsumptio praepositiva* or *anticipatione della nota*. For example:

Diese Figur kann von dem Accent wegen der Verwandtschafft kaum unterschieden werden, als nur hierinne, neml. daβ der Accent meist im Anfange und Ende einer Noten gebrauchet, diese Figur aber sonst in vielsylbigten Wörtern kann angebracht werden. Die andere Art kann genennet werden Subsumptio post positiva oder in Vocal-Sachen Anticipatione della syllaba, auch Errare. Z.E.

Because of the similarity, this figure can hardly be distinguished from the *accentus*, except, namely, that the *accentus* is mostly used at the beginning and end of a note; this figure can also be employed, however, in multisyllable words. The second form can be called *subsumptio post positiva* or *anticipatione della syllaba* in vocal music, also *errare*. For example:

Walther (*Lexicon*)
Cercar della Nota ein Suchen der Note, heisset: wenn zwischen 2 per tertias auf- oder absteigenden Substantial-Noten, noch eine eingerücket, und in der execution gantz gelinde mitgenommen wird; ist also von dem Accent, wegen der Verwandschafft, kaum zu unterscheiden, nur daβ dieser meist im Anfange, und am Ende einer Note gebraucht wird; das Cercar della Nota aber auch sonst in vielsyllbichten Worten angebracht werden kan.

The *cercar della nota*, a searching for the note, occurs when, between two ascending or descending regular notes separated by a third, yet another is inserted and is very gently executed in performance. Because of the similarity, it is hardly distinguishable from the *accentus*, except that the *accentus* is mostly used at the beginning and end of a note, the *cercar della nota*, however, can also be employed in multisyllable words.

SUPERJECTIO: see *ACCENTUS*

SUPPLEMENTUM: see *PARAGOGE*

SUSPENSIO: a delayed introduction of a composition's principal thematic material.

The musical-rhetorical *suspensio* has little in common with the harmonic suspension, a device covered by figures such as *anticipatio*, *ligatura*, *retardatio*, *synaeresis*, and *syncopatio*. Scheibe, who first introduces the *suspensio* into the musical *Figurenlehre*, followed by Forkel, models his definition of the figure on Gottsched's rhetorical definition. Characteristic of many of his figures, Scheibe's *suspensio* concerns the arrangement or *dispositio* of the composition. The figure is used to structure an entire movement or composition rather than to embellish a particular passage or subject. Although the *suspensio* is not to be found in musical *Figurenlehren* before the eighteenth century, it is a familiar rhetorical device since antiquity. Quintilian identifies such a delay with a similar term, *sustentatio*.[1] While he does not indicate the point in an oration at which the figure is to be employed, both Gottsched and Scheibe specify that the *suspensio* is to be used at the beginning of a work. This is further clarified through Scheibe's lengthy illustrations. Both Scheibe and Forkel emphasize that the *suspensio* is not to be confused with the *dubitatio*. The *suspensio* is not to cause uncertainty or doubt in the listener but is to heighten expectations or suspense. The listener must be convinced that the composition has a definite direction, even though the intended goal is not initially perceptible.

Quintilian (*Institutio* IX.ii.22)

Deinde, cum diu suspendisset iudicum animos, subiecit, quod multo esset improbius. Hoc Celsus sustentationem vocat.

And then, after he held the judges in suspense for some time, he added something much worse. This Celsus calls *sustentatio*.

---

1. In his translation of Quintilian's *Institutio*, H. E. Butler translates *sustentationem* with *suspensio*.

Gottsched (*Dichtkunst* p.334)
Es folgt itzo das Aufhalten (Suspensio) als die XVIII. Figur, wenn man nämlich eine Rede ganz von weitem anfängt, und eine gute Weile durch viele Umschweife fortführet: daß der Leser oder Zuhörer nicht gleich weis, was der Poet haben will, sondern das Ende erwarten muß; wo sich der Ausgang zum Labyrinthe, von sich selbst zeiget. Dieser Kunstgriff ist sehr gut, die Leute aufmerksam zu machen.

Next follows the delay or *suspensio* which occurs when an oration begins from a remote point and progresses for a considerable time through numerous digressions in such a manner that the reader or listener cannot immediately discern the intention of the poet, but must await the end where the exit from the labyrinth becomes self-evident. This figure is well suited to make the listeners attentive.

Scheibe (*Critischer Musicus* p.694)
Die IXte Figur ist das Aufhalten, (Suspensio,) wenn man einen Satz ganz von weitem anfängt, und eine gute Weile durch viele Umschweife fortführet, daß der Zuhörer nicht gleich weis, was des Componisten eigentliche Meynung ist, sondern den Schluß erwarten muß, wo sich die Auflösung von sich selbst zeiget. Man muß diese Figur nicht mit dem Zweifel verwechseln, der gewissermaßen eine Aehnlichkeit mit ihr hat. Sie betrifft nicht die Ungewißheit der Tonart, aus welcher man setzet, als welches ein eigentliches Wesen des Zweifels ist, sondern sie betrifft die Einrichtung des Anfangs eines Stückes. So läßt man sehr oft ein Recitativ mit einem Geräusche der Instrumenten anfangen, ohne darinnen einen gewissen Satz zum Grunde zu legen; und der Zuhörer wird so lange aufgehalten, bis endlich die Singestimme eintritt, und die Erklärung der vorhergegangenen Umschweife entdecket. So läßt man ferner in Concerten sehr oft einen langsamen Satz mit einer starken und schwärmenden Modulation der Geigen anheben, bis endlich das Concert-Instrument mit einer angenehmen Melodie eintritt, und die vorhergegangenen fremden und umschweifenden Sätze der Geigen damit verbindet. Dieses pflegt man auch mit veränderten Umständen in geschwinden Sätzen zu thun: daß man nämlich ein Concert mit einer ganz fremden Art von Melodie anfängt, die mehr einer Sym-

The next figure is the delay or *suspensio* which occurs when a passage begins from a remote point and progresses for a considerable time through numerous digressions in such a manner that the listener cannot immediately discern the intention of the composer but must await the end where the resolution becomes self-evident. This figure is not to be confused with the *dubitatio*, which has a certain similarity to it. The *suspensio* does not concern an uncertainty in the intended tonality, which is the essence of the *dubitatio*, but rather concerns the arrangement of the opening of a piece. Frequently, a recitative is allowed to begin with a flurry of instruments without an indication of a specific subject. The listener is held in suspense up to the point of the singer's entry, when the explanation of the preceding digression is discovered. Furthermore a slow movement in a concerto very frequently begins with a powerful and enthusiastic passage for the strings until finally the concerto instrument enters with a pleasant melody, incorporating the preceding foreign and digressing string passage. This is also customary in altered circumstances in fast movements, where, for example, the concerto begins with a completely foreign kind of melody more suitable to a symphony. The listener cannot judge with certainty what he is about to hear until the concerto voice finally enters alone

phonie gemäß ist, und daß der Zuhörer nicht eher gewiß urtheilen kann, was er zu hören bekommen wird, als bis sich endlich die Concertstimme mit ihren eigenen, oder aus den vorhergehenden genommenen Sätzen, allein hören läßt. . . . Es ist also die vornehmste Eigenschaft des Aufhaltens, die Zuhörer in Aufmerksamkeit zu setzen, als wozu sie insonderheit geschickt ist.

with its own theme or one based on the preceding material. . . . It is the distinguishing property of the *suspensio* to move the listener to attentiveness, for which the figure is particularly well suited.

Forkel (*Geschichte der Musik* p.57)
Die Suspension (das Aufhalten) besteht darin, daß man einen Satz durch viele Umwege so fortführt, daß der Zuhörer die Absicht desselben erst am Ende merkt. Diese Figur muß nicht mit der Dubitation verwechselt werden, mit welcher sie einige Aehnlichkeit zu haben scheint. Denn sie ist eigentlich Ausdruck einer Verzögerung, nicht aber einer Ungewißheit.

Through the *suspensio* or delay, a passage is advanced through numerous digressions in such fashion that the listener perceives the purpose of the passage only at the end. This figure is not to be confused with the *dubitatio*, with which it appears to have some similarity. For the *suspensio* is, in fact, an expression of delay, not, however, of uncertainty.

SUSPIRATIO, STENASMUS: a musical expression of a sigh through a rest.

The expressive use of pauses to reflect the text is a well-established practice in Renaissance music.[1] The various musical figures of silence can be classified into two categories: those signifying a breaking off or rupture of the musical line (*abruptio*, *ellipsis*, *tmesis*), and those signifying the ensuing silence (*aposiopesis*, *homoioptoton*, *homoioteleuton*, *pausa*), including *suspiratio* or *stenasmus*. The *suspiratio* or *stenasmus* (from *suspirare*, *stenazo*, to sigh, groan) refers to a specific use of rests within a composition employed to express sighs, gasps, or affections of sighing or longing. The terms do not appear as rhetorical figures; expressions of silence as such would fall under the domain of *elocutio* and would not be a part of the formal structure of an oration. In contrast, musical pauses must be notated in the composition.

1. See *Pausa*.

Kircher discusses the figure twice in his *Musurgia*, first under *pausa* and again under *climax*. While the inclusion of *suspiratio* with *pausa* is self-evident, its connection to the *climax* is explained through the example which the two figures share: "As the deer pants for the water brooks, so my soul pants for Thee, O God."[1] Here the *suspiratio* is to express both the panting as well as the affection of longing (*suspirantis animi affectus*). The figure functions as the musical source for both the specific image as well as the intended affection. As he explains in his definition, eighth and sixteenth rests are also called *suspiria* because they are used to express such sighing and groaning. Vogt's definition of *stenasmus* is found only in his introductory glossary. Here he also lists *tmesis*, describing it as a division of a suspension through short rests or *suspiria*. In his later discussion of the *figurae ideales* he defines *aposiopesis* and *tmesis*, examples of both categories of figures of silence.[2] His definition and example of the *aposiopesis* describe brief silences in the vocal line, expressing a question (*interrogatio*) and reflecting the understanding of the brief *suspiratio* rather than the more common understanding of *aposiopesis* as a general pause.

Printz and Walther define *figura suspirans* simply as a modified *figura corta* in which the longer first note is shortened by half through a rest. As in all of his definitions, Printz does not wish to identify text-expressive devices but simply methods of embellishment. Walther defines the term with the same intentions. It is significant that Walther does not list the term under *suspirans* but rather *figura*, implying that it is simply a notational device. The two categories of expressive or affective figures of silence are represented in his *Lexicon* by *abruptio* and *aposiopesis*.

Kircher (*Musurgia* L.8, pp.144, 145)

Ad hanc revocari potest στεναɑμὸς sive suspiratio, dum per pausas fusas, aut

At this point the *stenasmus* or *suspiratio* can be mentioned, through which we ex-

---

1. Psalm 42.1 (*New American Standard* translation). While rests in the passage exemplify the *suspiratio*, the rising progression is an example of the *climax*. See *Climax*, *Gradatio*.

2. The second definition of *tmesis*—"a splintered passage"— is illustrated through a musical example to the text *suspiro ad te* ("I sigh/pant/long for you"), an example which would do equally well to illustrate a *stenasmus* or *suspiratio*. See *Tmesis*.

semifusas, quae & ideo suspiria vocantur, gementis, & suspirantis animae affectus exprimimus.

press affections of groaning or sighing with eighth or sixteenth rests, which are therefore called *suspiria*.

Ad hanc revocari potest stenasmus id est suspiratio, quae variis suspiriis per pausas, suspirantis animi affectus naturaliter exprimit.

At this point the *stenasmus* or *suspiratio* can be recalled, which naturally expresses affections of sighing through various sighs created through pauses.

Printz (*Phrynis Mytilenaeus* pt.2, p.60)
Figura suspirans ist nichts anders / als eine Figura Corta, welche an statt der förden längern Noten / eine halb so grosse Pause und eine denen andern beyden gleiche Noten hat.

The *figura suspirans* is nothing other than a *figura corta* which, instead of its first longer note, has a pause half its duration and a note of equal duration to the other two notes.

Janovka (*Clavis* p.55)
Ad hanc revocari potest Stenasmus, id est suspiratio, quae variis suspiriis per pausas, suspirantis animi affectus naturaliter exprimit.

At this point the *stenasmus* or *suspiratio* can be mentioned, which naturally expresses affections of sighing through various sighs created through pauses.

Vogt (*Conclave* p.7)
Stenasmus, tractus in cantu suspirando, gemendo.

Stenasmus is a sighing, groaning passage in a composition.

Walther (*Lexicon*)
Figura suspirans ist eben was Figura corta, nur daβ sie, an statt der vordern längern Note, eine halb so grosse Pause, und drauf eine den andern beyden gleiche Note hat.

The *figura suspirans* is like a *figura corta* except that, instead of the first longer note, it has a pause half its duration, followed by a note of equal duration to the other two notes.

SYMBLEMA: see *TRANSITUS*

SYMPLOCE: see *COMPLEXIO*

SYNAERESIS: (1) a suspension or syncopation; (2) a placement of two syllables per note, or two notes per syllable.

Of the two musical definitions which *synaeresis* receives, Vogt's description comes closest to the rhetorical understanding of the figure. Parallel to a grammatical contraction, two syllables can be fused to correspond to one note in the music. Likewise, two notes can accompany one syllable, hardly an unusual occurrence in vocal music. Burmeister introduces *synaeresis* in his *Musica Autoschediastike* as the preferred term for *syncopa*, explaining that it is a conglutination or contraction of two parts into one. In choosing the rhetorical over the traditional musical term, Burmeister intends to establish a closer link between the two disciplines. In fact, the rhetorical device of *synaeresis* is a more accurate description of the musical device than is the rhetorical *syncopa*: while *syncopa* signifies an omission of a letter or syllable, *synaeresis* signifies a fusion.

Burmeister defines the term only toward the end of his definition of *syncopa*, without making any reference to the placement or resolution of dissonances. Thus the *synaeresis* can be understood as a rhythmic suspension or syncopation, not necessarily including a dissonance or harmonic suspension. In the *syncopa* definition in his *Hypomnematum*, Burmeister differentiates between these two forms as being "relatively" and "absolutely" consonant. His musical example, common to both treatises, includes suspensions with and without dissonances, some being purely rhythmic, others combining rhythmic and harmonic displacements. Whether Burmeister wishes to differentiate between these two forms of syncopation with the terms *syncopa* and *synaeresis*, or whether he wishes to replace *syncopa* with *synaeresis* altogether is not clear. In any event, in his *Musica Poetica* Burmeister returns to the customary term, only including *synaeresis* in the heading to his *syncopa* definition without mentioning the term again in the description of the device.

Susenbrotus (*Epitome* p.24)

Synaeresis Συναίρεσις est quoties ex duabus syllabis inter modulandum compactis, sit una.	A *synaeresis* occurs when one syllable is created out of two, compressing the rhythmic meter.

Burmeister (*Musica Autoschediastike*)

Pro syncopa malim usurpari Syneresin, quae est duarum partium in unam conglutinatio. συναίρεσις contractionem vel	Instead of *syncopa* I would prefer to use *syneresis*, which is a fusion of two parts into one. *Synaeresis* signifies a contrac-

compositionem significat. Cuius hocesto exemplum in quo simul & semel omnium generum ferme exempla, quibus similia, omnium autorum carmina, vix pauca exhibent, sunt delineata.

tion or compounding. Following is an example of this figure, delineating nearly every form of the figure all at the same time. Similar examples can be found with little difficulty in compositions of all composers.

Vogt (*Conclave* p.152)

Sinaeresis cum duae notae uno situ pro una Syllaba, vel duae Syllabae pro una nota ponuntur, ut:

A *synaeresis* occurs when two notes are placed for one syllable or two syllables are placed for one note, as in:

SYNATHROISMUS: see *CONGERIES*

SYNCOPATIO, LIGATURA: a suspension, with or without a resulting dissonance.

The suspension is one of the earliest devices described by music theorists as a means of artfully fashioning and embellishing a composition.[1] The figure is associated with rhetoric as early as the sixteenth century through both its designation with a rhetorical term and its use as a text-expressive device. Dressler, who establishes a number of parallels between music and rhetoric, highlights the *syncopatio*, in addition to

1. The term "suspension" is normally used as the English translation of *syncopatio/sycopa* throughout this text on the grounds that, like *syncopatio*, "suspension" implies a "harmonic syncopation" with an ensuing dissonance. The English term "syncopation," on the other hand, is normally understood as a rhythmic shift or irregularity, without necessarily implying harmonic irregularities.

fuga and *clausula*, as *ornamenta* (i.e., figures) which distinguish the work of Clemens. Calvisius considers the suspension most useful "in varying the music and explaining the sense of the text."[1] Burmeister then adopts the well-known musical device along with its name into his *Figurenlehre*, including it among the *figurae harmoniae*. Whether the suspension occurs in one or numerous voices, it can only be perceived, either harmonically, rhythmically, or both, in the context of the entire structure. Burmeister similarly classifies the passing-note dissonance, *symblema*, describing it as the antithesis of *syncopa*. While the *symblema* incurs a dissonance on a weak beat, the *syncopa* generates one on a strong beat.

In his *Musica Autoschediastike* he introduces the term *synaeresis* as an alternative to *syncopa* but includes the same musical example used in his *Hypomnematum*. In choosing this rhetorical term over the traditional musical term, Burmeister intends not only to establish a closer link between the two disciplines but also to adopt a term which most clearly describes the musical phenomenon. In fact, the rhetorical device of *synaeresis* is a more accurate description of the musical device than is the rhetorical *syncopa*: while *syncopa* signifies an omission of a letter or syllable, *synaeresis* signifies a fusion of syllables.[2] Similarly, the musical *syncopa* is consistently described as a fusion of notes resulting in a shift in rhythm rather than as a certain omission. Burmeister may also have been disturbed by the literal meaning of *syncopa* as a strike or attack in describing a musical ornament. In spite of his apparent reservations about the term, he returns to using it exclusively in his *Musica Poetica* definition.

Nucius inaugurates a new classification of the musical figures in his *Figurenlehre*, distinguishing between those figures which are essentially technical musical devices and those which are more closely linked to the text- and affection-expressive rhetorical figures. Nucius, Thuringus, Kircher, and Janovka identify these categories as *figurae principales* and *figurae minus principales*, respectively. Thuringus, who adopts a great deal of Nucius's writings, makes significant changes to the classification

---

1. ". . . ad variandam Harmoniam et ad energian textus demonstrandam." *Melopoiia* (Erfurt, 1592) ch.12; cited in Ruhnke, *Burmeister*, 138.
2. See *Synaeresis*.

of the figures. In addition to substantially increasing the number of musical-rhetorical *figurae minus principales*, he removes the *syncopatio* from this category and places it among the "principal" figures, along with *fuga* and *transitus*. Thuringus's grouping of the figures is then adopted by Kircher and Janovka, as well as Bernhard and Walther, who rename the categories as *figurae fundamentales* and *figurae superficiales*. At the close of the Baroque era these three "principal" or "fundamental" compositional devices are still regarded as a unit, even though their importance as text- and affection-expressive figures is questioned. Scheibe describes them in an appendage to his *Figurenlehre* as merely elementary rules of musical composition.

Kircher like Thuringus counts the *syncopatio* among the *figurae principales*. Because he explains this device earlier in his *Musurgia*, he only mentions it in passing in the chapter dealing with these figures. Janovka, on the other hand, who adopts Kircher's *Figurenlehre* virtually verbatim, defines the *syncopatio* at some length under the *figurae principales*. He also points out that the Greek term is translated into Latin with *ferio, verbero*, meaning to strike, beat, assail. The *syncopatio* flogs the beat, as it were, assailing the established measure of the *tactus*. This focus on the irregularity of the rhythm rather than the dissonances which might ensue is underscored by his explanation that the *syncopatio* can occur with or without dissonances, depending on whether only one voice or all voices are rhythmically shifted or altered.

True to his concept of the musical-rhetorical figures, Bernhard highlights the dissonant elements of the *syncopatio* or *ligatura*. The term *ligatura* is a familiar term since medieval music theory, signifying the "binding" (*ligare*) of two or more *breves* in thirteenth-century modal notation. This concept of binding or tying two notes together to form one ligature is transferred to the suspension. Although Walther uses both terms in his *Praecepta*, he chooses to describe the terms *syncope* and *ligatura* with their original definitions in his *Lexicon*. Both Bernhard and Walther also list further forms of the *syncopatio*. In a *quasi-transitus* the syncopated note is articulated anew, either on the strong beat (i.e., the dissonance) or immediately thereafter, before resolving. As his examples indicate, it can also anticipate the resolution in situations involving a coincidental harmonic change by anticipating the next melody note before the bass moves. Such a combination of *syncopatio* with other figures is frequently mentioned by Bernhard, including in his definitions of *superjectio*, *subsumtio*, *multiplicatio*, *prolongatio*, *ellipsis*, *mora*, and *heterolepsis*. Similar frequent mention is made of the *transitus*, reinforcing Bernhard's intention to explain the various harmonic irregularities as *licentiae* or deviations which are nonetheless based on traditional compositional devices. Walther lists two further types of *syncopatio* in his *Lexicon*: the *syncope consonans aequivagans*, in which all voices are simultaneously syncopated, thereby avoiding any dissonance, and the *syncope consonans desolata*, in which only one voice is syncopated but without incurring a dissonance. The "consonant syncopation" is already included in Janovka's definition of the figure (*sine dissonantiarum commissione*) and is also suggested by Burmeister in his discussion and example of the *synaeresis*. Because of Bernhard's concentration on dissonance use, he does not discuss such consonant syncopations.

The *syncopatio* is discussed once more in Scheibe's *Figurenlehre*, albeit only in a footnote. The constant evolution of the concept of the musical-rhetorical figures is reflected in the relative importance assigned to the *syncopatio*. By the end of the Baroque era the suspension along with imitative counterpoint (*fuga*) and passing dissonances lose their position as principal and fundamental methods of structuring and ornamenting a composition. The primacy of the structural *figurae principales* or *fundamentales* gives way to the expressive and affective musical-rhetorical figures through which a composer, in Forkel's words, is able to individualize general sentiments.

Susenbrotus (*Epitome* p.22)

Syncope, est cum litera vel syllabe e dictionis medio tollitur.

The *syncope* occurs when a letter or syllable is removed from the middle of a word.

Burmeister (*Hypomnematum*)

Syncopa est Symblemati contrarium, sit licet vicinum ornamentum, duas partes alicujus tactus vel integri vel dimidii; vel etiam quadrantis, in aliqua voce coagmentans, quarum posterior pars ex contractione, relative consonat, quam mox in locum demissum proxime vicinum consonantia subsequitur congruens, cum universa structura, quae non procul a natura clausularum abest. Relativa con-

The *syncopa* is opposite to the *symblema* but allows a related ornament. It occurs when two parts of a certain whole, half, or quarter *tactus* within one voice are joined. The latter part of this contraction results in a *relativa consonantia* which is pleasantly followed by the lower neighboring consonance so that the entire structure does not deviate far from the nature of the cadence. A *relativa con-*

sonantia est, quae, licet cum iis quibus annexa est ad perpendiculum videatur dissonare, atque ob id pro discordantia haberi possit, non tamen propter Syncopen dissonat. Absoluta est quae cum omnibus sonis ad perpendiculum connexa, consonat.

sonantia is one which, although it seems to be dissonant with those notes with which it is vertically aligned and on this account could be held for a dissonance, nonetheless is not dissonant because of the *syncopa*. An *absoluta consonantia* is one which is consonant with all the notes with which it is vertically combined.

Burmeister (*Musica Poetica* p.60)
Syncopa συνκοπὴ contrario modo se habet ad Symblema. Syncopa committit Dissonantiam in Initio Tactus Minoris, vel etjam Majoris. Dissonantia autem illa est Dissonantia relativa, & pars soni praecedentis tactus, cum qua illa est per Syncopationem in unum aliquod integrum conglutinata. Diversae etjam partes in quoddam totum contrabuntur, quae ratione aequalitatis tactuum & in eis connexionum concordantiam dissolutae esse deberent.

The *syncopa* is opposite in character to the *symblema*. The *syncopa* causes a dissonance at the beginning of a *tactus minoris* or *majoris*. However, that dissonance, as a part of the *tactus* of the preceding note, is a *dissonantia relativa*, inasmuch as it is fused into a pure [consonance] through the *syncopa*. Also, diverse parts are combined into a whole which, through the requirements of both a regular *tactus* and in themselves being agreeing consonances, must be resolved.

Nucius (*Musices Poeticae* p.G3^r)
Quid est Syncopatio? Cum contra tactum plures Semibreves notae diutius protractae, tandem in clausulam abeunt, ac usurpatur creberrime in Discantu, in caeteris non ita frequenter: figura omnibus notissima, ideo exemplo non indiget.

What is a *syncopatio*? When numerous *semibreves* are extended against the *tactus* but finally resolve in the cadence. It is used more frequently in the discant than in the other voices. As this figure is most familiar to everyone, it therefore requires no example.

Thuringus (*Opusculum* p.119)
Sesquitur iam tertia figura principalis, quae est Syncopatio, figura omnibus notissima. Quid vocant Musici Syncopationem? Cum majores notulae inclusae minoribus contra tactum incedunt, quae ratio & artificiosum & gratum & suavem reddit cantum; usurpatur celeberrime in Discantu, in caeteris non ita frequenter.

And now follows the third *figura principalis*, the *syncopatio*, a figure most familiar to all. What do composers call a *syncopatio*? When longer confined notes are advanced against the *tactus* through shorter ones, which renders an artful, agreeable, and pleasant composition. It is used more frequently in the discant than in other voices.

Kircher (*Musurgia* L.5, p.368)
Secunda figura est Syncopatio, de qua cum abundantissime in alio capitulo particulari actum fit, supervacaneum esse arbitror, ea denuo repetere.

The second [*principalis*] figure is the *syncopatio*, which was discussed in great detail in another chapter. I find it to be superfluous to repeat it here again.

Bernhard (*Tractatus* p.67)

Die Syncopation, welche etliche eine Ligatur nennen ist, wenn eine rückende Note gegen eine Consonantz und Dissonantz stehet. NB. Unter die rückenden Noten gehören auch die durch einen Punkt vermehrten. Daher soll die rückende Note gegen ihren ersten Theil eine Consonantz, und gegen den anderen Theil eine Dissonantz haben. . . . Die auff die rückende folget muβ eine Secunde fallen und consoniren.

The *syncopatio*, which some call *ligatura*, occurs when a rhythmically shifted note stands against a consonance and a dissonance. NB: notes extended through a dot are also considered among the shifted ones. Therefore a shifted note is to have a consonance against its first part and a dissonance against its second part. . . . The note following the shifted note must fall a second and be consonant.

(*Tractatus* p.70)

Quasi-Syncopatio ist der gebundenen. . . Stimme Aufflösung. Die richtet sich allerdings nach denen Regeln der Syncopation, und hat keine statt wo dieselbe nicht seyn kan. Sie wird aber selten gebraucht, doch zum meisten in der Quarta, als welche doch nicht so sehr von der natur der Dissonantzen participiret.

The *quasi-syncopatio* is a subdivision of the tied or shifted note. However, it follows the rules of the *syncopatio* and has no place where the *syncopatio* may not occur. It is seldom used, yet usually with a fourth, as the fourth does not share the nature of dissonances to the same extent.

(*Tractatus* p.77)

Syncopatio catachrestica ist, wenn eine Syncopatio nicht, wie die Regel erfordert, durch eine folgende Consonantz, so eine Secunde tieffer ist, resolviret wird. Und ist dreyerley: Entweder die gebundene Stimme fält zwar eine Secunde aber nicht in eine Consonatz. . . . Wo das erste Theil der rückenden Note nicht recht völlig consoniret, ist die andere Art. Oder die Note, so auff die rückende folget, fält nicht eine Secunde.

The *syncopatio catachrestica* occurs when a *syncopatio* is not resolved through a subsequent consonance a second lower, as the rule requires. It is of three kinds: the tied note may, in fact, fall a second but not to a consonance. . . . Second, the first part of the shifted note is not entirely consonant. Third, the note following the shifted note does not fall a second.

Bernhard (*Bericht* p.144)

Ligatura, sonst auch Syncopatio genand, ist, wenn eine rückende Note gegen einer Consonans und Dissonans zu finden. In solcher Ligatur ist folgendes zu beobachten: 1) daß sie sich rücken müße, 2) daß ihre Helffte gut, die andere schlimm sey. 3) daß die nächste auf die rückende folgende Note eine Secunda niedriger stehe. Die Rückung ist entweder offenbar . . . oder wird durch einen Punct an der Note hengend verstanden.

The *ligatura*, also called *syncopatio*, occurs when a shifted note is placed against a consonance and a dissonance. The following is to be observed in such a *ligatura*: (1) it must be a rhythmically shifted note; (2) its one half must be good, the other bad; (3) the note following the shifted note must stand a second lower. The rhythmic shift must either be clearly evident . . . or it is implied through a dot added after the note.

Janovka (*Clavis* p.47)

Syncopatio seu Syncopsis vox a verbo graeco Syncopo, quod latine ferio seu verbero in latinum translata, sic dicta, quod notae sic contra tactum expressae & decantatae tactum mensurantis quasi feriant vel verberent; Tactus enim aequaliter mensuratur, notae autem Syncopatae inaequaliter, sed contra eum quasi franguntur. Unde definitur, quod sit irregularis notae ad Tactum facta applicatio, propter minorem notam praecedentem. Dupliciter fieri solet: primo sine dissonantiarum commissione, quae tamen improprie Syncopatio dicitur. Secundo dissonantiarum interventione.

The *syncopatio* or *Syncopsis*, from the Greek word *Syncopo*, translated into Latin as *ferio* (to strike) or *verbero* (to assail), is thus called because the notes are expressed and sung against the *tactus* in such a manner as if to strike against or assail the measured beat. For the *tactus* is measured equally, but syncopated notes are unequal and are shattered, as it were, against the *tactus*. It is therefore defined as an addition to the *tactus* of an irregular note through a preceding shorter note. This occurs in two forms: first, without causing dissonances, which are nevertheless called *syncopatio improprie*; second, with intervening dissonances.

Walther (*Praecepta* p.140)

Syncopatio oder Ligatura ist, wenn die Noten wieder den Tact tractiret werden, und so lange inaequaliter einhergehen, biß sie mit dem Tacte wieder in Ordnung kommen. Dicitur a συνκόπτω, i.e. verbero, ferio, quia notulae sic contra tactum expresse et decantatae, tactum qs. feriunt: Tactus n. aequaliter mensuratur, notulae autem syncopatae non aequaliter, sed contra eum tractantur. Diese Rückung geschicht entweder cum oder sine Dissonantiarum intermixtione. Sine Dissonantiarum intermixtione entstehet syncopatio auf folgende und andere dergl. Art.

The *syncopatio* or *ligatura* occurs when notes are placed against the beat and remain unequal until such time as they are once again brought into agreement with the beat. *Syncopatio*, from *synkopto*, *verbero*, *ferio*, occurs when notes are expressed and sung against the beat in such a manner as if to strike against the beat, resulting in an unequally measured *tactus* through the unequal syncopated notes which are placed against it. This shift occurs either with or without intermingled dissonances. A *syncopatio* without intermingled dissonances occurs in the following and other similar manners:

Cum Dissonantiarum intermixtione entstehet syncopatio auf 4ley Art und weise: worbey zu observiren, 1) Wie die Consonantien sich in Dissonantien verändern, und 2) Wie diese hinwiederum in Consonantien sich resolviren. 1) Da dann, was das erste anlanget, wohl zu mercken ist, daβ alle Dissonantien . . . vom vorhergehenden Satze schon liegen müβen; . . . 2) muβ die syncopirte Note sich in thesi des Tactes gemeiniglich anfangen, und in arsi deβelben sich wieder enden; oder eine neue Syncopation wieder anheben. . . . 3) muβ die syncopirte Note mit der vorher gehenden entweder gleich, oder kürtzer; niemahls aber länger seyn. Was nun zum andern, neml. Resolutionem Dissonantiarum, anlanget, sind solche in folgenden also angebracht, daβ dasjenige, was auβer angeführten Gängen solte gefunden werden, nicht aller Dings vor zuläβig zu halten.

A *syncopatio* with intermingled dissonances occurs in four forms with following considerations: (1) how the consonances are altered into dissonances, and (2) how the dissonances are again resolved into consonances. Regarding the first point, it must be carefully noted that (1) all dissonant notes must already be in place from the preceding harmony; . . . (2) the syncopated note normally must begin on an upbeat and end on a downbeat of a *tactus* or begin a new *syncopatio*; . . . (3) the syncopated note must be of equal duration or shorter but never longer than the preceding note. Regarding the other point, namely the resolution of the dissonances, the following discussion will present this in such a manner that progressions apart from the presented ones cannot be considered admissible.

Walther (*Lexicon*)

Syncopatio oder syncope . . . vom Griechischen Verbo συνκόπτω, ferio, verbero, ich schlage; bedeutet eine wieder den Tact angebrachte Rück- oder Zertheilung einer Note, so ein Semibrevis, Minima oder Semiminima seyn kan.

Syncopatio or *syncope*, from the Greek *synkopto*, *ferio*, *verbero*, I strike, signifies a shifting or division of a note placed against the beat through either a *semibrevis*, *minima*, or *semiminima*.

Syncopatio catachrestica, ist: wenn eine dissonirende Note nicht, wie es sonst die Regel erfordert, durch eine folgende consonirende, die um ein Grad tiefer liegt, andere, fremdere, weitentlegenere, und höhere Consonanz, auch wohl gar durch eine abermahlige Dissonanz, einen Ausweg suchet.

The *syncopatio catachrestica* occurs when a dissonant note is not resolved according to the rule through a following consonance which lies one step lower but which seeks an evasion through another, foreign, distant, and higher consonance or even through yet another dissonance.

Syncope consonans aequivagans, oder syncopatio sine dissonantiarum inter-

The *syncope consonans aequivagans* or *syncopatio sine dissonantiarum inter-*

mixtione, ist: wenn alle Stimmen zugleich ohne dissonanz sich rücken, und wieder den Tact gehen.

mixtione (without intermingled dissonances) occurs when all voices are shifted simultaneously and are placed against the beat without incurring a dissonance.

Syncope consonans desolata ist: wenn nur eine Stimme, und zwar ohne dissonanz sich rücket.

The *syncope consonans* occurs when only one voice is shifted without incurring a dissonance.

Syncope consono-dissonans ist: wenn der erste Theil der Note, so wieder den Tact gehet, consoniret, der zweyte Theil aber derselben dissoniret, worauf wieder eine Consonanz folget, welche die syncopirte Stimme mit ordentlichen Absteigen machet. Diese ist wiederum zweyerley: Tactualiter dissecta und Realiter dissecta. Jene behält die syncopirte oder wieder den Tact gehende Note gantz: diese aber zertheilet sie wegen des Texts würcklich.

The *syncope consono-dissonans* occurs when the first part of the note which goes against the beat is consonant, its second part, is dissonant, followed by another consonance which descends one step from the syncopated note. This is of two forms: *tactualiter dissecta* and *realiter dissecta*. In the first case, the syncopated note which stands against the beat remains intact. In the second case, the note is subdivided to accommodate the text.

Scheibe (*Critischer Musicus* p.698)

Ligatura und Syncopatio, oder Syncope, die Bindung, ist, wenn aus zwo Noten

The *ligatura* (*syncopatio* or *syncope*), the tie, occurs when one note is constructed

eine gemachet wird, also daβ wider die gewöhnliche Beschaffenheit oder Eintheilung des Taktes, eine accentuirte Note an die unaccentuirte Note gebunden ist. Diese Figur dienet eigentlich dazu, den Gebrauch der Dissonanzen angenehmer und lieblicher zu machen; wiewohl sie auch sehr oft nur bey den Consonanzen gebrauchet wird. Sonst nennet man sie auch eine zierliche Rückung des Taktes.

out of two by tying an accented note to an unaccented one against the normal structure or division of the beat. This figure actually serves to make the use of dissonances more agreeable and pleasant, although it is also often used only with consonances. It is furthermore also called a graceful shifting of the beat.

SYNONYMIA: an altered or modified repetition of a musical idea.

The *synonymia* is first mentioned in Ahle's *Figurenlehre*. His point of departure is not a musical device but rather the rhetorical figures found in the text which are to receive musical expression or consideration. The composer is to observe not only the figures which can be transferred from the literary to the musical medium but indeed all rhetorical figures found in the text. He is to apply the rhetorical *Figurenlehre*, constructing literary figures in the text and then observing them in his setting when appropriate. It is in this spirit that Ahle includes the *synonymia*. Walther cites Ahle in his *Praecepta* regarding the use of rhetorical figures. In his discussion of setting the text, Walther encourages the composer to "employ various rhetorical figures in elaborating a text." However, in listing and defining the musical-rhetorical figures to be used in a composition, Walther does not mention *synonymia*. In his *Lexicon* Walther includes all of Ahle's figures except for *asyndeton*, *polysyndeton* (a lack or excess of conjunctions), and *synonymia*. Presumably these are omitted due to the difficulty in expressing these rhetorical devices in the music.

Mattheson is the first author to lend *synonymia* a musical interpretation. In his discussion of the *loci topici*, specifically the *locus notationis*, Mattheson suggests that a composer might draw ideas for his *inventio* from the notes themselves: "In like manner [to words and letters], yea, even more successfully and fittingly, the formation and placement of the notes as sounding letters lead us to innumerable alterations, of which especially the following four procedures are to be singled out: (1) through the duration of the notes; (2) through inversions or exchanges; (3) through repetitions or answers; and (4) through canonic progressions."[1] Mattheson then equates various altered repetitions or the fugal *repercussio*, a modified or tonal answer to the fugal subject, with rhetorical *clausulae synonymae*. Just as it is possible to restate a certain linguistic idea in an altered form, so too can a musical idea be modified. Thus *synonymia* is more of a process than a specific device, incorporating numerous forms of altered repetition and having a great deal in common with the general *imitatio*.[2]

Forkel is much more explicit in his description of a musical *synonymia*. Like Mattheson, he does not discuss the device in the context of the musical-rhetorical figures. Unlike Mattheson, however, he deals with "synonymous expressions" in his discussion of the musical *dispositio* rather than *inventio*. Forkel applies the concept of the musical-rhetorical figures to larger portions of a composition, resulting in an understanding of these devices as methods for structuring the composition rather than only elaborating its parts. Synonymous expressions can be used to execute subdivisions (*Zergliederungen*) of a principal theme. In his example of a synonymous expression, Forkel restates a given passage through a harmonic variant, similar to his example of "individualizations of general sentiments."[3] While the *distributio* is a method of subdividing or dissecting a principal theme, the *synonymia* or synonymous form of expression is the method used to vary these dissected parts.

Quintilian (*Institutio* IX.iii.45)

Aliquando, sicut in geminatione verborum diximus, initia quoque et clausulae sententiarum aliis, sed non alio tendentibus verbis inter se consonant. . . . Hoc alii συνωνυμίαν, alii disiunctionem vocant, utrumque, etiamsi est diversum, recte; nam est nominum idem significantium separatio.

Occasionally, as was stated regarding the repetition of words, the beginnings and endings of sentences correspond to each other through various words with the same meaning. . . . This some call *synonymia* and others *disiunctio*. And although the terms are different, they are both correct, for the *synonymia* signifies different words with the same meaning.

---

1. "Eben also . . . führen uns auch die Gestalt und Stelle der Noten, als Klang-Buchstaben, zu schier unzehligen Veränderungen, bey welchen man sich insonderheit diese vier Wege belieben läßt: 1) durch die Geltung der Noten; 2) durch die Verkehr- oder Verwechselung; 3) durch die Wiederholung oder den Wiederschlag; und 4) durch die canonischen Gänge." *Capellmeister*, 124.

2. See *Mimesis*.

3. See *Distributio*.

Gottsched (*Redekunst* p.278)
Synonymia. Wenn man etliche gleich vielheissende Wörter setzt.

Synonymia. When a number of words with the same meaning are used.

Gottsched (*Dichtkunst* p.326)
Zur XIten kann die Verdoppelung (Synonymia) einer und derselben Sache, die aber mit ganz andern Worten geschieht, gezogen werden. Einer, der im Affecte steht, bemüht sich seinen Lesern und Zuhörern die Sachen recht einzuprägen und einzutrichtern. Daher sagt er ihnen auch wohl einerley Ding etlichemal, nur immer mit andern Ausdrückungen.

The next figure is the doubling (*synonymia*) of one and the same thought but with entirely different words. An impassioned person endeavors to influence and persuade his readers and listeners of his thoughts. He will therefore also say the same thing a number of times but always with different expressions.

Ahle (*Sommer-Gespräche* p.17)
Setzet er weiter: singet / rühmet und lobet; oder: jauchzet / singet / rühmet und lobet; so ist es eine Synonymia.

Were he further to set: sing, glorify, and praise; or rejoice, sing, glorify, and praise, it would be a *synonymia.*

Walther (*Praecepta* p.158)
Es mag zwar wohl ein Componist in elaborirung eines textes unterschiedl. rhetorische Figuren anwenden (vid: Joh. Georg Ahlens musical. Sommer Gespräche par: 16 u. 17) Z.E. die Epizeuxin, als die gebräuchlichste und emphatischste: die Anaphoram, Synonymiam, Anadiplosin, Epistrophen, Epanalepsin, u.s.f.

A composer can also well employ different rhetorical figures in elaborating a text (see Ahle's *Musicalische Sommer-Gespräche*, pp.16 and 17). For example, the *epizeuxis*, which is the most common and emphatic, the *anaphora*, *synonymia*, *anadiplosis*, *epistrophe*, *epanalepsis*, an so on.

Mattheson (*Capellmeister* p.124f.)
Der dritte Weg, darauf uns diese Notations-Quelle der Erfindung führet, begreifft die Wiederholungen, mit ihrem Kunst-Worte clausulae synonymae genannt, oder was man sonst in fugirten Sachen den Wiederschlag nennet, d.i. wenn ich einen gewissen Satz in andre Höhe oder Tiefe versetze.

The third method suggested by this notational source [*locus notationis*] of *inventio* encompasses the repetitions, known by the art word *clausulae synonymae* or what is otherwise called *Wiederschlag* (repercussion) in fugal pieces, that is, when a certain passage is transferred to higher or lower placements.

Forkel (*Geschichte der Musik* p.51)
Die Zergliederungen eines Hauptsatzes dienen dazu, ihn von allen seinen verschiedenen Seiten und Gesichtspunkten zu zeigen. . . . Die Absicht eines Tonstücks kann seyn: eine individuelle, oder eine allgemeine Empfindung zu schildern. In beyden Fällen sind der Beziehungen und Verhältnisse so viele, daβ die

The subdivisions [*distributio*] of a principal theme serve to examine the musical material from all sides. . . . A composition's intention can be to express either an individual or a general sentiment. In both cases the relationships and circumstances are so diverse that the sentiments cannot be sufficiently clarified

Empfindung ohne Auflösung in ihre einzelne Theile nicht deutlich genug werden kann. Man bedient sich zu dieser Auflösung eben so wie in der Sprache, mehrerley Mittel; wir haben z.B. auch in der Musik synonymische Ausdrücke, Umschreibungen verschiedener Arten, Versetzungen u.s.f. ja sogar eine Individualisirung allgemeiner Empfindungen läßt sich in den musikalischen Ausdrücken denken. Synonymische Ausdrücke sind zwar der Hauptbedeutung nach einerley; können aber doch eine Empfindung von irgend einer andern Seite blos dadurch zeigen, daß sie einen kleinen Nebenumstand daran ausdrücken. Folgende zwey Takte:

without dissolving them into their separate parts. Such a dissolution employs devices similar to linguistic ones: for example, in music we also have synonymous expressions, diverse forms of restatement, displacements, and so on. Even an individualization of general sentiments can be musically expressed. Although synonymous expressions are of the same general meaning, they can each only illustrate a sentiment from their particular perspective by expressing a small incidental detail relating to the whole. The following two bars:

sind der Hauptbedeutung nach völlig einerley; demohngeachtet modificiren sie den Gedanken so, daß das Ohr weit geneigter ist, ihn für einen neuen als für den nemlichen Gedanken zu nehmen. Die Umschreibung erweitert einen kurzen Satz, sammelt seine meisten nächsten Merkmale auf, und sucht ihn dadurch deutlicher zu machen. So würde z.B. der [folgende] Satz durch diese Umschreibung folgende Gestalt bekommen:

are completely identical in their general meaning. In spite of that they modify the expression in such a manner that the ear is far more inclined to consider it a new expression rather than the same one. Such a restatement expands a short passage, gathers its most significant features, and thereby seeks to lend it greater clarity. For example, the following progression can be rewritten to give it the following form:

TENUTA: see *RIBATTUTA*

TERTIA DEFICIENS: see *CONSONANTIAE IMPROPRIAE*

TIRATA: a rapid scalar passage, spanning a fourth to an octave or more.

The *tirata* is a musical embellishment belonging to the category of *Manieren* (Mattheson) or *figurae simplices* (Spiess). Printz and Walther differentiate between four variants of the ornament: a *tirata mezzo* consists of only a short run, spanning no more than a fourth; the *tirata defectiva, perfecta,* and *aucta* span at least a fifth, exactly an octave, and more than an octave, respectively. While Printz's examples indicate a rapid figure, Walther allows the *tirata* also to be constructed of slowly moving notes. He translates the Italian term with *Zug* (a tug, stroke) or *Strich* (a dash, line), mentioning in his definition that the figure can also refer especially to a rapid succession of notes. Mattheson sarcastically refutes Brossard's and his disciples' interpretation (clearly implying Walther, who frequently cites Brossard) of the *tirata* as a "leisurely" progression, insisting that the device consists of a "tirade" of notes, "vigorously bolting upwards or downwards" like a spear throw or bow-shot.

Although Mattheson regards *Manieren* as ornamental embellishments which are added to the music by the performer, they can also be used to lend the music a great deal more emphasis. Such an expressive and affective use of a *Manier* is illustrated in his discussion of the *accentus*. A similar expressiveness is expected of the *tirata*. Like the *accentus*, the *tirata* can also assume both a text-expressive and affective role, particularly when employed in conjunction with a text which is related to the figure's name. In Handel's oratorio *Saul*, Saul's javelin throw at David, occurring five bars into the second section of the aria *A serpent in my bosom warm'd* (Act I), is vividly portrayed in the music, bringing the aria to an abrupt stop. Here the *tirata* is not a simple *Manier* improvised by the musician but rather becomes an affective expression of *hypotyposis*.

Printz (*Phrynis Mytilenaeus* pt.2, p.49)

Tirata meza ist eine Figur, so in vier ordentlich auff- oder absteigenden geschwinden Noten bestehet. Sie ist entweder Adscendens, so ordentlich hinauff

The *tirata meza* is a figure consisting of four stepwise, rapidly ascending or descending notes. It is either *adscendens*, which runs upwards by step, or *descen-*

lauffet / oder Descendens, so ordentlich hinunter fähret.

dens, which runs downwards by step.

(*Phrynis Mytilenaeus* pt.2, p.64)
Tirata ist / wenn etliche ordentlich-auff- oder ablauffende Figuren ordentlich in nechst-folgenden Clavibus an einander gehangen werden. Sie ist entweder Defectiva, oder Perfecta, oder Aucta. Defectiva ist / welche zwar die Quint überschreitet / doch die Octav nicht erreichet. Perfecta ist / welche gerad in Octavam laufft. Aucta ist / welche die Octav überschreitet.

The *tirata* occurs when a number of similarly stepwise ascending or descending running figures are linked together at their subsequent pitches. It can be either *defectiva*, *perfecta*, or *aucta*. *Defectiva* refers to a *tirata* which exceeds a fifth but does not reach the octave. *Perfecta* refers to a *tirata* which spans an octave exactly. *Aucta* refers to a *tirata* which exceeds an octave.

Walther (*Lexicon*)
Tirata [ital.] Tirade [gall.] bedeutet einen Zug oder Strich, und überhaupt eine Reihe vieler Noten von einerley Geltung, die so wohl auf- als absteigend einander gradatim folgen.

Tirata or *tirade* means a stroke or line, and especially a row of numerous notes of the same duration which either ascend or descend by step.

Die mit dem A bezeichnete Art heisset: Tirata di Semiminime; und die mit dem B. Tirata di legature; insonderheit aber: wenn nurbesagte Reihe Noten aus vielen Achteln oder Sechzehntheilen bestehet, vor welchen fast allezeit eine Sechzehntheil-Pause hergehet, und auf welche ordinairement eine grössere Note folget. Man theilet sie in vier Sorten, die 1.) Tirata mezza, oder mezza Tirata, bestehet aufs höchste aus drey oder vier zweygeschwäntzten Noten, und machet demnach mit der drauf folgenden Note entweder ein quart- oder quint-intervallum

Example A is called *tirata di semiminime*, the other *tirata di legature*. Specifically, however, the figure consists of a row of eighth or sixteenth notes, almost always preceded by a sixteenth rest and followed by a note of longer duration. There are four kinds of *tirata*: (1) the *tirata mezza* or *mezza tirata*, consisting at most of three or four sixteenth notes which span a fourth or fifth, including the following note; (2) the *tirata defectiva*, which in fact actually exceeds the fifth but does not reach an octave; (3) the *tirata perfecta*, which fulfills the octave com-

aus. Die 2.) Tirata defectiva überschreitet zwar würcklich das quint-intervallum; erreichet aber die Octav nicht. Die 3.) Tirata perfecta erreichet die Octav vollkommen, so, daß keine Note mehr, weder drüber noch drunter vorkommt; und die 4.) Tirata aucta oder excedens überschreitet die Grentzen der Octav um einige Noten.

pletely, so that neither a note more or a note less appears; and (4) the *tirata aucta* or *excedens*, which exceeds the range of an octave by a few notes.

Mattheson (*Capellmeister* p.117)
Nun kommen wir zur Tirata, welche bey itzigen Zeiten auf gewisse Weise einen stärckern Gebrauch hat, als die vorhergehende Manier, und eigentlich einen Schuß oder Pfeilwurff, nicht aber, wie die meisten Ausleger wollen, einen Zug oder Strich bedeutet, weil die Stimme nicht bloßhin gezogen oder gestrichen wird, sondern mit Macht herauf oder herunter schiesset, und ein gar schnelles Schleuffen, gemeiniglich in Pans Quint, auch wol in die Octav, doch seltener anstellet. Daher ich denn das gemächliche Auf- und Niederziehen der Sing-Leiter (Scalae) in lauter halben Schlägen mit diesem Tiraten-Nahmen unmöglich belegen kan, wie Brossard, und einige seiner Jünger thun, ohne ihn zu nennen: indem dabey weder schleuffen noch lauffen, weder Zug noch Strich, vielweniger etwas, das einem Spieß-Schuß, Pfeil-Wurff oder dergleichen ähnlich wäre, sondern ein gantz spanischer Gang, Fuß vor Fuß, zu erblicken ist. Nun folgen Muster von rechten Tiraten; wobey sich von ungefehr auch ein Halbcirckel meldet.

We now come to the *tirata*, which to a certain degree finds stronger use nowadays than the previous figure [*circulo mezzo*]. It actually means a shot or spear throw, and not a stroke or line, as most commentators insist, for the voice is not simply pulled through or lined in but forcefully bolts upward or downward, resulting in a rapid spurting commonly exceeding a fifth, and at times, albeit less frequently, even encompassing an octave. It is therefore impossible for me to assign the name *tirata* to such a leisurely scale passage, ascending or descending only in half notes, as Brossard and some of his disciples (without naming him) do. For it contains no spurting or running, neither stroke nor line, much less something which resembles a spear throw, bowshot, or the like, but rather appears to be a most ordinary and plodding progression. Now follow examples of real *tirate*, intermingled by chance with a *circulo mezzo.*

Spiess (*Tractatus* p.156)
Tirata, bedeutet überhaupt eine Reihe vieler Noten von einerley Geltung, die sowohl auf- als absteigend einander gradatim folgen. Walther v. Tirata. Die Noten können frey oder gebunden seyn.

Tirata specifically signifies a row of numerous notes of the same duration which either ascend or descend by step. See Walther, *Tirata.* The notes can be free or tied. Moreover, a *tirata* is *perfetta* if it

Ubringens ist Tirata perfetta, so die Octavam: Mezza, so sie nur die Quintam erreichet.

spans an octave and *mezza* if it spans a fifth.

TMESIS: a sudden interruption or fragmentation of the melody through rests.

Both the musical and the rhetorical *tmesis* signify a fragmentation, reflecting the literal meaning of the word as a cut or incision. While intervening words interrupt a compound word through the rhetorical figure, inserted pauses interrupt a note through the musical figure. The interruption of the word *suspiro* (I sigh) in the musical example provided by Vogt and Spiess results in a simultaneous musical and rhetorical *tmesis*: both the word (albeit not a compound one) and the melody are interrupted through rests. In Vogt's first definition, found in his introductory glossary, the figure is described as a suspension interrupted by *suspiria.* As Kircher explains in his definition of *suspiratio*, eighth and sixteenth rests are also called *suspiria* because they are used to express such sighing and groaning. In the musical example in his second definition of *tmesis* Vogt then illustrates how the suspensions in the vocal line are "splintered" through interrupting rests or *suspiria.*

The various musical figures of silence can be classified into two categories: those signifying a breaking off or rupture of the musical line, including *abruptio*, *ellipsis*, and *tmesis*, and those signifying an ensuing silence, including *aposiopesis*, *homoioptoton*, *homoioteleuton*, *pausa*, and *suspiratio*. Although the *tmesis* and *suspiratio* represent the two contrasting categories of figures of silence, they are both applied to individual melodic lines rather than to the entire musical texture. In contrast, the *abruptio* and the *aposiopesis*, also representing the two categories of silence figures, affect all the voices of a composition, the *abruptio* indicating a breaking off in all the voices, and the *aposiopesis* signifying a general pause.

Susenbrotus (*Epitome* p.35)
Tmesis Τμῆσις Diacope Διακοπή est unius dictionis compositae divisio, una dictione pluribue interiectis, Latine Sectio, sive Intercisio. Mancinellus: Dat Tmesim partes in binas dictio secta.

The *tmesis* or *diacope* signifies the division of a compound word through the interjection of one or more other words. It is called *sectio* or *intercisio* (a cutting) in Latin. According to Mancinellus, *tmesis* is a word divided into two parts.

Vogt (*Conclave* p.7)
Tmema vel Tmesis, sectio syncopatica, suspiria.

Tmema or *Tmesis*, the division of a *syncopatio* with a short rest (*suspiria*).

(*Conclave* p.152)
Tmesis sectio. Fit sparsim per periodos, ut hoc modo:

The *tmesis* or *sectio* (a cutting) consists of a splintered passage, as in the following example:

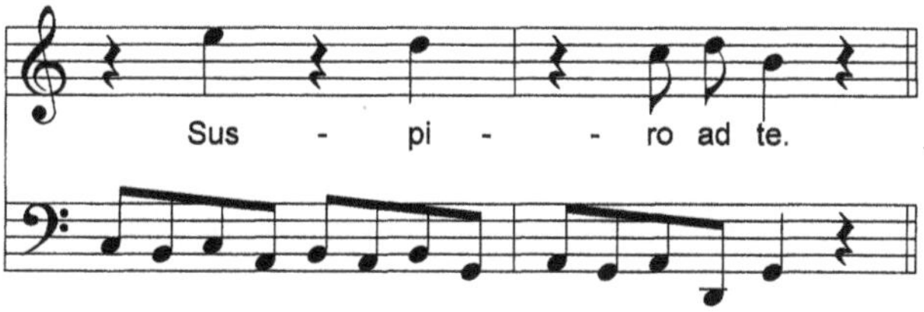

Spiess (*Tractatus* p.156)
Tmesis, Sectio, Abschnitt, geschicht, wie und wann es der Text oder Affect erfordert. v.g. in dem Wort Suspiro:

The *Tmesis*, *sectio*, cutting, occurs whenever and wherever the text or the affection demands, as in the example to the word *suspiro* (sigh).

TRANSGRESSIO: see *METABASIS*

TRANSITUS, CELERITAS, COMMISSURA, DEMINUTIO, SYMBLEMA: a dissonant or passing note between two consonant ones, on either the strong or the weak beat.

Throughout the centuries, the passing note has been described with a variety of terms, a number of them having roots in classical rhetoric. The term *transitus* has a long tradition in music and rhetoric, going back to antiquity in both disciplines.[1] In rhetoric *transitus* as well as *transitio* are used in reference to a transition from one part of the oration to another. In accordance with the general rhetorical thrust of his writings, Mattheson adopts this rhetorical understanding as one of the musical definitions of *transitus*, corresponding to Susenbrotus's *transitio* or *metabasis*.[2] Although Mattheson generally uses the related term *transitus* in its common musical understanding (a passing note), in his discussion of the musical *dispositio* the term *transitus* is used to indicate "a transition, through which the foregoing is connected to the following."[3] Here he refers to a specific bass note immediately repeated an octave higher following a cadential note marked with a fermata and forming an upbeat to the following phrase. The repeated note thereby "recalls" what has just been uttered while at the same time introducing the subsequent thought, an exact parallel to the rhetorical *metabasis* or *transitio*. As a translation of the term *metabole*, *transitus* can also refer to a change in poetic meter. The term is also used adverbially: *per transitum* (in passing), signifying a brief or quick reference. In describing Greek music theory, *transitus* is used to define changes in the tetrachord, *tonus*, or *ethos*. Medieval music theory adapted the term to refer to the change from the plagal to its authentic mode. *Transitus* is also used in reference to unusual melodic progressions, particularly the dissonances leading from an imperfect to a perfect consonance, especially the sixth to the octave. This use of the term is particularly significant with Gaffurius, who uses the compound term *celer transitus* to describe such a transitory dissonance.[4] At this point, the terminology for the passing dissonance begins to proliferate. The term *transitus* is used in Italy (in addition to *cattiva*) throughout the sixteenth century. In the following century, Marco Scacchi uses the term

---

1. P. Cahn, "Transitus," *Handwörterbuch der musikalischen Terminologie*. This detailed and helpful study, which provides much of the above background, traces the history of *transitus* as well as the terms *celeritas* and *commissura*.

2. See *Metabasis*.

3. "Da ist ein Transitus oder Uibergang, Krafft dessen das vorige mit dem folgenden an einander gefüget, und von jenem zu diesem herüber getreten wird." *Capellmeister*, 238.

4. "Quae vero per sincopam et ipso rursus celeri transitu latet discordantia admittitur in contrapuncto." *Practica musicae* (Milan, 1496); cited in Cahn, "Transitus," 5.

in reference not only to the passing dissonance between an imperfect and perfect consonance but between any intervals. Bernhard, who was significantly influenced by Scacchi, particularly regarding the question of musical styles, then introduces the term into his own *Figurenlehren*. With that, *transitus* replaces *celeritas* and *commissura*, two terms for the passing dissonance which had become established terminology in German circles since the sixteenth century.

The term *celer* (*celeritas*) is introduced through Gaffurius's description of the brevity of the *transitus*. In similar language Gallus Dressler describes the quickly passing dissonance, using, however, only the term *celeritas*.[1] Although *celeritas* becomes widely adopted—it is used by Calvisius and Lippius—Burmeister and Nucius do not choose to use it. Rather it is Thuringus who is the first to include the term in a *Figurenlehre*, citing it in addition to Burmeister's terms, *commissura* and *symblema*. Kircher, who likewise mentions all three terms, and Thuringus favor Burmeister's term *commissura* in their description of the figure. Besides its use by Crüger and Herbst,[2] *celeritas* is mentioned once again in Walther's *Lexicon*, where he simply refers to the term "*commissura*." With Bernhard, the term *transitus* replaces all other Latin and Greek terminology, itself to be eventually replaced by vernacular expressions.

Burmeister selects *commissura*, along with its Greek translation, *symblema*, to define the passing dissonance. Like *transitus*, the term *commissura* appears in classical sources, where it is used not as a figure but rather simply to describe the unpleasant collision of ending and beginning consonants of subsequent words.[3] The word *commissura* is then used by Froschius (1535) in his description of a dissonance which connects two consonances. Together with its Greek translation, *symblema*, *commissura* is then instituted as a musical term by Burmeister.

---

1. "Quibus rationibus admittuntur? Duabus rationibus: videlicet syncopatione et celeritate"(*Praecepta musicae poeticae*, Magdeburg, 1563). Ibid., 6.

2. "Was ist Celeritas, oder Geschwindigkeit: Hiebevor ist meldung geschehen / daβ die dissonantiae, damit sie nicht also hart gehöret / auff zweyerley wieβ können verdeckt und verduschet werden / als erstlich durch die Syncopation. . . . Darnach durch Celeritatem und Geschwindigkeit / das ist: Wann viel kleinere Noten / gegen einer grössern in einem Tact mensurirt und gesungen werden / und gradatim, Staffel weiβ geschwind durchlauffen." Herbst, *Musica poetica*, 27.

3. Quintilian, IX.iv.37.

Unlike *transitus*, which refers to the "passing" nature of the dissonance (from *transire*, to pass over), or *celeritas*, which emphasizes the brevity of the dissonance (*celeritas*, swiftness), the terms *symblema* or *commissura* focus on the binding or connecting function of the interjected dissonance (*commissura*, connection, joint, knot). Not only does the *commissura* link consonances with dissonances, but it presents a passage which simultaneously consists of consonances and dissonances. In each of Burmeister's definitions, not one but two voices are to feature parallel passing notes, consonant to each other but dissonant to the sustained accompanying notes. Because the *commissura* thereby affects the entire structure of the composition, Burmeister includes it among the *figurae harmoniae*. Burmeister clearly prefers *symblema* to *commissura*, on account of the implied association with classical Greek rhetoric. The choice of these terms over *transitus* or *celeritas* also points to Burmeister's wish to establish the ornamental use of dissonance in his *Figurenlehre*. Dissonance is not simply to be endured or excused but is to be included to avoid boredom on the part of the listeners.[1] Burmeister only admits the passing dissonance on the unaccented beat. However, should the dissonance pass too quickly, as in the case of the *symblema minus* (which occurs within a *tactus*), it will not affect the listener significantly and therefore cannot be considered a *figura hamoniae*. This justification stands in direct contrast to the idea of the *celeritas*, explaining why Burmeister could not accept that term. Nucius adopts the term *commissura* without mentioning its Greek equivalent. Instead of differentiating between a longer and shorter sounding dissonance, Nucius distinguishes between dissonances either on or following an accented beat: *commissura directa* and *cadens*. Thuringus and Kircher make the same distinctions, but list *commissura*, *symblema*, and *celeritas* as equivalent terms. Thuringus, Kircher, and Walther (*Praecepta*) explicitly contradict Burmeister's limitation of the passing dissonance to notes of longer duration, stating that "all notes of short duration are permissible as *commissurae*," but that the *semibrevis* is not allowed "because its duration is too long." Like Nucius, Thuringus and Kircher also list the *commissura* as one of the *figurae principales*, the principal or fundamen-

1. Ruhnke, *Burmeister*, 134ff.

tal devices of contrapuntal composition.

Bernhard also lists the figure as a basic contrapuntal device or ornament: the *transitus* is one of the *figurae fundamentales* used in the *stylus gravis*. While his *transitus* corresponds to the *commissura cadens*, he defines the *quasi-transitus* in his *Tractatus* parallel to the *commissura directa*, with the dissonance falling on the beat. In the same treatise he lists the *transitus inversus* as a figure used in the modern *stylus theatralis*. Although it is also understood as a dissonance on the beat, it can be approached by leap instead of only by step, and normally has the dissonance extended through the *multiplicatio*, thereby becoming a more expressive and "modern" figure. In his *Bericht*, Bernhard uses the terms *transitus regularis* (unaccented dissonance) and *irregularis* (accented dissonance) to describe the passing note. The term *quasi-transitus* is here used to describe the earlier *transitus inversus*. Thus the *quasi-transitus* is now included in the *figurae superficiales*.

Bernhard's discussion of the figures is marked by a concern to link the expressive and dissonant musical devices to the established compositional rules. Even the *transitus* is to be traced to its source, which he does through the use of the term *Deminution*: through the "diminution" of a consonance into two smaller entities, the original consonance and a neighboring dissonance, Bernhard establishes the "original" note and underscores the "passing" nature of the dissonance. His intention to establish the "root" of a figure is not only revealed in his *Deminution* explanation but is particularly significant in his explanation of numerous other figures which are derived from or associated with the *transitus*, namely *superjectio*, *anticipatio*, *variatio*, *multiplicatio*, *prolongatio*, *ellipsis*, and *heterolepsis*. The explanation of these figures frequently includes their musical examples, along with an unornamented example with traditional passing notes and the remark: "It should be thus."

The passing dissonance is regarded as one of the three *principales* or *fundamentales* figures (in addition to *fuga* and *syncopatio*) throughout the seventeenth century, being considered one of the basic devices used to embellish or figurate a composition. With the increased emphasis on affection and text expression in the following century, these figures lose their preeminent *ornatus* position to the more expressive *movere*-oriented musical-rhetorical figures. Thus the *transitus* is mentioned only *in transitu* by Scheibe, who defines the device in a footnote at the close of his extensive *Figurenlehre*. He reminds the reader that the *transitus*, together with the suspension and fugue, belong much more to the "general and elementary rules of composition" and not to an expressive *Figurenlehre*.

Burmeister (*Hypomnematum*)
Symblema sive Commissura est quando alicui parti tactus majori adjiciuntur minores, quae illi in valore respondent, ita, ut prima illarum concors sit, secunda discors & sic reliquae consequenter per vices, quo manifesta deprehendatur per mixtio sive commissura consonantium & dissonantium sonorum, per proxima loca, ut sunt semitonium, & tonum, &c. se subsequentium, nihil harmoniae derogans.

The *symblema* or *commissura* occurs when notes of smaller duration are added to notes of longer duration in a certain part of the *tactus*, which appear in such fashion that their first part forms a consonance, their second a dissonance, with the following notes alternating back to a consonance. The *permixtio* or *commissura* is clearly perceived through this alternation of neighboring consonant and dissonant semitones and whole tones, without detracting from the *harmonia*.

Burmeister (*Musica Autoschediastike*)
Symblema Σύμϐλημα est concordantiarum & dissonantiarum commissura quae sic se habet: Principio vel parte priori tactus minoris (ut quidam vocant) hoc est ejus mensurae, quae omnium est usitatissima, & quae ex duabus aequalibus partibus depressione scil. & elevatione constat, quarum altera prae altera plus temporis non requirit, concordantiae omnes se habent in omnibus vocibus harmoniae, ut absolutae concordantiae; Fine vero vel parte posteriori non omnes voces se in syntaxi habent ut concordantiae absolutae, sed quaedam tantum. Quae inter se concordes sunt harum alterae moventur & quidem motu pari, reliquae prorsus ad aliquot tactus persistunt.

The *symblema* is a combination [*commissura*] of consonances and dissonances as follows: it is most common in the beginning or prior part of a weak beat (as some call it) and consists of two parallel descending or ascending parts of equal duration. The consonances in all voices of the composition behave like absolute consonances. However, at the end or the last part of the beat, all voices do not behave according to the syntax of absolute consonances but rather only to a certain extent. Among themselves the voices are consonant, either those progressing in parallel motion, or the other remaining voices which hold through the beat.

Burmeister (*Musica Poetica* p.60)
Symblema σύμϐλημα est Concordantiarum & Dissonantiarum commissura, quae hac ratione fit: Omnes Concordantiae se habent in omnibus Harmoniae vocibus ut absolutae Concordantiae, idque in Principio, vel parte priori tactus dimidia. In Fine vero vel parte tactus dimidia posteriori non omnes vo-

The *symblema* is a combination of consonances and dissonances occurring as follows: all the consonances behave like absolute consonances in all the voices of the composition in the beginning or first half of the beat. However, in the end or last part of the beat, not all voices behave according to the syntax of absolute con-

ces se in syntaxi habent, ut Concordantiae absolutae, sed quaedam tantum. Quae inter se concordes sunt, hae aut moventur, & quidem motu pari; aut prorsus ad aliquot tactus persistunt. . . . Id majus Symblema dicitur: Minus est quando talis commissura fit sub dimidio tactus, quod quia non ita afficit, pro Figura & Ornamento non reputatur. Exemplum hoc esto.

sonances but rather only to a certain extent. Among themselves the voices are consonant, either progressing in parallel motion, or holding through the entire beat. . . . This is called a *symblema majus*. A *symblema minus* occurs when this combination [*commissura*] appears within the middle of the beat. It is not considered among the *figura* or *ornamenta* because it does not affect [the listener] in the same manner.

Nucius (*Musices Poeticae* p.F4[v])

Quid est Commissura? Commissuram vocant Musici, cum dissonantia aliqua propter praecedentem & sequentem consonantiam excusatur. Est que duplex: Directa & Cadens.

What is a *commissura*? Musicians define *commissura* as a certain dissonance which is excused because of a preceding and following consonance. It is of two kinds: *directa* and *cadens*.

Quid est Commissura Directa? Quando cum depressione tactus dissonantia, aurium quidem sensu percepta, propter sequentem concordantiam, tamen admittitur, qualiter in omnibus formalibus clausulis & syncopationibus fieri solet.

What is a *commissura directa*? When the ear perceives a dissonance on the downbeat that is nonetheless admitted on account of the following consonance, which usually occurs in all formal cadences and in *syncopationes*.

Quid est Commissura Cadens? Cum prior pars tactus consona est, posterior vero dissonat, qui positus propter sequentem consonantiam tamen admittitur, ac contingit plaerunque in gradationibus. Hujus generis Commissurae extra omnem clausularum & syncopationis rationem contingunt, & fugis saepe sunt aptissimae.

What is a *commissura cadens*? When the first part of the *tactus* is consonant and the last part is dissonant, which is nonetheless admitted on account of the following consonance. It is often used in a *gradatio*. These kinds of *commissura* occur particularly in all cadences and *syncopationes*, and are especially appropriate in *fugae*.

Thuringus (*Opusculum* p.98)
Commissura, quae & symblema vel celeritas dicitur, est, quando notulae etiamsi dissonae, harmoniam tamen absque offensione aurium artificiose ingrediuntur. Vel, est cum dissonantia in minimis contrapuncto inseritur, & committitur in elevatione tactus. In commissura admittuntur omnes minores notulae, ut sunt: minimae, semiminimae, fusae, semifusae: Semibrevis autem non admittitur, quia justo tardior est.

The *commissura*, also called *symblema* or *celeritas*, occurs when dissonant notes are artfully integrated into the composition without, however, offending the ears, or when dissonances are inserted into the counterpoint on an upbeat through *minimae*. All notes of short duration are permissible as *commissurae*, including *minimae*, *semiminimae*, *fusae*, and *semifusae*. The *semibrevis*, however, is not permissible because its duration is too long.

Quotuplex est Commissura? Duplex: Directa Cadens. Directa est: Quando cum depressione tactus dissonantia, aurium quidem sensu percepta, propter sequentem concordantiam, tamen admittitur, qualiter in omnibus formalibus clausulis & syncopationibus fieri solet. Quae est Commissura cadens? Cum prior pars tactus consona est, posterior vero dissonat, hoc est, quae fiat in elevatione non in deprehensione tactus: qui positus propter sequentem Consonantiam tamen admittitur, ac contingit plerumque in gradationibus ascendendo vel descendendo.

How many forms of *commissura* are there? Two: *directa* and *cadens*. *Directa* occurs when the ear perceives a dissonance on the downbeat that is nonetheless admitted on account of the following consonance, which usually occurs in all formal cadences and in *syncopationes*. What is a *commissura cadens*? When the first part of the *tactus* is consonant and the last part is dissonant, that is, when it occurs in an upbeat rather than a downbeat, which is nonetheless admitted on account of the following consonance. It is often used in an ascending or descending *gradatio*.

Kircher (*Musurgia* L.5, p.366)
Commissura, quae & σύμβλημα, vel celeritas dicitur, est quando notulae etiamsi dissonae, harmoniam tamen absque aurium offensione artificiose ingrediuntur, vel est cum dissonantiae in minimis Contrapuncto, & in elevatione tactus committuntur. Admittuntur autem in commissura omnes minores notulae, uti sunt minimae, semiminimae, fusae, semifusae; Semibrevis autem non admittitur, quia tardior est. Est autem commissura

The *commissura*, also called *symblema* or *celeritas*, occurs when dissonant notes are artfully integrated into the composition without, however, offending the ears, or it occurs when dissonances are incurred in an upbeat in the counterpoint through *minimae*. All notes of short duration are permissible as *commissurae*, including *minimae*, *semiminimae*, *fusae*, and *semifusae*. The *semibrevis*, however, is not permissible because its duration is

duplex, directa, & cadens; Illa est quando ad thesin mensurae, sive depressionem tactus dissonantia aurium quodam sensu percepta, propter sequentem tamen concordantiam admittitur, hanc recentiores apto vocabulo Resolutionem vocant; quod videlicet, nota brevis, aut semibrevis in minimas particulas, tam consonas, quam dissonas resolvatur, cuius in praecedenti tractatu de contrapuncto amplissima, & perfrequens facta est mentio. Cadens commissura est cum prior pars tactus consona est, posterior dissona, hoc est, quae fit in elevatione non in depressione tactus, qui positus propter sequentem & sic dissonantia consonantiam bona redditur, & contingit, plerumque in grandioribus notis ascendendo, & descendendo, ut in sequenti paradigmato apparet.

too long. The *commissura* is of two kinds, *directa* and *cadens*. *Directa* occurs when the ear perceives a dissonance on the downbeat that is nonetheless admitted on account of the following consonance. Recent theorists fittingly call this a *resolutio*, which it clearly is, as a *brevis* or *semibrevis* is dissoved into smaller dissonant and consonant *minimae*. This was very clearly and frequently mentioned in the preceding chapter on counterpoint. The *cadens commissura* occurs when the first part of the *tactus* is consonant and the second part is dissonant, that is, when it occurs in an upbeat and not in a downbeat. A dissonance placed in such fashion is restored to health through a following consonance. It is frequently applied to ascending and descending notes of longer duration, as the following example illustrates:

Bernhard (*Tractatus* p.64)

Transitus welchen man auch Deminution heißen kan, ist: wenn zwischen 2 Consonirenden Noten, so alle beyde numero impari das Subjectum einsehen, eine dissonirende Note numero pari im nächsten Intervallo oben oder unten gleichsam durchschleichet. Daher sollen alle ungerade Theile des Tactes aus Consonantzen bestehen. . . . In Tripla muß die erste gut seyn, hernach kan die andere oder 3te /: nicht alle beyde :/ dissoniren, doch kan in Rückungen die erste Note in Tripla auch dissoniren, und denn ist es mehr Syncopatio als Transitus. Auff die Consonantz soll die Dissonantz in dem nächsten Intervallo unten oder oben seyn, und wiederum im nächsten Intervallo eine Consonantz haben. Die andere Stimme so dagegen ist, soll langsame Noten haben also daß eine Consonantz und Dissonantz einer Note solcher Stimme . . . gleich gelte.

The *transitus*, which can also be called *Deminution*, occurs when a dissonant note on an even-numbered [weak] beat slips by, as it were, on a higher or lower interval between two consonant notes of the subject on odd-numbered [strong] beats. Hence all strong beats of the measure are to consist of consonances. . . . In triple time the first part should be consonant, after which the second or third (but not both) can be dissonant. In rhythmic shifts the first part of a triple measure can also be dissonant, in which case it is more of a *syncopatio* than *transitus*. The dissonance is to follow the consonance at the neighboring higher or lower pitch, followed by a consonance at the next pitch. The voice which is set against the *transitus* should have slow notes of such duration that the consonance and dissonance of the one voice equals one longer note of such another voice.

(*Tractatus* p.65)

Quasi-Transitus ist, wenn eine falsche

The *quasi-transitus* occurs when a disso-

Note den Regeln des vorigen Transitus zu wieder loco impari stehet als

nant note is placed on an odd [strong] beat, contrary to the rules of the preceding *transitus*, as follows:

(*Tractatus* p.86)

Transitus inversus ist, wenn das erste Theil eines Tactes im Transitu böse, das andere gut ist. Welcher darum in Stylo recitativo zugelaßen, weil darinnen kein Tact gebraucht wird, und also nicht observiret wird, welches deßen erste oder andere Helffte ist. Diese Figur wird gleichwohl niemals ohne die Multiplication angetroffen.

The *transitus inversus* occurs when the first part of a *tactus* with a *transitus* is dissonant and the second is consonant, which is allowed in the *stylus recitativus* because the beat is not used there, and therefore it is not perceived which is the first or the second half of the *tactus*. Furthermore, this figure is never encountered without the *multiplicatio*.

Bernhard (*Bericht* p.146)

Transitus, welchen ich sonst auch Deminution geheißen, ist, wenn zwischen zweyen guten Noten eine falsche im nächsten Intervallo ist. Und ist zweyerley, Regularis vel Irregularis. Regel oder Unregelmäßig. Transitus regularis ist, wenn die anschlagende Note consonans, die andere aber Dissonans ist. Bey diesem Transitu ist zu mercken 1) daß alle ungeraden Theile des Tacts aus Consonantien bestehen sollen, denn das heiße ich die anschlagenden Noten. . . . 2) Daß auff die Consonans eine Dissonans im nächsten Intervallo folge, und auf eine Dissonans abermal eine Consonans im nächsten Intervallo.

The *transitus*, which I also call *Deminution*, occurs when a dissonant note is set between two consonant notes in the neighboring pitch. It is of two kinds: *regularis* and *irregularis*. A *transitus regularis* occurs when the note on the beat is consonant, the other, however, dissonant. In this kind of *transitus* it is to be observed (1) that all uneven parts of the measure consist of consonances, which I call "striking notes" (on the beat) . . . and (2) that a consonance is to be followed by a dissonance in the neighboring pitch, and the dissonance again by a consonance in the neighboring pitch.

Transitus Irregularis ist, wenn die anschlagende Note falsch, die folgende aber gut ist. Die Transitus Irregulares sollen 1) selten gebrauchet werden, 2) die verkleinerten Noten in Transitu irregulari sollen nur herunter, nicht aber hinauffgehen. 3) Es soll eine kleine falsche Note anschlagen, eine [gleiche] andere aber, die Secunda niedriger fallende, sie gut machen.

The *transitus irregularis* occurs when the note on the beat is dissonant but the following one is consonant. These *transitus irregulares* (1) should seldom be used; (2) the shortened notes of the *transitus irregularis* should only descend and not ascend; (3) a short dissonant note should be on the beat, and a second note of equal duration should fall a second, resolving the first note.

(*Bericht* p.152)
Quasitransitus ist, wenn wieder die Regul des Transitus, die Dissonanz anschläget. Und wird nur in Stylo Recitativo zugelaßen, weil daselbst kein Tact observiret wird. Alß:

The *quasi-transitus* occurs when a dissonance is placed on the beat, contrary to the rule of the *transitus*. It is only permitted in the *stylus recitativus*, because in that style the *tactus* is not observed, as:

Walther (*Praecepta* p.150)
Transitus, sonsten auch Commissura genannt, ist, wenn eine Stimme stille hält, und die andere sich beweget dergestalt, daß regulariter zwischen zweyen wohl klingenden Noten eine dissonirende sich befindet. Der Transitus ist zweyerley, Regularis et Irregularis. Transitus regularis ist, wenn die in thesi stehende Note

The *transitus*, otherwise called *commissura*, occurs when one voice remains stationary while the other moves in such a manner that, as a rule, a dissonance is placed between two consonant notes. The *transitus* is of two kinds: *regularis* and *irregularis*. The *transitus regularis* occurs when the note on the beat is conso-

gegen die andere Stimme consoniret, und die in arsi stehende Note dissoniret. Observatio 1) Der Transitus hat nur statt in notis minoribus; als minimis, semiminimis, fusis und semifusis; nicht aber in majoribus, als maximis, longis, brevibus und semibrevibus: weil diese in ihren sedibus zu lange bleiben, und resolutionem harmonicam über die Zeit aufhalten. 2) Die Noten müßen allein gradatim, nicht aber saltuatim, auf oder niederwarts steigen. 3) Alle ungerade Theile des Tacts (welches eben thesis ist) müßen aus Consonantien bestehen.

nant against the other voice and the note after the beat is dissonant. The following is to be observed: (1) the *transitus* is only to occur with shorter notes, such as *minimae, semiminimae, fusae*, and *semifusae*, but not with longer notes such as *maximae, longae, breves*, and *semibreves*, for these remain too long in their place and excessively delay the harmonic resolution; (2) the notes must only ascend or descend by step and not by leap; (3) all uneven parts of the measure (which are downbeats or *in thesis*) must be consonant.

Transitus irregularis ist, wenn die in thesi befindl. Note dissoniret, und die in arsi stehet consoniret. Observatio 1) Die dissonirende Noten sollen nur herunter, und nicht aufwarts gehen, (es geschehe denn nicht gar zu offt in geschwinden Sachen) 2) Unter vier kleinen gleichgeltenden Noten (denn in größern gehet es nicht an) können die ersten beyden, und die letzte consoniren, und nur die dritte dissoniren.

The *transitus irregularis* occurs when the note on the beat is dissonant and the note following the beat is consonant. The following is to be observed: (1) the dissonant notes should only descend and not ascend, except if this happens not too frequently in faster pieces; (2) in figurations of four rapid notes of equal duration (for this does not apply to slower notes) the first two and last notes can be consonant, only the third note being dissonant.

Walther (*Lexicon*)

Commissura heisset: wenn zwischen zwo gegen eine Ober- oder Unter-Stimme consonirenden Noten, eine dissonirende, und zwar im nechsten intervallo, zu stehen kommt.

Commissura means the placement of a dissonant note in the neighboring pitch between two notes which are consonant against another upper or lower voice.

Commissura cadens, oder, wie Goclenius hat, cedens, ist: wenn die in thesi stehend Note consoniret, und die in arsi dissoniret.

A *commissura cadens*, or as Goclenius calls it, *cedens*, occurs when the note on the beat is consonant and the note after the beat is dissonant.

Commissura directa ist: wenn die in thesi stehende Note dissoniret, hingegen die in arsi consoniret.

A *commissura directa* occurs when the note on the beat is dissonant while the note after the beat is consonant.

Symblema σύμβλημα von συμβάλλων, welches Wort unter andern auch: committere aliquos, i.e. sibi invicem inimicos reddere, Feindschafft unter einander stifften, bedeutet. Und in eben diesem Verstande wird diese Figur auf lateinisch auch Commissura genennet, und von Rückungen oder syncopationibus, item

Symblema, from *symballon*, a word meaning, among other things, to perpetrate something, that is, to mutually incite hostility or to cause enmity among oneselves. And in this particular understanding the figure is translated with the Latin term *commissura* and refers to rhythmic shifts or *syncopationes* and their passing

von solchen durchgehenden Noten gebrauchet, die beyderseits dergleichen dissoniernd darstellen. conf. Commissura.

notes, both of which incur dissonances. See *Commissura*.

Transitus ein Durchgang; wenn nemlich die in arsi stehende Noten dissoniren.

The *transitus* is a passing note, occurring when the notes in an upbeat [weak beat] are dissonant.

Mattheson (*Capellmeister* p.118)
Durchgang wird bey sehr vielen Lehrern für Passaggio genommen; oder wenigstens legen sie das Wort Passaggio von einem Durchgange gantz natürlich aus. Transitus heiβt auch sonst, wenn einige in den Ober-Stimmen vorkommende Klänge mit dem Basse nicht wol übereinstimmen und dennoch mit durchlauffen. Bey unsrer vorhabenden Materie ist der vermeinte Durchgang gantz was anders, und findet sich in den Grund-Noten der aufgeschriebenen ordentlichen einstimmigen Melodie, alwo er nur mit einem schnellen Triller und einer hurtigen Drehung gezieret wird.

The passing note [*Durchgang, transitus*] is understood by many teachers as a *passaggio*; at least they wish to derive the meaning of *passaggio* quite naturally from a passing note. *Transitus* also means when a number of notes in the melody do not agree properly with the bass but nonetheless proceed along. Our present discussion [of embellishing *Manieren*] regards the passing note as something completely different. It is found in the principal notes of the notated regular melody voice, where it is ornamented with a fast trill and a rapid turn.

(*Capellmeister* p.238)
Da ist ein Transitus oder Uibergang, Krafft dessen das vorige mit dem folgenden an einander gefüget, und von jenem zu diesem herüber getreten wird.

There [*] is a *transitus* or transition, through which the previous material is connected with the following, progressing from the one to the other.

Scheibe (*Critischer Musicus* p.698)
Transitus, oder der Durchgang ist, wenn mehr als eine Note neben einander auf- oder absteigend gegen eine in einer an-

The *transitus* or passing note occurs when two or more subsequent, neighboring, ascending or descending notes stand

dem Stimme befindliche Note zu stehen kommen. Die eine Note ist alsdann als die anschlagende, von der die Zusammenstimmung entsteht, anzusehen; die andere Note hingegen ist die durchgehende. Da aber auch sehr oft von der durchgehenden Note die Harmonie entspringt: so ist annoch zu merken, daβ wenn die accentuirte Note, als die anschlagende, die Harmonie machet, solches Transitus regularis genennet wird. Ist aber die unaccentuirte, oder die durchgehende Note der Grund der Harmonie: so heiβt solches Transitus irregularis. In diesem letztern Falle aber ist die erstere Note, ob sie schon accentuirt ist, doch nur als ein Vorschlag der folgenden Note zu betrachten.

against one note in another voice. The note which forms the harmony is considered the striking [*anschlagende*] note, while the other is the passing note. However, as the harmony is also frequently derived out of the passing note, the following, moreover, is to be mentioned. When the accented or striking note produces the harmony, it is known as a *transitus regularis*. However, should the unaccented or passing note form the basis of the harmony, it is called a *transitus irregularis*. In this latter case, however, the first note, even if it is accented, is only to be considered as an *accentus* [*Vorschlag*] to the following note.

TRANSUMPTIO: see *METALEPSIS*

TREMOLO, TRILLO: (1) an instrumental or vocal trembling on one note, resulting in a wavering pitch or vibrato; (2) a rapid reiteration of one note; (3) a rapid alternation of two adjacent notes; a trill.

The confusion in terminology regarding these two ornaments can be traced back to inconsistent use of the terms in early-seventeenth-century Italy. The oscillating ornament is called *tremolo* by Ganassi, Diruta, and Bovicelli and *trillo* by Cavalieri, Frescobaldi, and Trabaci. Furthermore, Conforto, Caccini, and Monteverdi use *trillo* to signify a rapid reiteration of one note.[1] Praetorius introduces the *tremolo* and *trillo* into German theoretical writings, defining the *tremolo* as the oscillating ornament, and *trillo* both as a reiteration of a note, according to Caccini, and a trembling note which cannot be notated but must be learned through living example. This understanding of the terms is then adopted by Herbst, Crüger, Bernhard, Printz, and other seventeenth-century theorists. Printz differentiates between these two forms of *trillo*, referring to the reiterated

---

1. See Neumann, *Ornamentation*, 287ff., for a detailed discussion of the terms *tremolo* and *trillo*.

and clearly articulated note as *trillo* and to the vibrato-like unarticulated reiteration as *trilletto*. In his *Trifolium* of 1691, Stierlein reverses the common terminology, defining the *tremulus* as a "trembling on one note" (*Beben in unisono*) and the *trillo* or *trilletto* as either a long or short trill on two distinct notes.[1] This gradually becomes the accepted understanding of the terms in the eighteenth century, as reflected in the definitions of Vogt, Walther, and Mattheson. Both Walther and Mattheson compare the *tremolo* to the organ tremulant, a mechanical device which alters the intensity of the wind pressure supplied to the organ pipes, causing a gentle vibrato. In spite of the different use of terminology, there seems to be general agreement on the structure of the oscillating trill. The vast majority of musical examples illustrate a trill which begins on the main note. Not until the growing influence of French ornamentation in the course of the early eighteenth century does the trill beginning on the upper note gain wider acceptance in German music, as indicated in Walther's *Lexicon*. "The musical evidence will underline the basic main-note character of the German trill during the whole period under consideration, with some qualifications only for its last few years."[2]

Praetorius (*Syntagma Musicum III* p.235)
Tremolo, vel Tremulo: Ist nichts anders / alß ein Zittern der Stimme uber einer Noten: die Organisten nennen es Mordanten oder Moderanten. Und dieses ist mehr uff Orgeln und Instrumenta pennata gerichtet / alß uff Menschen Stimmen.

A *tremolo* or *tremulo* is nothing other than a trembling of the voice over a note, which organists call *mordants* or *moderants*. This is more appropriate in music written for the organ and other instruments than for the human voice.

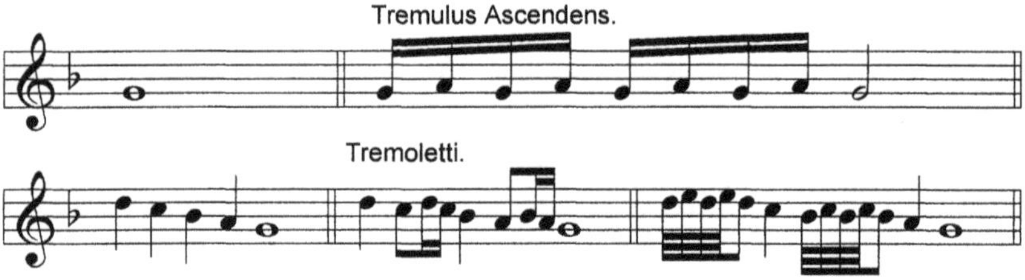

(*Syntagma Musicum III* p.237)
Trillo: Ist zweyerley: Der eine geschiehet

The *trillo* is of two kinds. The first occurs

1. Ibid., 299.
2. Ibid., 304.

in Unisono, entweder auff einer Linien oder im Spatio; Wann viel geschwinde Noten nacheinander repetiret werden.

in unisono, either on the same line or space, when numerous rapid notes are successively repeated.

Der Ander Trillo ist uff unterschiedenen Arten gerichtet. Und ob zwar einen Trillo recht zu formiren, unmüglich ist außm vorgeschriebenen zu lernen / es sey dann / das es viva Praeceptoris voce & ope geschehe / und einem vorgesungen und vorgemacht werde / darmit es einer vom andern / gleich wie ein Vogel vom andern observiren lerne. . . . Jedoch hab ich etliche Arten alhier obiter mit bey zusetzen nötig erachtet / damit die noch zur zeit unwissende Tyrones, nur in etwas sehen und wissen mögen was ohngefehr ein Trillo genennet werde.

The second form of *trillo* is formed in diverse manners. And although it is impossible to learn how to form such a *trillo* from written examples, except that it occur through live example by having it sung and illustrated that one can learn it from another as do the birds, . . . nonetheless I have considered it necessary to include a number of its forms, in order that the at this time yet uninformed students catch a glimpse and understanding of approximately what is referred to as a *trillo.*

Printz (*Phrynis Mytilenaeus* pt.2, p.48)
Tremolo ist ein scharffes Zittern der Stimme über einer grössern Noten / so die nechste Clavem mit berühret. Er ist entweder verkürtzt oder verlängert / jener bestehet in vier geschwinden Noten / dieser in mehrern. Beyde seyn entweder auffsteigend oder absteigend.

The *tremolo* is a sharp trembling of the voice over a longer note which touches the neighboring note. It is either short or long, the former consisting of four rapid notes, the latter of more notes. Both forms are either ascending or descending.

(*Phrynis Mytilenaeus* pt.2, p.63)
Schwebende einfache Figuren seyn nur zwo / nehmlich Trillo und Trilletto. Trillo ist ein Zittern der Stimme in einer Clave

There are only two simple hovering figures, namely *trillo* and *trilletto.* A *trillo* is a trembling of the voice on one pitch

über einer grössern Noten / als daß das Anschlagen zwar scharff seyn / iedoch mit sonderbarer Manier geschehen solle: Welches nicht recht beschrieben werden kan / sondern mit lebendiger Stimme gewiesen werden muß. Trilletto aber ist nur eine Bebung der Stimme / so viel linder / als Trillo, und fast gar nicht angeschlagen wird. Auf denen Saiten geschicht er mit einem offtwiederholeten Niederdrücken / und doch nicht gäntzlicher Aufflassung der Saite von eben dem Finger / der sonst denselben Ton verursacht: Hergegen wird Trillo verursacht / durch ein offt-wiederholetes Drucken und gäntzliches Aufflassen der Saite von dem nechstfolgenden Finger: Welches beydes auff denen Geigen / unter Wärung eines einzigen Strichs geschehen solle.

over a longer note in which the notes are crisply articulated, yet in an extraordinary manner which cannot be properly explained but must be illustrated with the live voice. A *trilletto* however is only a trembling of the voice which is much gentler than a *trillo* and is hardly articulated. On stringed instruments this occurs with an often repeated depression of the finger yet without completely releasing the string which otherwise produces the note. In contrast, the *trillo* is produced through an often repeated depression and complete release of the string by the neighboring finger. Both of these figures are to be played on violins using a single stroke of the bow.

Vogt (*Conclave* p.7)

Tremula largo tremens in eodem tono vox.

The *tremula* is a voice slowly trembling on the same note.

Trilla, celer inter duas notas vicinas vicissitudinarius cursus.

The *trilla* is a rapid alternating movement between two neighboring notes.

Walther (*Lexicon*)

Tremolo oder Tremulo und abbrevirt. Trem. bedeutet, daß auf besaiteten und mit Bogen zu tractirenden Instrumenten, viele in einerley Tone vorkommende Noten, mit einem zitternden Striche absolvirt werden sollen, um den Orgel-Tremulanten zu imitiren; manchmal aber auch, nebst seinem Diminutivo Tremoletto, ein Trillo.

Tremolo or *tremulo*, abbreviated with *trem.*, refers to the playing on bowed, stringed instruments of numerous notes at the same pitch in one, trembling stroke, which is to imitate an organ tremulant. Besides its diminutive, *tremoletto*, it at times also means a *trillo*.

Trillo, ist eine Sing- und Spiel-Manier, zu deren expression (nach Beschaffenheit der Vorzeichnung) entweder die secunda major oder minor gebraucht, und diese mit der auf dem Papier gesetzten, und mit einer tr, oder t bezeichneten Note, wechselsweise behende und scharff angeschlagen wird; jedoch dergestalt, daß man bey der höhern Note anhebet, und bey der tiefern als gegenwärtigen, Note

The *trillo* is a vocal or instrumental embellishment indicated with a *tr* or *t* which alternates either a major or minor second (according to the key signature) with the written note in a rapid and sharply articulated fashion. It is executed in such a manner that one begins on the higher note and ends on the lower, given note. *Trilletto* is the diminutive of *trillo* and means a short *trillo*.

aufhöret. Trilletto ist das Diminutivum von Trillo, und bedeutet: daβ es kurz gemacht werden soll.

Mattheson (*Capellmeister* p.114)

Der Tremolo oder das Beben der Stimme ist weder der so genannte Mordant, wie ihrer viele meinen, noch irgend eine auf andre Art aus zween Klängen bestehende Figur, nach Printzens irrigem Angeben und ungültigem Exempel; sondern die allergelindeste Schwebung auf einem eintzigen festgesetzten Ton, dabey meines Erachtens das Oberzünglein des Halses (epiglottis) durch eine gar sanffte Bewegung oder Mäβigung des Athems, das meiste thun muβ: so wie auf Instrumenten die blosse Lenckung der Fingerspitzen, ohne von der Stelle zu weichen, gewisser maassen eben das ausrichtet, absonderlich auf Lauten, Geigen und Clavichordien, die gnugsam beweisen, daβ mehr nicht, als ein eintziger Haupt-Klang, dazu erfordert wird. Wer die Tremulanten in den Orgelwercken kennet, wird wissen, daβ bloβ der zitternde Wind daselbst die Sache ausmacht. . . . Auf Geigen kan dergleichen Zittern auch mit den Bögen in einem Strich, auf einem Ton bewerckstelliget werden; ohn daβ man dazu einen zweiten nöthig hat.

The *tremolo* or the trembling of a voice is neither the so called mordant, as many think, nor any other kind of figure constructed out of two notes, as Printz suggests with his erroneous definition and invalid example. Rather it is a most gentle trembling on one single note, best produced in my opinion by a movement of the epiglottis through a very gentle tempering of the breath. On instruments the same effect is produced by a simple pivot of the fingertips without changing location, especially on lutes, violins, and clavichords. This sufficiently proves that not more than one principal note is needed to express the ornament. Whoever is familiar with organ tremulants will know that such a device only requires trembling wind pressure. . . . Such a trembling can also be produced on one note with violins through one stroke of the bow, without requiring a second one.

Man muβ also den Tremolo im geringsten nicht mit dem Trillo und Trilletto vermischen: wie fast alle alte Lehrer in ihren Schrifften gethan haben: denn die letztgenannten Zierrathen bestehen in einem scharffen und deutlichen Schlagen zweener zusammenliegender oder benachbarter, und mit einander auf das hurtigste unverwechselnder Klänge; wie denn auch das Trillo von dem Trilletto sonst in keinem Stücke unterschieden ist, als in der Länge und Kürtze ihrer Dauer, die bey dem letzten nur sehr klein ist.

One must not in the least confuse the *tremolo* with the *trillo* and *trilletto*, as almost all previous authors have done in their treatises. For the latter ornaments consist of a sharp and clear, rapid striking of two identifiable adjacent or neighboring notes. Furthermore, the *trillo* is in no respect different from the *trilletto*, except in the length or brevity of their duration, which is very short in the latter.

VARIATIO, COLORATURA, DIMINUTIO, PASSAGGIO: an ornamentation of a melodic passage with a variety of embellishments.

Free or improvised melodic ornamentation has a long history in Western music, predating and inspiring the development of polyphonic music. With the rise of independent instrumental music through the Renaissance and Baroque eras, a parallel growth in methods and techniques of free ornamentation can also be witnessed.[1] Although this phenomenon has little to do with the musical-rhetorical figures, a number of the embellishments, *figurae simplices*, or *Manieren* which are used in free ornamentation do appear in various *Figurenlehren*. Both the process and the result of applying the *figurae simplices* to an unornamented melodic line is termed variously as *variatio*, *diminutio*, *coloratura*, and *passaggio*.[2] Of interest is Mattheson's footnote that the *Manieren*, known as *diminutionem notarum*, are called *Variation* in the vernacular. Frequently the definitions either implicitly or explicitly emphasize the need to preserve the original outline of the melody, stating either that the figurations occur between two principal notes or that the original melody not be obscured. In some definitions authors explicitly refer to the use of the *figurae simplices*, while at other times the embellishments are described in more general terms.

The embellishment of a melodic passage through various *figurae simplices* is termed *diminutio* or *coloratura* by Praetorius, *passaggio* by Vogt, and *variatio* by Spiess. All three authors use their respective terms as general headings for the specific ornamental figures. Praetorius lists the *passaggio*, consisting of any ascending or descending steps or leaps, as a specific form of *diminutio*, while Spiess lists *diminutio* as a specific form of *variatio*.

Printz also differentiates between terms. Like Vogt, he uses *passaggio* to denote embellishment through various running *figures simplices*. His *variatio* refers to all conceivable kinds of variation. He subdivides *variatio* into two kinds, variation or embellishment in the strict

---

1. For a thorough discussion of free ornamentation, see Neumann, *Ornamentation*, esp. pt. 9, "Free Ornamentation," 523ff.

2. *Diminutio* appears both as a synonym for *coloratura* and *passaggio* as well as a form of embellishment in its own right. See *Diminutio*.

sense (*in stricta significatione*), which would seem to coincide with *passaggio*, and in the broad sense (*in lata significatione*), which involves variation not only through the figures, including *schematoides*, but also through transposition, change of mode, rhythmic meter, genus, density, number, and spread of voices or instruments, instrumentation, and the concertante arrangement of choirs and instruments.[1]

Bernhard, who does not use the term *diminutio*,[2] equates the terms *variatio*, *coloratura*, and *passaggio*, describing the device as a form of embellishment which can involve other figures, particularly running figurations constructed out of various forms of *transitus*. In contrast to most of his other figures which modify the composition through various forms of dissonance, the *variatio* is understood as a figure employed to fill in the space between intervals, "rushing to the following principal note with all kinds of steps and leaps." As such, it is not understood as a general process of embellishment but rather as a specific figuration which might also involve other figures.

Janovka and Walther use the various terms interchangeably, listing *coloratura*, *diminutio*, and *passaggio* separately in their dictionaries; Walther also lists *variatio*. While he equates *diminutio* and *coloratura* in his *diminutio* definition, he understands *coloratura* as a device which employs virtually all forms of figuration, including not only the *figures simplices* but also *diminutio* and *variatio*. Similarly, his *passaggio* definition, which refers both to Printz and Brossard, includes the use of various *figurae simplices*. Unlike the *coloratura*, *diminutio*, and *variatio* however, the *passaggio* is not described as a method of figuration but as a figure in itself, which is not to extend beyond the limit of one breath.

In his early composition treatise, Scheibe defines *variatio* as the subdivision of a longer dissonant note into numerous notes of shorter

---

1. "Es geschicht aber solche Variatio fürnehmlich auff achterley Weise: 1. Figuris, 2. Schematöidibus, oder Modulis Figuris similibus, 3. Transpositione ejusdem Moduli in alias Claves, 4. Modis progrediendi Simplicibus und Compositis, oder Varia Compositione Pedum Rhythmicorum, 5. Generibus Modulationum, 6. Vocibus humanis, earumque Crassitudine, Multitudine und Latitudine, 7. Instrumentis, eorumque Crassitudine, Multitudine, Latitudine und variis Speciebus, und 8. Choris Concertantibus & Complementalibus." *Phrynis Mytilenaeus*, pt.2, 46.

2. Bernhard suggests that the term *Deminution* can be used instead of *transitus* to denote a passing dissonance. See *Transitus*.

duration. This definition coincides with Bernhard's and Walther's description of *multiplicatio*.[1]

Praetorius (*Syntagma Musicum III* p.232)
Fürs ander muβ ein Sänger rechte Wissenschafft haben / die Diminutiones (so sonsten in gemein Coloraturen genennet werden) lieblich und Apposite zu formiren. Diminutio aber ist / wenn eine grössere Nota in viel andere geschwinde und kleinere Noten resolviret und gebrochen wird. Dieser sind nun unterschiedliche Arten und Modi: Deren etliche Gradatim nacheinander folgende / geschehen: als / Accentus, Tremulo, Gruppi und Tirata.

Second [in addition to a good voice], the singer must possess the expertise to appropriately and graciously execute the *diminutiones*, otherwise generally called *coloraturen*. *Diminutio* signifies a dissolving or breaking up of a longer note into numerous faster and smaller notes, and can occur in various forms and methods, including in successive stepwise fashion, as for example the *accentus*, *tremulo*, *gruppi*, and *tirata*.

(*Syntagma Musicum III* p.240)
Passaggi. Sind geschwinde Läuffe / welche beydes Gradatim und auch Saltuatim durch alle Intervalla, wo wol ascendendo alβ descendendo, uber den Noten so etwas gelten / gesetzet und gemacht werden.

Passaggi are rapid runs progressing by step or by leap through all ascending or descending intervals, applied to notes of substantial duration.

Bernhard (*Tractatus* p.73)
Variatio, von denen Italiänern Passaggio und insgemein Coloratura genant, ist; wenn ein Intervallum durch mehrere kleinere Noten geändert wird, also, daβ anstatt einer groβen Note mehr kleinere durch allerhand Gänge und Sprünge zu der nächstfolgenden Note eilen. Diese Figura ist so reich, daβ alle ihre Exempel anzuführen ohnmöglich. Jedoch ist das Intervallum, dadurch man zur nächsten Note schreitet, entweder Secundae, Tertiae, Quartae, Quintae, Sextae oder Octavae, selten aber Septimae. . . . Auch diese Variationes können noch weiter variiret werden, durch kleine Noten. Und wird ein Verständiger ohn mein Anzeigen leicht sehen, daβ der Transitus und Quasi-Transitus das vornehmste in Pas-

The *variatio*, called *passaggio* by the Italians and generally known as *coloratura*, occurs when an interval is altered through numerous shorter notes in such fashion that, instead of the longer note, numerous shorter notes rush to the following [principal] note through all kinds of runs and leaps. This figure is so abundant that it is impossible to list all its examples. Even so, the interval through which one progresses to the next note is either a second, third, fourth, fifth, sixth, or octave, but seldom a seventh. . . . These *variationes* can be varied still further through shorter notes. A knowledgeable person will easily see without my indication that the *transitus* and *quasi-transitus* have best results in *passaggi*,

1. See *Multiplicatio*.

sagen verrichten, der Accentus zuweilen darzukomme, bißweilen auch die Subsumtio, und andere vorhergehends gewiesene Figuren.

and at times the *accentus*, occasionally the *subsumtio*, and other previously mentioned figures are added.

Bernhard (*Bericht* p.149)
Variatio, sonst Passagio genennet, ist, wenn anstad einer großen Note mehr kleinere und in unterschiedlichen Clavibus sich ereignen, welche zu der nachfolgenden Note eilen.

The *variatio*, otherwise called *passaggio*, occurs when, instead of a longer note, numerous shorter ones at various pitches are introduced which rush to the following note.

Printz (*Phrynis Mytilenaeus* pt.2, p.46)
Hier aber ist zu wissen / daß das Wort Variatio bey denen Musicis auff zweyerley Weise gebraucht wird / nemlich late und stricte. In stricta Significatione ist Variatio eine künstliche Veränderung eines vorgegebenen Moduli, da man dieses allezeit in jener mercken und abnehmen kan. In lata Significatione aber ist Variatio eine jede Veränderung eines Moduli, es werde gleich dieser in jener vermercket oder nicht.

It should be known that the word *variatio* is used in two ways by musicians, namely in both a broad and a strict sense. In a strict sense, *variatio* refers to an artful alteration [figuration] of a given melodic passage, yet in which the original melody is always noticed and recognized. In a broad sense, *variatio* signifies any kind of alteration of a melodic passage whether it includes the former kind or not.

(*Phrynis Mytilenaeus* pt.2, p.65)
Passaggio ist / wenn etliche lauffende Figuren / jedoch anders als in Tirata und Circulo zusammen gesetzt werden: Item, wenn Circuli, Tirate, Bombilantes und einfache lauffende / viel oder wenig zusammen gesetzt werden.

A *passaggio* occurs when a number of running figures are combined, yet in a different manner from the *tirata* or *circulo*. Likewise, when many or few *circuli, tirate, bombilantes*, and other simple running figures are combined.

Janovka (*Clavis* p.23)
Colloraturae sunt cursus aliqui in cantu parvi, qui Diminutiones aliter etiam vocantur, eo quod nota in qua aut loco cujus fiunt, diminuatur, seu in minores dissolvatur.

Colloraturae, otherwise also called *diminutiones*, are various short runs in the melody which are generated through reducing or breaking up a note in itself or its place into smaller notes.

Janovka (*Clavis* p.34)
Diminutiones. vide Colloraturae

Diminutiones. See *Colloraturae*.

Janovka (*Clavis* p.96)
Passagae (vocabulum Italicum) dicuntur diminutiones seu colloraturae aut pulchri celeres a tertia, quarta, aut quandoque etiam quinta clavi sursum celerrime facti alique cursus.

Passagae, an Italian term for *diminutiones* or *colloraturae*, are any delightful rapid and most quickly executed runs through the interval of a third, fourth, or even up to a fifth.

Vogt (*Conclave* p.148)
Omnes hae figurae ad faciendum passagio conducunt: atque si passagio Italicum est, in ordinatam phantasiam resolvi potest. Imo habita phantasia his figuris variatur. Vide exemplum:

All these *figurae* [*simplices*] can serve to make a *passaggio*. Moreover, the Italian *passaggio* is such that it can reveal the arranged *phantasia*. Indeed, the structure of the *phantasia* is varied through these *figurae* [*simplices*], as in the example:

Walther (*Praecepta* p.153)
Variatio. Sonsten auch Passagio genannt ist, wenn an statt einer groβen und langen Note, allerhand geschwinde Läufflein gemacht werden.

The *variatio*, otherwise also called *passaggio*, occurs when, instead of a larger and longer note, numerous rapid runs are formulated.

Walther (*Lexicon*)
Coloratura, pl. Colorature (ital.) ist das gemeine und sehr bekannte Wort, so man allen geschwinden Figuren, als: den Circoli mezzi, Tremoli, Trilli, Diminutione, Variationi, und andern überhaupt beyzulegen pflegt, weil sie fein bunt und farbicht aussehen.

Coloratura, *colorature* is the common and very familiar word used in reference to all rapid figures, such as the *circoli mezzi*, *tremoli*, *trilli*, *diminutione*, *variationi*, and generally all other figures on account of their colorful appearance.

Diminutio ist eben was Coloratura, wenn man nemlich eine groβe Note in viel kleine zertheilet. Es gibt deren vielerley Arten, als: 1) gradatim gehende, dergleichen

The *diminutio* has the same meaning as *coloratura*, namely, the division of a long note into numerous shorter ones. This can be accomplished either through the many

die Trilli, Tremoli, Tremoletti, Groppi, Circoli mezzi, Fioretti, Tirate, Ribattuti di gola, u.s.f. sind 2) Saltuatim eingerichtete, nemlich um eine Terz, Quart, Quint, u.s.f. springende. Ehemahls hieß auch Diminutio, wenn der Tact um den dritten Theil, oder um die Helffte geschwinder, als ordinair gewöhnlich, gegeben wurde.

stepwise ornaments, such as *trilli, tremoli, tremoletti, groppi, circoli mezzi, fioretti, tirate, ribattuti di gola*, and similar figures, or through figures which leap by a third, fourth, fifth, etc. Previously, *diminutio* also referred to the acceleration of the established *tactus* by a third or a half.

Passaggio [ital.] Passage [gall.] ist, wenn etliche lauffende Figuren anders als in Tirata und Circolo zusammen gesetzt werden. it. wenn Circoli, Tiratae bombilantes und einfach lauffende, viel oder wenig einander unmittelbar folgen. s. Printzens Compendium Signatoriae & Modulatoriae vocalis, pag. 53. oder, nach Brossards Beschreibung, eine Reihe Gesang, aus vielen kleinen Noten, als Achteln, Sechzehentheilen etc. bestehend, so 1. 2. oder aufs längste 3 Tacte währet. s. dessen Dictionaire, p.89. Am 303ten Blatte erkläret er es durch Morceau de Chant; und giebt dadurch zu verstehen: daß eine Passage nicht länger seyn solle, als man in einem Athem verrichten könne; gleich einem Bissen (morceau) den man auf einmal ins Maul nimmt.

A *passaggio* . . . occurs when a number of running figures are combined, yet in a different manner from the *tirata* or *circulo*. Likewise, when many or few *circuli, tiratae, bombilantes*, and other simple running figures immediately follow each other. See Printz's *Compendium*, p.53. According to Brossard's description, a *passage* is a row of numerous smaller notes such as eighths and sixteenths extending over one, two, or at the most three measures. See his *Dictionnaire*, p.89. On page 303 he explains it through *morceau de chant*, where he states that a *passage* should not extend beyond the limit of one breath, just like the bite of food (*morceau*) which one takes at one time.

Variazione [ital.] Variation [gall.] Variatio [lat.] heisset: wenn eine schlechte Sing- oder Spiel-Melodie durch Anbringung kleinerer Noten verändert und ausgeschmücket wird, doch so, daß man dennoch die Grund-Melodie mercket und verstehet.

Variatio . . . occurs when an unadorned vocal or instrumental melody is altered and embellished through the introduction of smaller notes, yet in such a manner that the principal melody notes can still be perceived and understood.

Mattheson (*Capellmeister* p.116)

Eigentlich ist es eine solche Figur, dadurch aus wenigen Grund-Noten gewisser maassen ihrer mehr, und kleinere (Man nennet dergleichen Zierrath durchgehends: Diminutionem Notarum; In der Pöbel-Sprache: eine Variation.) gemacht werden.

In fact, it [*circolo mezzo*] is such a figure, which occurs when numerous additional smaller notes, in a sense, are generated out of a few principal notes. [Footnote:] All such embellishments are called *diminutionem notarum*; known as *Variation* in the vernacular.

Scheibe (*Compendium*)

Variatio ist, wenn ich nemlich die Dis-

The *variatio* occurs when the dissonances

sonanz vor der Resolution durch kleinere Noten variire.

before a resolution are varied through smaller notes.

Spiess (*Tractatus* p.156)
Variatio, Veränderung, heisset, wann eine Sing- oder Spihl-Melodia durch Anbringung kleinerer Noten veränderet und ausgeschmücket wird, doch so, daß man dannoch die Grund-Melodey oder Grund-Satz mercket, verstehet, und beybehaltet. Es geschehen aber die Variationes theils durch Verklein- und Verminderung der Noten (Diminutione Notarum) theils durch kleine, grosse, gleiche, ungleiche Läuffe, Sprüng etc. welche auch Figurae simplices genennet, und gleich jetzt sollen fürgestellet werden, so, wie Maurit Vogt fol. 147. & seqq gibt. Sie heissen mit ihren welschen Kunst-Wörtern, Figura Curta, Groppo, Circolo, Tirata, Messanza oder Misticanza, Tenuta, Ribattuta etc.

The *variatio* or alteration occurs when an unadorned vocal or instrumental melody is altered and embellished through the introduction of smaller notes, yet in such a manner that the principal melody notes or theme is still perceived, understood, and retained. These *variationes* are the result partly of a lessening or diminution of the notes' durations (called *diminutione notarum*), partly through smaller, larger, equal, and unequal runs and leaps, which are also called *figurae simplices.* These are now to be introduced as Vogt did. They are given the Italian terminology of *Figura Curta*, *Groppo*, *Circolo*, *Tirata*, *Messanza* or *Misticanza*, *Tenuta*, *Ribattuta*, etc.

Appendices

Appendix 1: Summary of Figure Definitions

Abruptio: a sudden and unexpected break in a musical composition.
Accentus, *Superjectio*: a preceding or succeeding upper or lower neighboring note, usually added to the written note by the performer.
Acciaccatura: an additional, dissonant note added to a chord, which is released immediately after its execution.
Anabasis, *Ascensus*: an ascending musical passage which expresses ascending or exalted images or affections.
Anadiplosis, *Reduplicatio*: (1) a repetition of a *mimesis*; (2) a repetition of the ending of one phrase at the beginning of the following one.
Analepsis: a repetition of a *noema* at the same pitch.
Anaphora, *Repetitio*: (1) a repeating bass line; ground bass; (2) a repetition of the opening phrase or motive in a number of successive passages; (3) a general repetition.
Anaploce: a repetition of a *noema*, particularly between choirs in a polychoral composition.
Anticipatio, *Praesumptio*: an additional upper or lower neighboring note following a principal note, prematurely introducing a note belonging to the subsequent harmony or chord.
Antimetabole: see *Hypallage*
Antistaechon: a substituted dissonance for an expected consonance, usually the result of the melody remaining on the same pitch while the bass implies harmonic changes.
Antistrophe: see *Hypallage*
Antithesis, *Antitheton*, *Contrapositum*: a musical expression of opposing affections, harmonies, or thematic material.
Apocope: an omitted or shortened final note in one voice of a composition.
Aposiopesis: a rest in one or all voices of a composition; a general pause.
Apotomia: an enharmonic rewriting of a semitone.
Ascensus: see *Anabasis*
Assimilatio, *Homoiosis*: a musical representation of the text's imagery.
Asyndeton: an omission of the appropriate conjunctions in a text.
Auxesis, *Incrementum*: successive repetitions of a musical passage which rise by step.
Bombus, *Bombi*, *Bombilans*: four identical notes in rapid succession.
Cadentia Duriuscula: a dissonance in the pre-penultimate harmony of a cadence.

Catabasis, *Descensus*: a descending musical passage which expresses descending, lowly, or negative images or affections.

Catachresis: see *Faux Bourdon*

Celeritas: see *Transitus*

Cercar della nota: see *Subsumptio*

Circulatio, *Circulo*, *Kyklosis*: a series of usually eight notes in a circular or sine wave formation.

Climax, *Gradatio*: (1) a sequence of notes in one voice repeated either at a higher or lower pitch; (2) two voices moving in ascending or descending parallel motion; (3) a gradual increase or rise in sound and pitch, creating a growth in intensity.

Coloratura: see *Variatio*

Commissura: see *Transitus*

Complexio, *Complexus*, *Symploce*: a musical passage which repeats its opening phrase at its conclusion.

Congeries, *Synathroismus*: an accumulation of alternating perfect and imperfect consonances, such as root-position and first-inversion triads.

Consonantiae Impropriae: false consonances, such as certain fourths, diminished or augmented fifths, augmented seconds, and diminished sevenths.

Contrapositio: see *Antithesis*

Corta: a three-note figure in which one note's duration equals the sum of the other two.

Deminutio: see *Transitus*

Descensus: see *Catabasis*

Diabasis: see *Metabasis*

Diminutio, *Meiosis*: (1) various elaborations of longer notes through subdivision into notes of lesser duration; (2) a restatement of thematic material in proportionally shorter note values.

Distributio: a musical-rhetorical process in which individual motifs or phrases of a theme or section of a composition are developed before proceeding to the following material.

Dubitatio: an intentionally ambiguous rhythmic or harmonic progression.

Ecphonesis: see *Exclamatio*

Ellipsis, *Synecdoche*: (1) an omission of an expected consonance; (2) an abrupt interruption in the music.

Emphasis: a musical passage which heightens or emphasizes the meaning of the text through various means.

Epanadiplosis, *Reduplicatio*: a restatement of the opening of a passage or phrase at its close.

Epanalepsis, *Resumptio*: (1) a frequent repetition of an expression; (2) a restatement of the opening of a passage at its close.

Epanodos, *Regressio*, *Reditus*: a retrograde repetition of a phrase.

Epiphora, *Epistrophe*: a repetition of the conclusion of one passage at the end of subsequent passages.

Epizeuxis: an immediate and emphatic repetition of a word, note, motif, or phrase.

Ethophonia: see *Mimesis*

Exclamatio, Ecphonesis: a musical exclamation, frequently associated with an exclamation in the text.

Extensio: a prolongation of a dissonance.

Faux Bourdon, Catachresis, Simul Procedentia: a musical passage characterized by successive sixth-chord progressions.

Fuga: (1) a compositional device in which a principal voice is imitated by subsequent voices; (2) a musical passage which employs *fuga* to vividly express chasing or fleeing.

Gradatio: see *Climax*

Groppo: a four-note motif in arch formation with a common first and third note.

Heterolepsis: an intrusion of one voice into the range of another.

Homoioptoton, Homoioteleuton: (1) a general pause in all voices (*aposiopesis*), either interrupting the composition (*homoioptoton*) or following a cadence (*homoioteleuton*); (2) similar endings of a number of subsequent passages.

Homoiosis: see *Assimilatio*

Hypallage: an inversion of the fugal theme.

Hyperbaton: a transfer of notes or phrases from their normal placement to a different location.

Hyperbole/Hypobole, Licentia: a transgression of the range or *ambitus* of a *modus*.

Hypotyposis: a vivid musical representation of images found in the accompanying text.

Imitatio: see *Mimesis*

Inchoatio Imperfecta: an omission of the opening consonance in the melody which is supplied by the *basso continuo* realization.

Incrementum: see *Auxesis*

Interrogatio: a musical question rendered variously through pauses, a rise at the end of the phrase or melody, or through imperfect or phrygian cadences.

Kyklosis: see *Circulatio*

Licentia: see *Hyperbole, Parrhesia*

Ligatura: see *Syncopatio*

Longinqua Distantia: a distance between two neighboring voices of a composition in excess of a twelfth.

Manubrium: see *Paragoge*

Messanza: a series of four notes of short duration, moving either by step or by leap.

Metabasis, Transgressio: a crossing of one voice by another.

Metalepsis, Transumptio: a *fuga* with a two-part subject, the parts alternating in the composition.

Mimesis, *Ethophonia*, *Imitatio*: (1) a repetition of a *noema* at a different pitch; (2) an approximate rather than strict imitation of a subject at different pitches.

Misticanza: see *Messanza*

Mora: a rising resolution of a *syncopatio* when a falling one is expected.

Multiplicatio: a subdivision of a longer dissonant note into two or more notes.

Mutatio Toni: an irregular alteration of the mode.

Noema: a homophonic passage within a contrapuntal texture.

Palilogia: a repetition of a theme, either at different pitches in various voices or on the same pitch in the same voice.

Paragoge, *Manubrium*, *Supplementum*: a cadenza or coda added over a pedal point at the end of a composition.

Parembole, *Interjectio*: a supplementary voice in a fugue which fills in the harmony by proceeding parallel to one of the fugue's regular voices.

Parenthesis: a musical representation of parentheses in the associated text.

Paronomasia: a repetition of a musical passage with certain additions or alterations for the sake of greater emphasis.

Parrhesia, *Licentia*: an insertion of a dissonance, such as a cross relation or tritone, on a weak beat.

Passaggio: see *Variatio*

Passus Duriusculus: a chromatically altered ascending or descending melodic line.

Pathopoeia: a musical passage which seeks to arouse a passionate affection through chromaticism or by some other means.

Pausa: a pause or rest in a musical composition.

Pleonasmus: (1) a prolongation of passing dissonances through suspensions; (2) four-part harmonized chant; *falso bordone*.

Polyptoton: a repetition of a melodic passage at different pitches.

Polysyndeton: an immediate repetition of an *emphasis* (*accentus*) in the same voice.

Prolepsis: see *Anticipatio*

Prolongatio: a passing dissonance or suspension of longer duration than the preceding consonance.

Prosopopoeia: see *Hypotyposis*, *Mimesis*, *Pathopoeia*

Quaesitio Notae: see *Subsumptio*

Quasi Transitus: see *Transitus*

Reduplicatio: see *Anadiplosis*, *Epanadiplosis*

Resumptio: see *Epanalepsis*

Repercussio: (1) a modified interval in a tonal fugal answer; (2) a tonal, inverted, or other modified fugal answer.

Repetitio: see *Anaphora*

Retardatio: (1) a suspension which is prolonged or which resolves by rising; (2) a delayed rather than anticipatory suspension.

Reticentia: see *Aposiopesis*
Ribattuta: an accelerating trill in dotted rhythm, used to embellish a *tenuta* or a note of extended duration.
Salti Composti: a four-note figuration consisting of three consonant leaps.
Salto Semplice: a consonant leap.
Saltus Duriusculus: a dissonant leap.
Schematoides: a figure which restructures a previous passage either through changing text underlay or through durational augmentation or diminution.
Sectio: see *Tmesis*
Sexta Superflua: see *Consonantiae Impropriae*
Simul Procedentia: see *Faux Bourdon*
Stenasmus: see *Suspiratio*
Subsumptio, *Quaesitio Notae* (*Cercar della nota*): various additions of lower neighboring notes.
Superjectio: see *Accentus*
Supplementum: see *Paragoge*
Suspensio: a delayed introduction of a composition's principal thematic material.
Suspiratio, *Stenasmus*: the musical expression of a sigh through a rest.
Symblema: see *Transitus*
Symploce: see *Complexio*
Synaeresis: (1) a suspension or syncopation; (2) a placement of two syllables per note, or two notes per syllable.
Synathroismus: see *Congeries*
Syncopatio, *Ligatura*: a suspension, with or without a resulting dissonance.
Synonymia: a repetition of a musical idea in an altered or modified form.
Tenuta: see *Ribattuta*
Tertia Deficiens: see *Consonantiae Impropriae*
Tirata: a rapid scalar passage spanning a fourth to an octave or more.
Tmesis, *Sectio*: a sudden interruption or fragmentation of the melody through rests.
Transgressio: see *Metabasis*
Transitus, *Celeritas*, *Commissura*, *Deminutio*, *Symblema*: a dissonant or passing note between two consonant ones, either on the strong or the weak beat.
Transumptio: see *Metalepsis*
Tremolo, *Trillo*: (1) an instrumental or vocal trembling on one note, resulting in a wavering pitch or vibrato; (2) a rapid reiteration of one note; (3) a rapid alternation of two adjacent notes; a trill.
Variatio, *Coloratura*, *Diminutio*, *Passaggio*: an ornamentation of a melodic passage with a variety of embellishments.

Appendix 2: Summary of Figures by Category

A. Figures of Melodic Repetition

Anadiplosis: a repetition of the ending of one phrase at the beginning of the following one.
Anaphora, Repetitio: (1) a repeating bass line; ground bass; (2) a repetition of the opening phrase or motive in a number of successive passages; (3) a general repetition.
Auxesis, Incrementum: successive repetitions of a musical passage which rise by step.
Climax, Gradatio: (1) a sequence of notes in one voice repeated at either a higher or lower pitch; (2) two voices moving in ascending or descending parallel motion; (3) a gradual increase or rise in sound and pitch, creating a growth in intensity.
Complexio, Complexus, Symploce: a musical passage which repeats its opening phrase at its conclusion.
Epanadiplosis, Reduplicatio: a restatement of the opening of a passage or phrase at its close.
Epanalepsis, Resumptio: (1) a frequent repetition of an expression; (2) a restatement of the opening of a passage at its close.
Epanodos, Regressio, Reditus: a retrograde repetition of a phrase.
Epiphora, Epistrophe, Homoioptoton: a repetition of the conclusion of one passage at the end of subsequent passages.
Epizeuxis: an immediate and emphatic repetition of a word, note, motif, or phrase.
Mimesis, Ethophonia, Imitatio: an approximate rather than strict imitation of a subject at different pitches.
Palilogia: a repetition of a theme, either at different pitches in various voices or on the same pitch in the same voice.
Polyptoton: a repetition of a melodic passage at different pitches.
Polysyndeton: an immediate repetition of an *emphasis* (*accentus*) in the same voice.
Synonymia: a repetition of a musical idea in an altered or modified form.

B. Figures of Harmonic Repetition; Fugal Figures

Anadiplosis: a repetition of a *mimesis*.
Analepsis: a repetition of a *noema* at the same pitch.
Anaploce: a repetition of a *noema*, particularly between choirs in a polychoral composition.

Fuga: a compositional device in which a principal voice is imitated by subsequent voices.

Hypallage, *Antimetabole*, *Antistrophe*: an inversion of the fugal theme.

Metalepsis, *Transumptio*: a *fuga* with a two-part subject, the parts alternating in the composition.

Mimesis: a repetition of a *noema* at a different pitch.

Parembole, *Interjectio*: a supplementary voice in a fugue which fills in the harmony by proceeding parallel to one of the fugue's regular voices.

Paronomasia: a repetition of a musical passage with certain additions or alterations for the sake of greater emphasis.

Repercussio: (1) a modified interval in a tonal fugal answer; (2) a tonal, inverted, or other modified fugal answer.

C. Figures of Representation and Depiction

Anabasis, *Ascensus*: an ascending musical passage which expresses ascending or exalted images or affections.

Antithesis, *Antitheton*, *Contrapositum*: a musical expression of opposing affections, harmonies, or thematic material.

Assimilatio, *Homoiosis*: a musical representation of the text's imagery.

Catabasis, *Descensus*: a descending musical passage which expresses descending, lowly, or negative images or affections.

Circulatio, *Circulo*, *Kyklosis*: a series of usually eight notes in a circular or sine wave formation.

Dubitatio: an intentionally ambiguous rhythmic or harmonic progression expressing doubt.

Emphasis: a musical passage which heightens or emphasizes the meaning of the text through various means.

Exclamatio, *Ecphonesis*: a musical exclamation, frequently associated with an exclamation in the text.

Fuga in alio sensu: a musical passage which employs *fuga* to vividly express chasing or fleeing.

Hypotyposis, *Prosopopoeia*: a vivid musical representation of images found in the accompanying text.

Interrogatio: a musical question rendered variously through pauses, a rise at the end of the phrase or melody, or through imperfect or phrygian cadences.

Metabasis, *Transgressio*: a crossing of one voice by another.

Noema: a homophonic passage within a contrapuntal texture, used for emphasis.

Parenthesis: a musical representation of parentheses in the associated text.

Pathopoeia: a musical passage which seeks to arouse a passionate affection through chromaticism or some other means.

D. Figures of Dissonance and Displacement

Antistaechon: a substituted dissonance for an expected consonance, usually the result of the melody remaining on the same pitch while the bass implies harmonic changes.
Apocope: an omitted or shortened final note in one voice of a composition.
Apotomia: an enharmonic rewriting of a semitone.
Asyndeton: an omission of the appropriate conjunctions in a text.
Cadentia Duriuscula: a dissonance in the pre-penultimate harmony of a cadence.
Congeries, *Synathroismus*: an accumulation of alternating perfect and imperfect consonances, such as root-position and first-inversion triads.
Consonantiae Impropriae: false consonances, such as certain fourths, diminished or augmented fifths, augmented seconds, and diminished sevenths.
Ellipsis, *Synecdoche*: (1) an omission of an expected consonance; (2) an abrupt interruption in the music.
Extensio: a prolongation of a dissonance.
Faux Bourdon, *Catachresis*, *Simul Procedentia*: a musical passage characterized by successive sixth-chord progressions.
Heterolepsis: an intrusion of one voice into the range of another.
Hyperbaton: a transfer of notes or phrases from their normal placement to a different location.
Hyperbole/Hypobole: a transgression of the range or *ambitus* of a *modus*.
Inchoatio Imperfecta: an omission of the opening consonance in the melody which is supplied by the *basso continuo* realization.
Longinqua Distantia: a distance between two neighboring voices of a composition in excess of a twelfth.
Mora: a rising resolution of a *syncopatio* when a falling one is expected.
Multiplicatio: a subdivision of a longer dissonant note into two or more notes.
Mutatio Toni: an irregular alteration of the mode.
Parrhesia, *Licentia*: an insertion of a dissonance, such as a cross relation or tritone, on a weak beat.
Passus Duriusculus: a chromatically altered ascending or descending melodic line.
Pleonasmus: (1) a prolongation of passing dissonances through suspensions; (2) four-part harmonized chant; *falso bordone.*
Prolongatio: a passing dissonance or suspension of longer duration than the preceding consonance.
Retardatio: (1) a suspension which is prolonged or which resolves by rising; (2) a delayed rather than anticipatory suspension.
Saltus Duriusculus: a dissonant leap.
Synaeresis: (1) a suspension or syncopation; (2) a placement of two syllables

per note, or two notes per syllable.

Syncopatio, *Ligatura*: a suspension, with or without a resulting dissonance.

Transitus, *Celeritas*, *Commissura*, *Deminutio*, *Symblema*: a dissonant or passing note between two consonant ones, either on the strong or the weak beat.

E. Figures of Interruption and Silence

Abruptio: a sudden and unexpected break in a musical composition.

Aposiopesis, *Reticentia*: a rest in one or all voices of a composition; a general pause.

Ellipsis, *Synecdoche*: (1) an omission of an expected consonance; (2) an abrupt interruption in the music.

Homoioptoton, *Homoioteleuton*: a general pause in all voices (*aposiopesis*), either interrupting the composition (*homoioptoton*) or following a cadence (*homoioteleuton*).

Pausa: a pause or rest in a musical composition.

Suspiratio, *Stenasmus*: a musical expression of a sigh through a rest.

Tmesis, *Sectio*: a sudden interruption or fragmentation of the melody through rests.

F. Figures of Melodic and Harmonic Ornamentation

Accentus, *Superjectio*: a preceding or succeeding upper or lower neighboring note, usually added to the written note by the performer.

Acciaccatura: an additional, dissonant note added to a chord, which is released immediately after its execution.

Anticipatio, *Praesumptio*, *Prolepsis*: an additional upper or lower neighboring note after a principal note, prematurely introducing a note belonging to the subsequent harmony or chord.

Bombus, *Bombi*, *Bombilans*: four identical notes in rapid succession.

Corta: a three-note figure, in which one note's duration equals the sum of the other two.

Groppo: a four-note motif in arch formation with a common first and third note.

Messanza, *Misticanza*: a series of four notes of short duration, moving either by step or by leap.

Ribattuta, *Tenuta*: an accelerating trill in dotted rhythm, used to embellish a *tenuta* or a note of extended duration.

Salti Composti: a four-note figuration consisting of three consonant leaps.

Salto Semplice: a consonant leap.

Subsumptio, *Quaesitio Notae (Cercar della nota)*: various additions of lower neighboring notes.
Tirata: a rapid scalar passage spanning a fourth to an octave or more.
Tremolo, *Trillo*: (1) an instrumental or vocal trembling on one note, resulting in a wavering pitch or vibrato; (2) a rapid reiteration of one note; (3) a rapid alternation of two adjacent notes; a trill.
Variatio, *Coloratura*, *Diminutio*, *Passaggio*: an ornamentation of a melodic passage with a variety of embellishments.

G. Miscellaneous Figures

Diminutio, *Meiosis*: (1) various elaborations of longer notes through subdivision into notes of lesser duration; (2) a restatement of thematic material in proportionally shorter note values.
Distributio: a musical-rhetorical process in which individual motifs or phrases of a theme or section of a composition are developed before proceeding to the following material.
Paragoge, *Manubrium*, *Supplementum*: a cadenza or coda added over a pedal point at the end of a composition.
Schematoides: a figure which restructures a previous passage either through changing text underlay or through durational augmentation or diminution.
Suspensio: a delayed introduction of a composition's principal thematic material.

Appendix 3: List of Figures by Author

(Authors are listed in alphabetical order, the figures in order of their appearance in the respective treatises.)

Ahle
epizeuxis
anaphora
synonymia
asyndeton
polysyndeton
anadiplosis
climax
epistrophe
epanalepsis
epanodos
antithesis
emphasis

Bernhard (*Tractatus*)
stylus gravis
transitus/deminutio
syncopatio
stylus luxurians communis
superjectio/accentus
anticipatio
subsumptio
variatio/passaggio/coloratura
multiplicatio
prolongatio

syncopatio catachrestica
passus duriusculus
mutatio toni
inchoatio imperfecta
longinqua distantia
consonantiae impropriae
quaesitio notae
cadentiae duriusculae

stylus luxurians theatralis

extensio
ellipsis
mora
abruptio
transitus inversus
heterolepsis
tertia deficiens
sexta superflua

BERNHARD (*Bericht*)

figurae fundamentales

syncopatio/ligatura
transitus/deminutio
(regularis, irregularis)

figurae superficiales

superjectio/accentus
subsumptio
variatio/passaggio
multiplicatio
ellipsis
retardatio
heterolepsis
quasitransitus
abruptio

BURMEISTER (*Hypomnematum*)

fuga realis
fuga imaginaria
hypallage
apocope
palilogia
paremobole
anaphora
noema
analepsis
metalepsis
mimesis
anadiplosis
symblema/commissura
syncopa
pleonasmus
auxesis
congeries
fauxbourdon
parrhesia
hyperbole
pathopoeia
hypotyposis
aposiopesis

BURMEISTER

(*Musica Autoschediastike,*
Musica Poetica)

figurae harmoniae

fuga realis
metalepsis
hypallage
apocope
noema
analepsis
mimesis
anadiplosis
symblema
syncopa/synaeresis
pleonasmus
auxesis
pathopoeia
hypotyposis
aposiopesis
anaploce

figurae melodiae

parembole
palilogia
climax
parrhesia
hyperbole
hypobole

figurae tam harmoniae quam melodiae

congeries/synathroismus
faux bourdon/
simul procedentia
anaphora
fuga imaginaria

(listed elsewhere)

supplementum

FORKEL

ellipsis
Wiederholung (repetitio)
paronomasia
suspensio

epistrophe
gradatio
dubitatio
Gegensatz (antithesis)
Zergliederung (distributio)
synonymia

JANOVKA

figurae principales
commissura
syncopatio
fuga

figurae minus principales
pausa
stenasmus/suspiratio
anaphora/repetitio
climax/gradatio
complexus
similiter desinens
antitheton/contrapositum
anabasis/ascensio
catabasis/descensus
circulatio
fuga (in alio sensu)
assimilatio
abruptio

(listed elsewhere)
falso bordone/pleonasmus
colloraturae
diminutiones
passagae

KIRCHER (*Liber* 5)

figurae principales
commissura/symblema/
celeritas
syncopatio
fuga (totalis, partialis)

figurae minus principales
(not defined)
pausa
repetitio
climax
complexus
anaphora
catachresis
noema
prosopopoeia
parrhesia
aposiopesis
paragoge
apocope

(*Liber* 8, defined)
pausa
stenasmus/suspiratio
anaphora/repetitio
climax/gradatio
symploce/complexus
homoioptoton/
similiter desinens
antitheton/contrapositum
anabasis/ascensio
catabasis/descensus
kyklosis/circulatio
fuga (in alio sensu)
homoiosis/assimilatio
abruptio

MATTHESON

Manieren (*Figurae cantionis*)
accent (Vorschlag,
Überschlag)
tremolo
trillo
trilletto
groppo
circolo mezzo
tirata
tenuta
ribattuta
Durchgang/transitus
mordant
acciacatura

(listed elsewhere)
synonymia
repercussio/refractio
emphasis
interrogatio
exclamatio
parenthesis
Fuge
imitatio

figurae cantus
epizeuxis/subjunctio
anaphora
epanalepsis
epistrophe
anadiplosis
paronomasia

polyptoton
antanaclasis
ploce
exclamatio
parrhesia
paradoxa
epamorthosis
paraleipsis
aposiopesis
apostrophe

NUCIUS

figurae principales
commissura (directa, cadens)
fuga (totalis, partialis)
repetitio

figurae minus principales
climax
complexio
homioteleuton
syncopatio

(listed elsewhere)
manubrium

PRINTZ

Einfache Figuren
variatio
accentus
tremolo
groppo
circulo mezo
tirata meza
bombi
salto semplice
salti composti
corta
messanza
suspirans
trillo
trilletto

Zusammengesetzte Figuren
circulo
tirata
bombilans
passagio
tremamento longo
mistichanza composta
pausa
schematoides

SCHEIBE (*Compendium*)
anticipatio
retardatio
variatio
generum Verwechselung

SCHEIBE (*Critischer Musicus*)
exclamatio
dubitatio
ellipsis
hyperbaton
repetitio
paronomasia
distributio
antithesis
suspensio
interrogatio
epistophe
gradatio

harmonische Figuren
transitus (regularis, irregularis)
sycopatio/ligatura
Fuge

SPIESS

figurae simplices
variatio
curta
groppo
circulo
circulo mezzo
tirata
messanza
tenuta
ribattuta
superjectio
trillo
mordent
acciaccatura

figurae
abruptio
accentus
anabasis/ascensus
catabasis/descensus
anaphora
antithesis/contrapositio
antistaechon
aposiopesis

accentus
anticipatio
retardatio
emphasis
ethophonia/mimesis
diminutio
imitatio
metabasis
tmesis/sectio

THURINGUS

figurae principales

commissura/symblema/
celeritas (directa, cadens)
fuga
syncopatio

figurae minus principales

pausa
repetitio/mimesis
climax/gradatio
complexio
anaphora
catachresis/fauxbourdon
noema
parthopoeia
parrhisia
aposiopesis (homioptoton/
homioteleuton)
paragoge
apocope

VOGT

figurae simplices

tremula
trilla
accentus
mezocircolo
curta
groppo
circulus
tirata
messanza
coulé
herbeccio
harpegiaturae
passaggio

figurae ideales

anabasis/ascensus
catabasis/descensus
anadiplosis
anaphora
antistaechon
antitheton
aposiopesis
apotomia
climax
ecphonesis
epanalepsis
ethophonia/mimesis
emphasis
polyptoton
polysyntheton
schematoides
metabasis
sinaeresis
stenasmus
tmesis/sectio

(listed elsewhere)

hypotyposis
prosopopoeia
prosonomasia

E. WALTHER

fuga
hypallage
climax
anadiplosis
hypotyposis
anaphora
mimesis
pathopoeia
syncope
paremoble
auxesis

J. G. WALTHER (*Praecepta*)

figurae fundamentales

syncopatio/ligatura
transitus/commissura
(regularis, irregularis)
fuga

figurae superficiales

superjectio/accentus
subsumptio
variatio
multiplicatio
ellipsis
retardatio
heterolepsis
abruptio

quasitransitus
(mentioned, but not defined)
epizeuxis
anaphora
synonymia
anadiplosis
epistrophe
epanalepsis

J. G. WALTHER (*Lexicon*)
abruptio
accentus
acciaccatura
anabasis
anadiplosis/reduplicatio
analepsis
anaphora
anticipatio notae
antithesis
antitheton
apocope
aposiopesis (homoeoteleuton, homoeoptoton)
apotome
auxesis
bombilans
bombo
catabasis
catachresis
cercar della nota
circolo
circulo mezzo
climax/gradatio
coloratura
commissura (cadens, directa)
complexio
corta
diminutio
ellipsis
epanadiplosis/reduplicatio
epanalepsis/resumptio
epanodos
epistrophe/epiphora
epizeuxis/adjunctio
exclamatio/ecphonesis
falso bordone
fauxbourdon
figura muta
fuga
groppo
messanza
mimesis/imitatio
mutatio
noema
palilogia
paragoge
parrhesia
passaggio
pausa
repercussio
retardatio
salti composti
salto semplice
superjectio
suspirans
symblema
sycopatio
tirata
transitus
tremolo
trillo
trilletto
variatio

APPENDIX 4: SUMMARY OF FIGURES BY AUTHOR

Abruptio: Bernhard, Janovka, Kircher, Spiess, Vogt, Walther
Accentus, *Superjectio*: Bernhard, Mattheson, Printz, Spiess, Walther
Acciaccatura: Mattheson, Spiess, Walther
Anabasis, *Ascensus*: Janovka, Kircher, Spiess, Vogt, Walther

Anadiplosis: Ahle, Burmeister, Mattheson, Vogt, Walther
Analepsis: Burmeister, Walther
Anaphora, Repetitio: Ahle, Burmeister, Forkel, Janovka, Kircher, Mattheson, Nucius, Scheibe, Spiess, Thuringus, Vogt, Walther
Anaploce: Burmeister
Anticipatio, Praesumptio: Bernhard, Scheibe, Spiess, Walther
Antimetabole: see *Hypallage*
Antistaechon: Spiess, Vogt
Antistrophe: see *Hypallage*
Antithesis, Antitheton, Contrapositum: Forkel, Janovka, Kircher, Mattheson, Scheibe, Spiess, Vogt, Walther
Apocope: Burmeister, Thuringus, Walther
Aposiopesis: Burmeister, Spiess, Thuringus, Vogt, Walther
Apotomia: Vogt, Walther
Ascensus: see *Anabasis*
Assimilatio, Homoiosis: Janovka, Kircher
Asyndeton: Ahle
Auxesis, Incrementum: Burmeister, Walther
Bombus, Bombi, Bombilans: Printz, Walther
Cadentia Duriuscula: Bernhard
Catabasis, Descensus: Janovka, Kircher, Spiess, Vogt, Walther
Catachresis: see *Faux Bourdon*
Celeritas: see *Transitus*
Cercar della nota: see *Subsumptio*
Circulatio, Circulo, Kyklosis: Janovka, Kircher, Mattheson, Printz, Spiess, Vogt, Walther
Climax, Gradatio: Ahle, Burmeister, Forkel, Janovka, Kircher, Nucius, Scheibe, Thuringus, Vogt, Walther
Coloratura: see *Variatio*
Commissura: see *Transitus*
Complexio, Complexus, Symploce: Janovka, Kircher, Nucius, Thuringus, Walther
Congeries, Synathroismus: Burmeister
Consonantiae Impropriae: Bernhard
Contrapositum: see *Antithesis*
Corta: Printz, Spiess, Walther
Deminutio: see *Transitus*
Descensus: see *Catabasis*
Diabasis: see *Metabasis*
Diminutio, Meiosis: see *Variatio*
Distributio: Forkel, Scheibe
Dubitatio: Forkel, Scheibe
Ecphonesis: see *Exclamatio*

Ellipsis, *Synecdoche*: Bernhard, Forkel, Scheibe, Walther
Emphasis: Mattheson, Spiess, Vogt
Epanadiplosis: Vogt, Walther
Epanalepsis: Ahle, Mattheson, Vogt, Walther
Epanodos, *Regressio*, *Reditus*: Ahle, Walther
Epiphora, *Epistrophe*: Ahle, Mattheson, Forkel, Scheibe, Walther
Epizeuxis: Ahle, Mattheson, Walther
Ethophonia: see *Mimesis*
Exclamatio, *Ecphonesis*: Mattheson, Praetorius, Scheibe, Vogt, Walther
Extensio: Bernhard, Walther
Faux Bourdon, *Catachresis*, *Simul Procedentia*: Burmeister, Janovka, Praetorius, Thuringus, Vogt, Walther, Werckmeister
Fuga: Burmeister, Janovka, Kircher, Mattheson, Nucius, Thuringus, Walther
Gradatio: see *Climax*
Groppo: Mattheson, Printz, Spiess, Walther
Heterolepsis: Bernhard, Walther
Homoioptoton, *Homoioteleuton*: Janovka, Kircher, Nucius, Thuringus, Walther
Homoiosis: see *Assimilatio*
Hypallage: Burmeister
Hyperbaton: Scheibe
Hyperbole/Hypobole: Burmeister
Hypotyposis: Burmeister, Vogt
Imitatio: see *Mimesis*
Inchoatio Imperfecta: Bernhard
Incrementum: see *Auxesis*
Interrogatio: Bernhard, Mattheson, Scheibe
Kyklosis: see *Circulatio*
Licentia: see *Hyperbole*, *Parrhesia*
Ligatura: see *Syncopatio*
Longinqua Distantia: Bernhard
Manubrium: see *Paragoge*
Messanza: Printz, Spiess, Walther
Metabasis, *Transgressio*: Spiess, Vogt
Metalepsis, *Transumptio*: Burmeister
Mimesis, *Ethophonia*, *Imitatio*: Burmeister, Mattheson, Spiess, Thuringus, Vogt, Walther
Misticanza: see *Messanza*
Mora: Bernhard
Multiplicatio: Bernhard, Walther
Mutatio Toni: Bernhard, Walther
Noema: Burmeister, Thuringus, Walther
Palilogia: Burmeister, Walther
Paragoge, *Manubrium*, *Supplementum*: Burmeister, Nucius, Thuringus, Walther

Parembole, *Interjectio*: Burmeister
Parenthesis: Mattheson
Paronomasia: Mattheson, Forkel, Scheibe
Parrhesia, *Licentia*: Bernhard, Burmeister, Herbst, Thuringus, Walther
Passaggio: see *Variatio*
Passus Duriusculus: Bernhard
Pathopoeia: Burmeister, Thuringus
Pausa: Janovka, Kircher, Printz, Thuringus, Walther
Pleonasmus: Burmeister, Janovka, Vogt
Polyptoton: Mattheson, Vogt
Polysyndeton: Ahle, Vogt
Prolepsis: see *Anticipatio*
Prolongatio: Bernhard
Prosopopoeia: Janovka, Kircher, Vogt
Quaesitio Notae: see *Subsumptio*
Quasi Transitus: see *Transitus*
Repercussio: Mattheson, Walther
Repetitio: see *Anaphora*
Retardatio: Bernhard, Scheibe, Spiess, Walther
Reticentia: see *Aposiopesis*
Ribattuta: Mattheson, Spiess
Salti Composti: Printz, Walther
Salto Semplice: Printz, Walther
Saltus Duriusculus: Bernhard
Schematoides: Printz, Vogt
Sectio: see *Tmesis*
Sexta Superflua: see *Consonantiae Impropriae*
Simul Procedentia: see *Faux Bourdon*
Stenasmus: see *Suspiratio*
Subsumptio, *Quaesitio Notae (Cercar della nota)*: Bernhard, Walther
Superjectio: see *Accentus*
Supplementum: see *Paragoge*
Suspensio: Forkel, Scheibe
Suspiratio, *Stenasmus*: Janovka, Kircher, Printz, Vogt, Walther
Symblema: see *Transitus*
Symploce: see *Complexio*
Synaeresis: Burmeister, Vogt
Synathroismus: see *Congeries*
Syncopatio, *Ligatura*: Bernhard, Burmeister, Janovka, Kircher, Nucius, Scheibe, Thuringus, Walther
Synonymia: Ahle, Forkel, Mattheson, Walther
Tenuta: see *Ribattuta*
Tertia Deficiens: see *Consonantiae Impropriae*

Tirata: Mattheson, Printz, Spiess, Walther
Tmesis, Sectio: Spiess, Vogt
Transgressio: see *Metabasis*
Transitus, Celeritas, Commissura, Deminutio, Symblema: Bernhard, Burmeister, Kircher, Mattheson, Nucius, Scheibe, Thuringus, Walther
Transumptio: see *Metalepsis*
Tremolo, Trillo: Mattheson, Praetorius, Printz, Vogt, Walther
Variatio, Coloratura, Diminutio, Passaggio: Bernhard, Janovka, Mattheson, Praetorius, Printz, Scheibe, Spiess, Vogt, Walther

BIBLIOGRAPHY

A. PRIMARY RHETORICAL SOURCES

Caldenbach, Christoph. *Compendium rhetorices*. Tübingen, 1682.
Cicero. *De Oratore*. Loeb Classical Library. London: Heinemann, 1949.
Descartes, René. *Les Passions de l'âme*. Paris: le Gras, 1649. Ed. G. Rodis Lewis. Paris: Librairie philosophique J. Vrin, 1966.
Ernesti, Johann Chr. *Lexicon technologiae Graecorum rhetoricae*. Leipzig, 1795. Facs. ed. Hildesheim: Olms, 1962.
———. *Lexicon technologiae latinorum rhetoricae*. Leipzig, 1797. Facs. ed. Hildesheim: Olms, 1962.
Gottsched, Johann Christoph. *Ausführliche Redekunst nach Anleitung der Greichen und Römer wie auch der neuern Ausländer*. Leipzig: Breitkopf, 1736. Facs. ed. Hildesheim: Olms, 1973.
———. *Versuch einer critischen Dichtkunst*. 4th ed. Leipzig, 1751.
Lamy, Bernhard. *La Rhétorique: ou, l'art de parler*. 4th ed. Paris: Delaulne, 1701.
Lippius, Johannes. *Philosophia verrae et sincerae sinopticae*. Erfurt, 1614.
Lossius, Lucas. *Erotemata Dialecticae et Rhetoricae Philippi Melanchthonis*. Leipzig, 1562.
Melanchton, Philipp. *Institutiones rhetoricae*. The Hague: Anshelm, 1521.
Peacham, Henry. *The Garden of Eloquence*. 2nd ed. London, 1593. Facs. ed. Gainesville FL: Crane, 1954.
Puttenham, George. *The Arte of English Poesie*. London: Field, 1589. New ed. Cambridge University Press, 1936; 1970.
Quintilian. *Institutio oratoria*. Eng. trans. H. E. Butler. London: Heinemann, 1921; Cambridge: Harvard University Press, 1966.
Susenbrotus, Johannes. *Epitome troporum ac schematum et grammaticorum et rhetorum*. Antwerp, 1566.
Vossius, Gerardus. *Commentatorium rhetoricorum*. Leiden, 1606.
———. *Institutiones rhetoricae*. 1630.
Weissenborn, M. Christoph. *Gründliche Einleitung zur teutschen und lateinischen Oratorie*. Dresden/Leipzig: Hübner, 1731.

B. SECONDARY RHETORICAL SOURCES

Arbusow, Leonid. *Colores rhetorici*. Göttingen: Vandenhoeck & Ruprecht, 1948.
Auerbach, Erich. "Figura." In *Gesammelte Aufsätze zur romanischen Philo-*

logie. Bern: Franke, 1967.
Barner, Wilfried. *Barockrhetorik: Untersuchungen zu ihren geschichtlichen Grundlagen*. Tübingen: Niemeyer, 1970.
Kehrein, Joseph. *Beispielsammlung in der Lehre von den Figuren und Tropen*. Berlin: Duncker & Humbolt, 1839.
Kennedy, George A. *Classical Rhetoric and Its Christian and Secular Tradition from Ancient to Modern Times*. Chapel Hill: University of North Carolina Press, 1980.
Kristeller, Paul O. *Renaissance Thought and Its Sources*. New York: Columbia University Press, 1979.
Lausberg, Heinrich. *Handbuch der literarischen Rhetorik*. Munich: Hueber, 1960.
Murphy, James. *A Synoptic History of Classical Rhetoric*. New York: Random House, 1972.
Sonnino, Lee A. *A Handbook to Sixteenth-Century Rhetoric*. London: Routledge & Kegan Paul, 1968.

C. Primary Musical Sources

Ahle, Johann G. *Musikalisches Frühlings-, Sommer-, Herbst-, und Winter-Gespräche*. Mühlhausen: Pauli und Brückner, 1695–1701.
Bach, C. P. E. *Versuch über die wahre Art, das Klavier zu spielen*. Berlin: 1753, 1762. Facs. ed. Leipzig: Breitkopf & Härtel, 1978.
Bacon, Francis. *Sylva Sylvarum; or, A naturall historie, in ten centuries*. London, 1627.
Bernhard, Christoph. *Tractatus compositionis augmentatus*; *Ausführlicher Bericht vom Gebrauche der Con- und Dissonantien*. New ed. In *Die Kompositionslehre Heinrich Schützens in der Fassung seines Schülers Chr. Bernhard*, ed. Joseph M. Müller-Blattau. Leipzig: Breitkopf & Härtel, 1926; 2nd ed., Kassel: Bärenreiter, 1963.
Burmeister, Joachim. *Hypomnematum musicae poeticae*. Rostock: S. Myliander, 1599.
———. *Musica autoschediastike*. Rostock: C. Reusner, 1601.
———. *Musica poetica*. Rostock: S. Myliander, 1606. Facs. ed. Kassel: Bärenreiter, 1955.
Butler, Charles. *The principles of musik*. London, 1636. Facs. ed. New York: Da Capo, 1970.
Calvisius, Seth. *Exercitationes musicae duae*. Leipzig, 1600, 1611.
———. *Melopoeia sive melodiae condendae ratio*. Erfurt, 1592.
Descartes, René. *Compendium musicae*. Utrecht, 1650; *Compendium of Music*. Trans. W. Robert. Rome: American Institute of Musicology, 1961.

Dressler, Gallus. *Praecepta musicae poeticae*. Magdeburg, 1563. New ed. Ed. B. Engelke. Magdeburg: Geschichtsblätter für Stadt und Land Magdeburg, 1914.

Forkel, Johann N. *Allgemeine Geschichte der Musik*. Göttingen, 1788. Facs. ed. Graz: Akademische Druck- und Verlagsanstalt, 1967.

Glareanus, Henricus. *Dodekachordon*. Basel, 1547. Facs. ed. Rome: American Institute of Musicology, 1965.

Heinichen, Johann D. *Der General-Bass in der Composition*. Hamburg, 1711. 2nd ed. Dresden, 1728. Facs. ed. Hildesheim: Olms, 1969.

Herbst, Johann Andreas. *Musica poetica sive compendium melopoeticum*. Nürnberg, 1643.

Janovka, Tomáš. *Clavis ad Thesaurum magnae artis musicae*. Prague, 1701. Facs. ed. Amsterdam: F. Knuf, 1973.

Kircher, Athanasius. *Musurgia Universalis sive ars magna consoni et dissoni*. Rome, 1650. Facs. ed. Hildesheim: Olms, 1970.

Krause, Christian. *Von der musikalischen Poesie*. Berlin, 1752.

Kuhnau, Johann. *Musicalische Vorstellung einiger Biblischer Historien*. Leipzig, 1700. New ed. Ed. K. Stone. New York: Broude Br., 1953.

Lippius, Johannes. *Disputatio musica tertia*. Wittenberg, 1610.

———. *Synopsis musicae nova*. Strassburg, 1612; *Synopsis of New Music*. Trans. Benito Rivera. Colorado Springs: Colorado College Music Press, 1977.

Listenius, Nikolaus. *Rudimenta musicae planae*. Wittenberg, 1533.

Lossius, Lukas. *Erotemata musicae practicae*. Nürnberg, 1563.

Marpurg, Friedrich. *Kritische Briefe über die Tonkunst*. Berlin, 1760–64. Facs. ed. Hildesheim: Olms, 1974.

Mattheson, Johann. *Critica musica*. Hamburg, 1722–25. Facs. ed. Amsterdam: F. Knuf, 1964.

———. *Das neu-eröffnete Orchestre*. Hamburg, 1713.

———. *Der vollkommene Capellmeister*. Hamburg, 1739. Facs. ed. Kassel: Bärenreiter, 1954.

Morely, Thomas. *A Plaine and Easie Introduction to Practicall Musicke*. London, 1597. New ed. Ed. R. A. Harman. New York: Norton, 1952.

Nucius, Johannes. *Musices poeticae sive de compositione cantus*. Niesse, 1613. Facs. ed. Kassel: Bärenreiter, 1976.

Praetorius, Michael. *Syntagma musicum III*. Wolffenbüttel: Holwein, 1619. Facs. ed. Kassel: Bärenreiter, 1958, 1978.

Printz, Wolfgang C. *Phrynis Mytilenaeus oder Satyrischer Componist*. Dresden/Leipzig, 1696.

Quantz, Johann. *Versuch einer Anweisung die Flöte traversiere zu spielen*. Berlin, 1752, 1789. Facs. ed. Kassel: Bärenreiter, 1953.

Rhaw, Georg. *Enchiridion musices*. Leipzig, 1518. Facs. ed. Kassel: Bärenreiter, 1951.

Scheibe, Johann. *Compendium musices theoretico-practicum*. Ca. 1730. New ed. In *Die deutsche Kompositionslehre des 18. Jahrhunderts*, ed. Peter Benary. Leipzig: Breitkopf & Härtel, 1961.

———. *Der critische Musicus*. Leipzig, 1745. Facs. ed. Hildesheim: Olms, 1970.

Speer, Daniel. *Vierfaches musicalisches Kleeblat*. Ulm, 1697.

Spiess, Meinrad. *Tractatus musicus compositorio-practicus*. Augsburg, 1745.

Thuringus, Joachim. *Opusculum bipartitum*. Berlin, 1624.

Tinctorus, Johannes. *Terminorum musicae diffinitorium*. 1495. In *Scriptorum de musica medii aevi*, ed. Charles Edmond Henri de Coussemaker. vol.4. Paris, 1876.

Vogt, Mauritius. *Conclave thesauri magnae artis musicae*. Prague, 1719.

Walther, Elias. *Dissertatio musica*. Tübingen, 1664.

Walther, Johann G. *Musicalisches Lexicon*. Leipzig, 1732. Facs. ed. Kassel: Bärenreiter, 1967.

———. *Praecepta der musicalischen Composition*. Ms 1708. New ed. Ed. P. Benary. Leipzig: Breitkopf & Härtel, 1955.

Werckmeister, Andreas. *Cribrum musicum oder musicalisches Sieb*. Quedlinburg, 1700. Facs. ed. *Hypomnemata musica und andere Schriften*. Hildesheim: Olms, 1970.

———. *Harmonologia musica*. Frankfurt/Leipzig, 1702. Facs. ed. *Hypomnemata musica und andere Schriften*. Hildesheim: Olms, 1970.

———. *Musicae mathematicae Hodegus curiosus*. Frankfurt/Leipzig, 1686.

———. *Musicalische Paradoxal-Discourse*. Quedlinburg, 1707. Facs. ed. *Hypomnemata musica und andere Schriften*. Hildesheim: Olms, 1970.

———. *Musicalisches Send-Schreiben*. Quedlinburg, 1700.

Zarlino, Giuseppe. *Le institutioni harmoniche*. Venice, 1558. Facs. ed. Ridgewood NJ: Gregg, 1966.

D. Secondary Musical Sources

Bartel, Dietrich. *Handbuch der musikalischen Figurenlehre*. Regensburg: Laaber, 1985.

Benary, Peter. *Die deutsche Kompositionslehre des 18. Jahrhunderts*. Leipzig: Breitkopf & Härtel, 1961.

Benitez, Vincent. "Musical-Rhetorical Figures in the Orgelbüchlein of J. S. Bach." *Bach* 18 (1987): 3–21.

Bianconi, Lorenzo. *Music in the Seventeenth Century*. Trans. David Bryant. Cambridge: Cambridge University Press, 1987.

Blume, Friedrich. *Renaissance and Baroque Music*. New York: Norton, 1967.

Bonds, Mark Evan. *Wordless Rhetoric: Musical Form and the Metaphor of the Oration*. Cambridge MA: Harvard University Press, 1991.

Brandes, Heinz. *Studien zur musikalischen Figurenlehre im 16. Jahrhundert*. Berlin: Triltsch & Huther, 1935.

Brown, Leslie E. "Oratorical Thought and the *Tragédie Lyrique*: A Consideration of Musical-Rhetorical Figures." *College Music Symposium* 20 (1980): 99–116.

Buelow, George J. "In Defence of J. A. Scheibe against J. S. Bach." *Proceedings of the Royal Musical Association* 101 (1974–75): 85.

———. "Johann Mattheson and the invention of the *Affektenlehre*." In *New Mattheson Studies*, ed. G. Buelow and H. J. Marx. Cambridge: Cambridge University Press, 1983.

———. "The *Loci Topici* and Affect in Late Baroque Music: Heinichen's Practical Demonstration." *Music Review* 27 (1966): 161–76.

———. "Music, Rhetoric, and the Concept of the Affections: A Selective Bibliography." *NOTES* 30 (1973): 250–59.

———. "Rhetoric and Music." In *The New Grove Dictionary of Music and Musicians*, ed. Stanley Sadie. London: Macmillan, 1980.

———. "Teaching Seventeenth-Century Concepts of Musical Form and Expression: An Aspect of Baroque Music." *College Music Symposium* 27 (1987): 1–13.

———. *Thorough-Bass Accompaniment according to Johann David Heinichen*. Rev. ed. Ann Arbor: UMI Research Press, 1986.

Buszin, Walter. *Luther on Music*. Pamphlet Series, no.3. Saint Paul MA: Lutheran Society for Worship, Music and the Arts, 1958. Originally published in *Musical Quarterly* 32 (1946).

Butler, Gregory. "The Fantasia as Musical Image." *Musical Quarterly* 60 (1974): 602–15.

———. "Fugue and Rhetoric." *Journal of Music Theory* 21 (1977): 49–109.

———. "Music and Rhetoric in Early Seventeenth-Century English Sources." *Musical Quarterly* 66 (1980): 53–64.

Cahn, Peter. "Retardatio, ritardando." In *Handwörterbuch der musikalischen Terminologie*. Wiesbaden: F. Steiner, 1972–.

———. "Transitus." In *Handwörterbuch der musikalischen Terminologie*. Wiesbaden: F. Steiner, 1972–.

Clerx, Suzanne. "Le 'Baroque' Musical." *Les Colloques de Wegimont* 4. Paris: Société d'éditions "Les Belles Lettres," 1963.

Dahlhaus, Carl. "Bach und der Zerfall der musikalischen Figurenlehre." *MUSICA* 42 (1988): 137–40.

———. "Christoph Bernhard und die Theorie der modalen Imitation." *Archiv für Musikwissenschaft* 21 (1964): 45–59.

———. "Die Figurae superficiales in den Traktaten Christoph Bernhards." In *Bericht über den Musikwissenschaftlichen Kongress Bamberg*.

Kassel: Bärenreiter, 1953. 135–38.

Dammann, Rolf. *Der Musikbegriff im deutschen Barock.* 2nd ed. Regensburg: Laaber, 1984.

Eggebrecht, Hans Heinrich. *Studien zur musikalischen Terminologie.* 2nd ed. Mainz: Verlag der Akademie der Wissenschaft und der Literatur, 1968.

———. "Über Bachs geschichtlichen Ort." In *Johann Sebastian Bach.* Wege der Forschung 170. Darmstadt: Wissenschaftliche Buchgesellschaft, 1970. 247–89.

———. "Walthers Musikalisches Lexikon in seinen terminologischen Partien." *Acta Musicologia* 29 (1957): 10–27.

———. "Zum Figur-Begriff der Musica poetica." *Archiv für Musikwissenschaft* 16 (1959): 57–69.

Federhofer, Helmut. "Christoph Bernhards Figurenlehre und die Dissonanz." *Musikforschung* 42 (1989): 110–27.

———. "Der strenge und freie Satz und sein Verhältnis zur Kompositionslehre von Heinrich Schütz in der Fassung seines Schülers Christoph Bernhard." In *Beiträge zur Musikalischen Gestaltanalyse.* Graz: Akademische Druck- u. Verlagsanstalt, 1950.

———. "Die Figurenlehre nach Christoph Bernhard und die Dissonanzbehandlung in Werken von Heinrich Schütz." In *Bericht über den Musikwissenschaftlichen Kongress Bamberg.* Kassel: Bärenreiter, 1953.

Federl, Ekkehard. "Der Tractatus Musicus des Pater Meinrad Spiess (1683–1761)." In *Festschrift Bruno Stäblein.* Kassel: Bärenreiter, 1967.

Feldmann, Fritz. "Das 'Opusculum biparitum' des Joachim Thuringus (1625) besonders in seinen Beziehungen zu Joh. Nucius (1613)." *Archiv für Musikwissenschaft* 15 (1958): 123–42.

———. "Mattheson und die Rhetorik." In *Kongress-Bericht.* Internationaler Musikwissenschaftlicher Kongress: Hamburg, 1956.

Fiebig, Folkert. "Christoph Bernhard und der stile moderno: Untersuchungen zu Leben und Werk." In *Hamburger Beiträge zur Musikwissenschaft* 22. Hamburg: Wagner, 1980.

Forchert, Arno. "Musik und Rhetorik im Barock." *Schütz Jahrbuch* 7–8 (1985–86): 5–21.

Göttert, Karl-Heinz. "Musik und Rhetorik: Eine wandlungsreiche Beziehung." *Concerto* 20 (1988): 12–20.

Greene, J. W. "Musical Rhetoric." *Diapason* 72 (1981): 6.

Gurlitt, Willibald. "Musik und Rhetorik." *Helicon* 5 (1944): 67–86.

Harrison, Daniel. "Rhetoric and Fugue: An Analytical Application." *Music Theory Spectrum* 12 (1990): 1–49.

Hilse, Walter. "The Treatises of Christoph Bernhard." In *Music Forum,* vol.3, ed. William Mitchell and Felix Selzer. New York: Columbia University Press, 1973.

Hoffmann-Axthelm, D. "Faburdon / fauxbourdon / falso bordone." In *Handwörterbuch der musikalischen Terminologie*. Wiesbaden: F. Steiner, 1972–.

Johnston, Gregory. "Musical-Rhetorical Prosopopoeia and the Animation of the Dead in Seventeenth-Century German Funeral Music." *Canadian University Music Review* 10 (1990): 12–39.

Kirkendale, Ursula. "The Source for Bach's *Musical Offering*: The *Institutio oratoria* of Quintilian." *Journal of the American Musicological Society* 33 (1980): 88–111.

Kirkendale, Warren. "*Circulatio*-Tradition, *Maria Lactans*, and Josquin as Musical Orator." *Acta Musicologica* 56 (1984): 69–92.

Kretzschmar, Hermann. "Allgemeines und Besonderes zur Affektenlehre." *Jahrbuch der Muskbibliothek Peters* (1911): 63–77; (1912): 65–78.

Krones, Hartmut. "Die Figurenlehre bei Bachs Amstvorgänger Johann Georg Ahle." *Österreichische Musikzeitschrift* 40 (1985): 89–99.

Le Huray, Peter. *Music and the Reformation in England 1549–1660*. Cambridge: Cambridge University Press, 1978.

Lenneberg, Hans. "Johann Mattheson on Affect and Rhetoric." *Journal for Music Theory* 2 (1958): 47–84, 193–236.

Lester, Joel. "The Recognition of Major and Minor Keys in German Theory: 1680–1730." *Journal of Music Theory* 22 (1978): 65–103.

Massenkeil, Günther. "Die Wiederholungsfiguren in den Oratorien G. Carissimis." *Archiv für Musikwissenschaft* 13 (1956).

———. "Zur Frage der Dissonanzbehandlung in der Musik des 17. Jahrhunderts." *Les Colloques de Wegimont* 4. Paris: Société d'éditions "Les Belles Lettres," 1963. 151–76.

Meier, Bernhard. *The Modes of Classical Vocal Polyphony*. New York: Broude Br., 1988.

Meyer, Siegfried. "Abweichungen von den Normen eines Modus als Mittel der Wortausdeutung." *Musica Disciplina* 42 (1988): 199–215.

Müller-Blattau, Joseph. *Die Kompositionslehre Heinrich Schützens in der Fassung seines Schülers Christoph Bernhard*. Kassel: Bärenreiter, 1963.

Neumann, Frederick. *Ornamentation in Baroque and Post-Baroque Music*. Princeton: Princeton University Press, 1978.

Palisca, Claude. "Beginnings of Baroque Music: Its Roots in Sixteenth-Century Theory and Polemics." Ph.D. diss., Harvard University, 1953.

———. *Baroque Music*. 3rd. ed. Englewood Cliffs NJ: Prentice Hall, 1991.

———. "Ut Oratoria Musica: The Rhetorical Basis of Musical Mannerism." In *The Meaning of Mannerism*, ed. F. Robinson and S. Nichols Jr. Hanover NH: University Press of New England, 1972. 37–65.

Pilszynski, Judith. "The Evolvement of the Humoral Doctine." *Medical Times* 92 (1964): 1009–14.

Ruhnke, Martin. *Joachim Burmeister: Ein Beitrag zur Musiklehre um 1600.* Kassel: Bärenreiter, 1955.

Schering, Arnold. "Die Lehre von den musikalischen Figuren." *Kirchenmusikalisches Jahrbuch* 21 (1908): 106–14.

Schmitz, Arnold. *Die Bildlichkeit in der wortgebundenen Musik J. S. Bachs.* Mainz: Schott, 1950.

———. "Figuren, musikalisch-rhetorische." In *Musik in Geschichte und Gegenwart.* Kassel: Bärenreiter, 1949. 4: 176–83.

———. "Die Figurenlehre in den theoretischen Werken Johann Gottfried Walthers." *Archiv für Musikwissenschaft* 9 (1952): 79–100.

———. "Die oratorische Kunst J. S. Bachs—Grundfragen und Grundlagen." In *Kongress-Bericht.* Zweiter Weltkongress der Musikbibliotheken, Lüneburg, 1950.

Serauky, Walter. "Affektenlehre." In *Music in Geschichte und Gegenwart.* Kassel: Bärenreiter, 1949. 1: 113–21.

Sevier, Z. *The Theoretical Works and Music of J. G. Ahle.* Ph.D. diss., University of North Carolina, 1974.

Söhngen, Oskar. *Theologie der Music.* Kassel: Johannes Stauda Verlag, 1967.

Steblin, Rita. *A History of Key Characteristics in the Eighteenth and Early Nineteenth Centuries.* Ann Arbor: University of Michigan Press, 1983.

Toussaint, Georg. "Die Anwendung der musikalisch-rhetorischen figuren in den Werken von Heinrich Schütz." Ph.D. diss., Mainz, 1950.

Unger, Hans-Heinrich. *Die Beziehungen zwischen Musik und Rhetorik im 16.–18. Jahrhundert.* Würzburg: Triltsch, 1941. Facs. ed. Hildesheim: Olms, 1969.

Vickers, Brian. "Figures of Rhetoric / Figures of Music?" *Rhetorica* 2 (1984): 1–44.

Waite, William. "Bernhard Lamy, Rhetorician of the Passions." In *Studies in Eighteenth-Century Music.* London: Allen & Unwin, 1970.

Willhelm, I. "Johann Adolph Scheibe: German Musical Thought in Transition." Ph.D. diss., University of Illinois, 1963.

Williams, Peter. "Encounters with the Chromatic Fourth." *Musical Times* 126 (1985): 276–78, 339–43.

———. "Figurenlehre from Monteverdi to Wagner." *Musical Times* 120 (1979): 476–79, 571–73, 648–50, 816–18.

———. "Need Organists Pay Attention to Theorists of Rhetoric?" *Diapason* 73 (1982): 3–4.

INDEX

Lightning Source UK Ltd.
Milton Keynes UK
UKHW010703201220
375546UK00001B/14

9 780803 212763